THEORY IN THE PACIFIC, THE PACIFIC IN THEORY

Theory in the Pacific, the Pacific in Theory explores the role of theory in Pacific archaeology and its interplay with archaeological theory worldwide.

The contributors assess how the practice of archaeology in Pacific contexts has led to particular types of theoretical enquiry and interest, and, more broadly, how the Pacific is conceptualised in the archaeological imagination. Long seen as a laboratory environment for the testing and refinement of social theory, the Pacific islands occupy a central place in global theoretical discourse. This volume highlights this role through an exploration of how Pacific models and exemplars have shaped, and continue to shape, approaches to the archaeological past. The authors evaluate key theoretical perspectives and explore current and future directions in Pacific archaeology. In doing so, attention is paid to the influence of Pacific people and environments in motivating and shaping theory-building.

Theory in the Pacific, the Pacific in Theory makes a significant contribution to our understanding of how theory develops attuned to the affordances and needs of specific contexts, and how those contexts promote reformulation and development of theory elsewhere. It will be fascinating to scholars and archaeologists interested in the Pacific region, as well as students of wider archaeological theory.

Tim Thomas is Senior Lecturer in the Archaeology programme at the University of Otago, New Zealand, specialising in the archaeological landscapes and material culture of the Solomon Islands, and longer-term processes of Pacific colonisation. A past editor of the *Journal of Pacific Archaeology*, his previous books include *Lapita: Ancestors and Descendants* (2009) and *Monuments and People in the Pacific* (2014).

THEORY IN THE PACIFIC, THE PACIFIC IN THEORY

Archaeological perspectives

Edited by Tim Thomas

Routledge
Taylor & Francis Group

LONDON AND NEW YORK

First published 2021
by Routledge
2 Park Square, Milton Park, Abingdon, Oxon OX14 4RN

and by Routledge
52 Vanderbilt Avenue, New York, NY 10017

Routledge is an imprint of the Taylor & Francis Group, an informa business

British Library Cataloguing-in-Publication Data
A catalogue record for this book is available from the British Library

Library of Congress Cataloging-in-Publication Data
Names: Thomas, Tim, 1971– editor.
Title: Theory in the Pacific, the Pacific in theory : archaeological perspectives / edited by Tim Thomas.
Description: Abingdon, Oxon ; New York, NY : Routledge, 2020. | Includes bibliographical references and index.
Identifiers: LCCN 2020006244 (print) | LCCN 2020006245 (ebook) | ISBN 9781138303546 (hbk) | ISBN 9781138303553 (pbk) | ISBN 9780203730973 (ebk)
Subjects: LCSH: Social archaeology–Islands of the Pacific. | Archaeology–Islands of the Pacific–Methodology. | Archaeology–Philosophy. | Excavations (Archaeology–Islands of the Pacific. | Islands of the Pacific–Antiquities.
Classification: LCC DU28 .T47 2020 (print) | LCC DU28 (ebook) | DDC 995–dc23
LC record available at https://lccn.loc.gov/2020006244
LC ebook record available at https://lccn.loc.gov/2020006245

ISBN: 978-1-138-30354-6 (hbk)
ISBN: 978-1-138-30355-3 (pbk)
ISBN: 978-0-203-73097-3 (ebk)

Typeset in Bembo
by Newgen Publishing UK

CONTENTS

FIGURES

TABLES

CONTRIBUTORS

Ethan E. Cochrane Associate Professor, Anthropology, School of Social Sciences, University of Auckland, Auckland, New Zealand.

Bruno David Professor, Monash Indigenous Studies Centre, Monash University, Clayton, Australia.

Tim Denham Associate Professor, School of Archaeology and Anthropology, Australian National University, Canberra, Australia.

Scott M. Fitzpatrick Professor, Department of Anthropology, University of Oregon, Eugene, Oregon, USA.

James L. Flexner Senior Lecturer in Historical Archaeology and Heritage, University of Sydney, Sydney, Australia.

Mark Golitko Assistant Professor, Department of Anthropology, University of Notre Dame, Notre Dame, Indiana, USA.

Jennifer G. Kahn Associate Professor, Anthropology, College of William & Mary, Williamsburg, Virginia, USA.

Patrick V. Kirch Chancellor's Professor Emeritus, Anthropology Department, University of California Berkeley, California, USA.

Matthew Leavesley Senior Lecturer, Department of Anthropology and Sociology, University of Papua New Guinea, Port Moresby, Papua New Guinea

Thomas P. Leppard Assistant Professor, Department of Anthropology, Florida State University, Tallahassee Florida, USA.

Yvonne Marshall Senior Lecturer, Archaeology, University of Southampton, Southampton, UK.

Ian J. McNiven Professor, Monash Indigenous Studies Centre, Monash University, Clayton, Australia.

Peter J. Sheppard Professor, Department of Anthropology, University of Auckland, Auckland, New Zealand.

Matthew Spriggs ARC Laureate Fellow & Professor of Archaeology, The Australian National University, Canberra, Australia.

Katherine Szabó Department of Archaeology, Max Planck Institute for the Science of Human History, Jena, Germany.

Tim Thomas Senior Lecturer, Archaeology Programme, School of Social Sciences, University of Otago, Dunedin, New Zealand.

Cynthia L. Van Gilder Department of Anthropology, Saint Mary's College of California, Moraga, California, USA.

1

THEORY IN THE PACIFIC, AND THE PACIFIC IN THEORY

Tim Thomas

Introduction

This book explores the role of theory in Pacific archaeology, and its interplay with archaeological theory worldwide. One goal in adopting a regional focus is to suggest an alternative to the perception of theoretical discourse traditionally emanating from a core group of Euro-American institutions. Rather than assume that archaeological theory is mostly the product of metropolitan thinkers exported for practical application around the globe, the book examines how regional practice, and conceptions of place, are entangled with the development of theory both locally and globally. As in other fieldwork-based or empirical disciplines, archaeologists develop theory out of encounters and experiments with matter in place. As such, theoretical perspectives are often attuned to the affordances and needs of specific contexts and assemblages. This leads to archaeologies with different regional characters and traditions (Lozny, 2011). These research traditions feed into, and feed on, a global trade in ideas, where regional attributes circulate as exemplars, sources of analogy and comparison, and fuel further theoretical development. In this way ideas, frameworks and philosophical concepts are extracted from the specifics of local contexts, and are rendered translatable to other settings, where they are used, tested and reworked. So, just as theory is not simply the top-down application of metropolitan frameworks, neither does it emerge fully formed from bottom–up regional practice. Theorising involves reciprocal comparison between circulating ideas and local materials, and so is a synthetic product that arises from diverse contexts of investigation and comparison. Indeed, regions, places and their definitional qualities might also be seen as the classificatory product of this comparative theorisation.

Historically, European encounters with Pacific landscapes and people have had a lasting impact on metropolitan ideas. In the human sciences island geographies provided clarity for the refinement and testing of theory, with their boundedness and diversity being touted as explanatory aids, facilitating the study of population relationships and influencing theories of race, social and cultural evolution, political organisation and human–environment relations. Conceived as a collection of island microcosms, the Pacific has long been a source region for theorisations of human progress and plight. As exemplified by the title of Bahn and Flenley's (1992) *Easter Island, Earth Island,* captioned 'a message from the past for the future of our planet', island societies have functioned as stand-ins for how we think about humanity as a whole. During the 20th century, Pacific archaeologists engaged productively with this vision, but also critiqued its assumptions, using local data and perspectives to do so. More recent post-colonial movements in archaeology and the broader social sciences have also looked to the Pacific in formulating approaches to decolonisation and indigenous research. Archaeologists increasingly display wariness about overtly metaphorical or analogical uses of Pacific pasts, in favour of studying them for their own sake and from local perspectives.

This history of productive encounter has awarded Pacific peoples and environments a symbolic and empirical explanatory value in the Western imagination that endures in discussions of social theory to this day. It is impossible to discuss archaeological theory in the Pacific without acknowledging its relationship to this broader history of thought. Pacific archaeology emerged during a long history of engagement with anthropology, history, biology, geography and other adjacent disciplines. Some of this history will become apparent in the various chapters of the book, but it is not our goal to provide a comprehensive account of interdisciplinary borrowing or to try to trace the origins of ideas as being from either inside or outside Pacific archaeology. Instead we are interested in how Pacific archaeology, and the Pacific itself, has been constituted as an arena for the exploration of theoretical perspectives, and has contributed to the definition and refinement of their benefits, successes and failings. Despite commonly voiced insecurities about the importation of theory into archaeology, theory has never truly obeyed disciplinary boundaries, and core concepts and approaches circulate widely in Euro-American thought. Considering the 'mobility of theory' (Lucas, 2015) in this way offers us the opportunity to configure an alternate theoretical landscape, where theory is not an abstract thing or structure that is transported between fixed disciplines or regions, but the process of working on ideas in practice.

To introduce the volume, then, I first discuss how theory and place interact, and how we can understand this relationship. I then turn to a historical overview of the establishment of the Pacific as an arena for theoretical development in archaeology as a branch of the human sciences. My focus is on how European theories of the Pacific defined the key research questions taken up by archaeologists and shaped an enduring role for the region in global archaeological discourse.

The place of theory

Generally, theory in archaeology is the means by which we interpret or explain observations garnered from the archaeological record. But not all archaeologists agree on what constitutes the theoretical – what theory is, or what it should do – and this is as true for archaeologists working in the Pacific as elsewhere. Some hold the view that theory must be a formal set of logical propositions, able to explain data and having definite empirical consequences amenable to testing and falsification. Others consider that since even fundamental assumptions about archaeological goals are influenced by theory, it is simply 'the order we choose to put facts in' (Johnson, 2006, p. 118). Either way, the view that theory is a distinct realm sitting apart from the realm of observations is orthodox, although, as we will see, even this is open to challenge.

According to the orthodox view, theory is what allows us to give structure to, and thus comprehend, the observed world, and so in some way is also prior to, or elevated above observation. For example, in both the hard sciences and social constructionist perspectives data are thought to be theory-laden – theory determines even what we consider counting as fact in the first place. Perhaps because of this elevation there is a tendency to rank theories hierarchically in terms of the amount of the world that they explain: weaker theories cover limited local phenomena, and are particularistic and mostly descriptive; stronger or ultimate theories are capable of bridging disparate phenomena, gathering them under the same explanatory scheme and revealing new perspectives and possibilities. Although emerging from practical observation, the best theory is accordingly seen to be abstract and transportable: not tied to any concrete case, but widely applicable anywhere (Pétursdóttir and Olsen, 2018, p. 104). The idea of regional or place-specific theory is rendered problematic or aberrant in this view, since theory should ideally be global and hegemonic. Clarke (1979, p. 154), for example, considered regionally diverse archaeologies to be a mark of a discipline in its infancy, suggesting that these would ultimately require integration.

This kind of framing naturally encourages a view that theory is distinct from practice and is a rarefied concern. We see this play out in strict empiricist rejections of the need for theory at all, but also in explicitly scientific approaches where rarefication is an essential constituent of truth claims. The positivist processual archaeologies stemming from the mid-20th-century scientific revolution clung to the ideal of grand, synthetic theorising, or at least the provision of a shared toolbox of concepts and axioms (Clarke, 1968, fig. 2; Binford, 1972). During the postprocessual critiques of the 1980s, the strongest defences of positivist approaches were mounted against suggestions that universalist theory might be influenced by local biases and politics, or devolve into a kind of 'ideopraxis' (Bintliff, 2011), as formulated most clearly in the counter-charge of relativism (Binford, 1987). From this perspective the only valid way of challenging theory is via falsification by data, or replacement with an alternative that better explains data.

However, it is perhaps the main lasting outcome of postprocessualism that the view of theory sketched in the preceding paragraphs has shifted. Almost all surveys of archaeological theory since the turn of the millennium identify a growing movement towards pragmatism and the acceptance of a diversity of approaches and perspectives. Rather than different theoretical perspectives being seen as necessarily hegemonic, oppositional, or successional, they are argued to be the product of, and thus suited to, different contexts of production: questions of different types and scales; evidence of different resolution and character; communities with different interests and needs (Preucel and Mrozowski, 2010). Hodder (2012a) identifies a 'community of discourses model' involving trade in the productive tensions that arise between different and competing perspectives. Harris and Cipola (2017) similarly argue that theoretical change is the product of ideas in ongoing dialogue rather than abrupt paradigm shifts.

This new pragmatism represents a turn away from the goal of a unified archaeological theory consisting of a shared toolbox of abstract concepts and axioms applicable anywhere. Although programmes of synthesis and integration and claims of universality still occur, Hodder (2012a, p. 5) notes that, in practice, archaeological theories are not abstract or wholly divorced from particular domains – they always seem to have a favoured region, timescale or data type. In a sense this is true of all disciplines with any kind of empirical interest (and of disciplinarity itself) – if theory emerges out of the need to explain or understand observations, then only certain arrangements of data provide the necessary context for explication, testing, or further exploration. Locally acquired data do not always accommodate explanatory models developed elsewhere. Canonical case studies, such as Darwin's Galápagos finches (adaptive radiation), or Flinders Petrie's predynastic Egyptian grave assemblages (seriation), come to exemplify a given theory, partly because they describe the sort of phenomena it explains, and the type of data it requires.

However, more than simply identifying that diverse theories divide the world into different explanatory domains, the general tenor of the new pragmatism is not to reiterate that data are theory-laden, but rather to stress that theory is also data-laden. If so, the question of how archetypes and original datasets constrain, inform or reveal the ontology of different theories, is mostly underexamined (Pétursdóttir and Olsen, 2018, p. 106). In historical reviews of regional archaeological traditions, there has long been an understanding that different theoretical issues assume prominence in different locations due to prevailing societal influences (Trigger and Glover, 1981), and there is acknowledgement that certain theoretical perspectives can remain relevant despite wider disciplinary trends due to local data-driven problems (Trigger, 1989). But there is less explicit consideration of the reciprocal influence of data and theory, or how particular encounters with, and conceptions of, place shape theoretical trajectories.

In a recent book, whose title *Theory in Africa, Africa in Theory* has inspired the current collection, Wynne-Jones and Fleisher (2015) propose that archaeological encounters with the African past, and African people, profoundly influenced the development of 'Western' archaeological theory. Ethno-archaeological engagements with African societies lie at the heart of the turn towards meaning-centred approaches during the postprocessual era (e.g. Hodder, 1982), such that the materiality of those societies 'actually created the space for postprocessualism to flourish theoretically in the West' (Wynne-Jones and Fleisher, 2015, p. 12). In particular, it was witnessing people in Africa using artefacts to express and manipulate social relations, as active material elements in locally generated systems of meaning, that encouraged Hodder, and others, to critique the grand, generalising goals of processual archaeology, and formulate the idea that archaeology, like politics, could be local (MacEachern, 1996, p. 273). But, while African peoples and their particular material and social concerns 'created post-processual ideas' their voices were subsequently written out of theory, or set off against it in post-colonial critiques that positioned Africans as subaltern opponents of supposedly Western discourse rather than its active participants and influencers (Wynne-Jones and Fleisher, 2015, p. 13). Despite the localised origins and localising implications of the theoretical insights derived from African fieldwork, these were still rendered mobile, and ultimately transformed into universal axioms. And despite the democratising intent of post-colonial critiques, Africans were themselves subsequently defined and delimited by subaltern theory.

The origins of postprocessualism are undoubtedly more complex than an original series of revelations in Africa, and theoretical influences from multiple directions have accumulated since the 1980s. Nevertheless, the way in which crucial moments of practical, local encounter with the archaeological record in the context of different social arrangements, ways of being and cultural geographies, can crystallise and promote theoretical development, bears more examination by archaeologists. Understanding the process of abstraction and generalisation, whereby core insights derived from such moments are given theoretical mobility by reducing their local characteristics, is equally necessary. The issue is not whether ideas should be allowed to escape their local origins to circulate as more generalised propositions or always remain parochial, but rather how mobility is produced, and the extent to which the origins of ideas are forgotten or obviated. The trick, going forward, will be to facilitate the mobility of theory, whilst also retaining a sense of its locality – that is, by acknowledging, rather than forgetting, its origins in place and with specific people, but without succumbing to essentialism. This is all the more necessary if we wish the discipline to become more cosmopolitan in accepting its multiple contributors and interlocutors, and their different perspectives and local situations (Meskell, 2009). Cosmopolitan perspectives are particularly pertinent in the Pacific, where archaeologists work in a post-colonial context requiring increasing consultation, acknowledgement and participation by local stakeholders, and which is also a region that has long functioned as a supply zone for the circulation of theoretical ideas and models of sociocultural forms.

Places in motion

One reason for the kind of 'forgetfulness' noted by Wynne-Jones and Fleisher is that archaeologists are typically highly attuned to, even anxious about, the applicability of 'external' theoretical ideas to their particular contexts of study. This is often revealed in debates about the uses and effects of ethnographic analogy (Wylie, 1985). Although debates about analogy in archaeology have focused on either its scientific rationale and inductive logic, or its morality and typological implications, they are also driven by a deeper anxiety about mixing contingent sociocultural attributes across time and space. In some sense anxiety stems from an incomplete separation of theory and empirics. If ideas are too closely associated with a definite time and place, if they carry too much cultural content, they fail to convince when applied elsewhere – leaving an opening for the double-sided critique of giving neither the source nor the subject of the analogy credit for its own historical particularity. Theoretical abstraction and the obviation of origins is thus a strategy for avoiding the doubts of analogy – and results in the kind of theoretical rarefication mentioned above.

Recent debates over the use of Pacific analogies and theoretical concepts derived from Pacific cases in interpretations of the European archaeological record illustrate some of these tensions. Matthew Spriggs, in particular, has critiqued the use of ethnographic examples to create 'ever more Pacific-looking European pasts' (2008, p. 538). Tilley's (1996) *An Ethnography of the Neolithic* is singled out for its use of examples of artefact personification and embodiment, gift exchange and death rituals from the Massim region of Papua New Guinea as a way of supporting interpretations of the archaeological record of Neolithic Sweden and Denmark. Gosden (1999, p. 8) finds that Tilley's version of the Neolithic has 'a distinctly Melanesian feel to it'. Similarly, Jones (2005) notes that the importation of Strathern's (1988) theory of relational personhood to disparate European Neolithic contexts – from Chapman's (2000) account of southeastern Europe, to studies by Fowler (2001; 2004) and Thomas (2002) in Britain – create a generalised picture of a single Neolithic with a 'Melanesian flavour' (Jones, 2005, p. 195). Fahlander, reviewing a recent account of these relational approaches, also expresses concern over the 'Melanesification of the past inherent in many relational archaeologies' (Fahlander, 2018, p. 642).

Spriggs's critique is particularistic and addresses the adequacy of modern Melanesian societies as appropriate analogues for the European past. Some wariness perhaps stems from the suspicion that these societies have been selected for their apparently authentic alterity, out of a Romantic primitivism. Spriggs undermines this by pointing to the extensive social change, population decline and economic reorganisation in Melanesian societies after early European contact and colonialism. For example, the classic Melanesian 'Big Man' model of political organisation (Sahlins, 1963), utilised in disparate archaeological contexts (Roscoe, 2000), is thought by Spriggs and others to largely be the product of colonial pacification. Hence, 'one has to ask who the colonial power in Neolithic Britain or Scandinavia was if we are going to use Big Man models to interpret that period' (Spriggs, 2008, p. 545). He argues that comparison should focus on continuous cultural sequences and processes rather than spot analogies built on inspiring counter-intuitives, noting a lack of engagement with the Melanesian archaeological record by those inspired by ethnographic case studies (2008, p. 547). Spriggs's (2016) own comparisons between European and Pacific archaeologies begin to rectify this, as do recent studies comparing Viking and Polynesian archaeological sequences (Ravn, 2018; Price, 2018; Price and Ljungkvist, 2018).

Nevertheless, early responses to Spriggs (2008) indicated that the impact of colonialism was overstated (Roscoe, 2009) or claimed that his critique relies on a model of analogy as static comparison of similarities, rather than an ongoing evaluation of differences and relevance (Ravn, 2011). Indeed, the colonial situation of Melanesian societies only matters if it is being claimed that the empirical similarity in question was produced by a similar causal sequence. This is not how Tilley and company claim to utilise Melanesian ethnography – instead they seek heuristic models of a functioning animism or relational personhood as a theoretical prompt to interpretation. The question of the commensurability of the source and subject of comparison is of less concern than that 'aspects of both are distinct from our own everyday modern experience' (Thomas, 2004, p. 241). Exoticism is partly the point then, but this is in response to a wariness about projecting modern Western ideas and assumptions into the past. This is a mirror image of anxieties about the use of ethnographic analogy. Pacific ethnographies are presumably preferable to comparing archaeological sequences because sources describing the latter are thought to be permeated by modernist assumptions. Spriggs (2008, p. 547) acknowledges a passing comment by Thomas (2004, p. 240) on the use of Marxism to define and compare past societies on the basis of their 'mode of production' – a classificatory endeavour whose terms are founded on a critique of 19th-century capitalism and early ethnological contrasts. Despite its generalisation in the mid-20th century, Marxism remained attuned to concepts of personhood, property ownership, labour and so on, rooted in industrial capitalism. In fact, the problems of applying such concepts to Melanesian societies were exactly the motivation for Strathern's alternative model of relational personhood – Marxist approaches (to gender particularly) assumed a theory of social action that responded to situations that simply did not exist in Melanesia, and so could only provide an exogenous analysis (Strathern, 1988, p. 138). Archaeologists in the Pacific are still working on exploring these tensions (e.g. Earle and Spriggs, 2015; see Spriggs (Chapter 8) and Flexner (Chapter 9)).

There is a hint here that the choice of either being bound by modern Western frameworks or of colouring the past with exotic ethnographic analogies is a false alternative. Theory generation is always the reciprocal product of comparison between prior understandings and assumptions (whatever their source) and new observations. The transformation of theoretical ideas is inherent to this process. The two key reasons for anxiety about the application of Melanesian models of relationality to the European past is that 1) the ideas are seen to be particularistic attributes of regional societies rather than generalisable theories, and 2) they are seen to be applied without transformation or accommodation to the new context. The same is true for doubts about the unreflexive usage of modernist assumptions. Ironically, Strathern's work, and the so-called New Melanesian Ethnography that it inspired, explicitly sought to deal with both of these issues in an anthropological context. Theories of the 'composite person' or the 'dividual' were not simply generated from indigenous concepts, or imposed from afar, but rather developed through the comparison of a complex history of perspectives in place (Englund and Yarrow, 2013). Strathern famously describes her account of Melanesia as a 'controlled fiction' (1988, p. 6), because it is 'an analysis from the point of view of

Western anthropological and feminist preoccupations of what Melanesian ideas might look like if they were to appear in the form of those preoccupations' (1988, p. 309). Hinging on a series of analytical contrasts between commodity and gift economies, individuals and dividuals, objectification and relationality, her work pursues a 'negative strategy' (Strathern, 1990) that uses Melanesia as a foil for the critique of pre-existing analytical assumptions. Strathern's model of gift exchange, for example, was based on Gregory's (1982) theoretical contrast between the Maussian gift (Melanesian) and the Marxist commodity (European). Mauss's (1990 [1925]) analytical category of the gift was itself the synthetic product of comparison between the modern market economy, the potlach, the Indian gift, *kula* exchange, and Māori notions of *hau*. The latter was based on New Zealand ethnologist Elsdon Best's (1909) reporting of Māori forest lore, most famously quoting a correspondent, Tamati Ranapiri. Widely referred to in essentialising terms as a 'Maori sage' (Sahlins, 1972, p. 150), Ranapiri was also known as Thomas Ransfield (Stewart, 2017): the son of an American whaler and a Māori woman; an advocate for his community in Māori-language newspapers; and in the late 1880s one of the founders of the Otaki-Māori [horse] Racing Club (Bull, 1989). This is not to suggest that the 'Melanesian gift' is inauthentic, but rather that it is thus a synthetic theoretical product developed out of a multi-sourced contrast between Western and other economies, whose hybridity goes all the way down to the worldly experience of its informants. It only becomes purified and regionalised as 'Melanesian' during its application in contexts that require reiteration of the originating contrast.

This entangled history is one of the reasons Strathern's theory of relationality has found such wide application – because it resonates with other projects that seek to question modernist assumptions and dichotomies. In this way 'Melanesia' escapes anachronism to become the vanguard of new theory. As such Strathern is often cited by archaeologists alongside works by Latour (1993) or Ingold (2000), and others making similar relational critiques of subject/object, culture/nature, dualisms (e.g. Hodder, 2012b; Thomas, 2019). Perhaps we can think of relationality as an example of what Moore (2004) refers to as 'concept-metaphors' – domain defining terms like agency, identity, gender or the person, which orient us towards areas of shared theoretical exchange. Such terms are the key theoretical devices of the postprocessual era, and since they are both abstract and indefinite without reference to specific cases, they serve to maintain a productive tension between universal claims and specific historical contexts. In describing her theoretical synthesis as a fiction, Strathern is acknowledging the status of anthropological theory as a tertiary product located between the Western philosophical tradition and various other ways of knowing and being (compare Gell, 1999, p. 34).

The production of archaeological theory is more complicated than ethnographic anthropology, because it adds the emplaced material record of past human activity as yet another dimension of contact and comparison. But the process of theory generation by way of reciprocal and transformative comparison is the same. We need to produce analyses critically engaged with how the Western tradition influences archaeological understanding, but also acknowledge how that tradition is simultaneously a 'tradition-in-the-making' influenced by its encounters with local material records and with other ideas, rather than circumscribed by its own pre-occupations. Recognising this is the solution to both anxieties about the trade in homogenising analogies, and the forgetting of local influence via generalising abstraction. The voices and interests of descendant communities mediated through emplaced analysis and reciprocal theoretical production can thus also inform and potentially reform the grounds of theoretical debate (Hirsch, 2014).

In the following I present a history of reciprocal theory generation in the context of external definitions of the Pacific and its past. I focus on how European encounters with Pacific peoples and geographies interacted with incipient theories of human origins and diversity and led to the formulation of the Pacific as an arena for the study of humanity. Pacific archaeology as an academic discipline is largely a post-Second World War phenomenon, but early scholars inherited, worked with and worked to escape, ideas and regional conceptions produced over a much longer history of European engagement. The very constitution of the Pacific as a geographical and cultural domain, with internal divisions, histories and relations, is one of these conceptual products, and one to which archaeologists continue to contribute. Indeed, many of the core dimensions by which the Pacific was first defined and understood permeate and inform the contours of contemporary archaeological debate. It is necessary to understand this history to recognise the significance of post-Second World War theoretical preoccupations.

Defining the Pacific

Historians and geographers have long recognised that contemporary notions of the Pacific (Fig. 1.1) as a classificatory region are largely an artefact of many centuries of European discourse (Spate, 1979; Lansdown 2006), albeit mediated and often challenged by practical engagements with the agency and nomenclatures of local inhabitants (Douglas, 2015). The region began as a purely imagined realm, based on speculative theories about the shape of the world beyond European experience. Aristotle's philosophical proofs of a spherical globe postulated a hidden southern antipodean landmass, balancing the northern continents. These lands were thought to be populated by 'antichthonic' inhabitants, the corresponding opposites of Europe's autochthones. Although this view was rejected by medieval Christianity, it was curated by theorists until the Renaissance when it was positioned on maps, first as *terra incognita*, but later as a hypothetical southern continent: *Terra Australis*. The latter was encouraged by Spanish and Portuguese voyages delimiting the western (the Moluccas or Spice Islands) and eastern (the Americas) edges of Oceania, and particularly Magellan's 1520–1 crossing of what he called the *Mare Pacificum*. Magellan encountered only one occupied island in the Pacific (Guam) but reported hearing the seas breaking against an unseen southern shore, reinforcing the notion that a continent awaited discovery (Douglas, 2010, pp. 181–6).

The Pacific thus began life as an abstract opposite, a hidden mirror-world to European ideas and ideals and, being initially empty of empirical content, it was

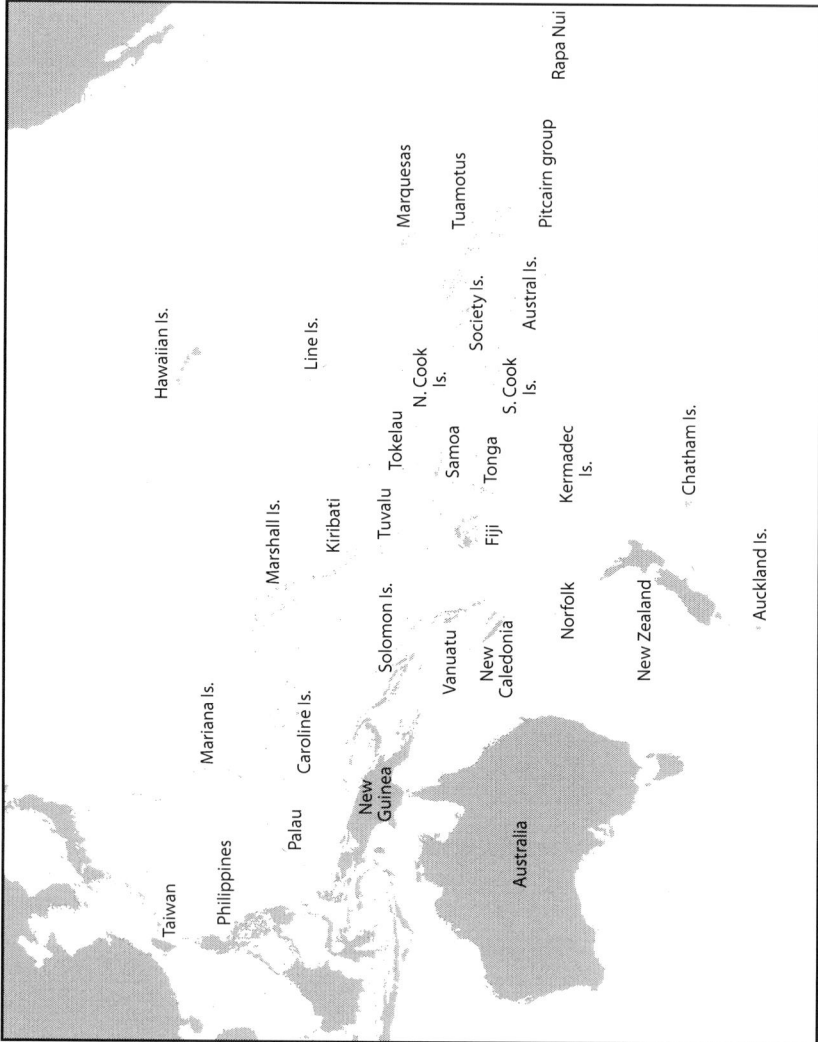

FIGURE 1.1 Map of the Pacific.

able to be filled with theoretical expectation. The trans-Pacific voyages of Alvaro de Mendaña and Pedro Fernández de Quirós (in 1567–9, 1595–7 and 1605–6), for example, were motivated by the Spanish conviction, fuelled by Inca legend, that vast riches and potential new colonies awaited discovery in the putative southern continent (Jack-Hinton, 1969). Instead of a continent they found islands (the Solomon Islands, Vanuatu, the Marquesas), and people who ultimately resisted their colonial efforts. As Douglas (2010, p. 180) notes, with increasing European incursion 'the empirical legacies of direct personal encounters and local knowledge began to infiltrate and complicate European theory and myth'. Such processes were increasingly formalised during the Enlightenment, and particularly after the voyages of Louis Antoine de Bougainville (1766–9) and Captain James Cook (1768–79) when traveller's accounts became more widely available.

Initially though, the writers of such accounts described Pacific peoples and landscapes 'through a haze of their own enchantments' (Salmond, 2009, p. 21), and were apt to cast observations in the mould of classical, biblical and romantic archetypes (Fig. 1.2) in line with prevailing neoclassicism (Smith, 1985). In fact, they were primed to do so by an already established association of tropical islands with archetypal models of Utopia or Eden, influenced by earlier Mediterranean and

FIGURE 1.2 Captn. Wallis, on his arrival at O'Taheite [Tahiti, June 1767], in conversation with Oberea the Queen, while her attendants are performing a favourite dance called the Timrodee.

Source: The New York Public Library Digital Collections. https://digitalcollections. nypl.org/items/e279ac80-f36a-0132-ce31-58d385a7bbd0

Caribbean exchanges (Grove, 1996). Joseph Banks, arriving with Cook on Tahiti in April 1769, for example, initially saw only 'an Arcadia' (Beaglehole, 1962, p. 252). A year earlier, Bougainville had found the Tahitian landscape reminiscent of the Elysian Fields, and compared local physiques to the classical gods, Hercules, Mars, and Venus. His accounts were suffused with eroticism (Harrison, 2012), and he ultimately named the island *Nouvelle Cythère* (New Kythira) after the island where the young Aphrodite had first washed ashore. Romantic primitivism permeated most aspects of description: staple tree crops like *Artocarpus* were referred to as 'bread' fruit, and the liquid in coconuts was 'milk' enabling observers to envision a paradise where bread and milk fell from the trees, and required no labour (Hawkesworth, 1773, p. 186).

Chroniclers of Enlightenment-era expeditions drew such observations into dialogue with metropolitan debates on the original state of human nature and the causes of worldwide diversity in customs and appearances. Publications such as Denis Diderot's *Supplément au Voyage de Bougainville* described explicit contrasts between Tahitian and European society at a time, immediately prior to the American and French Revolutions, when emerging public discourse sought to escape the structures of feudal society (Lansdown, 2006 pp. 64–109). As such, a key concern was whether civilisation corrupted or improved the natural qualities of humanity, and locations like Tahiti seemed to provide 'a way of catching live, as it were, aspects of Europe's own prehistory' (Howe, 2003, p. 247). Initially, explorers' accounts seemed to disprove Hobbesian postulations that the past of humanity consisted of a brutish, competitive, savagery only improved by civilisation, and confirm that it was a natural state unspoilt by the longings and miseries of modern life. But opinion quickly shifted to reflect that, while 'Tahiti proved that there was once a Golden Age; Tahiti also proved that it had long passed away' (Smith, 1985, p. 44). Not only did explorers witness rapid change and express anxiety over their own corrupting influence, but they also noticed material traces of internal change – Cook and Forster, for example, saw the toppled statuary of Rapa Nui (Easter Island), as 'monuments of antiquity' and the melancholic 'remains of better times'. As such, the Pacific increasingly occupied European thought 'not as a symbol of the normality of human happiness but as a symbol of its transience' (Smith, 1985, p. 44).

Regions, races and replacement

The apparently fragile nature of insular societies encouraged notions that they were ideal contexts for understanding social progress and change, and this was also facilitated by a comparative perspective afforded by their scattered geographical distribution. Explorers' ships became research tools in a comparative endeavour – travelling laboratories collecting samples of variation. The naturalists aboard Cook's ships included prominent students and correspondents of Carl Linnaeus, whose formalised system of biological classification promised an all-encompassing model through which to understand global diversity. Pre-Enlightenment explorers followed the biblical monogenic convention that all of humanity descended from

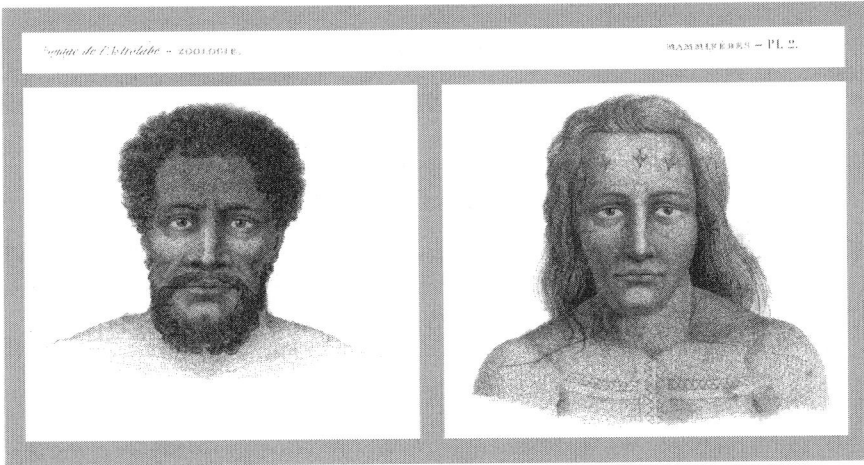

FIGURE 1.3 Early explorers described two races in the Pacific, and these were formally classified in the 'Mammals' section of Quoy and Gaimard's zoological appendix to Dumont d'Urville's *Voyage de l'Astrolabe*. *Left:* Naturel des Iles Viti (Race Noire [Black Race]). *Right:* Naturel de Iles Tikopia (Race Jaune [Yellow Race]) (D'Urville, 1830, Zoology, vol. 1, pl. 2).

Source: The New York Public Library Digital Collections. https://digitalcollections. nypl.org/items/510d47da-8da1-a3d9-e040-e00a18064a99

a common stock, being categorically distinct from, and superior to, the lower animals – accordingly, human differences were seen to be merely the product of environment, and improvement was possible. But Linnaeus classified humans and animals within the same natural domain, and after the 1770s differences among people were increasingly theorised as the product of biologically determined, and distinct, races (Douglas, 2008).

The German naturalist Johann Reinhold Forster, having sailed on Cook's second voyage of 1772–5, identified in the Pacific 'two great varieties of people', whose presence and differences were explained by the displacement of an 'aboriginal black race' by successive migrations of more civilized 'ancient Malays' (Forster, 1778, pp. 227–84). Although Forster did not consider these to be biological races in the modern sense, his observations were soon organised as such (Fig. 1.3) under the influence of the new racial taxonomies (Douglas, 2010, p. 201). The most enduring scheme was formalised in 1832 by Dumont d'Urville, a French naval naturalist with extensive experience in the Pacific. Inspired by Forster's account, as well as his own experiences, Dumont d'Urville defined a four-part regional geography for the Pacific based largely on racial markers (Fig. 1.4). Melanesia was his name for the area occupied by a 'black race' described as 'very inferior' in physical, political, moral and intellectual terms to a 'yellow' or 'coppery' race divided into two groups living in areas defined as Polynesia and Micronesia. Sense was made of this distribution by connecting it to already defined Malaysia and Australasia by way of a

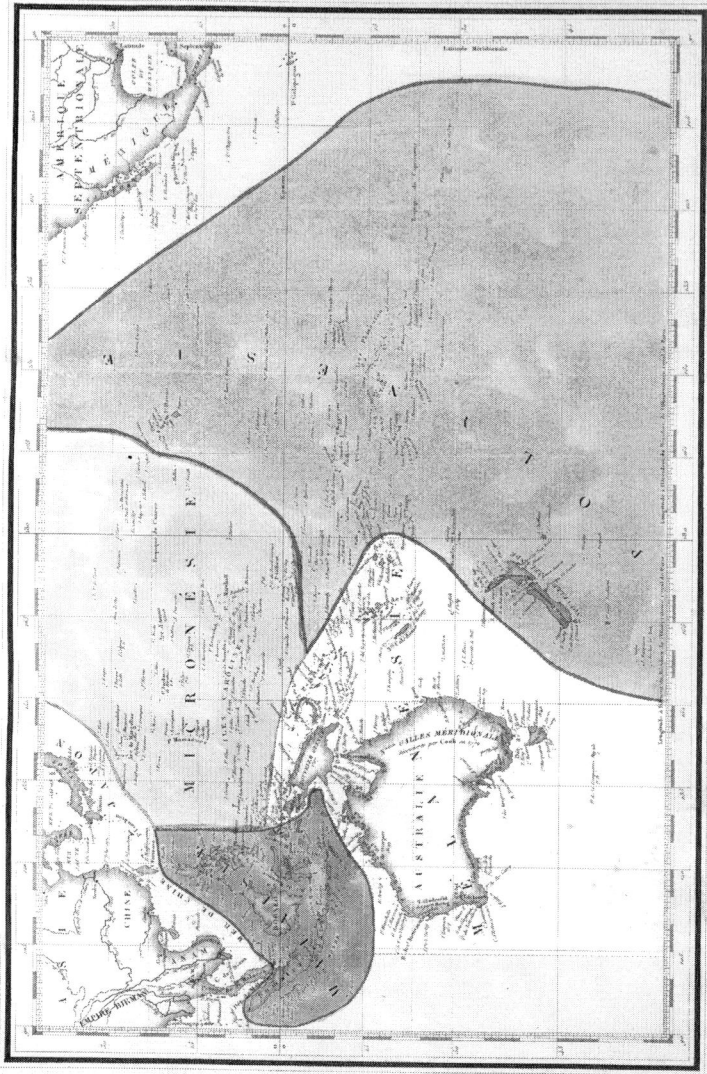

FIGURE 1.4 Dumont D'Urville's Oceania, divided into Malaysia, Melanesia, Micronesia and Polynesia (1830).

Source: The New York Public Library Digital Collections. https://digitalcollections.nypl.org

conjectural history of migrations. Australians were at the base of his racial hierarchy as 'the primitive and natural state of the Melanesian race' and thus representative of the first occupants of Oceania. Polynesians and Micronesians had subsequently invaded from Malaysia. The replacement of the darker skinned race by the lighter was considered the 'natural order' (Tcherkézoff, 2003; Douglas, 2010).

Dumont d'Urville's scheme was widely adopted and became the core framework for subsequent descriptions of the Pacific, and despite dissatisfaction with its racism, doubts about its accuracy, and various attempts at replacement, it remains dominant (Clark, 2003). In 19th-century Europe and America, its typological structure facilitated the incorporation of travellers' observations into unilineal evolutionary models by Tylor, Morgan, and Spencer (e.g. Gardner, 2008). Whilst these explained human types in terms of varying intellectual and cultural progress, ethnologists in the Pacific took the narratives of racial migration and replacement underlying Dumont d'Urville's classification as their explanation for regional differences. Debate essentially came to focus on the question of Polynesian origins. Initially at least, Melanesians were considered either to be autochthonous or linked to ancient 'negrito' or 'pygmy' migrations from Africa, and thus served mostly as a relict, primitive foil for this question (Ballard, 2006). Narratives of population replacement were deeply compelling for settler societies in the region, allowing European colonialism to be narrated as part of an eternal, natural process (Howe, 2003). Consequently, replacement models prevailed, where waves of racial migration functioned as progressive civilising steps. These have come to be known regionally as 'two-stratum' theories (Barber, 1995), although in most instances they postulated more than two migrations and became increasingly convoluted through time.

Archaeological evidence made little contribution to such theories, but in New Zealand Julius Haast proposed a two-stratum account of the local archaeological sequence after a series of excavations in Canterbury and Otago. A key site was Moa-Bone Point Cave where bones of the extinct ratite, moa, were found associated with flaked stone tools in the lowest levels. Above these deposits were shell midden layers with polished or ground stone tools. To explain the change Haast drew inspiration from Boucher de Perthes's discovery of stone tools associated with extinct animals in France, and John Lubbock's Palaeolithic and Neolithic subdivisions of the European Stone Age, arguing that the lower layers were produced by Palaeolithic 'moa-hunters', and the upper by invading Neolithic 'shellfish eaters' who became the Polynesian Māori encountered by Europeans. The moa-hunters were argued to be autochthones rather than migrants since it was 'rather difficult to conceive that a people in such a low state of civilization could have built canoes' and their distribution, and that of the moa, suggested the previous existence of land bridges or a submerged Pacific continent (Haast, 1871, 1874). The proposition was immediately controversial since Alexander McKay, who had been employed to excavate by Haast, suggested a contradictory interpretation: the moa-hunters were ancestors of the modern Māori, and had hunted moa to extinction soon after their arrival (McKay, 1874).

By the 1890s the latter view of the evidence had prevailed, but the idea of a pre-Māori people was not at all abandoned. New ethnological syntheses of Polynesian oral traditions superseded archaeological evidence. Indigenous traditions of migration and rumours of dark-skinned forest folk (*maruiwi, manahune*) were taken as evidence for population replacement. The two most prominent advocates were the ethnologists S. Percy Smith and Abraham Fornander, who believed Polynesians were an Aryan race driven by the eastward advance of peoples from the Indian subcontinent, through Southeast Asia into the Pacific. In New Zealand, Smith, along with Elsdon Best, crudely blended oral traditions into a simple, coherent narrative in which a primitive, dark-skinned people of Melanesian origin, known as the Maruiwi (or Moriori), had been exterminated by, or inter-married with, the superior Polynesian Māori, except on the remote Chatham Islands where a small enclave remained. Māori were held to have arrived in a Great Fleet of seven canoes in AD 1350 (Barber, 1995; Howe, 2003).

In Melanesia meanwhile, growing awareness of linguistic and ethnological diversity had encouraged a more complex view of population origins. Language, culture and biology were drawn on freely to supply traits for classification. By the late 19th century, the term 'Melanesian' increasingly described only communities living on the coastal fringes and islands of the region (Ray, 1895) – that is, Austronesian-speaking communities. Non-Austronesian-speaking areas of New Guinea and off-shore islands, whose languages are often as distinct from each other as they are from Austronesian languages, were distinguished as being inhabited by 'Papuans' – a race aboriginal to the region and perhaps connected to Australians, but considered superior to them (Urry, 1998; Ballard, 2008). Coastal Melanesians were understood to be a 'mixed' race perhaps with Papuan ancestry, but certainly influenced by subsequent migration from the west. Robert Codrington's (1891) major synthetic account of Island Melanesia, for example, noted that 'two currents of influence have poured and are pouring into' the region, including an ancient current marked by the distribution of betel-nut, and a 'modern and more direct' (pp. 1–2) influence brought by Polynesian settlers and marked by the distribution of kava root. Seligman (1909) proposed a distinction between the older, more primitive 'Papuans' of mainland New Guinea, and more recent and advanced 'Papuo-Melanesians' of its coastal fringes and islands. A.C. Haddon (1909, pp. 20–1) thought he could identify an even earlier and more primitive pygmy 'Papuan Negritoid' race in the interior of New Guinea (Urry, 1998).

Culture history

These classificatory observations were given theoretical structure by the German *Kulturhistorischen* school founded in the emerging geographic ethnology of F. Ratzel and L. Frobenius, which drew Oceania into a global culture history of diffusing *Kulturkreise* ('culture circles'). Each *Kulturkreis* was occupied by a *Kulturkomplex* ('cultural complex') made up of traits that travelled together in unity. Fritz Graebner (1905) traced six such circles in Oceania, arguing that it was possible to infer their 'culture strata', or relative ages of arrival – beginning with Tasmanians and ending with Polynesians. These geographic approaches were subsequently refined with the addition of cultural ecology by Franz Boas, who took them to the United States where they influenced C. Wissler, A.L. Kroeber and others. German culture history made its way into European archaeology via the work of V. Gordon Childe. Both routes subsequently influenced the first generation of professional archaeologists in the Pacific trained in the British and American traditions.

Culture history in early 20th-century sociocultural anthropology gradually pried apart the link between cultural traits and biology, such that racial and psychological theories of unilineal evolution were replaced with essentially cultural diffusionist models (e.g. Boas, 1901). In British social anthropology, diffusionist explanations had emerged during the first truly ethnographic expeditions to the Pacific. Whilst these had begun with evolutionary questions in mind, the island context and the results of fieldwork encouraged a shift in explanation (Urry, 1998; Kuklick, 1994). W.H.R. Rivers, for example, who participated in A.C. Haddon's Cambridge Anthropological Expedition to Torres Straits, and returned to the Pacific in 1907–8 with an intent to study the evolution of kinship structures, ended up producing a diffusionist account of the *History of Melanesian Society* (Rivers, 1914). Rivers thought a migrating 'kava-people' from Indonesia had replaced or blended with a more ancient 'betel-people' who had occupied the region as far as Fiji, and that underlying both of these was the shadow of an aboriginal population he called the 'dual people'. Witnessing first-hand patterns of trade, material change and mobility in the colonial Pacific, Rivers grew to think population movements and interactions disguised evolutionary change, and thus required sorting out prior to the study of internal development (Rivers, 1914, vol. 2, pp. 1–2; Thomas, 2014a). Nevertheless, in explicit contrast to Graebner, Rivers modelled diffusion by migration as an 'evolutionary' process in which small numbers of immigrants gradually influenced interconnected social institutions. Change depended on a complex series of adoptions and transformations, in the context of existing social and environmental conditions, rather than being the mechanical introduction and replacement of packages of things, languages and institutions (Rivers, 1914, vol. 2, pp. 3–5).

In archaeological culture history the separation of cultural traits from biology was partial, and it took some time before debates about migration, population replacement and the empirical unity of cultural complexes became important in the Pacific, and mostly only in Melanesian archaeology (see below). In Polynesia the question of population origins settled on a model of branching and development from a single founding population, so processes of internal change grew dominant. Two-stratum views in Polynesia were challenged by comparative material culture analyses and archaeological excavations in the first half of the 20th century, but racial preconceptions were only gradually discarded. In New Zealand, H.D. Skinner, who had studied under Haddon and Rivers at Cambridge, refuted the proposition that an earlier Melanesian stratum had preceded the Māori, using 'somatic' evolutionary changes in material culture assemblages (adzes particularly) to demonstrate continuity, and placed this within a diffusionist framework, incorporating Clark Wissler's age-area approach (Skinner 1921; 1924). Te Rangi Hiroa in *Vikings of the Sunrise* (Buck, 1938) also rejected a primal stratum of Melanesians, and indeed refused any influence at all, arguing that Polynesians resulted from the mixture of a Caucasian and a Mongoloid population in Asia, and had voyaged to Polynesia via a Micronesian route that skirted Melanesia. So, despite challenging the two-stratum view, these critiques nevertheless reinforced existing racial distinctions by repudiating any Melanesian influence on Polynesian people or culture.

Roger Duff's excavations at Wairau Bar (Duff, 1956) solidified a growing understanding of the essential coherence and foundational status of East Polynesian culture, as well as its adaptive transformation in New Zealand, but like others he linked his findings to the broader narrative of external Polynesian origins in Southeast Asia and utilised Smith's Great Fleet chronology for the New Zealand sequence (Duff, 1959). It was not until the first generation of professionally trained archaeologists began working in New Zealand, and radiocarbon dating became available, that earlier ethnological or 'traditionalist' frameworks were abandoned (Golson, 1986). Jack Golson, a Cambridge graduate who had studied under Grahame Clark, established the independence of archaeology and oral tradition (Golson, 1960) and developed a culture-historical sequence for New Zealand based on changes in artefact form (Golson, 1959). Although heavily influenced by V. Gordon Childe, Golson adopted the terminology of Willey and Phillips (1958) to define a 'genetic' sequence of two chronological phases, with regional aspects, within the same cultural tradition. Roger Green, who had studied with Gordon Willey at Harvard, subsequently developed a more dynamic account of culture change based on interdependent relationships in cultural ecology, subsistence and settlement pattern under conditions of colonisation, albeit within the same typological paradigm (Green, 1963).

In the wake of the Second World War, new relevance of the tropical Pacific for American geopolitical strategy led to increased research interest, and this included archaeological surveys that began to provide evidence challenging the long-term distinctiveness of Melanesians and Polynesians. The Californian anthropologist Edward W. Gifford, who had extensive salvage ethnographic experience working with Kroeber in California and W.C. McKern in Tonga, led archaeological expeditions to Fiji in 1947 and New Caledonia in 1952. Although explicitly searching for evidence of 'a succession of cultures' (Gifford, 1951, p. 189), this work instead established an early ceramic horizon across the region dating back some 2800 years. Jack Golson later synthesised these findings, comparing them to his own work in Samoa, and other evidence from the Bismarck Archipelago, to propose an early 'community of culture' (now known as Lapita) that crossed the Melanesia-Polynesia boundary in prehistory (Golson, 1961). As with his previous synthesis in New Zealand, this was an explicitly culture-historical formulation, where an archaeological culture was defined by the regular association of artefact traits: 'This community is expressed in terms of variants of the same pottery tradition and should logically, on the basis of discoveries in Samoa and observations on Tonga, be expressed in terms of adzes too' (Golson, 1961, p. 176). The archaeological relevance of ethnologically defined cultural areas was thus questioned, facilitating a shift towards mapping artefact-based cultural traditions with temporally unstable geographic boundaries.

Nevertheless, Golson accommodated the prevailing view that Polynesians and Melanesians were biologically distinct by proposing that the Lapita horizon was

'Ancestral to the historic Western Polynesian cultures' (p. 176) but antedated the arrival of Melanesians. In other words, the previous order of history was inverted (Clark, 2003) – a culture Ancestral to Polynesians first colonised the remote Pacific but was subsequently replaced as far east as Fiji by a second wave of 'Melanesian' migrants, here understood to be nearly equivalent to what the previous generation had called 'Papuans'. On the other hand, the discovery of Pleistocene-age archaeological sites in New Guinea and Australia subsequently reinforced the status of Papuans as the original inhabitants of that area, and hence the initially assumed order of arrival was preserved in the far western Pacific.

At first there was some expectation that the Lapita horizon might even constitute a Polynesian cultural package, the sites being 'transit camps' documenting a trail of rapid migration from southeast Asia to Tonga-Samoa, but it quickly became apparent that Lapita sites to the west lacked key Polynesian traits such as quadrangular cross-sectioned adzes (instead resembling 'Melanesian' forms). External Polynesian origins were thus unlikely, and by 1971 Les Groube was able to confidently state that Polynesian culture was an internal development in West Polynesia from a Lapita founding culture (Groube, 1971), a view that prevails to this day (see Kirch, Chapter 4).

Golson's definition of Lapita as a community of culture was subsequently further extended to include subsistence and settlement patterns (again by Green), and in this form came to be known as the 'Lapita Cultural Complex' (Green, 1982; Spriggs, 1984). Peter Bellwood formally linked this complex to a theory of an ethnolinguistic migration fuelled by the spread of Neolithic horticulture, whose signature was seen in the distribution of the Austronesian languages from Taiwan through Island Southeast Asia to Polynesia (e.g. Bellwood, 1984, pp. 113–14). These were people of 'Mongoloid' affinity, distinct from indigenous 'Australoid' and 'Negrito' hunter-gatherers already resident in New Guinea and Australia (Bellwood, 1980, p. 176). The ethnolinguistic model solidified the association of Lapita with Polynesian origins, and also reinforced expectations of post-Lapita population replacement as far as Fiji, to account for Island Melanesian ethnographic and racial characteristics. A ceramic signature of this migration was thought by many to be found in a putative pan-Melanesian 'incised and applied-relief tradition' of post-Lapita pottery (Spriggs, 1997; Bedford and Clark, 2001).

By this time, archaeology had firmly replaced earlier ethnological methods of establishing population origins and sociocultural anthropology turned to other problems, but the old divisions continued to influence both. At about the same time that archaeologists were questioning the temporal validity of the Polynesia-Melanesia boundary from a culture-historical perspective, Sahlins (1958; 1963) reframed its ethnographic significance as a contrast of evolutionary differences in political organisation. Polynesia was characterised by stratified chiefdoms, with institutionalised power established through the inheritance of office and rank. Regional variations constituted a series of historical transformations of a 'single genus' from an Ancestral source (Sahlins, 1958, p. ix). Melanesia, in contrast, was characterised by egalitarian big-man societies, where power resided in personal demonstration, and produced groupings resistant to integration. No sequence of historical transformation was postulated for the latter societies, since they were framed as belonging to an 'under-developed' or 'truncated' branch of social evolution. This, perhaps inadvertently, buttressed an image of Melanesia as a disparate collection of timeless, primitive societies, also promulgated by large numbers of highly localised Melanesian ethnographies produced in the wake of Malinowski (1922). Subsequent critiques of Sahlins's model focused less on its evolutionary framework than its regional accuracy, noting contradictory cases and suggesting that he had compared 'Polynesian ideology with Melanesian practice' (Douglas, 1979, p. 27).

Disassembling regions, unpacking culture

The diversity of Melanesia, and a feeling that geographic regions failed to encapsulate variant forms of social organisation, led to a growing sense among some sociocultural anthropologists that large-scale regional categories had outlived their utility. By the 1980s post-colonial critiques of evolutionary typologies and the generally ahistorical framing and primitivism of traditional ethnography coalesced into arguments that Melanesia was a particularly dubious category (Thomas, 1989). This was, of course, undermined somewhat by the subsequent prominence of Strathern's (1988) theoretical vision of Melanesia as a useful relational mirror for Euro-American thought practices, and indeed by newly independent post-colonial nation states adopting Melanesia as a unifying identity term (Lawson, 2013). Nevertheless, Roger Green organised these critiques in relation to archaeological data, arguing that 'Melanesia' should be disestablished as an analytical category because the region is not 'ethnographically, linguistically, or biologically tied together by any overwhelming or obviously unifying factors' (Green, 1991a, p. 499).

Green proposed instead the utilisation of a series of historically important bio-geographic boundaries to capture the basic structure of population history – a proposition that has much in common with culture-historical models but incorporates changing environmental relationships. The growing corpus of archaeological sites of Pleistocene age discovered in Australia, New Guinea and the Bismarck Archipelago had forced a consideration of the changing underlying biogeographical context of human occupation in the Pacific over the longer term. Green proposed that 'Ancient Near Oceania', located between the Huxley-Wallace Line and the eastern end of the Solomon Islands archipelago, captured a region of short water gaps and large continental islands first colonised '45,000 or more years ago by populations of *Homo sapiens*' (1991a, p. 496). 'Island Southeast Asia', 'Australia' and 'Modern Near Oceania' (i.e. New Guinea to the Solomon Islands) only became three distinct regions about 6000 years ago. The emergence or arrival of the Lapita cultural complex in the latter region over 3000 years ago exemplified a series of developments that 'at last allowed people to move from Modern Near Oceania into Remote Oceania' (p. 498) – the latter being the region beyond the Solomon Islands, whose colonisation required voyages out of sight of land. The Andesite Line, marking the edge of the Pacific Plate, was the final boundary, crossed only by Polynesians in the final phase of Pacific colonisation (Fig. 1.5).

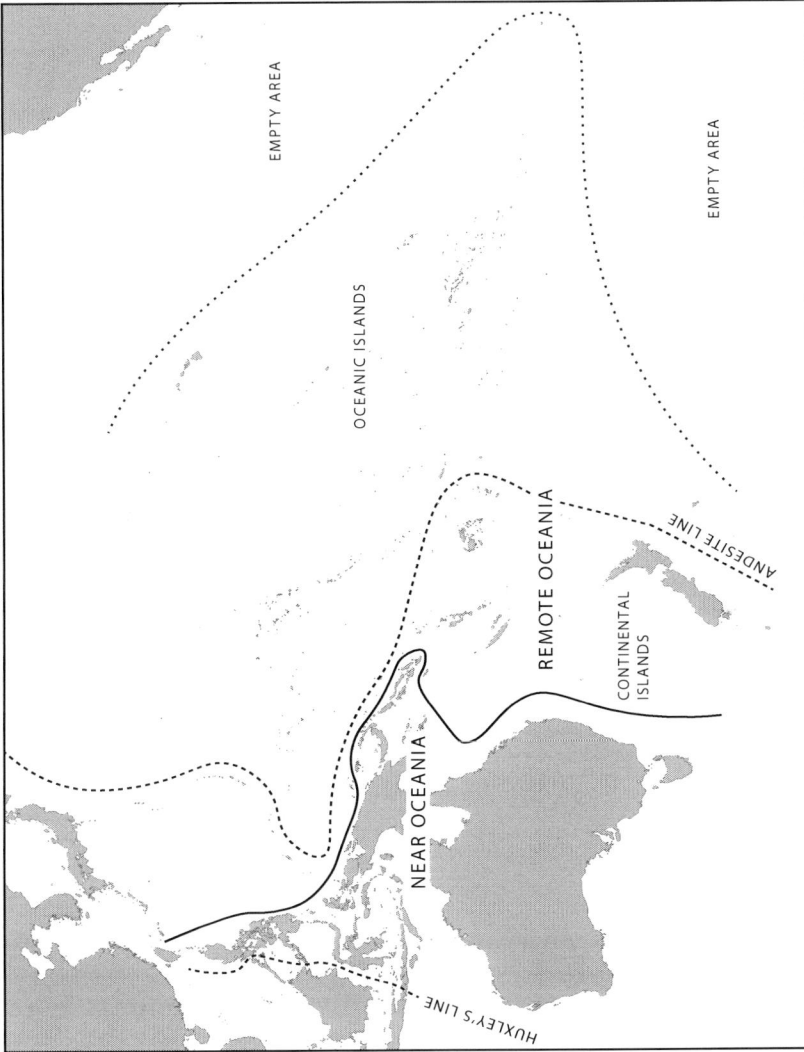

FIGURE 1.5 Near and Remote Oceania, as defined by Green (1991b).

Green's argument, often simplified as a contrast between Near and Remote Oceania, has been widely accepted by Pacific archaeologists due to its integration of environmental, geographic, cultural and chronological dimensions. Arguably though, it provided a replacement terminology more than a way of resolving underlying conceptual tensions in the Melanesia, Polynesia, Micronesia division. In particular, the colonisation of Ancient Near Oceania and the later colonisation of Remote Oceania could still be envisioned as the spatial layering of biologically, linguistically and culturally distinct populations – roughly corresponding to the ancestors of diverse Papuans and more homogeneous Polynesians (or non-Austronesians and Austronesians in linguistic terms) (Terrell et al., 2001).

Discomfort with the theoretical sufficiency, racial essentialism and progressivist implications of ethnolinguistic migration as an explanatory device (Terrell, 1986) provoked considerable debate in the 1980s and 1990s. Debate focused on the issue of whether the archaeological record of Lapita could be derived from earlier sequences in the New Guinea/Bismarcks region, or whether it mostly represented an immigrant Southeast Asian population with a 'Neolithic' culture (Allen, 1984; Allen and White, 1989; Terrell and Welsch, 1997). The discovery of an independent centre of agriculture in New Guinea (see Denham, Chapter 10), evidence of pre-Lapita voyaging and lithic exchange, amongst other things, encouraged arguments that Lapita may have been an indigenous development, or at least the product of a complex assortment of influences and acquisitions over the long term rather than a single introduced package. The acquisition of Lapita pottery was perhaps just the 'barium meal' that made this long-term assembly at last visible as a cultural complex (Allen and White, 1989, p. 142).

Connected to, and recapitulating, wider debates about the mechanisms of Neolithic transitions worldwide (Bellwood, 2004; Robb, 2013), the Lapita case provoked a similar diversification of models. Green (1991b) himself proposed a compromise solution that disaggregated components of the cultural complex into elements: those *introduced* by migrants from Southeast Asia; those *integrated* with pre-existing cultures in the Bismarck Archipelago; and those locally *innovated* during cultural interaction and development (a 'Triple-I' model). More-or-less attenuated views of the package-like character of Lapita were subsequently proposed (Spriggs, 1997). One recent review suggests Lapita cultural elements were introduced by the 'constant movement of people and goods between communities for a range of purposes and of varying duration and distance without necessarily involving permanent residential relocations' (Specht et al., 2014, p. 92). These alternative explanatory strategies extended to other cases. Bedford and Clark (2001) for example, mounted a similar argument against the proposed post-Lapita 'Melanesianising' migration associated with the incised and applied-relief tradition. Clark (2003) suggests that post-Lapita diversity in Island Melanesia was the product of a complex set of economic and political interactions and gene-flow, rather than a migratory wave. Bedford and Spriggs (2018) similarly argue for a continuing process of long-distance interaction rather than a simple dispersal event.

These critiques thus established a contrast between culture-historical models of migration and ethnolinguistic replacement, and models of cultural assembly by way of social interaction and diffusion. Insofar as the latter models accommodate any degree of migration (such as in Green's Triple-I model), they resemble the arguments of W.H.R. Rivers noted above. However, more strident variants seek to avoid the use of migration as an explanatory device at all and try to work around any classificatory need for talk of 'peoples', 'populations' or ethnolinguistic groups (Terrell, 2018). For this reason, they usually avoid incorporating, or attempting to explain, extant distributions of language and biological variation. Specht et al. (2014, p. 119) for example, explicitly exclude consideration of historical linguistics and human genetics from their argument that Lapita did not comprise a unified package, on the grounds that these information sources lack the chronological precision of archaeological data. It is also a conservative strategy, because while there is general acceptance amongst Pacific archaeologists of the Boasian argument that biology, language and culture may not track the same scale or pattern of population history (e.g. Bellwood, 2013, p. 18), in practice taxonomies constructed for these have traditionally been co-dependent. Archaeologists, historical linguists and population geneticists routinely reconsider interpretations in light of new arguments in their counterpart disciplines (e.g. Walworth, 2014; Bedford et al., 2018). As Kirch and Green's (2001, p. 42) 'triangulation' method implies, archaeological, linguistic and genetic data, despite having different 'polygons of error', are viewed as the fossil traces of the same coherent history involving aggregates of culture, language and biology. In contrast, restricting discussion to purely archaeological evidence is to imply that we should model culture as an assembly of changing 'practices', with their own histories irrespective of the genetic or linguistic heritage of the people engaged therein. Communities of practice emerge from co-involvement and investment in the ontological salience and efficacy of various available ideas and technologies, and it is such communities that produce the enduring spatiotemporal patterns of the archaeological record (Thomas, 2009).

These implications are underdeveloped however, and studies that simply trace the diverse origins of various practices or traits do not preclude their assembly occurring alongside or within the context of migration. Theoretical specification of the causal nexus and archaeological signature of the various sociocultural processes by which traits can be disseminated or brought together has never been properly refined in the Pacific. In the absence of better theorised alternatives many Pacific archaeologists still favour ethnolinguistic group migration as a valid way of characterising the Lapita phenomenon (Kirch, 2017, pp. 78–81). Migration fits within the inherited episteme described in the above historical overview, where change is thought of as transformational rather than a process of incremental sorting (see Cochrane, Chapter 3). Island geographies with long water-gaps perhaps encourage such explanations because islands can be envisaged as natural objects with relatively bounded populations whose occupancy was achieved via distinct founding events (particularly in the remote Pacific/Polynesia). This notion of boundedness in turn encourages the possibility of population replacement. But it is here that the mode of explanation betrays the more dubious aspects of its inheritance and reveals its conceptual limits.

In a recent genomic study of the population history of Vanuatu, for example, Posth et al., (2018) describe a gradual genetic shift through time from a Lapita founding population with mostly 'East Asian' genetic ancestry (Austronesian) to a contemporary population with mostly 'Near Oceanian' genetic ancestry (Papuan). But, despite this being an 'extended and incremental process' involving probably small numbers of mostly men, and no major linguistic change, it is still referred to as a 'population replacement' and a 'massive demographic change' in which 'Oceanic speaking Lapita peoples were genetically replaced by a population closely related to Papuan-speaking Baining people'. In a subsequent debate forum on the findings, archaeologists displayed corresponding confusion over the results and expressed concerns about the political implications of the notion of replacement in the context of post-colonial politics (Bedford et al., 2018). In reply, Posth et al. (2019) reaffirmed the complexity of the incremental process they envisage, but also noted that it had singular cultural effects in terms of the introduction of head binding, penis sheaths and other characteristically 'Papuan' cultural elements to Vanuatu. They reach the limits of their conceptual terminology when they envisage a 'dual or multiple-stranded heritage' for contemporary Vanuatu people but insist 'replacement' is the most appropriate descriptor (2019, p. 60).

These debates arise out of an awareness of the problematic history of theories of population origins in the Pacific, and the enduring colonial obsession with establishing the genealogy, and hence precedence, of ethno-biological groupings. Insofar as geneticists adopt the language, categories and conceptual models of this history, they inherit its problems, and potentially blur distinctions between the unique character of their own data and older biological classifications. But archaeologists in the region have also only just begun to turn from mapping the origins of categorical populations to theorising the many sociocultural processes by which people and things came to be distributed. Unlike those working in continental settings, island archaeologists cannot do without some model of human dispersal, but origin narratives, as we have seen, tend to conflate the empirical fact of migration with its role in explanation. One way of avoiding the problematic political consequences and cultural loading of such conflations is to resist fitting new data to old narratives and instead use it to create new theory. We might also reframe the political aspects of origin narratives as part of the object of study: if migration and the ways people establish ties to place are seen as components of the broader phenomenon of colonisation, their political consequences can be incorporated as part of the domain requiring explanation (see Thomas, Chapter 7). Nevertheless, only a closer study of the processes and practices of migration, mobility, interaction and the dissemination or adoption of culture will facilitate better theorisation of what we take to be meant by a complex, multiple-stranded heritage.

Regional abstractions

The ongoing involvement of archaeologists in debates about population relationships in the Pacific has contributed to a growing sensitivity to the effects of our regional abstractions – and particularly biases introduced by regionally bound thinking (e.g. Flexner et al., 2019). There is perhaps less awareness of how classificatory regions and places are produced via processes of reciprocal theory generation and practical application. Debates about the relative role of ethnolinguistic migration versus long-term cultural assembly, for example, have been framed as an empirical question of Lapita origins in the western Pacific. Polynesia has largely remained isolated from these debates, and a model of ethnolinguistic migration and adaptive radiation has never been seriously threatened there. The regional Melanesia-Polynesia contrast is thus rewritten in contrasting theoretical models for how cultural diversity is generated. While archaeologists today typically state that they now use the terms Melanesia, Polynesia and Micronesia to simply describe convenient geographic regions rather than to imply anything about ethnolinguistic groups (Kirch, 2017, p. 4), in fact it is still very common to organise research using these categories (Rainbird, 2004; Spriggs, 1997; Leclerc and Flexner, 2019). Irrespective of these terms being 'merely' geographic descriptors the effect is to encircle abstract populations with coherent, if not distinct, histories – whatever boundaries were crossed in the past, the story always ends up in the same place. Spriggs (2019, p. 9) finds an essential narrative similarity between *Kulturkreis* archaeologist/ethnologist Heine-Geldern's (1932) account of Austronesian migrations and Bellwood's (2017) recent survey, suggesting that the concepts underlying master narratives remain much the same. His advice that we need to be more self-conscious about the inherited ways archaeology creates its objects and puts them into relationships is well taken. Contributors to this book explore a variety of ways that this can be done.

Book structure

In Chapter 2, Leppard and Fitzpatrick review the role of the Pacific in the wider field of global island archaeology, where islands have been seen as uniquely productive contexts for the study of human behaviour, diversity and relationships with the environment. As noted above, Pacific exploration encouraged a view of islands as natural laboratories for the investigation of humanity's past. This was given systematic significance after the work of Charles Darwin in the Galápagos Islands and Alfred Russel Wallace in Indonesia and Malaysia, where insularity provided the necessary context to refine evolutionary theory and biogeography. Later, zoologists such as A.C. Haddon, who had embarked on field expeditions to the Pacific to collect specimens and find evidence of intermediate species change, turned to the study of human populations in the region, modelling ethnographic work on the methods of the field naturalist (Kuklick, 1994; 1996). From this point on, Pacific islands became the epitome target of anthropology, providing myriad 'experiments in cultural adaptation and evolutionary development' (Sahlins, 1963, p. 285), where each culture could be theorised as illustrating 'species variations within the genus' (Sahlins, 1957, p. 291).

Like diffusionism, evolutionary theory was thus native to anthropological study in the Pacific, and its re-emergence in the school of cultural ecology exemplified by the early work of Sahlins was a key inspiration for American-trained archaeologists working in the region. Cochrane (Chapter 3), reviews this history from its early roots in unilineal progressivist models, through a late 20th-century focus on processes of adaptation, to more recent selectionist archaeologies. The Pacific, and Polynesia particularly, has been a testing-ground for differences of explanatory approach between the latter two strains of evolutionary archaeology. Patrick Kirch and Roger Green refined the adaptationist approach, identifying mechanisms of cultural change such as colonisation, adaptation to changing environments, development of intensive production and social conflict and competition (e.g. Kirch, 1984). In Chapter 4, Kirch reviews and reflects on the theoretical foundations of this work and justifies its phylogenetic, or branching tree-like, view of cultural radiation and network decay. In contrast, the selectionist school repudiates 'intentional' or Lamarckian causes of cultural change, believing instead that change occurs as cultural traits are sorted according to their differential performance characteristics by higher-scale non-intentional processes. This strand of evolutionary theory draws inspiration from the work of Robert Dunnell (1980), and several of his students (and their students in turn) have carried out research programmes in the Pacific.

Phylogenetic models of cultural variation require some mechanism of population division and isolation in order to create and sustain branching cultural traditions. Island colonisation sequences provide branching events, while island boundedness and separation provide conditions of isolation. But were island societies ever insular? A highly influential paper by Epeli Hau'ofa (1993) proposed a locally conceived alternative: instead of tiny islands isolated by a vast ocean, he suggested a sea-oriented vision of Oceania composed of historically inflected island networks integrated by trading and cultural exchange systems. Archaeologists, particularly those working in Near Oceania, found that this networked model of 'seascapes' (Gosden and Pavlides, 1994) resonated with arguments that interaction, rather than isolation, is the fundamental dimension of social life in the Pacific (Terrell et al., 1997). Interaction was believed to thwart our ability to conceptualise history as a family tree, with cultural exchange producing an entangled or 'reticulate' network of relations, growing like a strangler fig occluding the branches of its host. Golitko (Chapter 5) discusses this debate, providing an overview of how network analysis and theory can contribute to understanding interaction systems, and finds that these can help us cast off some colonial baggage. Szabo and colleagues (Chapter 6), discuss patterns of interaction and polythetic assemblage relationships in the Circum-New Guinea region, similarly challenging the notion of cultural packages and exploring the limits of bounded geographical thinking.

Debates over the application of phylogenetic and network models to the Pacific past have tended to frame this as an empirical problem, where fidelity of dataset to model is a test for deciding whether branching or interaction had the greatest historical influence. Such approaches are often equivocal because both processes will usually have a proximity structure (i.e. nearby groups will be more similar due to recent branching or frequent interaction) and so geographically patterned data will tend to make equal sense in either model. Viewed as a dualistic alternative the contrast produces a problem of anthropological indeterminacy, where populations have either history or relations, but these cannot be seen at the same time. Newer phylogenetic-network methods attempt to avoid this problem but continue under the same data-fitting programme (Cochrane and Lipo, 2010).

Underlying such patterns, however, are long-term human–environment relationships, the dimensions of which can be understood from a variety of theoretical perspectives. In Chapter 7, Thomas reviews theoretical approaches to island colonisation that do not study it as a simple branching event in population history, but rather as a longer-term process that can be examined at different scales – from the broad factors governing the pacing and direction of range shifts, to the finer-grained social, economic and political dimensions of spatial organisation and place-making. Such a perspective takes migration away from its role as the explanatory agent in genealogical history and reframes it as a component of landscape production.

Colonisation is also about power, and control over place. Sahlins's cultural ecology of political organisation in the Pacific is again relevant here, in that it inspired archaeological investigations of the emergence of social stratification (Kirch, 1984; Earle, 1997). Spriggs (Chapter 8), Flexner (Chapter 9) and Denham (Chapter 10), address different aspects of the theoretical legacy of European thinking about power, inequality and the evolutionary ranking of Pacific societies. Spriggs refines an enduring Marxist approach to political economy, discussing the role of prestige practices in creating avenues for the emergence of inequality. Flexner discusses recent anarchist perspectives on the role of resistance to power in creating 'societies against the state'. This reformulates the unilineal image of acephalous Melanesian societies as truncated or somehow blocked from achieving more complex organisations, as an intentional resistance to domination. Denham rethinks teleological models that link the inception of agriculture to increasing socio-political hierarchy, drawing on research in New Guinea where egalitarian societies prevail. Rather than utilise higher-level abstractions like 'domestication' which bundle assumptions about sedentism, complexity and ecology, Denham suggests instead a theorisation of 'agricultural practices' as our best way of avoiding teleology.

An early question in Pacific archaeology was whether political entities corresponding to the units identified by ethnographers, such as 'tribes' or 'chiefdoms', could be identified. Settlement pattern archaeology was the main theoretical framework for such work. In New Zealand, archaeologists working in the wake of Roger Green's early settlement pattern studies grew increasingly sceptical that this was possible. Māori society was not neatly divided into parcels, but rather comprised a mosaic of local groups who variously coalesced and split, producing a time-averaged record of sites with multiple occupations and uses (Allen, 1996; Holdaway, 2004). In tropical Polynesia, however, the existence of above-ground architectural stonework features was seen to provide a more fixed record facilitating structural inferences (Weisler and Kirch, 1985). Archaeologists in Melanesia have theorised a midway position in which the architectural record is viewed as the temporally emergent product of underlying ontologies and practices (Thomas, 2014b). Kahn, in Chapter 11, discusses settlement pattern approaches to political stratification in the Society Islands, finding direct correspondences between ethnohistorical accounts and archaeological data, but also envisaging a process in which architecture is involved in the reworking of social structure, rather than being simply its product.

At this scale a finer-grained social archaeology positioned between the interests of ethnography and archaeology becomes possible. Van Gilder (Chapter 12) considers the history and potential for an archaeology of gender in the Pacific. Utilising a rich, late period, archaeological record of household level spatial organisation in Hawai'i, she traces gender-based patterns in foodways and task differentiation to critique the projection of post-colonial assumptions and assumed norms into the past.

Social archaeology in the Pacific is enhanced by the availability of the ethnohistorical record, although archaeologists have debated its utility. Sheppard (Chapter 13) reviews these debates and identifies how archaeologists have framed the relationship between indigenous oral histories and archaeological data, as well as the role of other ethnographic materials in archaeological interpretation. In light of the use of Pacific ethnography for analogical purposes by archaeologists in Europe and elsewhere, it is interesting to note that Pacific archaeologists rarely deploy explicit cross-regional analogies, favouring relatively close temporal and cultural associations. One reason is that the period of European contact is usually conceived of as the 'ethnographic endpoint' (Kirch, 1984, p. 6) or culmination of island sequences, and hence is a developmental target rather than a model for the past. Nevertheless, implicit ethnographic analogy permeates archaeological understandings of food productions systems, fishing practices, artefact function and settlement patterns in the Pacific.

Oral histories have often been regarded as more problematic, referring to a culturally constructed past essentially distinct from the archaeological past. This argument distances the interests of archaeologists from those of local descendant communities. In contrast, recent explorations of the intersection of oral history and archaeology (Kirch, 2018) have opened space for community-driven archaeological practice, and a role for indigenous archaeology (O'Regan, 2010; Mills and Kawelu, 2013; Kawelu, 2014; Phillips and Allen, 2016). Although the role of Pasifika people in archaeological research has a long practical history increasingly acknowledged in co-authorship and processes of community consultation, there has been less explicit exploration of a role for indigenous theory in archaeology. While ethnographically translated Pacific concepts have made their way into archaeology (e.g. 'Melanesian relationality', *mana, tapu*), this is mostly limited to specific cases of interpretation. But true parity will not be achieved without 'bringing local conceptualizations into archaeological practice in ways that guide interpretation at a theoretical level' (Lilley, 2009, p. 49).

Drawing on recent New Zealand Māori scholarship and attempts to forge decolonised methodologies in the broader social sciences, Marshall (Chapter 14) takes a core Polynesian concept, *whakapapa*, and examines how it may be deployed in the role of theory in an archaeological context. Indigenous theories often resonate with Western theories and, because of this, are often absorbed by existing concepts (e.g. *whakapapa* vs. genealogy). Taking indigenous theory seriously entails refusing this strategy and instead exploring aspects that cannot be encompassed. Marshall contrasts *whakapapa* to the genealogical and evolutionary concepts so pervasive in archaeological thinking about the Pacific and finds therein an alternative way of theorising phenomena. The practical ontology of *whakapapa* directs attention away from the simple object categories of culture history, towards a more relationally focused social archaeology.

The future of theory in Pacific archaeology may well lie in this more explicitly cosmopolitan approach, drawing together places, contexts and ideas from a variety of sources, and putting these into productive contrast. This is not the same thing as 'applying' local ideas to the archaeological record, or even holding these up as exemplars of alterity to reveal the limits of Western conceptions. Rather it is about producing new forms of theory during transformative encounters. Instead of making new data tread old paths this may yet create new versions of theory in the Pacific, and new versions of the Pacific in theory.

References

Allen, H., 1996. Horde and hapu: The reification of kinship and residence in prehistoric Aboriginal and Māori settlement organisation. In: J. Davidson, G. Irwin, B.F. Leach, A. Pawley and D. Brown, eds. *Oceanic Culture History: Essays in Honour of Roger Green*. Dunedin: New Zealand Journal of Archaeology, pp. 657–674.

Allen, J., 1984. In search of the Lapita homeland: reconstructing the prehistory of the Bismarck Archipelago. *Journal of Pacific History*, 19(4), pp. 186–201.

Allen, J. and White, J.P., 1989. The Lapita homeland: some new data and an interpretation. *Journal of the Polynesian Society*, 98(2), pp. 129–46.

Bahn, P.G. and Flenley, J.R., 1992. *Easter Island, Earth Island*. London: Thames & Hudson.

Ballard, C., 2006. Strange alliance: pygmies in the colonial imaginary. *World Archaeology*, 38(1), pp. 133–151.

Ballard, C., 2008. 'Oceanic Negroes': British anthropology of Papuans, 1820–1869. In: C. Ballard and B. Douglas, eds. *Foreign Bodies, Oceania and the Science of Race 1750–1940*. Canberra: ANU Press, pp. 157–202.

Barber, I., 1995. Constructions of change: a history of early Maori culture sequences. *Journal of the Polynesian Society*, 104(4), pp. 357–396.

Beaglehole, J.C., 1962. *The Endeavour Journal of Joseph Banks, 1768–1771*. Sydney: Trustees of the Public Library of New South Wales in association with Angus & Robertson.

Bedford, S., Blust, R., Burley, D.V., Cox, M., Kirch, P.V., Matisoo-Smith, E., Naess, Å., Pawley, A., Sand, C. and Sheppard, P., 2018. Ancient DNA and its contribution to understanding the human history of the Pacific Islands. *Archaeology in Oceania*, 53(3), pp. 205–219.

Bedford, S. and Clark, G., 2001. The rise and rise of the incised and applied relief tradition: a review and reassessment. In: G.R. Clark, A. Anderson and T. Vunidilo, eds. *The Archaeology of Lapita Dispersal in Oceania: Papers from the Fourth Lapita Conference, June 2000*, Canberra, Australia . Canberra: Pandanus Books, pp. 61–74.

Bedford, S. and Spriggs, M., 2018. The archaeology of Vanuatu: 3,000 years of history across islands of ash and coral. In: E. Cochrane and T.L. Hunt, eds. *The Oxford Handbook of Prehistoric Oceania*. Oxford: Oxford University Press, pp. 162–184.

Bellwood, P., 1980. The peopling of the Pacific. *Scientific American*, 243(5), pp. 174–185.

Bellwood, P., 1984. A hypothesis for Austronesian origins. *Asian Perspectives*, 26(1), pp. 107–117.

Bellwood, P., 2004. *First Farmers: The Origins of Agricultural Societies*. Malden, MA: Wiley-Blackwell.

Bellwood, P., 2013. *First Migrants: Ancient Migration in Global Perspective*. Malden, MA: Wiley-Blackwell.

Bellwood, P., 2017. *First Islanders: Prehistory and Human Migration in Island Southeast Asia*. Oxford: Wiley-Blackwell.

Best, E., 1909. Art. LII. – Maori Forest Lore: Being some Account of Native Forest Lore and Woodcraft, as also of many Myths, Rites, Customs, and Superstitions connected with the Flora and Fauna of the Tuhoe or Urewera District. Part III. *Transactions and Proceedings of the New Zealand Institute*, 42, pp. 433–481.

Binford, L.R., 1972. *An Archaeological Perspective*. New York; London: Seminar Press.

Binford, L.R., 1987. Data, relativism and archaeological science. *Man*, 22(3), pp. 391–404.

Bintliff, J., 2011. The death of archaeological theory? In: J. Bintliff and M. Pearce, eds. *The Death of Archaeological Theory?* Oxford: Oxbow Books, pp. 7–22.

Boas, F., 1901. The mind of primitive man. *Journal of American Folklore*, 14(52), pp. 1–11.

Buck, P.H., 1938. *Vikings of the Sunrise*. New York: F.A. Stokes Co.

Bull, A., 1989. *The Otaki-Maori Racing Club: A History 1886–1990*. Otaki: Otaki-Maori Racing Club.

Chapman, J., 2000. *Fragmentation in Archaeology: People, Places, and Broken Objects in the Prehistory of South-Eastern Europe*. London: Routledge.

Clark, G., 2003. Shards of meaning: archaeology and the Melanesia-Polynesia divide. *Journal of Pacific History*, 38(2), pp. 197–215.

Clarke, D.L., 1968. *Analytical Archaeology*. London: Methuen.

Clarke, D.L., 1979. *Analytical Archaeologist: Collected Papers of David L. Clarke*. London: Academic Press.

Cochrane, E.E. and Lipo, C.P., 2010. Phylogenetic analyses of Lapita decoration do not support branching evolution or regional population structure during colonization of Remote Oceania. *Philosophical Transactions of the Royal Society B: Biological Sciences*, 365(1559), pp. 3889–3902.

Codrington, R.H., 1891. *The Melanesians: Studies in their Anthropology and Folklore*. Oxford: Clarendon Press.

Douglas, B., 1979. Rank, power, authority: a reassessment of traditional leadership in South Pacific societies. *Journal of Pacific History*, 14(1), pp. 2–27.

Douglas, B., 2008. Climate to crania: science and the racialization of human difference. In: B. Douglas and C. Ballard, eds. *Foreign Bodies, Oceania and the Science of Race 1750–1940*. Canberra: ANU Press, pp. 33–96.

Douglas, B., 2010. Terra Australis to Oceania. *Journal of Pacific History*, 45(2), pp. 179–210.

Douglas, B., 2015. Agency, affect, and local knowledge in the exploration of Oceania. In: S. Konishi, M. Nugent and T. Shellam, eds. *Indigenous Intermediaries, New Perspectives on Exploration Archives*. Canberra: ANU Press, pp. 103–130.

Duff, R., 1956. *The Moa-Hunter Period of Maori Culture*. 2nd edition. Wellington: NZ Government Printer.

Duff, R., 1959. Neolithic adzes of Eastern Polynesia. In: J. D. Freeman and W. R. Geddes, eds. *Anthropology in the South Seas: Essays Presented to H.D. Skinner*. New Plymouth: Thomas Avery & Sons, pp. 121–147.

Dunnell, R.C., 1980. Evolutionary theory and archaeology. *Advances in Archaeological Method and Theory*, 3, pp. 35–99.

Dumont d'Urville, J.-S.-C., 1830. *Voyage de la corvette l'Astrolabe exécuté par ordre du roi, pendant les années 1826-1827-1828-1829*. Paris: J. Tastu.

Earle, T., 1997. *How Chiefs Come to Power: The Political Economy in Prehistory*. Stanford, CA: Stanford University Press.

Earle, T. and Spriggs, M., 2015. Political economy in prehistory: a Marxist approach to Pacific sequences. *Current Anthropology*, 56(4), pp. 515–544.

Englund, H. and Yarrow, T., 2013. The place of theory: rights, networks, and ethnographic comparison. *Social Analysis: The International Journal of Social and Cultural Practice*, 57(3), pp. 132–149.

Fahlander, F., 2018. Book review: Oliver J.T. Harris and Craig Cipolla. *Archaeological Theory in the New Millennium: Introducing Current Perspectives*. *European Journal of Archaeology*, 21(4), pp. 640–643.

Forster, J.R., 1778. *Observations Made During a Voyage Round the World: On Physical Geography, Natural History, and Ethnic Philosophy*. London: G. Robinson.

Fowler, C., 2001. Personhood and social relations in the British Neolithic with a study from the Isle of Man. *Journal of Material Culture*, 6(2), pp. 137–163.

Fowler, C., 2004. *The Archaeology of Personhood: An Anthropological Approach*. London: Routledge.

Gardner, H., 2008. The origin of kinship in Oceania: Lewis Henry Morgan and Lorimer Fison. *Oceania*, 78(2), pp. 137–150.

Gregory, C., 1982. *Gifts and Commodities*. London: Academic Press

Gell, A., 1999. Strathernograms, or, the semiotics of mixed metaphors. In: A. Gell and E. Hirsch, eds. *The Art of Anthropology: Essays and Diagrams*. London: Althone Press, pp. 29–75.

Gifford, E.W., 1951. *Archaeological Excavations in Fiji*. Berkeley, CA: University of California Press.

Golson, J., 1959. Culture change in prehistoric New Zealand. In: J. D. Freeman and W. R. Geddes, eds. *Anthropology in the South Seas: Essays Presented to H.D. Skinner*. New Plymouth: Thomas Avery & Sons, pp. 29–74.

Golson, J., 1960. Archaeology, tradition, and myth in New Zealand prehistory. *Journal of the Polynesian Society*, 69(4), pp. 380–402.

Golson, J., 1961. D. Report on New Zealand, Western Polynesia, New Caledonia, and Fiji. *Asian Perspectives*, 5(2), pp. 166–180.

Golson, J., 1986. Old guards and new waves: reflections on antipodean archaeology 1954–1975. *Archaeology in Oceania*, 21(1), pp. 2–12.

Gosden, C. and Pavlides, C., 1994. Are islands insular? Landscape vs. seascape in the case of the Arawe Islands, Papua New Guinea. *Archaeology in Oceania*, 29(3), pp. 162–171.

Graebner, F., 1905. Kulturkreise und Kulturschichten in Ozeanien. *Zeitschrift für Ethnologie*, 37(1), pp. 28–53.

Green, R.C., 1963. *A Review of the Prehistoric Sequence of the Auckland Province*. Auckland: New Zealand Archaeological Association.

Green, R.C., 1982. Models for the Lapita cultural complex: an evaluation of some current proposals. *New Zealand Journal of Archaeology*, 4(1), pp. 7–19.

Green, R.C., 1991a. The Lapita cultural complex: current evidence and proposed models. In: P. Bellwood, ed. *Indo-Pacific Prehistory 1990: Proceedings for the 14th Congress of the Indo-Pacific Prehistory Association*. Canberra: Indo Pacific Prehistory Association, pp. 295–305.

Green, R.C., 1991b. Near and Remote Oceania – disestablishing 'Melanesia' in culture history. In: A. Pawley, ed. *Man and a Half: Essays in Pacific Anthropology and Ethnobiology in Honour of Ralph Bulmer*. Auckland: Polynesian Society, pp. 491–502.

Groube, L.M., 1971. Tonga, Lapita pottery, and Polynesian origins. *Journal of the Polynesian Society*, 80(3), pp. 278–316.

Grove, R.H., 1996. *Green Imperialism: Colonial Expansion, Tropical Island Edens and the Origins of Environmentalism, 1600–1860.* Cambridge: Cambridge University Press.

Haast, J., 1871. Moas and moahunters. Address to the Philosophical Institute of Canterbury. *Transactions and Proceedings of the New Zealand Institute*, 4, pp. 66–107.

Haast, J., 1874. Researches and excavations carried on in and near the Moa-bone Point Cave, Sumner Road, in the year 1872. *Transactions and Proceedings of the New Zealand Institute*, 7, pp. 91–98.

Haddon, A.C., 1909. *The Races of Man and their Distribution*. London: Milner.

Harris, O.J.T. and Cipolla, C., 2017. *Archaeological Theory in the New Millennium: Introducing Current Perspectives*. London: Routledge.

Harrison, C.E., 2012. Replotting the ethnographic romance: revolutionary Frenchmen in the Pacific, 1768–1804. *Journal of the History of Sexuality*, 21(1), pp. 39–59.

Hau'ofa, E., 1993. Our sea of islands. In: E. Waddell, V. Naidu, and E. Hau'ofa, eds. *A New Oceania: Rediscovering our Sea of Islands*, Suva, Fiji: School of Social and Economic Development, University of the South Pacific, pp. 2–16.

Hawkesworth, J., 1773. *An account of the voyages undertaken by the order of His present Majesty for making discoveries in the Southern Hemisphere, and successively performed by Commodore Byron, Captain Wallis, Captain Carteret, and Captain Cook, in the Dolphin, the Swallow, and the Endeavour: drawn up from the journals which were kept by the several commanders, and from the papers of Joseph Banks, esq.* London: Printed for W. Strahan & T. Cadell.

Heine-Geldern, R., 1932. Urheimat und früheste wanderungen der Austronesier. *Anthropos*, 27(3/4), pp. 543–619.

Hirsch, E., 2014. Melanesian ethnography and the comparative project of anthropology: reflection on Strathern's analogical approach. *Theory, Culture and Society*, 31(2–3), pp. 39–64.

Hodder, I., 1982. *Symbols in Action: Ethnoarchaeological Studies of Material Culture*. Cambridge: Cambridge University Press.

Hodder, I., 2012a. Introduction: contemporary theoretical debate in archaeology. In: I. Hodder, ed. *Archaeological Theory Today*. Cambridge: Polity Press, pp. 1–14.

Hodder, I., 2012b. *Entangled: An Archaeology of the Relationships between Humans and Things*. Malden, MA: Wiley-Blackwell.

Holdaway, S., 2004. Theory: aspect and phase. In: S.J. Holdaway and L. Furey, eds. *Change through Time: 50 Years of New Zealand Archaeology*. Auckland: New Zealand Archaeological Association, pp. 9–28.

Howe, K.R., 2003. *The Quest for Origins: Who First Discovered and Settled New Zealand the Pacific Islands?* Honolulu: University of Hawaii Press.

Ingold, T., 2000. *The Perception of the Environment: Essays in Livelihood, Dwelling and Skill*. London: Routledge.

Jack-Hinton, C., 1969. *The Search for the Islands of Solomon 1567–1838*. Oxford: Clarendon Press.

Johnson, M., 2006. *Archaeological Theory: An Introduction*. Chichester: John Wiley & Sons.

Jones, A., 2005. Lives in fragments? Personhood and the European Neolithic. *Journal of Social Archaeology*, 5(2), pp. 193–224.

Kawelu, K., 2014. In their own voices: contemporary native Hawaiian and archaeological narratives about Hawaiian archaeology. *The Contemporary Pacific*, 26(1), pp. 31–62.

Kirch, P.V., 1984. *The Evolution of the Polynesian Chiefdoms*. Cambridge: Cambridge University Press.

Kirch, P.V., 2017. *On the Road of the Winds: An Archaeological History of the Pacific Islands before European Contact*. 2nd edition. Berkeley, CA: University of California Press.

Kirch, P.V., 2018. Voices on the wind, traces in the earth: integrating oral narrative and archaeology in Polynesian history. *Journal of the Polynesian Society*, 127(3), pp. 275–306.

Kirch, P.V. and Green, R.C., 2001. *Hawaiki, Ancestral Polynesia: An Essay in Historical Anthropology*. Cambridge: Cambridge University Press.

Kuklick, H., 1994. The color blue: from research in the Torres Strait to an ecology of human behavior. In: R.M. MacLeod and P.F. Rehbock, eds. *Darwin's Laboratory: Evolutionary Theory and Natural History in the Pacific*. Honolulu: University of Hawaii Press, pp. 339–366.

Kuklick, H., 1996. Islands in the Pacific: Darwinian biogeography and British anthropology. *American Ethnologist*, 23(3), pp. 611–638.

Lansdown, R., 2006. *Strangers in the South Seas: The Idea of the Pacific in Western Thought: An Anthology*. Honolulu: University of Hawaii Press.

Latour, B., 1993. *We Have Never Been Modern*. Cambridge, MA: Harvard University Press.

Lawson, S., 2013. 'Melanesia' the history and politics of an idea. *Journal of Pacific History*, 48(1), pp. 1–22.

Leclerc, M. and Flexner, J., 2019. *Archaeologies of Island Melanesia: Current Approaches to Landscapes, Exchange and Practice*. Canberra: ANU Press.

Lilley, I., 2009. Strangers and brothers? Heritage, human rights, and cosmopolitan archaeology in Oceania. In: L. Meskell, ed. *Cosmopolitan Archaeologies*. Durham, NC: Duke University Press, pp. 48–67.

Lozny, L.R. ed., 2011. *Comparative Archaeologies: A Sociological View of the Science of the Past*. New York: Springer-Verlag.

Lucas, G., 2015. The mobility of theory. *Current Swedish Archaeology*, 23, pp. 13–31.

MacEachern, S., 1996. Foreign countries: the development of ethnoarchaeology in sub-Saharan Africa. *Journal of World Prehistory*, 10(3), pp. 243–304.

Malinowski, B., 1922. *Argonauts of the Western Pacific*. London: George Routledge & Sons.

Mauss, M., 1990 [1925]. *The Gift: The Form and Reason for Exchange in Archaic Societies*. London: W.W. Norton.

McKay, A., 1874. On the identity of the Moa-hunters with the present Maori race. *Transactions and Proceedings of the New Zealand Institute*, 7, pp. 98–105.

Meskell, L., 2009. Introduction: cosmopolitan heritage ethics. In: L. Meskell, ed. *Cosmopolitan Archaeologies*. Durham, NC: Duke University Press, pp. 1–27.

Mills, P.R. and Kawelu, K.L., 2013. Decolonizing heritage management in Hawai'i. *Advances in Anthropology*, 3(3), pp. 127–132.

Moore, H.L., 2004. Global anxieties: concept-metaphors and pre-theoretical commitments in anthropology. *Anthropological Theory*, 4(1), pp. 71–88.

O'Regan, G., 2010. Working for my own. In: G. Nicholas, ed. *Being and Becoming Indigenous Archaeologists*. Walnut Creek, CA: Left Coast Press, pp. 235–245.

Pétursdóttir, Þ. and Olsen, B., 2018. Theory adrift: the matter of archaeological theorizing. *Journal of Social Archaeology*, 18(1), pp. 97–117.

Phillips, C. and Allen, H. eds., 2016. *Bridging the Divide: Indigenous Communities and Archaeology into the 21st Century*. London: Routledge.

Posth, C., Nägele, K., Colleran, H., Valentin, F., Bedford, S., Gray, R., Krause, J. and Powell, A., 2019. Response to 'Ancient DNA and its contribution to understanding the human history of the Pacific Islands' (Bedford et al. 2018). *Archaeology in Oceania*, 54(1), pp. 57–61.

Posth, C., Nägele, K., Colleran, H., Valentin, F., Bedford, S., Kami, K.W., Shing, R., Buckley, H., Kinaston, R., Walworth, M., Clark, G.R., Reepmeyer, C., Flexner, J., Maric, T., Moser, J., Gresky, J., Kiko, L., Robson, K.J., Auckland, K., Oppenheimer, S.J., Hill, A.V.S., Mentzer,

A.J., Zech, J., Petchey, F., Roberts, P., Jeong, C., Gray, R.D., Krause, J. and Powell, A., 2018. Language continuity despite population replacement in Remote Oceania. *Nature Ecology and Evolution*, 2(4), pp. 731–740.

Preucel, R.W. and Mrozowski, S.A., 2010. *Contemporary Archaeology in Theory: The New Pragmatism*. Malden, MA: John Wiley & Sons.

Price, N., 2018. Distant Vikings: a manifesto. *Acta Archaeologica*, 89(1), pp. 113–132.

Price, N. and Ljungkvist, J., 2018. Polynesians of the Atlantic? Precedents, potentials, and pitfalls in Oceanic analogies of the Vikings. *Danish Journal of Archaeology*, 7(2), pp. 133–138.

Rainbird, P., 2004. *The Archaeology of Micronesia*. Cambridge: Cambridge University Press.

Ravn, M., 2011. Ethnographic analogy from the Pacific: just as analogical as any other analogy. *World Archaeology*, 43(4), pp. 716–725.

Ravn, M., 2018. Roads to complexity: Hawaiians and Vikings compared. *Danish Journal of Archaeology*, 7(2), pp. 119–132.

Ray, S.H., 1895. The languages of British New Guinea. *Journal of the Anthropological Institute of Great Britain and Ireland*, 24, pp. 15–39.

Rivers, W.H.R., 1914. *The History of Melanesian Society*, vols. 1 and 2. Cambridge: Cambridge University Press.

Robb, J., 2013. Material culture, landscapes of action, and emergent causation: a new model for the origins of the European Neolithic. *Current Anthropology*, 54(6), pp. 657–683.

Roscoe, P., 2000. New Guinea leadership as ethnographic analogy: a critical review. *Journal of Archaeological Method and Theory*, 7(2), pp. 79–126.

Roscoe, P., 2009. On the 'pacification' of the European Neolithic: ethnographic analogy and the neglect of history. *World Archaeology*, 41(4), pp. 578–588.

Sahlins, M., 1958. *Social Stratification in Polynesia*. Seattle, WA: University of Washington Press.

Sahlins, M., 1957. Differentiation by adaptation in Polynesian societies. *Journal of the Polynesian Society*, 66(3), pp. 291–300.

Sahlins, M., 1963. Poor man, rich man, big-man, chief: political types in Melanesia and Polynesia. *Comparative Studies in Society and History*, 5(3), pp. 285–303.

Sahlins, M., 1972. *Stone Age Economics*. New York: Academic Press.

Salmond, A., 2009. *Aphrodite's Island: The European Discovery of Tahiti*. Berkeley, CA: University of California Press.

Seligmann, C.G., 1909. A classification of the natives of British New Guinea. *Journal of the Royal Anthropological Institute of Great Britain and Ireland*, 39, pp. 246–275.

Skinner, H.D., 1921. Culture areas in New Zealand. *Journal of the Polynesian Society*, 30(2/ 118), pp. 71–78.

Skinner, H.D., 1924. The origin and relationships of Maori material culture and decorative art. *Journal of the Polynesian Society*, 33(132), pp. 229–243.

Smith, B., 1985. *European Vision and the South Pacific*. New Haven, CT: Yale University Press.

Spate, O.H.K., 1979. *The Spanish Lake*. Canberra: ANU Press.

Specht, J., Denham, T., Goff, J. and Terrell, J.E., 2014. Deconstructing the Lapita cultural complex in the Bismarck Archipelago. *Journal of Archaeological Research*, 22(2), pp. 89–140.

Spriggs, M., 1984. The Lapita cultural complex: origins, distribution, contemporaries and successors. *Journal of Pacific History*, 19(4), pp. 202–223.

Spriggs, M., 1997. *The Island Melanesians*. Oxford: Blackwell.

Spriggs, M., 2008. Ethnographic parallels and the denial of history. *World Archaeology*, 40(4), pp. 538–552.

Spriggs, M., 2016a. Lapita and the linearbandkeramik: what can a comparative approach tell us about either? In: L. Amkreutz, F. Haack, D. Hofmann and I. van Wijk, eds. *Something out of the Ordinary? Interpreting Diversity in the Early Neolithic Linearbandkeramik and Beyond.* Newcastle upon Tyne: Cambridge Scholars Publishing, pp. 481–504.

Spriggs, M., 2019. Towards a history of Melanesian archaeological practices. In: M. Leclerc and J. Flexner, eds. *Archaeologies of Island Melanesia: Current Approaches to Landscapes, Exchange and Practice.* Canberra: ANU Press, pp. 9–32.

Stewart, G., 2017. The 'hau' of research: Mauss meets kaupapa Māori. *Journal of World Philosophies*, 2(1), pp. 1–11.

Strathern, M., 1988. *The Gender of the Gift.* Berkeley and Los Angeles, CA: University of California Press.

Strathern, M., 1990. Negative strategies in Melanesia. In: R. Fardon, ed. *Localizing Strategies: Regional Traditions of Ethnographic Writing.* Edinburgh: Scottish Academic Press.

Tcherkézoff, S., 2003. A long and unfortunate voyage towards the 'invention' of the Melanesia/Polynesia distinction 1595–1832. *Journal of Pacific History*, 38(2), pp. 175–196.

Terrell, J.E., 1986. *Prehistory in the Pacific Islands.* Cambridge: Cambridge University Press.

Terrell, J.E., 2018. Understanding Lapita as history. In: E. Cochrane and T.L. Hunt, eds. *The Oxford Handbook of Prehistoric Oceania.* Oxford: Oxford University Press, pp. 112–132.

Terrell, J.E. and Welsch, R.L., 1997. Lapita and the temporal geography of prehistory. *Antiquity*, 71(273), pp. 548–572.

Terrell, J.E., Hunt, T.L. and Gosden, C., 1997. The dimensions of social life in the Pacific: human diversity and the myth of the primitive isolate. *Current Anthropology*, 38(2), pp. 155–195.

Terrell, J.E., Kelly, K.M. and Rainbird, P., 2001. Foregone conclusions? In search of Papuans and Austronesians. *Current Anthropology*, 42(1), pp. 97–124.

Thomas, J., 2002. Archaeology's humanism and the materiality of the body. In: Y. Hamilakis, M. Pluciennik and S. Tarlow, eds. *Thinking through the Body: Archaeologies of Corporeality.* Boston, MA: Springer, pp. 29–45.

Thomas, J., 2004. *Archaeology and Modernity.* London: Routledge.

Thomas, N., 1989. The force of ethnology: origins and significance of the Melanesia-Polynesia division. *Current Anthropology*, 30, pp. 27–41.

Thomas, T. 2009. Communities of practice in the archaeological record of New Georgia, Rendova and Tetepare. In: Sheppard, P., Thomas, T., and G. Summerhayes, eds, *Lapita: Ancestors and Descendants.* NZAA Monograph 28. Auckland: New Zealand Archaeological Association, pp. 119–145.

Thomas, T., 2014a. Objects and photographs from the Percy Sladen Trust Expedition. In: E. Hviding and C. Berg, eds. *The Ethnographic Experiment: A.M. Hocart and W.H.R. Rivers in Island Melanesia, 1908.* Oxford: Berghahn Books, pp. 252–281.

Thomas, T., 2014b. Shrines in the landscape of New Georgia. In: H. Martinsson–Wallin and T. Thomas, eds. *Monuments and People in the Pacific.* Studies in Global Archaeology 20. Uppsala: Uppsala Universitet. pp. 47–76.

Thomas, T., 2019. Axes of entanglement in the New Georgia group, Solomon Islands. In: M. Leclerc and J. Flexner, eds. *Archaeologies of Island Melanesia: Current Approaches to Landscapes, Exchange and Practice.* Canberra: ANU Press, pp. 103–116.

Tilley, C., 1996. *An Ethnography of the Neolithic: Early Prehistoric Societies in Southern Scandinavia.* Cambridge: Cambridge University Press.

Trigger, B. and Glover, I., 1981. Editorial. *World Archaeology*, 13(2), pp. 133–137.

Trigger, B.G., 1989. *A History of Archaeological Thought.* Cambridge: Cambridge University Press.

Urry, J., 1998. Making sense of diversity and complexity: the ethnological context and consequences of the Torres Strait Expedition and the Oceanic phase in British anthropology, 1890–1935. In: A. Herle and S. Rouse, eds. *Cambridge and the Torres Strait: Centenary Essays on the 1898 Anthropological Expedition*. Cambridge: Cambridge University Press, pp. 201–233.

Walworth, M., 2014. Eastern Polynesian: the linguistic evidence revisited. *Oceanic Linguistics*, 53(2), pp. 256–272.

Weisler, M. and Kirch, P.V., 1985. The structure of settlement space in a Polynesian chiefdom. *New Zealand Journal of Archaeology*, 7, pp. 129–158.

Willey, G.R. and Phillips, P., 1958. *Method and Theory in American Archaeology*. Chicago, IL: University of Chicago Press.

Wylie, A., 1985. The reaction against analogy. *Advances in Archaeological Method and Theory*, 8, pp. 63–111.

Wynne-Jones, S. and Fleisher, J., 2015. Theory in Africa, Africa in theory. In: S. Wynne-Jones and J. Fleisher, eds. *Theory in Africa, Africa in Theory: Locating Meaning in Archaeology*. London: Routledge, pp. 3–18.

2

THEORY BEYOND THE CALM OCEAN?

The Pacific contribution to global island archaeology

Thomas P. Leppard and Scott M. Fitzpatrick

Introduction

In this chapter, we consider the impact of bodies of theory that initially developed within Pacific archaeology but have greatly influenced areas outside of the region. This means, in practice, exploring the extent to which 'island archaeology' reflects the central concerns of the archaeology of the insular Pacific. We are interested in intellectual and historiographic genealogies – how did recurrent themes and concepts cross-pollinate between various island-focused prehistoric archaeologies in the 20th century, and what has this meant for island archaeology in the 21st century? We consider in particular the relationship between Mediterranean, Caribbean and Pacific archaeology, as our primary areas of specialisation, addressing why archaeology as practised in the Pacific has had an impact in one (the Mediterranean), but a reduced impact in the other (the Caribbean) of the major 'theatres' of global island archaeology, assessing why these barriers remained relatively intellectually impermeable until quite recently. In drawing these disparate themes together, we reflect on current theoretical trends within island archaeology; which, in this analysis, seems to be a cohesive body of inter-related interests, research concerns and theoretical approaches, rather than a monolithic and homogeneous approach.

Island archaeology as scholarly discourse

Island archaeology can be said to differ from archaeology simply undertaken on islands, in that its practitioners view insular contexts as uniquely productive places in which to study the generalities and specificities of human behaviour by virtue of the constraints imposed on human populations due to insularity (e.g. Broodbank, 2018; DiNapoli and Leppard, 2018; Fitzpatrick, 2004; Fitzpatrick and Anderson, 2008; Fitzpatrick and Keegan, 2007; Fitzpatrick et al., 2015; Fitzpatrick, 2018a;

Keegan and Diamond, 1987; Kirch, 1997a). Archaeological research on islands, of course, has a long history, whereas island archaeology as a formalised field of study only emerged during the second half of the 20th century. In its current form, global island archaeology may loosely be characterised as having a series of key concerns or emphases that are especially characteristic (but cf. Broodbank, 2018). Fitzpatrick and colleagues (Erlandson and Fitzpatrick, 2006; Fitzpatrick et al., 2015) have identified some of these:

> (1) the antiquity of coastal adaptions and maritime dispersals; (2) variation in marine or coastal productivity; (3) development of specialization maritime technologies and capabilities; (4) underwater archaeology and drowned terrestrial landscapes; (5) cultural responses to insularity, isolation and circumscription; (6) cultural contacts and historical processes; (7) human impacts and historical ecology in island and coastal ecosystems; (8) conservation and management of island and coastal sites; (9) the expanding methodological toolkit available to island and coastal archaeologists; (10) aquatic or maritime influences on symbolic expression …; (11) contributions to biogeography and ecology; (12) philosophical dilemmas on islands as units of analysis; and (13) islands as case studies for understanding human diasporas.
>
> *(Fitzpatrick, 2018a, p. 210)*

Ignoring the methodological components of this list, the remaining core concerns clearly derive from the relatively unusual types of environment that islands represent, as 'relatively small, discrete types of habitat surrounded by spatially extensive qualitatively divergent habitat' (Leppard, 2017, p. 556). Accordingly, we might then suggest that the main, animating concerns of island archaeology derive ultimately from: the capacity of oceans and seas to inhibit or promote interaction and connectivity between human communities; the ecodynamics of colonising humans and biotas impoverished by the constraints that this relative isolation imposes on ecological and evolutionary processes; the resulting degree of human interconnectivity or lack of it; and the social and cultural dimensions of this connectivity – not just how it can be measured, but how travel and movement itself were (or were not) major concerns of the cultural lives of islanders before the modern era. These themes, we contend, can clearly be traced in early Pacific archaeology, and have come to characterise island archaeology more generally, if differentially. We explore what has diffused intellectually, and what has not, below.

Before embarking on our brief odyssey around island archaeology, we should note the degree to which 'global island archaeology' is still primarily a subset of archaeological research that occurs in the Pacific – to the extent that such research is aware of itself as part of a broader, comparative intellectual project. More than a decade ago, Cherry (2004) noted the degree to which Mediterranean island archaeology, despite having absorbed – as we show – some of the central concerns that also characterised its Pacific cousin, was still under-represented in publishing formats dominated by Pacific archaeologists. A brief and non-scientific survey of the *Journal of Island and Coastal Archaeology*[1] (arguably the main forum for anthropological archaeologists with an explicit interest in comparative island archaeology) suggests this trend remains. Of the 136 papers published in volumes 1 to 13 that deal with the archaeology of an identifiable island group (rather than methodological, comparative or theoretical issues), 58 per cent were drawn from the Pacific, and only 5 per cent from the Mediterranean (indeed, the Caribbean was better represented at 13 per cent, but the advent of this journal post-dates the intellectual *glasnost* of the Caribbean subfield in the 2000s; see below). This is not to suggest that Mediterranean island archaeologists do not publish comparable data or interpretations, but they largely do so in different formats (e.g. the *Journal of Mediterranean Archaeology*, the *Journal of European Archaeology*, *Mediterranean Archaeology and Archaeometry*, and the house journals (*Hesperia, PBSR, ABSA*) of what are known as the foreign schools of archaeology located in various Mediterranean capitals). This underscores the continuing relevance of Renfrew's (1980) point about the 'great divide', but we do not wish to pursue this further here beyond stressing the extent to which this division has affected the development of island archaeology in various theatres; rather, we simply emphasise that 'island archaeology' as a coherent sub-discipline might not unfairly be said to most frequently occur in the Pacific.

Island archaeology as Pacific archaeology?

Isolates to laboratories

The Pacific is a prodigious oceanic space, containing some of the most isolated (by various metrics) fragments of land on the planet. It is then unsurprising that the effects of these vast distances on the human organism and its cultural behaviours have been of profound interest to Pacific archaeologists and anthropologists. The literature in this vein is voluminous, and a review is beyond our capacity here. Rather, we aim to sketch the major trends that made a theoretical and conceptual impact beyond the Pacific.

There was early, sporadic interest within British anthropology in how Pacific isolation might drive unusual cultural attributes. A.C. Haddon's Torres Strait work, in particular, revolved around his emerging interest in isolation driving endemic cultural processes comparable to biological dynamics, and Kuklick (1996) traces this interest to Haddon's personal and professional exposure to Darwin's early exponents. Haddon's interest in cultural isolation was matched by some of his contemporaries in what was a small and intimate field (e.g. Rivers, 1913). Yet this early Anglophone interest in isolation and biological comparanda to a large extent faded into the scenery in the major, foundational works of British social anthropology (e.g. Malinowksi, 1922). Subsequent to this loss of interest, and aside from occasional references (e.g. Mead, 1928), it was arguably Sahlins's paper *Esoteric Efflorescence in Easter Island* (1955) that next sought to explicitly account for unique cultural behaviours as a function of isolation, with notable archaeological manifestations.

In attempting to explain the development of the practice of erecting the famous *moai* statues on Rapa Nui/Easter Island, Sahlins envisaged a generalised Polynesian socio-ecological dynamic existing in an insular tropical Pacific environmental niche. This relationship was conceptualised by Sahlins as an idealised norm (1955, pp. 1047–1049), a benchmark disrupted by the extreme isolation and (for Remote Oceania) unusually temperate climate of Rapa Nui. The interaction between an established socio-economic system and novel environment created new cultural and behavioural forms – the 'esoteric efflorescence' of the paper's title. Vitally, it is the geographic and ecological properties of the island that are both limiting and enabling factors; its relative isolation mitigating against cultural and/or genetic flow between the source population and Rapa Nui.

Sahlins's key contribution is that the condition of insularity and its associated properties (in this case, relative environmental depauperation and distance from other communities) may have transformative effects on culture. The notion of cultural isolation, as a condition related to or paralleling genetic isolation, subsequently had an increasingly profound influence in Pacific archaeology. Sahlins's paper was followed rapidly by Goodenough's (1957) more theoretically explicit formulation of the problem, which also noted the capacity of cultural isolation to permit the construction of cultural phylogenies. This was in the context of Mead – in her introduction to Goodenough's paper, a published version of his 1956 AAAS paper and building on her earlier observations (1928) – explicitly connecting insularity with the notion of the 'laboratory' in a manner not seen since Haddon's early work (Mead, 1957). These contributions were followed by a clear recognition that biological and cultural processes might fruitfully be understood to be equally sensitive to the same dimensions of variability: distance, area and heterogeneity (Vayda and Rappaport, 1963).

The interest in how isolation constrains and drives cultural change clearly echoes parallel interests in the biological sciences regarding how, in particular, separation ultimately drives allopatric speciation. Within an insular context, this work was first codified by MacArthur and Wilson as the theory of island biogeography (MacArthur and Wilson, 1963; 1967). This theory – primarily concerned with how specific geographies can drive specific ecological and evolutionary processes – has in turn spawned and influenced numerous subfields, including community ecology and conservation biology (see Leppard, 2018), but in the Pacific it also served to reinforce extant trends in the archaeological literature towards overt emphasis on isolation as a conditioning factor. Potential parallels between biological and cultural processes have remained enormously influential in Pacific archaeology; to constrain an otherwise lengthy discussion, we acknowledge this but do not consider the natural science literature in detail (and, in any case, it is clear that by the mid-1950s Pacific anthropologists had already grasped the significance of isolation for cultural diversity, even if lacking the explanatory framework that island biogeography established in the 1960s). Suffice it to say that, through the 1970s and 1980s, the concept of the island laboratory retained traction, even if related components of the phylogenetic model were simultaneously beginning to be challenged (Clark and

Terrell, 1978; Terrell, 1977a). Kirch (1980) and Hunt (1987) both emphasised the advantages of the island as a 'laboratory', referring to the work of MacArthur and Wilson (as well as to Diamond and Simberloff, the latter Wilson's student and both central figures in the 'Single Large or Several Small' (SLOSS) debates in conservation biology), and the impact of island-laboratory thinking persisted into the late 1980s (e.g. Kirch and Green, 1987).

Explicit interest in isolation and distance as a conditioning factor in human behaviour appeared in the Mediterranean literature comparatively early (see Cherry and Leppard, 2014, for a fuller historiography of Mediterranean island archaeology); earlier, in fact, than the first global overview of the implications of island biogeography for colonisation studies (Keegan and Diamond, 1987). Evans (1973; 1977) was arguably drawing on the sophisticated Pacific scholarship, although his references are opaque. The foundational 1973 paper (deriving from the 1971 Sheffield conference organised by Renfrew) cites no literature, although by 1977 it is clear that Evans had read Vayda and Rappaport (1963). It was John Cherry, however, who, in a series of influential papers, explicitly introduced island biogeographic theory to Mediterranean island archaeology (Cherry, 1981; 1984; 1985). Cherry was especially interested in how the geographic configuration of insular landscapes might – or might not – influence colonisation dynamics. This concrete interest in the confluence of human behaviour and environmental organisation, viewed through a lens provided by theory from the life sciences, was revolutionary in Mediterranean archaeology (we note in passing that the patterns identified in this research still appear to broadly obtain, some three and half decades later: Dawson, 2014). Crucially, Cherry's interest in the application of island biogeographic theory brought burgeoning Mediterranean island archaeology into line with established trends in the Pacific scholarship. This is despite the fact that Cherry (pers. comm.) was drawing less on Pacific archaeology and more on lessons that Edward O. Wilson in particular derived from his Pacific entomological fieldwork and distilled in his work with Robert MacArthur, as well as Wilson's subsequent work in the Florida Keys (Simberloff and Wilson, 1969; 1970). Renfrew, Cherry's doctoral supervisor, was also utilising Pacific models in his attempts to better understand prehistoric Mediterranean political organisation and economy (Renfrew, 1973, pp. 155–166), but in so doing was engaging more closely with the Pacific literature on archaeological parallels of ethnographically attested chiefly societies, rather than on island archaeology or island biogeography *per se*.

This paradigm shift – part of the broader arrival of the New Archaeology in Mediterranean prehistory, and the move away from culture history approaches – dominated Mediterranean island archaeology for the next decade, exemplified by the ongoing work of Cherry (1990), but also Held (1989a; 1989b; 1993), Gómez Bellard (1995) and Patton (1996). Held and Gómez Bellard in particular attempted to use explicitly biogeographic approaches to address conceptual challenges in Mediterranean archaeology; the apparent cultural isolation of Cyprus during the Early and Middle Holocene (Held, 1989a; 1993), and the aberrantly late colonisation of Ibiza and Formentera in the western Mediterranean (Gómez Bellard,

1995; Cherry and Leppard, 2018a). The influence of Evans's and Cherry's work is evident, and these papers fit well into the Mediterranean biogeographic paradigm, which had matured by the 1990s, coming to dominate the aspect of Mediterranean island archaeology that was explicitly concerned with theory. Indeed, in going beyond insular geography and geometry to consider the environmental and biotic dynamics of small islands, Gómez Bellard anticipated some of the major concerns of Mediterranean island archaeology into the new millennium; specifically, how insular environmental properties can render islands more or less attractive to colonists (Cherry and Leppard, 2018b).

The ubiquity of connectivity: networks and voyaging

Just as Pacific models utilising biogeographic principles were paralleled in Mediterranean island archaeology, so was the reaction against these models. The phylogenetic tendency within Pacific prehistory met with broad and sustained critique in the late 1980s and 1990s (see Cochrane and Hunt 2018); with it, the island-laboratory model was also exposed to criticism. Isolation as a driver of cultural change was especially singled out. In particular, debate focused on whether distance and isolation represented an ontological fact that constrained human action; or whether 'isolation' was culturally specific, an epistemological construct rather than a deterministic constraint.

Terrell (1986) had already challenged the intrinsic isolation model, but a paper by Gosden and Pavlides on their work in the Arawe Islands (1994) explicitly rejected what they called the 'development-in-isolation' model. They instead proposed that prehistoric Oceanic societies maintained large-scale and long-distance interaction networks that rendered the isolationist perspective insufficient for explaining cultural evolutionary models (Hau'ofa, 1993). This was followed by a substantive intervention by Terrell, Hunt and Gosden (1997), who aimed in part to demonstrate that 'isolation' in the pre-Contact Pacific was essentially a construct of Pacific archaeology as a discipline, failing to reflect the lived Pacific experience and replete with worryingly colonialist and essentialising assumptions (this article perhaps being best understood in a wider landscape of increasing concern with decolonising Pacific scholarship and building a critique of Western concepts of 'race', which were strongly tied to isolation and cultural proxies, e.g. Hau'ofa, 1993; Terrell, et al., 2001). This debate, to some extent, has continued into the new millennium (e.g. Fitzpatrick, et al., 2007; Fitzpatrick and Anderson, 2008; Boomert and Bright, 2007). Its main contours have been described elsewhere (Hunt and Fitzhugh, 1997; Cochrane and Hunt, 2018), and one of us (Leppard, 2015, pp. 721–722) has argued that this dichotomy itself (isolation vs. interconnectivity) ignores the fact that environmental and demographic dynamism likely altered the thresholds of tolerable isolation during the occupation histories of Pacific islands. We are, then, less interested in the continuing repercussions of this contention, and more in its immediate impact beyond Pacific archaeology. In the Mediterranean, this impact was substantial.

Paul Rainbird, himself a Pacific (Micronesian) archaeologist, introduced the most stringent form of Pacific critique of island archaeology as informed by biological and isolationist models to the Mediterranean (Rainbird, 1999). The critique – expanded upon in a slim volume titled *The Archaeology of Islands* (Rainbird, 2007) – reads, two decades later, as a useful but overstated corrective, and one that was largely derivative from Pacific scholarship. Rainbird castigated Mediterranean island archaeologists for their reliance on interpretive frameworks drawn from the other sciences, and urged instead an island archaeology that recognised the intrinsic connectivity of island groups as well as the importance of 'seascapes', a term borrowed from Gosden and Pavlides (1994). Responses to his paper, published in the *Journal of Mediterranean Archaeology*, underscore how divisive this corrective was.

It is hard to assess the impact of Rainbird's critique, as Cherry and Leppard (2014) note, in part because it appears not to have established a distinct approach to Mediterranean island archaeology. The paper is broadly cited, but only a minority of these are positive citations by Mediterranean scholars. Instead, the work of Cyprian Broodbank – a student of Cherry – has proven more influential. Broodbank, prior and subsequent to Rainbird's critique, developed a more nuanced, distinctive and arguably richer approach to Mediterranean island archaeology. In a series of papers, Broodbank drew eclectically on Pacific models and ethnographic parallels more broadly, while approaching the Mediterranean in its own terms (Broodbank, 1989; 1992; 1993; 2000a). He emphasised the social dimensions of long-distance maritime travel, pointing to its association in the Early Bronze Age Aegean with high-status goods and suggesting that it may have been a source of social capital. This important series of contributions was followed by a major synthetic treatment that still arguably represents the high-water mark of mature Mediterranean island archaeology, enriched by the social critique, but still drawing explanatory power from the models offered by biogeography (Broodbank, 2000b). Broodbank united various strands of explanation – drawing on, for example, Terrell's (1977b) early use of graph theory and proximal point analysis as well as target/distance ratios and the work of Keegan and Diamond (1987) – to provide a varied analysis of early island colonisation and occupation. This was undertaken along multiple dimensions, considering spatial dynamics, the archaeology of watercraft, ideational and symbolic aspects of human perceptions of landscape, along with detailed artefact and typological studies, woven into a compelling narrative.

The approach adopted by Broodbank – one that draws judiciously but broadly on various bodies of theory – appears to have become essentially the norm in Mediterranean island archaeology, which remains markedly undogmatic. Much of the scholarship is now concerned with what we might understand as the social and material aspects of relative isolation and long-distance travel (Robb, 2001; Dawson, 2006; Farr, 2006; van Dommelen and Knapp, 2010; Vella, 2016), and less on the biological and cultural restrictions imposed by insularity; but the overall tenor has more in common with Broodbank and less with Rainbird. We do not wish to dwell extensively on this here, however, at the risk of a lengthy discourse on how mobility and connectivity as themes have come to dominate Mediterranean prehistory more generally. More importantly for present purposes, it becomes apparent from the foregoing discussion that Mediterranean island archaeology has seen paradigm shifts broadly comparable to (and derived largely from) those witnessed in the Pacific: from an interest in using biological and biogeographic models to, in part, a reaction against this. This is a clear example of endemic Pacific theoretical concerns informing wider island archaeology. The degree to which biogeographic thought and the reaction against it permeated other island theatres has, however, been considerably variable.

Connectivity and isolation in Caribbean island archaeology

The influence of Pacific theory as regards the island-laboratory simile on Caribbean island archaeology has been more complex – rather than an early cross-fertilisation of ideas, the Caribbean has arguably arrived late to global island archaeology. One of us (Fitzpatrick, 2004) has already explored the apparent parochialism of Caribbean archaeology in the 20th century. In terms of intellectual content, there is little evidence of the arrival of biologically informed interpretive frameworks in the Caribbean during the 1980s and 1990s. The exception is the well-cited paper by Keegan and Diamond (1987), the first author being a Caribbean specialist, but this paper was more influential beyond the Caribbean than within.

This resistance to bodies of theory developed elsewhere can in part be ascribed to the nature of the Caribbean academy. The region draws from scholarship that is necessarily polyglot and continues to be infused with various national conceptions of archaeology. This contrasts with largely monoglot Pacific scholarship, which, except for Francophone scholarship (Dotte-Sarout, 2017), leans towards Anglo-Americanist anthropological archaeology. Even if islands-as-laboratories and biogeographic reasoning were pervasive elsewhere, they were largely so only in Anglophone academic circles (at least until the 1990s). This resistance can also be ascribed, however, to the nature of the dominant research agendas that emerged in Caribbean archaeology after the 1950s and that derived largely from the work of Irving Rouse (Keegan, 2007).

Rouse was primarily concerned with large-scale chrono-typological structures (Rouse, 1985; 1986; 1989). In particular, he was interested in defining ceramic styles as chronological markers, and subsequent large-scale excavations were aimed at refining the relationship between established stratigraphic sequences and ceramic typologies. This led to the foundation of the classic series (and sub-series) convention – Casimiroid, Ortoirioid (Archaic), replaced by Saladoid, Ostionoid, Troumassoid and ultimately Suazoid (Ceramic Age) – a scheme which covered the entirety of the insular Caribbean (interestingly, this approach led Kirch (1978; 1981), a graduate student at Yale studying under Rouse, to use this same Caribbean convention in the Pacific, which led to the short-lived use of the term 'Lapitoid' to describe the initial foray of Austronesian speaking groups into Remote Oceania). The series/subseries method was intrinsically classificatory and culture historical; indeed, Keegan (2007) records Rouse's antipathy to the New Archaeology. Rouse, writing in the context of an issue of a journal dedicated solely to island archaeology, was certainly aware of the foundational literature of island biogeography and the burgeoning development of island archaeology itself (Rouse 1977, p. 8; cf. Kirch, 1978; 1981). For him, however, the key issues were not the capacity of insularity to promote new behaviours or to foster certain kinds of socio-cultural process, but defining the cultural suites, associated with discrete migratory waves, which transcended and linked islands. Perhaps perversely, in an edition of a journal in which Evans (1977) was laying out the future for Mediterranean island archaeology centred around the island as a unit of investigation, Rouse was describing the cultural series as the basic unit of analysis; even if subseries reflected different island contexts, Rouse provided no explanatory mechanism to link environmental and cultural processes. Clearly, he saw his scheme as one that was generally applicable – hence the ambitious scope of his major work on migration and its relationship to culture and culture change (1986), a scope which included the Pacific. But that static relationship between migration and material culture relied, in the Rousian scheme, on a *deus ex machina*, a gap that the New Archaeology had attempted to fill.

This is not to say that Caribbean archaeologists were unaware either of Pacific archaeology, or on the focus on adaptation as a theoretical tool to bridge environment and cultural dynamics (e.g. Goodwin, 1978; Veloz Maggiolo, 1976–1977; Watters, 1980; 1981). Nonetheless, in the Caribbean the sea has tended to be viewed as a connector rather than an insulator, driving (in particular) migration episodes and cultural transmission (Hofman et al., 2008), though various chronological disparities in how the Antilles seem to have been colonised (or not) in the past remain intriguing questions (Fitzpatrick, 2006; 2015). Accordingly, it is perhaps no surprise that criticism of isolationist models has emerged from the Caribbean (Boomert and Bright, 2007). Nor should it be surprising that, with the reaction *against* biogeographic and biologically informed models in global island archaeology, Caribbean archaeology has emerged as a major sub-theatre – one in which the nature of cultural and demographic flows is of profound interest (*inter alia* Curet, 2005; Fitzpatrick and Ross, 2010; Keegan and Hofman, 2017; Hofman et al., 2010, 2014; Hofman and van Duijvenbode, 2011). The Caribbean has also been home to cutting-edge research exploring animal translocation, agricultural development (Reid, 2018), and inter-island movement from an archaeological science perspective (e.g. Giovas, 2017a; 2017b; Laffoon et al., 2017a, 2017b), similar to Pacific trends, but distinct from the Mediterranean.

It can be seen that the degree of influence Pacific Island archaeology has exerted elsewhere is largely context-dependent. With the arrival of the New Archaeology in the Mediterranean in the 1970s, conditions were arguably ripe for the absorption or replication of processual models, which were major features of Pacific anthropological archaeology (noting of course that the isolationist models in the Pacific pre-date Binford's major contributions in the 1960s). In the Caribbean, by contrast, Rouse's legacy fit poorly with processual models of endogenous cultural dynamics, and only with the advent of the critique of biogeographic and isolationist approaches in the 1990s and 2000s could Caribbean scholarship be fully integrated into a loosely defined global island archaeology.

Human–island ecodynamics

Island palaeoenvironments and historical ecology

In this chapter we have been mainly concerned with charting the spread and impacts of bodies of theory that: (a) were developed within Pacific archaeology; and (b) had effects on island archaeology as undertaken elsewhere. In understanding the main intellectual preoccupations of current global island archaeology, however, we note in passing a field of study from outside island archaeology, which has nonetheless become essentially ubiquitous in insular archaeology: historical ecology.

We have discussed the early interest in the Pacific in understanding biological models as having explanatory potential with regard to culture change. This was matched by and related to a keen interest in the transformative capacity of island environments with regard to human behaviour. This interest arguably derived from the same source as the prevailing emphasis on isolation – a recognition that, in their ecosystemic fragility and geological life histories, oceanic islands represent a relatively rare type of environment, one that might drive otherwise aberrant adaptive processes. In *Man's Place in the Island Ecosystem* (Fosberg, 1963a), papers by Fosberg (1963b) and others (Vayda and Rappaport, 1963) place great importance on islands as niches, which are frequently remote and generally resource-poor (although certain resources may be present in abundance). Crucially, Fosberg suggests that insular *adaptation* – not simply isolation – may result in 'archaic, bizarre, or possibly ill-adapted [cultural] forms' (1963b, p. 5). Here, Fosberg (1963a, b) connects behavioural and cultural plasticity with environmental parameters, a characteristic feature of the New Archaeology, but well ahead of its time in the early 1960s.

In Fosberg's conception, this process is essentially bi-directional – humans adapt to their environments, but there is feedback from environmental conditions to human behaviour, which is then conditioned by the nature and organisation of the environment. Fosberg (1963b) is interested in a deterministic relationship, then, in which environmental organisation remains essentially constant. By contrast, historical ecology and allied approaches emphasise the dynamic, recursive relationship between organisms and their environments: humans physically and permanently alter material and organic conditions around them, but as they do so these altered conditions then reframe human choices, limiting some strategies and facilitating others. First articulated by Deevey (1964), historical ecology as a sub-discipline that straddled natural and human sciences was more fully developed in the work of Balée (1988) and Crumley (1994), although Karl Butzer's (1996; 2012) conceptualisation of human ecology also clearly implied long-term recursive dynamics, especially in the Mediterranean. Considering the longitudinal assumptions of historical ecology (i.e. the visibility of recursive dynamics in various proxies, both organic and inorganic), it is unsurprising that it has been incorporated into archaeological thought more generally. But this is especially true of the archaeology of islands, and again, the Pacific witnessed this development comparatively early, particularly, but not only, in the work of Patrick Kirch (Kirch and Hunt, 1997; Kirch, 1997a; 1997b; 2004). This turn towards a recognition of dynamic human–environment processes has further been codified in terms of (a) coupled and (b) model systems – the dual recognition that humans are: (i) integrated components of multi-dimensional bio-physical systems with emergent properties; and (ii) that islands should be peculiarly exemplary of the functioning of such systems at scales that lend themselves to study and quantification (e.g. DiNapoli and Leppard, 2018; Vitousek, 2002; Kirch, 2007a; 2007b).

This concern – with dynamic, longitudinally observable feedbacks between cultural and natural processes – has filtered through to the other island theatres under discussion. The Caribbean has seen a relatively recent, but critically important, move toward developing substantial research programmes that adopt an historical ecological perspective, building on an established tradition of exemplary zooarchaeological research (Giovas, 2017a; 2017b; 2018; Giovas et al., 2012; Keegan et al., 2003; LeFebvre, 2007; Newsom and Wing, 2004; Steadman and Jones, 2006; Steadman et al., 2017; Wing, 2001; Wing and Wing, 2001) that incorporates palaeoenvironmental data, which has seen a major uptick in research recently (Bain et al., 2018; Caffrey and Horn, 2015; Castilla-Beltrán et al., 2018; Siegel et al., 2015; Siegel, 2018; van Hengstum et al., 2018), and substantial historical accounts (Fitzpatrick, 2018b; Fitzpatrick and Keegan, 2007). These broader syntheses have been used to challenge as well as buttress models drawn from archaeological data (Cooke et al., 2017; Siegel et al., 2015). Mediterranean island archaeology has incorporated the explicit lessons of historical ecology more gradually, but island archaeologists are increasingly viewing cultural and biological dynamics on islands as coupled systems (Ghilardi and Lespez, 2017; Sureda et al., 2017). In general, then, although historical ecology approaches (and allied concepts such as model and coupled systems, and human ecology) did not originate in the Pacific, their adoption there can be argued to have had a profound influence over how island archaeology outside the Pacific is conducted, with human–environment dynamics a major research theme in global island archaeology (Braje et al., 2012; 2015; Erlandson et al., 2008; Rick and Erlandson, 2008).

Conclusions

The Pacific contribution to global island archaeology

Before concluding, it is important to emphasise the necessary limitations of this chapter. We have not – by virtue of a lack of familiarity with the subfields – considered the impact of Pacific island archaeology in the archaeology of the Indian Ocean or North Atlantic, save to the extent that the research problems animating these subfields are those of global island archaeology more generally. Nor have we considered the contribution of Pacific archaeology and anthropology to Neo-Evolutionary theory, and in particular the conceptualisation of ranked societies within that theory (Sahlins, 1958; 1963; Kirch, 1984); not because social organisation and the emergence of complexity have not been concerns in other island theatres (they demonstrably have been, and theory from the Pacific has been integral; e.g.

Renfrew, 1973, pp. 155–166), but because models developed in the Pacific and by Pacific anthropologists have had such a broad, general impact in how we conceive of canonical social forms, and in particular chiefly societies, as well as now being the focus of substantial critique (Pauketat, 2007; Yoffee, 2005). There is little space here to do more than simply acknowledge this, and to ponder whether the current preoccupation of global island archaeology with: (a) the social dimensions of connectivity; and (b) human–island ecodynamics has obscured the seemingly genuine tendency for islands to generate surprisingly diverse and hierarchical forms of social organisation.

It has also not been our intention here to evaluate whether or not island archaeology, or indeed Pacific archaeology, is in any sense a valid intellectual enterprise. Having charted island archaeology's outgrowth from yet continued orbit around the Pacific, however, it seems important to at least consider this disciplinary genealogy in the light of Broodbank's recent (2018) challenge: does island archaeology matter? That is, has its descent from Pacific island archaeology and its diversification in and enrichment from other arenas strengthened it, making it a methodologically robust and intellectually coherent valued member of a wider anthropological archaeology? Broodbank (2018) conceptualises the possible means of buttressing the importance of island archaeology under three signs: intrinsic value, comparative value, and potential contributions to a global deep history. We focus here on comparative value, as we are sympathetic to the intrinsically valuable nature of island archaeology, and the possibility of a global deep history is well beyond our scope.

In charting the debt of global island archaeology to Pacific archaeology, we have tried to emphasise that island archaeologists generally remain preoccupied by: (a) the broad spectrum of biological, behavioural and cultural effects engendered by the physical separation of island communities (including how this separation has been obviated); and (b) the dynamic nature of the interaction between humans and highly responsive (sensitive) island environments. These shared concerns provide a general coherence to global island archaeology in the face of otherwise massive area- and academy-specific divergence. It is this coherence, we suggest, that lends global island archaeology its analytic power when it comes to comparison (cf. Smith, 2011): do comparable types of physical organisation encourage parallel adaptive processes in otherwise unrelated contexts (Leppard, 2017), or are the specificities of adaptation to island environments subtly different in each instance? As island archaeology matures as a field of study, answering anthropological questions of this sort will become increasingly viable, accentuating the relevance of global island archaeology for archaeologists more generally interested in comparison.

Future directions

Global island archaeology is, as we have seen, substantially concerned with how insularity conditions or drives human behaviour – in particular, and deriving from trail-blazing Pacific scholarship and theory, whether insularity isolates or connects communities (Fitzpatrick and Anderson, 2008; Lape, 2004; Moss, 2004). We conclude by reflecting on major methodological advances in the archaeological sciences, which are revolutionising our understanding of the composition and dynamics of human communities: aDNA sequencing, Bayesian modelling of radiocarbon dates, and stable isotope chemistry. In all three instances (excepting perhaps the latter), Pacific island archaeology was ahead of global island archaeology more generally. The importance of these techniques for island archaeologists in particular is their power to: (a) constrain temporal horizons; and (b) illuminate the composition of funerary populations in terms of homogeneity and potentially origination. This has major implications for resolving, in particular, issues relating to chronologies of colonisation and the biological composition of colonising communities.

These techniques are already having decisive impacts within island archaeology. In one instance (the study of the Lapita phenomenon), sequencing can be combined with Bayesian approaches to provide a clearer image of a colonisation phenomenon. Modelling by Rieth and Athens (2017) indicates a tightly constrained window for the first colonisation of the remote Pacific, with Lapita colonisation of the Bismarcks either immediately prior to or contemporaneous with the arrival in the Marianas of populations also characterised by an incised redware tradition (between c.3400 and 3100 BP). Skoglund et al. (2016), having sequenced the genomes of three individuals from the Lapita Teouma cemetery in southern Vanuatu, posit a relationship between Lapita genetic composition and indigenous Philippine and Taiwanese genomes. They also suggest little admixture of indigenous Papuan genetic material in the Lapita sample. This limited evidence for genetic admixing may reflect comparatively rapid dispersal into Remote Oceania from ISEA, rather than a gradual process, and this is bolstered to an extent by the refined chronology. We caution that results from recent aDNA research in the Pacific are too limited at present to fully demonstrate how population origins and movements were structured, but we are hopeful that future studies will help resolve many of these lingering questions.

Clearly, there are methodological and interpretive issues which require resolving; but the increasingly high spatial and temporal resolution that archaeological science offers as regards demographic phenomena (and not only via material proxies, but via human biochemistry itself) will transform how we understand dynamics of movement and separation in island contexts, necessitating new theoretical frameworks to order and interpret increasingly voluminous biochemical provenience data. Once again, the Pacific will likely be leading paradigm change within global island archaeology, though with an increasing contribution from other regions that have been influenced by decades of scholarship focused on islands, island societies and societal change.

Acknowledgements

We are enormously grateful to Tim Thomas for his patience as an Editor in awaiting our chapter. We also thank Tim, as well as Bill Keegan, for their constructive comments on an earlier draft on this chapter. In particular, Tim drew our attention to Haddon's interest in isolation in his Torres Strait work, of which we were previously unaware, and Bill broadened and nuanced our Caribbean perspective. John Cherry provided critical feedback and contextualisation, for which we are very grateful.

Note

1 This includes articles, reports, notes and forum pieces, but not editorials, reviews, review essays or responses to forum pieces. It also does not include methodological, theoretical or comparative contributions or contributions which deal with coasts. Perhaps unfairly, it considers research on Oceania, the California Channel Islands, and the subduction arcs of East Asia as 'Pacific', but excludes those islands traditionally considered to fall within Island Southeast Asia. In full disclosure, one of us (SMF) is the founding co-editor of this journal.

References

Bain, A., Faucher, A.M., Kennedy, L.M., LeBlanc, A.R., Burn, M.J., Boger, R. and Perdikaris, S., 2018. Landscape transformation during Ceramic Age and Colonial occupations of Barbuda, West Indies. *Environmental Archaeology*, 23(1), pp. 36–46.

Balée, W., ed., 1998. *Advances in Historical Ecology*. New York: Columbia University Press.

Boomert, A. and Bright, A., 2007. Island archaeology: in search of a new horizon. *Island Studies Journal*, 2, pp. 3–26.

Braje, T.J., Rick, T.C. and Erlandson, J.M., 2012. A trans-Holocene historical ecological record of shellfish harvesting on California's Northern Channel Islands. *Quaternary International*, 264, pp. 109–120.

Braje, T.J., Rick, T.C., Erlandson, J.M., Rogers-Bennett, L. and Catton, C.A., 2015. Historical ecology can inform restoration site selection: the case of black abalone (*Haliotis cracherodii*) along California's Channel Islands. *Aquatic Conservation*, 26, pp. 470–481.

Broodbank, C., 1989. The longboat and society in the Cyclades in the Keros-Syros culture. *American Journal of Archaeology*, 93(3), pp. 319–337.

Broodbank, C., 1992. Colonization and culture in the Neolithic and Early Bronze Age Cyclades. *American Journal of Archaeology*, 96(2), p. 341.

Broodbank, C., 1993. Ulysses without sails: trade, distance, knowledge and power in the early Cyclades. *World Archaeology*, 24(3), pp. 315–331.

Broodbank, C., 2000a. Perspectives on an Early Bronze Age island centre: an analysis of pottery from Daskaleio-Kavos (Keros) in the Cyclades. *Oxford Journal of Archaeology*, 19(4), pp. 323–342.

Broodbank, C., 2000b. *An Island Archaeology of the Early Cyclades*. Cambridge: Cambridge University Press.

Broodbank, C., 2018. Does island archaeology matter? In: A.R. Knodell and T.P. Leppard, eds. *Regional Approaches to Society and Complexity: Studies in Honor of John F. Cherry*. Sheffield: Equinox, pp. 188–206.

Butzer, K., 1996. Ecology in the long view: settlement histories, agrosystemic strategies, and ecological performance. *Journal of Field Archaeology*, 23(2), pp. 141–150.

Butzer, K., 2012. Collapse, environment, and society. *Proceedings of the National Academy of Sciences*, 109(10), pp. 3632–3639.

Caffrey, M.A. and Horn, S.P., 2015. Long-term fire trends in Hispaniola and Puerto Rico from sedimentary charcoal: A comparison of three records. *The Professional Geographer*, 67(2), pp. 229–241.

Castilla-Beltrán, A., Hooghiemstra, H., Hoogland, M.L., Pagán-Jiménez, J., van Geel, B., Field, M.H., Prins, M., Donders, T., Malatesta, E.H., Hung, J.U. and McMichael, C.H., 2018. Columbus' footprint in Hispaniola: a paleoenvironmental record of indigenous and colonial impacts on the landscape of the central Cibao Valley, northern Dominican Republic. *Anthropocene,* 22, pp. 66–80.

Cherry, J.F., 1981 Pattern and process in the earliest colonization of the Mediterranean islands. *Proceedings of the Prehistoric Society,* 47, pp. 41–68.

Cherry, J.F., 1984. The initial colonization of the West Mediterranean islands in the light of island biogeography and paleogeography. In: W. Waldren, R. Chapman, J. Lewthwaite and R.-C. Kennard, eds. *The Deyà Conference of Prehistory: Early Settlement in the Western Mediterranean Islands and the Peripheral Areas* (BAR International Series 229, 4 vols). Oxford: Oxbow, pp. 7–28.

Cherry, J.F., 1985. Islands out of the stream: isolation and interaction in early East Mediterranean insular prehistory. In: A.B. Knapp and T. Stech, eds. *Prehistoric Production and Exchange: The Aegean and Eastern Mediterranean* (UCLA Institute of Archaeology Monograph 25). Los Angeles, CA: Cotsen Institute of Archaeology, pp. 12–29.

Cherry, J.F., 1990. The first colonization of the Mediterranean islands: a review of recent research. *Journal of Mediterranean Archaeology,* 3, pp. 145–221.

Cherry, J.F., 2004. Mediterranean island archaeology: what's different and what's new? In: S.M. Fitzpatrick, ed. *Voyages of Discovery: The Archaeology of Islands.* Westport, CT: Praeger, pp. 233–248.

Cherry, J.F. and Leppard, T.P., 2014. A little history of Mediterranean island prehistory. In: A.B. Knapp and P. van Dommelen, eds. *The Cambridge Prehistory of the Bronze Age–Iron Age Mediterranean.* Cambridge: Cambridge University Press, pp. 10–24.

Cherry, J.F. and Leppard, T.P., 2018a. The Balearic paradox: why were the islands colonized so late? *Pyrenae: Journal of Western Mediterranean Prehistory and Antiquity,* 49(1), pp. 49–70.

Cherry, J.F. and Leppard, T.P., 2018b. Patterning and its causation in the pre-Neolithic colonization of the Mediterranean islands (Late Pleistocene to Early Holocene). *Journal of Island and Coastal Archaeology,* 13(2), pp. 191–205.

Clark, J.T. and Terrell, J., 1978. Archaeology in Oceania. *Annual Review of Anthropology,* 7, pp. 293–319.

Cochrane, E.E. and Hunt, T.L., 2018. The archaeology of prehistoric Oceania. In: E.E. Cochrane and T.L. Hunt, eds. *The Oxford Handbook of Prehistoric Oceania.* Oxford: Oxford University Press, pp. 1–26.

Cooke, S.B., Dávalos, L.M., Mychajliw, A.M., Turvey, S.T. and Upham, N.T., 2017. Anthropogenic extinction dominates Holocene declines of West Indian mammals. *Annual Review of Ecology, Evolution, and Systematics,* 48, pp. 301–327.

Crumley, C.L., ed. 1994. *Historical Ecology: Cultural Knowledge and Changing Landscapes.* Santa Fe, NM: SAR Press.

Curet, A., 2005. *Caribbean Paleodemography: Population, Culture History, and Sociopolitical Processes in Ancient Puerto Rico.* Tuscaloosa, AL: University of Alabama Press.

Dawson, H., 2006. Understanding colonization: adaptation strategies in the central Mediterranean islands. *Accordia Research Papers,* 10, pp. 35–60.

Dawson, H., 2014. *Mediterranean Voyages: The Archaeology of Island Colonisation and Abandonment.* Walnut Creek, CA: Left Coast Press.

Deevey, E.S., 1964. General and historical ecology. *BioScience,* 14(7), pp. 33–35.

DiNapoli, R. and Leppard, T.P., 2018. Islands as model environments. *Journal of Island and Coastal Archaeology,* 13(2), pp. 157–160.

Dotte-Sarout, E., 2017. How dare our 'prehistoric' have a prehistory of their own?! The interplay of historical and biographical contexts in early French archaeology of the Pacific. *Journal of Pacific Archaeology*, 8(1), pp. 23–34.

Erlandson, J.M. and Fitzpatrick, S.M., 2006. Oceans, islands, and coasts: current perspectives on the role of the sea in human prehistory. *Journal of Island and Coastal Archaeology*, 1(1), pp. 5–32.

Erlandson, J.M., Rick, T.C. Braje, T.J., Steinberg, A. and Vellanoweth, R.L., 2008. Human impacts on ancient shellfish: a 10,000 year record from San Miguel Island, California. *Journal of Archaeological Science*, 35, pp. 2144–2152.

Evans, J.D., 1973. Islands as laboratories of culture change. In: C. Renfrew, ed. *The Explanation of Culture Change: Models in Prehistory*. London: Duckworth, pp. 517–520.

Evans, J.D., 1977. Island archaeology in the Mediterranean: problems and opportunities. *World Archaeology*, 9(1), pp. 12–26.

Farr, H., 2006. Seafaring as social action. *Journal of Maritime Archaeology*, 1(1), pp. 85–99.

Fitzhugh, B. and Hunt, T.L., 1997. Introduction: islands as laboratories: archaeological research in comparative perspective. *Human Ecology*, 25(3): 379–383.

Fitzpatrick, S.M., 2004. *Quo vadis* Caribbean archaeology? The future of the discipline in an international forum. *Caribbean Journal of Science*, 40(3), pp. 281–290.

Fitzpatrick, S.M., 2006. A critical approach to 14C dating in the Caribbean: Using chrono-metric hygiene to evaluate chronological control and prehistoric settlement. *Latin American Antiquity*, 17(4), pp. 389–418.

Fitzpatrick, S.M., 2015. The Pre-Columbian Caribbean: Colonization, Population Dispersal, and Island Adaptations. *PaleoAmerica*, 1(4), pp. 305–331.

Fitzpatrick, S.M., 2018a. Islands in the comparative stream: the importance of inter-island analogies to archaeological discourse. In: A.R. Knodell and T.P. Leppard, eds. *Regional Approaches to Society and Complexity: Studies in Honor of John F. Cherry*. Sheffield: Equinox, pp. 207–224.

Fitzpatrick, S.M., 2018b. Comparative perspectives on pre-Columbian farming in the Caribbean as seen through the lens of historical ecology. In: B. Reid, ed. *The Archaeology of Caribbean and Circum-Caribbean Farmers (6000 BC–AD 1500)*, London: Routledge, pp. 63–82.

Fitzpatrick, S.M., and Anderson, A., 2008. Islands of isolation: archaeology and the power of aquatic perimeters. *Journal of Island and Coastal Archaeology*, 3(1), pp. 4–16.

Fitzpatrick, S.M. and Keegan, W.F., 2007. Human impacts and adaptations in the Caribbean Islands: An historical ecology approach. *Earth and Environmental Science Transactions of the Royal Society of Edinburgh*, 98(1), pp. 29–45.

Fitzpatrick, S.M. and Ross, A.H., eds. 2010. *Island Shores, Distant Pasts: Archaeological and Biological Approaches to the Pre-Columbian Settlement of the Caribbean*. Gainesville, FL: University Press of Florida.

Fitzpatrick, S.M., Erlandson, J.M, Anderson, A. and Kirch, P.V., 2007. Straw boats and the pro-verbial sea: a response to 'Island Archaeology: In Search of a new Horizon'. *Island Studies Journal*, 2(2), pp. 229–238.

Fitzpatrick, S.M., Rick, T.C. and Erlandson, J.M., 2015. Recent progress, trends, and developments in island and coastal archaeology. *Journal of Island and Coastal Archaeology*, 10(1), pp. 3–27.

Fosberg, F.R., ed. 1963a. *Man's Place in the Island Ecosystem*. Honolulu: Bishop Museum Press.

Fosberg, F.R., 1963b. The island ecosystem. In: F.R. Fosberg, ed. *Man's Place in the Island Ecosystem*. Honolulu: Bishop Museum Press, pp. 1–6.

Ghilardi, M. and Lespez, L., 2017. Geoarchaeology of the Mediterranean islands: from 'lost worlds' to vibrant places. *Journal of Archaeological Science: Reports,* 12, pp. 735–740.

Giovas, C.M., 2017a. Continental connections and insular distributions: deer bone artifacts of the Precolumbian West Indies – a review and synthesis with new records. *Latin American Antiquity,* 29(1), pp. 27–43.

Giovas, C.M., 2017b. The beasts at large: perennial questions and new paradigms for Caribbean translocation research. Part I: Ethnozoogeography of mammals. *Environmental Archaeology,* 24(2), pp. 182–198. doi: 10.1080/14614103.2017.1315208.

Giovas, C.M., 2018. Pre-Columbian Amerindian lifeways at the Sabazan site, Carriacou, West Indies. *The Journal of Island and Coastal Archaeology,* 13(2), pp. 161–190.

Giovas, C.M., LeFebvre, M.J. and Fitzpatrick, S.M., 2012. New records for prehistoric introduction of Neotropical mammals to the West Indies: evidence from Carriacou, Lesser Antilles. *Journal of Biogeography,* 39(3), pp. 476–487.

Gómez Bellard, C., 1995. The first colonization of Ibiza and Formentera (Balearic Islands, Spain): some more islands out of the stream? *World Archaeology,* 26, pp. 442–455.

Goodwin, R.C., 1978. Demographic change and the crab-shell economy. *Proceedings of the Eighth International Congress for the Study of Pre-Columbian Cultures of the Lesser Antilles.* Tempe, AZ: Arizona State University, pp. 45–68.

Goodenough, W., 1957. Oceania and the problem of controls in the study of cultural and human evolution. *Journal of the Polynesian Society,* 66, pp. 146–155.

Gosden, C. and Pavlides, C., 1994. Are islands insular? Landscape vs. seascape in the case of the Arawe Islands, Papua New Guinea. *Archaeology in Oceania,* 29, pp. 162–171.

Hau'ofa, E., 1993. Our sea of islands. In: E. Waddell, V. Naidu and E. Hau'ofa, eds. *A New Oceania: Rediscovering our Sea of Islands.* Suva, Fiji: University of the South Pacific, pp. 2–16.

Held, S.O., 1989a. Colonization cycles on Cyprus I: the biogeographic and palaeontological foundations of early prehistoric settlement. *Report of the Department of Antiquities, Cyprus,* 1989, pp. 7–28.

Held, S.O., 1989b. Early Prehistoric Island Archaeology in Cyprus: Configurations of Formative Culture Growth from the Pleistocene/Holocene Boundary to the mid-3rd Millennium BC. Unpublished PhD dissertation, Institute of Archaeology, University College London.

Held, S.O., 1993. Insularity as a modifier of culture change: the case of prehistoric Cyprus. *Bulletin of the American School ls of Oriental Research,* 292, pp. 25–33.

Hofman, C.L. and van Duijvenbode, A., eds. 2011. *Communities in Contact: Essays in Archaeology, Ethnohistory, and Ethnography of the Amerindian Circum-Caribbean.* Leiden: Sidestone Press.

Hofman, C.L., Bright, A.J., Hoogland, M.L. and Keegan, W.F., 2008. Attractive ideas, desirable goods: examining the Late Ceramic Age relationships between Greater and Lesser Antillean societies. *Journal of Island and Coastal Archaeology,* 3(1), pp. 17–34.

Hofman, C.L., Bright, A.J. and Rodríguez Ramos, R., 2010. Crossing the Caribbean Sea: towards a holistic view of pre-colonial mobility and exchange. *Journal of Caribbean Archaeology,* special number 3, pp. 1–18.

Hofman, C.L., Mol, A.A.A., Hoogland, M.L.P. and Valcarel Rojas, R., 2014. State of encounters: migration, mobility and interaction in the pre-colonial and early colonial Caribbean. *World Archaeology,* 46(4), pp. 590–609.

Hunt, T.L., 1987. Patterns of human interaction and evolutionary divergence in the Fiji Islands. *Journal of the Polynesian Society,* 96(3), pp. 299–334.

Keegan, W.F., 2007. *Benjamin Irving Rouse 1913–2006: A Biographical Memoir.* Washington, DC: National Academy of Sciences.

Keegan, W.F. and Diamond, J.M., 1987. Colonization of islands by humans: a biogeographical perspective. *Advances in Archaeological Method and Theory*, 10, pp. 49–92.

Keegan, W.F. and Hofman, C.L., 2017. *The Caribbean before Columbus.* Oxford: Oxford University Press.

Keegan, W.F., Portell, R.W. and Slapcinsky, J., 2003. Changes in invertebrate taxa at two pre-Columbian sites in southwestern Jamaica, AD 800–1500. *Journal of Archaeological Science*, 30(12), pp. 1607–1617.

Kirch, P.V., 1978. The Lapitoid period in west Polynesia: excavations and survey in Niuatoputapu, Tonga. *Journal of Field Archaeology*, 5(1), pp. 1–13.

Kirch, P.V., 1980. Polynesian prehistory: cultural adaptation in island ecosystems. *American Scientist*, 63, pp. 39–48.

Kirch, P.V., 1981. Lapitoid settlements of Futuna and Alofi, western Polynesia. *Archaeology in Oceania*, 16(3), pp. 127–143.

Kirch, P.V., 1984. *The Evolution of the Polynesian Chiefdoms.* Cambridge: Cambridge University Press.

Kirch, P.V., 1997a. Microcosmic histories: island perspectives on 'global' change. *American Anthropologist*, 99(1), pp. 30–42.

Kirch, P.V., 1997b. Introduction: the environmental history of oceanic islands. In: P.V. Kirch and T.L. Hunt, eds. *Historical Ecology in the Pacific Islands: Prehistoric Environmental and Landscape Change.* New Haven, CT: Yale University Press, pp. 1–21.

Kirch, P.V., 2004. Oceanic islands: microcosms of 'global change'. In: C.L. Redman, S.R. James, P.R. Fish and J.D. Rogers, eds. *The Archaeology of Global Change: The Impact of Humans on their Environment.* Washington, DC: Smithsonian Press, pp. 13–27.

Kirch, P.V., 2007a. Hawaii as a model system for human ecodynamics. *American Anthropologist*, 109(1), pp. 8–26.

Kirch, P.V., 2007b. Three islands and an archipelago: reciprocal interactions between humans and island ecosystems in Polynesia. *Earth and Environmental Science Transactions of The Royal Society of Edinburgh*, 98(1), pp. 85–99.

Kirch, P.V. and Green, R.C., 1987. History, phylogeny, and evolution in Polynesia. *Current Anthropology*, 28(4), pp. 161–186.

Kirch, P.V. and Hunt, T.L., eds. 1997. *Historical Ecology in the Pacific Islands: Prehistoric Environmental and Landscape Change.* New Haven, CT: Yale University Press.

Kuklick, H., 1996. Islands in the Pacific: Darwinian biogeography and British anthropology. *American Ethnologist*, 23(3), pp. 611–638.

Laffoon J.E., Hoogland, M.L.P., Davies, G.R. and Hofman, C.L., 2017a. A multi-isotope investigation of human and dog mobility and diet in the pre-colonial Antilles. *Environmental Archaeology*, 24(2), pp. 132–148. doi: 10.1080/14614103.2017.1322831

Laffoon J.E., Sonnemann, T.F., Shafie, T., Hofman, C.L., Brandes, U. and Davies, G.R., 2017b. Investigating human geographic origins using dual-isotope (87Sr/86Sr, δ18O) assignment approaches. *PloS One*, 12(2), e0172562.

Lape, P.V., 2004. The isolation metaphor in island archaeology. In: S.M. Fitzpatrick, ed., *Voyages of Discovery: The Archaeology of Islands*, Westport, CT: Praeger, pp. 223–232.

LeFebvre, M.J., 2007. Zooarchaeological analysis of prehistoric vertebrate exploitation at the Grand Bay Site, Carriacou, West Indies. *Coral Reefs*, 26(4), pp. 931–944.

Leppard, T.P., 2015. Adaptive responses to demographic fragility: mitigating stochastic effects in early island colonization. *Human Ecology*, 43(5), pp. 721–734.

Leppard, T.P., 2017. The biophysical effects of Neolithic island colonization: general dynamics and sociocultural implications. *Human Ecology*, 45(5), pp. 555–568.

Leppard, T.P., 2018. Unique challenges in archipelagos: examples from the Mediterranean and Pacific islands. In: P. Siegel, ed. *Island Historical Ecology: Socionatural Landscapes across the Caribbean Sea.* New York: Berghahn, pp. 15–33.

MacArthur, R.H. and Wilson, E.O., 1963. An equilibrium theory of insular zoogeography. *Evolution*, 17, pp. 373–387.

MacArthur, R.H. and Wilson, E.O., 1967. *The Theory of Island Biogeography*. Princeton, NJ: Princeton University Press.

Malinowski, B., 1922. *Argonauts of the Western Pacific*. London: Routledge.

Mead, M., 1928. *Coming of Age in Samoa*. New York: Morrow Quill.

Mead, M., 1957. Introduction to Polynesia as a laboratory for the development of models in the study of cultural evolution. *Journal of the Polynesian Society*, 66, p. 145.

Moss, M.L., 2004. Island societies are not always insular: Tlingit territories in the Alexander Archipelago and the adjacent Alaska mainland. In: S.M. Fitzpatrick, ed. *Voyages of Discovery: The Archaeology of Islands*, Westport, CT: Praeger. pp. 165–183.

Newsom, L.A. and Wing, E., 2004. *On Land and Sea: Native American Uses of Biological Resources in the West Indies*. Tuscaloosa, AL: University of Alabama Press.

Patton, M., 1996. *Islands in Time: Island Sociogeography and Mediterranean Prehistory*. London: Routledge.

Pauketat, T., 2007. *Chiefdoms and Other Archaeological Delusions*. Lanham, MD: AltaMira Press.

Rainbird, P., 1999. Islands out of time: towards a critique of island archaeology. *Journal of Mediterranean Archaeology*, 12(2), pp. 216–234.

Rainbird, P., 2007. *The Archaeology of Islands*. Cambridge: Cambridge University Press.

Reid, B., ed., 2018. *The Archaeology of Caribbean and Circum-Caribbean Farmers (6000 BC–AD 1500)*. London: Routledge.

Renfrew, C., 1973. *Before Civilization: The Radiocarbon Revolution and Prehistoric Europe*. London: Jonathan Cape.

Renfrew, C., 1980. The great tradition versus the great divide: archaeology as anthropology? *American Journal of Archaeology*, 84, pp. 287–298.

Rick, T.C. and Erlandson, J.M., eds, 2008. *Human Impacts on Ancient Marine Ecosystems: A Global Perspective*. Berkeley and Los Angeles, CA: University of California Press.

Rieth, T.M. and Athens, J.S., 2017. Late Holocene human expansion into Near and Remote Oceania: a Bayesian Model of the chronologies of the Mariana Islands and Bismarck Archipelago. *Journal of Island and Coastal Archaeology*, 14(1), pp. 5–16. doi: 10.1080/15564894.2017.1331939

Rivers, W., 1913. Report on anthropological research outside America. In: W. Rivers, A. Jenks and S. Morley, eds. *The Present Constitution and Future Needs of the Science of Anthropology*. Washington, DC: Carnegie Institution, pp. 5–28.

Robb, J., 2001. Island identities: ritual, travel, and the creation of difference in Neolithic Malta. *European Journal of Archaeology*, 4(2), pp. 175–202.

Rouse, I., 1977. Pattern and process in West Indian archaeology. *World Archaeology*, 9(1), pp. 1–11.

Rouse, I., 1985. Arawakan phylogeny, Caribbean chronology, and their implications for the study of population movement. *Antropológica*, 63–4, pp. 9–21.

Rouse, I., 1986. *Migrations in Prehistory: Inferring Population Movement from Cultural Remains*. New Haven, CT: Yale University Press.

Rouse, I., 1989. People and cultures of the Saladoid frontier in the Greater Antilles. In: P. Siegel, ed. *Early Ceramic Population Lifeways and Adaptive Strategies in the Caribbean* (BAR International Series 506). Oxford: British Archaeological Reports, pp. 383–403.

Sahlins, M., 1955. Esoteric efflorescence in Easter Island. *American Anthropologist*, 57, pp. 1045–1052.

Sahlins, M., 1958. *Social Stratification in Polynesia*. Seattle, WA: University of Washington Press.

Sahlins, M., 1963. Poor man, rich man, big-man, chief: political types in Melanesia and Polynesia. *Comparative Studies in Society and History*, 5(3), pp. 285–303.

Siegel, P.E., ed. 2018. *Island Historical Ecology: Socionatural Landscapes of the Eastern and Southern Caribbean*. Oxford and New York: Berghahn.

Siegel, P.E., Jones, J.G., Pearsall, D.M., Dunning, N.P., Farrell, P., Duncan, N.A. Curtis, J.H. and Singh, S.K., 2015. Palaeoenvironmental evidence for first human colonization of the eastern Caribbean. *Quaternary Science Reviews,* 129, pp. 275–295.

Simberloff, D. and Wilson, E., 1969. Experimental zoogeography of islands: The colonization of empty islands. *Ecology,* 50(2), pp. 278–296.

Simberloff, D., and Wilson, E., 1970. Experimental zoogeography of islands: a two-year record of colonization. *Ecology,* 51(5), pp. 934–937.

Skoglund, P., Posth, C., Sirak, K., Spriggs, M., Valentin, F., Bedford, S., Clark, G.R., Reepmeyer, C., Petchey, F., Fernandes, D., Fu, Q., Harney, E., Lipson, M., Mallick, S., Novak, M., Rohland, N., Stewardson, K., Abdullah, S., Cox, M.P., Friedlaender, F.R., Friedlaender, J.S., Kivisild, T., Koki, G., Kusuma, P., Merriwether, D.A., Ricaut, F.-X, Wee, J.T.S., Patterson, N., Krause, J., Pinhasi, R., and Reich, D., 2016. Genomic insights into the peopling of the Southwest Pacific. *Nature,* 538, pp. 510–513.

Smith, M.E, ed. 2011. *The Comparative Archaeology of Complex Societies.* Cambridge: Cambridge University Press.

Steadman, D.W. and Jones, S., 2006. Long-term trends in prehistoric fishing and hunting on Tobago, West Indies. *Latin American Antiquity,* 17(3), pp. 316–334.

Steadman, D.W., Singleton, H.M., Delancy, K.M., Albury, N.A., Soto-Centeno, J.A., Gough, H., Duncan, N., Franklin, J. and Keegan, W.F., 2017. Late Holocene historical ecology: the timing of vertebrate extirpation on Crooked Island, Commonwealth of The Bahamas. *Journal of Island and Coastal Archaeology,* 12(4), pp. 572–584.

Sureda, P., Camarós, E., Cueto, M., Teira, L.C., Aceituno, F.J., Albero, D., Álvarez-Fernández, E., Bofill, M., López-Dóriga, I., Marín, D., Masclans, A., Picornell, L., Revelles, J. and Burjachs, F., 2017. Surviving on the isle of Formentera (Balearic Islands): adaptation of economic behaviour by Bronze Age first settlers to an extreme insular environment. *Journal of Archaeological Science: Reports,* 12, pp. 860–875.

Terrell, J.E., 1977a. Biology, biogeography, and man. *World Archaeology,* 8, pp. 237–247.

Terrell, J.E., 1977b. *Human Biogeography in the Solomon Islands.* Chicago, IL: Field Museum of Natural History.

Terrell, J.E., 1986. *Prehistory in the Pacific Islands.* Cambridge: Cambridge University Press.

Terrell, J.E., Hunt, T.L. and Gosden, C., 1997. The dimensions of social life in the Pacific: human diversity and the myth of the primitive isolate. *Current Anthropology,* 38(2), pp. 155–195.

Terrell, J.E., Kelly, K. and Rainbird, P., 2001. Foregone conclusions? In search of 'Papuans' and 'Austronesians'. *Current Anthropology,* 42(1), pp. 97–124.

van Dommelen, P. and Knapp, A.B., eds, 2010. *Material Connections in the Ancient Mediterranean: Mobility, Materiality and Mediterranean Identities.* London: Routledge.

van Hengstum, P.J., Maale, G., Donnelly, J.P., Albury, N.A, Onac, B.P., Sullivan, R.M., Winkler, T.S., Tamalavage, A.E. and MacDonald, D., 2018. Drought in the northern Bahamas from 3300 to 2500 years ago. *Quaternary Science Reviews,* 186, pp. 169–185.

Vayda, A.P. and Rappaport, R.A., 1963. Island cultures. In: F.R. Fosberg, ed. *Man's Place in the Island Ecosystem.* Honolulu: Bishop Museum Press, pp. 133–144.

Vella, C., 2016. Manipulated connectivity in island isolation: Maltese prehistoric stone tool technology and procurement strategies across the fourth and third millennia BC. *Journal of Island and Coastal Archaeology,* 11(3), pp. 344–363.

Veloz Maggiolo, M., 1976–7. *Medioambiente y adaptación humana en la prehistoria de Santo Domingo* (2 vols). Santiago: Ediciones de Taller.

Vitousek, P.M., 2002. Oceanic islands as model systems for ecological studies. *Journal of Biogeography,* 29(5–6), pp. 773–582.

Watters, D., 1980. Transect surveying and prehistoric site locations on Barbuda and Montserrat, Leeward Islands, West Indies. Unpublished PhD dissertation, Department of Anthropology, University of Pittsburgh.

Watters, D., 1981. Relating oceanography to Antillean archaeology: implications from Oceania. *Journal of New World Archaeology,* 5, pp. 3–12.

Wing, E.S., 2001. The sustainability of resources used by Native Americans on four Caribbean islands. *International Journal of Osteoarchaeology,* 11(1–2), pp. 112–126.

Wing, S. and Wing, E., 2001. Prehistoric fisheries in the Caribbean. *Coral Reefs,* 20(1), pp. 1–8.

Yoffee, N., 2005. *Myths of the Archaic State: Evolution of the Earliest Cities, States, and Civilizations.* Cambridge: Cambridge University Press.

3

PACIFIC ISLAND ARCHAEOLOGY AND EVOLUTIONARY THEORY

Ethan E. Cochrane

Introduction

The Pacific Islands have been a crucible for the development of evolutionary concepts in archaeology and anthropology that are now used world-wide. Pacific researchers' experimentations with evolution (e.g. Sahlins, 1960) were originally based upon the cultural evolution of 19th-century scholars, and their ladder of evolutionary progress. Since the 1970s, however, and under some influence from Americanist New Archaeology (O'Brien et al., 2005), evolutionary research in the region dismissed the more strident, progressivist Victorian ideas and focused increasingly on both adaptive processes that might explain the functioning of past societies (e.g. Kirch, 1980) and ecological models applied to human behaviour (e.g. Anderson, 1981). Later still, another evolutionary framework in the Pacific (e.g. Allen, 1996) developed from a mixture of mathematical models of cultural trait transmission (e.g. Cavalli-Sforza and Feldman, 1981; Boyd and Richerson, 1985) and a generalisation of evolutionary concepts beyond biology (e.g. Dunnell, 1978).

This chapter outlines the use of evolutionary theory in Pacific Island archaeology, noting the points of commonality and divergences of thought in the most prominent evolutionary frameworks. The next section reviews these frameworks in the Pacific and focuses on their most important theoretical contributions. The earliest framework, the Ladder of Cultural Evolution, while tinged with dubious notions of progress, emphasised the importance of phylogenetic history or cultural relatedness, and encouraged theorising on processes of societal change. A framework focused on phylogenetic history and adaptation emerged from ladder-like approaches but developed and expanded both a range of adaptive processes to account for the similarities and differences amongst populations, and sophisticated techniques to generate hypotheses of cultural or phylogenetic relatedness. A third framework, focused on selection, drift and related artefact classifications privileges explanations that invoke evolutionary processes, complementary to proximate processes. Proximate processes refer to the socio-natural dynamics that generate the costs and benefits associated with variants of a behavioural type, while evolutionary processes refer to the sorting mechanisms, such as selection, that act on those costs and benefits to generate behavioural distributions through time and space (Winterhalder and Smith, 2000, pp. 52–54).

The final section compares two frameworks' explanation of a pivotal event, the Lapita migration from Near to Remote Oceania. This comparison demonstrates the application of proximate and evolutionary mechanisms and the recognition of phylogeny, but also proposes that robust explanations should employ descriptions of the archaeological record using units, artefact types or other classes, that are explicitly linked to evolutionary theory.

Evolutionary theories in the Pacific

Like many attempts at intellectual categorisation, the following division of evolutionary frameworks in Pacific Island archaeology is meant to highlight distinguishing features, but these frameworks are sometimes combined in single analyses or bodies of work.

The ladder of cultural evolution: stages and adaptive advances

The evolutionary concepts first used to explain variation in Pacific Island material culture and practices derive from a ladder-like view of cultural evolution. In this view, populations occupy different rungs on a ladder of increasing complexity or progress. For example, d'Urville's (1832) widely used division of the Pacific into Melanesia, Micronesia and Polynesia included an assumption that the people in these geographic regions were of differing social and political complexities, with Polynesians the most advanced and Melanesians the least (Clark, 2003, pp. 157–158). However, the idea that populations of different complexity were evidence of processes of evolutionary development was not elaborated for several more decades until Spencer (1855, 1857, 1873) prominently argued that human social development, from lower forms to higher forms, was caused by the cultural inheritance of human inventions and a force leading to perfection or progress (Freeman, 1974). Rungs on the ladder of progress were also given labels including Morgan's (1877) savagery, barbarism and civilisation that fit with the age-system of European archaeology popular at the time (Dunnell, 1988).

The ladder-like view of cultural evolution is distinct from Darwinian evolution (Fig. 3.1) and is not built upon the latter's theoretical assumptions of variation, transmission and selection (Blute, 1979; Dunnell, 1980; Mesoudi, 2016). Instead, and despite the use of phrases such as 'survival of the fittest' by 19th-century cultural evolutionists, the ladder-like view of cultural evolution is transformational, and not based on a Darwinian selection process (contra Carneiro, 2003, pp. 68–73). In the transformational view explanations state the processes by which one societal

Spencerian Evolution

Darwinian Evolution

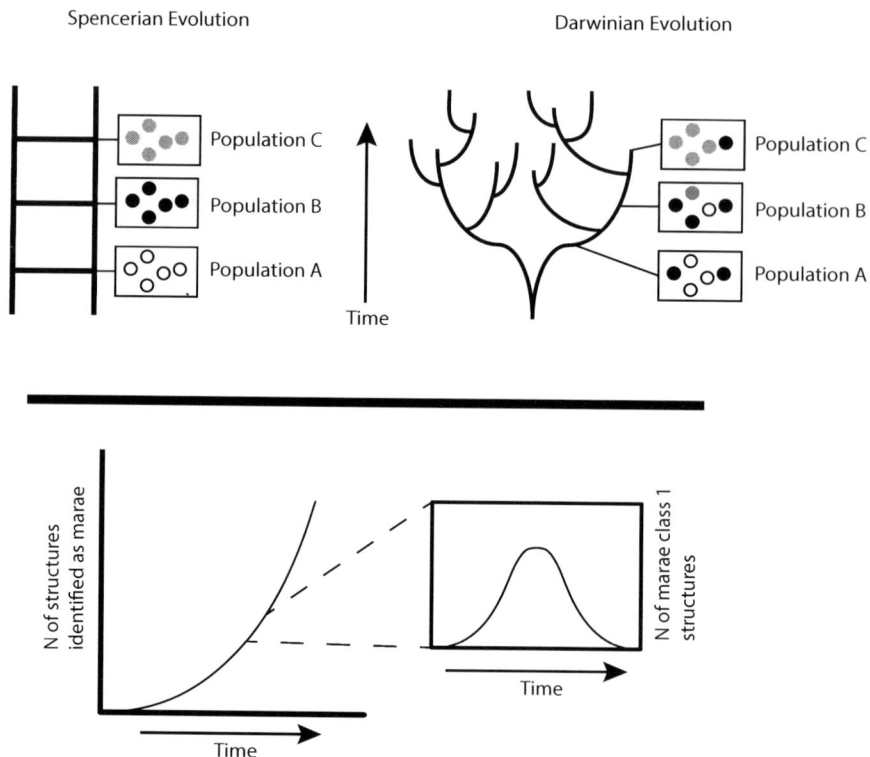

FIGURE 3.1 Comparison of Darwinian evolutionary and ladder-like cultural evolutionary perspectives on change. *Top left:* the transformational approach to variation within types. *Top right:* the Darwinian approach to variation within types (after Mesoudi, 2016, fig. 2.1, and Medawar, 1953, figs. 4, 5). *Bottom:* distributions (exponential on left, monotonic on right) produced by archaeologist-constructed cultural trait classes ('marae' and the finer-grained 'marae class 1') are the focus of explanation in evolutionary archaeology (after Cochrane, 2001, fig. 10.2).

type transforms to another. Tylor (1870), as an example of the time, suggested technology transfer might explain the transformation of a tribe, a low rung on the ladder, to a higher civilisation. Even with more rungs or finer-grained types – incipient and simple chiefdoms (Steponaitis, 1978; Earle, 1987), archaic and modern states (Marcus and Feinman, 1998) – the explanatory focus remains the processes whereby one finer-grained type transforms to another. In the transformational view, societal types exist in the sense that explanations account for how these types originate.

This contrasts with some explanations in Darwinian evolution where types do not exist independent of the analyst, but are conceptualised and constructed as measurement units (Mayr, 1959), the artificiality of which is obvious if you imagine types in the human lineage, an *H. erectus*, for example, birthing an

H. sapiens. Using a similar approach in archaeology, types are constructed and used to characterise variant distributions in the archaeological record (Cochrane, 2001) and it is these variant distributions that are the focus of explanation (Fig. 3.1). As types are a product of archaeological classification procedures, their origin is a non-question.

The influence of 19th-century cultural evolutionism on Americanist archaeology and ethnology was dimmed by Boas's focus (e.g. 1911) on the particularistic aspects of cultures. By the mid-20th century, however, ladder-like cultural evolution was rekindled by Leslie White who linked Spencer's nebulously defined force of progress to specific empirical variation across populations. White clearly associated cultural evolution with the amount of energy extracted from the environment by populations:

> Social systems are but the social form of expression of technological control over the forces of nature. Social evolution is therefore a function of technological development. Social systems evolve as the amount of energy harnessed per capita per year increases, other factors remaining constant. This is to say, they become more differentiated structurally, more specialized functionally, and as a consequence of differentiation and specialization, special mechanisms of integration and regulation are developed.
>
> *(White, 1959, pp. 144–145; see also White, 1943)*

Sahlins described White's proposal as general evolution, the focus of which is 'the determination and explanation of the successive transformations of culture through its several stages of overall progress' (1960, p. 29). General evolution, Sahlins also argued, was distinct from specific evolution, which was concerned with adaptation within cultural lineages, for example, how the diversification of production systems in related Polynesian chiefdoms show adaptive advances (Sahlins, 1958). Specific evolution was also related to Steward's (1955) multilinear cultural evolution that investigated similarities between cultural traditions to identify adaptive regularities (e.g. patrilineal bands), particularly those associated with certain environments. In contrast to Steward, however, Sahlins considered a complete explanation of culture to include both specific and general evolution as 'the former is a connected, historic sequence of forms, the latter a sequence of stages exemplified by forms of a given order of development' (Sahlins, 1960, p. 33).

Nevertheless, Sahlins (1958) focused on specific evolution in his study of social stratification in Polynesia where he identified adaptive regularities, in large part, by the number of status levels present, and grouped them into three types (from greater to fewer status levels): ramage systems, descent-line systems and atoll systems. Since it was not possible to generate data on productivity or per capita energy extraction in these societies (as White's proposal required), Sahlins argued that variation in surplus food production, measured by the spatial scale and frequency of its distribution, is a valid proxy for per capita energy extraction (Sahlins, 1958, pp. 107–110, table 1). He concluded that societies with greater social stratification, with ramage systems for example, had greater surplus, and therefore greater per capita energy extraction, confirming White's general evolutionary thesis.

White's notion that more evolved societies should also exhibit relatively greater structural differentiation and functional specialisation was also suggested by Sahlins and others (e.g. Service, 1962) working in the Pacific. For example, Sahlins described how more highly developed chiefdoms should have a greater number of cultural sub-systems and more specialised sub-systems than less developed tribes (Sahlins, 1960, pp. 21–22 and pp. 35–37; 1972).

While mid-century cultural evolutionists correlated societal stages with productivity measured in various ways, the processes that cause societies to become more productive and transform from one rung on the ladder to the next have been continuously, if somewhat infrequently, debated (Carneiro, 2003, pp. 155–156). These processes, such as Goldman's (1955) inherent status rivalry, Friedman's (1981) structuralist transformation, Kirch's (1984) competition in limited environments, Earle's (1997) political economy and the culturally specific rules or social logic of Flannery and Marcus (2012), all include individuals, groups or societies adapting to new socio–natural environments. Current archaeological research that privileges these processes relies, at least in part, upon emic perspectives or human motivations to explain cultural evolution and changes in cultural complexity (e.g. Kirch, 2010; Lepofsky and Kahn, 2011; Clark, 2017; Quintus and Cochrane, 2018).

Ladder-like cultural evolution has influenced archaeological thinking on the processes that may explain changes in cultural complexity, but ladder-like cultural evolution is also widely employed in Pacific archaeology in another way. The general characteristics of a rung on the ladder, a societal type, are used to culturally reconstruct a time-space portion of the archaeological record as representing, for example, a tribe or chiefdom. The association of some characteristic of the archaeological record with a particular type – monumental architecture with chiefdoms, for example – aids in the reconstruction of other aspects of ancient society (e.g. Stevenson, 2002; Wallin and Solsvik, 2010). Clark et al. (2008), for example, suggest that the cultural chronology of monumental tomb constructions and harbour modifications at Lapaha, Tonga, supports a pre-AD 1450 date for marine transport associated with 'inasi, the first-fruits ceremony found in many Pacific chiefdoms. Tongan chiefs 'may have been using the 'inasi and other ceremonies to promote social cohesion among local and non-local groups in the newly constituted and geographically dispersed chiefdom' (Clark et al., 2008, p. 1006). Other aspects of chiefdom society have been reconstructed at various times and places from the Pacific island archaeological record including alliances between New Caledonia chiefdoms (Sand et al., 2003), the possible dual sacred and secular leadership roles in ancient Samoa (Wallin and Martinsson-Wallin, 2007), and attached specialist carvers in Rapa Nui (Simpson et al., 2018).

Leonard and Jones (1987) pointed out a potential problem with this cultural reconstruction approach over 30 years ago after analysing the data within Murdock's (1967) *Ethnographic Atlas*, and focusing on three variables: community organisation, settlement pattern and class stratification. They demonstrated that the values within these variables that typically define cultural evolutionary stages – for example, the segmented communities, complex settlements and dual stratification of chiefdoms – do not often appear as a package within particular ethnographically described societies (Leonard and Jones, 1987, table 1). In other words, using an archaeologically visible trait, such as monumental architecture, to infer additional, less easily observed traits of particular societal types, can lead to unrecognised errors, a problem occasionally identified in the Pacific (Sand, 2002) and elsewhere (Wengrow and Graeber, 2015; Hildebrand et al., 2018).

Phylogenetic history and adaptation: the legacy of islands as laboratories

In his discussion of specific and general evolution, Sahlins described the study of specific evolution of cultures as the examination of cultural traits 'arising through adaptation' (Sahlins, 1960, p. 25) within phylogenetically related societies. According to Sahlins when a group enters a new environment, traits arising through adaptation are synthesised from the group's previous traits, or are diffused from other groups, or both (Sahlins, 1960, p. 24). These ideas were developed in the Pacific most prominently by Kirch (1984) in his seminal book *The Evolution of the Polynesian Chiefdoms* (see also Kirch and Green, 1987; Kirch and Green, 2001). Kirch argued that the culturally related societies of Polynesia provide an opportunity to investigate how variation in environments, interaction and demography have influenced traits arising through adaptation in separate, but related societies.

The focus on adaptation is a defining feature of this approach. Adaptation is typically conceptualised as a proximate, ecological process whereby entities, such as human groups, continuously achieve a better fit with their changing environment (cf. Steward, 1955; Kirch, 1980). This privileges systems-like explanations, which are a component of evolutionary explanations in general, and identify how the values within a set of interrelated variables change (e.g. Kirch et al., 2012). These explanations are compatible with selection processes as they focus on the adaptive function of an evolved system, but they do not demonstrate why one system evolved relative to another (Dunnell, 1980). To illustrate the latter question, consider several behaviours explained as adaptive systems that minimise potentially lethal competition between groups over limited resources: Rapa Nui moai construction and costly signalling (DiNapoli et al., 2018); settlement locations in Fiji and economic defendability (Field, 2004); subsistence and flexible territories in the Channel Islands (Kennett and Clifford, 2004). To determine the evolutionary processes that resulted in a particular system – costly signalling and not economic defendability, for example – requires identifying the chronological and spatial history of behavioural alternatives and their relative fitnesses. Although such research has rarely occurred, Allen's (2011) study of different political systems provides a structure for this kind of analysis.

Various conceptual frameworks are used to generate explanations of societies as adaptive systems with Political Economy and Human Behavioural Ecology frameworks particularly prevalent in Pacific research. Political Economy frameworks focus on types of individuals, such as elites, and their variable ability to draw on different sources of power 'to strategically direct (and resist) the actions of social groups' (Earle, 1997, p. 208). Earle argues that three sources of power – economic, military and ideological – are most important for explaining changes in cultural complexity and control in societies. Natural environments and historical circumstances will also shape the use of particular power sources (Earle, 1997). Reviewing the history of Political Economy frameworks, Earle (1997, pp. 68–70) distinguishes those that are 'voluntarist, adaptationist theories' from 'coercive, political' ones. The former describe societies where elites and non-elites perform different, integrated roles that create an adaptive system, for example, chiefly management of collective water-rights for commoner farmers. The latter describe societies where different types of individuals variously compel others, or resist, through use of power. In fact, both kinds of Political Economy frameworks are adaptationist in the sense that the explanations generated consider the behaviour of types of individuals as interrelated with the variables of changing natural and social environment. In Hawaii, for example, the political economy of 600 or more years ago was based on control of staple finance (crops) in an area where agricultural productivity was high and could be increased through means of landesque capital. Contrastingly, in the Thy region of Denmark during the Neolithic-Bronze Age transition, the political economy was based on control of wealth finance (cattle) that could be easily moved and exchanged in a natural environment with little possibility for control of crop-based staple finance (Earle 1997). Political Economy frameworks are also adaptationist in that they typically produce system-like explanations and conceptualise culture as comprised of sets of interrelated variables, such that change in one variable may affect others (e.g. Earle, 1997, figure 6.1).

Human Behavioural Ecology (HBE) frameworks may also form the foundation for adaptive explanations in the Pacific (DiNapoli and Morrison 2017). In archaeology, HBE frameworks have long-assumed that relevant human variation is patterned by natural selection acting upon the distribution of fitness-related behaviours in particular social-ecological contexts (Irons, 1979; Smith and Winterhalder, 1992; Bird and O'Connell, 2006). Two additional assumptions are important: first, behaviours in a population are assumed to be a product of inheritance, but the type of inheritance, genetic or cultural, is not relevant (the phenotypic gambit; Smith and Winterhalder, 1992; Codding and Bird, 2015); second, HBE explanations are typically based on either optimisation (Macarthur and Pianka, 1966) or game-theory methods (Lewontin, 1961). When using optimisation methods, the distribution of individuals' behaviours is predicted to optimise some currency, such as net caloric return of hunted animals. The Prey Choice Model, for example, can be used to explain variable frequencies of hunted animals in a diachronic deposit by calculating the weights of different taxa (e.g. Morrison and Cochrane, 2008). Game-theory methods are used to predict the distribution of behaviours in a population when the fitness of a behaviour is influenced by the probabilities of interactions between different behaviour-types in a population. The Hawk-Dove model, for example, can be used to explain the distribution of aggressive and acquiescent behaviours in a population when the chances of aggressive-aggressive, aggressive-acquiescent and acquiescent-acquiescent interactions vary. Hayman (2019) has used this model to investigate the changing numbers of competitors for high-status titles in ancient Tonga relative to those who acquiesce at less potential cost, but therefore receive lower titles (cf. Aswani and Graves, 1998).

HBE, Political Economy and other adaptationist evolutionary research in Pacific archaeology often examines different systems that share phylogenetic history or cultural relatedness (e.g. Kirch, 1990; Allen, 2011; DiNapoli et al., 2018). Phylogenetic history may distinguish analogous or convergent similarity from homologous similarity or similarity that is a product of relatedness (Binford, 1968; Kirch and Green, 1987). Phylogenetic history is typically reconstructed either quantitatively using linguistic (e.g. Gray et al., 2009) or, less commonly, artefact data (e.g. Cochrane, 2015), or comparatively using historical linguistic methods (e.g. Blust, 1995) or artefact types (e.g. Emory, 1946).

For archaeologists, phylogenetic relationships, irrespective of how they are generated, are typically a valuable aid in archaeological interpretations. Gray and Jordan (2000), for example, constructed quantitative linguistic phylogenies to evaluate competing hypotheses concerning Lapita migration and Pawley (2018) used comparative linguistic methods to propose a particular settlement history for Fiji-West Polynesia. While archaeological interpretation of various phylogenies has proven popular (e.g. Green, 1966; Kirch and Green, 1987; Pawley, 1996; Sheppard and Walter, 2006; Burley, 2013) there are two frequently voiced concerns (Dewar, 1995; Terrell et al., 1997; Moore, 2001). One is the degree of isomorphism between language phylogenies and the phylogenetic relationships defined by human biology or artefact traditions. This amounts to the significant argument that language, culture and biology might not travel together down the same evolutionary pathways (see comments in Bedford et al., 2018). The other concern is that the branching relationships required by many phylogenetic methods might be inappropriate models to investigate cultural change (Collard et al., 2006). One remedy for the first concern is to construct phylogenies based on different realms of human variation, languages and artefacts for example, and identify mismatches that require explanation (Tehrani et al., 2010). The concern that branching models of relatedness are inappropriate can be approached as an empirical problem with branching and reticulate models applied to the same data (e.g. Cochrane and Lipo, 2010; Shennan et al., 2015).

Phylogenetic relationships are also investigated to determine if similarities in different populations are homologous, such as shared Ancestral traits, or if similarities are analogous, arising due to independent invention, among other possible processes. Distinguishing between the two is known as Galton's problem (Mace and Pagel, 1994) and has been investigated in the Pacific with reference to agriculture techniques, as well as fishhooks (e.g. Allen, 1992; Pfeffer, 2001), and ceramics (e.g. Winter et al., 2012). Considering agricultural techniques, the processes that explain similarities in the origins and distribution of raised beds (Kirch and

Lepofsky, 1993), simple flooding (Kuhlken, 1994, p. 364; McCoy and Graves, 2010, p. 94), windbreak farming (McCoy and Graves, 2010, p. 94) and lithic mulch cultivation (Barber, 2010, p. 76) are all debated with specific proposals based variably on reconstructed proto-lexemes, archaeological chronologies and distances between island groups.

Reconstructing the cultural characteristics of Ancestral societies at the branch points or nodes of cultural phylogenies is another focus of phylogenetic history and adaptation research. This has been pursued by Kirch and Green (1987, 2001) using a triangulation approach whereby controlled comparison across different domains of human variation – ethnography, linguistics, material culture and biology – is used to develop cultural reconstructions. Beginning with a comparative linguistic phylogeny, they propose that Ancestral Polynesian Society, the population from which East Polynesian groups radiated, was likely situated in Tonga, Samoa and some of their nearby islands. Using both lexical reconstruction of proto-Polynesian language, and comparative ethnography, Kirch and Green reconstruct, for example, the spatial segregation of domestic activities and argue that separate cooking and dwelling structures existed in the region and time period (i.e. about 2300–1000 BP), although there is currently no archaeological evidence of this (Kirch and Green, 2001, p. 196). A related research programme using quantitative approaches to phylogenetic reconstruction has recently emerged. This research uses linguistic trees produced within a Bayesian framework to estimate the likelihood of particular proto-language stages, and concomitantly, the likelihood that certain concepts or social forms represented by reconstructed lexemes were present (e.g. Currie et al., 2010; Kushnick et al., 2014).

Selection, drift and other evolutionary mechanisms

The most recent evolutionary approach to be applied in the Pacific focuses on mechanisms such as selection, drift and other cultural transmission processes to explain the distribution of archaeological (e.g. Graves and Cachola-Abad, 1996; O'Connor et al., 2017) and ethnographic traits (e.g. Rogers and Ehrlich, 2008). This framework, typically called evolutionary archaeology (Shennan, 2008), and sometimes cultural evolution, a label confusingly similar to mid-20th-century work, derives from two intellectual lineages. The first is quantitative cultural transmission research beginning about the 1970s (e.g. Cavalli-Sforza and Feldman, 1981; Lumsden and Wilson, 1981; Boyd and Richerson, 1985), a programme later termed dual-inheritance theory or gene-culture co-evolution. The second lineage includes research focused on drift and selection applied to explicitly constructed artefact classes (e.g. Dunnell, 1978, 1992). Both lineages are also inter-woven with human behavioural ecology (Broughton and O'Connell, 1999; O'Brien and Lyman, 2002).

Evolutionary archaeology research in the Pacific (and elsewhere) regularly uses artefact classes specifically created to investigate mechanisms defined in evolution theory (Graves and Ladefoged, 1995; Cochrane, 2002; Morrison, 2012). These artefact classes are the types by which variation in the archaeological record is quantified to produce variant distributions. Archaeological variant distributions are then compared with the distributional expectations of evolutionary mechanisms to determine if a specific mechanism, such as drift, is an adequate explanation. The comparison of empirical distributions and theoretical expectations facilitates evaluation of artefact classification as the arbitrary decisions in classification must be justified relative to the proposed evolutionary mechanisms (Lipo, 2001; Glatz et al., 2011). Cochrane (2009), for example, evaluated variously defined Fijian ceramic classes for their ability to track drift processes by examining class criteria against theoretical expectations of continuous distributions and others.

Allen's (1996) work on ancient fishhooks is an excellent example of creating specific artefact classes to investigate evolutionary mechanisms. By using hook types whose definitional criteria are hypothesised to largely measure the results of cultural transmission, Allen was able to show stochastic (i.e. drift) change over time in hook-type abundances from particular islands. After classifying the same hooks with criteria hypothesised to track variation in fishing environments, she demonstrated that the distribution of these hook types in different populations is likely explained by selection and adaptation to different prey types. Applying a similar classification-focused approach to ethnographic variation in canoes, Rogers and Ehrlich (2008) argued that decorative canoe traits such as prow carvings change rapidly, as predicted by drift, and more than functional traits such as outrigger attachment types whose distribution is explained by selection and adaptation.

As artefact classes in evolutionary archaeology are designed to investigate evolutionary mechanisms they will not necessarily match emic or ethnohistoric classes. Allen's (1996) fishhook types, for example, might not be recognised as such by ancient fishers. While these artefact types may or may not have emic reality, their usefulness is evaluated by both justifying the assumptions that underlie their construction, why for example might fishhook head morphology track transmission, and by their ability to produce empirical patterns that can be compared to theoretical expectations. In comparison, other evolutionary frameworks sometimes use observational units proposed to map onto past emically meaningful variation. For example, Kahn and Kirch's (2011; Kahn, 2015) Political Economy explanations of variation in Society Islands temple architecture employ culturally relevant types drawn from ethnohistory such as shrines, *marae*, community-level *marae*, particular kinds of priestly dwellings and structures in which sacred objects were stored. They argue that greater architectural complexity over time and increasing spatial differentiation of these emic architectural types resulted from increasing elite manipulation of ideology and control of staple finance. Cochrane (2015) also examined temple architecture across the Society Islands and Polynesia, but his approach to archaeological classification was based on expectations for the architectural variables whose distribution would be patterned predominantly by transmission and drift. Briefly, these expectations include that frequencies of different values in variables should be independent, they should not be correlated with different environments and they should vary spatially and temporally. Cochrane's resulting architectural classes do not match emic categories, but the analysis based on them indicates widespread transmission of ideas across East Polynesia, a finding supported by other recent evolutionary archaeology and artefact sourcing studies (e.g. Weisler et al., 2016; O'Connor et al., 2017).

A case study of two approaches

A case study comparing different evolutionary frameworks applied to the Pacific archaeological record will serve to highlight points of similarity and divergence and suggest how multiple frameworks might be used to produce better explanations. The archaeological record of initial migration from Near to Remote Oceania has long been a significant research issue in Pacific Island archaeology and two recent evolutionary studies have attempted to explain this population movement: Earle and Spriggs's (2015) Political Economy explanation and Cochrane's (2018) selection-based approach.

Evidence for the initial migration of populations from Near to Remote Oceania (Fig. 3.2) is based on the distribution of Lapita ceramics, an intricately decorated earthenware. These ceramics appear in the Bismarck Archipelago, without local precedent, most likely between 3535–3234 cal BP (95% probability, Rieth and Athens, 2017). After a pause, the ceramics appear with the first human colonists in southwestern Remote Oceania between 3000 cal BP (Sheppard, 2011) for islands in the west like Vanuatu and New Caledonia, and 2750 cal BP for Samoa (Petchey, 2001), the farthest eastern island colonised at the time. These colonists crossed the Near-Remote Oceanic biogeographic boundary that, in part, kept humans and other species confined to the west for approximately 50,000 years (Green, 1991).

Before Lapita pottery appears in Near Oceania, populations there had a long history of hunting and gathering, mid-Holocene agriculture and arboriculture, and animal management, as well as tuber and aroid use beginning in the Pleistocene. After the appearance of Lapita ceramics and associated material culture in Near Oceania these subsistence practices continued at new Lapita occupations and at locations with both pre-Lapita and Lapita deposits (Kirch, 1997, pp. 203–205; Lentfer and Torrence, 2007). A suite of domesticated Asian animals also appear in Near Oceania during and after the advent of Lapita pottery.

After voyaging to Remote Oceania, the Lapita ceramic-producing populations encountered new plants, animals and landscapes and the colonists targeted these rich resources (Nagaoka, 1988; Steadman et al., 2002; Valentin et al., 2010). They also brought crops such as bananas, and taro, that had a multi-millennia history of human use in Near Oceania (Horrocks and Bedford, 2005; Horrocks and Nunn, 2007; Fall, 2010). Some domesticated or commensal Asian animals also accompanied the colonists (Matisoo-Smith, 2007). There is a substantially greater number of Lapita deposits in Remote Oceania compared to Near Oceania (Anderson et al., 2001).

Those groups who left for Remote Oceania initially maintained contact with Near Oceanic populations as evidenced by obsidian transport and the similar,

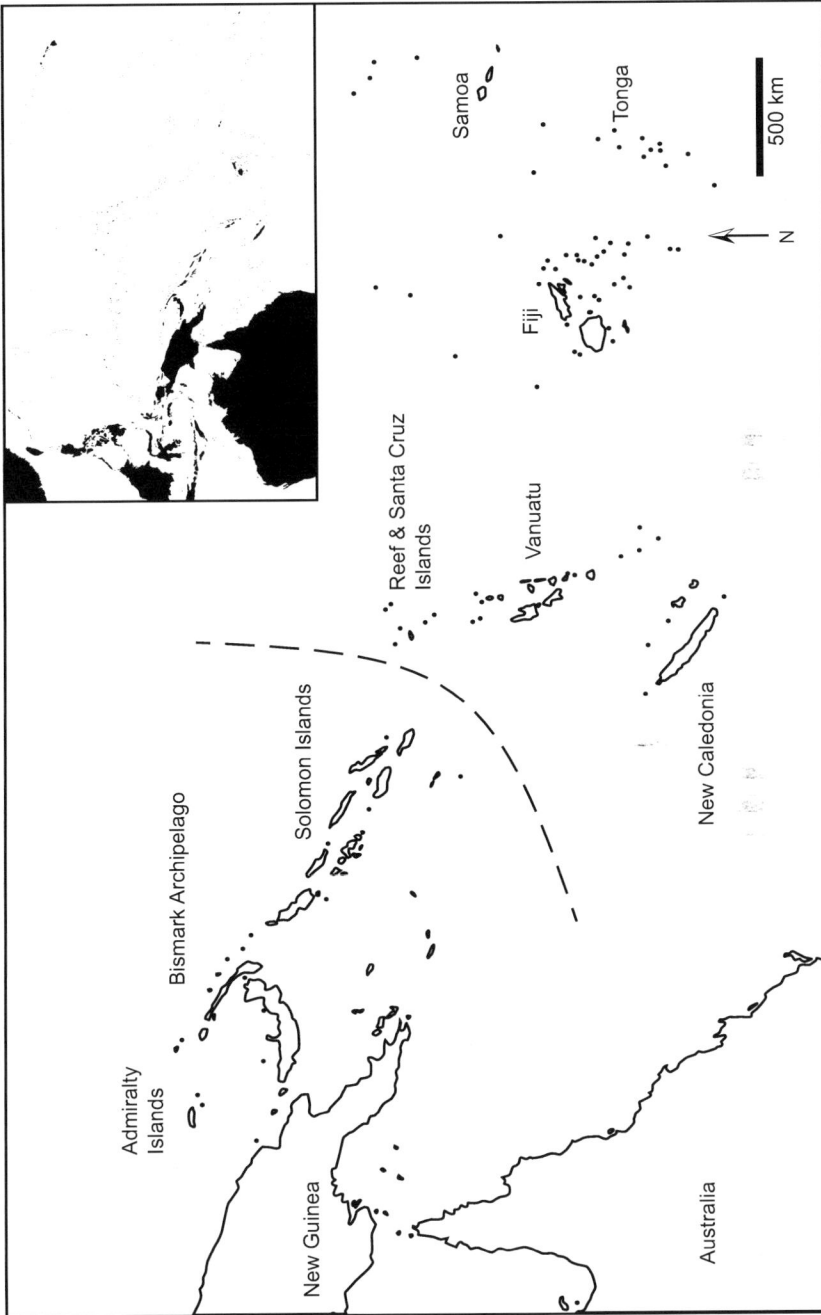

FIGURE 3.2 Near and Remote Oceania separated by the dashed line. Australia shown, but not considered Near Oceania.

Source: map by Ethan Cochrane

intricate Lapita pottery decorations repeated on locally made pottery (Dickinson, 2006) in both regions. By approximately 2700 cal BP this movement between populations had largely stopped, both within Remote Oceania and between the regions, as evidenced by the lack of artefact transport, and the replacement of commonly decorated Lapita pottery with different, archipelago-specific styles in Remote Oceania.

A political economy explanation of Lapita movement

Earle and Spriggs (2015) develop a Political Economy explanation of Lapita movement to Remote Oceania focusing on differential access to power within society. They propose that differential access begins with bottlenecks or the 'constriction points in commodity chains that offer an aspiring leader the opportunity to limit access, thus creating ownership over resources, technologies, or knowledge' (Earle and Spriggs, 2015, p. 517). Once an aspiring leader has restricted others' access to a resource she or he can more easily extract surplus from the resource to underwrite control of economic, military or ideological power sources. Earle and Spriggs note that the archaeological application of Political Economy requires the identification of important resources and their constriction points by focusing on the objects which move through ancient economies.

Earle and Spriggs apply this strategy to the Lapita case through an emic approach to unit formation, in particular relying on Pacific ethnography and cross-cultural comparison to determine what archaeological types would correspond to prestige items, Lapita pots, shell ornaments and bird feathers for example. They argue, however, that the nature of Lapita prestige items, including the widespread Lapita pots, limited their control, with a similar lack of constriction points and opportunities for control of staple finance. In contrast, they point out that knowledge of long-distance voyaging and the ability to colonise new lands, and with new opportunities for trade, was a knowledge-resource that was not available to all and whose distribution and use might be controlled by a minority. If use of this knowledge was a somewhat competitive arena, this, in part, explains Lapita migration 'to search out undiscovered islands that could offer easy subsistence, exchangeable products, and a basis for leaders to establish themselves independently' (Earle and Spriggs, 2015, p. 518).

A selection-based explanation of Lapita movement

Cochrane's (2018) explanation of the Lapita migration is different from Earle and Spriggs (2015). Instead of assuming a relevant explanatory process is individuals' use of power to direct and resist groups, Cochrane divides explanations into ultimate-evolutionary and proximate-adaptive causes. In the former the relative advantage of cultural traits causes their differential transmission (i.e. replication) over time and across space. That is, trait distributions are explained by selection. The Remote Oceanic Lapita trait or trait-suite includes a focus on hunting and gathering, and long-distance maritime movement, while the Near Oceanic trait-suite includes less focus on both hunting and gathering, and long-distance movement. If there is no differential transmission of these trait-suites, then selection is probably not implicated in Lapita movement into Remote Oceania. For proximate-adaptive explanations, adaptation or the changing correlations of traits and environments is a system-level explanation. These correlations can be explained by physiological responses, learned and flexible behaviours or some combination. And such correlations are triggered by other changes in the system, such as environmental change, technological change or social changes.

To apply this framework, Cochrane develops a method to identify the archaeological signatures of different movement types, such as range-expansion or range shift, with the distribution of these types predicted by both evolutionary and adaptive processes in different environments. Cochrane argues that the Lapita migration is a range-expansion and the greater rate of replication of Lapita trait-suites in Remote Oceania compared to Near Oceania indicates selection. The differential replication of Lapita trait-suites in Near and Remote Oceania can also be explained as a proximate system-like process with alterations in both regional weather patterns and canoe technology that changed the costs and benefits of long-distance voyaging. In short, 'While climate change and innovation in voyaging technology lowered the cost of movement for Lapita populations, selection processes related to environmental variation and demography explain the relatively greater rate of Lapita deposition in Remote Oceania' (Cochrane, 2018, p. 543). Importantly, there are several empirical observations that would refute or challenge this explanation. If for example, there is not a greater rate of Lapita trait-suite replication in Remote Oceania compared to Near Oceania, then selection is not a valid explanation.

Conclusion

The selection-based approach and the Political Economy approach to Lapita migration encapsulate many of the salient characteristics of various evolutionary approaches in the Pacific, highlight the differences and suggest where they might be combined for mutual benefit. Evolutionary approaches in the Pacific can be broadly divided into adaptationist, system-focused frameworks and selectionist, transmission-focused frameworks. As has been recognised for decades (Mayr, 1961), a complete evolutionary explanation of behaviour, in this case past behaviour fossilised in the archaeological record, should ideally include both kinds of explanations. To exemplify the possibilities, Cochrane's explanation of Lapita migration does not delve into the proximate social triggers that may have kick-started the movement. It is here that a Political Economy and cross-cultural approach might identify more social competitive processes and associated archaeological units by which to investigate the evolution of range-expansion and other movement types. A selection-based approach might identify the evolutionary mechanisms that explain the probable phylogenetic relatedness of populations such as the pre-Lapita ceramic-using groups in Island Southeast Asia, Lapita populations and the descendant populations of the Pacific whose hierarchical social systems are often the focus of Political Economy research. Such a division of labour mirrors Mesoudi et al.'s (2006) unified approach to the evolutionary study of culture. Here, Political Economy is cast in the role of micro-evolutionary studies with selection-based approaches investigating macro-evolution.

All evolutionary approaches often espouse a concern with scientific explanations, but what this means differs between frameworks. Minimally science uses theory or ideas to explain the distribution of empirical phenomena, in this case the archaeological record, and potential scientific explanations should be empirically testable. That is, explanations should be constructed in such a way that one can envision an empirical observation that would falsify them. All evolutionary approaches should strive for this, lest we construct unverifiable stories.

Acknowledgements

This research was partly funded by the Royal Society Te Apārangi Marsden Fund (contract UOA1709). The comments of Robert DiNapoli, Thegn Ladefoged, Tim Thomas and an anonymous reviewer improved the manuscript.

References

Allen, M.S., 1992. Temporal variation in polynesian fishing strategies: the southern Cook Islands in regional perspective. *Asian Perspectives*, 31, pp. 183–204.

Allen, M.S., 1996. Style and function in East-Polynesian fishhooks. *Antiquity*, 70, pp. 97–116.

Allen, M.S., 2011. Oscillating climate and socio-political process: the case of the Marquesan Chiefdom, Polynesia. *Antiquity*, 84, pp. 86–102.

Anderson, A.J., 1981. A model of prehistoric collecting on the rocky shore. *Journal of Archaeological Science*, 8, pp. 109–120.

Anderson, A., Bedford, S., Clark, G.R., Lilley, I., Sand, C., Summerhayes, G.R. and Torrence, R., 2001. An inventory of Lapita sites containing dentate-stamped pottery. In: G.A. Clark, A.J. Anderson, and T.S. Vunidilo, eds. *The Archaeology of Lapita Dispersal in Oceania*. Canberra: Pandanus Books, pp. 1–14.

Aswani, S. and Graves, M.W., 1998. Tongan sociopolitical evolution. *Asian Perspectives*, 37, pp. 135–164.

Barber, I., 2010. Diffusion or innovation? Explaining lithic agronomy on the southern Polynesian margins. *World Archaeology*, 42, pp. 74–89.

Bedford, S., Blust, R., Burley, D.V., Cox, M., Kirch, P.V., Matisoo-Smith, E., Næss, Å., Pawley, A., Sand, C. and Sheppard, P., 2018. Ancient DNA and its contribution to understanding the human history of the Pacific Islands. *Archaeology in Oceania*, 53, pp. 205–219.

Binford, L.R., 1968. Archaeological perspectives. In: S.R. Binford and L.R. Binford, eds. *New Perspectives in Archaeology*. Chicago, IL: Aldine Publishing Co., pp. 5–32

Bird, D. and O'Connell, J., 2006. Behavioral ecology and archaeology. *Journal of Archaeological Research*, 14, pp. 143–188.

Blust, R., 1995. The prehistory of the Austronesian-speaking peoples: a view from language. *Journal of World Prehistory*, 9, pp. 453–510.

Blute, M., 1979. Sociocultural evolutionism: an untried theory. *Behavioral Science*, 24, pp. 46–59.

Boas, F., 1911. *The Mind of Primitive Man.* New York: Macmillan Co.

Boyd, R. and Richerson, P.J., 1985. *Culture and the Evolutionary Process.* Chicago, IL: University of Chicago Press.

Broughton, J.M. and O'Connell, J.F., 1999. On evolutionary ecology, selectionist archaeology, and behavioral archaeology. *American Antiquity,* 64, pp. 153–165.

Burley, D.V., 2013. Fijian polygenesis and the Melanesian/Polynesian divide. *Current Anthropology,* 54, pp. 436–462.

Carneiro, R.L., 2003. *Evolutionism in Cultural Anthropology: A Critical History.* Boulder, CO: Westview Press.

Cavalli-Sforza, L.L. and Feldman, M.W., 1981. *Cultural Transmission and Evolution: A Quantitative Approach.* Princeton, NJ: Princeton University Press.

Clark, G., 2017. The Tongan maritime state. In: T. Hodos, ed. *The Routledge Handbook of Archaeology and Globalization.* New York: Routledge, pp. 283–300.

Clark, G.R., 2003. Shards of meaning: archaeology and the Melanesia–Polynesia divide. *Journal of Pacific History,* 38, pp. 197–215.

Clark, G.R., Burley, D.V. and Murray, T., 2008. Monumentality and the development of the Tongan maritime chiefdom. *Antiquity,* 82, pp. 994–1008.

Cochrane, E.E., 2001. Style, function, and systematic empiricism: the conflation of process and pattern. In: T.D. Hurt and G.F.M. Rakita, eds. *Style and Function: Conceptual Issues in Evolutionary Archaeology.* Westport, CT: Bergin & Garvey, pp. 183–202.

Cochrane, E.E., 2002. Separating time and space in archaeological landscapes: an example from windward Society Islands ceremonial architecture. In: T.N. Ladefoged and M.W. Graves, eds. *Pacific Landscapes: Archaeological Approaches.* Los Osos, CA: Easter Island Foundation Press, pp. 189–209.

Cochrane, E.E., 2009. *The Evolutionary Archaeology of Ceramic Diversity in Ancient Fiji.* Oxford: Archaeopress.

Cochrane, E.E., 2015. Phylogenetic analysis of Polynesian ritual architecture suggests extensive cultural sharing and innovation. *Journal of the Polynesian Society,* 124, pp. 7–46.

Cochrane, E.E., 2018. The evolution of migration: the case of Lapita in the southwest Pacific. *Journal of Archaeological Method and Theory,* 25, pp. 520–558.

Cochrane, E.E. and Lipo, C.P., 2010. Phylogenetic analyses of Lapita decoration do not support branching evolution or regional population structure during colonization of Remote Oceania. *Philosophical Transactions of the Royal Society B: Biological Sciences,* 365, pp. 3889–3902.

Codding, B.F. and Bird, D.W., 2015. Behavioral ecology and the future of archaeological science. *Journal of Archaeological Science,* 56, pp. 9–20.

Collard, M., Shennan, S.J. and Tehrani, J.J., 2006. Branching, blending, and the evolution of cultural similarities and differences among human populations. *Evolution and Human Behavior,* 27, pp. 169–184.

Currie, T.E., Greenhill, S.J., Gray, R.D., Hasegawa, T. and Mace, R., 2010. Rise and fall of political complexity in island South-East Asia and the Pacific. *Nature,* 467, pp. 801–804.

d'Urville, D., 1832. Notice sur les îles du Grand Océan et sur l'origine des peuples qui les habitent. *Société de Géographie Bulletin,* 17, pp. 1–21.

Dewar, R.E., 1995. Of nets and trees: untangling the reticulate and dendritic in Madagascar's prehistory. *World Archaeology,* 26, pp. 301–318.

Dickinson, W.R., 2006. *Temper Sands in Prehistoric Oceanian Pottery: Geotectonics, Sedimentology, Petrography, and Provenance.* Boulder, CO: Geological Society of America.

DiNapoli, R.J. and Morrison, A.E., 2017. Human behavioural ecology and Pacific archaeology. *Archaeology in Oceania,* 52: 1–12.

DiNapoli, R.J., Morrison, A.E., Lipo, C.P., Hunt, T.L. and Lane, B.G., 2018. East Polynesian islands as models of cultural divergence: the case of Rapa Nui and Rapa Iti. *Journal of Island and Coastal Archaeology*, 13(2), pp. 206–223.

Dunnell, R.C., 1978. Style and function: a fundamental dichotomy. *American Antiquity*, 43, pp. 192–202.

Dunnell, R.C., 1980. Evolutionary theory and archaeology. In: M.B. Schiffer, ed. *Advances in Archaeological Method and Theory*. New York: Academic Press, pp. 35–99.

Dunnell, R.C., 1988. The concept of progress in cultural evolution. In: M.H. Nitecki, ed. *Evolutionary Progress*. Chicago, IL: University of Chicago Press, pp. 169–194.

Dunnell, R.C., 1992. Archaeology and evolutionary science. In: L. Wandsnider, ed. *Quandaries and Quests: Visions of Archaeology's Future*. Carbondale, IL: Southern Illinois University Press, pp. 209–224.

Earle, T., 1997. *How Chiefs Come to Power: The Political Economy in Prehistory*. Stanford, CA: Stanford University Press.

Earle, T. and Spriggs, M., 2015. Political economy in prehistory: a Marxist approach to Pacific sequences. *Current Anthropology*, 56, pp. 515–544.

Earle, T.K., 1987. Chiefdoms in archaeological and ethnohistorical perspective. *Annual review of Anthropology*, 16, pp. 279–308.

Emory, K.P., 1946. Eastern Polynesia, its Cultural Relationships. PhD dissertation, Yale.

Fall, P., 2010. Pollen evidence for plant introductions in a Polynesian tropical island ecosystem, Kingdom of Tonga. In: S.G. Haberle, J. Stevenson, and M. Prebble, eds. *Altered Ecologies: Fire, Climate and Human Influence on Terrestrial Landscapes*. Canberra: Australia National University, pp. 253–271.

Field, J., 2004. Environmental and climatic considerations: a hypothesis for conflict and the emergence of social complexity in Fijian prehistory. *Journal of Anthropological Archaeology*, 23, pp. 79–99.

Flannery, K.V. and Marcus, J., 2012. *The Creation of Inequality: How our Prehistoric Ancestors Set the Stage for Monarchy, Slavery, and Empire*, Cambridge, MA: Harvard University Press.

Freeman, D., 1974. The evolutionary theories of Charles Darwin and Herbert Spencer. *Current Anthropology*, 15, pp. 211–237.

Friedman, J., 1981. Notes on structure and history in Oceania. *Folk. Dansk Ethnografisk Tidsskrift Kobenhavn*, 23, pp. 275–295.

Glatz, C., Kandler, A. and Steele, J., 2011. Cultural selection, drift, and ceramic diversity at Boğazköy-Hattusa. In: E.E. Cochrane and A. Gardner, eds. *Evolutionary and Interpretive Archaeologies*. Walnut Creek, CA: Left Coast Press, pp. 199–225.

Goldman, I., 1955. Status rivalry and cultural evolution in Polynesia. *American Anthropologist*, 57, pp. 680–697.

Graves, M.W. and Cachola-Abad, C.K., 1996. Seriation as a method of chronologically ordering architectural design traits: an example from Hawai'i. *Archaeology in Oceania*, 31, pp. 19–32.

Graves, M.W. and Ladefoged, T.N., 1995. The evolutionary significance of ceremonial architecture. In: P.A. Teltser, ed. *Evolutionary Archaeology: Methodological Issues*. Tucson, AZ: University of Arizona Press, pp. 149–174.

Gray, R.D., Drummond, A.J. and Greenhill, S.J., 2009. Language phylogenies reveal expansion pulses and pauses in Pacific settlement. *Science*, 323, pp. 479–483.

Gray, R.D. and Jordan, F.M., 2000. Language trees support the express-train sequence of Austronesian expansion. *Nature*, 405, pp. 1052–1055.

Green, R.C., 1966. Linguistic subgrouping within Polynesia: the implications for prehistoric settlement. *Journal of the Polynesian Society*, 75, pp. 6–38.

Green, R.C., 1991. Near and Remote Oceania: disestablishing 'Melanesia' in culture history. In: A.K. Pawley, ed. *Man and a Half: Essays in Pacific Anthropology and Ethnobiology in Honour of Ralph Bulmer.* Auckland: Polynesian Society, pp. 491–502.

Hayman, J.M.H., 2019. Islands in an Empire: The Tongan Maritime Chiefdom in Evolutionary Perspective. Master's thesis, University of Auckland.

Hildebrand, E.A., Grillo, K.M., Sawchuk, E.A., Pfeiffer, S.K., Conyers, L.B., Goldstein, S.T., Hill, A.C., Janzen, A., Klehm, C.E., Helper, M., Kiura, P., Ndiema, E., Ngugi, C., Shea, J.J. and Wang, H., 2018. A monumental cemetery built by eastern Africa's first herders near Lake Turkana, Kenya. *Proceedings of the National Academy of Sciences,* 115, pp. 8942–8947.

Horrocks, M. and Bedford, S., 2005. Microfossil analysis of Lapita deposits in Vanuatu reveals introduced *Araceae* (Aroids). *Archaeology in Oceania,* 40, pp. 67–74.

Horrocks, M. and Nunn, P.D., 2007. Evidence for introduced taro (*Colocasia esculenta*) and lesser yam (*Dioscorea esculenta*) in Lapita-era (c.3050–2500 cal. yr BP) deposits from Bourewa, southwest Viti Levu Island, Fiji. *Journal of Archaeological Science,* 34, pp. 739–748.

Irons, W., 1979. Natural selection, adaptation, and human social behavior. In: N.A. Chagnon and W. Irons, eds. *Evolutionary Biology and Human Social Behavior.* North Scituate, MA: Duxbury Press, pp. 4–39.

Kahn, J.G., 2015. Identifying residences of ritual practitioners in the archaeological record as a proxy for social complexity. *Journal of Anthropological Archaeology,* 40, pp. 59–81.

Kahn, J.G. and Kirch, P.V., 2011. Monumentality and the materialization of ideology in Central Eastern Polynesia. *Archaeology in Oceania,* 46, pp. 93–104.

Kennett, D.J. and Clifford, R.A., 2004. Flexible strategies for resource defense on the northern Channel Islands of California: an agent-based model. In: S.M. Fitzpatrick and A. Anderson, eds. *Voyages of Discovery: The Archaeology of Islands.* Westport, CT: Praeger, pp. 21–50.

Kirch, P.V., 1980. The archaeological study of adaptation: theoretical and methodological issues. In: M.B. Schiffer, ed. *Advances in Archaeological Method and Theory.* New York: Academic Press, pp. 101–156.

Kirch, P.V., 1984. *The Evolution of the Polynesian Chiefdoms.* Cambridge: Cambridge University Press.

Kirch, P.V., 1990. Monumental architecture and power in Polynesian chiefdoms: a comparison of Tonga and Hawaii. *World Archaeology,* 22, pp. 206–222.

Kirch, P.V., 1997. *The Lapita Peoples.* Cambridge, MA: Blackwell.

Kirch, P.V., 2010. *How Chiefs Became Kings: Divine Kingship and the Rise of Archaic States in Ancient Hawai'i,* Berkeley, CA: University of California Press.

Kirch, P.V., Asner, G., Chadwick, O.A., Field, J., Ladefoged, T., Lee, C., Puleston, C., Tuljapurkar, S. and Vitousek, P.M., 2012. Building and testing models of long-term agricultural intensification and population dynamics: a case study from the Leeward Kohala Field System, Hawai'i. *Ecological Modelling,* 227, pp. 18–28.

Kirch, P.V. and Green, R.C., 1987. History, phylogeny, and evolution in Polynesia. *Current Anthropology,* 28, pp. 431–456.

Kirch, P.V. and Green, R.C., 2001. *Hawaiki, Ancestral Polynesia: An Essay in Historical Anthropology.* Cambridge: Cambridge University Press.

Kirch, P.V. and Lepofsky, D., 1993. Polynesian irrigation: archaeological and linguistic evidence for origins and development. *Asian Perspectives,* 32, pp. 183–204.

Kuhlken, R.T., 1994. Agricultural Terracing in the Fiji Islands. PhD dissertation, Louisiana State University and Agricultural and Mechanical College.

Kushnick, G., Gray, R.D. and Jordan, F.M., 2014. The sequential evolution of land tenure norms. *Evolution and Human Behavior,* 35, pp. 309–318.

Lentfer, C.J. and Torrence, R., 2007. Holocene volcanic activity, vegetation succession, and ancient human land use: unraveling the interactions on Garua Island, Papua New Guinea. *Review of Palaeobotany and Palynology,* 143, pp. 83–105.

Leonard, R.D. and Jones, G.T., 1987. Elements of an inclusive evolutionary model for archaeology. *Journal of Anthropological Archaeology,* 6, pp. 199–219.

Lepofsky, D. and Kahn, J., 2011. Cultivating an ecological and social balance: elite demands and commoner knowledge in ancient ma'ohi agriculture, Society Islands. *American Anthropologist,* 113, pp. 319–335.

Lewontin, R.C., 1961. Evolution and the theory of games. *Journal of Theoretical Biology,* 1, pp. 382–403.

Lipo, C.P., 2001. *Science, Style, and the Study of Community Structure: An Example from the Central Mississippi River Valley.* Oxford: Hadrian Books.

Lumsden, C. and Wilson, E.O., 1981. *Genes, Mind, and Culture.* Cambridge, MA: Harvard University Press.

MacArthur, R.H. and Pianka, E.R., 1966. On optimal use of a patchy environment. *The American Naturalist,* 100, pp. 603–609.

Mace, R. and Pagel, M., 1994. The comparative method in anthropology. *Current Anthropology,* 35, pp. 549–564.

Marcus, J. and Feinman, G.M., 1998. Introduction. In: G.M. Feinman and J. Marcus, eds., *Archaic States.* Santa Fe, NM: School for Advanced Research, pp. 3–13.

Matisoo-Smith, E.A., 2007. Animal translocations, genetic variation and the human settlement of the Pacific. In: J.S. Friedlaender, ed., *Genes, Language and Culture History in the Southwest Pacific.* Oxford: Oxford University Press, pp. 157–170.

Mayr, E., 1959. Darwin and evolutionary theory in biology. In: B.J. Meggers, ed. *Evolution and Anthropology: A Centennial Appraisal.* Washington, DC: Anthropological Society of Washington, pp. 1–10.

Mayr, E., 1961. Cause and effect in biology. *Science,* 134, pp. 1501–1506.

McCoy, M. and Graves, M.W., 2010. The role of agricultural innovation on Pacific islands: a case study from Hawai'i Island. *World Archaeology,* 42, pp. 90–107.

Medawar, P., 1953. A commentary on Lamarckism. Reprinted in: P. Medawar, *The Uniqueness of the Individual.* New York: Dover, 1957, pp. 79–107.

Mesoudi, A., 2016. Cultural evolution: a review of theory, findings and controversies. *Evolutionary Biology,* 43, pp. 481–497.

Mesoudi, A., Whiten, A. and Laland, K.N., 2006. Towards a unified science of cultural evolution. *Behavioral and Brain Sciences,* 29, pp. 329–383.

Moore, J.H., 2001. Ethnogenetic patterns in native North America. In: J.E. Terrell, ed. *Archaeology, Language and History: Essays on Culture and* Ethnicity. Westport, CT: Bergin & Garvey, pp. 30–56.

Morgan, L.H., 1877. *Ancient Society.* New York: Henry Holt.

Morrison, A.E., 2012. An Archaeological Analysis of Rapa Nui Settlement Structure: A Multi-Scalar Approach. PhD, University of Hawaii.

Morrison, A.E. and Cochrane, E.E., 2008. Investigating shellfish deposition and landscape history at the Natia Beach site, Fiji. *Journal of Archaeological Science,* 35, pp. 2387–2399.

Murdock, G.P., 1967. *Ethnographic Atlas.* Pittsburgh, PA: University of Pittsburgh Press.

Nagaoka, L., 1988. Lapita subsistence: the evidence of non-fish archaeofaunal remains. In: P.V. Kirch and T.L. Hunt, eds. *Archaeology of the Lapita Cultural Complex: A Critical Review.* Seattle, WA: Thomas Burke Memorial Washington State Museum, pp. 117–153.

O'Brien, M.J. and Lyman, R.L., 2002. Evolutionary archaeology: current status and future prospects. *Evolutionary Anthropology,* 11, pp. 26–36.

O'Brien, M.J., Lyman, R.L. and Schiffer, M.B., 2005. *Archaeology as a Process: Processualism and its Progeny*. Salt Lake City, UT: University of Utah Press.

O'Connor, J.T., White, F.J. and Hunt, T.L., 2017. Fishhook variability and cultural transmission in East Polynesia. *Archaeology in Oceania*, 52, pp. 32–44.

Pawley, A.K., 2018. Linguistic evidence as a window into the prehistory of Oceania. In: E.E. Cochrane, and T.L. Hunt, eds. *The Oxford Handbook of Prehistoric Oceania*. Oxford: Oxford University Press, pp. 302–335.

Pawley, A.K., 1996. On the Polynesian subgroup as a problem for Irwin's continuous settlement hypothesis. In: J. Davidson, G. Irwin, F. Leach, A.K. Pawley, and D. Brown, eds. *Oceanic Culture History: Essays in Honour of Roger Green*. Dunedin: New Zealand Archaeological Association, pp. 387–410.

Petchey, F.J., 2001. Radiocarbon determinations from the Mulifauna Lapita site, Upolu, western Samoa. *Radiocarbon* 43, pp. 63–68.

Pfeffer, M.T., 2001. The engineering and evolution of Hawaiian fishhooks. In: T.L. Hunt, C.P Lipo, and S.L. Sterling, eds. *Posing Questions for a Scientific Archaeology*. Westport, CT: Bergin & Garvey, pp. 73–96.

Quintus, S. and Cochrane, E.E., 2018. The prevalence and importance of niche in agricultural development in Polynesia. *Journal of Anthropological Archaeology*, 51, pp. 173–186.

Rieth, T.M. and Athens, J.S., 2017. Late Holocene human expansion into Near and Remote Oceania: a Bayesian model of the chronologies of the Mariana Islands and Bismarck Archipelago. *Journal of Island and Coastal Archaeology*, 14, pp. 1–12.

Rogers, D.S. and Ehrlich, P.R., 2008. Natural selection and cultural rates of change. *Proceedings of the National Academy of Sciences*, 105, pp. 3416–3420.

Sahlins, M.D., 1958. *Social Stratification in Polynesia*. Seattle, WA: University of Washington Press.

Sahlins, M.D., 1960. Evolution: Specific and General. In: M.D. Sahlins and E.R. Service, eds. *Evolution and Culture*. Ann Arbor, MI: University of Michigan Press, pp. 12–44.

Sahlins, M.D., 1972. *Stone Age Economics*. Chicago, IL: Aldine.

Sand, C., 2002. Melanesian tribes vs. Polynesian chiefdoms: recent archaeological assessment of a classic model of sociopolitical types in Oceania. *Asian Perspectives*, 41, pp. 284–296.

Sand, C., Bolé, J. and Ouetcho, A., 2003. Prehistory and its perception in a Melanesian Archipelago: the New Caledonia example. *Antiquity*, 77, pp. 505–519.

Service, E.R., 1962. *Primitive Social Organization*. New York: Random House.

Shennan, S., 2008. Evolution in archaeology. *Annual Review of Anthropology*, 37, pp. 75–91.

Shennan, S.J., Crema, E.R. and Kerig, T., 2015. Isolation-by-distance, homophily, and 'core' vs. 'package' cultural evolution models in Neolithic Europe. *Evolution and Human Behavior*, 36, pp. 103–109.

Sheppard, P.J., 2011. Lapita colonization across the Near/Remote Oceania boundary. *Current Anthropology*, 52, pp. 799–840.

Sheppard, P.J. and Walter, R., 2006. A revised model of Solomon Islands culture history. *Journal of the Polynesian Society*, 115, pp. 47–76.

Simpson, D.F.J., Van Tilburg, J.A. and Dussubieux, L., 2018. Geochemical and radiometric analyses of archaeological remains from Easter Island's *moai* (statue) quarry reveal prehistoric timing, provenance, and use of fine–grain basaltic resources. *Journal of Pacific Archaeology*, 9, pp. 12–34.

Smith, E.A. and Winterhalder, B., 1992. Natural selection and decision making: some fundamental principles. In: E.A. Smith and B. Winterhalder, eds. *Evolutionary Ecology and Human Behavior*. New York: Aldine De Gruyter, pp. 25–60.

Spencer, H., 1855. *The Principles of Psychology*. London: Longman, Brown, Green & Longmans.

Spencer, H., 1857. Progress: its law and cause. *Westminster Review*, 67, pp. 445–485.

Spencer, H., 1873. The study of sociology, no. XVI: conclusion. *Contemporary Review,* 22, pp. 663–677.

Steadman, D.W., Plourde, A. and Burley, D.V., 2002. Prehistoric butchery and consumption of birds in the Kingdom of Tonga, South Pacific. *Journal of Archaeological Science,* 29, pp. 571–584.

Steponaitis, V., 1978. Location theory and complex chiefdoms. In: B. Smith, ed. *Mississippian Settlement Patterns.* New York: Academic Press, pp. 417–453.

Stevenson, C., 2002. Territorial divisions on Easter Island in the 16th century: evidence from the distribution of ceremonial architecture. In: T.N. Ladefoged and M.W. Graves, eds. *Pacific Landscapes: Archaeological Approaches.* Los Osos, CA: Easter Island Foundation Press.

Steward, J.H., 1955. *Theory of Cultural Change.* Chicago, IL: University of Illinois Press.

Tehrani, J.J., Collard, M. and Shennan, S.J., 2010. The cophylogeny of populations and cultures: reconstructing the evolution of Iranian tribal craft traditions using trees and jungles. *Philosophical Transactions of the Royal Society B: Biological Sciences,* 365, pp. 3865–3874.

Terrell, J., Hunt, T.L. and Gosden, C., 1997. The dimensions of social life in the Pacific: human diversity and the myth of the primitive isolate. *Current Anthropology,* 38, pp. 155–195.

Tylor, E.B., 1870. *Researches into the Early History of Mankind and the Development of Civilizations.* London: John Murray.

Valentin, F., Buckley, H.R., Herrscher, E., Kinaston, R., Bedford, S., Spriggs, M., Hawkins, S. and Neal, K., 2010. Lapita subsistence strategies and food consumption patterns in the community of Teouma (Efate, Vanuatu). *Journal of Archaeological Science,* 37, pp. 1820–1829.

Wallin, P. and Martinsson-Wallin, H., 2007. Settlement patterns: social and ritual space in prehistoric Samoa. *Archaeology in Oceania,* 42 (suppl.), pp. 83–89.

Wallin, P. and Solsvik, R., 2010. Marae reflections: on the evolution of stratified chiefdoms in the leeward Society Islands. *Archaeology in Oceania,* 45, pp. 86–93.

Weisler, M.I., Bolhar, R., Ma, J., St Pierre, E., Sheppard, P.J., Walter, R.K., Feng, Y., Zhao, J.-X. and Kirch, P.V., 2016. Cook Island artifact geochemistry demonstrates spatial and temporal extent of pre-European interarchipelago voyaging in East Polynesia. *Proceedings of the National Academy of Sciences,* 113, pp. 8150–8155.

Wengrow, D. and Graeber, D., 2015. Farewell to the 'childhood of man': ritual, seasonality, and the origins of inequality. *Journal of the Royal Anthropological Institute,* 21, pp. 597–619.

White, L.A. 1943., Energy and the evolution of culture. *American Anthropologist,* 45, pp. 335–356.

White, L.A., 1959. *The Evolution of Culture.* New York: McGraw-Hill.

Winter, O., Clark, G.R., Anderson, A. and Lindahl, A., 2012. Austronesian sailing to the northern Marianas, a comment on Hung et al. (2011). *Antiquity,* 86, pp. 898–914.

Winterhalder, B. and Smith, E.A., 2000. Analyzing adaptive strategies: Human behavioral ecology at twenty-five. *Evolutionary Anthropology,* 9, pp. 51–72.

4

CONTROLLED COMPARISON AND THE PHYLOGENETIC MODEL IN POLYNESIAN CULTURE HISTORY

Patrick V. Kirch

The method of 'controlled comparison' has a long tradition in anthropology. In 1997, cultural anthropologist Ward Goodenough wrote that 'Anthropologists have long recognized that cultural traditions in different societies can be related phylo-genetically in that they derive historically from a common Ancestral tradition in the same way that languages can be related phylogenetically' (1997, p. 16). He noted, however, that some methodological problems remained for convincingly establishing such phylogenetic relations for cultural traditions. Goodenough suggested that 'Remote Oceania, where we have reason to assume that nearly all existing cultural traditions are phylogenetically related, offers possibilities for comparative study to illustrate the methodological issues to be resolved' (1997, p. 16). In this chapter, I address those methodological issues, and what archaeologists in particular have done to develop the tools necessary to resolve them, unleashing the full power of controlled comparison.

The dendritic versus reticulate debate in prehistory

A long-standing debate among archaeologists focuses on whether the emergence of new and different cultures, 'ethnogenesis' as it is sometimes termed, should best be viewed as a matter of dendritic splitting (as in a family tree), or the outcome of com-plex, reticulate interactions. John Moore (1994a, 1994b), for example, challenged the branching or dendritic view, arguing that rhizotic or reticulate processes of ethnogenesis were more frequent in human prehistory. Moore's 'ethnogenetic' approach was influenced by his ethnohistorical research among Native American populations in southeastern North America, where he demonstrated historical fusion as well as fission among groups such as the Lakota and Cheyenne. However, Moore did not entirely reject a phylogenetic or dendritic model, pointing specific-ally to Polynesia as one region where such models are both appropriate and useful (Moore, 1994b, p. 14).

Ruth Mace and Mark Pagel (1994) argued that the application of a formal comparative method within historical anthropology called for an explicitly phylogenetic approach:

> the validity of comparative methods for anthropology depends upon correctly counting independent instances of cultural change. Independent instances of cultural change, in turn, cannot be identified without the construction of a phylogeny (or cladogram) showing the patterns of hierarchical descent of the cultures being studied.
>
> *(1994, p. 551)*

But Mace and Pagel also recognised that the construction of cultural phylogenies is not identical to the process of phylogeny construction in biology, due to 'horizontal transmission' between human cultures, this being another term for what anthropologists (and linguists) have long called 'diffusion' or 'borrowing'.

Dendritic versus rhizotic – or phylogenetic versus ethnogenetic – models have been explicitly debated by historical anthropologists working within the vast Austronesian-speaking region, including Polynesia. Bellwood et al. (1995) argued for the application of a phylogenetic model to the entire Austronesian-speaking region. For Madagascar, Dewar (1995) argued the relative strengths of reticulate versus dendritic processes in that island's cultural history. In contrast, John Terrell and colleagues (Terrell, 1986; 1988; Welsch et al., 1992; Welsch and Terrell, 1994; Welsch, 1996) insisted that no phylogenetic patterning is discernible in Near Oceania. Terrell et al. (1997) extended this argument to the whole of Oceania, seeing the Pacific as a sea of islands criss-crossed by so many reticulate pathways of interaction so as to doom any attempt at inferring cultural phylogeny. Yet Terrell's own New Guinea research (Terrell et al., 1997) failed to support this contention. Rather, as Moore and Romney (1994; 1996; Roberts et al., 1995) showed, the New Guinea case yields strong correlations between language and culture, even though much horizontal transmission between Austronesian and Non-Austronesian cultures clearly occurred over the past 3,500 years.

Bellwood (1996) cast the phylogeny versus reticulation debate more broadly, arguing that while both approaches have their place in the repertoire of historical anthropology, much depends on the temporal and spatial scales at play. As Bellwood puts it:

> Large-scale and fairly integrated colonizations *did* happen in prehistory; human cultures and languages can, to varying degrees depending upon time and space coordinates, be organized in phylogenetic arrays. The generation of human diversity in the past has not been entirely reticulate and dependent on processes of *in situ* interaction between peoples of different ethno-linguistic background. Neither has it been entirely radiative and dependent upon adaptation in isolation. But to rule out phylogeny as of *any* significance in the patterning of difference and similarity between human cultures is surely no more than a 'whimsical view'.
>
> *(Bellwood, 1996, p. 888)*

Controlled comparison in Polynesia

In his seminal volume, *Western Polynesia: A Study in Cultural Differentiation*, Edwin G. Burrows (1938; 1940) drew explicitly on Sapir's (1916) methodology for historical reconstruction, and firmly established Polynesia as an exemplary cultural area for controlled comparison. Burrows, however, worked at a time that archaeological methods in Polynesia were still primitive (stratigraphic excavation lay in the future), and in particular lacked any method for direct dating. Similarly, historical linguistic analyses of relationships between Polynesian languages were not yet well understood. Thus, Burrows confined his research to the comparative distribution of cultural 'traits', such as material culture, kinship systems, cosmogony and religious beliefs. Nonetheless, Burrows was able to deduce a series of 'historical processes which had apparently brought about the differentiation of western from central-marginal Polynesia' (1938, p. 92). These processes included diffusion, local development and abandonment or rejection of specific cultural traits.

Goodenough (1957) was the next to call for comparative research in Oceania, noting the suitability of the region for controlled studies. Marshall Sahlins (1958) produced just such a comparative study of Polynesia, theoretically situated within a cultural evolutionary framework (Sahlins and Service, 1960). Sahlins invoked a phylogenetic analogy by describing Polynesian cultures as 'members of a single cultural genus that has filled in and adapted to a variety of local habitats' (1958, p. ix). It was not phylogenetic analysis *per se*, however, or the reconstruction of historical processes within Polynesia that interested Sahlins. Nor were such historical issues the main concern of Goldman (1955; 1970), who like Sahlins regarded Polynesia as a group of genetically related societies well suited for comparative analysis. Goldman (1970) did incorporate newly emerging archaeological data into his study, which along with oral traditions and related historical records, provided historical context for his analysis of the Polynesian 'status system'. The pioneering studies of Sahlins and Goldman relied almost exclusively on *synchronic* data, that is, the ethnographic and ethnohistoric record. As a consequence, particular ethnographic endpoints in their evolutionary schemes inevitably stood as exemplars of putative earlier stages in the historical process. In Goldman's case, for example, the 'Traditional' societies of Tikopia, Pukapuka or Ontong-Java appeared to represent an original, Ancestral form of Polynesian society. But as we know, ethnographically attested societies are not the changeless descendants of their ancestors, even though they may have been culturally conservative.

For historical anthropologists, the problem lies in distinguishing *homologous* traits (whose age must then be determined in some manner) from *synologous* traits (resulting from later borrowing), as well as from those recurring *regularities* that 'transcend culture' (Goldman, 1970, p. xi), reflecting more general (*analogous*) processes. Such analogous processes and properties were the focus of some New Archaeologists whose research agendas were more process-oriented than historical. Identification of well-established regularities within a culture region allow one to test the utility of cross-cultural generalisations grounded in ethnography and whose basis is usually statistical (see Mace and Pagel, 1994).

Kirch (1980; 1984) tackled historical change within Polynesia using an explicitly comparative and evolutionary approach, privileging the archaeological evidence that had accumulated from the mid-1950s through the 1970s, rather than relying exclusively on the ethnographic record used by scholars from Burrows to Sahlins and Goldman. Kirch's approach (1984, pp. 5–8) was that of a 'study of internal differentiation of Polynesian societies' designed to draw on the power of holistic anthropology:

> Precisely because Polynesia as a region consists of a series of discrete, but historically related societies – all derived from a common ancestor – and because there was direct historical continuity between the 'ethnographic present' and the prehistoric past, we are in an excellent position to draw upon ethnohistoric, ethnographic, and linguistic data, as well as upon strictly archaeological evidence in an attempt to understand the region's prehistory. The Polynesian ethnographic baseline does not provide mere analogies for the interpretation of archaeological data; it illuminates directly the *endpoints* of indigenous developmental sequences.
>
> *(Kirch 1984, p. 5)*

Kirch used a graphic model, reproduced here as Fig. 4.1, to illustrate the process of cultural differentiation within Polynesia. This was in fundamentally a phylogenetic model, in which the ethnographically attested Polynesian cultures and societies were seen as having been derived from a proto-group that Kirch termed 'Ancestral Polynesian Society' (abbreviated APS in the diagram). Although emphasis was placed on a series of successive colonisation events (migrations out of the original APS homeland, and out of later daughter communities), and on the effects of subsequent isolation between descendant populations, Kirch did not ignore cultural contact and borrowing between island groups (as depicted by the double-arrow linking W_3 and X_3 in the diagram).

Kirch argued that knowledge of the APS 'baseline' was necessary in order to assess later historical changes in the descendant cultural traditions within Polynesia. Only by first having some idea of the social and technological bases of APS would it be feasible to determine which later features were retentions, adaptations or elaborations of older patterns, and which were entirely new innovations, borrowing or, at times, convergences. Kirch drew upon evidence from both archaeology and linguistics (lexical reconstructions) to outline important aspects of APS, including technology, production systems and social relations (Kirch, 1984, pp. 53–69).

A major advance in the development of an explicitly phylogenetic approach was the 1987 article by Kirch and Green, drawing upon the 'genetic' model outlined by Kim Romney (1957), and on improvements to that model proposed by Vogt (1964) in its application to the Maya. The direct impetus to the Kirch and Green article on phylogeny in Polynesia was the monograph by Flannery and Marcus, *The Cloud People* (1983).

ISLAND A   ISLAND B   ISLAND C   ISLAND D

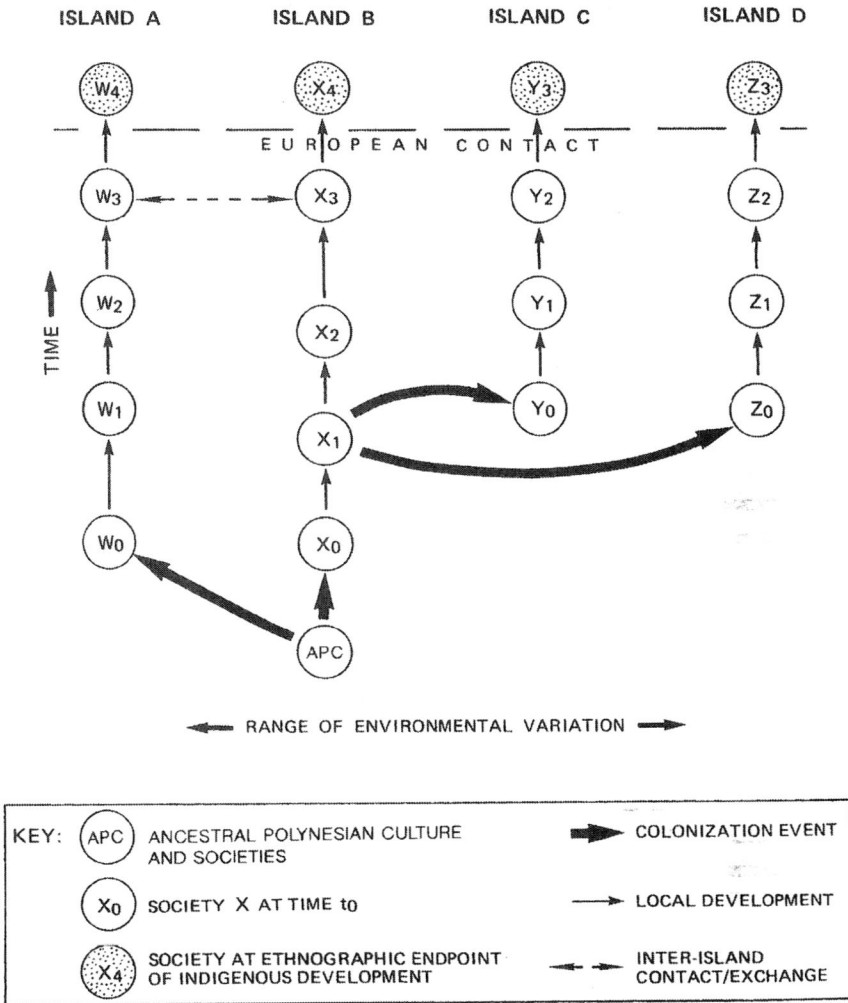

RANGE OF ENVIRONMENTAL VARIATION

KEY:

APC — ANCESTRAL POLYNESIAN CULTURE AND SOCIETIES

X_0 — SOCIETY X AT TIME t_0

X_4 — SOCIETY AT ETHNOGRAPHIC ENDPOINT OF INDIGENOUS DEVELOPMENT

COLONIZATION EVENT

LOCAL DEVELOPMENT

INTER-ISLAND CONTACT/EXCHANGE

FIGURE 4.1 Kirch's 1984 model of phylogenetic differentiation in Polynesia.

Source: P.V. Kirch, *Evolution of the Polynesian Chiefdoms* (1984, fig. 1). © Cambridge University Press 1984. Reproduced with permission of Cambridge University Press through PLSclear.

The phylogenetic model: background and development

Kim Romney (1957) had been the first to delineate specific criteria for cultural phylogenetic units, drawing upon Fred Eggan's proposals (1954) regarding controlled comparison in anthropology (see also Goodenough, 1957). Romney rightly observed that there is no necessary correspondence between language, biology and culture, but that when these variables 'do show significant concordance in their distribution this may well represent an important historical fact, namely that the explanation for their concordance can be traced to a common point somewhere in the past' (1957, p. 36). Romney then proceeded to outline what he termed the 'genetic model':

> The genetic model takes as its segment of cultural history a group of tribes which are set off from all other groups by sharing a common physical type, possessing common systemic patterns, and speaking genetically related languages. It is assumed that correspondence among these three factors indicates a common historical tradition at some time in the past for these tribes. We shall designate this segment of cultural history as the 'genetic unit' and it includes the Ancestral group and all intermediate groups, as well as the tribes in the ethnographic present. The genetic unit represents a substantive segment of cultural history while the term 'genetic model' refers to the conceptual framework which serves as a tool to order the data.
>
> *(Romney, 1957, p. 36)*

Evon Vogt (1964) expanded and refined Romney's seminal proposals in an introductory essay to a volume on Maya cultural development (see also Vogt, 1994). Vogt pointed out that a 'common historical tradition' in an area such as the Maya, would need to be defined on the *independent* criteria of (1) a common physical (i.e. biological) type, (2) common systemic cultural patterns and (3) genetically related languages. Vogt explicitly compared the 'genetic model' to models of adaptive radiation in biology:

> In brief, the genetic model assumes that genetically related tribes, as determined by related languages, physical types, and systemic patterns, are derived from a small proto-group with a proto-culture at some time in the past. The model resembles that of the zoologist who views a certain species of animal as evolving and making an adaptive adjustment to a given ecological niche and then radiating from this point as the population expands into neighboring ecological niches. As the population moves into different ecological settings, further adaptive variations occur in the species. But these variations are traceable to the Ancestral animal, or, in other words, back to the proto-type.
>
> In the genetic model, as applied to human populations, we assume that a small proto-group succeeds in adapting itself efficiently to a certain ecological niche and in developing certain basic systemic patterns which constitute the basic aspects of the proto-culture. If the adaptation proves to be efficient, the population expands, and the group begins to radiate from this point of dispersal. As members split off from the proto-group and move into neighboring ecological niches, they make appropriate adaptations to these new situations and begin to differentiate – that is, there are adaptive variations from the proto-type over time as the members of the genetic unit spread from the dispersal area.
>
> *(Vogt, 1964, pp. 11–12)*

Vogt moved the discussion of the genetic model beyond a strictly theoretical concept by outlining explicit methodological steps and procedures for its application in historical anthropology. Vogt advocated 'the combined use of a number of linguistic, archaeological, physical anthropological, ethnological, and historical methods bringing to bear the full range of anthropological data as these become available from field and archival research' (1964, p. 12). Primacy was accorded to linguistic evidence, with a crucial first step being 'the definition of genetic units in terms of genetically related languages'. As Sanders put it in a review of Vogt's essay: 'Methodologically speaking, the basis of defining such genetic units should be linguistic because of the relative exactness of linguistic methods as compared to those of ethnography and archaeology' (Sanders, 1966).

Vogt's methods for applying the genetic model to a specific 'segment of cultural history' entailed eight steps (1964, pp. 10–13):

(1) plot the geographical distribution of related languages;
(2) calculate time depth, using lexicostatistics and glottochronology;
(3) locate the dispersal area and spread of the proto-group;
(4) reconstruct the proto-language and proto-culture using the linguistic methods of lexical reconstruction;
(5) use archaeological data to test specific hypotheses generated by steps 3 and 4;
(6) check the sequences of divergence derived from linguistic and archaeological analyses with the independent evidence of physical or biological anthropology;
(7) use ethnohistorical materials to 'provide readings on the various branches of the genetic unit' between the time of first European contact to the present; and
(8) add ethnographic data on contemporary communities to 'map variations in systemic patterns that have survived from earlier time levels and to detect cultural "drifts" or trends that are still occurring in these living systems'.

These eight steps constitute an integrated methodology for delineating a phylogenetic unit, whose various branches have diverged from a common ancestor, according to a historical sequence that can be defined in time and space.

Despite its potential, Vogt's research strategy was not widely applied, in part because cultural anthropologists had by then largely abandoned their prior interests in historical and evolutionary issues. Flannery and Marcus (1983), however, used Romney and Vogt's genetic model in their path-breaking study of evolutionary divergence among the Zapotec and Mixtec peoples of Mesoamerica. Kirch and Green, independently reading this monograph, were inspired to collaborate on a joint application of the phylogenetic model to Polynesia (Kirch and Green, 1987).

History and phylogeny in Polynesia

In their 1987 article, Kirch and Green found it necessary to address inadequacies in Vogt's (1964; 1994) methods, especially Vogt's proposed reliance upon lexicostatistics and glottochronology to determine the subgrouping relationships among a region's languages, and to calculate the time depth of cultural differentiation. Kirch and Green were aware that historical linguists in the Pacific had recognised that a strictly lexicostatistical approach (e.g. Dyen, 1965) could not determine language subgrouping relationships as accurately as the classic comparative method of historical linguistics. They also saw that glottochronology was similarly flawed.

Kirch and Green (1987) therefore based their subgrouping model for Polynesian languages *not* on lexicostatistics, but on the comparative analysis of phonology, lexicon and morphology as had been developed by the linguists Biggs (1971; 1972), Pawley (1966; 1967), and others. This subgrouping model was based on *shared innovations* (as opposed to retentions, or generalised similarity), a methodological advance comparable to the paradigm shift from phenetic to cladistic methods in biology. And, rather than relying on glottochronology to calculate the time depth of differentiation (as Vogt had proposed), Kirch and Green used the radiocarbon dating chronology that had been developed for Polynesia (Green, 1981).

Kirch and Green's use of the 'genetic comparative method' in historical linguistics (as opposed to lexicostatistics) was critical because, in Polynesia, this method provides both robust models of subgrouping as well as a well-attested set of lexical reconstructions. The same is true at higher levels in the Austronesian language family, where the comparative method yields both the major *Oceanic* subgroup (Pawley and Ross, 1993, pp. 433–434), and various internal subgroups within it (Ross, 1988; Pawley and Ross, 1993, pp. 439–440, fig. 2; Green, 1997, fig. 4).

Kirch and Green (1987) also put forward some 'initial propositions' regarding 'evolutionary process' within the Polynesian region. They emphasised the importance of 'establishing homologies, thus clearing the path for the analysis of evolutionary process' (1987, p. 432), finding inspiration in Gould's assertions regarding the 'triumph of homology, or why history matters' (Gould, 1986). In Gould's succinct phrasing,

> once we map homologies properly, we can finally begin to ask interesting biological questions about function and development – that is, we can use morphology for its intrinsic sources of enlightenment, and not as an inherently flawed measure of genealogical relationships.
>
> *(Gould, 1986, p. 68)*

Although Gould wrote as a biologist, his arguments apply equally to issues of cultural evolution. Determining the sequence of phylogenetic divergence within Polynesian societies, and then reconstructing as thoroughly as possible the baseline of Ancestral Polynesian culture, opens up possibilities for rigorous analyses of cultural evolutionary process.

Kirch and Green (1987) outlined several 'mechanisms of divergence', 'parallel evolutionary processes' and processes of 'convergence', which they argued had been significant in Polynesia. Among potential mechanisms of divergence, they offered: (1) isolation; (2) founder effect or drift; (3) colonisation, including adaptation to new and contrastive environments; (4) long-term environmental selection resulting both from natural and from human-induced environmental changes; and (5) external contact. Among the parallel evolutionary processes they proposed were: (1) demographic factors, such as a cultural analogue of the r/K selection continuum in evolutionary ecology; (2) intensification and specialisation of production; and (3) increased competition over time. Kirch and Green also commented on the 'analogic emergence of similar traits or structures' in Polynesian societies that had not been in direct contact with each other, and where such structures were therefore likely to be convergences. For example, the European contact-era societies of Tonga and Hawai'i were the most highly stratified societies anywhere within the Polynesian region, with strongly hierarchical political systems (Clark, 2016; Kirch, 1984, pp. 217–263; Kirch, 2010). Tonga and Hawai'i share such remarkable parallels as a sacred-secular dual paramountship and land tenure systems in which district chiefs held large estates (the Tongan *tofi'a* and Hawaiian *ahupua'a*) on which the common people were alienated from hereditary land rights. In both societies, commoners maintained rights of usufruct through offerings of labour and tribute to the chiefs. Yet these two contact-era systems of political organisation and land tenure, despite their structural similarities, clearly represent *convergent* developments rather than retentions from an earlier history. These two societies had undergone parallel historical processes, such as the growth of large and dense populations, accompanied by agricultural intensification. In contrast, certain concepts of chiefship in both Hawaiian and Tongan society (such as the association of chiefs with the related concepts of *mana* and *tapu*), are undoubtedly homologous, being shared retentions from an Ancestral Polynesian social structure.

While foregrounding the determination of homology, Kirch and Green did not neglect the potential for inter-island contacts, noting that 'isolation is relative in Oceania, and external contact played varying roles in the evolutionary trajectories of specific societies' (Kirch and Green, 1987, p. 442). They opined that 'relatively few Oceanic islands were ever fully isolated', and that many societies were known to have been linked by complex networks of external exchange.

Triangulation and the phylogenetic model

Partly in response to certain critiques of their 1987 paper, Kirch and Green resolved to refine their phylogenetic model, resulting in a 375-page book, *Hawaiki, Ancestral Polynesia* (Kirch and Green, 2001). This required the development of what they called the *triangulation method* for integrating data from the disciplines of historical linguistics, archaeology, comparative ethnology and biological anthropology. The term 'triangulation' derives metaphorically from the classic method of surveying by triangulation, in which sightings are taken from two or more points along an established baseline to an unlocated point which one wishes to fix in space. As these sightings converge on that point, a triangle or 'polygon of error' is defined, within which the actual point lies. By metaphorical extension, the 'sight-lines' are those provided by the independent evidence of historical linguistics, archaeology, comparative ethnography, biological anthropology or even oral traditions. As independent lines of evidence converge and cross-check each other, the polygon of error decreases in size and historical reconstruction becomes increasingly accurate.

The triangulation method brings to bear two distinct classes of evidence: (1) those that are truly *diachronic* in that they derive directly from past events and can be positioned in real chronological time; and (2) those that permit the construction of relative time sequences through systematic comparison of *synchronic* materials. The analytical power of triangulation – and the robustness of the historical reconstructions derived from it – requires that the relevant sub-disciplinary methods, inferences and conclusions be respected and treated *independently*, based exclusively on the evidence from each field. The philosopher of science Alison Wylie (1989; 1992), discussing problems of confirmation in archaeology, noted that employing independent sources of data for any given reconstructive-evaluative argument ensures that the constituent arguments are not merely *mutually reinforcing* but also *mutually constraining*. In short,

> if diverse evidential strands all converge on a given hypothesis – if you can use different means to triangulate on the same postulated set of conditions or events – then you may be able to provide it decisive, if never irreversible, support simply because it is so implausible that the convergence should be the result of compensatory error in all the influences establishing its evidential support.
>
> *(Wylie, 1992, p. 28)*

Reconstructing Ancestral Polynesian culture and society

The linguistic phylogeny or internal subgrouping of the Polynesian languages is now among the best understood of any subset within the Austronesian language family (Biggs, 1971; Clark, 1979; Green, 1966; Marck, 2000; Pawley, 1966; Wilson, 1985; Walworth, 2014). The thirty-six extant Polynesian languages are most closely related to Fijian and Rotuman, with which they form the next higher-order subgroup of Oceanic languages, Central Pacific. Proto Central-Pacific is regarded as the language spoken by the Eastern Lapita colonists of the Fiji–Tonga–Samoa area. Fairly soon after the settlement of the Fiji–Tonga region, Proto Central-Pacific began to differentiate into distinct Proto Fijic and Proto Tokalau-Polynesian languages (Geraghty, 1983). Continued change within the latter linkage led to successive language interstages within the Tonga-Samoa region.

Figure 4.2 shows a widely accepted model of the internal relationships of the Polynesian languages, allowing one to infer that all known Polynesian languages

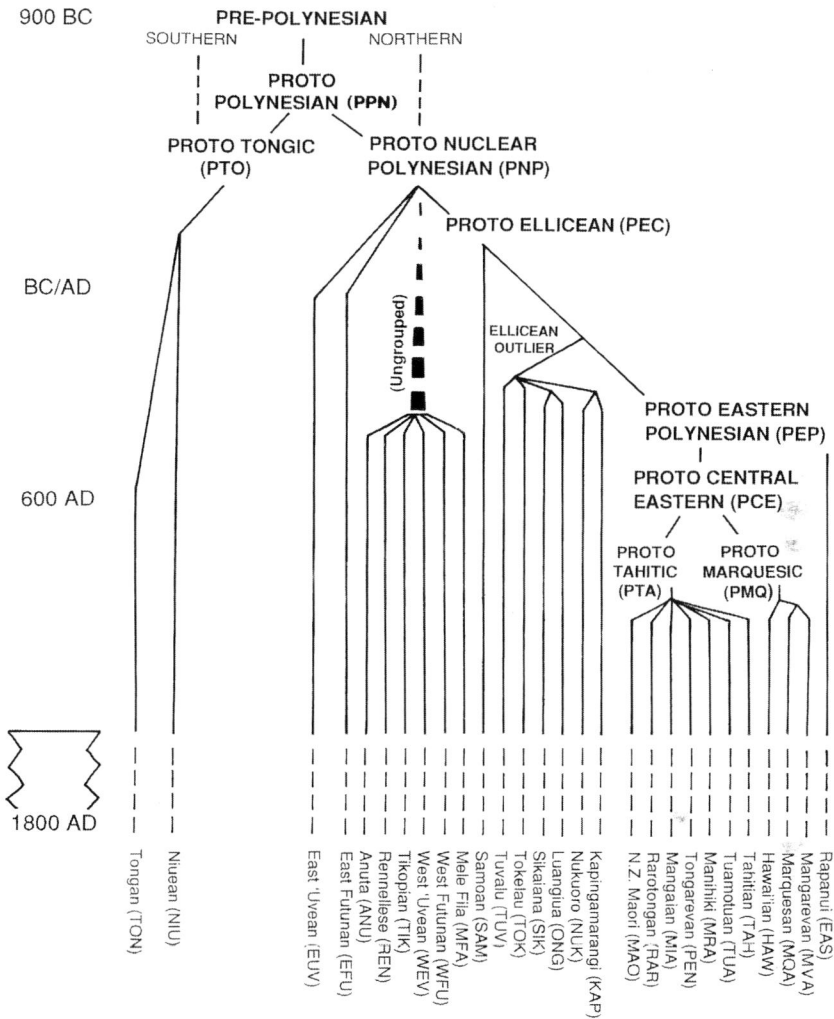

FIGURE 4.2 The 'family tree' or subgrouping model of the Polynesian languages used by Kirch and Green in their phylogenetic model of Polynesian culture history.

Source: from P.V. Kirch and R. Green, *Hawaiki, Ancestral Polynesia: An Essay in Historical Anthropology* (2001, fig. 3.5). © Cambridge University Press 2001. Reproduced with permission of Cambridge University Press through PLSclear.

can be traced back to Proto Polynesian, and confirming the existence of a mono-phyletic unit. The branching structure of this tree likewise provides a model for successive stages in the differentiation of Polynesian subgroups. While the early split of Proto Polynesian into Proto Tongic and Proto Nuclear Polynesian branches must have occurred within the Tonga–Samoa region, subsequent splits in the tree would have resulted from populations moving out of this core region, primarily into Eastern Polynesia, as well as the Polynesian Outliers.

Biological anthropology also affirms the essential homogeneity of Polynesian populations. Distinct morphological features have long been recognised as denoting a common Polynesian phenotype, such as large body size and a high incidence of the 'rocker jaw' and of a strongly 'pentagonally' shaped cranium (Houghton, 1996). Studies of metrical and nonmetrical traits (Pietrusewsky (1970; 1996), and more recently genetic studies, including DNA sequencing, reinforce this homogeneity within the Polynesian genotype (Hill and Serjeantson, 1989; Kayser et al., 2006; Merriwether et al., 1999). This high degree of biological homogeneity is thought to have resulted from a population bottleneck during the initial colonisation of Fiji and Western Polynesia (Kelly, 1996; Martinson, 1996; Martinson et al., 1993), resulting in the well-known founder effect.

Comparative ethnography – the third line of evidence regarding Polynesian relationships – likewise documents widely shared, systemic cultural patterns inherited by Polynesian cultures from their common ancestor (Sahlins, 1958; Goldman, 1970; Howard and Borofsky, 1989). These shared patterns range from basic kinds of social groups and land tenure patterns, to religious concepts (*mana* and *tapu*), cosmogonic origin myths and the ubiquitous presence of hereditary chiefship, as well as more prosaic aspects of material culture (Burrows, 1938).

As a phyletic unit, Polynesia is particularly well suited to the application of the phylogenetic approach. Some aspects of this early culture – such as artefacts, diet or settlement patterns – are directly evidenced by archaeological materials, in addition to being inferred from linguistic reconstructions and comparative ethnography. However, the power of the triangulation method is that it permits the historical anthropologist to also reconstruct aspects of culture that do not leave material traces, such as social and political organisation, religious concepts or calendrical systems.

Kirch and Green (2001) applied a phylogenetic model to Polynesia, and systematically used the triangulation method to reconstruct Ancestral Polynesian culture, during the time frame of the middle to late first millennium BC. Archaeologically, this early phase is attested by more than twenty-five sites, each representing a social community. All were small hamlets or villages, mostly situated on or near the coast. A mixed horticultural-maritime economy, including the cultivation of tuber and root crops such as taro and yams, and tree crops such as coconut, breadfruit, bananas, vi apple and Tahitian Chestnut, is attested both by direct archaeobotanical and faunal remains and by linguistic reconstructions. While pigs, dogs and chickens were present in small numbers, fish and shellfish provided most of the protein in the Ancestral Polynesian diet, augmented by hunting birds. Linguistic reconstructions indicate a wide range of fishing methods, as well as more than 150 terms for different kinds of fish (Clark, 1991; Hooper, 1994).

Direct archaeological evidence reveals that Ancestral Polynesians made plain ware pottery (largely simple bowls and cups), adzes of *Tridacna* shell and (increasingly over time) of basalt, one-piece fishhooks of *Turbo* shell, beads and rings of

Conus shell, hammerstones, files or abraders of sea-urchin spine and of coral or pumice, and amorphous scrapers or other ad hoc tools made from flakes of basalt or obsidian. But a much greater range of material culture emerges when the triangulation method is applied, extending the reconstructions to objects made of wood or vegetable fibres that generally do not preserve in the archaeological record. These include mats woven from coconut and *Pandanus* leaves, wooden bowls and containers, coconut water bottles, baskets and clothing (loincloths and skirts) made from paper mulberry bark (*Broussonetia papyrifera*) and other plants. Fishing gear included poles and lines, along with several kinds of nets made from *Pipturus* bark cordage. Dwellings and cook-houses alike were fashioned with stout timber posts and rafters and thatched with sago palm or *Pandanus* leaves.

The archaeological record is largely mute with respect to kinship, social organisation and religion, and here again triangulation permits the development of semantic history hypotheses for a wide range of lexically attested concepts (Green, 1994). Marck (2000), for example, reconstructed Proto Polynesian kinship terminology. Kirch and Green (2001, pp. 201–236) determined that the primary social group in Ancestral Polynesia was the *kainanga (the asterisk denoting a reconstructed term), a unilineal descent group whose members traced their lineage back to a founding ancestor (*tupunga). The head of a *kainanga was the *qariki, in most cases a senior (ranking) male, who served as the group's secular and ritual leader. During the Ancestral Polynesian stage, there does not appear to have been a separate status category of priest. However, special terms can be reconstructed for an expert or knowledgeable craftsperson (*tufunga), sea expert or navigator (*tautai) and warrior (*toa). The *kainga was a smaller, a co-residential social group holding an estate of land as well as other tangible and intangible property and rights.

Triangulation also permits the reconstruction of Ancestral Polynesian religious concepts, their calendar and their ritual cycle. The pan-Polynesian concepts of *tapu (sacredness) and *mana (spiritual power) were central to their belief system (Shore, 1989). Ancestors, from whom *mana flowed, were arguably at the core of Ancestral Polynesian ritual life. Functionally diversified anthropomorphic gods – such as Tāne, Tū and Rongo, so well-known from Eastern Polynesian societies, were not part of the Ancestral Polynesian cosmology, but were a later, early Eastern Polynesian innovation, accompanied by changes in ritual architecture and the beginnings of a formal priesthood. Only Tangaloa was known as a deity to the Ancestral Polynesians, who also recounted the great doing of a culture hero, Maui, who performed magical feats such as fishing islands from the deep or snaring the sun.

The psychoactive *kava* plant (*Piper methysticum*), domesticated in Vanuatu and presumably carried to the Tonga-Samoa region by the Lapita colonisers, played a role in Ancestral Polynesian ritual, due to the trancelike state it induced. There are at least ten Proto Polynesian words dealing with kinds of ritual, prayer and rite, and there is a hint of an important ceremonial feast, perhaps a first-fruits ritual. The year was organised around a lunar calendar of thirteen months, indexed to the rising and setting of the star cluster Pleiades (*Mata-liki) and to the annual spawning of the reproductive segments of the *palolo sea worm. The lunar month names are concerned in large part with the annual wet-dry seasonality critical to the planting and harvesting of the yam crop.

The above paragraphs merely sketch out how the triangulation method – constrained by the phylogenetic approach – allows for a richly textured reconstruction of Ancestral Polynesian culture. It demonstrates the power of a *holistic* historical anthropology, integrating the evidence of archaeology with that obtained from its sister disciplines of linguistics, comparative ethnography and biological anthropology.

Isolation, interaction and cultural phylogeny

Critics have pointed to interisland and interarchipelago interaction as posing insurmountable problems for a phylogenetic approach to Polynesian (or indeed, Oceanic) prehistory (e.g. Terrell et al., 1997; Hunt et al., 1998). To be sure, rapid isolation is unlikely to have been the case during the early stages of human colonisation in the Fiji-Tonga-Samoa region. Instead of an A $\rightarrow$ B $\rightarrow$ C sequence of colonisation with discrete breaks, the formation of linked communities and dialect chains is more plausible. Kirch and Green (2001) argued that a gradual process of network-breaking best accounts for the formation of dialectal and cultural differentiation within the Polynesian homeland. But what of later, and continued, contact or interaction among related Polynesian societies? Would such interaction, combined with 'horizontal trait transmission' such as lexical borrowing, or the diffusion of technological innovations, lead to a total masking of the phylogenetic signals of shared ancestry and inheritance? Hunt et al. argued that phylogenetic 'trees reflect an unknown and *unknowable* mixture of ancestry and later sharing' (1998, p. 3; their emphasis).

Terrell et al. (1997) opine that Pacific Island societies have never been 'primitive isolates', and that some degree of interaction and communication has always been present between island communities. This is indisputable. Kirch (1986) offered a detailed analysis of Tikopia as an example of 'inter-island contact in the transformation of an island society'. Arguing that islands were rarely, if ever, closed systems, Kirch wrote that 'even in the more geographically remote islands of Eastern Polynesia, the notion that island societies developed *in vacuo*, as it were, deserves on recent evidence to be seriously questioned' (1986, p. 33). The issue is not whether contact or interaction occurred, but what effects it had on island languages, cultures and gene pools. Did interaction inevitably and inexorably lead to the dissolution of patterns of homologous traits, fatally undermining a phylogenetic model?

Ethnohistoric and ethnographic evidence for interaction within the Polynesian region shows that degrees of isolation varied significantly. Despite oral narratives of an earlier period of two-way voyages between Hawai'i and an Ancestral land called Kahiki, for example, the Hawaiians had not been in contact with other Polynesian groups for at least several centuries prior to Cook's arrival in 1778 (Cachola-Abad, 1993). Similarly, there is no evidence that the Rapa Nui people had maintained regular communication with other islands after the period of initial settlement by their founding ancestor Hotu Matu'a (Métraux, 1940). New Zealand, too, had been isolated for some time prior to European voyaging. Thus, the marginal sectors of Eastern Polynesia, set off from the core by open ocean distances ranging from 2,000 to 4,000 km, had not been in regular contact with the Eastern Polynesian homeland for many centuries at least.

The situation was different in the tropical core of Polynesia, where interisland distances were typically in the range of 200–600 km. Two major spheres of regular interisland voyaging are well documented ethnohistorically: (1) a formal exchange system linking Tonga with Samoa and other Western Polynesian islands, and with Fiji; and (2) a less formalised system linking the Society Islands, directly or indirectly, with the Tuamotus, Australs, Marquesas and southern Cooks. The Tongan system is sometimes known as the 'Tongan maritime empire' (Kaeppler, 1978; Kirch, 1984, pp. 217–242; Hage and Harary, 1991, pp. 16–20). The Tongan exchange network was operated by a small number of Tongan elites and involved the transfer of prestige goods (such as mats and feathers) and the marriage of limited numbers of high-ranking spouses. The central Eastern Polynesian network is less well documented, but also involved elites and was probably restricted to prestige goods. Neither of these systems involved large numbers of people (or non-elites), or high-frequency movement of goods and materials. Thus, the impacts of such exchange were principally confined to the elite sectors of society, where they doubtless influenced political affairs and, at times, religious ideology.

That such interisland contacts did *not* lead to wholesale horizontal transmission of traits (linguistic or cultural) – thus swamping out any phylogenetic signal – is obvious in that the several interacting groups maintained distinctive languages and cultural patterns. Despite limited inter-marriage between high-ranking Tongan males and Samoan chiefly women, Tongans and Samoans retained their own cultural distinctiveness (as in barkcloth designs, club forms or monumental architecture, to name just a few examples). Tongan and Samoan languages, likewise, remained discrete and distinctively separate, even though there was some borrowing. Marck (2000, p. 107) identified ninety-nine words in the 'metropolitan Western Polynesian vocabulary which may constitute post Proto Tongic and/or post-Proto Nuclear Polynesian borrowings around Western Polynesia'. While significant, this hardly constitutes massive linguistic impact. The same can be said for the maintenance of cultural and linguistic differences among the central Eastern Polynesian cultures. Indeed, various Polynesian groups *consciously* maintained distinctive cultural and linguistic identities, quite the opposite of willy-nilly borrowing of every new word or thing they heard or saw on voyages to other islands.

Contrary to the assertion of Hunt et al. (1998) that the 'mixture of ancestry and later sharing' is 'unknowable', historical linguists and archaeologists have good empirical methods for determining historical contacts between groups. In historical linguistics, 'borrowing' of words can be detected through the presence of irregular sound correspondences, and sometimes 'doublets', resulting in what Biggs termed 'direct and indirect inheritance' in his classic study of Rotuman (Biggs, 1965). Given the ethnohistoric evidence for the Tongan 'maritime empire', one predicts the presence of Tongan loan words in the languages of other groups with whom the Tongans interacted; this is precisely the case (Clark, 1979, p. 264; Biggs, 1980; Dye, 1980, p. 352; Marck, 2000, pp. 110–112). Indeed, with East 'Uvea, which was conquered and politically dominated by the Tongans for some centuries, extensive lexical change did occur, although Pawley (1967) could still determine convincingly that 'Uvean was fundamentally a Samoic language with a heavy Tongan overlay. The respective contributions of ancestry or shared inheritance could be unambiguously separated from those of culture-contact.

The development of geochemical methods for sourcing prehistoric artefacts, such as both non-destructive and destructive XRF techniques, has now permitted Polynesian archaeologists to begin to empirically trace ancient spheres of interaction between islands and archipelagos (Weisler, 1997). Weisler et al. (2016), for example, have demonstrated the movement of basalt adzes from sources as distant as Samoa, the Marquesas and Rurutu (Austral Islands) to Mangaia in the Southern Cook Islands. This demonstration that small quantities of stone artefacts were transported from one island or archipelago to another implies exactly the kinds of relatively low-frequency, elite-centred voyaging demonstrated by the ethnohistoric record.

To sum up, while regular patterns of interaction characterised parts of Polynesia, other more geographically remote sectors were significantly isolated. Where interaction was ongoing and is ethnographically described, it mostly involved small numbers of elites. Furthermore, the claim that the effects of interaction are 'unknowable' is unfounded. Linguists, archaeologists and biological anthropologists have each developed and tested empirical methods to track interaction, and the correspondence between the results of their independent analyses is striking. We need only point to the kinds of deep divisions within Polynesia, so well analysed by Burrows (1938; see table 3.1), to realise that interaction did not produce a homogenised culture. The major and pervasive distinctions between Western and Eastern Polynesia are sufficient to differentiate two major clades or branches within the Polynesian phylogeny. Polynesian societies were never 'primitive isolates', nor were they a panmictic mélange. Their history, as defined by shared ancestry, by innovation and by interaction, is both real and knowable.

Advances in the application of the phylogenetic model

In this chapter, I have focused on the history and development of a phylogenetic model in the context of long-standing anthropological interests in controlled comparison, with particular reference to Polynesia, culminating in Kirch and Green's (2001) treatise on Ancestral Polynesia. A phylogenetic approach in Pacific prehistory, however, has continued to develop and flourish since that work was published, incorporating both new data and new methods. While a thorough review of these developments is beyond my purview, a brief discussion of some examples seems appropriate.

The phylogenetic model applied by Kirch and Green (1987, 2001) in Polynesia used as its foundation the family tree or subgrouping model of Polynesian languages

(Fig. 4.2) as worked out by Biggs, Pawley, Clark and other linguists using the classical methods of comparative historical linguistics. These methods are sound, yielding abundantly attested phylogenies based on sets of shared innovations in lexicon and grammar; their drawback is that they are slow, and require painstaking application. It took Biggs and his students several decades to achieve the baseline that Kirch and Green used as the foundation for their reconstruction of Ancestral Polynesian culture. An alternative approach emerged in the early 2000s, with the work of Russell Gray and colleagues, applying new computational methods derived from biological phylogenetics to large linguistic data sets extending beyond Polynesia and encompassing the entire Austronesian language family (Gray and Jordan, 2000; Gray et al., 2009; 2013). They not only detected a strong phylogenetic signal inherent in these data but found that this lent strong support to what has been called 'the fast train' hypothesis of a rapid spread of Austronesian-speaking peoples into Remote Oceania (Gray and Jordan, 2000). Refinements in this approach, using a Bayesian statistical approach, further demonstrated that the Austronesian expansion into the Pacific world occurred as a series of 'pulses and pauses' (Gray et al., 2009), a model that correlates quite well both with the classical linguistic evidence and with the emerging data from recent archaeological research in Near and Remote Oceania.

The development of a phylogeny – whether by traditional linguistic methods or by the new computational approaches – should not, however, be seen as an end result but rather as the means of advancing further research. Just as Kirch and Green (2001) used their phylogeny to address the task of reconstructing Ancestral Polynesian culture, Gray and colleagues have recently used their computationally derived Austronesian phylogeny to test several provocative hypotheses regarding cultural evolution. In one case (Watts et al., 2015), they have used the Austronesian phylogenetic model to test the hypothesis of whether religious systems incorporating 'moralizing high gods' drove the evolution of socio-political complexity, or emerged following the development of such complexity. In another recent study, Sheehan et al. (2018), investigate the causal links between socio-political hierarchy and the development of landesque capital intensive agriculture, finding that this relationship was broadly reciprocal, with 'political complexity … more of a driver than a result of intensification'. These recent applications of a phylogenetic model testify to the continuing power of this approach to drive new research into fundamental questions regarding cultural evolution.

Finally, recent advances in biological anthropology also have important implications for advancing phylogenetic approaches that seek to achieve the long-standing goal of an integrative holistic anthropology. The phylogenetic model, as conceived by Vogt (1964), recognised that physical anthropology (as the subfield was then known) could be a potential contributor (see Vogt's step 6) of information of the divergence of a 'segment of cultural history'. In practical terms, however, the physical anthropology of Vogt's time was far too primitive in its methods (largely limited to statistical analyses of phenotypic variation) to make a substantive contribution. Even when Kirch and Green (1987; 2001) applied a phylogenetic model to Polynesia, biological anthropology was only in the first stages of the molecular revolution that has now transformed the field, and played no significant role in their work. This situation, however, has now changed dramatically, with not only mtDNA and Y-chromosome mapping of populations across Oceania, but even whole genome sequencing of archaeologically recovered individuals (aDNA sequencing).

With these advances in molecular biological anthropology comes the potential to compare phylogenetic models based on language diversity (whether by traditional or computational methods) with models derived from the analysis of genetic population diversity – both modern and as reflected by samples of individuals who lived and died at different times in the past. The tremendous potential for taking the phylogenetic approach in Pacific prehistory to an entirely new level of sophistication is evident in just two recent applications of aDNA analysis in Remote Oceania (Liston et al., 2018; Posth et al., 2018). What both of these studies demonstrate is that, in spite of a complex history of continuing movement of people down the island arcs of Melanesia into Vanuatu, beginning with initial Lapita (Austronesian) expansion and continuing with later episodes involving populations with a greater genetic component of 'Papuan' ancestry, the phylogenetic signals of this process can be disentangled. As Liston et al. (2018) note, such analyses are capable of highlighting 'a history of multiple episodes of migration and mixture in shaping the human diversity of Oceania'.

To conclude, a phylogenetic approach to Pacific prehistory is not only alive and well, but is rapidly advancing in new theoretical and methodological directions that we could not have conceived of just a few years ago. Rather than an intractable, 'tangled bank' whose complex history could never be uncovered, the history of the human settlement of the Pacific islands, as well as the later history of multiple interactions between island societies, is ultimately knowable, at least in its major trends and configurations. As Hurles et al. stated several years ago: 'Oceanic prehistory is not simple, but it is tractable. There is a strong phylogenetic signal, together with some reticulation, for both languages and genetics' (2003, p. 539).

Acknowledgements

This chapter is an update to material in chapters 1 and 2 of Kirch and Green (2001), *Hawaiki, Ancestral Polynesia: An Essay in Historical Anthropology*. I must here express my deep gratitude and respect for my former colleague and collaborator, the late Professor Roger Green. The development of a phylogenetic approach to Polynesian prehistory was truly a joint – and wonderfully enjoyable – collaboration between the two of us.

References

Bellwood, P., 1996. Phylogeny *vs* reticulation in prehistory. *Antiquity,* 70, pp. 881–90.
Bellwood, P., Fox, J.J. and Tryon, D., 1995. The Austronesians in history: common origins and diverse transformations. In: P. Bellwood, J.J. Fox and D. Tryon, eds. *The Austronesians: Historical and Comparative Perspectives.* Canberra: Australian National University, pp. 1–16.

Biggs, B., 1965. Direct and indirect inheritance in Rotuman. *Lingua,* 14, pp. 383–415.

Biggs, B., 1971. The languages of Polynesia. In: T.A. Sebeok, ed. *Current Trends in Linguistics,* vol. 8, part 1, *Linguistics in Oceania.* The Hague: Mouton, pp. 466–505.

Biggs, B., 1972. The implications of linguistic subgrouping with special reference to Polynesia. In: R.C. Green and M. Kelly, eds. *Oceanic Culture History,* vol. 3, Pacific Anthropological Records 13. Honolulu: Bishop Museum, pp. 143–52.

Biggs, B., 1980. The position of East 'Uvean and Anutan in the Polynesian language family. *Te Reo,* 23, pp. 115–134.

Burrows, E.G., 1938. *Western Polynesia: A Study in Cultural Differentiation.* Goteborg: Etnologiska Studier 7.

Burrows, E.G., 1940. Culture areas in Polynesia. *Journal of the Polynesian Society,* 49, pp. 349–363.

Cachola-Abad, C.K., 1993. Evaluating the orthodox dual settlement model for the Hawaiian Islands: an analysis of artefact distribution and Hawaiian oral traditions. In: M.W. Graves and R.C. Green, eds. *The Evolution and Organization of Prehistoric Society in Polynesia.* Auckland: New Zealand Archaeological Association Monograph 19, pp. 13–32.

Clark, G., 2016. Chiefly tombs, lineage history, and the ancient Tongan state. *Journal of Island and Coastal Archaeology,* 11, pp. 326–343.

Clark, R., 1979. Language. In: J.D. Jennings, ed. *The Prehistory of Polynesia,* Cambridge, MA: Harvard University Press, pp. 249–270.

Clark, R., 1991. Fingota/Fangota: shellfish and fishing in Polynesia. In: A. Pawley, ed. *Man and a Half: Essays in Pacific Anthropology and Ethnobiology in Honour of Ralph Bulmer.* Auckland: Polynesian Society, pp. 78–83.

Dewar, R., 1995. Of nets and trees: untangling the reticulate and dendritic in Madagascar's prehistory. *World Archaeology,* 26, pp. 301–318.

Dye, T., 1980. The linguistic position of Niuafo'ou. *Journal of the Polynesian Society,* 89, pp. 349–357.

Dyen, I., 1965. A Lexicostatistical Classification of the Austronesian Languages. International Journal of American Linguistics Memoir 19. Bloomington, IN: Waverly Press.

Eggan, F., 1954. Social anthropology and the method of controlled comparison. *American Anthropologist,* 56, pp. 743–63.

Flannery, K.V. and Marcus, J., eds. 1983. *The Cloud People: Divergent Evolution of the Zapotec and Mixtec Civilizations.* New York: Academic Press.

Geraghty, P., 1983. *The History of the Fijian Languages.* Oceanic Linguistics Special Publication 19. Honolulu: University of Hawaii Press.

Goldman, I., 1955. Status rivalry and cultural evolution in Polynesia. *American Anthropologist,* 57, pp. 680–697.

Goldman, I., 1970. *Ancient Polynesian Society.* Chicago, IL: University of Chicago Press.

Goodenough, W.H., 1957. Oceania and the problem of controls in the study of cultural and human evolution. *Journal of the Polynesian Society,* 66, pp. 146–155.

Goodenough, W.H., 1997. Phylogenetically related cultural traditions. *Cross-Cultural Research,* 31, pp. 16–26.

Gould, S.J., 1986. Evolution and the triumph of homology, or why history matters. *American Scientist,* 74, pp. 60–69.

Gray, R.D., Drummond, A.J. and Greenhill, J.S., 2009. Language phylogenies reveal expansion pulses and pauses in Pacific settlement. *Science,* 323, pp. 479–483.

Gray, R.D., Greenhill, J.S. and Atkinson, Q.D., 2013. Phylogenetic models of language change: three new questions. In: P.J. Richerson and Morten H. Christiansen, eds. *Cultural Evolution: Society, Technology, Language, and Religion.* Cambridge, MA: MIT Press, pp. 285–302.

Gray, R.D. and Jordan, F.M., 2000. Language trees support the express-train sequence of Austronesian expansion. *Nature,* 405, pp. 1052–1055.

Green, R.C. 1966. Linguistic subgrouping within Polynesia: the implications for prehistoric settlement. *Journal of the Polynesian Society,* 75, pp. 6–38.

Green, R.C. 1981. Location of the Polynesian homeland: a continuing problem. In: J. Hollyman and A. Pawley, eds. *Studies in Pacific Languages and Cultures, in Honour of Bruce Biggs.* Auckland: Linguistic Society of New Zealand, pp. 133–158.

Green, R.C. 1994. Archaeological problems with the use of linguistic evidence in the reconstruction of rank, status and social organization in Ancestral Polynesian society. In: A.K. Pawley and M.D. Ross, eds. *Austronesian Terminologies: Continuity and Change,* Pacific Linguistics C-127. Canberra: Australian National University, pp. 171–184.

Green, R.C., 1997. Linguistic, biological, and cultural origins of the initial inhabitants of Remote Oceania. *New Zealand Journal of Archaeology,* 17, pp. 5–27.

Hage, P. and Harary, F., 1991. *Exchange in Oceania: A Graph Theoretic Approach.* Oxford: Clarendon Press.

Hill, A.V.S. and Serjeantson, S.W., eds. 1989. *The Colonization of the Pacific: A Genetic Trail.* Oxford: Clarendon Press.

Hooper, R., 1994. Reconstructing Proto Polynesian fish names. In: A.K. Pawley and M.D. Ross, eds. *Austronesian Terminologies: Continuity and Change,* Pacific Linguistics C-127. Canberra: Australian National University, pp. 185–230.

Houghton, P. 1996. *People of the Great Ocean: Aspects of Human Biology of the Early Pacific.* Cambridge: Cambridge University Press.

Howard, A. and Borofsky, R., eds. 1989. *Developments in Polynesian Ethnology.* Honolulu: University of Hawaii Press.

Hunt, T., Lipo, C. and Madsen, M., 1998. The flaws of phylogeny as history: a Pacific Islands case study. Paper presented at the Society for American Archaeology annual meeting, March 1998 (Seattle). Accessed from: https://www.researchgate.net/publication/256317382_The_Flaws_of_Phylogeny_as_History_A_Pacific_Islands_Case_Study

Hurles, M.E., Matisoo-Smith, E., Gray, R.D. and Penny, D., 2003. Untangling Oceanic settlement: the edge of the knowable. *Trends in Ecology and Evolution,* 18, pp. 531–540.

Kaeppler, A., 1978. Exchange patterns in goods and spouses: Fiji, Tonga, and Samoa. *Mankind,* 11, pp. 246–252.

Kayser, M., Brauer, S., Cordaux, R., Casto, A., Lao, O., Zhivotovsky, L.A. Moyse-Faurie, C., Rutledge, R.B., Schiefenhoevel, W., Gil, D., Lin, A.A., Underhill, P.A., Oefner, P.J., Trent, R.J. and Stoneking, M., 2006. Melanesian and Asian origins of Polynesians: mtDNA and Y chromosome gradients across the Pacific. *Molecular Biological Evolution* 23, pp. 2234–2244.

Kelly, K.M., 1996. The end of the trail: the genetic basis for deriving the Polynesian peoples from Austronesian speaking palaeopopulations of Melanesian Near Oceania. In: J. Davidson, G. Irwin, F. Leach, A. Pawley and D. Brown, eds. *Oceanic Culture History: Essays in Honour of Roger Green.* Dunedin: New Zealand Journal of Archaeology Special Publication, pp. 365–76.

Kirch, P.V., 1980. Polynesian prehistory: cultural adaptation in island ecosystems. *American Scientist,* 68, pp. 39–48.

Kirch, P.V., 1984. *The Evolution of the Polynesian Chiefdoms.* Cambridge: Cambridge University Press.

Kirch, P.V., 1986. Exchange systems and inter-island contact in the transformation of an island society: the Tikopia case. In: P. V. Kirch, ed. *Island Societies: Archaeological Approaches in Evolution and Transformation.* Cambridge: Cambridge University Press, pp. 33–41.

Kirch, P.V., 2010. *How Chiefs Became Kings: Divine Kingship and the Rise of Archaic States in Ancient Hawai'i*. Berkeley, CA: University of California Press.

Kirch, P.V. and Green, R.C., 2001. *Hawaiki, Ancestral Polynesia: An Essay in Historical Anthropology*. Cambridge: Cambridge University Press.

Kirch, P.V. and Green, R.C., 1987. History, phylogeny, and evolution in Polynesia. *Current Anthropology*, 28, pp. 431–443, 452–456.

Lipson, M., Skoglund, P., Spriggs, M., Valentin, F., Bedford, S., Shing, R., Buckley, H., Phillip, I., Ward, G.K., Mallick, S., Rohland, N., Broomandkhoshbacht, N., Cheronet, O., Ferry, M., Harper, T.K., Michel, M., Oppenheimer, J., Sirak, K., Stewardson, K., Auckland, K., Hill, A.V.S., Maitland, K., Oppenheimer, S.J., Parks, T., Robson, K., Williams, T.N., Kennett, D.J., Mentzer, A.J., Pinhasi, R. and Reich, D., 2018. Population turnover in Remote Oceanic shortly after initial settlement. *Current Biology*. doi: 10.1016/j.cub.2018.02.051.

Mace, R., and Pagel, M., 1994. The comparative method in anthropology. *Current Anthropology*, 35, pp. 549–564.

Marck, J., 2000. *Topics in Polynesian Language and Culture History*. Pacific Linguistics 504. Canberra: Australian National University.

Martinson, J.J. 1996. Molecular perspectives on the colonisation of the Pacific. In: A.J. Boyce and C.G.N. Mascie-Taylor, eds. *Molecular Biology and Human Diversity*. Cambridge: Cambridge University Press, pp. 171–195.

Martinson, J.J., Harding, R.M., Philippon, G., Flye Sainte-Marie, F., Roux, J., Boyce, A.J. and Clegg, J.B., 1993. Demographic reductions and genetic bottlenecks in humans: minisatellite allel distributions in Oceania. *Human Genetics*, 91, pp. 445–450.

Métraux, A., 1940. *Ethnology of Easter Island*. Bernice P. Bishop Museum Bulletin 160. Honolulu: Bernice P. Bishop Museum.

Merriwether, D.A., Friedlaender, J.S., Mediavilla, J., Mgone, C., Gentz, F. and Ferrell, R.E., 1999. Mitochondrial DNA variation is an indicator of Austronesian influence in Island Melanesia. *American Journal of Physical Anthropology*, 110, pp. 243–270.

Moore, C. and Romney, A.K., 1994. Material culture, geographic propinquity, and linguistic affiliation on the north coast of New Guinea: a reanalysis of Welsch, Terrell, and Nadolski (1992). *American Anthropologist*, 96, pp. 370–396.

Moore, C. and Romney, A.K., 1996. Will the 'real' data please stand up? Reply to Welsch (1996). *Journal of Quantitative Anthropology*, 6, pp. 235–261.

Moore, J.H., 1994a. Putting anthropology back together again: the ethnogenetic critique of cladistic theory. *American Anthropologist*, 96, pp. 925–948.

Moore, J.H., 1994b. Ethnogenetic theories of human evolution. *Research and Exploration*, 10, pp. 10–23.

Pawley, A., 1966. Polynesian languages: a subgrouping based on shared innovations in morphology. *Journal of the Polynesian Society*, 75, pp. 39–64.

Pawley, A., 1967. The relationships of Polynesian outlier languages. *Journal of the Polynesian Society*, 76, pp. 259–296.

Pawley, A. and Ross, M., 1993. Austronesian historical linguistics and culture history. *Annual Review of Anthropology*, 22, pp. 425–459.

Pietrusewsky, M., 1970. An osteological view of indigenous populations in Oceania. In: R.C. Green and M. Kelly, eds. *Studies in Oceanic Culture History*, vol. 1, Pacific Anthropological Records 11. Honolulu: Bishop Museum, pp. 1–12.

Pietrusewsky, M., 1996. The physical anthropology of Polynesia: a review of some cranial and skeletal studies. In: J. Davidson, G. Irwin, F. Leach, A. Pawley and D. Brown, eds. *Oceanic Culture History: Essays in Honour of Roger Green*, Dunedin: New Zealand Journal of Archaeology Special Publication, pp. 343–353.

Posth, C., Nagele, K., Colleran, H.,Valentin, F., Bedfor, S., Kami, K.W., Shing, R., Buckley, H., Kinaston, R.,Walworth, M., Clark, G.R., Reepmeyer, C., Flexner, J., Maric, T., Moser, J., Gresky, J., Kilo, L., Robson, K.J., Auckland, K., Oppenheimer, S.J., Hill, A.V.S., Mentzer, A.J., Zech, J., Petchy, F., Roberts, P., Jeong, C., Gray, R.D., Krause, J. and Powell, A., 2018. Language continuity despite population replacement in Remote Oceania. *Nature Ecology and Evolution.* doi: 10.1038/s41559-018-0498-2

Roberts, J.M., Moore, C.C. and Romney, A.K., 1995. Predicting similarity in material culture among New Guinea villages from propinquity and language. *Current Anthropology,* 36, pp. 769–788.

Romney, A.K., 1957. The genetic model and Uto-Aztecan time perspective. *Davidson Journal of Anthropology,* 3, pp. 35–41.

Ross, M., 1988. *Proto Oceanic and the Austronesian Languages of Western Melanesia,* Pacific Linguistics C-98. Canberra: Australian National University.

Sahlins, M., 1958. *Social Stratification in Polynesia.* Seattle, WA: American Ethnological Society.

Sahlins, M. and Service, E., eds. 1960. *Evolution and Culture.* Ann Arbor, MI: University of Michigan Press.

Sanders, W.T., 1966. Review of Desarrollo Cultural de los Mayas, edited by E. Z. Vogt and A. Ruz L. [Mexico City: Universidad Nacional Autonoma de Mexico 1964]. *American Anthropologist,* 68, pp. 1068–1071.

Sapir, E., 1916. *Time Perspective in Aboriginal American Culture: A Study in Method.* Department of Mines, Geological Survey Memoir 90, Anthropological Series 13. Ottawa: Government Printing Bureau.

Sheehan, O., Watts, J., Gray, R. and Atkinson, Q., 2018. The coevolution of landesque capital intensive agriculture and sociopolitical hierarchy. *Proceedings of the National Academy of Sciences, USA,* 115 (14), pp. 3628–3633.

Sheppard, P.J., Walter, R. and Parker, R.J., 1997. Basalt sourcing and the development of Cook Island exchange systems. In: M.I. Weisler, ed. *Prehistoric Long-Distance Interaction in Oceania: An Interdisciplinary Approach.* Auckland: New Zealand Archaeological Association Monograph 21, pp. 85–110.

Shore, B., 1989. *Mana* and *tapu.* In: A. Howard and R. Borofsky, eds. *Developments in Polynesian Ethnology.* Honolulu: University of Hawaii Press, pp. 137–173.

Terrell, J.E., 1986. *Prehistory in the Pacific Islands.* Cambridge: Cambridge University Press.

Terrell, J.E., 1988. History as a family tree, history as an entangled bank. *Antiquity,* 62, pp. 642–657.

Terrell, J.E., Hunt, T.L. and Gosden, C., 1997. The dimensions of social life in the Pacific: human diversity and the myth of the primitive isolate. *Current Anthropology,* 38, pp. 155–196.

Vogt, E.Z., 1964. The genetic model and Maya cultural development. In: E.Z. Vogt and A. Ruz L., eds. *Desarrollo Cultural de los Mayas.* Mexico City: Universidad Nacional Autonoma de Mexico, pp. 9–48.

Vogt, E.Z., 1994. On the application of the phylogenetic model to the Maya. In: R.J. DeMallie and A. Ortiz, eds. *North American Indian Anthropology: Essays on Society and Culture.* Norman, OK: University of Oklahoma Press, pp. 377–414.

Walter, R., 1998. *Anai'o: The Archaeology of a Fourteenth Century Polynesian Community in the Cook Islands.* Auckland: New Zealand Archaeological Association Monograph 22.

Walworth, M., 2014. Eastern Polynesian: the linguistic evidence revisited. *Oceanic Linguistics* 53, pp. 256–272.

Watts, J., Greenhill, S.J., Atkinson, Q.D., Currie, T.E., Bulbulia, J. and Gray, R.D., 2015. Broad supernatural punishment but not moralizing high gods precede the evolution of political complexity in Austronesia. *Proceedings of the Royal Society B,* 282, pp. 2014–2556.

Weisler, M., ed. 1997. *Prehistoric Long-Distance Interaction in Oceania: An Interdisciplinary Approach.* New Zealand Archaeological Association Monograph 21. Auckland: New Zealand Archaeological Association.

Weisler, Marshall I., Bolhar, R., Ma, J., St Pierre, E., Sheppard, P., Walter, R.K., Feng, Y., Zhao, J. and Kirch, P.V., 2016. Cook Island artifact geochemistry demonstrates spatial and temporal extent of pre-European interarchipelago voyaging in East Polynesia. *Proceedings of the National Academy of Sciences, USA,* 113, pp. 8150–8155.

Welsch, R.L., 1996. Language, culture, and data on the North Coast of New Guinea. *Journal of Quantitative Anthropology,* 6, pp. 209–234.

Welsch, R. and Terrell, J.E., 1994. Reply to Moore and Romney. *American Anthropologist,* 96, pp. 392–396.

Welsch, R., Terrell, J. and Nadloski, J.A., 1992. Language and culture on the north coast of New Guinea. *American Anthropologist,* 94, pp. 568–600.

Wilson, W., 1985. Evidence for an outlier source for the Proto Eastern Polynesian pronominal system. *Oceanic Linguistics,* 24, pp. 85–133.

Wylie, A., 1989. Archaeological cables and tacking: the implications of practice for Bernstein's 'Options beyond objectivism and relativism'. *Philosophy of the Social Sciences,* 19, pp. 1–18.

Wylie, A., 1992. The interplay of evidential constraints and political interests: recent archaeological research on gender. *American Antiquity,* 57, pp. 15–35.

5

PACIFIC ETHNOGRAPHY, ARCHAEOLOGY AND THE PATTERN OF GLOBAL PREHISTORIC SOCIAL LIFE

Mark Golitko

Introduction

It would not be much of an overstatement to suggest that most of anthropological social theory, particularly during the formative period of the discipline, draws heavily on studies of the Pacific Islands and its peoples. Across the domains of economy, subsistence, kinship, technology and political systems, different peoples and places in Oceania have provided models of human behaviour upon which general anthropological understanding and specific archaeological interpretations are based. In part, this reflects a vision of the Pacific and its people as a natural experiment in adaptation to a diversity of environments and circumstances in the absence of the complications of contact between these diverse and far-flung communities. While Oceania geographically spans about one-third of the globe, it is a world of islands and relatively small populations. Island density decreases, and inter-island spacing increases, the further eastward one moves from mainland Asia.

The larger and more closely spaced islands of the southwestern Pacific ('Near Oceania', Fig. 5.1) have played a particularly important role in anthropological and archaeological understandings of non-industrial social life. It is a region where the intensity of inter-community and inter-island voyaging and exchange was noted during first encounters by explorers, colonial officials and ethnographers (Spriggs, 1997). Bronislaw Malinowski's *Argonauts of the Western Pacific* (1961, originally published 1922) may be the best-known description of inter-community exchange and interaction in the entire anthropological canon. Most archaeology students either read it during their graduate training or are familiar with the book through its repeated mention in other sources. Malinowski's descriptions of the *kula* exchange cycle of the Massim region of New Guinea present exchange and voyaging as the fundamental fabric of social life in the region. Margaret Mead (1970, p. 21) similarly wrote of the region that 'the simplest peoples think in terms of the

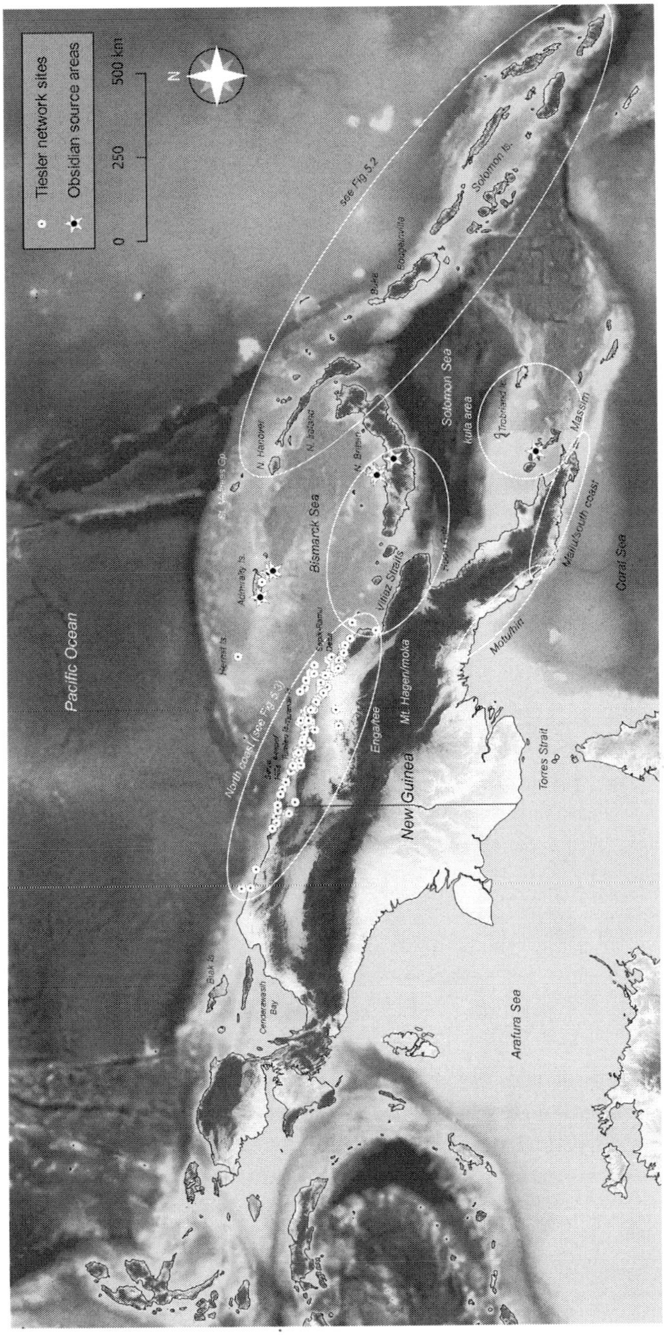

FIGURE 5.1 Near Oceania, showing places and exchange/trade systems discussed in the text.

constant interchange, not only of material things, but also of techniques and non-material traits'.

Yet, simultaneously, the southwestern Pacific has been seen as a world of isolated, self-sufficient communities with little contact with – and indeed, a great deal of hostility towards – their neighbours, diverging in custom, language and biology over time. On northern New Guinea, Lutkehaus and Roscoe term this contradictory representation of Pacific Islanders the 'Sepik Paradox' (Lutkehaus and Roscoe, 1987, p. 579), yet the lessons to be drawn from the Oceanic ethnographic and archaeological record globally also reflect a contentious debate over what the human past was like, and what the Pacific record can tell us about it.

Pacific ethnography and socio-economic theory

The early importance of Pacific ethnography to social theory

Early social theorists in the emerging disciplines of political science, sociology and anthropology were interested in the mechanisms that hold society together, particularly in the absence of formal governments. Influenced by contemporary understandings of Darwinian evolution, early anthropological writers like Morgan and Spencer developed unilineal evolutionary frameworks in which different peoples represented particular stages of social evolution based on their perceived level of technological, cultural and racial sophistication. Drawing on loose biological analogies, these scholars argued that these successive stages represented increases in complexity – an increase in the number of interacting and interdependent parts or units (Trigger, 1989, p. 145).

Mid–late 19th-century social theorists also speculated on past human society, drawing on these idealised stages of social evolution and complexity. Most wrote within the context of 'primitivist' economic thinking, arguing that people in non-Western society worked only as much as needed to survive. Overproduction and exchange occurred only due to absolute necessity or the actions of colonial companies or governments (Oka and Kusimba, 2008, pp. 343–344). Karl Marx and his collaborator Friedrich Engels were (and remain) particularly influential in this regard. They argued that modern capitalism undermined the true nature of human sociality, in which work and production took place within the structure of community social bonds (Marx, 1978a, pp. 74–75). These early communities were self-sufficient and egalitarian, with the individual subsumed by community identity and needs – specialised production and exchange developed only later, ultimately developing into a means of moving goods against labour to build capital (Engels, 1972, pp. 46–47; Marx, 1978b, pp. 265, 273).

The French sociologist Emile Durkheim similarly argued that pre-modern society was unspecialised, held together by commonality of conscience ('mechanical solidarity'), and divided only into equivalent units such as moieties or clans. In contrast, the modern world was, in Durkheim's view, held together by specialisation, exchange and economic interdependency ('organic solidarity'). Inter-community isolation in the pre-modern world contributed to the development of distinct races of humankind, while organic solidarity tended to erode biological and cultural differences between communities (Durkheim, 1966, pp. 54–55, 304–309).

While Durkheim occasionally drew on the Pacific anthropological record (particularly Tonga and Tahiti), his student Marcel Mauss drew heavily on the Oceanic record in his analysis of gifting, including the Maori concept of *hau* – a spiritual obligation embodied in the gifting or exchange of goods that transcends the material transaction itself and becomes a social obligation. Mauss argued for exchange as a 'total social phenomenon', linked to all areas of social life and essential to the structuring of society (Mauss, 1967, pp. 36, 77–79). Malinowski (1961, pp. 157, 168) similarly argued against economic primitivism and, influenced by Mauss, saw the *kula* cycle as a total social phenomenon encompassing social relationships, myth, magic and politics. Malinowski noted that society in the Trobriands was not comprised of identical, self-sufficient social units, but instead spanned different political forms and ecologies, and transcended ethnic and linguistic boundaries. While structured by the cyclical symbolic transaction of *kula* valuables (*vaygu'a*) – armshells (*mwali*) and shell necklaces (*soulava*) – the *kula* cycle also entailed commercial bargaining over foodstuffs and specialised craft products like pottery, axes and shell ornaments (Malinowski, 1961, p. 168). For Malinowski, *kula* was part of the very structure of human functional adaptation to island life.

The Pacific and post-war social theory

By the mid-20th century, economic debate in anthropology moved on from the 'primitivist/modernist' debate to disagreements between 'substantivists' (who followed Mauss and Malinowski in viewing exchange as a socially embedded institution in pre-modern society) and 'formalists' (who utilised modern economic theory to interpret pre-modern exchange). Substantivism was largely associated with the work of the economic historian Karl Polanyi and his students (Fusfield, 1957; Polanyi, 1957). They argued for economics as a socially and culturally embedded phenomenon, not an outgrowth of human nature as argued in the field of formal economics.

Polanyi and his circle distinguished between 'exchange' and 'trade' – the former transfers of objects that manifest a set of lasting social ties, the later a commercialised and equal set of exchanges creating no lasting social obligations (Ambrose, 1976, p. 351). Polanyi (1957, pp. 257–270) also defined three types of transactions, which have become standard concepts for most archaeologists: reciprocity, redistribution and market exchange. While the influence of Malinowski and Mauss is readily evident, Polanyi and his school downplayed the more commercial transactions (referred to as *Gimwali* in Sinaketa, where Malinowski spent most of his time while in the Trobriands) that occur simultaneously alongside the exchange of *kula* valuables (Malinowski, 1961, p. 96; Oka and Kusimba, 2008, p. 343). Reciprocity and redistribution thus became associated with 'primitive' and pre-modern society, and market systems and trade with modern states.

As ethnography and archaeology moved out of their respective culture-historical phases and into concerns with cultural ecology after the Second World War, Pacific ethnography remained a critical source of theorising. The work of Marshall Sahlins was particularly influential in archaeology. Sahlins established a multi-lineal, neo-evolutionary political and economic categorisation of Pacific societies (Sahlins, 1963, pp. 285–287). He argued that, far from the 'total social phenomenon' envisioned by Malinowski, religion, magic and exchange are super-structural features that follow from different systems of food production and land tenure. In a return to primitivist theory, Sahlins argued that, in egalitarian society, households produce for their own needs, do not exchange regularly and systematically under-produce relative to their hypothetical potential. Surplus production occurs only in the context of political competition (in Melanesia by 'big men', in much of Polynesia by hereditary chiefs), and egalitarian communities either eventually develop hierarchy and exchange or are dominated by more hierarchical neighbours (Sahlins, 1972, pp. 51, 65). As he wrote of what he termed the domestic mode of production (DMP) (1972, p. 95), 'The domestic mode anticipates no social or material relations between households except that they are alike', and more broadly (1972, p. 86), 'economically, primitive society is founded on an antisociety'.

The views of Polanyi and Sahlins remained influential within archaeology during its 'new' or 'processual' movement of the 1950s–1970s. Processual archaeologists followed their Marxist view of social domains beyond production and subsistence as super-structural elements of social life, tied into explicit stages of social reorganisation (e.g. Renfrew, 1969; Service, 1962). During the 1960s, systems-theory based approaches came into vogue as a means of understanding how these super-structural elements helped to regulate the basic work of producing enough food. Systems based models of exchange are readily evident in both Harding's (1967) ethnography of the Vitiaz Straits region and Rapaport's (1968) study of the Maring of highland New Guinea, and were employed to model social evolution in the SW Pacific (e.g. Friedman, 1982; Allen, 1984; 1985) and beyond. For instance, Pires-Ferreira and Flannery (1976) drew directly on work by Sahlins, Harding and Rapaport in developing archaeological models of exchange and social integration for the Formative Oaxaca valley, while Dalton (1977) and Earle (1977) both drew heavily on Pacific ethnography as the basis for general models of exchange and social evolution.

Perhaps because industrialised Europeans had no comparable indigenous ethno-graphically documented 'stone-age' society to make comparisons to, models drawn from the Pacific were transplanted wholesale to the European Neolithic. During the 1970s, archaeologists invoked the *kula* to explain exchange of *spondylus* shell ornaments between early Neolithic communities (Schackleton and Renfrew, 1970, p. 1064), and status competition between big men to explain exchange of axes and other prestige goods. The DMP was at one time taken as a general model for social life in early European agricultural communities, so that in 1977 for instance, Milisauskas (1977, p. 309) argued that early Neolithic *Linearbankeramik* (LBK) households were self-sufficient with little or no motivation to maintain extensive inter-community ties.

Language, material culture and human history

The end of the culture-historical period and beginning of the processual paradigm in Anglo-American archaeology changed focus from understanding how prehistoric events shaped the modern distribution of culture and language to understanding local sequences of socio-economic development. However, in the Pacific, historical linguistics remained a basic research paradigm, particularly with regard to the distinction between Austronesian and non-Austronesian speakers (Terrell et al., 2001). In the late 1980s, these ongoing Pacific concerns with the role of language as a framework for understanding the past re-entered the archaeological discourse on a global scale. In 1987, Colin Renfrew published *Archaeology and Language*, arguing that the beginnings of agriculture in the Near East and resulting population growth created great ethnolinguistic migrations that spread related Indo-European languages across the Eurasian landmass.

During the 1990s, Renfrew and other scholars applied this argument globally, proposing the 'farming-language dispersal hypothesis' (FLDH) to explain the modern distributions of large language families (Bellwood, 2001). The possible connection between rice agriculture in east Asia and a rapid dispersal of Austronesian speakers was already an established component of Pacific archaeological explanation (Spriggs, 2011) and putative expansions of other larger language groupings like the Trans-New Guinea phylum on mainland New Guinea were quickly incorporated into the FLDH framework and associated with particular material signatures.

A central assumption of the FLDH is that language phylogenies and the archaeological material record tell the same story of the human past. Branching events inferred from historical language phylogenies represent historical events that can be historically and geographically mapped via the appearance and spread of archaeological material cultures or styles (e.g. Lapita in the Pacific, or LBK in central Europe). Recent tests of the FLDH using both modern and ancient DNA in the Pacific (e.g. Bergström et al., 2017; Skoglund et al., 2016) and globally (e.g. Allentoft et al., 2015) similarly treat the archaeological culture as a meaningful unit of analysis for parsing out human biological and linguistic history.

Testing the 'myth of the primitive isolate'

Both ecologists and anthropologists have used Pacific islands as repeated natural experiments to study adaptation and cultural, linguistic and biological diversification (Kirch and Green, 1987; Terrell, 1976; Terrell et al., 1997). Given the large number (c.1200 or more) of languages spoken on New Guinea, and a long history of documenting and collecting its material culture, the island is one of the few places in the world where statistically robust comparisons of language and material culture can be made.

In 1992, Welsch, Terrell and Nadolski published a paper examining statistical associations between language, material culture and geographical distance (as a proxy for interaction likelihood) on the Sepik coast of northern New Guinea, a linguistically diverse area even by the standards of the SW Pacific (Wurm et al., 1983). They drew on a large collection of material culture acquired by the Field Museum of Natural History between 1900 and 1913 from thirty-one communities in the area between modern-day Jayapura and Madang, representing some fifty-five languages belonging to eight families, including both Austronesian and non-Austronesian languages. They found no significant association between language and material culture after controlling for distance, arguing as a consequence that archaeological material culture should not be treated as a reliable indicator of spoken language in the past (Welsch et al., 1992).

Their paper generated vigorous debate about the association between language and material culture, and a number of new analyses of New Guinean material culture. Roberts and colleagues (1995) re-examined the same dataset using different statistical methods, and concluded that language and geography both equally contribute to variance in material culture, while Shennan and Collard (2005) argue that language might account for up to 70 per cent of variance in material culture in the Sepik dataset. Yet another recent reanalysis by von Cramon-Taubadel and Lycett (2018) provides support for Welsch and colleagues' original interpretation, as does a reanalysis by Terrell (2010a).

Fyfe and Bolton have examined stylistic and technological variation in arrows (made by men) and *bilums* (net bags, made by women) in the Upper Sepik and parts of the central Highlands. They also found no association between language and material cultural patterning once distance is accounted for, although noting that *bilum* variability is more strongly geographically patterned than for arrows, likely because women are less mobile on average than men in most of New Guinea (Fyfe, 2009; Fyfe and Bolton, 2011). In another, less statistically formal study of war shields, Craig and colleagues (2008) were able to identify individual stylistic elements that are unique to particular language areas, though not universal to speakers of any given language.

Of course, these analyses can only document the relationship between material culture and linguistic diversity in the relatively recent past. Given the standard evolutionary formula 'isolation + time = diversity', the large number of languages spoken in Near Oceania seems to suggest a long history of relative isolation between speech communities, resulting perhaps from both geographical (mountains, water, jungle) and social factors. As Allen writes:

> Before white contact, Papua New Guinea communities were small and very localized. With few exceptions they could provide for themselves all their subsistence requirements from within their own territory. Many men travelled no further than a few kilometers from their birthplaces all their lives. Travel was discouraged by rugged terrain and hostile neighbors. Nevertheless, the country was criss-crossed with well established trade routes …
>
> *(Allen, 1983, p. 19)*

A number of scholars have argued that the level of inter-community interaction and sharing of ideas observed ethnographically occurred only after colonial pacification ended persistent inter-community conflict (Dalton, 1977, pp. 200–221).

Prehistoric social life in Near Oceania

Unlike ethnography, SW Pacific archaeology started late, with the first shovels entering the ground only in the later 1950s. Most early studies were concerned with developing local cultural sequences and understanding the antiquity of ethnographically documented cultural patterns (e.g. Ambrose, 1976). While Malinowski (1961, p. 510) argued that the *kula* was an ancient phenomenon, archaeologists studying the Pacific quickly grew dissatisfied with ahistorical functionalist accounts of Pacific social life (Kirch, 1991, p. 141). The ensuing decades of archaeological research have concretely demonstrated the relatively shallow time depth of most ethnographic patterns of interaction and exchange. Both formalised/ceremonial trade circuits like the *kula* (Irwin, 1983; Irwin et al., 2019), *hiri* (Allen 1984; Irwin 1978; 1983), *moka* and *tee* (Feil, 1987, pp. 25–27; Spriggs, 2008) as well as less formalised networks like that present in the Vitiaz Straits (Harding, 1967; Lilley, 2004) appear to be developments of the last 300–500 years at most.

Like archaeologists elsewhere during the 1960s and 1970s, archaeologists in the Pacific worked within a neo-evolutionary framework as they constructed diachronic models of exchange. Unlike their Anglo-American colleagues working elsewhere, Pacific archaeologists were at the same time heavily influenced by historical linguistics. When archaeologists first recognised that Lapita ceramics (dating to c.3500–1900 BP) were present in both the islands of Near Oceania and across the divide into Remote Oceania, they linked Lapita to the spread of Austronesian languages.

As putative ancestors of Polynesians, the makers of Lapita pottery are often argued to have lived in more hierarchical social systems then their Papuan-speaking neighbours, possessed more advanced voyaging technology (outrigger canoes with sprit-sails), and specialised in the production of prestige goods including elaborately decorated ceramics and shell ornaments (Ambrose, 1978; Friedman, 1982). As Kirch writes,

> A rapid and widespread intensification and formalization of external exchange occurred throughout lowland Melanesia between the early second millennium and the close of the first millennium BC. In the Bismarck Archipelago, this development is associated with the appearance of the Lapita Cultural Complex. In the Massim and coastal Papua, the beginnings of formal long-distance exchange are associated with a putative migration of Austronesian speakers (possibly derived from Lapita) around 2000 BP.
>
> *(Kirch, 1991, p. 155)*

On both stylistic and compositional grounds, archaeologists demonstrated that Lapita sites contain substantial amounts of non-local materials, including pottery from other Lapita communities and obsidian transported over vast distances. Obsidian from the Willaumez peninsula of New Britain occurs in archaeological sites stretching from Borneo to Tonga, up to 4500 km from its source (Summerhayes, 2009, p. 116). The paradigm that emerged out of the 1970s and 1980s envisioned Austronesian-speaking Lapita communities as the origin point for the development of the complex networks of exchange that characterised the region at the time of European contact (Tiesler, 1969/1970, p. 116). These Lapita period social links eventually contracted into more localised networks characterised by increasingly specialised production, extensive movement of foodstuffs (Allen, 1984; Harding, 1994), and monopolisation of trade by both inland and coastal middlemen (Lipset, 1985; Schwartz 1963, pp. 77–78) after about 2000 BP (Friedman, 1982). The high diversity of non-Austronesian languages was an outcome of millennia of isolation before contact with Austronesians.

If this neo-evolutionary framework seemed to fit the available data at one time, new data are beginning to push back evidence for extensive transport of materials much earlier into prehistory. Near the end of the Holocene Thermal Maximum (c.7000–6000 BP), inhabitants of the Bismarck Archipelago began to produce distinctive stemmed obsidian tools. These were widely transported throughout Near Oceania, reaching the New Guinea Highlands, Buka, the Massim region and possibly as far west as Biak Island in modern West Papua (Summerhayes, 2009, pp. 115–116; Torrence et al., 2013). Stone mortars and pestles believed to date to the mid-Holocene (c.6000–3000 BP) appear in the same areas (Torrence and Swadling, 2008, p. 604) and may relate to the spread of taro horticulture and tree crops like bananas throughout the lowlands of Near Oceania (Swadling, 2004) and surrounding island archipelagos (Donohue and Denham, 2010).

Torrence and Swadling (2008, p. 613) suggest that Lapita ceramics may have been just one more material moved through pre-existing social networks. However, at present, most obsidian stemmed tools and mortars and pestles are undated. Taphonomic factors (many sites dating to this period may be deeply buried under more recent sediments) and site visibility issues (principally the lack of ceramics by which to identify pre-Lapita deposits) have hindered a detailed understanding of when such longer distance links first appeared. Translocation of phalangers to the Bismarcks and shorter distance exchanges of obsidian hint at yet earlier patterns of interaction between mainland New Guinea and within Island Melanesia near the Last Glacial Maximum (c.22,000–24,000 BP), but could alternatively reflect higher mobility and direct procurement by Pleistocene foragers (Summerhayes, 2009, p. 115).

Archaeological network analysis and a relational past

If complexity refers to dense interconnections between communities and individuals, then arguably the SW Pacific has been socially complex for at least the last 6,000 years. Torrence (2011, p. 38) expresses hope that further Pacific research 'could open up the past to different interpretations that help the discipline as a whole finally make the crucial break from progressivist social evolutionary theory'. What models or theories to use, and how to link these to the archaeological record, are by no means certain. Perusal of the archaeological literature on exchange in the Pacific shows that archaeologists developed few if any formal models of exchange and interaction after the early 1980s.

This turn away from formalism in archaeology reflects a general trend as the discipline emerged from the height of its processual phase. In the ensuing decades, archaeologists studying interaction and exchange have resorted to vague notions of 'culture contact', or 'interaction spheres', seemingly drawn from the culture-historical period of the discipline (Golitko, 2019, p. 90). Arguably, without formal models, it is difficult to determine what the archaeological record is telling us based on the prehistoric distribution of obsidian, pottery or shell ornaments. For instance, what might be the expected impact of new sailing technology on the distribution of obsidian, or changes in population density and abandonment of communities during natural disasters? How might differences in resource availability affect local demand for particular goods, and how are we to model stochastic changes in the structure of interaction? At present, archaeologists have few tools to address these issues.

One possible solution lies in the emerging field of network analysis and science. Such analysis has a long history in the social sciences, bringing together structuralism with the formal mathematics of graph theory (Freeman, 2004). The network concept (first developed in the 1930s) appears to have been employed relatively early in the Pacific. For instance, in 1956, Mead and Schwartz (quoted in Schwartz, 1963, p. 59) wrote:

> If instead of asking a Manus, 'to what do you belong?' one asks, 'what are your roads?', the answer is a network of various degrees of intimacy covering all adjacent villages of the Manus linguistic group, and a series of trade friends in faraway villages.

Despite this early beginning, network methods do not appear to have been widely adopted by ethnographers of the Pacific, although Harding (1967, p. 16) for instance used the visual language of graphs to schematically map trade relationships in the Vitiaz Straits.

The Pacific also produced the earliest applications of graph theory and network analysis to the archaeological record (Kirch, 1991, p. 145). In 1974, influenced by work in island biogeography and locational geography, John Terrell developed a method he termed 'proximal point analysis' to model plausible links between islands in the Solomons chain (Fig. 5.2). Islands were treated either as single nodes (small islands) or as a series of nodes (for larger islands) connected to their three closest geographical neighbours. He found that this very simple model produced a reasonable overlap with ethnographically documented patterns of exchange (Terrell, 1976,

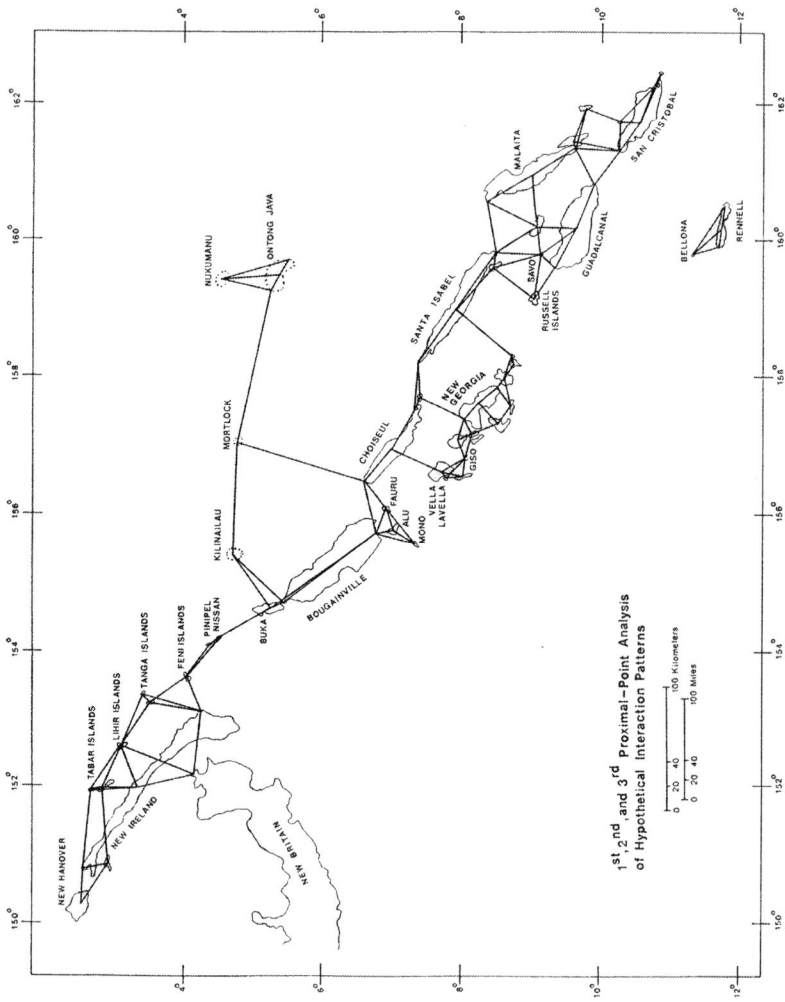

FIGURE 5.2 Third order proximal point analysis of hypothetical interaction patterns in the Solomon Island chain.

Source: originally published in Terrell (1976, p. 11), © Oceania Publications, used with permission.

pp. 10–12). Around the same time, Geoff Irwin applied formal metrics developed within the emerging discipline of social network analysis (SNA) to understand transformations in trade patterns along the south coast of Papua New Guinea as reconstructed by chemical ceramic sourcing (Irwin, 1978; 1983). Also during the latter 1970s, the anthropologist Per Hage and graph theorist Frank Harary mod-elled both the structure and hypothetical evolution of the *kula* cycle using graph theoretical mathematics and Markov chain modelling (Hage et al., 1986).

Explanation in these studies follows the central tenet of network analysis and theory – that the attributes and actions of individual actors/nodes in a network are constrained by the structure of relationships in which they are embedded (Brughmans, 2013, pp. 632–633). Hage and Harary, for instance, linked hierarchy and wealth to favourable positioning in the *kula* ring, while in a later study, Hunt (1989) pointed to the network centrality of the St Matthias group as aiding the rapid spread of Lapita ceramics to other parts of the Bismarck Archipelago.

Network analysis had little contemporary influence in archaeology, particularly outside of island settings. Whether this reflected broader theoretical trends away from structuralism, the difficulty of defining nodes and network ties outside of island settings or the relative marginality of Pacific archaeology to the broader discipline is unclear. However, after major developments in the study of complex networks in physics and the social sciences during the late 1990s and early 2000s, the net-work concept and related methods began a rapid ascent in archaeological practice (Brughmans, 2013, p. 631; Peeples, 2019), including in the Pacific (Cochrane and Lipo, 2010; Ladefoged et al., 2019; Terrell, 2010a; 2010b). Network studies carried out in the Pacific laid the groundwork for most subsequent archaeological network analysis, including deductive modelling approaches (Terrell, Hage, and colleagues), inductive networks based on either stylistic or sourcing data (Irwin) and diachronic models of network change (Hage and colleagues).

Diversity in a networked world

If complex interactions have been the norm in Near Oceania for the last 6,000 years, why is there so much linguistic and cultural diversity? This is by no means an easy question to answer, but a combination of ethnographic theory and network struc-tural properties might provide some insight.

If many studies of the Pacific equate historical linguistic phylogenies with 'his-tory' (e.g. von Cramon-Taubadel and Lycett, 2018) that need only be validated using material culture and genetics, the rich SW Pacific socio-linguistic tradition suggests that language may play a much different role in a networked social world. In much of the SW Pacific, multilingualism is the rule rather than the exception (Dutton, 1982; Sankoff, 1980, pp. 95–133). In some places, children stay for a time with their parent's trade friends/partners as 'wards', during which time they learn the language of that village and gain knowledge of the broader social world they will have to navigate as adults (May and Tuckson, 2000, p. 165; Schwartz, 1963). Trade languages or pidgins (often based on the languages of important middleman communities) likely also have a long history in Near Oceania (Dutton, 1982). Multilingualism can contribute to rapid language switching at the community level (Sankoff, 1980, pp. 95–133), and in the long term, language borrowing appears to be a common process in much of the SW Pacific. As Donohue and Denham (2010, p. 229) note, most Austronesian languages spoken near New Guinea exhibit high rates of Papuan loan words, which in some cases make up nearly the entire vocabulary. It is by no means certain that the diversity of languages spoken there implies that Oceanic peoples lived in relative isolation from one another until recently.

As an area of both high language diversity and a long history of ethnographic documentation, the Sepik coast provides a reasonable example of how ethnography and network analysis might be combined to understand the relationship between cultural diversity and interactive structure. Connections between communities on the Sepik coast were compiled by Tiesler (1969/1970), including all communities in Welsch and colleagues' original study of language and material cultural patterning. Figure 5.3 represents recorded marriage, kinship and trade/exchange relationships between these communities.

The system that is revealed has little tendency towards clustering by language, other than when geographic proximity and language happen to coincide, as noted by Terrell (2010a). While most links are relatively local and short distance (consistent with Allen's statement regarding the short distances most people travelled), Murik traders (Lipset, 1985) ventured as far west as Arop (c.240 km) and as far east as Monumbo (c.105 km) (Tiesler, 1969/1970). Tumleo Island pottery was exchanged over a similar area, though often transported by neighbouring Ali Islanders (May and Tuckson, 2000, p. 307).

To the east, further connections with Bilbil and Siassi traders linked the north coast to New Britain and the Solomon Islands (Harding, 1967), while Manus traders regularly visited the offshore islands of the north coast (Ambrose, 1976; 1978). Through these links, obsidian from both New Britain and the Admiralty Group reached as far west as Aitape and Tumleo Island. Via the Torricelli Mountains and Sepik River valley, coastal products moved into the central New Guinea Highlands (Swadling, 2010). Notably, no single good or style maps the entire social world of inter-community engagement – Tumleo Island pottery, for instance, is primarily limited to a c.300 km stretch of coast between the Serra Hills and Sepik–Ramu Delta, and other specialised products have similarly limited distributions. In archaeological terms, it is unclear that the distribution of a single material like New Britain obsidian or style like Lapita provides an accurate mapping of the total social world people of the time occupied. At the same time, goods and ideas can spread over quite vast distances, despite the majority of links being relatively short distance.

Despite the ease of moving people, goods or ideas from one community to another, very few of the possible links between communities on the north coast are present. The network is highly geographically structured and clustered, with particular intermediary communities (e.g. Murik, Munumbo) linking more highly clustered areas of the coast to one another. Such patterning, reminiscent of a so-called 'small world' (Brughmans, 2013, p. 643), likely partially explains how distinct

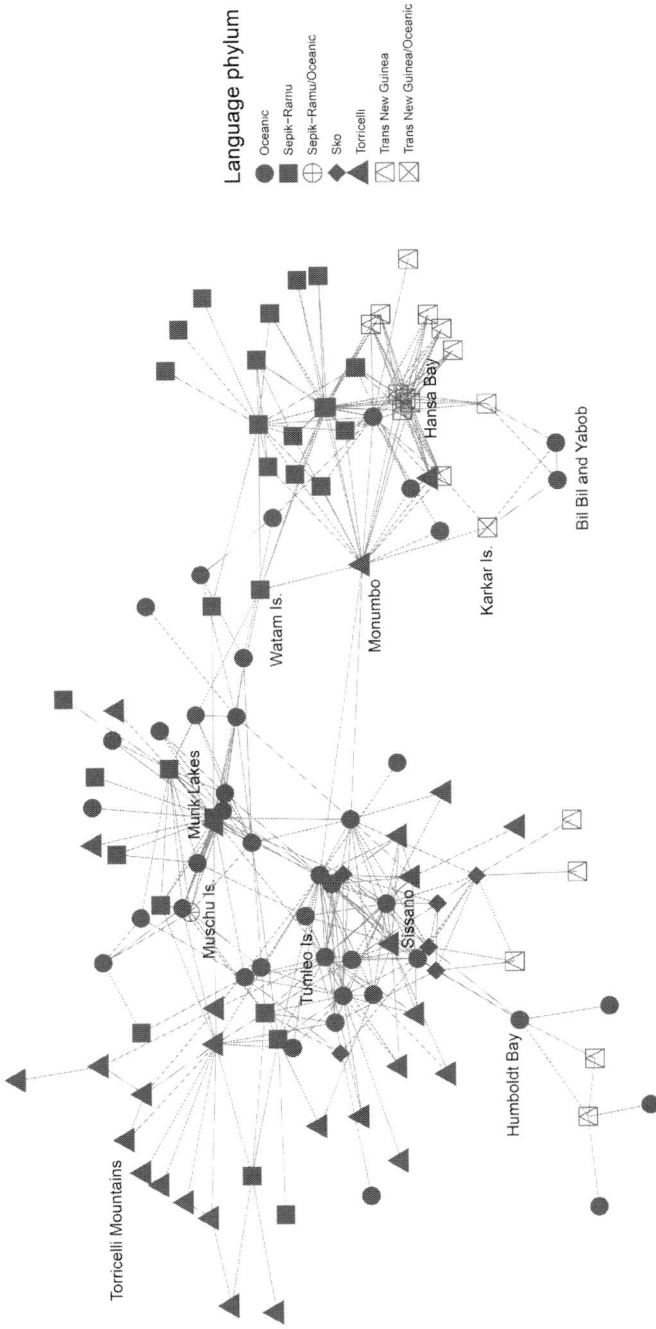

FIGURE 5.3 Network graph of ethnographically documented interactions on the north coast of New Guinea and parts of the Sepik River valley during the early 20th century, with nodes coded by language phylum. Data from Tiesler (1969/1970), Mead (1968) and Wurm et al. (1983).

practices may be maintained within particular areas of the coast where interaction is more frequent despite the whole coast being linked into a broad 'community of culture' (Terrell, 2010a, p. 17).

Colonial administrators had a relatively high degree of control on the Sepik coast during the period in which ethnographers and others documented this social world. However, stylistic and compositional studies of archaeological material culture from archaeological sites in the area between the Serra Hills and Tarawai Island (Fig. 5.1) document little if any significant change in the distribution of materials during the last millennium. Obsidian from the Admiralties and New Britain reached the coast at consistent frequencies (as did Fergusson Island obsidian from the Massim on occasion) (Golitko et al., 2013) and Tumleo Island pottery was traded within the entirety of its ethnographic distribution (Golitko and Terrell, 2012).

However, like other documented patterns of exchange in the SW Pacific, the situation on the Sepik coast was not timeless. Obsidian frequencies at north coast sites between 2000–1000 BP differ from those of the last millennium (Golitko et al., 2013), suggesting differences in either network structure or how materials moved through social ties, although still indicating wide-ranging social ties reaching to the Admiralties and New Britain. Mid-Holocene stone mortars and pestles occur along the length of the New Guinea north coast, but obsidian stemmed tools are on present knowledge largely absent west of the Sepik-Ramu delta. At the time, this delta was the mouth of a large inland sea (Torrence and Swadling, 2008, p. 602).

The social impacts of such major environmental transformations, including postulated high population densities in the Sepik-Ramu, likely had significant impacts on where people lived and how they spatially interacted. It could be, for instance, that high population densities in the Sepik-Ramu largely diverted the flow of goods southward such that obsidian did not reach other parts of the north coast, while less dense social connections to communities further to the west still allowed the spread of mortar and pestle styles (Swadling, 2010, pp. 146–147). Such a model (or a variety of others) could be tested by modifying the baseline ethnographic network, and the flow of goods through the resulting network modelled to see which conditions and changes produce plausible matches to archaeological data.

While shifting network structure may account for at least some of the variable patterning observed in the archaeological record, it is also worth remembering that the mere presence of a tie between two places may not automatically lead to the transmission of a particular set of cultural practices. Future modelling of cultural diversity should take into account the fact that variable motivations, beliefs and attitudes may contribute to whether a style or material spreads or not, or how much any given individual or community chooses to participate in the broader social world around them. At times, ancient inhabitants of the Pacific islands may also have chosen to maintain particular unique manners of speech and custom as a sign of social distinctiveness while simultaneously engaging in intense exchanges of other ideas, goods and marriage partners (e.g. Dutton, 1982; Roscoe, 1989; 1996).

Conclusion

Debate continues between scholars who conceptualise the past as a story of linked linguistic, cultural and biological divergence (Gray et al., 2010; Steele et al., 2010), and those who argue for a reticulated, interactive social world in which cultural, linguistic and biological diversity need not tell the same story (Moore, 1994; Terrell, 1988). The Pacific islands remain key playing fields on which these debates about the structure of the human past take place.

Ethnographic analogy as a means of archaeological theorising fell out of favour as interpretive and critical approaches came to dominate both cultural anthropology and archaeology in the 1980s and later. Direct comparison with social models developed in the Southwestern Pacific likewise fell out of favour with European archaeologists of other theoretical persuasions, who have come to recognise both the importance and complexity of long-distance exchange systems and existence of inequality in increasingly early stages of prehistory (e.g. Bentley et al., 2012). Yet it seems likely that ethnographies of the Pacific will continue to exert influence over broader archaeological theory and practice whatever the future theoretical directions of the discipline. As Spriggs (2008, pp. 542–543) notes, post-modern archaeologists in Europe, even while rejecting controlled ethnographic comparisons, have continued to use Pacific examples as ad hoc metaphors for what social life might have been like during prehistory.

Such uncritical application of ethnographic models remains a problem – Spriggs (2008, pp. 548–549) suggests that key aspects of social life in the Pacific during the late 19th and early 20th century (e.g. big man systems, marriage patterns) may have resulted from colonialism. For instance, population densities may have been significantly higher prior to European contact – it is quite possible that the systematic underproduction argued by Sahlins was an outcome of rapid population decline rather than symptomatic of all 'primitive' economics. Roscoe (2009, p. 579) is more optimistic, suggesting that colonialism was but one more factor playing into a long history of social and economic change.

While archaeologists globally should acknowledge their debt to the Pacific as a source of theory and models, they also should read Pacific archaeology to understand regional sequences of change, within which ethnographic observation represents a brief moment in time. The last seven decades of archaeological research in the Pacific have demonstrated that ethnographic accounts do not document timeless patterns of social life. On the other hand, it is also clear that archaeology can never provide the level of detail and nuance that observation of living communities can. The value of the Pacific ethnographic record (from an archaeological standpoint) lies in its ability to provide well-understood baseline models of behaviour against which to compare the prehistoric record.

It will be difficult to realise this potential of the Oceanic record if Pacific archaeologists themselves do not play a significant role in developing new models of the past based on detailed understanding of prehistoric sequences and the ethnographic patterns that emerged from them. Given the increasing evidence for intensive interaction between communities well before colonial intervention, and likely well before the appearance of Lapita pottery, these models and theories apparently must simultaneously incorporate both patterned bio-cultural diversity, and variably structured wide-ranging sociality.

Acknowledgements

I would like to thank Tim Thomas for inviting me to contribute to this volume, and John Edward Terrell, Rahul Oka and Sylvia Vatuk for many conversations over the years that contributed to the ideas presented here.

References

Allen, B., 1983. Human geography of Papua New Guinea. *Journal of Human Evolution*, 12, pp. 3–23.

Allen, J., 1984. Pots and poor princes: a multidimensional approach to the role of pottery trading in coastal Papua. In: S.E. van der Leeuw and A.C. Prichard, eds. *The Many Dimensions of Pottery: Ceramics in Archaeology and Anthropology*. Amsterdam: Amsterdam Institute for Pre- and Proto-History. pp. 407–463.

Allen, J., 1985. Comments on complexity and trade: a view from Melanesia. *Archaeology in Oceania*, 20(2), pp. 49–57.

Allentoft, M.E., Sikora, M., Sjögren, K.-G., Rasmussen, S., Rasmussen, M., Stenderup, J., Damgaard, P.B., Schroeder, H., Ahlström, T., Vinner, L., Malaspinas, A.-S., Margaryan, A., Higham, T., Chivall, D., Lynnerup, N., Harvig, L., Baron, J., Della Casa, P., Dabrowski, P., Duffy, P.R., Ebel, A.V., Epimakhov, A., Frei, K., Furmanek, M., Gralak, T., Gromov, A., Gronkiewicz, S., Grupe, G., Hajdu, T., Jarysz, R., Khartanovich, V., Khokhlov, A., Kill, V., Kolář, J., Kriiska, A., Lasak, I., Longhi, C., McGlynn, G., Merkevicius, A., Merkyte, I., Metspalu, M., Mkrtchyan, R., Moiseyev, V., Paja, L., Pálfi, G., Pokutta, D., Pospieszny, L, Price, T.D., Saag, L., Sablin, M., Shishlina, N., Smrčka, V., Seonov, V.I., Szeverényi, V., Tóth, G., Trifanova, S.V., Varul, L., Vicze, M., Yepiskoposyan, L., Zhitenev, V., Orlando, L., Sicheritz-Pontén, T., Brunak, S., Nielsen, R., Kristiansen, K. and Willerslev, E., 2015. Population genomics of Bronze Age Eurasia. *Nature*, 522, pp. 167–172.

Ambrose, W.R., 1976. Obsidian and its prehistoric distribution in Melanesia. In: N. Barnard, ed. *The Proceedings of a Symposium on Scientific Methods of Research in the Study of Ancient Chines Bronzes and Southeast Asian Metal and Other Archaeological Artifacts, October 6–10, 1975*. Melbourne: National Gallery of Victoria, pp. 351–378.

Ambrose, W.R., 1978. The loneliness of the long distance trader in Melanesia. *Mankind*, 11, pp. 326–333.

Bellwood, P., 2001. Early agriculturalist population diasporas? Farming, languages, and genes. *Annual Review of Anthropology*, 30, pp. 181–207.

Bentley, R.A., Bickle, P., Fibiger, L., Nowell, G.M., Dale, C.W., Hedges, R.E.M., Hamilton, J., Wahl, J., Francken, M., Grupe, G., Lenneis, E., Teschler-Nicola, M., Arbogast, R.M., Hofmann, D. and Whittle, A. 2012. Community differentiation and kinship among Europe's first farmers. *PNAS*, 109(24), pp. 9326–9330.

Bergström, A., Oppenheimer, S.J., Mentzer, A.J., Auckland, K., Robson, K., Attenborough, R., Alpers, M.P., Koki, G., Pomat, W., Siba, P., Xue, Y., Sandhu, M.S. and Tyler-Smith, C., 2017. A Neolithic expansion, but strong genetic structure, in the independent history of New Guinea. *Science*, 357, pp. 1160–1163.

Brughmans, T., 2013. Thinking through networks: a review of formal network methods in archaeology. *Journal of Archaeological Method and Theory,* 20, pp. 623–662.

Cochrane, E.E. and Lipo, C.P., 2010. Phylogenetic analyses of Lapita decoration do not support branching evolution or regional population structure during colonization of Remote Oceania. *Philosophical Transactions of the Royal Society B: Biological Sciences,* 365, pp. 3889–3902.

Craig, B., Lewis, G. and Mitchell, W.E., 2008. War shields of the Torricelli Mountains, West Sepik Province, Papua New Guinea. *Oceania,* 78(3), pp. 241–259.

Dalton, G., 1977. Aboriginal economies in stateless societies. In: T.K. Earle and J.E. Ericson, eds. *Exchange Systems in Prehistory.* New York: Academic Press, pp. 191–212.

Donohue, M. and Denham, T., 2010. Farming and language in island Southeast Asia: reframing Austronesian history. *Current Anthropology,* 51(2), pp. 223–256.

Durkheim, E., 1966. *The Division of Labor in Society.* New York: Free Press.

Dutton, T., 1982. The Melanesian response to linguistic diversity: the Papuan example. In: R.J. May and H. Nelson, eds. *Melanesia: Beyond Diversity,* vol. 1. Canberra: Research School of Pacific Studies, the Australian National University, pp. 251–261.

Earle, T.K., 1977. A reappraisal of redistribution: complex Hawaiian chiefdoms. In: T.K. Earle and J.E. Ericson, eds. *Exchange Systems in Prehistory.* New York: Academic Press, pp. 213–229.

Engels, F., 1972. *The Origin of the Family, Private Property and the State, in the Light of the Researches of Lewis H. Morgan.* New York: International Publishers.

Feil, D.K., 1987. *The Evolution of Highland Papua New Guinea Societies.* Cambridge: Cambridge University Press.

Freeman, L.C., 2004. *The Development of Social Network Analysis: A Study in the Sociology of Science.* Vancouver: Empirical Press.

Friedman, J., 1982. Catastrophe and continuity in social evolution. In: C. Renfrew, M.J. Rowlands, and B.A. Segraves, eds. *Theory and Explanation in Archaeology.* New York: Academic Press, pp. 175–196.

Fusfield, D.B., 1957. Economic theory misplaced: livelihood in primitive society. In: K. Polanyi, C.M. Arensberg and H.H. Pearson, eds. *Trade and Market in the Early Empires: Economies in History and Theory.* Glencoe, IL: Free Press, pp. 342–356.

Fyfe, A., 2009. Exploring spatial relationships between material culture and language. *Oceania,* 79(2), pp. 121–161.

Fyfe, A. and Bolton, J., 2011. An analysis of arrow and string bag craft variability in the Upper Sepik and Central New Guinea. *Oceania,* 81(3), pp. 259–279.

Gray, R.D., Bryant, D. and Greenhill, S.J., 2010. On the shape and fabric of human history. *Philosophical Transactions of the Royal Society B: Biological Sciences,* 365, pp. 3923–3933.

Golitko, M., 2019. The potential of obsidian 'Big Data'. *UISPP Journal,* 2(1), pp. 83–98.

Golitko, M. and Terrell, J.E., 2012. Mapping prehistoric social fields on the Sepik coast of Papua New Guinea: ceramic compositional analysis using laser ablation-inductively coupled plasma-mass spectrometry. *Journal of Archaeological Science,* 39, pp. 3568–3580.

Golitko, M., Schauer, M. and Terrell, J.E., 2013. Obsidian acquisition on the Sepik coast of northern Papua New Guinea during the last two millennia. In: G. Summerhayes and H. Buckley, eds. *Pacific Archaeology: Documenting the Past 50,000 Years.* Dunedin: University of Otago, pp. 43–57.

Hage, P., Harary, F. and James, B., 1986. Wealth and hierarchy in the Kula Ring. *American Anthropologist,* 88(1), pp. 108–115.

Harding, T.G., 1967. *Voyagers of the Vitiaz Strait: A Study of a New Guinea Trade System.* Seattle, WA, and London: University of Washington Press.

Harding, T.G., 1994. Precolonial New Guinea trade. *Ethnology,* 33(2), pp. 101–125.

Hunt, T.L., 1989. *Lapita Ceramic Exchange in the Mussau Islands, Papua New Guinea.* Seattle, WA: University of Washington.

Irwin, G.J., 1978. Pots and entrepôts: a study of settlement, trade and the development of economic specialization in Papuan Prehistory. *World Archaeology,* 9(3), pp. 299–319.

Irwin, G.J., 1983. Chieftainship, kula and trade in Massim prehistory. In: J.W. Leach and E. Leach, eds. *The Kula: New Perspectives on Massim Exchange.* Cambridge: Cambridge University Press, pp. 29–72.

Irwin, G., Shaw, B. and McAlister, A., 2019. The origins of the Kula Ring: archaeological and maritime perspectives from the southern Massim and Mailu areas of Papua New Guinea. *Archaeology in Oceania,* 54(1), pp. 1–16.

Kirch, P.V., 1990. Specialization and exchange in the Lapita complex of Oceania (1600–500 B.C.). *Asian Perspectives,* 29(2), pp. 117–133.

Kirch, P.V., 1991. Prehistoric exchange in Western Melanesia. *Annual Review of Anthropology,* 20, pp. 141–165.

Kirch, P.V. and Green, R.C., 1987. History, phylogeny, and evolution in Polynesia. *Current Anthropology,* 28(4), pp. 431–456.

Ladefoged, T.N., Gemmell, C., McCoy, M., Jorgensen, A., Glover, H., Stevenson, C. and O'Neale, D., 2019. Social network analysis of obsidian artefacts and Māori interaction in northern Aotearoa New Zealand. *PLoS ONE,* 14(3), e0212941.

Lilley, I., 2004. Trade and culture history across the Vitiaz Strait, Papua New Guinea: the emerging post-Lapita coastal sequence. *Records of the Australian Museum,* suppl. 29, pp. 89–96.

Lipset, D.M., 1985. Seafaring Sepiks: ecology, warfare, and prestige in Murik trade. *Research in Economic Anthropology,* 7, pp. 67–94.

Lutkehaus, N. and Roscoe, P., 1987. Sepik culture history: variation, innovation, and synthesis. *Current Anthropology,* 28(4), pp. 577–581.

Malinowski, B., 1961. *Argonauts of the Western Pacific: An Account of Native Enterprise and Adventure in the Archipelagos of Melanesian New Guinea.* New York: E.P. Dutton & Co.

Marx, K., 1978a. Economic and philosophic manuscripts of 1844. In: R.C. Tucker, ed. *The Marx-Engels Reader,* 2nd edition. New York and London: W.W. Norton & Co., pp. 66–101.

Marx, K., 1978b. The Grundrisse, sections E and F. In: R.C. Tucker, ed. *The Marx-Engels Reader,* 2nd edition. New York and London: W.W. Norton & Co., pp. 261–278.

Mauss, M., 1967. *The Gift: Forms and Functions of Exchange in Archaic Society.* New York: W.W. Norton & Co.

May, P. and Tuckson, M., 2000. *The Traditional Pottery of Papua New Guinea.* Honolulu: University of Hawai'i Press.

Mead, M., 1968. *The Mountain Arapesh III: Stream of Events in Alitoa.* Garden City, NY: Natural History Press.

Mead, M., 1970. *The Mountain Arapesh II: Arts and Supernaturalism.* Garden City, NY: Natural History Press.

Milisauskas, S., 1977. Adaptations of the early Neolithic farmers in Central Europe. In: C.E. Cleland, ed. *For the Director: Research Essays in Honor of James B. Griffen.* Ann Arbor, MI: Museum of Anthropology, University of Michigan, pp. 295–316.

Moore, J.H., 1994. Putting anthropology back together again: the ethnogenetic critique of cladistic theory. *American Anthropologist,* 96(4), pp. 925–948.

Oka, R. and Kusimba, C.M., 2008. The archaeology of trading systems, part 1: towards a new trade synthesis. *Journal of Archaeological Research,* 16, pp. 339–395.

Peeples, M.A., 2019. Finding a place for networks in archaeology. *Journal of Archaeological Research,* 27, pp. 451–499.

Pires-Ferreira, J.W. and Flannery, K.V., 1976. Ethnographic models for formative exchange. In: K.V. Flannery, ed. *The Early Mesoamerican Village*. New York: Academic Press, pp. 286–291.

Polanyi, K., 1957. The economy as instituted process. In: K. Polanyi, C.M. Arensberg and H.H. Pearson, eds. *Trade and Market in the Early Empires: Economies in History and Theory*. Glencoe, IL: Free Press, pp. 243–270.

Rappaport, R.A., 1968. *Pigs for the Ancestors: Ritual in the Ecology of a New Guinea People*. New Haven, CT, and London: Yale University Press.

Renfrew, C., 1969. Trade and culture process in European prehistory. *Current Anthropology*, 10(2/3), pp. 151–169.

Renfrew, C., 1987. *Archaeology and Language: The Puzzle of Indo-European Origins*. Cambridge: Cambridge University Press.

Roberts, J.M. Jr., Moore, C.C. and Kimball Romney, A., 1995. Predicting similarity in material culture among New Guinea Villages from propinquity and language: a log-linear approach. *Current Anthropology*, 36(5), pp. 769–788.

Roscoe, P.B. 1989. The pig and the long yam: the expansion of a Sepik cultural complex. *Ethnology*, 28(3), pp. 219–231.

Roscoe, P., 1996. War and society in Sepik New Guinea. *Journal of the Royal Anthropological Institute*, 2(4), pp. 645–666.

Roscoe, P., 2009. On the 'pacification' of the European Neolithic: ethnographic analogy and the neglect of history. *World Archaeology*, 41(4), pp. 578–588.

Sahlins, M.D., 1963. Poor man, rich man, big-man, chief: political types in Melanesia and Polynesia. *Comparative Studies in Society and History*, 5, pp. 285–303.

Sahlins, M.D., 1972. *Stone Age Economics*. New York: Aldine Publishing Co.

Sankoff, G., 1980. *The Social Life of Language*. Philadelphia, PA: University of Pennsylvania Press.

Schwartz, T., 1963. Systems of areal integration: some considerations based on the Admiralty Islands of northern Melanesia. *Anthropological Forum*, 1(1), pp. 56–97.

Service, E.R., 1962. *Primitive Social Organization: An Evolutionary Perspective*, 2nd edition. New York: Random House.

Schackleton, N. and Renfrew, C., 1970. Neolithic trade routes re-aligned by oxygen isotope analysis. *Nature*, 228, pp. 1062–1065.

Shennan, S. and Collard, M., 2005. Investing processes of cultural evolution on the north coast of New Guinea with multivariate and cladistic analyses. In: R. Mace, C.J. Holden and S. Shennan, eds. *The Evolution of Cultural Diversity: A Phylogenetic Approach*. Walnut Creek, CA: Left Coast Press, pp. 133–164.

Skoglund, P., Posth, C., Sirak, K., Spriggs, M., Valentin, F., Bedford, S., Clark, G.R., Reepmeyer, C., Petchey, F., Fernandes, D., Fu, Q., Harney, H., Lipson, M., Mallick, S., Novak, M., Rohland, N., Stewardson, K., Abdullah, S., Cox, M.P., Friedlaender, F.R., Friedlaender, J.S., Kivisild, T., Koki, G., Kusuma, P., Merriwether, D.A., Ricaut, F.-X., Wee, J.T.S., Patterson, N., Krause, J., Pinhasi, R. and Reich, D., 2016. Genomic insights into the peopling of the Southwest Pacific. *Nature*, 538, pp. 510–513.

Spriggs, M., 1997. *The Island Melanesians*. Oxford: Blackwell.

Spriggs, M., 2008. Ethnographic parallels and the denial of history. *World Archaeology*, 40, pp. 538–552.

Spriggs, M., 2011. Archaeology and the Austronesian expansion: where are we now? *Antiquity*, 85, pp. 510–528.

Steele, J., Jordan, P. and Cochrane, E., 2010. Evolutionary approaches to cultural and linguistic diversity. *Philosophical Transactions of the Royal Society: Biological Sciences B*, 365, pp. 3781–3785.

Summerhayes, G.R., 2009. Obsidian network patterns in Melanesia: Sources, characterisation and distribution. *IPPA Bulletin,* 29, pp. 109–124.

Swadling, P., 2004. Stone mortar and pestle distribution in New Britain revisited. *Records of the Australian Museum,* suppl. 29, pp. 157–161.

Swadling, P., 2010. The impact of a dynamic environmental past on trade routes and language distributions in the lower-middle Sepik. In: J. Bowden, N.P. Himmelmann and M. Ross, eds. *A Journey through Austronesian and Papuan Linguistic and Cultural Space: Papers in Honour of Andrew Pawley.* Canberra: Pacific Linguistics, pp. 141–157.

Terrell, J., 1976. Island biogeography and man in Melanesia. *Archaeology and Physical Anthropology in Oceania,* 11(1), pp. 1–17.

Terrell, J., 1988. History as a family tree, history as an entangled bank: constructing images and interpretations of prehistory in the South Pacific. *Antiquity,* 62, pp. 642–657.

Terrell, J.E., 2010a. Language and material culture on the Sepik Coast of Papua New Guinea: using social network analysis to simulate, graph, identify, and analyze social and cultural boundaries between communities. *Journal of Island and Coastal Archaeology,* 5, pp. 3–32.

Terrell, J.E., 2010b. Social network analysis of the genetic structure of Pacific Islanders. *Annals of Human Genetics,* 74, pp. 211–232.

Terrell, J.E., Hunt, T.L. and Gosden, C., 1997. The dimensions of social life in the Pacific: human diversity and the myth of the primitive isolate. *Current Anthropology,* 38(2), pp. 155–195.

Terrell, J.E., Kelly, K.M. and Rainbird, P., 2001. Foregone conclusions? In search of 'Papuans' and 'Austronesians'. *Current Anthropology,* 42(1), pp. 97–123.

Tiesler, F., 1969/1970. Die intertribalen Beziehungen an der Nordküste Neuguineas im Gebiet der Kleinen Shouten-Inseln. *Abhandlungen und Berichte des Staatlischen Museums für Völkerkunde Dresden,* 30/31, pp. 1–195.

Torrence, R. and Swadling, P., 2008. Social networks and the spread of Lapita. *Antiquity,* 82, pp. 600–616.

Torrence, R., 2011. Finding the right question: learning from stone tools on the Willaumez Peninsula, Papua New Guinea. *Archaeology in Oceania,* 46, pp. 29–41.

Torrence, R., Kelloway, S. and White, P., 2013. Stemmed tools, social interaction, and voyaging in early-mid Holocene Papua New Guinea. *Journal of Island and Coastal Archaeology,* 8(2), pp. 278–310.

Trigger, B.G., 1989. *A History of Archaeological Thought.* Cambridge: Cambridge University Press.

von Cramon-Taubadel, N. and Lycett, S.J., 2018. Assessing the relative impact of historical divergence and inter-group transmission on cultural patterns: a method from evolutionary ecology. *Philosophical Transactions of the Royal Society B: Biological Sciences,* 373, 20170054.

Welsch, R.L., Terrell, J. and Nadolski, J.A., 1992. Language and culture on the north coast of New Guinea. *American Anthropologist,* 94(3), pp. 568–600.

Wurm, S.A., Hattori, S., Baumann, T. and Gakushiin, N., 1983. *Language Atlas of the Pacific Area, Part 2.* Canberra: Australian Academy of the Humanities.

6

PRECERAMIC SHELL-WORKING, CAUTION BAY AND THE CIRCUM-NEW GUINEA ARCHIPELAGO

Katherine Szabó, Bruno David, Ian J. McNiven and Matthew Leavesley

In a series of papers published in the early 2000s, mammologist Tom Heinsohn drew together historical, archaeological and zoological evidence to consider the temporality and directionality of human-mediated translocations of vertebrate faunas to, from and within the New Guinea region (Heinsohn, 2001; 2003; Heinsohn and Hope, 2006). From the earliest archaeologically demonstrated translocations of cuscus possums (*Phalanger orientalis*) from New Britain to New Ireland around 20,000 years ago (Allen et al., 1989) (see Fig. 6.1), through the likely early Holocene human-mediated movements of forest wallaby (*Dorcopsis muelleri*) from western New Guinea to northern Maluku (Flannery et al., 1998; Hull et al., 2019),[1] to records of historical and contemporary animal translocations, Heinsohn built up evidence for a world of constant connections and movements (see also McNiven and Hitchcock, 2004). Although the majority of animal translocations in the recent past derived from Asia west of the Wallace Line, archaeologically attested cases prior to the introduction of Asian domesticates tended to radiate out from the New Guinea mainland to the surrounding archipelagos. In recognition of the fact that the redistribution of animals by human agents did not fall into a 'Southeast Asian story' west of New Guinea and a 'Melanesian' one to the north and east, he coined a new geographical term: the Circum-New Guinea Archipelago.

The Circum-New Guinea Archipelago, as laid out by Heinsohn (2001; 2003), drew together the islands of Wallacea south of the Philippines and western Island Melanesia around the landmass of New Guinea. For analytical reasons, these islands and archipelagos around the New Guinea mainland were broken into six regions: the Lesser Sunda Islands, Sulawesi, Maluku, the Bismarck Archipelago, the islands off the southeastern tip of New Guinea and the Solomon Islands. He mapped specific instances of animal translocations through time, and their directionality. While the precise location of source areas within New Guinea, and the conditions which underpinned movement, are not clear from Heinsohn's work,

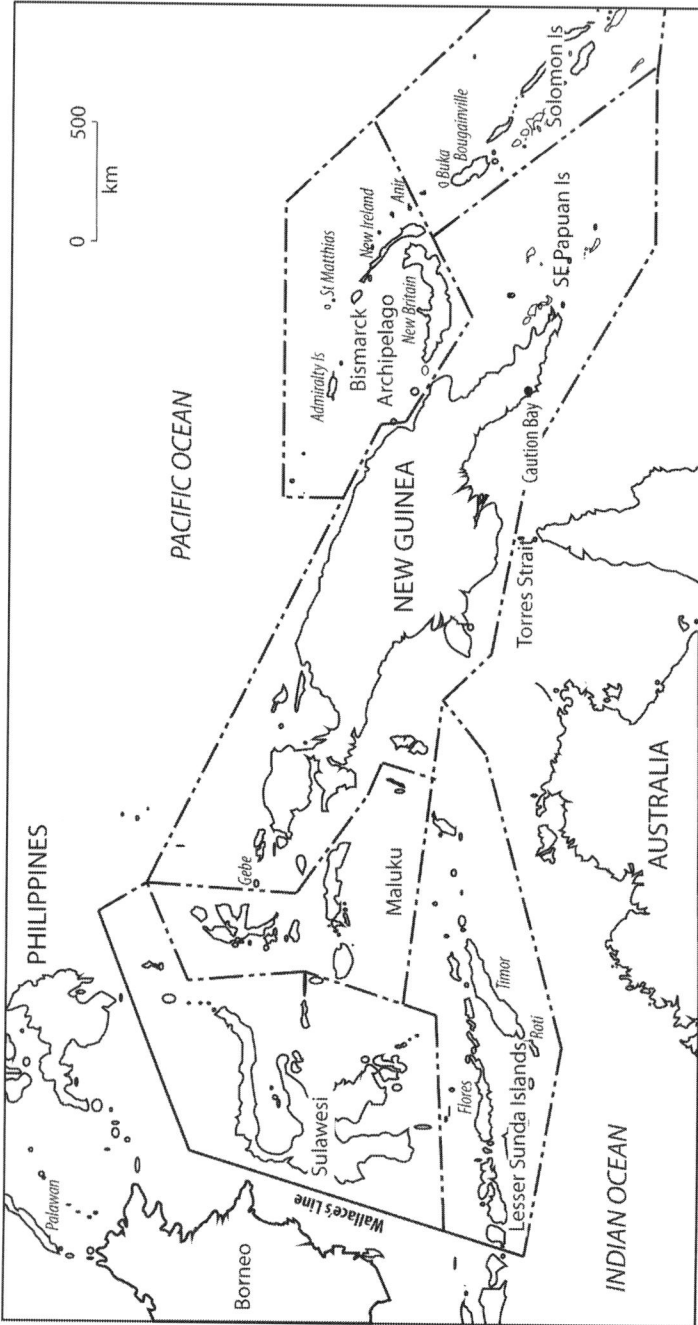

FIGURE 6.1 Map of the Circum-New Guinea Archipelago, as defined by Heinsohn (2003).

what *is* clear is that there is movement between the mainland and islands around the entire coastline of New Guinea. What is also clear is that such movements happened consistently over a sustained period of time from the late Pleistocene (in some locations) or early to mid-Holocene (in other locations) onwards. This is as true for the islands to the west of New Guinea as for those to the north, south and east.

Although the concept of a Circum-New Guinea Archipelago has rarely been used in the archaeological literature (but see White, 2004), its already-demonstrated pathways and connections provide a useful heuristic for thinking about broader cultural connections and relationships; one that pays little heed to the modern and, as far as the preceramic archaeology is concerned, artificial political geography of the region which severs the region bilaterally into 'Southeast Asia' and 'Melanesia'. Here, specifically, we find the idea of a Circum-New Guinea Archipelago useful for thinking about the nature and constituent parts of a recently excavated archaeological worked shell assemblage from the southeast coast of New Guinea.

For decades, those with an interest in the archaeology of the Lapita Cultural Complex have debated whether these distinctive archaeological materials arrived fully formed in the Bismarck Archipelago of northern New Guinea via the migration of Austronesian-speaking peoples from Island Southeast Asia, or whether they emerged *in situ* in the Bismarcks. A compromise position sees a blending of the two options (Green, 1991; 2000; 2003). Through all of this, however, few have considered the potential validity of the underlying geographic divisions themselves. 'Island Southeast Asia', stretching from Taiwan through the Philippines, Borneo and Indonesia, is mostly explicitly or implicitly seen as being synonymous with a rather fluidly defined Austronesian Neolithic and treated as a broadly unitary category (e.g. Bellwood, 2006; Spriggs, 1996 – but see Spriggs, 2011 for an equivocal treatment of Island Southeast Asia). To the east, the Bismarck Archipelago, including surrounding island groups such as the Admiralty Islands and St Matthias Group, is also generally treated as an analytical unit, with evidence from the various islands being discussed as a whole (e.g. Allen, 2003). The central article that explicitly challenges the conceptual framework of these analytical divisions (Allen and Gosden, 1996) also proceeds to consider the evidence within their geographical bounds. While some have attempted to draw the large island of New Guinea into discussions (e.g. Terrell, 2004a; 2004b; Torrence and Swadling, 2008), the ephemeral evidence for the presence of Lapita sites there has meant that such approaches have not tended to gain general traction. Swadling's (1996) research on the extension of Southeast Asian traders eastwards along the south coast of New Guinea over the past 500 years certainly reveals that the geographical boundedness of our understandings of interaction spheres and cultural influences need to be reconceptualised (see also McNiven, 2017).

While the archaeological evidence to date has tended to align with the notion of these broad geographical spheres, the recent discovery of a number of Late Lapita deposits in the Caution Bay area of southeast mainland Papua New Guinea has engendered more discussion about the relationship of a Late Lapita pottery tradition to the Early Papuan Pottery (EPP) complex than about how the Caution Bay Lapita sites came to be in southeast New Guinea in the first place, and what this may mean for Lapita spatio-temporal dynamics (e.g. Irwin, 2012; Specht, 2012). Only one contributor to an *Australian Archaeology* forum on the Caution Bay finds grappled with what the new evidence may mean for understanding Lapita internal connections and relationships, as well as pointing to the potential significance of pre-Lapita layers at several Caution Bay sites (Sand, 2012; see also Skelly and David, 2017).

Excavations at Caution Bay along the southeast coast of mainland New Guinea have been undertaken in 122 archaeological sites that together cover the past 6,000 years of cultural history. Both preceramic and ceramic assemblages are present. Tanamu 1 (PNG National Museum and Art Gallery site code ABHA) is one of these sites (Fig. 6.2), its preceramic assemblage of worked shell forming the basis of the following discussion.

In the absence of any regional formulations of preceramic worked shell technologies in line with either particular geographical areas or recognised socio-cultural groups, we here investigate similarities and differences in shell-working technologies and types across the Circum-New Guinea Archipelago through time, and what these may mean for the configurations of preceramic cultural traditions and geographies. Given the extremely scattered and partial nature of current understandings of large areas of the Circum-New Guinea Archipelago, this analysis of worked shell assemblages acts as a launching point from which to explore the broader region's spatial history.

Background: Tanamu 1 excavations and chronology

Excavations undertaken on the south coast of the Papua New Guinea mainland, 20 km northwest of Port Moresby, have uncovered a series of mid- to late Holocene archaeological sites (David et al., 2011; McNiven et al., 2011). Some are single-phase deposits, but a number include multiple ceramic horizons, some also with substantial preceramic habitation. Tanamu 1 is one such site, with excavations exposing three major cultural horizons – Stratigraphic Units (SUs) 1, 3 and 5–6 – separated by two largely sterile layers – SUs 2 and 4 – and the underlying SU7 containing more sparse cultural deposits (Fig. 6.3). Full details of the excavations, deposits and the worked shell assemblage are currently in preparation (David et al., in prep), but the main salient details are presented here.

Tanamu 1 is located in a stable but exposed coastal sand dune forming a low and narrow, north-northwest to south-southeast trending spit. This grassy area is bounded by extensive mangrove forest to the northwest and open tidal mudflats to the southwest. The present ground surface at Tanamu 1 sits 5 m above the high-water mark.

Excavations focused on two contiguous 1 m × 1 m squares (A and B), around which a series of peripheral squares was also dug. The two main squares were excavated in average 2.1 ± 0.5 cm-thick arbitrary Excavation Units (XUs) following the stratigraphy where visible during excavation. The excavations reached a maximum depth of 2.84 m and revealed seven major Stratigraphic Units (SUs)

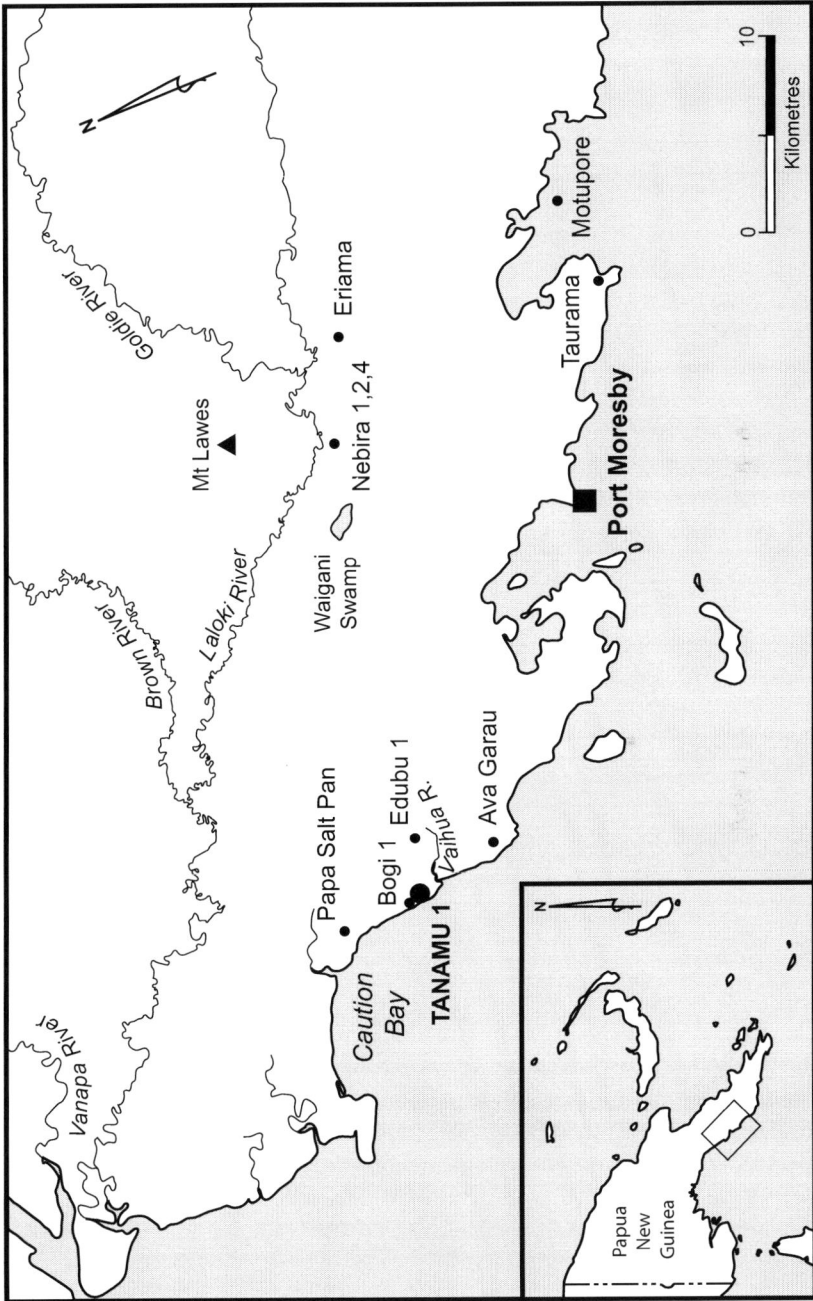

FIGURE 6.2 Map showing the location of Caution Bay and Tanamu 1.

(Fig. 6.3). The major SUs are sub-horizontal layers of moderately consolidated and compact sand. There are no signs of major post-depositional disturbance or mixing of materials between SUs, including a total absence of intrusive postholes.

Fifty-nine accelerator mass spectrometry (AMS) radiocarbon determinations were obtained from Squares A and B, each on a single piece of charcoal or *Anadara antiquata* or *Gafrarium tumidum* shell whose species-specific ΔR values have been measured specifically for Caution Bay (Petchey et al., 2013). The dates are in good chronostratigraphic order, and none of these calibrated radiocarbon ages show age-depth reversals between the preceramic and earliest ceramic levels. The complete list of AMS determinations and detailed stratigraphic drawings and photographs will be published in David et al. (in prep.), with the total range for each relevant SU, calibrated and reported at 2σ, being presented here.

Over 1,000 pottery sherds were excavated from Squares A and B, with all large (≥3 cm-long) sherds deriving from the upper 74 cm of the sequence (see Fig. 6.3), down to the base of SU3. Seven very small (<3 cm-long, most only a few millimetres long) sherds were recovered from SU4 down to a maximum depth of 94 cm. There is no evidence from the ceramics for the downward movement of SU3 cultural material into underlying preceramic strata beyond the mid-levels of SU4. All cultural material from SU5 downwards, on the basis of radiocarbon determinations, is associated with a series of dates ranging from 3902 to 5200 cal BP (2σ) and is preceramic in nature.

Shell is found throughout the Tanamu 1 deposits and is generally in a good state of preservation, with peak concentrations recorded for the three dense cultural layers (SU1, SU3 and SU5). Worked shell is strongly associated with the deeper deposits, with nearly all objects and worked fragments having a preceramic association.

Tanamu 1 worked shell: identification and analytical methods

A small number of shell artefacts was recognised and bagged separately during the course of the excavations, but the majority of the worked shell material was encountered during post-fieldwork midden analysis. None of the shell material retained in the 2.1 mm mesh sieves was discarded in the field, and all sieved materials were sorted in controlled laboratory conditions. During initial laboratory shell identifications, any piece of shell that appeared worked, as well as all material deriving from molluscan taxa well-known regionally as raw materials for shell artefact production, including *Conus* spp., *Rochia nilotica* (= *Trochus niloticus*), *Tridacna* spp. and pearl oyster fragments (Pteriidae and Isognomidae), were separated for further detailed examination. All pieces of potentially worked shell were studied using a Dino-Lite Premiere AM7013MT digital microscope under 10–60× magnification.

While some forms of cultural modification, such as grinding facets and drilled holes, are fairly straightforward to discern and describe, the application of techniques such as direct or indirect percussion, pressure flaking or the hewing out of sections

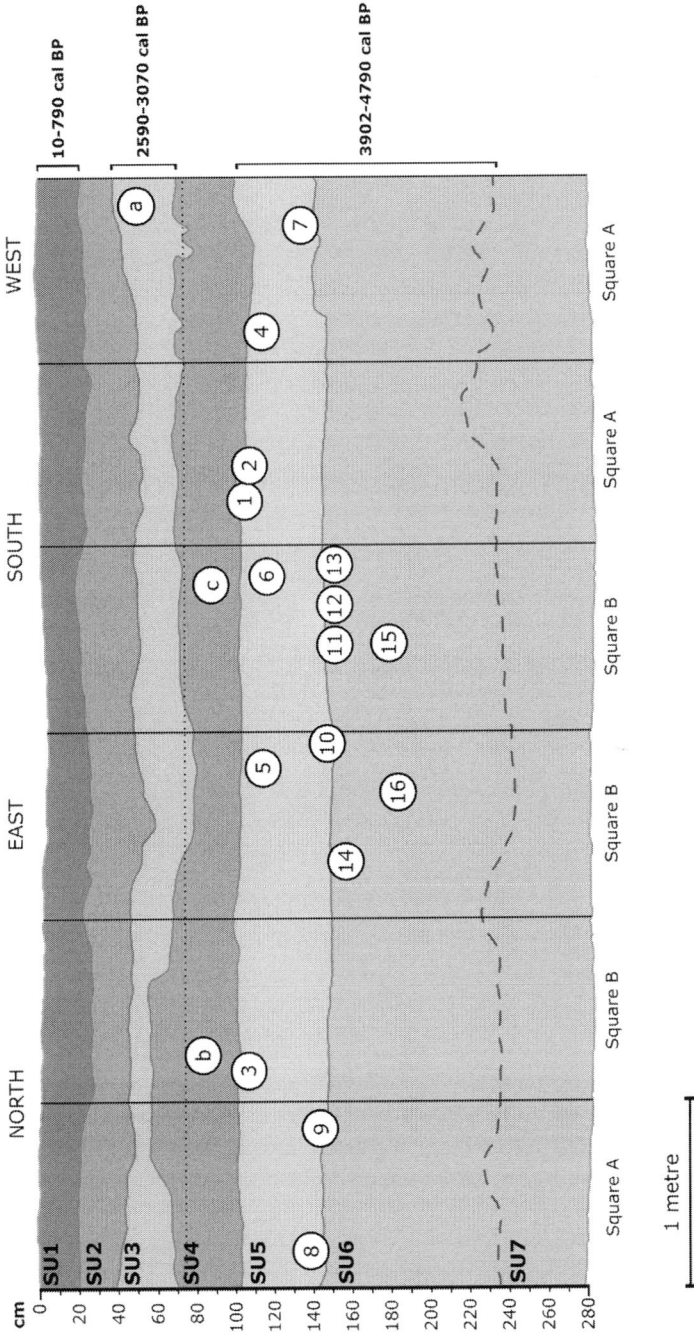

FIGURE 6.3 Stratigraphic profile of Squares A and B, Tanamu 1, showing the range of AMS radiocarbon dates for each of the main cultural stratigraphic units (SUs) and worked shell locations by depth. The dotted line at 74 cm depth shows the lowest extent of larger pottery sherds. Only seven small fragments of pottery were found below this depth to a maximum depth of 94 cm.

Source: figure by Brent Koppel.

of shell can be more difficult to distinguish from natural and meat-extraction breakage patterns or wear and tear as a result of the action of taphonomic processes. The identification of such modifications needs to be informed by a consideration of the way in which the shell is composed at the microstructural level, which can vary considerably between families. Further discussion of such microstructural variations and their consequences for the identification of shell working can be found in Szabó (2005; 2008; 2013).

Sixteen shell artefacts were identified associated with strictly preceramic contexts in SU5 and SU6 (numbered 1–16 in Fig. 6.3). A further three shell artefacts were recovered from levels above SU5 (numbered a–c in Fig. 6.3), with Artefact 'a' being associated with the ceramic SU3 deposits and 'b' and 'c' of possible ceramic association. Only direct AMS radiocarbon dating of these artefacts 'b' and 'c' would firmly establish their chronological association, for they were excavated at the interface of preceramic and ceramic levels. The preceramic shell artefacts (1–16) are described in full below.

Preceramic shell artefact assemblage

Shell artefacts associated with preceramic radiocarbon dates derive from both SU5 and SU6. The radiocarbon sequences from these two SUs are distinct, with SU6 being systematically older than SU5. There is no evidence of downward displacement from SU5 to SU6. Given the temporally distinct nature of SU5 and SU6, we will discuss the shell artefact assemblages of the two layers separately to maintain chronostratigraphic resolution.

Stratigraphic Unit 6 (SU6) shell artefacts

There are six shell artefacts from SU6 which takes in radiocarbon ages spanning from 4240 to 4790 cal BP (2σ). This group includes three fragments of *Rochia nilotica* ring preform, a small, drilled annular bead in *Nautilus* sp., a perforated *Oliva* cf. *irisans*, and an adze produced in *Conus* sp. (see Table 6.1 for exact provenances).

The lowermost artefact, associated with an AMS radiocarbon determination of 4420–4790 cal. BP (2σ) from the same XU, is an adze constructed from a triangular portion of the robust body whorl of a large *Conus* sp. shell (Fig. 6.4a). The bevel is located at the spire/posterior end of the shell and has been ground on a single facet on the inner shell surface. Light abrasion accentuated by use-wear on the opposing outer shell surface has created a slightly curved acute cutting edge.

A few centimetres above the adze, a complete *Oliva* cf. *irisans* shell with a hewn perforation through the ventral surface of the body whorl and the apex manually removed (Fig. 6.4b) was recovered. The outer lip and anterior portion of the aperture have been smoothed and rounded through use.

Twenty centimetres above the *O.* cf. *irisans* artefact, also in Square B, a small, perforated disc bead in *Nautilus* sp. shell was identified (Fig. 6.4c). The thickness and

TABLE 6.1 Shell artefacts recovered from the preceramic units at Tanamu 1

SU	XU	Depth (cm)	Square	Artefact number★	Material	Artefact type
5	48	101–102.5	A	1	*Conus* cf. *eburneus*	Abraded spire
5	49	102.5–104.7	A	2	Bivalve sp.	Ground disc bead
5	53	110.4–112.3	B	3	*Vasticardium vertebratum*	Perforated valve
5	55	117–119	A	4	*Conus* sp.	Ground spire
5	55	117–119	B	5	*Monetaria annulus*	Abraded fragment
5	57	119–122	B	6	*Rochia nilotica*	Ring preform fragment
5	61	129–132	A	7	*Rochia nilotica*	Ring preform fragment
5	64	136–139	A	8	*Placuna placenta*	Hewn perforated disc
5	66	141–144	A	9	*Conus* cf. *pulicarius*	Ground spire
5	68	143–144	B	10	*Vasticardium vertebratum*	Perforated valve
6	71	147–149	B	11	*Rochia nilotica*	Ring preform fragment
6	71	147–149	B	12	*Rochia nilotica*	Ring preform fragment
6	71	147–149	B	13	*Rochia nilotica*	Ring preform fragment
6	75	155–157	B	14	*Nautilus* sp.	Disc bead
6	85	175–177	B	15	*Oliva* cf. *irisans*	Perforated shell
6	89	183–185	B	16	*Conus* sp.	Adze

★The artefact numbers given correspond to those placed on the stratigraphic section shown in Fig. 6.3.

structure indicate that it has been cut out of the main body whorl of the shell rather than from one of the inner septal walls that divide the shell into interconnected buoyancy chambers. The bead is entirely nacreous, with the outer cream and brown layer of the shell having been removed. The central perforation has been countersunk. Rounding around the periphery of the bead as well as edge of the perforation indicates that the bead was used.

Also in Square B SU6 were three fragments of preforms of large rings produced in *Rochia nilotica* (Fig. 6.4d–f). It is possible that all three pieces derive from the same artefact, but none of the extant pieces conjoin. The three ring preform fragments all show evidence of having been chipped out of the shell with a sharp point, as well as exhibiting varying degrees of subsequent grinding and abrasion. The largest example (Fig. 6.4d) is ground flat on the second whorl edge. The two smaller examples (Fig. 6.4e and 6.4f) have both split at the suture-line which separates the whorls of the shell during production. The artefact shown in Fig. 6.3e has also been abraded around the periphery – one of the final stages in *R. nilotica* ring production.

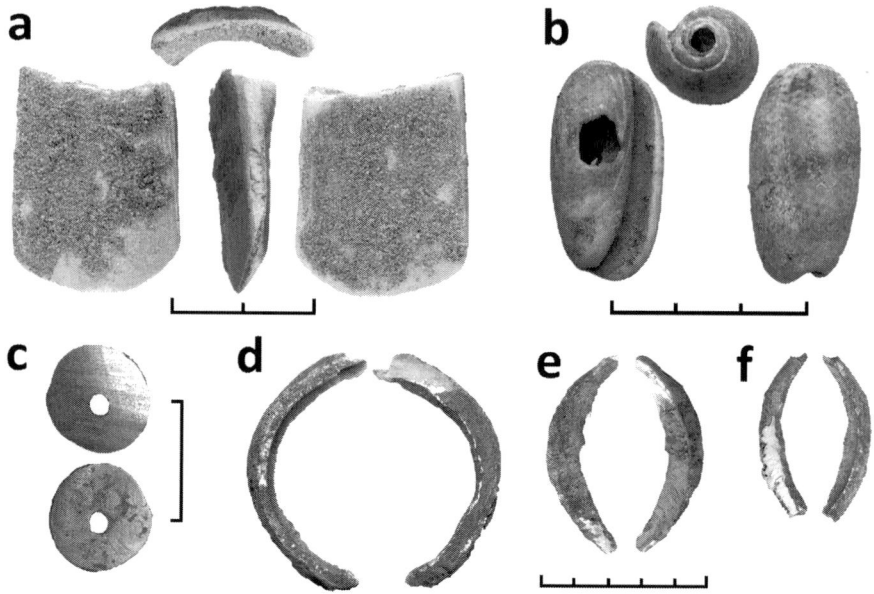

FIGURE 6.4 Shell artefacts recovered from Stratigraphic Unit 6 (SU6): (a) *Conus* sp. adze; (b) perforated *Oliva* cf. *irisans*; (c) annular *Nautilus* sp. bead; (d–f) *Rochia nilotica* ring preform fragments. Scale bars are in centimeter increments.

Source: photographs by Brent Koppel.

Stratigraphic Unit 5 (SU5) shell artefacts

A range of shell artefacts was recovered from SU5, and associated AMS dates span from 3920 to 4420 cal. BP (2σ). This group includes two pierced valves of the bivalve cockle *Vasticardium vertebratum*, two ground *Conus* spp. spires, two further fragments of *R. nilotica* ring preform, a large hewn disc made from a valve of the Windowpane Oyster *Placuna placenta*, an abraded piece of the small cowrie species *Monetaria annulus* and a small disc bead likely produced from a species of bivalve (see Table 6.1 for exact provenances).

Two complete right valves of the cockle species *V. vertebratum* with perforations hewn near the hinge and use-wear on the valve bodies were recovered from SU5 in Square B, with one recovered from near the top of the layer (XU53) (Fig. 6.5a) and one near the bottom (XU68) (Fig. 6.5b). The XU68 example has two distinctive zones of wear on the body. The first zone is the elevated ribs in the central, most inflated portion of the valve exterior where the small ridges of the ribs have been abraded smooth. The wear in this zone contrasts with the rough texture of the ribs elsewhere on the valve, and the pattern of wear suggests that the valve has seen prolonged use involving a smoothing or burnishing action. The second zone of wear is along the central portion of the ventral margin, where the tips of the ribs have been abraded into flattened facets. This pattern of wear implies that the valve

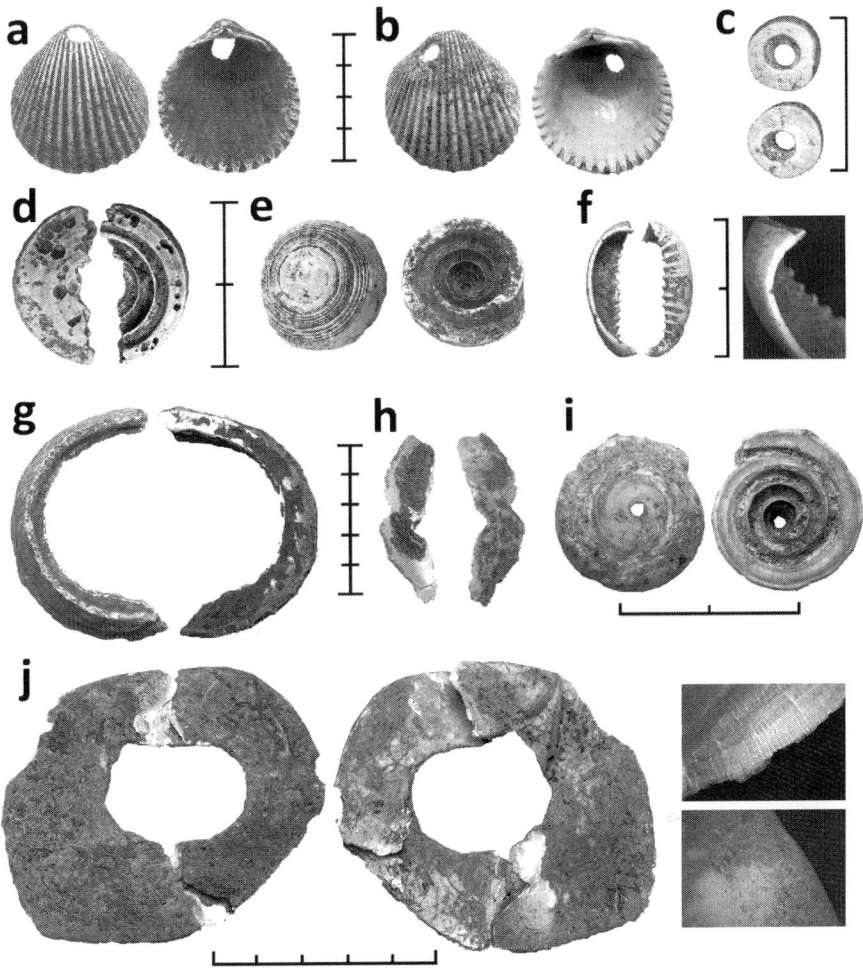

FIGURE 6.5 Shell artefacts recovered from Stratigraphic Unit 5 (SU5): (a) Pierced *Vasticardium vertebratum* valve from Square B XU53 (110–112 cm depth); (b) Pierced *V. vertebratum* valve from Square B XU68 (143–144 cm depth); (c) Fully ground disc bead; (d) Ground *Conus* sp. spire; (e) Abraded *Conus* cf. *eburneus* spire; (f) Abraded *Monetaria annulus*; (f inset) detail of abraded area of *M. annulus* artefact magnified 35×; (g) Fragment of *Rochia nilotica* ring preform from Square B XU57 (117–122 cm depth); (h) Fragment of *R. nilotica* ring preform from Square A XU61 (129–132 cm depth); (i) Ground *Conus* cf. *pulicarius* spire; (j) hewn *Placuna placenta* disc; (j inset top) ventral margin of a modern *P. placenta* valve collected from northern Australia showing its lamellar and acute nature, magnified 35×; and (j inset bottom) hewn edge of the *P. placenta* disc from Tanamu 1 showing edge-rounding, magnified 35×. Scale bars are in centimetre increments.

Source: macro photographs by Brent Koppel; micro photographs by Katherine Szabó.

has been held at the hinge area, with the opposing ventral margin being used in a scraping, cutting or abrading action. The XU53 valve does not show the same use-wear pattern at the ventral margin, but does have the smoothed wear patch along the ribs of the most inflated zone of the valve. There is little sign of wear around the perforation of either valve.

Three worked *Conus* spp. spires were identified from within the Square A SU5 deposits. Half of a fully ground *Conus* sp. spire was recovered from XU55 (Fig. 6.5d). Although the condition of the artefact appears poor, the damage visible on both faces was a feature of the original material and not the result of the action of post-depositional processes. The extensive pitting and boreholes have been caused by boring sponges (*Cliona* spp.) and small worms that excavate into shell and other calcareous materials (Vermeij, 1993). Both faces and the periphery of the spire have been extensively ground.

The detached spire of a *Conus* cf. *eburneus* from XU48 (Fig. 6.5e) shows less intensive working than the example from XU55. There is no evidence of grinding on a grindstone, but the apex and central spire area have been intentionally abraded using a freehand abrading tool. The outer spire sculpture and the break surfaces at the body whorl are still relatively crisp, ruling out the action of general weathering and mechanical taphonomic processes.

Another *Conus* spire artefact, this example deriving from a *Conus* cf. *pulicarius* shell, was recovered from the XU66 midden material (Fig. 6.5i). The spire has been detached from the body of the shell, and the break surface has been ground on a single facet. The apex and central spire on the opposing face have also been ground on a single facet. The grinding of the elevated spire would have produced a small central perforation, but close examination of the hole indicates that it was enlarged through drilling from the outer spire face.

Two further fragments of *R. nilotica* ring preform were identified from within the SU5 deposits; one from XU57 (Fig. 6.5g) and one from XU61 (Fig. 6.5h). Again, there is no evidence that the two fragments refit, or that either refit with any of the three fragments recovered from SU6. Both SU5 fragments show evidence of being chipped into a preform, but neither shows evidence of the grinding or abrasion that usually follows this first step in the ring production reduction sequence.

A worked half shell of the small species of cowrie *Monetaria annulus* was recovered from Square B XU55 (Fig. 6.5f). The dorsum of the shell has been removed and the fracture surface has been abraded smooth. The curved form of the abraded surface indicates that a freehand abrader, such as a volcanic pebble or piece of branch coral, was used, as opposed to the use of a grinding slab which would produce a flat facet (Fig. 6.5f inset).

A fragile disc of a near-complete *Placuna placenta* valve with a central perfor-ation hewn out was recovered in two conjoining fragments from Square A XU64 (Fig. 6.5j). *P. placenta* shells are typically very thin and comprised of foliated calcite sheets c.6 μm thick with only c.1 per cent organic matter being incorporated into the shell matrix (Li and Ortiz, 2013). In contrast to the natural edges of *P. placenta* valves, which are very lamellar and acute (see Fig. 6.5j top inset), the outer margins of the Tanamu 1 disc have been trimmed (Fig. 6.5j lower inset). The irregularity of the outline of the central perforation indicates rough cutting, but the abrasive action of the cutting itself has dulled and rounded the exposed edges.

A small (4.32 mm maximum diameter), fully ground disc bead was recovered from Square A XU49 (Fig. 6.5c). The central perforation has been countersunk with wide bevels on each face, indicating the use of a fairly obtuse drill-bit. The periphery has been fully freehand abraded and is thus convex although entirely smooth. Growth structures and directions of the shell, visible under magnification, confirm that the bead was not manufactured from a gastropod spire and that the raw material is most likely a bivalve, but the complete removal of surface features precludes a more specific identification.

Tanamu 1 worked shell within the context of preceramic and early ceramic Circum-New Guinea Archipelago

There are, conservatively, 10,000 species of mollusc in the Tropical Indo-West Pacific marine province. Thus, while some types of artefacts may be more suited to being produced in particular sorts of shell, such as adzes in *Tridacna* spp. giant clam, choices always exist. Coincidence in raw material choice is notable, and the more idiosyncratic or complex the object morphology, raw material choice or style of working, the less chance there is of a totally independent evolution (see also Torrence and Swadling, 2008). However, these typological principles do not necessarily discriminate between a relationship between objects across time or space due to a shared ancestry, shared ideas or technological transfer. These ideas and their theoretical underpinnings are addressed at length in Szabó (2005). Nevertheless, for our purposes we wish to isolate potential relationships of any type, with the nature and structure of any relationships being a secondary question. To this end we assess how the Tanamu 1 worked shell assemblage fits within the broader preceramic and early ceramic Circum-New Guinea Archipelago context.

Widespread across much of the temporal and geographic range of early ceramic sites of the eastern Circum-New Guinea Archipelago region (Kirch, 1988; Szabó, 2010), large chipped and abraded rings in *R. nilotica* are one of the few shell artefact types broadly acknowledged as having a preceramic presence in the same locale (Gosden et al., 1994; Green, 2000) as well as rare occurrences in East Timor (Glover, 1986). A single example from the Maluku region of the western Circum-New Guinea Archipelago, dated to between 3300 and 2200 BP (Bellwood et al., 1998), is one of the rare ceramic-associated occurrences in the western Circum-New Guinea Archipelago.

The use of *Conus* spp. is strongly associated with early ceramic sites of the eastern Circum-New Guinea Archipelago, where it is the overwhelmingly dominant raw material used for shell artefact production (Szabó, 2010). Preceramic instances of *Conus* spp. artefacts across the Circum-New Guinea Archipelago, or indeed in the islands further west, are extremely rare. Ground and perforated spires are locally common in the islands to the west of the Circum-New Guinea

Archipelago (Borneo and Palawan, e.g. Fox, 1970; Szabó and Ramirez, 2010; Szabó et al., 2013), but their frequent presence in mixed mortuary contexts makes assigning an age range difficult. They are certainly present in Metal Age (c.2200–1000 BP) deposits, and also seem to occasionally occur in preceding pre-Metal ceramic-associated burials, although a date for the first appearance in the west is elusive. Two detached *Conus* sp. spires recovered from excavations on islands off the coast of Timor are of unclear age and the photographs show no clear signs of working (Mahirta, 2009). In the northeastern zone of the Circum–New Guinea Archipelago, one example was identified from pre-Lapita deposits dating to c.4500–5000 BP in New Britain (Gosden et al., 1994) and a second example was directly AMS radiocarbon dated to c.7500 BP (Spriggs, 2001). Confusingly, a number of later ceramic-associated examples in the literature appear to be unfinished rings rather than true disc artefacts, thereby distorting any querying of distributions of types (Szabó, 2010).

To date, adzes produced in *Conus* sp. have been restricted to ceramic-associated sites of the eastern Circum–New Guinea Archipelago, so the Tanamu 1 occurrence provides the first preceramic association. On current evidence, *Conus* spp. adzes are most common in early ceramic deposits, with six reported for the site of Kamgot on Babase Island off the east coast of New Ireland (Szabó and Summerhayes, 2002; Szabó, 2005).

The other artefact that has only been associated with ceramic-associated deposits of the eastern Circum–New Guinea Archipelago to date is the *Placuna placenta* disc. As with the *Conus* sp. adze, the site of Kamgot contains the other known example (Szabó and Summerhayes, 2002). Originally tentatively identified as *Hyotissa hyotis* at Kamgot, it has since been positively identified as *Placuna placenta*. It is a rare raw material regionally, with the only other Pacific record of the use of *P. placenta* being a preceramic shaped valve fragment from Pamwak, Manus Island (Szabó, 2005).

Currently the best-reported evidence for disc bead production in *Nautilus* shell comes from Timor-Leste (Glover, 1986; O'Connor, 2010; Langley et al., 2016). Although the beads occur throughout the various Holocene levels of sites, direct AMS radiocarbon dates on three examples have all returned early Holocene determinations (O'Connor, 2010). *Nautilus* working in Timor-Leste is reported for the Pleistocene, although recorded fragments do not align with a bead *chaîne opératoire* (Langley et al., 2016). Current data suggest that *Nautilus* beads were produced in Timor-Leste throughout the early and mid-Holocene, with little apparent change in form through time.

Recent excavations on Rote and Sawu Islands off the coast of Timor have also produced *Nautilus* sp. beads from a number of rockshelter sites. None have been directly dated, and although some occur within dated preceramic contexts, their production and use has been associated with the Neolithic (Mahirta, 2009). *Nautilus* beads have been identified at other sites in the Lesser Sunda islands, including Liang Toge on Flores (Glover, 1986), scored and cut fragments from Holocene levels at Liang Bua also on Flores (van den Bergh et al., 2009), and Pleistocene and Holocene fragments from Golo Cave in Maluku (Szabó et al., 2007; Parkinson,

2016). To the west of the Circum-New Guinea Archipelago, *Nautilus* disc beads are also reported for Sodong Cave on Java, Greater Sunda islands (Glover, 1986).

In the northeastern zone of the Circum-New Guinea Archipelago, cut pieces of *Nautilus* sp. shell have been identified from preceramic levels at multiples sites on Buka and on Manus Island (Spriggs, 2001; Szabó, 2005). Within ceramic-associated assemblages of the eastern Circum-New Guinea Archipelago, worked *Nautilus* shell is uncommon. Cut fragments have been identified from the site of Kamgot (Szabó, 2005), but the only examples of finished beads are from the New Caledonian site of St Maurice-Vatcha in Remote Oceania (Szabó, 2005).

Perforated *Oliva* spp. shells are not a form of artefact associated with ceramic sites of the eastern Circum-New Guinea Archipelago, but they have been recorded across the Circum-New Guinea Archipelago range in preceramic sites. Pierced *Oliva* spp. beads associated with preceramic levels have been recovered from multiple sites on Timor-Leste with direct AMS radiocarbon dating demonstrating an antiquity for this form back to the late Pleistocene (Glover, 1986; O'Connor, 2010; Langley and O'Connor, 2016). *Oliva* spp. beads were also recovered from excavations at rockshelter sites in Rote and Sawu Islands near Timor, with broadly mid- to late-Holocene associations (Mahirta, 2009). *Oliva* spp. beads to the west of the Circum-New Guinea Archipelago are always in association with Metal Age deposits (Szabó et al., 2013).

To the northeast, excavations on Buka unearthed two *Oliva* spp. shells with the apices removed: one in preceramic levels and the other from the base of a ceramic context (Wickler, 1990). Both were produced on the large species *Oliva carneola* (Szabó, 2005). Originally these finds were classified as ceramic-associated (Wickler, 1990), but direct AMS radiocarbon dating (Spriggs, 2001) on a number of associated artefacts demonstrates that most are indeed preceramic in age.

Pierced bivalves and fragments of cowrie are difficult to discuss due to the tendency of assuming an artefactual function merely through the presence of breakage (e.g. see Spenneman, 1993). Very rarely is use-wear convincingly recorded to confirm a shell's use as an artefact, and thus it is generally unclear whether reported occurrences are valid or spurious. Despite this, worthy of note is a small collection of pierced bivalves from Timor-Leste, including a pierced *Vasticardium* (= *Cardium*) valve with traces of red ochre in the interior. The horizon containing this valve was dated to c.5700 BP (Glover, 1986). A single pierced *Vasticardium* shell has also been recovered with a burial in Alor, north of Timor, dated to c.11,500 cal BP (O'Connor et al., 2017).

Although larger species of cowrie modified for use as peelers and scrapers have been consistently reported at ceramic-associated sites, only a single site (Kamgot, New Ireland) has reported a small *M. annulus* modified through abrading the dorsum away as seen at Tanamu 1 (Szabó and Summerhayes, 2002). The earliest small cowries recovered from a regional archaeological context are the three *M. moneta* shells with the dorsa removed that are considered 'probably humanly made' (White, 1972) from the Kafiavana site in the Papua New Guinea highlands. The horizon from which the shells were excavated was dated to 9290 ± 140 BP on a pooled sample of midden bone (White, 1972).

The small, fully ground bead appears to have no Circum-New Guinea Archipelago analogues to either the east or west of Tanamu 1. The only unidentified disc bead from a preceramic context is from Matenbek on New Ireland, and was recovered from a layer below a date of ~6000 BP (J. Allen pers. comm., 2015). Morphological and technological details are difficult to extract from the single published photograph (Smith and Allen, 1999).

Tanamu 1 in Circum-New Guinea Archipelago space and time

Turning to what these disjointed temporal and geographical similarities (and dissimilarities) may mean, it is clear that the Tanamu 1 preceramic worked shell assemblage shares broad elements in common with other contemporaneous and earlier sites in the Circum-New Guinea Archipelago region. *Nautilus* and *Oliva* working are well represented in the western Circum-New Guinea Archipelago, and in particular Timor-Leste, but there are also examples towards the northeast in the less-intensively sampled Bismarcks, Admiralties and northern Solomons. This is suggestive of a broad common cultural stratum, and the Pleistocene dates associated with these from Timor-Leste and Maluku demonstrate considerable antiquity. Also represented across the Circum-New Guinea Archipelago, but with more abundant evidence deriving from the northeastern Bismarcks and northern Solomons zones, is the manufacture of *Rochia nilotica* rings. The current lack of evidence for preceramic *Rochia* working from Maluku and islands to the west of the Circum-New Guinea Archipelago, and the minimal and non-securely dated evidence from Timor-Leste, perhaps points towards an origin for *Rochia* ring production in the northeastern Circum-New Guinea Archipelago. Queries over the recognition and accurate reporting of worked *Monetaria annulus* and pierced bivalves such as *Vasticardium vertebratum* currently make any serious commentaries about analogues for the finds at Tanamu 1 specious.

Although the ubiquitous *Conus* sp. ring form so characteristic of Lapita deposits is absent from the Tanamu 1 preceramic worked shell assemblage, the equally distinctive *Conus* adze form is present. Given the near-total absence of worked *Conus* spp. across Circum-New Guinea Archipelago preceramic assemblages, the occurrence of the adze and further artefacts in *Conus* at Tanamu 1 are notable. Also of note is the presence of the fragile hewn disc in *Placuna placenta*; hitherto an idiosyncratic object only recorded for the early ceramic New Ireland site of Kamgot. What previously appeared to be a unique local innovation (Szabó and Summerhayes, 2002) might now be recognised as a more general form with its own spatio-temporal distribution.

Drawing all of these strands together it is clear that: (1) the Tanamu 1 preceramic worked shell assemblage sits comfortably within what we know of preceramic shell-working across the wider Circum-New Guinea Archipelago; (2) some elements of the Tanamu 1 assemblage group most comfortably with Circum-New Guinea Archipelago sites in the west and northwest (e.g. *Nautilus* working), while other elements align more closely with Circum-New Guinea Archipelago traditions of the northeast (e.g. *Rochia* ring production); (3) further elements have no known relationship at all to other preceramic Circum-New Guinea Archipelago assemblages, but instead link strongly with later northeasterly ceramic traditions (e.g. *Conus* adze and *P. placenta* disc production). These various threads of connection in different directions tell us a variety of things. First, although shared traditions in shell-working can be observed across the preceramic Circum-New Guinea Archipelago, they are not homogeneous. Indeed, even when similar traditions are manifest in different areas, the intensity of expression can differ markedly. Such is the case with the focus on *Oliva* and *Nautilus* bead production in Timor-Leste as opposed to the low-level occurrences of the working of these materials in the Bismarcks and northern Solomons, with an inverse geographical case relating to *Rochia* rings. Secondly, the complete absence of *Conus* adzes and *P. placenta* discs elsewhere in the broader regional preceramic record strongly suggests a connection with later-emergent ceramic-associated traditions to the northeast. Both materials are uncommon in preceramic shell-working, and both forms and associated working techniques are prescriptive and distinctive. This implies that coastal southeast New Guinea is directly, or indirectly, linked to later ceramic traditions in the Bismarcks in ways we do not yet understand.

The Circum-New Guinea Archipelago as a tool for thinking

When Heinsohn mapped out the long and complex history of human-mediated animal translocations ('ethnophoresy' in Heinsohn's terminology) from and between the islands surrounding the landmass of New Guinea (2001; 2003), he implicitly did much more than establish a new important ecological mechanism for faunal dispersal. He demonstrated a widespread shared tradition of human mobility and the movement of economic – and sometimes non-economic – goods of considerable longevity. He showed that there was clear knowledge of landscapes, their resources, and probably peoples, beyond immediate areas of residence. Furthermore, ideas of human 'adaptation' were stretched to accommodate something more akin to niche construction; right around the Circum-New Guinea Archipelago people fashioned their landscapes to suit their wants and needs. Islands were not bounded or isolated and people were not necessarily constrained by local affordances, and indeed, the 'transported landscapes' of economic plants and animals carried out into Remote Oceania can be viewed as a later extension of these approaches (Kirch, 1982). These observations grounded in the nature of animal translocations also have repercussions for shell-working: with a profusion of potential raw materials available, convergences between assemblages in terms of raw materials, technologies and morphologies are rarely likely to be coincidental.

Methodologically, Heinsohn more explicitly did two key things: (1) he started with a mapping out of the evidence, and (2) he dissolved the *a priori* modern boundary between 'Southeast Asia' and 'Melanesia'. The consideration of the Tanamu 1 preceramic worked shell here demonstrates that there is merit in taking a similar approach. There are clearly lines of connection between Caution Bay and other locales around the Circum-New Guinea Archipelago – whether Ancestral (homology) or born of enduring interaction. The Tanamu 1 preceramic worked shell does not map onto that of any other locale precisely, but draws on elements of several to produce a distinctive composite. More than that, it also connects forward in time through highly specific artefacts to link into the earliest ceramic-bearing assemblages of the Bismarck Archipelago.

At present there are too many gaps, both chronologically and geographically, to say how different locales may be connected with each other at different points in time. But Tanamu 1 and associated sites in Caution Bay ought to reorient long-standing debates by enfolding the south coast of New Guinea not simply as a receiver of culture from elsewhere, but as a node of importance in the Circum-New Guinea Archipelago.

Epilogue

At a recent conference of the Australian Archaeological Association, an Australian archaeologist was overheard referring to Lapita as 'Repeater' (in reference to the stagnant nature of the debate) intoned with equal parts irritability and despair. Indeed, upon rereading Allen and Gosden (1996), the structure of the debate about 'Lapita origins' still seems very familiar. Additional material has been infused and chronologies have been refined, arguments have become more detailed and nuanced (e.g. Specht et al., 2014), but the structure of the discussions is largely the same. An attempt was made here to take on the challenge laid down by Allen and Gosden (1996) and Torrence and Swadling's (2008) data-driven analyses incorporating the New Guinea mainland and islands, and to try to see past the bounded nature of the geographical categories that frame our questions; the precocious presence and nature of the Caution Bay preceramic (and ceramic) assemblages help to facilitate this. Viewing the region through the lens of the Circum-New Guinea Archipelago reorients the way in which evidence is considered. There are as many ways to do this as there are ways to envision geography, but as the modern proverb says: 'if you always do what you've always done, you'll always get what you've always gotten'.

Acknowledgements

We thank the ARC Centre of Excellence for Australian Biodiversity and Heritage, the Monash Indigenous Studies Centre at Monash University, and the Department of Anthropology and Sociology at the University of Papua New Guinea, under whose auspices this research was undertaken. The analysis of the Tanamu 1 worked shell material was undertaken by Szabó as part of her Australian Research Council Future Fellowship (FT140100504) research with additional research by Claire Perrette. Brent Koppel assisted with aspects of analysis and figure preparation.

Note

1 Although the early Holocene dating of *Dorcopsis* from archaeological contexts on Halmahera and Gebe, Maluku, has been confirmed (Hull et al., 2019), they and others (e.g. O'Connor, 2015) query whether it is indeed a human translocation given the lack of Pleistocene bone assemblages. The position is maintained here, as it is in sections of Hull et al. (2019), that the absence of Pleistocene bone at Gebe Cave cannot be dismissed as a taphonomically mediated absence, as well-preserved marine shell is present throughout the Pleistocene deposits to bedrock. Unless a specific taphonomic process which eliminates bone but leaves shell unscathed can be pinpointed for the site, the absence of Pleistocene bone at Golo appears to be real, and the sudden appearance of vertebrate remains in the early Holocene is stratigraphically stark. Interestingly, the Pleistocene deposits at Leang Sarru, on the small impoverished Talaud Islands, show the same pattern of a large assemblage of marine invertebrate remains and a complete absence of bone (Tanudirjo, 2001; Ono et al., 2010).

References

Allen, J., 2003. Discovering the Pleistocene in Island Melanesia. In: C. Sand, ed. *Pacific Archaeology: Assessments and Prospects*. Nouméa: Le Cahiers de l'Archéologie en Nouvelle-Calédonie, pp. 33–42.

Allen, J. and Gosden, C., 1996. Spheres of interaction and integration: modelling the culture history of the Bismarck Archipelago. In: J. Davidson, G. Irwin, F. Leach, A. Pawley and D. Brown eds. *Oceanic Culture History: Essays in Honour of Roger Green*. Dunedin: New Zealand Journal of Archaeology Special Publication, pp. 183–197.

Allen, J., Gosden, C. and White, J.P., 1989. Human Pleistocene adaptations in the tropical island Pacific: recent evidence from New Ireland, a Greater Australian outlier. *Antiquity*, 63, pp. 548–561.

Bellwood, P., Nitihaminoto, G., Irwin, G., Gunadi, Waluyo, A. and Tanudirjo, D., 1998. 35,000 years of prehistory in the Northern Moluccas. In: G.-J. Bartstra (ed.), *Bird's Head Approaches: Irian Jaya Studies, A Programme for Interdisciplinary Research*, Modern Quaternary Research in Southeast Asia 15. Rotterdam: Balkema, pp. 233–275.

Bellwood, P. 2006. The early movements of Austronesian-speaking peoples in the Indonesian region. In: T. Simanjuntak, I.H.E. Pojoh and M. Hisyam, eds. *Austronesian Diaspora and the Ethnogenesis of People in the Indonesian Archipelago*. Jakarta: Indonesian Institute of Sciences, International Center for Prehistoric an Austronesian Studies, Indonesian National Committee for UNESCO, pp. 61–82.

David, B., McNiven, I.J., Richards, T., Connaughton, S.P., Leavesley, M., Barker, B. and Rowe, C., 2011. Lapita sites in the Central Province of mainland Papua New Guinea. *World Archaeology*, 43, pp. 576–593.

David, B., Szabó, K., Ash, J. and McNiven, I.J. eds. In prep. *Lapita to Post-Lapita Transformations at Caution Bay, Papua New Guinea*. Oxford: Archaeopress.

Flannery, T., Bellwood, P., White, J.P., Ennis, T., Irwin, G., Schubert, K. and Balasubramaniam, S., 1998. Mammals from Holocene archaeological deposits on Gebe and Morotai Islands, Northern Moluccas, Indonesia. *Australian Mammalogy*, 20, pp. 391–400.

Fox, R., 1970. *The Tabon Caves*. Manila: National Museum of the Philippines.

Glover, I., 1986. *Archaeology in Eastern Timor, 1966–67*. Canberra: Research School of Pacific Studies, Australian National University.

Gosden . C., Webb, J., Marshall, B. and Summerhayes, G., 1994. Lolmo Cave: a mid- to late Holocene site, Arawe Islands, West New Britain Province, Papua New Guinea. *Asian Perspectives*, 33, pp. 97–119.

Green, R.C., 1991. The Lapita cultural complex: current evidence and proposed models. *Bulletin of the Indo-Pacific Prehistory Association,* 11, pp. 295–305.

Green, R.C., 2000. Lapita and the cultural model for intrusion, integration and innovation. In: A. Anderson and T. Murray, eds. *Australian Archaeologist: Collected papers in honour of Jim Allen.* Canberra: Pandanus Books, pp. 372–392.

Green, R.C., 2003. The Lapita horizon and traditions: signature for one set of oceanic migrations. In: C. Sand, ed. *Pacific Archaeology: Assessments and Prospects.* Nouméa: Les Cahiers de l'Archéologie en Nouvelle Calédonie 15, pp. 95–120.

Heinsohn, T., 2001. Human influences on vertebrate zoogeography: animal translocation and biological invasions across and to the east of Wallace's Line. In: I. Metcalfe, J.M.B. Smith, M. Morwood and I. Davidson, eds, *Faunal and Floral Migrations and Evolution in SE Asia-Australasia.* Lisse: A.A. Balkema, pp. 154–170.

Heinsohn, T., 2003. Animal translocation: long-term human influences on the vertebrate zoogeography of Australasia (natural dispersal versus ethnophoresy). *Australian Zoologist,* 32, pp. 351–376.

Heinsohn, T. and Hope, G., 2006. The Torresian connections: zoogeography of New Guinea. In: J.R. Merrick, M. Archer, G.M. Hickey and M.S.Y. Lee, eds. *Evolution and Biogeography of Australasian Vertebrates.* Oatlands: Auscipub, pp. 71–93.

Hull, J.R., Piper , P., Irwin, G., Szabó, K., Oertle , A. and Bellwood, P., 2019. Observations on the Northern Moluccan excavated animal bone and shell collections. In: *The Spice Islands in prehistory: archaeology in the Northern Moluccas, Indonesia.* Canberra: ANU Press, pp. 135–165.

Irwin, G., 2012. Some comments and questions about newly discovered Lapita sites at Caution Bay, near Port Moresby, and the implications for New Guinea prehistory. *Australian Archaeology,* 75, pp. 8–12.

Kirch, P.V., 1982. Transported landscapes. *Natural History,* 91, pp. 32–35.

Kirch, P.V., 1988. Long-distance exchange and island colonization: the Lapita case. *Norwegian Archaeological Review,* 21, pp. 103–117.

Langley, M. and O'Connor, S., 2016. An enduring shell artefact tradition from Timor-Leste: *oliva* bead production from the Pleistocene to late Holocene at Jerimalai, Lene Hara and Matja Kuru 1 and 2. *PLoS ONE,* 11, e0161071. doi: 10.137 1/journalpone. 0161071.

Langley, M., O'Connor, S. and Piotto, E., 2016. 42,000-year-old worked and pigment-stained *Nautilus* shell from Jerimalai (Timor-Leste): evidence for an early coastal adaptation in ISEA. *Journal of Human Evolution,* 97, pp. 1–16.

Li, L. and Ortiz, C., 2013. Biological design for simultaneous optical transparency and mechanical robustness in the shell of *Placuna placenta. Advanced Materials,* 25, pp. 2344–2350.

Mahirta, 2009. *Prehistoric Human Occupation on Rote and Sawu Islands, Nusa Tenggara Timur, Indonesia.* BAR International Series 1935. Oxford: Archaeopress.

McNiven, I.J., 2017. Edges of worlds: Torres Strait Islander peripheral participation in ancient globalizations. In: T. Hodos, ed. *The Routledge Handbook of Globalization and Archaeology.* New York: Routledge, pp. 319–334.

McNiven, I.J, David, B., Richards, T., Aplin, K., Asmussen, B., Mialanes, J., Leavesley, M., Faulkner, P. and Ulm, S., 2011. New direction in human colonisation of the Pacific: Lapita settlement of south coast New Guinea. *Australian Archaeology,* 72, pp. 1–6.

McNiven, I.J. and Hitchcock, G., 2004. Torres Strait Islander marine subsistence specialisation and terrestrial animal translocation. In: I.J. McNiven and M. Quinnell, eds. *Torres Strait Archaeology and Material Culture.* Memoirs of the Queensland Museum, Cultural Heritage Series 3. Brisbane: Queensland Museum, pp. 105–162.

O'Connor, S., 2006. Unpacking the Island Southeast Asian Neolithic cultural package, and finding local complexity. In: E.A. Bacus, I.C. Glover and V.C. Pigott, eds, *Uncovering Southeast Asia's Past: Selected Papers from the Tenth Biennial Conference of the European Association of Southeast Asian Archaeologists, London, 14th–17th September 2004*. Singapore: National University Press, pp. 74–87.

O'Connor, S., 2010. Continuity in Shell Artefact Production in Holocene East Timor. In: B. Bellina, E.A. Bacus, T.O. Price and J. Wisseman Christie, eds, *50 Years of Archaeology in Southeast Asia: Essays in Honour of Ian Glover*. Bangkok: River Books, pp. 218–233.

O'Connor, S., 2015. Rethinking the Neolithic in Island Southeast Asia, with particular reference to the archaeology of Timor-Leste and Sulawesi. *Archipel. Études Interdisciplinaires Sur Le Monde Insulindien*, 90, pp. 15–47.

O'Connor, S., Mahirta, Samper Carro, S.C., Hawkins, S., Kealy, S., Louys, J. and Wood, R., 2017. Fishing in life and death: Pleistocene fish-hooks from a burial context on Alor Island, Indonesia. *Antiquity*, 91, pp. 1451–1468.

Ono, R., Soegondho, S. and Yoneda, M., 2010. Changing marine exploitation during late Pleistocene in Northern Wallacea: shell remains from Leang Sarru rockshelter in Talaud Islands. *Asian Perspectives,* 48, pp. 318–341.

Parkinson, G., 2016. Establishing Traces for the Working of *Nautilus* shells in Prehistory. Unpublished BSc thesis. Wollongong, University of Wollongong.

Petchey, F., Ulm, S., David, B., McNiven, I.J., Asmussen, B., Tomkins, H., Dolby, N., Aplin, K., Richards, T., Rowe, C., Leavesley, M. and Mandui, H., 2013. High-resolution radiocarbon dating of marine materials in archaeological contexts: radiocarbon marine reservoir variability between *Anadara, Gafrarium, Batissa, Polymesoda* spp. and Echinoidea at Caution Bay, southern coastal Papua New Guinea. *Archaeological and Anthropological Sciences,* 5, pp. 69–80.

Sand, C., 2012. Comment as part of Forum: Some comments and questions about newly discovered Lapita sites at Caution Bay, near Port Moresby, and the implications for New Guinea prehistory. *Australian Archaeology,* 75, pp. 14–15.

Skelly, R.J. and David, B., 2017. *Hiri: Archaeology of Long-Distance Maritime Trade along the South Coast of Papua New Guinea*. Honolulu: University of Hawai'i Press.

Smith, A. and Allen, J., 1999. Pleistocene shell technologies: evidence from Island Melanesia. In: J. Hall and I. McNiven, eds. *Australian Coastal Archaeology*. Canberra: ANH Publications, Australian National University, pp. 291–297.

Specht, J., 2012. Caution Bay and Lapita pottery: cautionary comments. *Australian Archaeology,* 75, pp. 3–7.

Specht, J., Denham, T., Goff, J. and Terrell, J.E., 2014. Deconstructing the Lapita cultural complex of the Bismarck Archipelago. *Journal of Archaeological Research,* 22, pp. 89–140.

Spennemann, D.R., 1993. Cowrie shell tools: fact or fiction? *Archaeology in Oceania*, 28, pp. 48–49.

Spriggs, M. 1996. What is southeast Asian about Lapita? In: T. Akazawa and E. Szathmary, eds. *Prehistoric Mongoloid Dispersals*. Oxford: Oxford University Press, pp. 324–348.

Spriggs, M., 2001. How AMS dating changed my life. In: M. Jones and P. Sheppard, eds. *Australasian Connections and New Directions: Proceedings of the 7th Australasian Archaeometry Conference*. Auckland: Department of Anthropology, University of Auckland, pp. 365–374.

Spriggs, M., 2003. Chronology of the Neolithic transition in Island Southeast Asia and the Western Pacific: a view from 2003. *Review of Archaeology*, 24, pp. 57–80.

Spriggs, M., 2011. Archaeology and the Austronesian expansion: where are we now? *Antiquity,* 85, pp. 510–528.

Swadling, P., 1996. *Plumes from Paradise: Trade Cycles in Outer Southeast Asia and their Impact on New Guinea and Nearby Islands until 1920.* Boroko: Papua New Guinea National Museum in association with Coorparoo, Robert Brown & Associates Pty Ltd.

Szabó, K., 2005. Technique and Practice: Shell-Working in the Western Pacific and Island Southeast Asia. PhD dissertation. Canberra, Archaeology and Natural History, Australian National University.

Szabó, K., 2008. Shell as a raw material: mechanical properties and working techniques in the Indo-West Pacific. *Archaeofauna,* 17, pp. 125–138.

Szabó, K., 2010. Shell artefacts and shell-working in the Lapita cultural complex. *Journal of Pacific Archaeology,* 1, pp. 115–127.

Szabó, K., 2013. Identifying worked shell: a consideration of methodological issues with particular reference to Pleistocene contexts. In: G. Bailey, K. Hardy and A. Camara, eds, *Shell Energy: Mollusc Shells as Coastal Resources.* Oxford: Oxbow, pp. 277–286.

Szabó, K., and Ramirez, H., 2009. Worked shell from Leta Cave, Palawan, Philippines. *Archaeology in Oceania,* 44, pp. 150–159.

Szabó, K. and Summerhayes, G.R., 2002. Worked shell artefacts: new data from early Lapita. In: S. Bedford, C. Sand and D. Burley, eds. *Fifty Years in the Field: Essays in Honour and Celebration of Richard Shutler Jr's Archaeological Career.* Auckland: New Zealand Archaeological Association, pp. 91–100.

Szabó, K., Brumm, A., Bellwood, P., 2007. Shell artefact production at 32,000–28,000 b.p. in Island Southeast Asia: thinking across media? *Current Anthropology,* 48, pp. 701–723.

Szabó, K., Cole, F., Lloyd-Smith, L., Barker, G., Piper, P., Cameron, J. and Doherty, C., 2013. The 'Metal Age' at the Niah Caves: c.2000–500 years ago. In: G. Barker, ed. *Rainforest Foraging and Farming in Island Southeast Asia: The Archaeology of the Niah Caves, Sarawak.* Cambridge: McDonald Institute Monographs, pp. 299–340.

Tanudirjo, D. 2001. Islands in between: Prehistory of the Northeastern Indonesian Archipelago. Unpublished Ph.D. thesis. Canberra, Australian National University.

Terrell, J.E., 2004a. Island models of reticulate evolution: the 'ancient lagoons' hypothesis. In: S.M. Fitzpatrick, ed. *Voyages of Discovery: The Archaeology of Islands.* Westport, CT: Praeger, pp. 203–222.

Terrell, J.E., 2004b. The 'sleeping giant' hypothesis and New Guinea's place in the prehistory of Greater Near Oceania. *World Archaeology,* 36, pp. 601–609.

Torrence, R. and Swadling, P., 2008. Social networks and the spread of Lapita. *Antiquity,* 82, pp. 600–616.

van den Bergh, G., Meijer, H.J.M., Rokus Awe Due, Morwood, M.J., Szabó, K., van den Hoek Ostende, L.W., Sutikna, T., Saptomo, E.W., Piper, P.J., and Dobney K.M., 2009. The Liang Bua faunal remains: a 95 k.yr. sequence from Flores, east Indonesia. *Journal of Human Evolution,* 57, pp. 527–537.

Vermeij, G.J., 1993. *A Natural History of Shells.* Princeton, NJ: Princeton University Press.

White, J.P., 1972. *Ol Tumbuna.* Canberra: Department of Prehistory, Research School of Pacific Studies, Australian National University.

White, J.P., 2004. Where the wild things are: prehistoric animal translocation in the Circum-New Guinea Archipelago. In: S.M. Fitzpatrick, ed. *Voyages of Discovery: The Archaeology of Islands.* Westport, CT: Praeger, pp. 147–164.

Wickler, S., 1990. Prehistoric Melanesian exchange and interaction: recent evidence from the Northern Solomon Islands. *Asian Perspectives,* 29, pp. 135–154.

7

PACIFIC COLONISATION AS PROCESS AND PRACTICE

Tim Thomas

Introduction

The human colonisation of the Pacific hemisphere is an enduring topic of enquiry in the archaeology of the region. Archaeologists have employed a wide variety of theoretical perspectives and evidence to gain insight into the problem, combining data from the archaeological record with computer simulation, experimental replication and ethnography, and deploying explanatory models ranging from simple culture history to behavioural ecology. Although romanticism and wonder at the sheer technological feat of Pacific colonisation have inspired this interest, the subject corresponds academically to a universalist goal of locating all people in a global history of human origins. In this respect Pacific colonisation has significance as the last major chapter in the terrestrial dispersal of our species. Connected at the tail end of the eastward spread of modern humans from Africa to Sahul, this is the story of the discovery and occupation of the last remaining fragments of land. However, notwithstanding the fact that water crossings and island occupation began in the Pleistocene, the colonisation of the remote Pacific was a recent phenomenon relative to the broader trends of hominin dispersal, being tied to the late Holocene emergence of domesticated production in Southeast Asia and the New Guinea region. In its last phases it required unprecedented techno-social systems – capable of long-range seafaring, navigation and the translocation of economic plants and animals. These factors distinguish the Pacific case from the incursion of earlier foraging populations into mostly continental environments, and this has had consequences in terms of how we conceptualise its relationship to broader patterns of colonisation.

To some extent its unusual characteristics have inhibited the theoretical and methodological approaches developed in the Pacific region from making a broader contribution to the study of colonisation beyond other instances of island dispersal (e.g. the Caribbean and Mediterranean). Barton et al. (2004, p. 138), for example, argue that the limited size of Pacific islands, their biological isolation and agricultural economies, make them special cases, distinct from forager colonisations of continental ecosystems, and thus less relevant to understanding global human dispersal processes. Certainly, most Pacific islands are diminutive and open water distances are extreme, accumulating into an area far beyond the size of standard archaeological regions of interest. The late Holocene colonisation episodes underlying the spread of Austronesian languages from Taiwan to Rapa Nui, for example, covered a linear distance of 15,000 km. Projecting this in the opposite direction would traverse all of China, India, the Middle East, northern Africa, and end up in the middle of the Atlantic. There is no other landscape that exhibits such an extreme ratio of habitable to uninhabitable space, such small target environments and vast intermediate distances.

Nevertheless, extreme cases are useful because they make clearly evident the effects of relevant parameters. Despite indicating the distinctiveness of islands, Barton et al. (2004) use optimal foraging theory to describe the colonisation of Europe and the Americas as a series of discontinuous jumps between highly ranked resource patches – effectively envisioning an archipelago of insular habitats. Indeed, the same approach has been applied to the Pacific (Kennett et al., 2006; O'Connell and Allen, 2012). Perhaps unsurprisingly given the connected origins of patch choice and island colonisation modelling (MacArthur and Pianka, 1966; MacArthur and Wilson, 1967), these are controlled by some of the same variables: the structure and geographic distribution of patches/islands; their relative size, resources and productivity; their accessibility. In continental landscapes many of these variables are cryptic at archaeological scales. Patch boundaries are not objectively observable since they are classically organism-defined (Wiens, 1976), and habitat fragments are, obviously, not entirely like islands (Wiens, 1995). But, whatever the empirics, the conceptual advantage of an archipelago model is that it facilitates clarification of the factors structuring population movement beyond a null assumption of incremental growth and encroachment. Conceptual and physical archipelagos define bounded and separated places from, to and between which populations can move. Thus, far from being determined solely by isolation, islands make connection and movement visible.

These heuristic advantages suggest that Pacific island colonisation might just as well be thought of as an exemplary context as an exceptional one. The characteristic extremes of island size and distance magnify underlying processes that can be difficult to see in many archaeological contexts. This is aided by the availability of relatively recent records of island colonisation in the Pacific, providing better temporal resolution of short-term processes due to the increased precision of younger dates. In continental settings that were colonised tens of thousands of years ago it can be impossible to discriminate between competing models because archaeological dates may have probability ranges spanning several millennia (Webb, 1998). Theoretically interesting components of the colonisation process – exploration, discovery, landscape learning, economic strategy and technology – become difficult or impossible to assess.

The Pacific is certainly not immune to the issue of theoretical expectations butting up against the temporal scale of archaeological records. Nevertheless, it may be possible to leverage the improved resolution brought by recency of colonisation to better understand its parameters, and benchmark reasonable expectations for other cases. Of course, even better resolution might be provided by textual records of recent historical colonisation (e.g. Pawson and Brooking, 2013). But these usually describe colonial contexts where newcomers were able to exploit existing indigenous knowledge bases in already-human landscapes, and consequently they serve as problematic models for the deeper past. The Pacific is a better middle ground, potentially allowing us to link insights from different time scales.

Scale

The issue of scale is pertinent because colonisation is an emergent phenomenon. Local-scale mobility decisions, based on fine-grained social, ecological and technological relationships, accumulate into the broader patterns of dispersal. Larger scale environmental parameters, geographic characteristics and demography provide boundary conditions shaping the emergence of these patterns. The Pacific is one of the few archaeological contexts where relevant ethnographic-scale information is available for its more recently settled parts (Cachola-Abad, 1993; Anderson, 2014; Walter and Reilly, 2018), sitting alongside rich archaeological data from first-settlement sites (Kirch, 2017, pp. 59, 82, 85–86, 201), large radiocarbon date databases (Wilmshurst et al., 2011a), and region-wide information on the environmental and technological parameters of travel (Irwin, 1992; Howe, 2006). Consequently, the Pacific is well-positioned as a context for the development of approaches to colonisation capable of theorising the phenomenon at multiple scales. In doing so, however, it will be important to be explicit about the target scale of explanations. This issue has not always been acknowledged or recognised by archaeologists working in the region.

Hypotheses about the impetus of colonising journeys, for example, often invoke at least three scales: an event-oriented focus on motivated individuals, such as visionary chiefs (Walter et al., 2017) or religious exiles (Anderson, 2006); a broader socio-cultural emphasis invoking cultural practice, technological innovation and politics (Irwin, 2008; Bellwood, 1996; Thomas, 2001); and a focus on the role of universal motive powers such as demography, ecological relationships and climatic variation (Bellwood, 2004; Kennett et al., 2006; Goodwin et al., 2014). But rather than seeing these as targeting different aspects of the phenomenon, it is more common to regard them as competing hypotheses. In a recent example, Bell et al. (2015) use Bayesian model selection to test four such hypotheses, comparing their fit to the colonisation dates of twenty-four pooled island groups. But the hypotheses in question do not all seek to explain the pan-Pacific order of colonisation: they range from archipelago accessibility measures (a good fit), to the presence/absence of social hierarchy in the recent past (a poor fit).

An alternative strategy adopted by some Pacific archaeologists is to categorise explanations according to evolutionary biologist Ernst Mayr's (1961) distinction between proximate and ultimate causes (Aswani and Graves, 1998; Kirch, 2010, p. 178; Cochrane, 2018, p. 524). Mayr considered these to be fundamentally different, rather than competing, explanatory targets. Proximate explanations explore how synchronic systems function, illuminating the physiological, social, environmental or other triggers of observed behaviour. Ultimate explanations, on the other hand, pursue why a given behaviour or system emerged at all, and thus focus on long-term evolutionary processes. The distinction usefully offers a framework for evaluating whether different explanations are true alternatives, or whether they simply address phenomena at different scales. But it also recalls long-standing debates in archaeology over the relative role and value of particularism and universalism, and similarly brings up questions of how explanatory scales relate to each other and whether they are of equal power. In biological convention there is an asymmetry to the distinction: evolution explains the existence of proximate drivers, but the reverse is untrue. For Mayr and other evolutionary biologists, this justified a focus on ultimate causes. Recently, this has been challenged by claims that some proximate processes can have evolutionary effects, and that this is particularly the case in the context of cultural evolution where proximate processes generating and reproducing variation create historical patterns that are not simply the result of differences in inclusive fitness (Laland et al., 2011, pp. 1514–1515; Sterelny, 2013). Indeed, because there are no pre-specified mechanical links between the performance of cultural traits and their reproduction, selection cannot usually be understood without reference to proximate socio-cultural factors. In these cases of 'reciprocal causation' the standard biological model could lead us to miss the systemic interplay of causal scales.

Allowing for reciprocal causation also helps avoid the tendency of particularising and universalising explanations to, respectively, over- and underdetermine a given case. Or, put differently, if Pacific colonisation is explained only at the scale of contingent historical events, we can be blind to general processes and seek to explain even the universal with the myriad particular. Alternatively, addressing the Pacific case solely at the scale of the universal would render it an eccentric example of transhistorical principles that explain all cases of organism dispersal, applying equally to sycamore trees and cane toads. The former renders history as a chaotic assortment of events, the latter drains historical phenomena of their socio-cultural particularity, outlining the necessary but being never sufficient. It is better to be inclusive in explanatory scope, since a fuller understanding of colonisation will come from tacking between scales, rather than diversification into distinct explanatory projects.

Defining colonisation

Before turning to a review of various explanatory strategies, it is worth considering how differences in conceptualisation of the domain of study may be responsible for differences of approach. Some evidence of this is suggested by the variable terminology used to characterise the phenomena in question: dispersal, migration, settlement, colonisation and so on. Often these terms are used nearly interchangeably, but they imply a variety of operations at different temporal and spatial scales, cover domains ranging from the political to the biological, and can refer to the actions of individuals, groups or entire populations. Efforts to define terms, such as Gamble's (1993, p. 7) distinction between migration as a short-time-scale event and colonisation as a longer term process, have not been widely adopted in the Pacific. Thus, where Walter et al., (2017) consider migration as a planned event, Cochrane (2018) considers migration an evolutionary-scale process.

Insofar as explicit frameworks and attendant terminologies have developed this has been in reference to culture-historical debates about the chronology of human arrival on islands, and whether this has detectable phases. Graves and Addison (1995), for example, argued that the 'discovery' of a novel island during an exploration phase could be modelled as being distinct from 'colonisation' or placement of settlements, and the subsequent 'establishment' of a long-term population. The goal was to define more or less archaeologically visible components of an incremental 'settlement process', thus providing a framework for the interpretation of radiocarbon date distributions (see also Irwin, 1992; Anderson, 1995). This view has subsequently been widely adopted, although the epistemological value of an early, largely invisible, discovery or exploration phase is still debated, since it is not falsifiable (Wilmshurst et al., 2011b). Migration is sometimes integrated into this framework as a term bracketing the transport phase of a settlement process, rather than as an ongoing form of human behaviour. Thus, Anderson and O'Connor (2008, p. 2) suggest we regard 'migration and colonisation' as 'the mobile and relatively sessile phases respectively of ... human settlement in oceanic landscapes'. This tracks the incrementalism of Graves and Addison's model, envisaging a settlement process in which populations become increasingly fixed in place, passing through phases to do so (see also Thomas, 2008, p. 102). Such models thus retain a chronological motivation and blend the accrual of the archaeological record with theorisation of the process in question.

Here I advocate a much broader view. Rather than being an occupation or sessile phase in a regional settlement process, colonisation is a long-term phenomenon encompassing most aspects of human–environment interactions. Colonisation is, at root, the process by which historical relationships are established between people and landscapes, and consequently involves the interaction of ecological, demographic, social, political and cultural dynamics through time. These interactions govern migration in the first place, as well as subsequent settlement and migratory behaviours, and hence they are encompassed in this same process. The arrival of people in novel environments is often framed as adaptation or 'landscape learning' (Rockman and Steele, 2003), but this clearly iterates through time – it involves continual adjustments whose tempo and effects depend on ecological interactions with subsistence needs, cultural traditions, demographic change, climate shifts (Anderson, 2013, pp. 72–73), and the flexibility of technological organisation (Nelson, 1991). These relationships define a taskscape (Ingold, 1993) influencing initial degrees of mobility and aggregation and patterns of resource use in a new landscape, but they are necessarily ongoing and have a history – they do not simply begin when people arrive and end when populations are permanently established. Indeed, the influx of people into a landscape may continue, although archaeological evidence of this is usually conceptualised as interaction. Equally, locations need not have permanent or settled populations to be colonised, since all landscapes have areas occasionally or seldom visited but still known, culturally evaluated, named and claimed as part of a territory. As such, colonisation is also about the formation of cultural ideas about landscapes, including the perception of space and distance during techno-social activity, and relations of knowledge and power. The political dimensions of colonisation include the role of power in structuring travel and access, and the development of ideological arguments connecting people to places. These ultimately serve to govern resources by establishing and maintaining territorial ranges and rights. By acknowledging these political components of colonisation, we are better able to make sense of local oral histories and origin narratives and their relationship to placemaking as well as to past events. Moreover, phenomena such as imperialism and colonialism (Gosden, 2004) become intelligible within the same analytical framework since they include the same recursive socio-political, cultural and ecological aspects of placemaking (Pawson and Brooking, 2013).

Conceptualised in this way, colonisation research becomes a framework for the study of landscape production, amenable to analysis at multiple scales with a variety of evidence types. It can certainly be about overarching processes governing population dispersal over long time scales, but it can also pay attention to the fine-grained processes by which people establish and maintain durable ties to place (e.g. Thomas et al., 2001). Moreover, such a framework facilitates our ability to properly understand the role and implications of archaeological accounts of colonisation in contemporary placemaking. Rather than simply provisioning data for modern political debates, archaeology can contribute to an understanding of how and why such debates occur (e.g. Thomas, 2009).

I return to these issues in the conclusion, but for most of this chapter focus on reviewing the dominant explanatory strategies in Pacific colonisation research. My primary theoretical goal is to advocate for a multi-scalar approach, integrating long-term process with socio-cultural practice.

Biogeographical perspectives

Because Pacific colonisation is a part of global human dispersal some of its characteristics conform broadly to patterns common to all species dispersals. Biological models have consequently featured prominently in archaeological explanations in the region. The best-known example is the important influence of MacArthur and Wilson's (1967) theory of island biogeography. Initially put to use by archaeologists working in the Solomon Islands (Irwin, 1973; Terrell, 1977; also a crucial field-site in the development of biogeography: Mayr, 1943), it was quickly integrated into colonisation research (Diamond, 1977; Keegan and Diamond, 1987; Terrell, 1986; Irwin, 1992).

MacArthur and Wilson provided an equilibrium theory whereby species richness on islands was modelled as a function of extinction rate versus immigration rate. Extinction rate was predicted to be correlated with island area, because larger islands provide a buffer against environmental risks and have more diverse habitats. Immigration rate was predicted to be correlated with the distance of islands from sources of dispersing individuals or propagules. Hence larger islands closer to continents have more diverse biota, and each subsequent sea barrier further reduces the biota of the next island. Consequently, geographic configuration, or island stepping-stone patterns, were also considered to be important.

In the Pacific the theory successfully predicts an isolation-related decline in environmental diversity from west to east, as islands become progressively smaller and further apart. This pattern and the variables of distance and size continue to influence the way archaeologists think about colonisation geography. For example, Green's (1991) influential framework identifies three biogeographic boundaries relevant to the timing of colonisation: (1) the Huxley-Wallace Line, defining the edge of the pre-Holocene continental landmass, and first crossed over 45,000 years ago; (2) Near/Remote Oceania, defining the boundary beyond which islands are no longer inter-visible, and crossed 3,000 years ago; and (3) the edge of the Pacific plate (or 'Andesite Line', marked most clearly by the Tonga trench), beyond which only non-continental, oceanic islands occur, and crossed 1,000 years ago. Each boundary is more severe in its environmental effects and required significant changes in subsistence strategies and seafaring technology (Green, 1991, pp. 496–499).

This west–east geographic configuration led Keegan and Diamond (1987) to argue that the Pacific was colonised by 'autocatalysis' – effectively a risk-reward system whereby the gradual increase in inter-island distances eastward shaped an expectation of always finding more islands and shifted perceptions of risk. In the remote Pacific archipelagos are consistently arranged on a northwest-southeast axis, perhaps also encouraging predictive journeys (Anderson, 2003, pp. 174–175). The role of broader island configuration effects is also apparent in Irwin's (1989, p. 168) idea of a 'voyaging nursery' in Near Oceania, where close islands in a region of predictable wind patterns and protection from cyclones provided relatively risk-free conditions for the development of seagoing skills. Irwin's (1992) model of subsequent search-and-return exploration and colonisation voyaging used derivations of inter-island distances and island sizes as key variables in determining the order of island discovery, as well as predicting subsequent degrees of interaction or abandonment. Inter-island distances alone had long been recognised as a key variable in colonisation timing (Biggs, 1972).

Comparing the spatial configuration of islands to the radiocarbon record of colonisation does suggest a strong relationship. As shown by the minimum spanning tree in Fig. 7.1, a path connecting every island in the Pacific by the shortest route effectively models stepping-stone distances from a source region in the west and approximates the archaeologically dated order of human arrival (Fig. 7.2). The mean and maximum branch lengths in regions defined by Green's (1991) biogeographic zones increase dramatically from west to east, suggesting there is also a

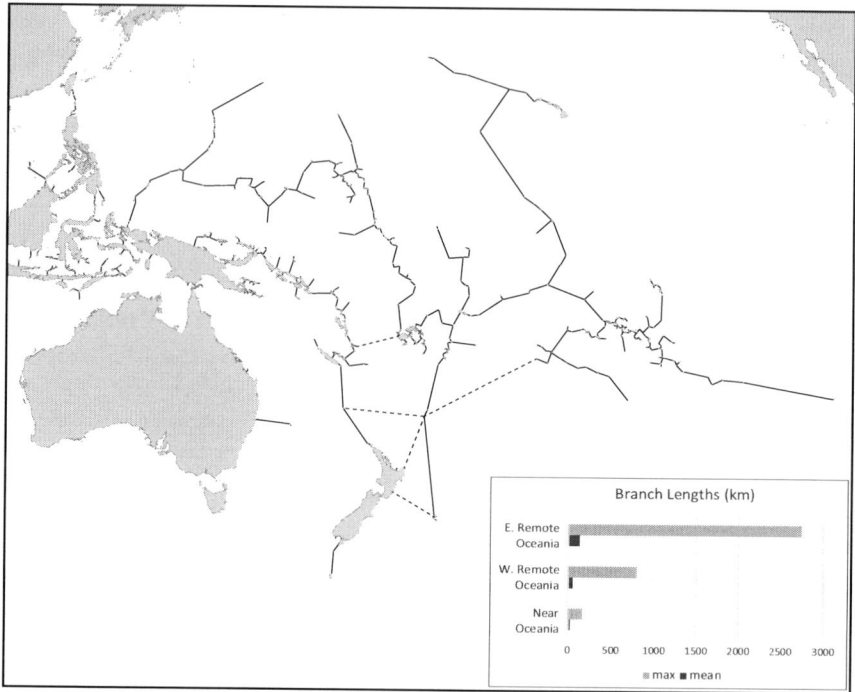

FIGURE 7.1 Minimum spanning tree connecting Pacific Islands >5 ha. Dotted lines indicate archaeologically likely colonisation pathways incompatible with computed tree. Tree calculated using Prim's algorithm in ArcGIS, from coastlines reduced to points at 5 km intervals.

strong relationship between timing and inter-island distances. There are some notable anomalies, however. The Fiji-Tonga-Samoa region was colonised during the Lapita expansion, from the Southeast Solomons–Vanuatu chain of islands, rather than via a stepping-stone route through Micronesia. This might be explained by other environmental factors: a mid-Holocene sea-level highstand meant that many low atolls across Micronesia were not habitable during the relevant period, and some not until as late as AD 1200 (Dickinson, 2004). The Polynesian Outlier communities on atolls immediately north of the Solomon Islands are another anomaly, but again late emergence, and late development of the techno-social adaptations to atoll environments, may be a factor. New Zealand, the Kermadecs and the Chatham Islands were colonised from central East Polynesia, rather than New Caledonia or Tonga. The proximity of New Zealand to New Caledonia (via Norfolk Island) has been often noted, but its much later colonisation date is usually explained by the fact that reaching New Zealand meant crossing new weather thresholds (Irwin, 1989, p. 185) with different wind patterns and sub-tropical to temperate climates.

Distance from source is a coarse measure of accessibility. As the anomalies indicate, other environmental factors have relevance, and these interact with modes

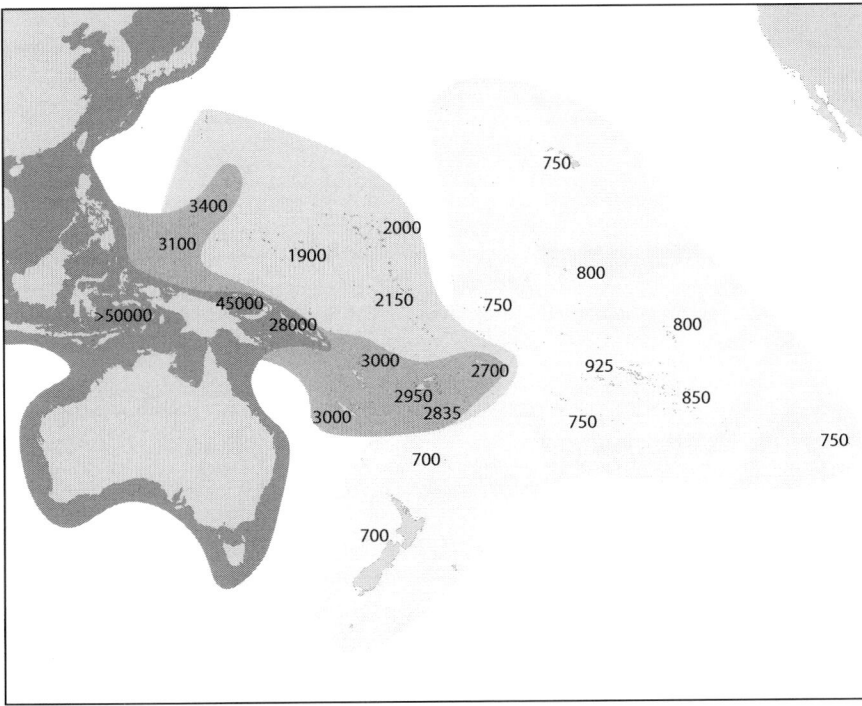

FIGURE 7.2 Pacific colonisation episodes. Simplified date estimates (cal BP) are shown (i.e. probabilities generally range several hundred years either side of date shown: see Reith and Cochrane, 2018, for recent discussion).

and technologies of travel. Irwin (2008) argues that the target angle presented by an island and the amount of sea surrounding it are measures more relevant to timing because they reflect variables in the task of island discovery voyaging. These measures are a function of island size, height and nearest-neighbour distances, which are all highly correlated in the region and follow the familiar west–east trend (Thomas, 2008).

Wind patterns and the direction of ocean currents are another important factor (Finney, 1985). Usually incorporated as deterministic variables in simulation modelling for weighing the likelihood of colonisation by drift (Levison et al., 1973) or for assessing viable sailing routes (Irwin, 1992; Montenegro et al., 2016), these are also important modifiers of distance for sail-driven craft. Trade winds in the central Pacific prevail from east to west (south-easterlies mostly), as do the major ocean currents – against the general direction of colonisation. Although Pacific sailing canoes could probably make headway up to 75° off the wind, the resulting path to an upwind target would require shallow (<15°) tacking, thus increasing the distance/time travelled by a factor of about four, only exacerbated by oppositional current flow (Finney, 1985, p. 10). Periodic reversals of the prevailing winds facilitating downwind eastward travel do occur however, particularly in the southern summer. In the South Pacific Convergence Zone, northerly and southerly winds occur in winter conditions with regular passing troughs, so that a canoe reaching across the wind can also make eastward progress (Finney et al., 1989). Nevertheless, in some regions certain routes between islands were only viable a few weeks of the year or necessitated lengthy and circuitous paths (Lewis, 1994).

Efforts to determine whether differential sailing conditions had any effect on the pace or order of colonisation indicate an important hurdle to reach islands east of Tonga-Samoa (Di Piazza et al., 2007; Montenegro et al., 2014). Di Piazza (2014) presents an innovative anamorphic map of the islands surrounding Samoa transformed from geographic coordinates to indicate sailing time, reflecting the fact that Pacific voyagers did not measure their world in Cartesian space but experienced it in terms of time and effort (Eckstein and Schwarz, 2019, pp. 36–37). Analysis indicates a pattern of increasing wind effect the longer the journey, particularly lengthening, and thus slowing, eastward travel. This pattern is true of wind-mediated accessibility across the wider Pacific, which again has cumulative effects from west to east (Weigelt and Kreft, 2013).

Early invocations of the above biogeographic parameters assumed constant propagation of colonists, such that success at reaching targets was paced only by external parameters interacting with the mode of travel (Irwin, 1992). As such they explained the relative order of island colonisation quite well, albeit with some anomalies. However, it is now apparent that they perform less well in explaining the tempo of colonisation, which was not constant. Re-evaluation of Pacific colonisation chronologies has demonstrated that eastward progress was extremely episodic (Fig. 7.2), with rapid expansions through, and long pauses at the edges of, the major biogeographic zones (Anderson, 2001).

Attempts to explain this within the parameters of seafaring technology and wind patterns suggest that longer term climate variations modulated periods of increased eastward voyaging, by changing the frequency of events such as the El Niño-Southern Oscillation (ENSO), which can weaken or reverse trade winds (Finney, 1985). Anderson et al. (2006) note that proxy reconstructions of centennial-scale increases in paleo-ENSO frequency compare tolerably well with the radiocarbon chronology of colonisation pulse periods. However, ENSO trade wind reversals mostly extend only as far as Fiji or travel northward to the equator. Moreover, the proxy records cited by Anderson et al. are no longer considered reliable, and alternatives are inconsistent in terms of both variance and timing (Schneider et al., 2018; Lu et al., 2018). Downwind routes into South Polynesia have also been proposed from modelled wind fields associated with the Medieval Climate Anomaly, again corresponding to some interpretations of colonisation date-ranges (Goodwin et al., 2014).

Although it is reasonable that long-term climate shifts periodically raised the floor of island accessibility, this does not explain colonisation pauses since favourable periods also occurred when no further eastward expansion took place (e.g. Anderson et al., 2006, fig. 3). Consequently, the data are better suited to an argument that eastward colonisation did not *require* upwind capabilities (Anderson,

2018, p. 487). But irrespective of whether canoes sailed to windward or not, multiple weather systems were crossed during colonisation episodes – particularly in the last major pulse, which saw voyages westward to the Polynesian Outliers, north to Hawaii, southwest to New Zealand and its outlying islands, as well as southeast through central East Polynesia to Rapa Nui and beyond. Post-colonisation interaction occurred in countervailing directions whatever the long-term wind frequency shifts (Allen, 2014; Rolett et al., 2015; Weisler and Walter, 2016). This multi-directional seafaring is better envisaged as being reliant on annual and decadal-scale surface wind variations than climate induced centennial-scale changes in directional frequency.

This still leaves the possibility that there was some punctuated sequence of technological development in voyaging canoes or practice governing temporal staging. The matter is subject to ongoing debate, and differences in assessment of the performance characteristics of ancient canoes generally derive from varying standards and weighting of evidence (Anderson, 2000; 2008; 2018; Finney, 2008; Irwin, 2008). Theoretically, they rely on phylogenetic and diffusionist inferences from ethnohistorical observations, as well as experimental and simulation data. Some evidence of west-to-east technological innovation is apparent, such as the advent of larger double-hull canoes with better performing hydrodynamics in Polynesia (Irwin and Flay, 2015), but ethnohistorical distribution patterns appear to be as much structured by environment and task-orientation as colonisation sequence (Beheim and Bell, 2011). Very occasional archaeological canoe finds support the notion that sophisticated voyaging canoes were in use in locations that lacked them at European contact (Johns et al., 2014), suggesting late period canoes are not a good model for the past. Again, this indicates a labile technology driven by use-context.

Demography and ecology

The base biogeographical parameters of island spatial configuration and travel conditions are thus not quite enough to sufficiently explain episodic colonisation. However, a consideration of the underlying demographic dynamics of range shifts may help. Most dispersals, whether at the species or community scale, have an episodic character, following a typical cycle of expansion, adaptation and retreat (Diamond, 1977). Despite its risks and costs, development of the ability and propensity to disperse is ubiquitous across organisms because it reduces population density related competition and inbreeding, mitigates against environmental stochasticity and provides access to new resources. Species dispersal is consequently always favoured over the long term and occurs up to the limits of available travel mechanisms and the distribution of viable habitats. An additional limiting factor is population feasibility at the frontier – a function of enough conspecifics being able to reach the same location and reproductive rates (i.e. Allee effects). Demographic density across the range thus influences the onset and cessation of colonisation episodes.

Demographic drivers of expansion have long been considered important in Pacific archaeology, chiefly in accounting for the distribution of Austronesian-speaking peoples. Bellwood (2013, pp. 178–209), particularly, argues for regional dispersal driven by a demographic transition in mainland China, resulting from adoption of food production and other Neolithic cultural attributes. The Lapita cultural complex in the Bismarck Archipelago is conventionally seen as the archaeological signature of this Neolithic expansion reaching the Pacific (Spriggs, 1997). However, insofar as this is a population growth or 'wave of advance' model, it is considered a poor fit for the rapid, punctuated colonisation of the islands of Remote Oceania (Green, 1982). Here the dispersal front is thought to have swept through the range ahead of any sequential filling-up of islands. In describing the Lapita case, Anderson (2001) notes that the spatial and temporal distribution of habitation sites implies a dual-phase process – a stable, sedentary phase in Near Oceania, where sites increased slowly and were occupied for longer, followed by an unstable, highly mobile phase during expansion into Remote Oceania, where sites increased rapidly, but were smaller and occupied for shorter periods. The same pattern probably repeats in Polynesia (Anderson, 2001, p. 21).

In explaining the difference, Anderson proposes that the initial stable phase involved slower, logistic population growth and aggregation towards carrying capacity prior to initiation of dispersal. In the Lapita case this may have been due to colonists arriving into an already populated Bismarck Archipelago, and thus experiencing space competition. In contrast, the later unstable phase involved expansion into unoccupied islands. Low densities there promoted exponential population growth and continued dispersal initiating at the first hint of resource stress, usually due to depletion of easily captured wild foods. These are labelled K-type and A-type dispersal respectively, using Keegan's (1995) behavioural–demographic version of MacArthur and Wilson's (1967) proposed continuum between density–regulated (K-selected) and non–density–regulated (r-selected) biological reproductive strategies (see also Kirch, 1984, pp. 86–87, 104–111).

We can expand on this a little here to identify the evolutionary processes usually thought to underlie these alternatives. Under density–regulated conditions life-history and ecological strategies that maximise carrying capacity (K) are favoured, promoting traits that enhance competition (e.g. long-term care of young, intensification of food production, defence of territory, etc.). When dispersal occurs different, density-independent, conditions prevail at the frontier – favouring strategies that maximise resource capture and benefit early arrivals, promoting fast population growth rates (r) and continued dispersal. Thus, a colonisation front (Fig. 7.3) can be thought of as a gradient between K-selective and r-selective environments (Phillips et al., 2010, p. 1620). Under the standard evolutionary model, the ultimate driver here is natural selection for lifetime reproductive success: over time different density conditions regulate the evolution of different reproduction-maximising strategies. However, this is not a viable cause of rapid, and relatively short-term, range expansions by species with long generational lengths, such as is the case for

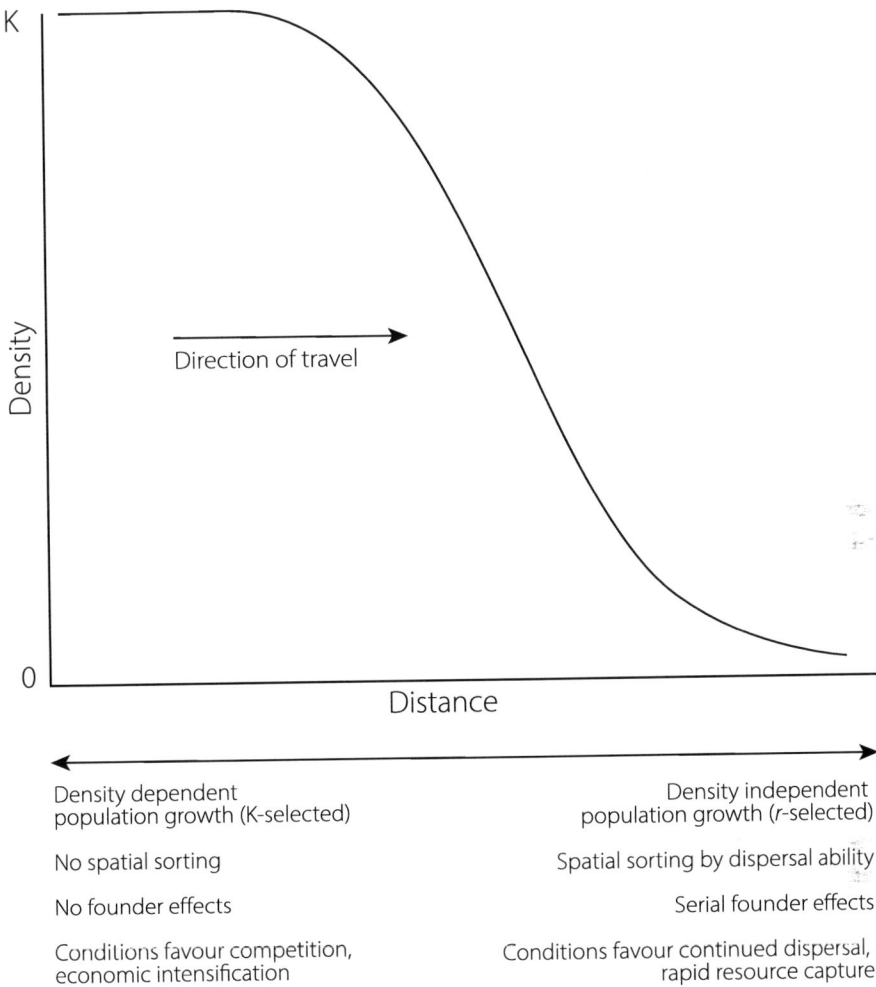

FIGURE 7.3 A colonisation dispersal front modelled as a gradient between K and r-selective sociodemographic environments.

human colonisation pulses in the Pacific. So, the model is generalised in cultural (Kirch, 1984, p. 86) or behavioural ecological (Anderson, 2001) terms: by assuming that similar patterns emerge when cultural/individual choices balance prevailing costs and rewards.

Rapid expansion is problematic for biologists too, and some have proposed that spatial sorting can operate to promote fast dispersal pulses irrespective of reproductive success (Shine et al., 2011). Given that the furthest edge of an expanding front must be populated by the most effective dispersers, high-performing variants of dispersal traits (e.g. body-types, or canoes and seafaring know-how in our case) are depleted at the core and concentrated at the frontier with every migrant's journey.

The more difficult the journey the stronger the sorting. During each successive advance further spatial sorting promotes the very traits that drive expansion, and it rapidly becomes a runaway process (Phillips et al., 2010). In biology the effect is sustained by assortive mating (sometimes called the 'Olympic village effect'), but it is also viable under cultural reproduction – island communities solely made up of successful seafarers are more likely to sustain and refine seafaring (see below). Spatial sorting is thus an alternative to temporal sorting (natural selection) in promoting rapid colonisation pulses.

Whatever the underlying mechanism, the Anderson/Keegan A-type (r-selected) dispersal model predicts colonisation occurring at increasing rates and in quite irregular spatial leaps, followed by slower, shorter distance backfilling. This irregularity is particularly evident during Lapita expansion into Remote Oceania (Sheppard, 2011), and perhaps follows a Lévy flight pattern typical of foraging behaviour (Lilley, 2008). Partly because of this, early archaeological accounts suggested Remote Oceanic colonists may have had an r-selected 'supertramp' or 'strandlooper' economy – skimming easily captured pristine and naïve wild food resources on the coasts of islands, until serial depletion necessitated a shift to terrestrial economies (Groube, 1971; Diamond, 1977; Clark and Terrell, 1978). Most early sites do show reliance on littoral zone food, but there is now abundant evidence of food production and domesticated animals, reducing the question to a matter of emphasis in contrast to later periods (Davidson and Leach, 2001; Horrocks and Bedford, 2005; Kinaston et al., 2014; Burley et al., 2018). Indeed, the colonisation of Remote Oceania is coincident with increased transition to food production in the region and was only sustainable due to the transport of domesticates to depauperate islands. Such niche construction was also likely a buffer for environmental unfamiliarity and uncertainty in novel environments. The foraging model works best in marginal habitats where food production is problematic, and it has been particularly useful in New Zealand where the early non-horticultural southern South Island had higher density sites and faster growing populations due to initial foraging success and increased mobility (Anderson, 2013; Brown and Crema, 2019).

Nevertheless, subsequent work drawing on this framework continues to emphasise resource distribution as a key factor in promoting rapid colonisation pulses. Patch choice models, for example, have been used to examine the arrival of foraging populations in Pleistocene Sahul (O'Connell and Allen, 2012) as well as food-producing horticulturalists in the wider Pacific (Kennett et al., 2006). These studies assume that dispersal results from conscious and continuing risk assessment of the density-dependent costs of either remaining in place and competing for resources or shifting to new habitat patches. Dispersal can thus occur long before carrying-capacity is reached, since the latter is not absolute, but rather a matter of changing system properties and perceptions. As well as habitat quality, various cultural interventions modify costs and risks, including the potential for technological innovations, social and political competition, and despotic behaviours (Kennett and Winterhalder, 2008). Under these parameters, patches are ranked, and this should be reflected in the chronological sequence of occupation and subsequent demographic distribution: higher-ranked habitats would be occupied earlier and develop larger populations than marginal habitats. The cumulative effect of ranking might tend towards an Ideal Free Distribution, an equilibrium state where no one has incentive to relocate (Kennett et al., 2006, pp. 269–270).

If islands themselves are considered patches there is some indication of ranking in the colonisation process. In Remote Oceania the leading edge of colonisation proceeded rapidly across the range, ahead of infilling moves to more ecologically marginal islands. Within archipelagos, larger resource-rich islands were occupied first. This is best documented in Tonga, where the earliest Lapita colonists occupied Tongatapu prior to a staged expansion to the smaller central and northern islands seventy to ninety years later (Burley et al., 2015). Most of the earliest East Polynesian sites are also found on the larger islands of archipelagos. Thomas (2008) argues that most East Polynesian islands have habitats only equivalent to the more marginal islands of the Western Pacific, potentially inhibiting their colonisation until after the latter had been occupied and feasible (or more generalist) subsistence strategies developed. Unfamiliar environments might thus produce friction slowing the pace of colonisation, whereas familiar environments might facilitate progress (e.g. Grollemund et al., 2015).

However, an obvious problem for a patch choice model in an island colonising context is that patch ranking depends on comparative environmental knowledge, and as such can only occur after discovery and familiarity is developed. Modelling has shown that lack of environmental knowledge, or foresight, can itself promote increased dispersal rates because colonists do not understand how to make deep use of available resources, whereas comprehensive knowledge promotes aggregation in choice locations (Wren et al., 2014). In contrast to evidence that larger, resource-rich islands attracted earlier colonisation, it is also the case that many extremely marginal and isolated islands in the Remote Pacific were colonised. The so-called 'Mystery Islands' are good examples – small, remote islands with poor resources that had populations during early expansion phases but were subsequently abandoned (Irwin, 1992, pp. 176–180). On the one hand this might reflect initial habitat choices being inevitably focused on short-term competitive benefits rather than long-term foresight, but it may also reflect a situation in which the context of colonisation voyaging flattened evaluation of relocation costs to invariance beyond the known horizon (Kennett et al., 2006, p. 272). When search costs are extremely high, ranking decisions could reduce to a binary evaluation of whether or not discovered land is considered habitable. Patch choice models reach their limit in such circumstances.

The Mystery Islands do, however, conform to expectations of A-type dispersal, since this will tend to produce hyper-dispersers who run ahead into unsustainable territory, initiating the retreat phase of colonisation cycles noted by Diamond (1977). During the Lapita expansion, this limit may have been reached in Samoa, where a single Lapita deposit and a handful of immediately post-Lapita plainware sites indicates a sparse founding population and possible period of abandonment

(Addison and Morrison, 2010). Cochrane (2018, p. 543) proposes that environmental unsuitability and the Allee effect may have reduced viability on this remote frontier. The extremities of East Polynesian colonisation exhibit similar characteristics: the Hawaiian chain to the north, the Pitcairn group to the east, New Zealand to the south and Norfolk to the west, all show signs of retreat at the margins. Henderson Island is a well-documented case of a resource-poor island that sustained a community only insofar as social and economic support was maintained with neighbouring Mangareva and Pitcairn (Weisler, 1995). As communities in the regional core high islands increasingly focused on internal competition, external long-distance relationships faltered and peripheral island communities who depended on these vanished (Weisler and Walter, 2016, p. 379). In New Zealand, colonists initially ranged well below the southern climate limit of Polynesian horticultural lifeways, travelling as far as the Auckland Islands, but activity declined in southern landscapes after wild-food resource depletion. The centre of population density subsequently shifted to the upper half of the North Island where horticulture was sustainable (Brown and Crema, 2019). In each of these cases, remote and/ or ecologically marginal habitat retreat occurred soon after the endpoint of colonisation pulses, coinciding with increasingly competition-focused socio-cultural processes becoming prevalent in core regions. The latter included intensification of horticulture, demarcation of territories, construction of fortifications, and other characteristically 'K-selected' phenomena.

A model derived from the study of biological dispersal patterns, invoking demographic and ecological parameters, thus appears to compare well with the episodic tempo of Pacific colonisation. However, as a cultural or behaviouralist generalisation from biological principles it remains mostly analogical, since it lacks the deterministic mechanics of the evolution of r/K strategies by natural selection. Even cultural selectionist variants (Cochrane, 2018) lack specification of a causal link between the theorised performance benefits of migration and a mechanism by which such behaviours would thereby necessarily increase in frequency. In behavioural-ecology variants, culturally mediated rational choices are assumed to cumulatively gravitate towards optimisation, with demographic patterns flowing on from those choices. But these supply no explicit theory of culture or society and, in fact, can only recognise such influences insofar as patterns *deviate* from a hypothetical optimum (i.e. a null model such as the Ideal Free Distribution). Although the patch choice variant posits the importance of social factors such as competition and despotism it inherits these from population biology (Fretwell, 1972, p. 98), where they are part of the kit of metaphors imported during the long history of reciprocal influence between neoclassical economics and evolutionary theory. It would be unfortunate if our only social theory amounted to a rediscovered Malthusian-Hobbesian political economy received through the naturalising filter of biology – the circular potential for which was recognised in the 1870s (Runkle, 1961, p. 111). Models of the social and cultural conditions, or communities of practice, sustaining seafaring and colonisation are consequently an important gap in broader scale explanations and require further consideration.

Politics and practice

There is a long tradition in the Pacific of thinking of island colonisation as a kind of reset that initiates experiments in social evolution on each island anew, facilitating a conceptualisation of early colonisation periods as being governed more by natural ecological processes (e.g. optimal foraging) than socio-cultural factors. But, in Remote Oceania at least, there is ample archaeological, linguistic and comparative ethnographic evidence that colonists preserved core principles of social organisation and tradition, transporting social landscapes (e.g. Kirch and Green, 2001, pp. 201–236). Bellwood (1996) has argued that fundamental social structures persisted and further developed during expansion into Remote Oceania, and that these had some reciprocal effect on colonisation. He finds that ranking and social hierarchy are common characteristics of most Austronesian-speaking communities. Historical linguistics implies that ascribed leadership and the ranking of senior and junior siblings, are traceable at least as far back as Lapita or linguistically defined 'Proto-Oceanic society' (Bellwood, 1996, p. 21). A corollary of ascribed ranking is reverence for, or deification of, kin-group founders, and Bellwood notes that there is a common 'founder focussed ideology' on many islands such that the 'highest traditional rank is held by the descendants of the first founders and the lineages founded by later arrivals have lesser ritual statuses' (1996, p. 25). Members of founding lineages legitimise their privileged access to the most productive land and other resources via ideological claims that they descend from, or embody, deified original ancestors whose appearance in the landscape was foundational, or world-making. This is reflected in the prevalence of '*waka* traditions', or tribal histories linking descendants to named origin canoes, particularly in the eastern Pacific.

Bellwood postulates that this pattern is the likely product of a self-reinforcing process of 'founder rank enhancement' under the conditions of island colonisation. The first arrivals in an unoccupied landscape might seek to protect their prior access to prime resources from subsequent arrivals by establishing rules of inheritance and primogeniture. However, under such ranked conditions junior siblings and secondary lineages would find it difficult to secure resources and prestige at home and so, in turn, seek their own land further afield. A founder-focused ideology thus provides both justification for control over resources, and a social impetus for further colonisation. Bellwood proposes that the effect was cumulative such that it explains a general west to east trend in the increasing occurrence of ascribed social ranking in Oceania (1996, p. 32). Consequently, and in contrast to an island laboratory model, Bellwood sees colonisation as a social evolutionary process occurring at the wider pan-Pacific scale, recalling an even longer tradition of drawing evolutionary contrasts between the western and eastern Pacific.

Founder rank enhancement is compatible with behavioural ecology insofar as it supplies a social context for resource competition and structures of control inspiring the onset of dispersal. Kennett and Winterhalder (2008), for example, echo Bellwood in suggesting that hierarchical subjugation and despotic control of land in West Polynesia initially stimulated East Polynesian colonisation. But, at the pan-Pacific scale, the argument does not fit well with current episodic colonisation chronologies since it supplies no reason for people to cease seeking founder rank enhancement for periods of a millennia or more. It is also questionable how well a demic model of stepwise community bifurcation fits rapid low-density periods of dispersal. During these phases, cooperation and continued input from homeland regions was probably necessary for social and demographic sustainability. Dispersing Lapita groups, for example, maintained a coherent pottery design system, perhaps reflecting formal inter-group contact, shared identity or even a 'supercommunity' (Gosden and Pavlides, 1994, p. 168). The decay of this system after several centuries of population establishment suggests the erosion of a network rather than a step-wise founding sequence of newly independent communities (Clark and Murray, 2006, p. 115).

In an earlier study, Hayden (1983) noted that founding communities are unlikely to have sustained hierarchies via elite resource control since population densities were low and resource access consequently high. Instead, political control might have focused on seafaring technology – particularly long-distance sailing craft, whose construction required several years of preparation, mobilised highly skilled labour and significant materials, and whose use called upon specialist knowledge and navigation skills (Thomas, 2001; Earle and Spriggs, 2015). Arguing that such projects were only possible under clear hierarchies of command, controlled by individuals of considerable wealth and power, Hayden (1983, pp. 127–130) like Bellwood, links this insight to an argument for colonisation being instrumental to the development of social complexity in the region (see Spriggs, Chapter 8).

In a different context, Alkire (1980) similarly identifies technical seafaring skills as a source of power: the control of knowledge by specialist navigators in the Central Caroline islands is held to have facilitated the emergence of polit-ical centralisation in the Yapese empire. But, Alkire also notes that the prestige of navigators competed with the political power of chiefs, whose status derived from their genealogical position based on founder ranking. In opposition to seafaring, this was primarily a 'people and land-based' authority (1980, p. 231). In other words, the contrast provided by Bellwood's and Hayden's theories turns upon a land versus sea dialectic common in Pacific power structures. These typically utilise a variety of oppositional symbolic associations (land-sea, female-male, cultivation-war, autochthonous-foreign: e.g. Sahlins, 1976), to characterise alternative arenas of power. Despite necessarily coexisting, one or another arena tends to assume priority in different socio-historical and environmental contexts.

Returning to the context of colonisation, it is useful to propose a generalisation based on the above: low-density dispersed or expanding communities promote the emergence of mobility-based power relations, while higher-density aggregations tend to focus on the politics of territorial units, boundaries and landesque capital. Transitions between these are not unidirectional, and the two arenas are necessarily entangled on islands – indeed, founder ideologies model contemporary land rights as an outcome of now mythical travel, and communities can remodel migratory histories to fit contemporary land-based political relations (see Alkire, 1984; Taonui,

2006). Some 'maritime empires' coordinated control over both territory and access routes (Petersen, 2000). However, given that Pacific colonisation involved long-term cyclical transitions between relative mobility and sessility, we can expect social organisation, and balances of power, to have followed suit.

In the atoll communities of central and eastern Micronesia, seafaring and navigation assumed more importance than perhaps anywhere else in the Pacific except during early pulses of colonisation. Because these groups (as well as Tuvalu and the northern Polynesian Outliers) potentially share some formal characteristics with the spatial and techno-social patterns of colonisation episodes, it is worth examining them briefly to understand better the potential relationships between seafaring and social power in contexts of spatial dispersion.

Seafaring politics and practice in dispersed island networks

Many dispersed archipelagos in the northwest Pacific sustain small communities organised in a handful of periodically mobile settlement areas per island, economically focused on marine resources and small-scale horticulture, but linked together by seafaring networks. Inter-island relationships are a necessary part of community sustainability, and in some cases, these facilitate population levels below what would otherwise be viable (Williamson and Sabath, 1984; Connell, 1986). In traditional Micronesia, kin groups were distributed across multiple islands and community relocation was common (D'Arcy, 2001, p. 173). Unsurprisingly, seafaring and wayfinding remain crucial technologies in atoll environments, and these were among the last places in the Pacific to retain traditional knowledge (Gladwin, 1970; Lewis, 1994; Genz, 2017). In marked contrast, people on the largely self-sufficient high volcanic islands of Micronesia lacked seafaring knowledge or relied on low islander specialists at the time of European contact (D'Arcy, 2006, p. 94).

As elsewhere in the Pacific, Micronesian seafaring skills were customarily the province of more-or-less formally recognised experts. Skills were maintained in transgenerational lineages, encompassing Ancestral spirits, living practitioners and apprentices. Ritual sanction (or spiritual efficacy) was pervasively necessary, called upon during rituals of canoe carving, rope lashing, canoe launching and navigation (D'Arcy, 2006). Lineages of navigators grew out of a core ontological assumption that worldly success derived from the maintenance of reciprocal (nurturing, familial) relationships with efficacious ancestor spirits (Petersen, 2009). As in wider Oceania, living persons made gifts to receive training and propitiate success, thereby becoming part of the lineage (e.g. Thomas, 2014, pp. 69–71). During voyages, spirits embodied in marine and bird life guided navigators, and canoes were embellished with motifs, such as stylised frigate bird tail and eye motifs on the prow and hull, conveying their efficacy (Genz, 2017, p. 213; Moyle, 2018). Navigators and fishermen were tattooed with similar designs, embodying that efficacy. In most atoll communities the centre of ritual life was the clan canoe house, which housed weather, fishing and navigation charms as well as canoes.

Ritual practice and secrecy facilitated the maintenance of relationships between experts, chiefs and the community. Some chiefs sought training in seafaring (Alkire, 1980), and intrepid navigators could attain status and prestige greater than that of a chief (Genz, 2017, p. 211). In this sense uncommon ritualised knowledge was certainly a form of power, leveraging and sustaining relations of dependency between chiefs, specialists and commoners (Thomas, 2001). But in many communities, this was likely 'soft power': navigators were admired, revered and given sustenance by the populace because they modelled values crucial to social reproduction (Gladwin, 1970). It is also worth noting that technological elaboration is a way of mitigating increasing risk but requires increasingly complex systems and effort to maintain. Given sufficient complexity, technological reproduction entails dedicated systems of training that become automatically exclusionary. In this sense seafaring could be better seen as a technological context through which specialisation and other power-inflected relations emerged, rather than just a case of enclaving by the power-hungry.

Nevertheless, seafaring clearly had an ideological dimension in that it sustained power relations by materialising them in necessary daily practice and by structuring spatial orders. This flowed into the way navigators were trained, and hence how seafaring persisted. The reproduction of technology is not simply about the transmission of normative forms or behaviours ('canoes', 'voyaging') but the cultivation of the skills and strategies responsible for producing them. Skill requires the guiding and shaping of practical experience and the replication of social relations, as much as the control and transmission of information (Ingold, 2000). Micronesian navigators learned during long and hierarchical apprenticeships, demanding the training and development of their haptic and kinaesthetic skills, as much as memorisation tasks and cognitive mapping (Genz, 2014). Detailed attention was paid to, and interacted with, the affordances of different environments – while Carolinian navigation focused on celestial observation, Marshallese navigators utilised wave interference patterns produced by the north-south alignment of that archipelago (Genz et al., 2009). Accordingly, repetitive practice was a necessary part of the structure of technological reproduction, and in turn, seafaring technology was only sustained insofar as it was necessary and able to be practised. Due to its complexity, danger and restrictions, seafaring was particularly susceptible to loss (D'Arcy, 2006, pp. 94–97) and thus only reproduced because it was an integrated part of the habitus of island life. As a body of practice that linked ecology, economics, social relationships, ritual and politics, seafaring was consequently the key techno-social structure through which atoll communities understood their worlds. As well as being ecologically necessary, it was the means by which space, relationships and identities were understood.

The main point of this review is to demonstrate that when small-scale dispersed communities engage in costly seafaring, this is facilitated and sustained through being practically integrated into subsistence, socio-political organisation, wider technological infrastructures and symbolic systems. This integration is reflected materially in the structure of landscape use and settlement space, foodways, tools and other technologies, as well as art and design systems. Ethnographically observed Micronesian atoll communities are perhaps at the extreme end of this integration, having refined highly sophisticated watercraft and methods of navigation in a unique context over many centuries of occupation. But atolls were not able to be colonised in the first place, and communities were not able to sustain themselves, without the development of these systems. Consequently, it is likely that some version of an integrated seafaring economy was present at first colonisation, and further refined subsequently. In contrast, occupants of high volcanic islands in the region were less dependent on external relations and offshore resources, and although necessary initially, the importance of seafaring declined. Instead, power relations increasingly turned to the definition of landed units, monumental construction projects, landscape transformation and other forms of competitive intensification (Kirch, 2017, pp. 164–183). In these locations, ancestry and place became the key foci of socio-political organisation (Rainbird, 2006, p. 315).

How do we relate these findings to colonisation processes? In terms of cultural ecology, the atolls and high island communities of Micronesia provide useful analogues for modelling the socio-cultural and political correlates of, respectively, A-type and K-type dispersal strategies. That is, a colonisation front transitioning from K-type to A-type dispersal entails not only a shift in demographic and economic strategies, but also necessitates socio-cultural and technological reorganisation. But there is a paradox here: if high-density, landed communities tend to develop socio-political strategies focused on territorial competition, it is difficult to see how they would spontaneously produce fully fledged systems of integrated seafaring. Put another way: if atoll colonisation required an integrated seafaring economy, how and where did this develop?

Marginal island network sorting

I think a broad answer lies in a model of long-term emergence given the affordances of patchwork geographies, and archipelago distributions. K-type dispersal on a large, resource rich landmass would promote slow, short-distance demic colonisation of favourable zones, including coastal fringes and, eventually, peripheral islands. Insofar as sustainable occupation of any of the latter necessitated a maritime economic focus and external social connections, marginal island networks would provide a context for the spatial sorting and further techno-social development of seafaring. Such development, and integrated systems ensuring its reproduction (habitus), would support A-type dispersal to available islands of similar or better resource base, up to the limits of accessibility and sustainability. Self-sustaining islands in the new range could subsequently transition to K-type strategies resulting in network decay. These, or remaining network fragments, would then serve as bases from which the process might begin anew. Over time this would cumulatively produce techno-social strategies capable of colonising ever more marginal islands (Fig. 7.4). Note that the overall pattern is scale independent, emerging relationally rather than as an outcome of some objective geographic limit or property.

A-type dispersal

A-type dispersal

A-type dispersal

K-type dispersal

K-type dispersal

Spatial Expansion

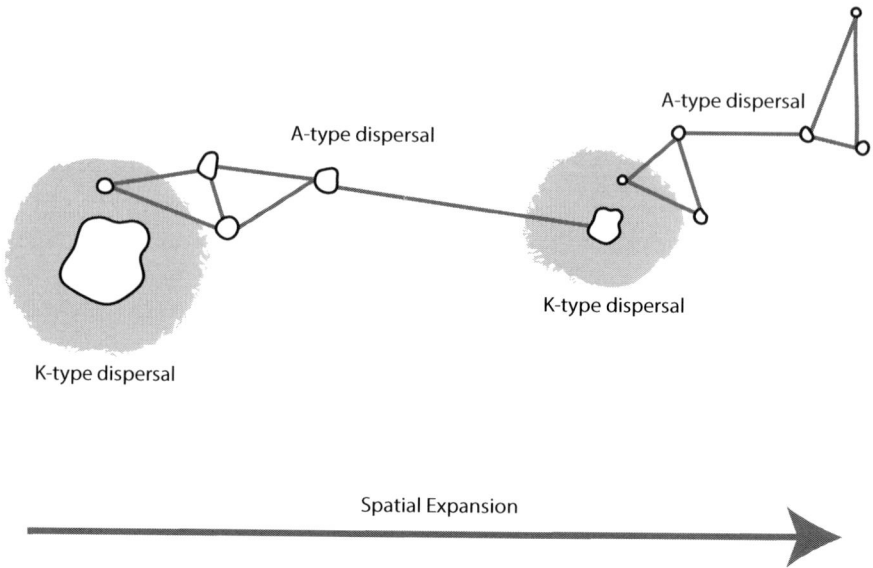

FIGURE 7.4 Marginal Island Network Sorting model of colonisation. Large landmasses radiate people under density-dependent conditions. Peripheral island communities curate seafaring and promote rapidly expanding networks under density-independent conditions.

A marginal island network sorting model compares well with the archaeological record of colonisation pulse episodes in the Pacific. I do not have the space here to supply a full account but will note some key characteristics of the record compatible with this model and the pattern of integrated seafaring seen in the ethnographic case. I focus on the Lapita and East Polynesian colonisation episodes.

The earliest Lapita sites occur on the coastal fringes and offshore islands (many <1 km²) of the Bismarck Archipelago, in positions that were either never previously occupied or had experienced an occupation hiatus (Specht, 2007). Settlements were hamlet-sized clusters of stilt-houses constructed over reef flats and lagoons, reflecting a maritime focus. Domesticated plants and animals were present, but reef-based and inshore fishing and collecting, and other forms of foraging, were important contributors to diets. Fishing technology was sophisticated and included trolling lures for taking offshore fish (Specht et al., 2014; Ono, 2010). Long-distance seafaring and social connectivity are indicated by inter-island transfers of obsidian, chert, oven stones and other materials. The spatial extent and volume of these transfers increased dramatically from patterns in the earlier Holocene (Summerhayes, 2009). Lapita pottery design coherence, and synchronised changes across sites, supports a model of persistent community interaction (Summerhayes, 2000). The meaning content of pottery design motifs is cryptic, but includes depictions of human faces, crouching body positions and split representation characteristic of ancestor spirit representations regionally (Chiu, 2007; Spriggs, 1990).

These depictions possibly blend with marine forms such as turtles and sea birds, including frigate bird motifs (Terrell and Schecter, 2009; Noury, 2017). Evidence of the curation of crania, and burials with pots decorated with such motifs (Bedford et al., 2007), echo ethnographically recorded Melanesian systems of ancestor veneration, and symbolic links between the efficacy of spirits and the efficacy of seagoing animal life (e.g. Thomas, 2013).

These characteristics are consistent with a maritime socio-cultural organisation, befitting a cultural complex that went on to colonise Remote Oceania. However, the marginal islands of the Bismarck Archipelago are not necessarily the original 'nursery' of long-distance seafaring: the Marianas were settled at about the same time, probably from a region between the Philippines and northern New Guinea (Hung et al., 2011; Fitzpatrick and Callaghan, 2013). The Bismarck Archipelago could be seen as a staging area (a marginal island network) whose sociogeography promoted further refinement and synthesis of existing patterns (Green, 1991). A second, Remote Oceanic, staging area in the Reef Islands is possible, since the earliest Lapita sites there have relatively large assemblages of obsidian imported from New Britain, probably reflecting continued or multiple arrivals (Sheppard, 1993). Direct transfers of pottery from the Reef Islands to locations such as Tongatapu suggest rapid onward journeys rather than incremental island hopping (Burley and Dickinson, 2010). However, Lapita sites in Remote Oceania were no longer inter-tidal stilt-house hamlets, and offshore fishing declined in favour of netting and spearing on the reef. These differences are probably related to the absence of prior inhabitants and changing environmental affordances, but they have broader implications for activity contexts and the importance of seafaring. Many of the islands colonised by Lapita communities in Remote Oceania were comparatively large, and after arrival there is a general pattern of demographic expansion and peripheral infilling moves, before network decay. Post-Lapita cultural sequences show increasing landscape intensification and regionalisation (Spriggs, 1997).

Subsequent to the spread of Lapita communities in Fiji–Tonga–Samoa 2900–2700 BP, further dispersal appears to have faltered until after 2000 BP when occupation of marginal islands in the chain of atolls to the Marshall Islands and east to Niue began to occur. Colonisation of East Polynesia began some 700–800 years later still. Like early Lapita sites, the earliest sites of central East Polynesia represent small coastal hamlets, in sheltered leeward positions near major reef passages, or in deep bays (Walter, 1996) – strategic points for access to sea and land. Compared to West Polynesia, there was an explosion of fishing technology and a consequent broadening of catch. Innovations in one-piece and compound shank fishhooks, trolling lures and harpoon heads occur, and consequently more canoe-based offshore and deep-water fishing. An abundance of strong pearlshell (*Pinctada margaritifera*) in the atolls and lagoons of early East Polynesia may have facilitated innovation, fuelling more time and energy spent offshore (Allen, 1992). Pearlshell was significant enough to be redistributed over long distances to islands lacking native stocks. The presence of harpoons indicates the capture of dolphin/porpoise, and possibly shark. Unique personal ornaments made from whale, seal and porpoise teeth (as well as pearlshell pendants or breastplates) are found accompanying burials in colonisation period sites (Walter, 1996, pp. 520–521) – perhaps suggesting some enduring link between deep-water activity and conceptions of personhood. A recent find of an early voyaging canoe in New Zealand has a sea turtle carved into the hull (Johns et al., 2014) – an animal whose migratory, seagoing life, and ability to cross the land-sea interface, was thought both human and godlike in many Polynesian cultures (Rolett, 1986).

Like the fishing kit there is a greater diversity of adze forms in early East Polynesia (Cleghorn, 1984). Again, this may be related to a reciprocal interplay between the affordances of changing materials (Oceanic basalts), and the techno-social context of colonisation: diversification may reflect increasing craft specialisation associated with changes in canoe production, and other woodworking tasks. The symbolic potential of adzes is well documented in Polynesia ethnographically, particularly in locations where canoe production was important. Preparations for canoe carving required the special procurement and consecration of adzes, and they feature in key traditions of mythic figures who transformed the materials of the forest into voyaging canoes and embarked on journeys of discovery (Handy, 1927, pp. 287–288; Henry, 1928). As well as the name of the ancestral canoe, the name of the ceremonial adze that carved it was sometimes commemorated in origin traditions, travelling aboard as the facilitator of its progress. These sorts of association may be why large, well-made adzes were deposited as grave goods in some early colonisation-era cemeteries.

Archaeologically, adzes provide evidence for inter-island connectivity during the East Polynesian colonisation period, with geochemical sourcing studies demonstrating long-distance artefact transfers (Weisler and Walter, 2016). Like pearlshell, the redistribution of adzes facilitated sustainability on islands lacking quality stone but imports also occurred even when local stone was available, suggesting a social impetus behind some of these interactions. Long-distance artefact transfers are largely confined to the period before AD 1450, after which inter-island networks contracted to the intra-archipelago scale. However, there is some evidence for slightly later persistence of imports on marginal islands: Mangaia, a raised reef island in the southern Cook Islands, has evidence of adze imports from Samoa and the Austral Islands into the AD 1600s, although even this is a retraction from the early period, which included importations from Eiao in the Marquesas, over 2,400 km away (Weisler et al., 2016; McAlister et al., 2013). As in other cases, Mangaia has its own sources of local basalt in the interior of the island.

In summary, both Lapita and East Polynesian episodes of colonisation produced archaeological evidence compatible with a model of an integrated maritime socio-cultural organisation, in which economic lifeways, social interaction, ritual and probably political structures were entangled with seafaring practice. During these periods, expansion was not propelled by exceptional one-way, one-off journeys, but rather by persistent networks and repetitive seafaring – and indeed repetitive practice is the only way that the technology required could be reproduced, sustained and developed, during episodes lasting several hundred years. Most journeys were no doubt near-shore and between known locations, but an increase in the frequency and duration of seaborne activity may have been enough, on its own, to increase the statistical likelihood of island discovery – in turn leading to network extension and further seafaring.

The cases differ in terms of their relative maritime emphasis and its degree of socio-cultural integration, and this corresponds to an eastward pattern of increasing seafaring distances, reduction in island size and diversity, and likely refinement of technology (Irwin and Flay, 2015). This is compatible with a marginal island sorting process; however, the exact geographic origins of the more developed East Polynesian pattern are currently uncertain. Early East Polynesian sites have coherent and distinctive artefact assemblages and include forms with no clear precedents on the larger islands of West Polynesia (Walter, 1996). Following the above model, it is possible that many of the initial developments occurred on the smaller islands of, or peripheral to, Fiji–Tonga–Samoa. Earlier movements into atoll environments northwest and northeast of Samoa/Tonga may have been important. A recent re-evaluation of linguistic relationships has proposed East Polynesian origins in the northern Polynesian outliers, near the Solomon Islands (Wilson, 2018). I consider this geographically unlikely, but during El Niño years wind patterns could certainly support a northern atoll route into central East Polynesia.

By AD 1450 most archaeological sequences in East Polynesia show signs of increasing population size, accompanied by a general trend towards inland settlement in rich agricultural landscapes. Although atoll communities (e.g. the Tuamotus) retained a networked maritime focus, in many locations the early diversity in fishing technology withdrew inshore, and adze-forms became less variable and more often locally made. Agricultural intensification, irrigation systems, field boundaries and monumental architectural projects are defining features of later periods on most high islands (Kirch, 2017, pp. 213–268). Fortifications also occur (Field and Lape, 2010). These trends reflect an increasing emphasis on the economic potential and politics of land, and it is in this context that methods of reckoning and establishing rights and powers over territory and its produce have more significance. Ideologies invoking arrival sequences, founding canoes and heroic voyaging ancestors are best seen as belonging to these methods if their primary function was to justify the privileged rights of ruling chiefs and their followers. But inasmuch as the prestige of chiefs derived from the deeds of voyaging ancestors, canoes and seafaring retained an association with power and the work of the gods. They would again have symbolic and practical political importance during episodes of polity expansion, naval raiding and trade network dominance during later periods (Kirch, 2010; Aswani and Graves, 1998). This, then, was not a one-way move towards landed sessility: as demonstrated elsewhere in the Pacific it was entirely possible for communities to transition away from inland regions and a political emphasis on agricultural production to form coastal chiefdoms whose politics centred on networks of maritime exchange and raiding (Thomas et al., 2001; Walter and Sheppard, 2006).

The wider point is that these transitions constitute different kinds of spatial order reflecting different modes of colonisation – understood here as the means by which people are organised in relation to their environment during the production of place. Biogeographic, ecological, techno-social, and cultural factors operating at, and entangled across, multiple scales influence the emergence of these spatial orders and environmental relations. The best understanding of colonisation will consequently emerge from multi-scalar approaches and integrated explanations that traverse such scales.

Conclusion

Colonisation is often thought of as a distinct realm of archaeological enquiry, concerned with population origins, migration and early adaptations, rather than longer term processes of landscape creation and changing politics of place. Indeed, above I have focused on the processes and practices by which unoccupied Pacific islands were first discovered and inhabited by humans. But in its broadest sense colonisation is about the many factors governing relationships between people and landscape, and as such is part of wider human–environment relations. From this perspective the politics of affiliation between people and place can be as much a part of colonisation research as histories of migration and adaptation.

However, an important goal of theorising colonisation as a longer term spatio-temporal process is to question frameworks in which the past is conceived as a collection of geographically demarcated, or place-based, sequences, each with its own beginning and end, each having different lengths (Bellwood, 2013, p. 7). Any kind of enduring movement or mobility is problematic under such regimes. Dispersal is rendered atypical, requiring a special cause that pushes or pulls migrants away from their definitional range, and is invariably seen as a brief event in between longer periods of adaptation in place. But if the alternative is to postulate perpetual movement whereby 'everyone is an immigrant' then this would only serve to disconnect people from place and frame their relationships as solely genealogical – defined by biogenetic substance rather than their co-involvement in a landscape. The world becomes a surface occupied by successive waves of immigrants who bring their identities with them as heritable material. Either view has disturbing implications – 'indigenous' people are rendered either ahistorical autochthones or mere occupants from elsewhere; they either have a history or a place, but not both. Needless to say, these alternatives are common discourses in versions of settler society colonialism ideologically justified by natural orders of progress and replacement (Ingold, 2000, p. 141; Howe, 2003).

On the face of it, Pacific founder focused narratives, which rank island clans in terms of the arrival sequence of apical ancestors, appear to conform to a genealogical view of history whereby the rights and identities of people are established by past events and are biologically inherited. Founder narratives produce a conical image of society radiating out from an event, inverting the fact that each person really has many ancestors. This is partly why such narratives are described as ideologies, and indeed there is a long history of debate in the Pacific surrounding the fictive or manipulated character of genealogies and founding traditions (Taonui, 2006, p. 35). But this is not necessarily the best way of thinking about them. For one thing, Pacific founder narratives often recount sequences of natural phenomena, places and things, as often as people, and cross island boundaries to describe networks of movement. Fox (1997) uses the term 'topogeny' to describe the way Pacific peoples understand landscapes as relational assemblages of places that materialise ancestral action in the features of the world. Topogenies recount the layering (lit. *whakapapa*) of historical action in place in order to explain the relational vitality and efficacy of knowledge, people and things, as much as their sources (Roberts, 2013). Retrospectively, these look like genealogies linked to spatial histories of movement, but in practice they emerge out of a theory of action: that contemporary efficacy is the product of reciprocal relationships with, and hence acknowledgement of, emplaced ancestors and prior actors (Thomas, 2009). Hence, genealogy and place are not mutually exclusive alternatives for defining people, but the products of ongoing action in the world.

My point is that topogeny may provide a useful model for colonisation, because people and place are viewed as the connected and emergent products of history. From a topogenic perspective colonisation is not simply a record of the movement of definitional populations between definitional places, but the ongoing spatio-temporal process of environmental involvement. Certainly, periods of dispersal and aggregation are part of this involvement, but only in retrospect is colonisation a history of travel, since in practice it is the process of world-making.

References

Addison, D.J. and Morrison, A.E., 2010. The Lapita settlement of Samoa: is a continuous occupation model appropriate. In: P. Wallin and H. Martinsson-Wallin, eds. *The Gotland Papers: Selected Papers from the VII International Conference on Easter Island and the Pacific: Migration, Identity, and Cultural Heritage*. Gotland: Gotland University Press, pp. 359–376.

Alkire, W.H., 1980. Technical knowledge and the evolution of political systems in the Central and Western Caroline Islands of Micronesia. *Canadian Journal of Anthropology*, 1(2), pp. 229–237.

Alkire, W.H., 1984. Central Carolinian oral narratives: indigenous migration theories and principles of order and rank. *Pacific Studies*, 7(2), pp. 1–14

Allen, M.S., 1992. Temporal variation in Polynesian fishing strategies: the Southern Cook Islands in regional perspective. *Asian Perspectives*, 31(2), pp. 183–204.

Allen, M.S., 2014. Marquesan colonisation chronologies and postcolonisation inter-action: implications for Hawaiian origins and the 'Marquesan Homeland' hypothesis. *Journal of Pacific Archaeology*, 5(2), pp. 1–17.

Anderson, A., 1995. Current approaches in East Polynesian colonisation research. *Journal of the Polynesian Society*, 104(1), pp. 110–132.

Anderson, A., 2000. Slow boats from China: issues in the prehistory of Indo-Pacific seafaring. In: S. O'Connor and P. Veth, eds. *East of Wallace's Line: Studies of Past and Present Maritime Cultures of the Indo-Pacific Region.* Modern Quaternary Research in Southeast Asia. Rotterdam: A.A. Balkema, pp. 13–50.

Anderson, A., 2001. Mobility models of Lapita migration. In: G. Clark, A. Anderson and T. Vunidilo, eds. *The Archaeology of Lapita Dispersal in Oceania: Papers from the Fourth Lapita Conference, June 2000, Canberra, Australia.* Canberra: Pandanus Press, pp. 15–24.

Anderson, A., 2003. Entering uncharted waters: models of initial colonization in Polynesia. In: M. Rockman and J. Steele, eds. *The Colonization of Unfamiliar Landscapes: The Archaeology of Adaptation.* London: Routledge, Taylor & Francis Group, pp. 169–189.

Anderson, A., 2006. Islands of exile: ideological motivation in maritime migration. *Journal of Island and Coastal Archaeology*, 1(1), pp. 33–47.

Anderson, A., 2008. Traditionalism, interaction, and long-distance seafaring in Polynesia. *Journal of Island and Coastal Archaeology*, 3(2), pp. 240–250.

Anderson, A., 2013. A fragile plenty: pre-European Māori and the New Zealand environment. In: E. Pawson and T. Brooking, eds. *Making a New Land: Environmental Histories of New Zealand.* Dunedin: Otago University Press, pp. 35–51.

Anderson, A., 2018. Seafaring in Remote Oceania: traditionalism and beyond in maritime technology and migration. In: E. Cochrane and T.L. Hunt, eds. *The Oxford Handbook of Prehistoric Oceania.* Oxford: Oxford University Press, pp. 473-492.

Anderson, A., Chappell, J., Gagan, M. and Grove, R., 2006. Prehistoric maritime migration in the Pacific Islands: an hypothesis of ENSO forcing. *The Holocene*, 16(1), pp. 1–6.

Anderson, A. and O'Connor, S., 2008. Indo-Pacific migration and colonization: introduction. *Asian Perspectives*, 47(1), pp. 2–11.

Anderson, A., Binney, J. and Harris, A., 2014. *Tangata Whenua: An Illustrated History.* Wellington: Bridget Williams Books.

Aswani, S. and Graves, M.W., 1998. The Tongan maritime expansion: a case in the evolutionary ecology of social complexity. *Asian Perspectives*, 37(2), pp. 135–164.

Barton, C.M., Schmich, S. and James, S.R., 2004. The ecology of human colonization in pristine landscapes. In: C.M. Barton, G.A. Clark, D.R. Yesner and G.A. Pearson, eds. *The Settlement of the American Continents: A Multidisciplinary Approach to Human Biogeography.* Tuscon, AZ: University of Arizona Press, pp. 138–161.

Bedford, S., Spriggs, M., Regenvanu, R., Macgregor, C., Kuautonga, T. and Sietz, M., 2007. The excavation, conservation and reconstruction of Lapita burial pots from the Teouma site, Efate, Central Vanuatu. In: *Oceanic Explorations: Lapita and Western Pacific Settlement.* Canberra: ANU Press, pp. 223–240.

Beheim, B.A. and Bell, A.V., 2011. Inheritance, ecology and the evolution of the canoes of east Oceania. *Proceedings of the Royal Society of London B: Biological Sciences*, 278(1721), pp. 3089–3095.

Bell, A.V., Currie, T.E., Irwin, G. and Bradbury, C., 2015. Driving factors in the colonization of Oceania: developing island-level statistical models to test competing hypotheses. *American Antiquity*, 80(2), pp. 397–407.

Bellwood, P., 1996. Hierarchy, founder ideology and Austronesian expansion. In: *Origins, Ancestry and Alliance.* Canberra: ANU Press, pp. 19–42.

Bellwood, P., 2004. *First Farmers: The Origins of Agricultural Societies.* Oxford: Blackwell.

Bellwood, P., 2013. *First Migrants: Ancient Migration in Global Perspective.* Malden, MA: Wiley-Blackwell.

Biggs, B., 1972. Implications of linguistic subgrouping with special reference to Polynesia. In: R.C. Green and M. Kelly, eds. *Studies in Oceanic Culture History,* vol. 3, Pacific Anthropological Records. Honolulu: B.P. Bishop Museum, pp. 143–160.

Brown, A.A. and Crema, E.R., 2019. Māori population growth in pre-contact New Zealand: regional population dynamics inferred from summed probability distributions of radiocarbon dates. *Journal of Island and Coastal Archaeology*, pp. 1–19. doi: 10.1080/15564894.2019.1605429

Burley, D., Edinborough, K., Weisler, M. and Zhao, J., 2015. Bayesian modeling and chronological precision for Polynesian settlement of Tonga. *PLOS ONE*, 10(3), e0120795. https://doi.org/10.1371/journal.pone.0120795

Burley, D.V. and Dickinson, W.R., 2010. Among Polynesia's first pots. *Journal of Archaeological Science*, 37(5), pp. 1020–1026.

Burley, D.V., Horrocks, M. and Weisler, M.I., 2018. Earliest evidence for pit cultivation provides insight on the nature of first Polynesian settlement. *Journal of Island and Coastal Archaeology*. doi: 10.1080/15564894.2018.1501441

Cachola Abad, C., 1993. Evaluating the orthodox dual settlement model for the Hawaiian Islands: an analysis of artefact distribution and Hawaiian oral traditions. In: M.W. Graves and R.C. Green, eds. *The Evolution and Organization of Prehistoric Society in Polynesia*. New Zealand Archaeological Association Monograph. Auckland: New Zealand Archaeological Association, pp. 13–32.

Chiu, S., 2007. Detailed analysis of Lapita face motifs: case studies from Reef/Santa Cruz Lapita sites and New Caledonia Lapita Site 13A. In: *Oceanic Explorations, Lapita and Western Pacific Settlement*. Canberra: ANU Press. pp. 241–264.

Clark, G. and Murray, T., 2006. Decay characteristics of the Eastern Lapita design system. *Archaeology in Oceania*, 41(3), pp. 107–117.

Clark, J.T. and Terrell, J., 1978. Archaeology in Oceania. *Annual Review of Anthropology*, 7(1), pp. 293–319.

Cleghorn, P.L., 1984. An historical review of Polynesian stone adze studies. *Journal of the Polynesian Society*, 93(4), pp. 399–421.

Cochrane, E.E., 2018. The evolution of migration: the case of Lapita in the southwest Pacific. *Journal of Archaeological Method and Theory*, 25(2), pp. 520–558.

Connell, J., 1986. Population, migration, and problems of atoll development in the South Pacific. *Pacific Studies,* 9(2), pp. 41–58.

D'Arcy, P., 2001. Connected by the sea: towards a regional history of the western Caroline Islands. *Journal of Pacific History*, 36(2), pp. 163–182.

D'Arcy, P., 2006. *The People of the Sea: Environment, Identity, and History in Oceania*. Honolulu: University of Hawaii Press.

Davidson, J. and Leach, F., 2001. The strandlooper concept and economic naivety. In: G.R. Clark, A.J. Anderson and T.Vunidilo, eds. *The Archaeology of Lapita Dispersal in Oceania: Papers from the Fourth Lapita Conference, June 2000, Canberra, Australia*. Canberra: Pandanus Books, pp. 115–123.

Di Piazza, A., 2014. An isochrone map of the prehistoric seascape around Samoa. *Geographical Research*, 52(1), pp. 74–84.

Di Piazza, A., Di Piazza, P. and Pearthree, E., 2007. Sailing virtual canoes across Oceania: revisiting island accessibility. *Journal of Archaeological Science*, 34(8), pp. 1219–1225.

Diamond, J.M., 1977. Colonization cycles in man and beast. *World Archaeology*, 8(3), pp. 249–261.

Dickinson, W.R., 2004. Impacts of eustasy and hydro-isostasy on the evolution and landforms of Pacific atolls. *Palaeogeography, Palaeoclimatology, Palaeoecology*, 213(3), pp. 251–269.

Earle, T. and Spriggs, M., 2015. Political economy in prehistory: a Marxist approach to Pacific sequences. *Current Anthropology*, 56(4), pp. 515–544.

Eckstein, L. and Schwarz, A., 2019. The making of Tupaia's map: a story of the extent and mastery of Polynesian navigation, competing systems of wayfinding on James Cook's

Endeavour, and the invention of an ingenious cartographic system. *Journal of Pacific History*, 54(1), pp. 1–95.

Field, J.S. and Lape, P.V., 2010. Paleoclimates and the emergence of fortifications in the tropical Pacific islands. *Journal of Anthropological Archaeology*, 29(1), pp. 113–124.

Finney, B., 2008. Contrasting visions of Polynesian voyaging canoes: comment on Atoll Anderson's 'Traditionalism, interaction and long-distance seafaring in Polynesia'. *Journal of Island and Coastal Archaeology*, 3(2), pp. 257–259.

Finney, B., Rhodes, R., Frost, P. and Thompson, N., 1989. Wait for the west wind. *Journal of the Polynesian Society*, 98(3), pp. 261–302.

Finney, B.R., 1985. Anomalous westerlies, El Niño, and the colonization of Polynesia. *American Anthropologist*, 87(1), pp. 9–26.

Fitzpatrick, S.M. and Callaghan, R.T., 2013. Estimating trajectories of colonisation to the Mariana Islands, western Pacific. *Antiquity*, 87(337), pp. 840–853.

Fox, J., 1997. Genealogy and topogeny: towards an ethnography of Rotinese ritual place names. In: *The Poetic Power of Place: Comparative Perspectives on Austronesian Ideas of Locality*. Canberra: Australian National University, pp. 89–100.

Fretwell, S.D., 1972. *Populations in a Seasonal Environment*. Princeton, NJ: Princeton University Press.

Gamble, C., 1993. *Timewalkers: The Prehistory of Global Colonization*. Stroud: Sutton Pub Ltd.

Genz, J., 2014. Complementarity of cognitive and experiential ways of knowing the ocean in Marshallese navigation. *Ethos*, 42(3), pp. 332–351.

Genz, J., Aucan, J., Merrifield, M., Finney, B., Joel, K. and Kelen, A., 2009. Wave navigation in the Marshall Islands: comparing indigenous and Western scientific knowledge of the Ocean. *Oceanography*, 22(2), pp. 234–245.

Genz, J.H., 2017. Without precedent: shifting protocols in the use of Rongelapese navigational knowledge. *Journal of the Polynesian Society*, 126(2), pp. 209–232.

Gladwin, T. and Gladwin, T., 1970. *East is a Big Bird: Navigation and Logic on Puluwat Atoll*. Cambridge, MA: Harvard University Press.

Goodwin, I.D., Browning, S.A. and Anderson, A.J., 2014. Climate windows for Polynesian voyaging to New Zealand and Easter Island. *Proceedings of the National Academy of Sciences of the United States of America*, 111(41), pp. 14716–14721.

Gosden, C., 2004. *Archaeology and Colonialism: Cultural Contact from 5000 BC to the Present*. Cambridge: Cambridge University Press.

Gosden, C. and Pavlides, C., 1994. Are islands insular? Landscape vs. seascape in the case of the Arawe Islands, Papua New Guinea. *Archaeology in Oceania*, 29(3), pp. 162–171.

Graves, M.W. and Addison, D.J., 1995. The Polynesian settlement of the Hawaiian archipelago: integrating models and methods in archaeological interpretation. *World Archaeology*, 26(3), pp. 380–399.

Green, R.C., 1982. Models for the Lapita cultural complex: an evaluation of some current proposals. *New Zealand Journal of Archaeology*, 4(1), pp. 7–19.

Green, R.C., 1991. Near and Remote Oceania: disestablishing 'Melanesia' in culture history. In: A. Pawley, ed. *Man and a Half: Essays in Pacific Anthropology and Ethnobiology in Honour of Ralph Bulmer*. Auckland: Polynesian Society, pp. 491–502.

Grollemund, R., Branford, S., Bostoen, K., Meade, A., Venditti, C. and Pagel, M., 2015. Bantu expansion shows that habitat alters the route and pace of human dispersals. *Proceedings of the National Academy of Sciences*, 112(43), 13296–13301; doi: 10.1073/pnas.1503793112

Groube, L.M., 1971. Tonga, Lapita pottery, and Polynesian origins. *Journal of the Polynesian Society*, 80(3), pp. 278–316.

Handy, E.S.C., 1927. *Polynesian Religion*. Bernice P. Bishop Museum Bulletin 35. Honolulu: Bernice P. Bishop Museum.

Hayden, B., 1983. Social characteristics of early Austronesian colonizers. *Bulletin of the Indo-Pacific Prehistory Association*, 4(0), pp. 123–134.

Henry, T. and Orsmond, J.M., 1928. *Ancient Tahiti*. Bernice P. Bishop Museum Bulletin 48. Honolulu: Bernice P. Bishop Museum.

Horrocks, M. and Bedford, S., 2005. Microfossil analysis of Lapita deposits in Vanuatu reveals introduced Araceae (aroids). *Archaeology in Oceania*, 40(2), pp. 67–74.

Howe, K.R., 2003. *The Quest for Origins: Who First Discovered and Settled New Zealand the Pacific Islands?* Honolulu: University of Hawaii Press.

Howe, P.K.R. ed. 2006. *Vaka Moana, Voyages of the Ancestors: The Discovery and Settlement of the Pacific*. Honolulu: University of Hawaii Press.

Hung, H., Carson, M.T., Bellwood, P., Campos, F.Z., Piper, P.J., Dizon, E., Bolunia, M.J.L.A., Oxenham, M. and Chi, Z., 2011. The first settlement of Remote Oceania: the Philippines to the Marianas. *Antiquity*, 85(329), pp. 909–926.

Ingold, T., 1993. The temporality of the landscape. *World Archaeology*, 25(2), pp. 152–174.

Ingold, T., 2000. *The Perception of the Environment: Essays in Livelihood, Dwelling and Skill*. London: Routledge.

Irwin, G., 1973. Man-land relationships in Melanesia: an investigation of prehistoric settlement in the islands of the Bougainville Strait. *Archaeology and Physical Anthropology in Oceania*, 8(3), pp. 226–252.

Irwin, G., 1989. Against, across and down the wind: a case for the systematic exploration of the remote Pacific islands. *Journal of the Polynesian Society*, 98(2), pp. 167–206.

Irwin, G., 1992. *The Prehistoric Exploration and Colonisation of the Pacific*. Cambridge: Cambridge University Press.

Irwin, G., 2008. Pacific seascapes, canoe performance, and a review of Lapita voyaging with regard to theories of migration. *Asian Perspectives*, 47(1), pp. 12–27.

Irwin, G. and Flay, R., 2015. Pacific colonisation and canoe performance: experiments in the science of sailing. *Journal of the Polynesian Society*, 124(4), pp. 419–443.

Johns, D.A., Irwin, G.J. and Sung, Y.K., 2014. An early sophisticated East Polynesian voyaging canoe discovered on New Zealand's coast. *Proceedings of the National Academy of Sciences*, 111(41), pp. 14728–14733.

Keegan, W.F., 1995. Modeling dispersal in the prehistoric West Indies. *World Archaeology*, 26(3), pp. 400–420.

Keegan, W.F. and Diamond, J.M., 1987. Colonization of islands by humans: a biogeographical perspective. *Advances in Archaeological Method and Theory*, 10, pp. 49–92.

Kennett, D.J., Anderson, A. and Winterhalder, B., 2006. The ideal free distribution, food production, and the colonization of Oceania. In: D.J. Kennett, and B. Winterhalder, eds. *Behavioral Ecology and the Transition to Agriculture*. Berkeley, CA: University of California Press, pp. 265–288.

Kennett, D.J. and Winterhalder, B., 2008. Demographic expansion, despotism and the colonisation of East and South Polynesia. In: G. Clark, F. Leach and S. O'Connor, eds. *Islands of Inquiry: Colonisation, Seafaring and the Archaeology of Maritime Landscapes*. Terra Australis 29. Canberra: ANU Press, pp. 87–96

Kinaston, R., Buckley, H., Valentin, F., Bedford, S., Spriggs, M., Hawkins, S. and Herrscher, E., 2014. Lapita diet in Remote Oceania: new stable isotope evidence from the 3000-year-old Teouma Site, Efate Island, Vanuatu. *PLOS ONE*, 9(3), e90376.

Kirch, P.V., 1984. *The Evolution of the Polynesian Chiefdoms*. Cambridge: Cambridge University Press.

Kirch, P.V., 2010. *How Chiefs Became Kings: Divine Kingship and the Rise of Archaic States in Ancient Hawai'i.* Berkeley, CA: University of California Press.

Kirch, P.V., 2017. *On the Road of the Winds: An Archaeological History of the Pacific Islands before European Contact.* 2nd edition. Berkeley, CA: University of California Press.

Kirch, P.V. and Green, R.C., 2001. *Hawaiki, Ancestral Polynesia: An Essay in Historical Anthropology.* Cambridge: Cambridge University Press.

Laland, K.N., Sterelny, K., Odling-Smee, J., Hoppitt, W. and Uller, T., 2011. Cause and effect in Biology revisited: is Mayr's proximate-ultimate dichotomy still useful? *Science,* 334(6062), pp. 1512–1516.

Levison, M.R., Ward, R.G. and Webb, J.W., 1973. *The Settlement of Polynesia: A Computer Simulation.* Minneapolis, MN: University of Minnesota Press.

Lewis, D., 1994. *We, the Navigators: The Ancient Art of Landfinding in the Pacific.* Honolulu: University of Hawaii Press.

Lilley, I., 2008. Flights of fancy: fractal geometry, the Lapita dispersal and punctuated colonisation in the Pacific. In: G. Clark, F. Leach and S. O'Connor, eds. *Islands of Inquiry: Colonisation, Seafaring and the Archaeology of Maritime Landscapes.* Terra Australis 29. Canberra: Pandanus Press, pp. 75–86.

Lu, Z., Liu, Z., Zhu, J. and Cobb, K.M., 2018. A review of paleo El Niño–Southern Oscillation. *Atmosphere,* 9(4), p. 130.

MacArthur, R.H. and Pianka, E.R., 1966. On optimal use of a patchy environment. *The American Naturalist,* 100(916), pp. 603–609.

MacArthur, R.H. and Wilson, E.O., 1967. *The Theory of Island Biogeography.* Princeton, NJ: Princeton University Press

Mayr, E., 1943. A journey to the Solomons. *Natural History,* 52, pp. 30–37.

Mayr, E., 1961. Cause and effect in biology: kinds of causes, predictability, and teleology are viewed by a practicing biologist. *Science,* 134(3489), pp. 1501–1506.

McAlister, A., Sheppard, P.J. and Allen, M.S., 2013. The identification of a Marquesan adze in the Cook Islands. *Journal of the Polynesian Society,* 122(3), pp. 257–273.

Montenegro, A., Callaghan, R.T. and Fitzpatrick, S.M., 2014. From west to east: environmental influences on the rate and pathways of Polynesian colonization. *The Holocene,* 24(2), pp. 242–256.

Montenegro, Á., Callaghan, R.T. and Fitzpatrick, S.M., 2016. Using seafaring simulations and shortest-hop trajectories to model the prehistoric colonization of Remote Oceania. *Proceedings of the National Academy of Sciences,* 113(45), pp. 12685–12690.

Moyle, R., 2018. Oral tradition and the canoe on Taku. *Journal of the Polynesian Society,* 127(2), p. 145.

Nelson, M.C., 1991. The study of technological organization. *Archaeological Method and Theory,* 3, pp. 57–100.

Noury, A., 2017. What is that bird? Pros and cons of the interpretation of Lapita pottery motifs. *Journal of Pacific Archaeology,* 8(2), pp. 79–87.

O'Connell, J.F. and Allen, J., 2012. The restaurant at the end of the universe: modelling the colonisation of Sahul. *Australian Archaeology,* 74, pp. 5–17.

Ono, R., 2010. Ethno-archaeology and early Austronesian fishing strategies in near-shore environments. *Journal of the Polynesian Society,* 119(3), pp. 269–314.

Pawson, E. and Brooking, T. eds, 2013. *Making a New Land: Environmental Histories of New Zealand.* Dunedin: Otago University Press.

Petersen, G., 2000. Indigenous island empires: Yap and Tonga considered. *Journal of Pacific History,* 35(1), pp. 5–27.

Petersen, G., 2009. *Traditional Micronesian Societies: Adaptation, Integration, and Political Organization.* Honolulu: University of Hawaii Press.

Phillips, B.L., Brown, G.P. and Shine, R., 2010. Life-history evolution in range-shifting populations. *Ecology*, 91(6), pp. 1617–1627.

Rainbird, P., 2006. The archaeology of the conical clan in Micronesia. In I. Lilley, ed. *Archaeology of Oceania: Australia and the Pacific Islands*, Oxford: Blackwell, pp. 302–317.

Rieth, T.M. and Cochrane, E.E., 2018. The chronology of colonization in Remote Oceania. In: E. Cochrane and T.L. Hunt, eds. *The Oxford Handbook of Prehistoric Oceania*. Oxford: Oxford University Press, pp. 133–161.

Roberts, M., 2013. Ways of seeing: whakapapa. *Sites: A Journal of Social Anthropology and Cultural Studies*, 10(1), pp. 93–120.

Rockman, M, S., J., 2003. *The Colonization of Unfamiliar Landscapes: The Archaeology of Adaptation*. London: Routledge.

Rolett, B.V., 1986. Turtles, priests, and the afterworld: a study in the iconographic interpretation of Polynesian petroglyphs. In: P.V. Kirch, ed. *Island Societies: Archaeological Approaches to Evolution and Transformation*. Cambridge: Cambridge University Press, pp. 78–87.

Rolett, B.V., West, E.W., Sinton, J.M. and Iovita, R., 2015. Ancient East Polynesian voyaging spheres: new evidence from the Vitaria adze quarry (Rurutu, Austral Islands). *Journal of Archaeological Science*, 53, pp. 459–471.

Runkle, G., 1961. Marxism and Charles Darwin. *Journal of Politics*, 23(1), pp. 108–126.

Sahlins, M., 1976. *Culture and Practical Reason*. Chicago, IL: University of Chicago Press.

Schneider, T., Hampel, H., Mosquera, P.V., Tylmann, W. and Grosjean, M., 2018. Paleo-ENSO revisited: Ecuadorian Lake Pallcacocha does not reveal a conclusive El Niño signal. *Global and Planetary Change*, 168, pp. 54–66.

Sheppard, P.J., 1993. Lapita lithics: trade/exchange and technology: a view from the Reefs/Santa Cruz. *Archaeology in Oceania*, 28(3), pp. 121–137.

Sheppard, P.J., 2011. Lapita colonization across the Near/Remote Oceania boundary. *Current Anthropology*, 52(6), pp. 799–840.

Shine, R., Brown, G.P. and Phillips, B.L., 2011. An evolutionary process that assembles phenotypes through space rather than through time. *Proceedings of the National Academy of Sciences*, 108(14), pp. 5708–5711.

Specht, J., 2007. Small islands in the big picture: the formative period of Lapita in the Bismarck Archipelago. In: S. Bedford, C. Sand and S. Connaughton, eds. *Oceanic Explorations: Lapita and Western Pacific Settlement*, Terra Australis 26. Canberra: ANU E-Press, pp. 51–70.

Specht, J., Denham, T., Goff, J. and Terrell, J.E., 2014. Deconstructing the Lapita cultural complex in the Bismarck Archipelago. *Journal of Archaeological Research*, 22(2), pp. 89–140.

Spriggs, M., 1990. The changing face of Lapita: transformations of a design. In: M. Spriggs, ed. *Lapita Design, Form and Composition. Proceedings of the Lapita Design Workshop, Canberra, Australia – December 1988*. Occasional Papers in Prehistory 19. Canberra: Australian National University, pp. 83–122.

Spriggs, M., 1997. *The Island Melanesians*. Oxford: Blackwell.

Sterelny, K., 2013. Cooperation in a complex world: the role of proximate factors in ultimate explanations. *Biological Theory*, 7(4), pp. 358–367.

Summerhayes, G., 2000. *Lapita Interaction*. Terra Australis 15. Canberra: Australian National University.

Summerhayes, G.R., 2009. Obsidian network patterns in Melanesia: sources, characterisation and distribution. *Bulletin of the Indo-Pacific Prehistory Association*, 29, pp. 109–123.

Taonui, R., 2006. Polynesian oral traditions. In: K.R. Howe, ed. *Vaka Moana: Voyages of the Ancestors*. Honolulu: University of Hawai'i Press, pp. 24–53.

Terrell, J., 1977. Human biogeography in the Solomon Islands. *Fieldiana Anthropology*, 68, pp. 1–47.

Terrell, J., 1986. *Prehistory in the Pacific Islands*. Cambridge: Cambridge University Press.

Terrell, J.E. and Schechter, E.M., 2009. The meaning and importance of the Lapita face motif. *Archaeology in Oceania*, 44(2), pp. 45–55.

Thomas, T., 2001. The social practice of colonisation: re-thinking prehistoric Polynesian migration. *People and Culture in Oceania*, 17, pp. 27–46.

Thomas, T., 2008. The long pause and the last pulse: mapping East Polynesian colonisation. In: G. Clark, F. Leach and S. O'Connor, eds. *Islands of Inquiry: Colonisation, Seafaring and the Archaeology of Maritime Landscapes*. Terra Australis 29. Canberra: ANU Press, pp. 97–112.

Thomas, T., 2009. Topogenic Forms in New Georgia, Solomon Islands. *Sites: A Journal of Social Anthropology and Cultural Studies*, 6(2), pp. 92–118.

Thomas, T. 2013. Sensory efficacy in the material culture of New Georgia, Solomon Islands. In: L. Bolton, N. Thomas, E. Bonshek, J. Adams and B. Burt, eds. Melanesia: *Art and Encounter*. London: British Museum Press, pp. 199–208.

Thomas, T., 2014. Shrines in the landscape of New Georgia. In: H. Martinsson–Wallin and T. Thomas, eds. *Monuments and People in the Pacific*. Studies in Global Archaeology 20. Uppsala: Uppsala Universitet, pp. 47–76.

Thomas, T., Sheppard, P. and Walter, R., 2001. Landscape, violence and social bodies: ritualized architecture in a Solomon Islands society. *Journal of the Royal Anthropological Institute*, 7(3), pp. 545–572.

Walter, R., 1996. What is the East Polynesian 'archaic'? A view from the Cook Islands. In: J. Davidson, G. Irwin, F. Leach, A. Pawley and D. Brown, eds. *Oceanic Culture History: Essays in Honour of Roger Green*. Dunedin: New Zealand Journal of Archaeology Special Publication, pp. 513–529.

Walter, R., Buckley, H., Jacomb, C. and Matisoo-Smith, E., 2017. Mass migration and the Polynesian settlement of New Zealand. *Journal of World Prehistory*, 30(4), pp. 351–376.

Walter, R. and Reilly, M., 2018. Ngā hekenga waka: migration and early settlement. In: M. Reilly, S. Duncan, G. Leoni and L. Paterson, eds. Te *Koparapara: An Introduction to the Māori World*. Auckland: Auckland University Press, pp. 65–85.

Walter, R. and Sheppard, P., 2006. Archaeology in Melanesia: a case study from the Western Province of the Solomon Islands. In: I. Lilley, ed. *Archaeology of Oceania: Australia and the Pacific Islands*. Oxford: Blackwell, pp. 137–159.

Webb, R.E., 1998. Problems with radiometric 'time'; dating the initial human colonization of Sahul. *Radiocarbon*, 40(2), pp. 749–758.

Weigelt, P. and Kreft, H., 2013. Quantifying island isolation: insights from global patterns of insular plant species richness. *Ecography*, 36, pp. 417–429.

Weisler, M.I., 1995. Henderson Island prehistory: colonization and extinction on a remote Polynesian island. *Biological Journal of the Linnaean Society*, 56(1–2), pp. 377–404.

Weisler, M.I. and Walter, R., 2016. East Polynesian connectivity. In: T. Hodos, ed. *The Routledge Handbook of Archaeology and Globalization*. Abingdon, Oxon: Routledge, pp. 369–386.

Wiens, J.A., 1976. Population responses to patchy environments. *Annual Review of Ecology and Systematics*, 7, pp. 81–120.

Wiens, J.A., 1995. Habitat fragmentation: island v landscape perspectives on bird conservation. *Ibis*, 137(s1), pp. S97–S104.

Williamson, I. and Sabath, M.D., 1984. Small population instability and island settlement patterns. *Human Ecology*, 12(1), pp. 21–34.

Wilmshurst, J.M., Hunt, T.L., Lipo, C.P. and Anderson, A.J., 2011a. High-precision radiocarbon dating shows recent and rapid initial human colonization of East Polynesia. *Proceedings of the National Academy of Sciences of the United States of America*, 108(5), pp. 1815–1820.

Wilmshurst, J.M., Hunt, T.L., Lipo, C.P. and Anderson, A.J., 2011b. Reply to Mulrooney, et al.: accepting lower precision radiocarbon dates results in longer colonization chronologies for East Polynesia. *Proceedings of the National Academy of Sciences of the United States of America*, 108(23), E195.

Wilson, W.H., 2018. The Northern Outliers–East Polynesian hypothesis expanded. *Journal of the Polynesian Society*, 127(4), pp. 389–423.

Wren, C.D., Xue, J.Z., Costopoulos, A. and Burke, A., 2014. The role of spatial foresight in models of hominin dispersal. *Journal of Human Evolution*, 69, pp. 70–78.

8

THE POLITICAL ECONOMY OF PRESTIGE PRACTICES IN THE PACIFIC

Understanding Lapita and after

Matthew Spriggs

Introduction

After situating the Lapita culture in time and space, this chapter examines the popular, but arguably under-interrogated, idea of prestige-good exchange as a theoretical building block in efforts to understand Pacific prehistory. It then delineates the concept of prestige practices contrasted with and complementary to that of prestige goods. It will examine the usefulness of both concepts in contemplating aspects of the Lapita culture of the Western Pacific, seen as – initially at least – being derived fairly directly from the spread of the Island Southeast Asian 'Neolithics', and most directly from Taiwan and first recognisable there some 5,000 or so years ago (Spriggs, 2011).

Lapita itself appears suddenly and fully formed in the Bismarck Archipelago off New Guinea in the centuries immediately preceding the start of the first millennium BCE. It is particularly distinguished by its highly decorated dentate-stamped pottery (Fig. 8.1), instantly recognisable as unique to this sole period of Pacific prehistory and reflecting a far-flung but relatively homogeneous cultural expression (Kirch, 1997). The initial Lapita expansion was undertaken by an East Asian migrant group (Skoglund et al., 2016). They moved through, and planted colonies among, existing Australo-Melanesian or Papuan populations in 'Near Oceania', consisting of those areas of the New Guinea and Solomon Islands region inhabited for 50,000 years or more. Initially there was minimal population mixing with these already-resident groups. After a short pause, Lapita colonists then moved out around 1000 BCE to settle the previously uninhabited island groups to the south and east. Beyond the main Solomons chain Lapita represents the culture of the initial human settlers of western 'Remote Oceania', the archipelagos of the Reefs-Santa Cruz Islands, Vanuatu, New Caledonia, Fiji, and the Western Polynesian region consisting of Tonga, Samoa, and Wallis and Futuna (Fig. 8.2). Lapita long-distance interactions

FIGURE 8.1 Dentate-stamped Lapita pottery from the Teouma site, Efate Island, Vanuatu, dating to approximately 1000 BCE.

Source: photo by Matthew Spriggs.

from the Bismarcks through to Western Polynesia occurred across some of the greatest distances found in Neolithic societies worldwide. The presentation here draws heavily on five recent papers examining aspects of the Lapita culture in comparative context (Earle and Spriggs, 2015; Spriggs, 2013; 2016a; 2016b; in press) to extend the ideas discussed in them.

Eastern Polynesia, including the three apices of the 'Polynesian triangle' of Hawaii, Easter Island, and New Zealand, is not part of our story. These archipelagos were settled in a much later series of exploratory pushes beginning only just over a thousand years ago. Another major Pacific Island story, again not covered here, is the initial exploration and settlement of northern Remote Oceania, commonly known as Micronesia, which began in Palau, the Mariana Islands, and possibly Yap at about the same time as the Lapita expansion and was carried out by culturally related Island Southeast Asian populations. The second edition of Kirch's Pacific archaeology text, *On the Road of the Winds*, gives up-to-date summaries of these other prehistories (Kirch, 2017).

Prestige-good systems in the Pacific?

In relation to Pacific archaeology, the concept of prestige goods exchange was first discussed by the anthropologist Jonathan Friedman in a paper containing a programmatic statement on the potential sociopolitical transformations of Pacific societies from a Lapita base (Friedman, 1981). The general concept of prestige-good systems had been originally elaborated in Kajsa Ekholm's (later Ekholm Friedman) historical analysis of the Kongo Kingdom in Central Africa (Ekholm, 1972; 1977) and was further developed as part of a general 'epigenetic model' of sociopolitical evolution by Friedman with the archaeologist Mike Rowlands (Friedman and

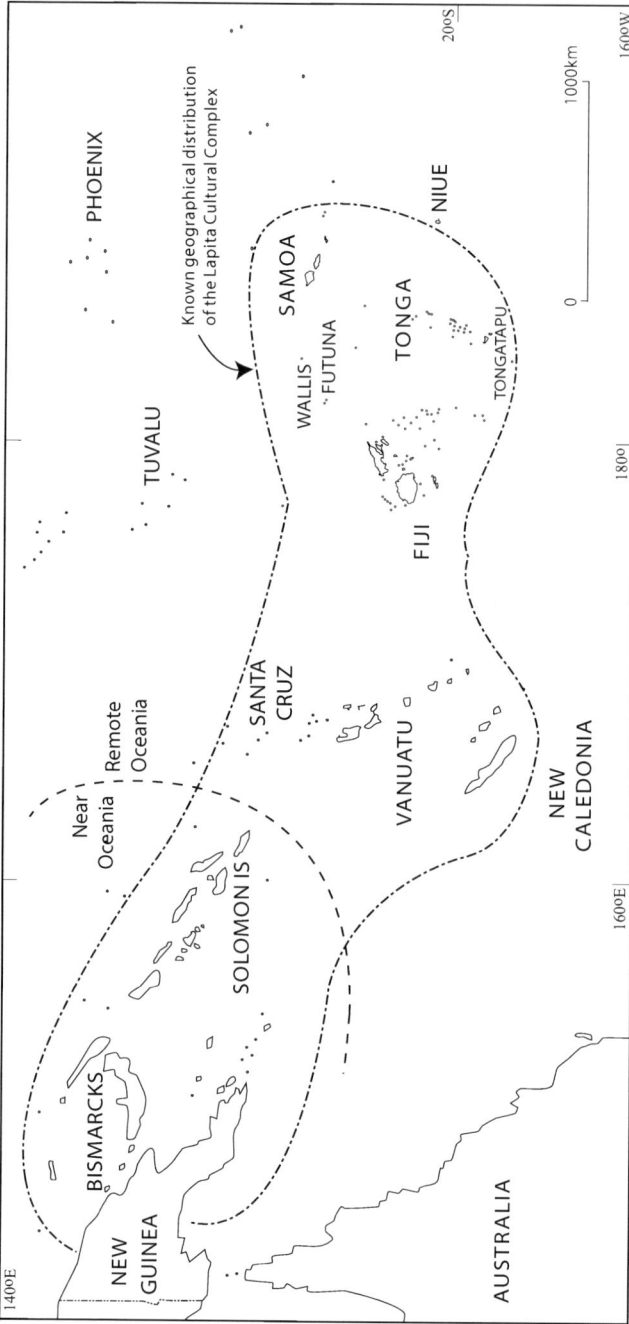

FIGURE 8.2 Distribution of the Lapita culture in the Western Pacific.

Source: map courtesy of Stuart Bedford.

Rowlands, 1977; cf. other papers in that volume). In a brief but highly influential essay, Friedman (1981; see also 1982), saw the potential importance of wealth objects in a Lapita political economy based on a system of prestige-good exchange, arguing that this was the basal system from which Oceanic societies ultimately derived.

Friedman's Oceanic model derived predominantly from ethnographic and ethnohistoric sources, with archaeology used in a more limited role. This was in terms of the presence or absence of supposed prestige goods, usually exotic, as evidence of direct historical connections between island groups. Examples included Lapita pottery generally and the presence of pottery in Eastern Polynesia uniquely in the Marquesas as suggesting this island group as the colonising site. Somewhat more surprisingly, Friedman invokes the presence of 'megalithic construction' betokening past prestige-good economies and being 'no longer a politically feasible investment' in big-man societies (1981, p. 292).

There were four components necessary for a prestige-good system. These were:

1. Generalised exchange
2. Monopoly over prestige-good imports that are necessary for marriage and other crucial payments, that is, for the social reproduction of local kin groups
3. A bilineal tendency in the kinship structure (asymmetrical)
4. A tendency to asymmetrical political dualism: religious versus political chiefs, original people versus invaders, female versus male, inside versus outside, and so on.

(Friedman, 1981, p. 281)

By necessity, the prestige-good system also implied the (?prior) existence of chiefs, glossed in Friedman's summary diagram as 'political hierarchy' (1981, fig. 4). The new formulation turned on its head any assumed evolutionary sequence from egalitarian societies to big-man societies to chiefdoms and then on to state-level societies in the Pacific. As later summarised, it was:

> based on a regional system approach in which an original prestige good-based system that was more or less maintained in Western Polynesia [Samoa and Tonga], parts of Micronesia [the Yapese empire] and Southern Melanesia [New Caledonia], developed into a locally stratified but regionally less integrated theocratic feudal organization in Eastern Polynesia and devolved, politically, into an intensely exchange-based but small-scale organization in Northern Melanesia where it led to what became known as a 'big-man' type of society.
>
> *(Ekholm Friedman and Friedman, 2008, p. 25)*

Friedman (1981, pp. 282–284) also included the Trobriand Islands of the Massim and the Admiralty Islands in Northern Melanesia as having preserved a prestige-good system until European contact. The Eastern Polynesian societies where 'theocratic feudalism' held sway were those of the Society and Hawaiian Islands where agricultural intensification, particularly irrigation, was possible. In other parts of Eastern Polynesia, where such intensification either was not possible or had reached or exceeded its environmental limits, political devolution had taken place – examples included island groups such as the Marquesas, Easter Island, and Mangaia in the Cook Islands (Friedman, 1981, p. 289). The big-man societies that were particularly singled out were those of the New Guinea Highlands, seen as likely devolved from prestige-good systems, and some Massim societies such as Goodenough Island, Siassi, and Dobu (Friedman, 1981, p. 280, fig. 4).

In Pacific archaeology the Ekholm and Friedman model was particularly taken up by Patrick Kirch (1984; 1986; 1988a and b; 1990; 1991; 1997, pp. 254–255; 2000, pp. 321–322) and Matthew Spriggs (1984; 1986; 1992; 1997, pp. 155–157), entering the archaeological mainstream where it has remained influential ever since (examples include Bellwood, 1996; Lilley, 1985; Sheppard, 1996; Torrence, 2004; among many others). The archaeological version of prestige-good systems was, of necessity, 'dumbed down' given the lack of any direct evidence for kinship systems and dualistic relations outside of oral traditions or ethnohistoric texts usually relating, at best, to the last few centuries prior to European contact in the region.

A somewhat similar model of exchange of 'primitive valuables', using some of the same Pacific sources as Friedman and with a much more extensive list of potential Lapita prestige goods, was promulgated by Brian Hayden in the early 1980s, seemingly independently given the lack of reference to Ekholm or Friedman's publications (Hayden, 1983). Hayden's main thrust, however, was to see Lapita groups as essentially specialist traders in an almost market-like system trading with elites perhaps as far away as coastal China. The expansion was driven by the search for new markets and new exotic resources (Hayden, 1983, p. 129)

Partly in response to its archaeological uptake, Thomas (1989, pp. 86–101) produced a spirited refutation of the (by now plural) 'prestige-goods' model, but the lack of any detailed alternative frameworks in that work meant that archaeologists felt able largely to ignore it. This was despite the undeniable point made by Thomas in relation to Friedman's model that: 'The standard evolutionary logic of taking one contemporary society as the primitive form of another is totally fallacious' (1989, p. 121, see also pp. 92–93). But, given the state of archaeological research in the Pacific when Friedman was writing, the logic was also probably inescapable as a first approximation.

As later rephrased by Earle (1997, 2017; see also D'Altroy and Earle, 1985), the basis for Lapita political economy might be better seen as a wealth finance system, in contrast to a staple finance system. Staple finance occurs through chiefly monopolisation and mobilisation of staple foods and other products, and was unlikely to have financed power relationships among Lapita groups because productive reefs and agricultural land would have been accessible to all on newly colonised islands. Consequently, there was no obvious 'bottleneck' that could be used by chiefs to exert control over the subsistence regime, no 'circumscribed population that cannot vote with its feet, moving to open lands elsewhere' (Earle, 2017, p. 11). Nor is there any evidence for monumental construction, and the lack of evidence for large-scale feasting suggests that local leaders could not easily mobilise staples for competitive displays (Earle and Spriggs, 2015).

In contrast, wealth finance 'involves the manufacture and procurement of special products (valuables, primitive money, and currency) that are used as means of payment' (D'Altroy and Earle, 1985, p. 188). These are channelled by the chief and are vital for the definition of status and identity. Potential Lapita 'prestige goods' listed by Hayden (1983, p. 128) include:

> Lapita ceramics, shell rings, shell bracelets, pig tusks, shark teeth and bone pendants, pearl shell disks, human skull tablets, tattooing chisels, round stone gaming disks, adzes made of rare rock types, obsidian and other unusual rocks as well as unusual fauna such as wallabies, plus an unknown number of perishable organic artifacts made of wood, fiber, cloth, skins and feathers.

Not all of these would seem to fit the bill of 'primitive valuables' or prestige goods subject to exchange over large areas. Even if they were highly valued, some of them are not easily tracked as such by archaeologists given the widespread distribution of many of the raw materials from which they were made. They do however provide a very useful list to be interrogated archaeologically.

Evidence for Lapita exchange of prestige items?

Let us examine some of these candidates for potentially exchanged prestige goods, starting with the iconic Lapita pots. The paradox of Lapita pots is that, despite very obvious similarities in decorative techniques and designs, often very broadly spread across the Lapita range, the pots themselves seem to have been rarely exchanged between islands except where lack of local clay sources necessitated such exchange. The most detailed study to date of Lapita pottery provenience showed that, of a sample of 112 reconstructible vessels from the Teouma site on Efate Island, Vanuatu, only 11% ($n=12$) were imported, at least 8% from the neighbouring archipelago of New Caledonia and some 3% from islands further north in the Vanuatu archipelago or beyond (Dickinson et al., 2013). There was nothing particularly unique about the exotic pots to distinguish them from the locally produced product constituting the other 89% of the inventory. Similarly, there was only very occasional movement of Lapita pots between the north and south coasts of New Britain, and along the south coast between the Arawe Islands and the Kandrian area (Summerhayes, 2003).

Marine-shell ornaments represent a diverse but standard inventory across the Lapita range (Szabo, 2010). Although some forms would have required considerable skill and time to make, no obvious bottleneck existed in their production or exchange as the same shell species were widespread across the Lapita range. There were, however, localised exceptions where marine substrates were not conducive to the growth of certain shell species, or where there was a lack of raised reefs containing fossil *Tridacnidae* shells, frequent sources of artefact raw materials in the western Pacific.

Use of colourful bird plumes is widespread in the Pacific as part of ritual costumes (Swadling, 1996), either attached directly onto the hair at the back or projecting from caps or other frameworks. Such feather headdresses are depicted in Lapita iconography (Spriggs, 2019), and among the faunal elements found at the Teouma Lapita site are examples of birds that are not usually known as food items but whose feathers are certainly valued, such as those of hawks, owls, and hornbills (Hawkins, 2015, pp. 204–209; Worthy et al., 2015, pp. 233, 235).

Based on ethnographic analogy, fine ceremonial pandanus mats and barkcloth could also have served as prestige goods, although they are unlikely to survive archaeologically. It has long been suggested that the geometric designs on Lapita pots could have derived from mat or basketry patterns (Casey, 1936; Ambrose, 2019).

Obsidian from Bismarck Archipelago sources (Summerhayes, 2009) is found across the Lapita range to at least Central Vanuatu, in quantities that suggest continued exchange for some time (Reepmeyer et al., 2010; Constantine et al., 2015). When Friedman (1981; 1982) originally categorised Lapita as a prestige-good economy, the only such item he could point to was obsidian. It has further been suggested that its appeal was because it represented in some symbolic way the Lapita homeland from whence it derived and it was thus seen as helping maintain social links back to the Bismarck Archipelago (Green, 1987).

This does not in itself, however, confirm obsidian as a prestige good. Rare specialised 'gravers' of obsidian are found in Lapita sites in Vanuatu, New Caledonia, the Reefs-Santa Cruz group, and the Bismarck Archipelago. They were used for tattooing with an application of charred plant or mineral pigments, which are found mixed with blood on their retouched points (Kononenko, 2012; Torrence et al., 2018). Most obsidian artefacts, however, consist of simple flakes, analysis of which does not suggest they were curated or conserved in any way that would imply intrinsic value, despite their wide distribution (Sheppard, 1993).

Hayden suggested adzes or other artefacts made from rare rock types (1983, p. 128) as potential prestige goods in Lapita. There is a jade artefact from the Sentani Lakes area of West Papua that has been found on an early Lapita site on Emirau (Mussau Group) in the Bismarcks (Harlow et al., 2012) that would certainly fit the bill. Polished stone adzes on the other hand, are generally small and simple in form, and, although they were sometimes exchanged between islands during the Lapita period, seem poor candidates as prestige goods.

Earle and Spriggs (2015) asked whether bottlenecks would have existed in a putative Lapita prestige-goods exchange system. They noted the point made above that potential prestige items, including decorated pottery, shell artefacts, feathers, obsidian and stone adzes all had local alternatives making them virtually uncontrollable.

Without bottlenecks the political economy of Lapita would have been largely open and contested. The one crucial exception seems to have been ownership of voyaging canoes, the technologically most complex item of Lapita material culture.

Hayden noted the 'large amounts of labor and materials' that had to be gathered and the skilled labour needed to construct a large voyaging canoe, an activity that could take one to three years. He also noted that 'average individuals would find the task of building such boats almost insurmountable' and suggested that only high-status individuals could mobilise the necessary capital and labour (Hayden, 1983, p. 127). Once constructed a voyaging canoe would allow control of the extra-island movement of persons and products.

The lure of an uninhabited island, where the otherwise never-to-succeed-to-power younger sons of chiefs could establish themselves as paramount, would have been a powerful incentive for undertaking the construction of such canoes (cf. Bellwood, 1996). Belonging to a chiefly family would ensure the power and influence needed to mount a colonising expedition. The potentially destabilising power plays of such younger sons may have encouraged family support for such a venture. Migration provided a political 'safety valve' in a strongly competitive and potentially conflictual situation (cf. Hayden, 1983, p. 125), drawing off as well younger more adventurous segments of the general population, particularly the always-restless young males.

In Earle and Spriggs's model, putative Lapita chiefs were able to monopolise long-distance travel because it was expensive (the 'costs' of canoe-building and skilled navigation) and required much ritual as well as technical preparation (Earle and Spriggs, 2015, p. 522). Such a monopolisation of long-distance canoe transport would have led to control over prestige goods as well as over provision of marriage partners, to the extent that this required recruitment from outside the immediately local area. They concluded, however, that it was in fact the maintenance of long-distance symbolic relationships that was actually significant for underwriting the political economy rather than the movement of material goods in Lapita.

From prestige goods to prestige practices

Earle and Spriggs (2015) implicitly made a distinction between tangible and intangible prestige goods. Intangible prestige goods included new rituals and dances, and technical and religious specialisations (the two usually go together in the Pacific) such as canoe-making, navigating, tattooing, adze manufacture and so on. Here I would like to go further and conceptualise the distinction differently: prestige goods ('tangible') versus prestige practices ('intangible'). To give a formal definition, prestige practices are those activities that enhance the sociopolitical status of an individual through the activation of often-esoteric knowledge systems and powers above and beyond the merely pragmatic skills used in the production of material items, transport systems or other communally recognised activities and/or performances.

A Google Scholar search brings up very few 'hits' for the term 'prestige practices' beyond listings of supposedly elite lawyers' offices. Among the few archaeologically relevant examples, usage is not consistent. The earliest archaeological reference to the term is by Mary Braithwaite (1984, p. 105) who seems closest to what is meant here in her 'ritual and prestige practices' and 'political and prestige activities'. But she gives no definition for the terms. She also uses the context-specific contrast between the 'traditional system of prestige and ritual practices' (1984, p. 103) and the 'new system of prestige and ritual' (1984, p. 106). Referring directly to Braithwaite's work, Bruce Trigger twice used the term 'prestige practices' (1985; 1993), but again provided no elaboration.

The concept seems then to have languished, at least by this name. There may well be some other terms that essentially mean the same thing. There is Hayden's (1995) discussion of 'prestige technologies' for instance, although on my reading that tends to assume that an individual chief controls the material output of these technologies and uses them strategically – a situation that does not necessarily follow from my definition as it underestimates the agency of the specialist producer. Hayden certainly described some of the prestige practices associated with canoe building, referencing Thompson and Taylor (1980, p. 21):

> Canoe builders were full-time specialists trained through a rigid system of apprenticeship and they occupied elevated social positions. This indicates the key role they played in sustaining the power of the elites. Similarly sail makers, wood carvers, and rope makers for boats had relatively high status, sometimes approaching the level of village chiefs.
>
> *(Hayden, 1983, p. 127)*

Perhaps the closest to what is envisaged here as prestige practices is Mary Helms's concept of 'skilled crafting' (Helms, 1993, p. 4). Her concept of 'craft' includes 'not only production of material goods … but also a number of other skilled abilities, including singing and instrumental musicianship, oratory and the activities of bards and poets, and dance, as well as hunting and navigation' (1993, p. 5). She also mentions in passing raiding and warfare, the work of religious practitioners such as shamans, priests, midwives, diviners and curers, and long-distance trade (1993, pp. 5–8). Her main point, taking off from her earlier book on long-distance travelling and the prestige that falls to those who undertake such travels (Helms, 1988), is to establish parallels between

> the qualities, values or symbolic meanings attributed to acts of skilled crafting and those attributed to long-distance acquisition. I view both areas of endeavor as acts of skilled practitioners, who are themselves accorded certain qualities and statuses for their capabilities.
>
> *(1993, p. 4)*

Again, as with Hayden above, she tends to put more stress on the putative chiefs who control these activities rather than the 'skilled practitioners' themselves. She also fetishises, in both her 1988 and 1993 works, long-distance trade as being the standard against which one measures 'skilled crafting', although I would see it as just one among many other possible prestige practices and would not privilege it in the way that Helms clearly does.

She sees travel and skilled crafting as comparable because they 'involve contact with some aspect of the outside realm by specialists whose activities mark them, too, as exceptional or liminal individuals by virtue of their involvement with the extraordinary outside world' (Helms, 1993, p. 8). Elsewhere she talks of skilled crafting involving 'the ritually defined manipulation of intangible forces aided by application of personal qualities and skills believed to be themselves derived from outside forces or beings' (1993, p. 17). Later, she talks of long-distance traders, religious practitioners, and skilled crafters as all engaging in 'politically and ideo-logically significant activities necessary for the continued reproduction of social life [that] require the transformative and expressive powers of society's skilled craftsmen for their safe and proper realization' (1993, p. 123). Many of the useful ethnographic and ethnohistoric examples she mentions, including several key Pacific references, describe what would be considered here as prestige practices. Helms fails, however, to break free from the close connection between rulers/patrons and the prestige practitioners/skilled crafters themselves. While chiefs may themselves be considered 'skilled crafters', either by engaging in some specialised activity directly or more broadly in their general role as chiefs, prestige practices do not depend per se on the prior existence of chiefs as the thrust of Helms's work would seem to assume.

One might ask why the addition of a (nearly) new term of prestige practices should be of benefit? Earle and Spriggs (2015, p. 522) suggested that Lapita society was peculiarly open and competitive, but I wonder if our problem was a too-monolithic idea of the nature and distribution of power in chiefdoms; the open and competitive nature of power witnessed in Lapita may well be the norm. 'Chief' is only one high-status role among many that might exist at any one time. A chief's power is perhaps more constantly on show in a community but when special events call upon special skills, the chief may have a very subsidiary role. Once 'chiefs' are identified, we tend to tick a box and close off any further analysis, whereas we should be seeking to identify further and perhaps independent prestigious roles within society; and, indeed, existing in societies without chiefs at all.

The agency of the skilled craftsperson or ritual specialist therefore needs to be considered far more than it usually is – Helms (1993) being the major exception – particularly as esoteric knowledge and spiritual power seem always to have been bound up with more pragmatic technical skills in the production of things and performances in Pacific cultures.

A particularly archaeological implication of prestige practices is that the material items produced may be incidental to the practice or performance itself, and of no value separate from it. Hence the ease by which early museum collectors acquired masks and ritual paraphernalia after particularly ceremonies were over. The highly decorated Malanggan masks of New Ireland are a prime example, found today in museums across the world, when traditionally they would have been burnt or left to rot in a cave after a single ceremonial use (Küchler, 2002).

The Lapita obsidian gravers may be a particularly stark clue in this regard (Torrence et al., 2018). It was the tattooists who were engaged in a prestige activity for which the obsidian artefacts are merely a proxy, rather than being prestige goods in and of themselves. This can be shown by the iconography on Lapita pots where geometric motifs within anthropomorphic head designs, as well as occasionally on modelled heads and possible figurines, appear to show tattooing patterns (Green, 1979; Summerhayes, 1998). Otherwise we might have no evidence beyond ethnographic analogy for the salience of this practice.

The anthropomorphic designs on the pots also often depict possibly feathered headdresses or skullcaps that were presumably used in ritual performances (Fig. 8.3); indeed it may be that one of the two 'faces' on double-face motifs in Lapita is meant

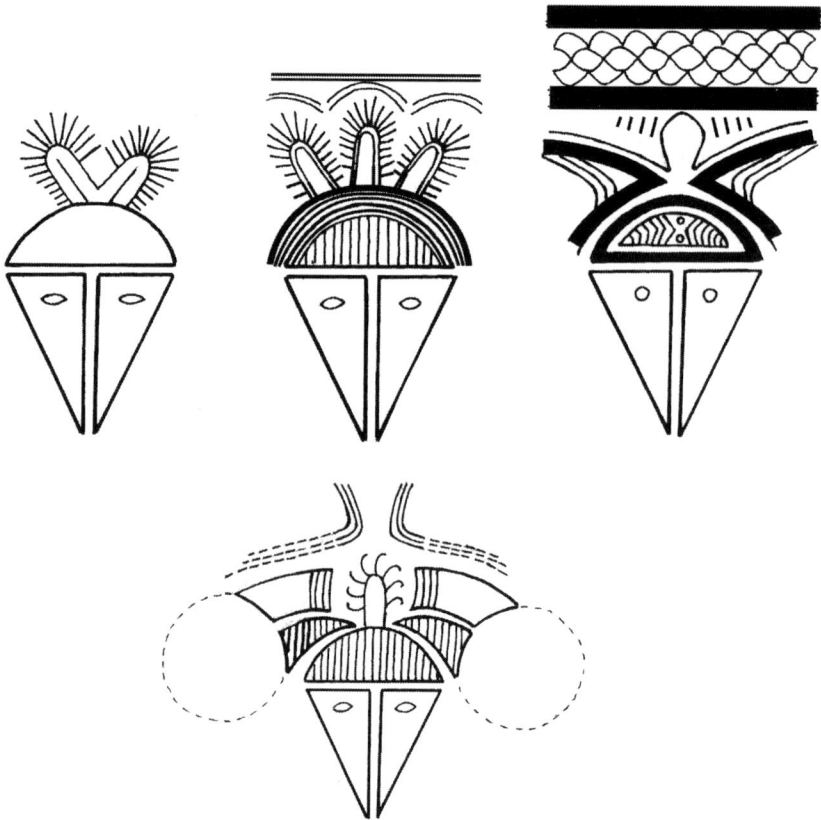

FIGURE 8.3 Possible feather headdress designs on Lapita pots. From Lapita WK0013, New Caledonia (a, b, d) and site SFB, Duke of York Islands, East New Britain (c). Motifs from Noury (2013, pp. 129–130), White (2007, p. 48J) and original drawings by Matthew Spriggs.

Source: Drawing by Siri Seule.

to represent a mask or headdress (Spriggs, 2019). There is also something significant happening beyond the fabrication of elaborately decorated dentate-stamped Lapita pots that provides additional information about ritual practice. Further episodes in the biographies of pots could occur, subsequent ritual acts where the original designs were over-painted and completely obscured by new designs. Evidence for such over-painting is hardly ever found except in fragmentary form as it tends to flake off, but a uniquely well-preserved example from Malakula in Vanuatu has survived (Bedford, 2006).

The ability to mount a colonising expedition to settle new archipelagos was not an option open to everyone. As noted earlier, the voyaging canoe is an extremely complex piece of technology, whose construction and navigation in the Pacific were universally associated with ritual and esoteric knowledge and practices. Access to canoes, navigation, food stores, and crews 'was determined by status, lineage and/ or which experts were in the service of which chiefs' (T. Thomas, 2001, p. 32). The key components were the canoe itself and the ability of navigators to find and refind islands, and of captains to bring the canoes to and from them safely. These navigation and handling skills were particularly necessary during the initial phases of Lapita settlement. This was in order to maintain links back to more populous centres for the supply of spouses and recruitment of followers when population densities in the new colonies were very low, to continue to access ritual specialists and specialties such as tattooing, and to acquire objects of exchange.

What have been identified as prestige goods, on the basis that they were exotic or highly decorated, may in fact have been mere props used as parts of prestige practices, and signs of such practices, rather than having any intrinsic value in themselves. There are many such practices that would have had exchange and prestige value in the settlement of the Pacific: being a boat-builder or navigator, the ability to mediate across languages and cultures that a scout or trader might possess, tattooing, wood carving, ritual specialisms of various kinds, healing and bone-setting, tactical skill in warfare and/or hunting, the magic of being the exemplary 'first farmer' in a region establishing a new settlement, of being a prospector and/ or stone axe maker, or being a handler of dead bodies. Being a chief is in itself a prestige practice, and one that has to be reinforced constantly through the performance of being and acting as a chief (cf. Earle and Spriggs, 2015, pp. 528–529), often involving successful organisation of feasts and rituals.

The end of Lapita

Recent ancient DNA evidence has demonstrated an almost complete population turnover, at least in Vanuatu, towards the end of Lapita, with the arrival of a second wave of Australo-Melanesian or Papuan settlement from the Bismarcks. The second wave were following the same migration pathway avoiding the main Solomon Island chain as had the initial Lapita push by mostly unadmixed First Remote Oceanians of East Asian origin (Lipson et al., 2018; Posth et al., 2018; cf. Skoglund et al., 2016). These second-wave migrants were also 'Lapita people' culturally, but perhaps had been so only for a generation or two. As they began to settle in and expand in numbers at the expense of the first wave, possibly because of greater resistance to malaria, the result was a genetic turnover (cf. Spriggs, 1997, pp. 158–159). As the immediate descendants of pre-Lapita Bismarck Archipelago groups, low density hunter-gatherers or non-intensive horticulturalists without domestic animals, they would likely have had a more egalitarian form of social organisation than the initial Lapita migrants to Vanuatu. Questions would inevitably have arisen among these second-wave migrants as to why they were reproducing what was still perhaps remembered as an originally alien set of beliefs and practices that were also still benefiting the same apex families descended from the original 'foreign' migrants into the Bismarcks. These second-wave settlers may have also re-evaluated aspects of their own previously more egalitarian culture and social organisation in a more positive light. In the Lapita homeland region itself this could have been through contacts with still non-acculturated groups that did not subscribe to a hierarchically ordered political economy. We might say that a shift (or even a reversion) in ethnicity occurred.

Towards the end of Lapita, long-distance contact disappears, and the design system on the pots simplified with increased regionalisation. Cultural diversification increased as the original Lapita 'super-community' (Gosden and Pavlides, 1994, p. 168) began to diversify, marking the end of an identifiable and widespread Lapita culture. Diverse pottery styles replaced Lapita across its extensive distribution, certain shell ornament types dropped out of use, and what were mutually intelligible dialects of early Oceanic Austronesian language began to break up into archipelago-specific subgroupings. Across its range, locally scattered Lapita pioneering populations, who had initially relied heavily on high levels of interaction, grew into larger self-sustaining communities (Pawley, 1981; Spriggs, 1997, pp. 152–162). As populations grew and became more locally rooted, the support for long-distance travel declined – spouses were available locally and exotic goods and knowledge were increasingly replaced by local equivalents.

The end of Lapita could have been as much about a crisis in identity and power relations as it was the loss of an originally imported iconography on pots; the two probably went together anyway. Without the 'bottleneck' of control over voyaging canoes and their journeys continuing to be of importance in a post-Lapita world, a major basis of chiefly power disappeared. Other prestige practices and roles also lost their salience.

In late Lapita and immediately post-Lapita sites in Vanuatu elaborate communal funerary rituals are replaced by simple and definitive inhumation (Valentin et al., 2011). The pots also change to become largely plain and indeed 'faceless', with a fading away too of the more elaborate vessel forms associated with Lapita fine ware. This seems to start to occur immediately as Lapita reached its geographical limits to the east in the Tongan and Samoan archipelagos of Western Polynesia. It may have been the fact of exploration and targeted migration by the original bearers of the Lapita culture that maintained the initial homogeneity of the design system.

Once that initial push out into the unknown had reached its limits, the need for continued back-reference to the 'homeland', perhaps for spouses, for support in establishing settlements, for reinforcement of prestige through goods and practices, seemed to contract progressively across the Lapita range; the Bismarck Archipelago thus claims some of the latest as well as the oldest Lapita dates. There is also a question of how acculturated the later second-wave carriers of the Lapita migration really were, or – to put it another way – how committed they may have been to maintaining its worldview and iconography.

Before the new biological evidence was available, of the origins of the earliest Lapita peoples being in Asia and the second wave as predominantly being Australo-Melanesian or Papuan, I had already referred to an increasing 'Melanesianization' of cultures in Island Melanesia post-Lapita (Spriggs, 1997, p. 159). Earle and Spriggs (2015, p. 523) also noted the archaeological evidence for an egalitarian turn in the political economy after the end of Lapita to a much less hierarchical system. Symptomatic of this is the lack of evidence of long-distance contacts; maintaining them was too costly compared to the benefits they may have originally brought. There was a transformation of both the subsistence and political economies, and with these transformations new ways of dealing with the problem of what to do with the young men after the earlier migratory 'safety valve' had gone. In parts of the Pacific competitive feasting and lengthy 'apprenticeships' through increasingly expensive grade-taking rituals provided safety valves, a theme developed in Earle and Spriggs (2015, pp. 523–524).

The comparison of archaeological sequences across transitions such as between Lapita and post-Lapita is instructive, as I have tried to point out in a series of papers comparing Lapita and its aftermath with the Neolithic Linearbandkeramik spread in Europe (Spriggs, 2016a), wider aspects of the prehistoric sequences of northern Europe (Spriggs, 2013), and more general examples of migration and rapid cultural spread (Spriggs, 2016b). These sequence comparisons, rather than the 'spot' analogies previously employed by scholars such as Friedman (1981), are a way to escape the strictures of Thomas (1989) concerning the use of contemporary societies as if they represented past evolutionary stages. Examining these parallels among archaeological sequences can help to build a truly comparative world archaeology, based on evolutionary and/or political economy models. This is an archaeology we need to engage with to help us 'think outside the box' of our own regional specialisations.

One parallel is in early Neolithic burial practices, as exemplified by the Lapita cemetery at Teouma on Efate in Vanuatu (for an overview see Bedford et al., 2010). The site revealed complex burial rites involving manipulating skeletons, such as by the removal of heads and other skeletal elements. This suggests extended revisiting of burials. Secondary burial in pottery vessels, paralleling practices in Island Southeast Asia at the same time, also occurred (Valentin et al., 2015). The cemetery was a place where ancestors were encountered directly, as they remained participants in a living cross-generational society (Valentin et al., 2011).

In contrast, in the cemeteries of the succeeding two millennia in Vanuatu, simple inhumation replaced these complex and multi-stagal Lapita rituals. The burial of intact bodies represents a shortening of mortuary activities to a single primary event, representing a changing societal relationship between the living and the dead. Descent rather than group membership was emphasised, and one can compare similar changes in British Neolithic funerary practices over time (J. Thomas, 2001). The late and post-Lapita concern was to establish land inheritance through descent from particular ancestors (Valentin et al., 2014), as access to land became an issue with rising population densities.

Conclusions

We should be giving as much attention to the performance of prestige practices as a bottleneck enabling direction and manipulation of the political economy as we do to control over putative prestige goods. The difficulty, however, is that many of these practices seem, at first sight, to be effectively archaeologically invisible. It is often hard in the material record of so-called 'chiefdoms' to point to convincing archaeological evidence for hierarchical organisation, something Earle and Spriggs (2015) found in the case of Lapita. But there is more evidence of such practices than initially one might think. Prestige practices are patterned behaviours that should leave patterned material traces. Evidence for them should be found in patterns of artefact distribution and deposition, rather than necessarily in the occurrence of specific items per se.

For instance, Earle and Spriggs had already speculated that obsidian was merely a sign of the movement and practice of skilled tattooists who were reproducing the Lapita design system not on pots, the form in which it survives to be found by archaeologists, but on people (Earle and Spriggs, 2015, p. 522). The obsidian merely accompanied their movements, rather than having any prestige value in and of itself. Similarly, there are occasional movements of decorated Lapita pots, between New Caledonia and Vanuatu for instance, but the vast majority of pots on almost all Lapita sites are made locally. They are clearly not being produced for long-distance exchange and so the rare presence of exotic pots in a site is thus a sign of something else – transport of their contents, perhaps as part of marriage or other ritual exchanges, or simply as convenient storage during voyages to undertake the same. Iconography on pottery and other items too can be used to reconstruct activities not otherwise preserved archaeologically such as tattooing, mat making and the production of masks, hats and feathered headdresses.

What happened after the initial spread of Lapita is instructive – a decrease in communal ritual, a major decline in the production of fine pottery, an increase in settlement size and a collapse of long-distance connections The rationale for sustaining long-distance exchange had disappeared; the immediate needs of the majority of the population could be met locally and the previously needed prestige goods and practices and the associated ideologies that justified those needs were no longer 'cost effective'. The result was a decidedly egalitarian turn in the post-Lapita societies of Vanuatu and presumably elsewhere in the Lapita realm.

Examples have been given in this chapter of archaeological materials that can be interpreted as signs of prestige practices rather than prestige-goods exchange. It is clearly necessary to give equal time to the idea of a political economy founded on the manipulation, exchange and control of prestige practices, rather than one solely based on material prestige goods that we (think we) identify in the archaeological record.

Acknowledgements

I dedicate this chapter to my friend and colleague Pat Kirch, who claimed to have retired but then recently took up a new university position in his natal Honolulu. It is developed from aspects of a paper delivered at the Trade Before Civilisation Conference at the University of Gothenburg, Sweden, organised by Ric Chacon and Kristian Kristiansen in 2016 and currently in press. It discusses in more detail some of the ideas first aired there. Stuart Bedford and Siri Seule are thanked for provision of figures. The chapter has also had the benefit of sage comments from Tim Earle and Tim Thomas that have hopefully improved its cogency.

References

Ambrose, W. 2019. Plaited textile expression in Lapita ceramic ornamentation. In: S. Bedford and M. Spriggs, eds. *Debating Lapita: Distribution, Chronology, Society and Subsistence.* Terra Australis. Canberra: ANU Press, pp. 241–256.

Bedford, S., 2006. The Pacific's earliest painted pottery: an added layer of intrigue to the Lapita debate and beyond. *Antiquity,* 80, pp. 544–557.

Bedford, S., Spriggs, M., Buckley, H., Valentin, F., Regenvanu, R. and Abong, M., 2010. Un cimetière de premier peuplement: le site de Teouma, Sud Efate, Vanuatu/A cemetery of first settlement: Teouma, South Efate, Vanuatu. In: C. Sand and S. Bedford, eds. *Lapita: Ancêtres Océaniens/Oceanic Ancestors.* Paris: Musée du Quai Branly/Somogy, pp. 140–161.

Bellwood, P., 1996. Hierarchy, founder ideology and Austronesian expansion. In: J.J. Fox and C. Sather, eds. *Origins, Ancestry and Alliance: Explorations in Austronesian Ethnography.* Canberra: Department of Anthropology, RSPacS, ANU, pp. 18–40.

Braithwaite, M., 1984. The past in the past. ritual and prestige in the prehistory of Wessex 2200–1400 BC: a new dimension to the archaeological evidence. In: D. Miller and C. Tilley, eds. *Ideology, Power and Prehistory.* Cambridge: Cambridge University Press, pp. 93–101.

Casey, D.A., 1936. Ethnological notes. *Memoirs of the National Museum of Victoria,* 9, pp. 90–97.

Constantine, A., Reepmeyer, C., Bedford, S., Spriggs, M. and Ravn, M., 2015. Obsidian distribution from a Lapita cemetery sheds light on its value to past societies. *Archaeology in Oceania,* 50, pp. 111–116.

D'Altroy, T.N. and Earle, T.K., 1985. Staple finance, wealth finance and storage in the Inka political economy. *Current Anthropology,* 26(2), pp. 187–206.

Dickinson, W., Bedford, S. and Spriggs, M., 2013. Petrography of temper sands in 112 reconstructed Lapita pottery vessels from Teouma (Efate): archaeological implications and relations to other Vanuatu tempers. *Journal of Pacific Archaeology*, 4(2), pp. 1–20.

Earle, T.K., 1997. *How Chiefs Come to Power: The Political Economy in Prehistory*. Stanford, CA: Stanford University Press.

Earle, T.K., 2017. *An Essay on Political Economies in Prehistory*. Beiträge zur Wirtschaftsarchäologie, 2. Bonn: Habelt-Verlag.

Earle, T.K. and Spriggs, M., 2015. Political economy in prehistory: a Marxist approach to Pacific sequences (with comments and reply). *Current Anthropology* 56(4), pp. 515–544.

Ekholm, K., 1972. *Power and Prestige: The Rise and Fall of the Kongo Kingdom*. Uppsala: Scriv Service.

Ekholm, K., 1977. External exchange and the transformation of Central African social systems. In: J. Friedman and M. Rowlands, eds. *The Evolution of Social Systems*. London: Duckworth, pp. 115–136.

Ekholm Friedman, K. and Friedman, J., 2008. *Historical Transformations: The Anthropology of Global Systems*. Lanham, MD: Altamira.

Friedman, J., 1981. Notes on structure and history in Oceania. *Folk*, 23, pp. 275–295.

Friedman, J., 1982. Catastrophe and continuity in social evolution. In: C. Renfrew, M.J. Rowlands and B.A. Segraves, eds. *Theory and Explanation in Archaeology: The Southampton Conference*. London: Academic Press, pp. 175–196.

Friedman, J. and Rowlands, M.J., 1977. Notes towards an epigenetic model of the evolution of 'Civilisation'. In: J. Friedman and M.J. Rowlands, eds. *The Evolution of Social Systems*. London: Duckworth, pp. 201–276.

Gosden, C. and Pavlides, C., 1994. Are islands insular? Landscape vs. seascape in the case of the Arawe Islands, Papua New Guinea. *Archaeology in Oceania*, 29, pp. 162–171.

Green, R., 1979. Early Lapita art from Polynesia and Island Melanesia: continuities in ceramic, barkcloth and tattoo decorations. In: S. Mead, ed. *Exploring the Visual Art of Oceania*. Honolulu: University of Hawaii Press, pp. 13–31.

Green, R.C., 1987. Obsidian results from the Lapita sites of the Reef/Santa Cruz Islands. In: W.R. Ambrose and J.M.J. Mummery, eds. *Archaeometry: Further Australasian Studies*. Canberra: Department of Prehistory, RSPacS, ANU and Australian National Gallery, pp. 239–249.

Harlow, G.E., Summerhayes, G.R., Davies, H.L. and Matisoo-Smith, L., 2012. A jade gouge from Emirau Island, Papua New Guinea (Early Lapita context, 3300 BP): a unique jadeitite. *European Journal of Mineralogy*, 24, pp. 391–399.

Hawkins, S., 2015. Human behavioural ecology, anthropogenic impact and subsistence change at the Teouma Lapita site, Central Vanuatu, 3000–2500 BP. Unpublished PhD thesis, Australian National University.

Hayden, B., 1983. Social characteristics of early Austronesian colonisers. *Bulletin of the Indo-Pacific Prehistory Association*, 4, pp. 123–134.

Hayden, B., 1995. The emergence of prestige technologies and pottery. In: W.K. Barnett and J.W. Hoopes, eds. *The Emergence of Pottery: Technology and Innovation in Ancient Societies*. Washington, DC, and London: Smithsonian Institution Press, pp. 257–265.

Helms, M.W., 1988. *Ulysses' Sail: An Ethnographic Odyssey of Power, Knowledge and Geographical Distance*. Princeton, NJ: Princeton University Press.

Helms, M.W., 1993. *Craft and the Kingly Ideal: Art, Trade and Power*. Austin, TX: University of Texas Press.

Kirch, P.V., 1984. *The Evolution of the Polynesian Chiefdoms*. Cambridge: Cambridge University Press.

Kirch, P.V., 1986. Exchange systems and inter-island contact in the transformation of an island society: the Tikopia case. In: P.V. Kirch, ed. *Island Societies: Archaeological Approaches to Evolution and Transformation*. Cambridge: Cambridge University Press, pp. 33–41.

Kirch, P.V., 1988a. Long-distance exchange and island colonization: the Lapita case. *Norwegian Archaeological Review*, 21(2), pp. 103–117.

Kirch, P.V., 1988b. The transformation of Polynesian societies: archaeological issues. In C. Cristino, P.Vargas, R. Izaurieta, and R. Budd, eds. *First International Congress, Easter Island and East Polynesia, Hanga Roa, Easter Island 1984*, vol. 1, *Archaeology*. Santiago: Universidad de Chile, Facultad de Arquitectura y Urbanismo, Instituto de Estudios, Isla de Pascua, pp. 1–12.

Kirch, P.V., 1990. The evolution of sociopolitical complexity in prehistoric Hawaii: an assessment of the archaeological evidence. *Journal of World Prehistory*, 4(3), pp. 311–345.

Kirch, P.V., 1991. Prehistoric exchange in Western Melanesia. *Annual Review of Anthropology*, 20, pp. 142–165.

Kirch, P.V., 1997. *The Lapita Peoples: Ancestors of the Oceanic World*. Oxford: Blackwell.

Kirch, P.V., 2000. *On the Road of the Winds: An Archaeological History of the Pacific Islands Before European Contact*. Berkeley, CA: University of California Press.

Kirch, P.V., 2017. *On the Road of the Winds: An Archaeological History of the Pacific Islands Before European Contact*. Revised and expanded edition. Berkeley, CA: University of California Press.

Kononenko, N., 2012. Middle and Late Holocene skin-working tools in Melanesia: tattooing and scarification. *Archaeology in Oceania*, 47(1), pp. 14–28.

Küchler, S., 2002. *Malanggan: Art, Memory and Sacrifice*. Oxford: Berg.

Lilley, I., 1985. Chiefs without Chiefdoms? Comments on prehistoric sociopolitical organization in Western Melanesia. *Archaeology in Oceania*, 20(2), pp. 60–65.

Lipson, M., Skoglund, P., Spriggs, M.,Valentin, F., Bedford, S., Shing, R., Phillip, I.,Ward, G.K., Mallick, S., Rohland, N., Broomandkhoshbacht, N., Cheronet, O., Ferry, M., Harper, T.K., Michel, M., Oppenheimer, J., Sirak, K., Stewardson, K., Auckland, K., Hill, A.V.S., Maitland, K., Oppenheimer, S.J., Parks, T., Robson, K., Williams, T.N., Kennett, D.J., Mentzer, A., Pinhasi, R. and Reich, D., 2018. Population turnover in Remote Oceania shortly after initial settlement. *Current Biology* 28(7), pp. 1157–1165 and supplementary information (doi.org:10.1016/j.cub.2018.02.051).

Pawley, A., 1981. Melanesian diversity and Polynesian homogeneity: a unified explanation for language. In: J. Hollyman and A. Pawley, eds. *Studies in Pacific Languages and Cultures in Honour of Bruce Biggs*. Auckland: Linguistic Society of New Zealand, pp. 269–309.

Posth, C., Nägele, K., Colleran, H.,Valentin, F., Bedford, S., Kami, K.W., Shing, R., Buckley, H., Kinaston, R.,Walworth, M., Clark, G.R., Reepmeyer, C., Flexner, J., Maric, T., Moser, J., Gresky, J., Kiko, L., Robson, K.J.,Auckland, K., Oppenheimer, S.J., Hill,A.V.S., Mentzer, A.J., Zech, J., Petchey, F., Roberts, P., Jeong, C., Gray, R.D., Krause, J. and Powell, A., 2018. Language continuity despite Population replacement in Remote Oceania. *Nature: Ecology and Evolution*, 2(Apr.), pp. 731–740 and supplementary information (doi.org/10.1038/s41559-018-0498-2).

Reepmeyer, C., Spriggs, M., Bedford, S. and Ambrose, W.C., 2010. Provenance and technology of lithic artefacts from the Teouma Lapita site,Vanuatu. *Asian Perspectives*, 49(1), pp. 205–225.

Sheppard, P.J., 1993. Lapita lithics: trade/exchange and technology: a view from the Reefs/Santa Cruz. *Archaeology in Oceania*, 28(3), pp. 121–137.

Sheppard, P.J., 1996. Hard rock: archaeological implications of chert sourcing in Near and Remote Oceania. In: J. Davidson, G. Irwin, F. Leach, A. Pawley, and D. Brown (eds),

Oceanic Culture History: Essays in Honour of Roger Green. Dunedin: New Zealand Journal of Archaeology, pp. 99–115.

Skoglund, P., Posth, C., Sirak, K., Spriggs, M., Valentin, F., Bedford, S., Clark, G.A., Reepmeyer, C., Fernandes, D., Fu, Q., Harney, E., Lipson, M., Mallick, S., Novak, M., Rohland, N., Stewardson, K., Abdullah, S., Cox, M.P., Friedlaender, F.R., Friedlaender, J.S., Kivisild, T., Koki, G., Kusuma, P., Merriwether, D.A., Ricaut, F.-X., Wee, J.T.S., Patterson, N., Krause, J., Pinhasi, R. and Reich, D., 2016. Genomic insights into the peopling of the Southwest Pacific. *Nature,* 538 (27 Oct.), pp. 510–513, and supplementary information (doi.org/10.1038/nature19844).

Spriggs, M., 1984. Another way of telling: Marxist perspectives in archaeology. In: M. Spriggs, ed. *Marxist Perspectives in Archaeology.* New Directions in Archaeology Series. Cambridge: Cambridge University Press, pp. 1–9.

Spriggs, M., 1986. Landscape, land use and political transformation in southern Melanesia. In: P.V. Kirch, ed. *Island Societies: Archaeological Approaches to Evolution and Transformation.* Cambridge: Cambridge University Press, pp. 6–19.

Spriggs, M., 1992. What happens to Lapita in Melanesia? In: J.C. Galipaud, ed. *Lapita et Peuplement: Actes du Colloque Lapita, Nouméa, Nouvelle-Calédonie, 1992.* Nouméa: ORSTOM, pp. 219–230.

Spriggs M., 1997. *The Island Melanesians.* Oxford: Blackwell.

Spriggs, M., 2011. Archaeology and the Austronesian expansion: where are we now? *Antiquity,* 85(328), pp. 510–528.

Spriggs, M., 2013. Leaving safe harbours: movement to immobility, homogeneity to diversification. A comparative archaeological sequence from the western Pacific. In: S. Bergerbrant and S. Sabatini, eds. *Counterpoint: Essays in Archaeology and Heritage Studies in Honour of Professor Kristian Kristiansen.* BAR International Series 2508. Oxford: Archaeopress, pp. 549–556.

Spriggs, M., 2016a. Lapita and the Linearbandkeramik: what can a comparative approach tell us about either? In: L. Amkreutz, F. Haack, D. Hofmann, and I. van Wijk (eds), *Something Out of the Ordinary? Interpreting Diversity in the Early Neolithic Linearbandkeramik Culture of Central and Western Europe.* Newcastle upon Tyne: Cambridge Scholars Publishing, pp. 481–504.

Spriggs, M., 2016b. Thoughts of a comparativist on past colonization, maritime interaction and cultural integration. In: H. Glørstad and L. Melheim, eds. *Interdisciplinary Perspectives on Past Colonization, Maritime Interaction and Cultural Integration.* New Directions in Anthropological Archaeology Series. Sheffield: Equinox Publishers, pp. 271–280.

Spriggs, M. 2019. The hat makes the man: masks, headdresses and skullcaps in Lapita iconography. In: S. Bedford and M. Spriggs, eds. *Debating Lapita: Distribution, Chronology, Society and Subsistence.* Terra Australis. Canberra: ANU Press, pp. 257–273.

Spriggs, M. In press. Lapita long-distance interactions in the Western Pacific: from prestige goods to prestige practices. In: R. Chacon and K. Kristiansen, eds. *Trade Before Civilisation.* Cambridge: Cambridge University Press.

Summerhayes, G.R., 1998. The face of Lapita. *Archaeology in Oceania,* 33, p. 100.

Summerhayes, G.R., 2003. Modelling differences between Lapita obsidian and pottery distribution patterns in the Bismarck Archipelago, PNG. In: C. Sand (ed.), *Pacific Archaeology: Assessments and Prospects. Proceedings of the International Conference for the 50th Anniversary of the First Lapita Excavation, July 2002, Koné-Nouméa.* Les Cahiers de L'Archéologie en Nouvelle-Calédonie, 15. Nouméa: Musée de Nouvelle-Calédonie, pp. 139–149.

Summerhayes, G.R., 2009. Obsidian network patterns in Melanesia: sources, characterisation and distribution. *Bulletin of the Indo-Pacific Prehistory Association,* 29, pp. 109–123.

Swadling, P., 1996. *Plumes from Paradise: Trade Cycles in Outer Southeast Asia and their Impact on New Guinea and Nearby Islands until 1920.* Boroko: PNG National Museum.

Szabo, K., 2010. Shell artefacts and shell-working within the Lapita cultural complex. *Journal of Pacific Archaeology,* 1, pp. 115–127.

Thomas, J., 2001. *Understanding the Neolithic.* London: Routledge.

Thomas, N., 1989. *Out of Time: History and Evolution in Anthropological Discourse.* Cambridge Studies in Social Anthropology. Cambridge: Cambridge University Press.

Thomas, T., 2001. The social practice of colonisation: re-thinking prehistoric Polynesian migration. *People and Culture in Oceania,* 17, pp. 27–46.

Thompson, J. and Taylor, A., 1980. *Polynesian Canoes and Navigation.* Laie, HI: Institute for Polynesian Studies.

Torrence, R., 2004. Pre-Lapita valuables in Island Melanesia. In: V. Attenbrow and R. Fullagar, eds. *A Pacific Odyssey: Archaeology and Anthropology in the Western Pacific. Papers in Honour of Jim Specht.* Records of the Australian Museum Supplement, 29, pp. 163–172.

Torrence, R., Kononenko, N., Sheppard, P., Allen, M.S., Bedford, S., Kirch, P. and Spriggs, M., 2018. Tattooing tools and the Lapita cultural complex. *Archaeology in Oceania,* 53(1), pp. 58–73.

Trigger, B., 1985. Marxism in archaeology: real or spurious? *Reviews in Anthropology,* 12(2), pp. 114–123.

Trigger, B., 1993. Marxism in contemporary Western archaeology. *Archaeological Method and Theory,* 5, pp. 159–200.

Valentin, F., Spriggs, M., Bedford, S. and Buckley, H., 2011. Vanuatu mortuary practices over three millennia: Lapita to the early European contact period. *Journal of Pacific Archaeology,* 2(2), pp. 49–65.

Valentin, F., Herrscher, E., Bedford, S., Spriggs, M. and Buckley, H., 2014. Evidence for social and cultural change in Central Vanuatu during the first millennium BC: comparing funerary and dietary patterns of the first and later generations at Teouma, Efate. *Journal of Island and Coastal Archaeology,* 9(3), pp. 381–399.

Valentin, F., Choi, J.-I., Lin, H., Bedford, S. and Spriggs, M., 2015. Three thousand year old jar burials at the Teouma cemetery (Vanuatu): a Southeast Asian-Lapita connection? In: S. Chiu, C. Sand and N. Hogg, eds. *The Lapita Cultural Complex in Time and Space: Expansion Routes, Chronologies and Typologies.* Archaeologia Pasifika, 3. Nouméa and Taipei: IANCP and Center for Archaeological Studies, Research Center for Humanities and Social Sciences, Academia Sinica, pp. 81–101.

Worthy, T., Hawkins, S., Bedford, S. and Spriggs, M., 2015. The avifauna from the Teouma Lapita site, Efate Island, Vanuatu, including a new genus and species of megapode. *Pacific Science,* 69(2), pp. 205–254.

9

ANARCHIST THEORY IN THE PACIFIC AND 'PACIFIC ANARCHISTS' IN ARCHAEOLOGICAL THOUGHT

James L. Flexner

Anarchists, Anarchy and Anarchism

The term *anarchist* has a decidedly etic ring to it in a Pacific context. It is not necessarily a term that would be easily recognised or identified with among Pacific communities. Indeed, many Pacific Islanders, particularly those that identify with postcolonial nation-states, would likely cringe at the notion of their societies representing 'anarchy'. But what do these terms really signify? I want to make it clear at the outset that the popular conception of anarchy and anarchists, characterised by violence and chaos, mischaracterises the broader tenets of anarchist thought and anarchist movements. Rather, the classical definitions of anarchy focus on principles of independence, self-realisation, egalitarianism and communal, spontaneous group organisation (e.g. Bakunin, 1950[1872; Kropotkin, 1902). One of the goals of much contemporary anarchist scholarship is to correct this misunderstanding by exploring the ways that non-state societies, far from representing chaos, are in fact examples of highly structured, if horizontal, forms of social organisation (Angelbeck and Grier, 2012; Bettinger, 2015[1]).

In this chapter, I will use the term 'anarchism' to signal that there are in fact many forms of anarchist thought and practice, and to avoid conflating Pacific Islander practices with contemporary, mostly Western political movements. Anarchism refers broadly to practices, structures, beliefs and attitudes that generally resist or prevent the emergence of coercive institutions, or the arbitrary accumulation of power by individuals (Borck and Sanger, 2017; Graeber, 2004).

In contrast to concepts like anarchism, indigenous terms like *tabu* and *mana*, once staples of the anthropological canon, remain nearly ubiquitous in Pacific scholarship (e.g. Tomlinson and Tengan, 2016), and introduced terms like 'chief' have, in many cases, been wholeheartedly adopted by Pacific Islanders as a signifier of social status (e.g. Earle and Spriggs, 2015, pp. 528–529). Yet anarchist thought, basically absent from scholarship in the region, has much to offer Pacific archaeology. Anarchist theories explore the alternative forms of order that have existed, exist in the present or could exist in the future, outside of the realms of state power.

Many Pacific Island societies, particularly in the area historically termed 'Melanesia', provide ethnohistorical examples of what anthropologists call 'societies against the state', that is, societies with built-in mechanisms to resist or creatively channel the forces of self-aggrandisement, coercive force and centralisation (e.g. Clastres, 1987; Scott, 2009). Archaeology offers a lens for exploring the long-term dynamics of these types of societies. The existence of these two lines of reasoning sets up a useful space for dialogue. Anarchist theoretical frameworks can expand the realm of possible thoughts used to interpret archaeological data. At the same time, the realities of past Pacific Islander lives might provide an interesting lens for reinterpreting some of the tenets of classical anarchist thought.

We need anarchism more than ever

To begin this discussion, it is worth asking, why engage with anarchism at all? A look at current events suggests the rise of dangerous far-right movements is becoming relatively common in global politics in the 21st century. Between the 'alt-right' in the USA, Brexit, the UK Independence Party, Marine Le Pen, *Alternativ fur Deutschland*, Erdogan, Bolsonaro, the Australia First party (and the list could go on), it is becoming clear that a politics driven by ethnonationalism, patriarchy and bolstering of entrenched social divisions is rearing its ugly head in many places. This is not to mention the worrying and obscene concentration of wealth and access to resources among a tiny percentage of the world's human population (for an anthropological exploration of these issues a quarter century ago see Rapaport, 1992). Anarchism provides a set of related philosophies and practices for combating these tendencies via projects aimed at dismantling capitalism, patriarchy and the state while 'prefiguring' a more egalitarian society, 'forming the structure of the new society within the shell of the old'.[2]

The term anarchism comes from Greek roots that mean (roughly), 'without rulers'. As Peter Kropotkin explained in *Encyclopedia Brittanica*, anarchy is:

> The name given to a principle or theory of life and conduct under which society is conceived without government – harmony in such a society being obtained, not by submission to law, or by obedience to any authority, but by free agreements concluded between the various groups, territorial and professional, freely constituted for the sake of production and consumption, as also for the satisfaction of the infinite variety of needs and aspirations of a civilized being.
>
> *(Quoted in Graeber, 2004, p. 1)*

Like James C. Scott (1998, p. 7; 2012, pp. xxii–xxiii), I do not necessarily see the state going anywhere in the next few years. In other words, we probably will not see the global dissolution of capitalism and states in our lifetime. But I think that the ideal of society conceived without government is an important one to keep in mind at this time, precisely because submission and obedience to authority are making life precarious for so many in so many places. Indeed, even in the Pacific, state suppression of local autonomy continues to produce social tension, inequality and violence, but also a variety of creative responses by Pacific Islanders (e.g. in West Papua; see Macleod, 2015). Anarchism provides a call to resistance.

Anarchism and Pacific archaeology

So, what does this have to do with archaeology? Surely the scientific study of the past has no need of revolutionary politics? Archaeologists have known for a long time (e.g. Shanks and Tilley, 1987) that our discipline is inherently political, and I am going to argue here that a revolutionary politics can be beneficial for arch-aeological thought and practice. Anarchist archaeology remains an emerging field within the discipline, as most publications on the topic have only appeared within the last ten years or so. This is in contrast to Marxist archaeology, which has a related interest in radical politics but a much longer history in the discipline going back at least to V. Gordon Childe (McGuire, 1992; Spriggs, 1984). Indeed, there is a longstanding, if not always agreeable, relationship between anarchism and Marxism, which dates back to the 19th-century labour movements that created the two schools of thought (Graham, 2015).

Other archaeological approaches, such as postcolonial (Lydon and Rizvi, 2010), community (Marshall, 2002) and indigenous (Smith and Wobst, eds., 2005) archaeologies, would also find affinities with anarchist archaeology because of their commitment to undermining and reframing orthodox narratives about the past and unequal practices in the present. There are also related conceptual terms, such as 'heterarchy' (Crumley, 1987) that challenge assumptions in archaeological narratives about power relations. Anarchist archaeology is not meant to supplant or replace any of these existing schools of thought. Rather, it provides a set of parallel concepts and rhetorical tools to supplement archaeology's already rich theoretical toolkit.

There is no one hegemonic 'anarchist archaeology' per se (this would be a very unanarchist thing to do). Rather, there is a variety of thinkers and practitioners working along similar lines, sometimes in conversation with each other (e.g. Black Trowel Collective, 2016), sometimes more independently. Anarchist archaeologies draw upon the classic works of Western anarchist thinkers, such as Bakunin (1950[1872]), Goldman (1969[1910]), Kropotkin (1902) and Proudhon (1994[1840]). They have also tended to take inspiration from anarchist anthropologists, in particular David Graeber (2004) and James C. Scott (1998; 2009). Where the earlier thinkers were more practically engaged with large-scale workers' movements, the anthropological approaches tend to be more theoretical in orientation (though see Graeber, 2013).

What anarchist archaeologies tend to have in common is two main threads, one theoretical and one practical (for recent summaries see Borck and Sanger, 2017; Flexner and Gonzalez-Tennant, 2018; Rathbone, 2017). The theoretical thread is based on a scepticism of narratives that valorise hierarchy, and a commitment to exploring evidence for cooperation, egalitarianism, mutual aid and resistance in the past. The practical thread involves applying the ideals of consensus-based behaviour in the present in the ways we act, in the field, the classroom and in relation to communities. This of course is not to deny that hierarchy exists, past or present. Rather the goal is to argue that where coercive and unjust hierarchies do exist, we have a responsibility to understand the ways that this kind of power worked in the past, how our narratives affect its interpretation in the present and how our behaviour can prefigure a more egalitarian future.

The long-term histories of indigenous societies in Island Melanesia offer a valuable example of what an anarchist approach can add to our theoretical understanding of the past. Simultaneously, the unique evolutionary trajectories of Island Melanesian societies themselves challenge Old World models for historical change. An orthodox civilisation narrative defines these societies by what they lacked before Europeans arrived in the region: there are no kings, no palaces, no urban settlements, no writing. If these cultures lacked what others developed, then clearly, they are 'less evolved' or did not have the same 'energy' as the classical civilisations of Mesopotamia, Egypt, Greece and Rome. While those of us in archaeology may think we have moved beyond this narrative (e.g. Golson, 1977, though I'm not always totally convinced that we are all the way there yet), the public largely has not.[3] People still seem to believe that human cultural evolution is a ladder rather than a tree.

An anarchist approach turns the civilisation narrative on its head. Anthropologist Pierre Clastres (1987) writes about 'societies against the state', noting that societies without fixed hierarchies make an active choice to prevent self-aggrandising individuals from acquiring too much power. Likewise, in *The Art of Not Being Governed*, James C. Scott (2009) describes the ways that the hill tribes of southeast Asia, inhabiting the mountainous region he calls 'Zomia' have created a 'non-state' space, that is a territory that can exist beyond the limits of the state's powers of surveillance, coercion and control. In short, where states do not evolve, one of the processes in play is an active choice to prevent their emergence.

Island Melanesia provides an excellent suite of case studies of societies against the state. Certainly this could be argued for the highlands of Papua New Guinea, which saw early settlement in the Pleistocene, followed by early and independent development of agriculture, but classic assumptions about what 'should come next' (cities, rulers, states) were never fulfilled (e.g. Denham, 2006; 2018; Golson et al., 2017; Gosden, 2010; Summerhayes et al., 2016). To repeat the mantra: on some level this was an active choice made by these societies and not a result of environmental limitation or some other deficiency. In the absence of centralised rulers, other forms of social relationships, artistic creativity and ritual expression flourished. While they may not have built palaces, New Guinea highlanders nonetheless created a remarkably complex way of life based on the production of agricultural surplus, complex exchange networks and the veneration of ancestral beings (e.g. Rapaport, 1984).

I have argued elsewhere that southern Vanuatu likewise represents a non-state space, particularly on the island of Tanna, which had a massively complex and heterarchical chiefly system (Flexner, 2014; see below). This non-hierarchical complexity proved baffling for European colonial agents, and likely contributed to the sometimes-violent encounters on the island. Arguments made by Spriggs (2008), Sand (2015) and others, that the ethnographic 'big men' societies of Melanesia reflect the major upheavals of colonialism, including the demographic catastrophe caused by introduced Western diseases, are well taken. However, I still think there is an argument to be made for a long-term anti-hierarchical structure for many Melanesian societies.

The story of Roi Mata from Vanuatu offers another useful case in point. Roi Mata was an individual who amassed great power in his lifetime, known from ethnographic and archaeological evidence (Ballard, 2016; Garanger, 1972, pp. 58–77; 1996), but in the end, he chose to sever his lineage rather than passing on his title, thus preventing this power from being passed on to a new generation (and possibly setting up a feedback loop towards centralisation).

This is not to say that Melanesian Islanders would have identified as 'anarchists'. Anarchism emerged from 19th-century labour movements in Europe and North America (though it does have more ancient antecedents in Western and non-Western contexts; Graham, 2005). What we can do is think about the ways that anarchist approaches to historiography, that is, those approaches that emphasise the centrality of resistance and advocate for a non-hierarchical evolutionary arrangement of human societies through time, might benefit the stories we tell. Further, as archaeologists we can consider the ways that our discipline's materials might inform and refine some of the tenets of classical as well as modern anarchism. The Pacific, and Island Melanesia in particular, provides a valuable archaeological perspective precisely because societies in the region followed such different pathways to social complexity, many of which eschewed or subverted entrenched hierarchies. Further, their social dynamics point not only to the arts of resistance, but also to the work of maintaining an egalitarian society (see below).

Sources of inspiration and argument: Darwin and Kropotkin

Much archaeological theory in the Pacific uses some combination of paradigms from the following schools of thought: functionalism (the idea that all human behaviour serves some material purpose), Darwinism (human history is the result of competition over resources and mates, as a result of which selection for traits and behaviours occurs), ecology (societies emerge from a synthesis of 'natural' and 'cultural' processes) and Marxism (history is a result of human struggle and class conflict). Each of these schools of thought offers important insights into the human past. However, many of the interpretations built on these theories can't be separated from the Western colonial and patriarchal assumptions that shaped the thoughts of the original theorists (arguably this is the case for many of the classical anarchists as well). As an example, we can compare the centrality of competition as a selective force, one of the tenets of classical Darwinism, with the centrality of cooperation in the writings of Kropotkin, one of the classical 19th-century anarchist thinkers who was also interested in evolution.

In *Origin of Species* (1849) and *The Descent of Man* (1871), Darwin laid out the basis for an evolutionary science that explained how related species emerged through the process of descent with modification. As part of his argument, Darwin makes two things necessary for the process to work: variability within a species, and competition, both between species and among individuals from the same species. Regarding social evolution, Darwin (1871, p. 154) claimed that, as with competing species, societies that were fitter for their environment inevitably supplanted those who were less fit (and the echoes of imperialist ideology cannot be ignored here).

As a counterpoint, Kropotkin (1902) offers a model for both biological and social evolution based on the principle of *Mutual Aid*. According to Kropotkin (1902, p. 5)

> though there is an immense amount of warfare and extermination going on amidst various species … there is, at the same time, as much, or perhaps even more, of mutual support, mutual aid, and mutual defence … Sociability is as much a law of nature as mutual struggle.

One of Kropotkin's major conclusions bears quoting at length:

> It is evident that no review of evolution can be complete, unless these two dominant currents [competition and mutual aid] are analyzed. However, the self-assertion of the individual or of groups of individuals, their struggles for superiority, and the conflicts which resulted therefrom, have already been analyzed, described, and glorified from time immemorial. In fact, up to the present time, this current alone has received attention from the epical poet, the annalist, the historian, and the sociologist [and here we can add at least some archaeologists]. History, such as it has hitherto been written, is almost entirely a description of the ways and means by which theocracy, military power, autocracy, and, later on, the richer classes' rule have been promoted, established, and maintained. The struggles between these forces make, in fact, the substance of history. We may thus take the knowledge of the individual factor in human history as granted – even though there is full room for a new study of the subject on the lines just alluded to; while, on the other side, the mutual-aid factor has been hitherto totally lost sight of; it was simply denied, or even scoffed at, by the writers of the present and past generation.
>
> *(Kropotkin, 1902, p. 295)*

A shifted focus that emphasises cooperative and consensus-based behaviours would be a beneficial way of reassessing some of our collective assumptions about the past (and indeed we can see this happening already, see e.g. DeMarrais, 2016). This is not to say that Darwin was 'wrong' by any means. The theory of natural selection remains one of the most powerful theoretical tools for the historical sciences. However, the focus on one kind of behavioural dynamic (competition) at the expense of others (cooperation and consensus), or assuming cooperative behaviour was engaged in only because it produces an optimising competitive advantage, offers a misleading view of past and present. We might suggest a re-evaluation of some of the implications of evolutionary thought in our understandings of past human societies.

Competition, cooperation and consensus in South Vanuatu chiefly societies

To explore the ways that anarchist thoughts about the arts of cooperation and resistance might be applied to Pacific archaeology, I turn to the island of Tanna in comparison with the neighbouring islands of Futuna, Erromango and Aneityum. It is worth noting at the outset that chiefly hierarchies and competition were intense in Vanuatu, often involving warfare and black magic. The chiefly systems themselves were quite variable across the archipelago. Feasting and pig sacrifices used to earn titles drove the 'grade-taking' ceremonial competitions of the north and centre. People constructed megalithic altars where grade-taking and other communal ceremonies took place in Malakula and neighbouring islands (Bedford, 2019; Layard, 1942). In the south, hydraulic chiefdoms evolved as powerful individuals sought control over massive irrigated terrace systems for growing taro (e.g. Earle and Spriggs, 2015, pp. 522–525; Spriggs, 1981).

Within southern Vanuatu, which is where Tanna is also located, there was local diversity in the forms and scale of chiefly hierarchies (e.g. Spriggs, 1986; Spriggs and Wickler, 1989). Tanna has the most complex, but also the most horizontally organised chiefly system of the southern Vanuatu islands. Tannese society has been described as 'atomistic', as the daily kava ritual involves the men retreating to independent corners of the *yimwayim* (or *imwarim* depending on the language area; large, open spaces framed by monumental banyan trees) to listen to the spirit of the intoxicating beverage (Brunton, 1979). Yet chiefly titles abound on Tanna. There is the chief who 'leads the canoe' (*yani neteta*; the second word both literally meaning canoe and referring to a land division), the talking chief (*yani en dete*), the chief who has the right to eat the head of the turtle, the hereditary chief (*yeremwanu*) who wears the feathers of the hawk (*kweriya*), and more (Bonnemaison, 1994, pp. 146–156; Douglas, 1996, p. 243; Guiart, 1956, pp. 15–17). Other men[4] of power included the *tupunas*, keepers of the magic stones that could both benefit (by making the yams grow, for example), and harm (by summoning storms or causing fatal illness), and the *narumin* who could predict the future and see the unknown (Bonnemaison, 1994, pp. 172–180; Guiart, 1956, pp. 63–72; Humphreys, 1926, pp. 70–71).

This proliferation of titles and roles in society was so great that a mid-20th-century survey of the island counted 601 'chiefs' against a total population of 6,937, or one chief among every eleven to twelve individuals (Guiart, 1956, p. 9). Titles could be gained and lost, and had to be defended. According to one of my friends on the island, the fighting over titles was so intense that it led a coalition of West Tanna chiefs to accept Christianity at the end of the 19th century in order to broker a peace, or at least reduce the fighting (and of course in the process they gained a new set of titles and powers through the Presbyterian Church; Iavis Nikiatu, pers. comm., 2013). Chiefs often have to publicly perform their roles through oration or song, showing they have the requisite knowledge to claim a title, while making sure they do not give their knowledge away to people who are unworthy (Lindstrom, 1990).

Much of Tannese art has been characterised as intangible, taking the form of song, dance and wordplay (Lindstrom, 1996). Nor did the Tannese usually build large structures in stone or other durable materials. However, the island's cultural landscape itself is arguably the greatest Tannese work of art. Tannese people invest in the ongoing creation of magically powered gardens that produce the staple yams and intoxicating kava, as well as the creation of the kava drinking and dancing grounds called *imwarim* or *yimwayim* (Bonnemaison, 1991; Brunton, 1989). That the Tannese did not generally build pyramids or other monuments should not be held against them, since they instead invested in producing a self-sustaining landscape of linked gardens, hamlets and gathering places (*imwarim*). If there is a form of Tannese monumentality, it is the *imwarim* themselves and the linked gardens with their yam mounds (*takwu*), which can be up to 2 m high and 20 m across, producing yams growing up to 1.5 m and weighing up to 22 kg (Turner, 1861, p. 87).

While the daily kava ritual might involve 'dissolution', the annual and seasonal dances and feasts (*nakwiari* and *nieri*) bring people together on the same grounds. These rituals involve the concentration of massive amounts of agricultural produce and those classic outcomes of surplus in Pacific societies, pigs. On the one hand, feasts were competitive events, and Spriggs (1986, pp. 16–18) argues that this kind of 'fighting with food' was one of the structuring mechanisms for Tanna's more heterarchical society. The flip side of this argument is that cooperation (and here we return to Kropotkin's perspective) was also critical to the functioning of these systems. After all, the chiefs who could draw on the largest numbers of kin, allies, friends and co-conspirators would be able to draw in the largest surplus, and their largesse in redistributing food and gifts would have in turn added to their prestige and authority. However, Tannese society is designed to resist any kind of runaway effects that would allow any singularly ambitious chief to make himself king of the island.

The description here largely draws on ethnographic and ethnohistoric observations. Aside from the pig bones, not much of these behaviours would be archaeologically 'visible' in the long term. However, there is an archaeological landscape on south Tanna that offers some clues about what to look for archaeologically in relation to these simultaneously cooperative and competitive events. The paired sites of Kwaraka and Anuikaraka consist of an apparently unique landscape of stone structures: walls, terraces and mounds. The mounds include a flat-topped form that may have been for habitation, and a conical form. Excavation of one of the conical mounds revealed that it was constructed from a single deposit of stone cobbles and dark sediment, rich with charcoal, red ochre (which was used as a pigment to decorate the body during dances), pig bones and fragments of large shellfish.

This deposit, from one of about seven similar mounds across Kwaraka and Anuikaraka, can be interpreted as being a result of communal behaviour. These kinds of mounds were likely formed by people cleaning the ground of stones and refuse either after or before a communal feasting and dancing event. The excavated example dates to the late 1600s or 1700s, so just prior to European contact on Tanna. The two sites are associated with an oral tradition of a *yeni en dete* called Iarisi. Iarisi is famous now for his connection to early Christianity in south Tanna (see Flexner et al., 2016; Flexner, 2016, pp. 66–73, 93–96 for a full description of the archaeology and oral history of Kwaraka and Anuikaraka). On Tanna, titles can be passed on, and chiefs hold not only the name, but also the accomplishments of previous bearers of the name (Lindstrom, 2011). Thus, the Iarisi who met the missionaries on neighbouring Aneityum was likely one of a series of men with the same title, which has continued to be passed on to the present. That Iarisi was and remains an influential chief may be due to his ability to bring people together, a process materialised in the remains of large communal feasts.

Neighbouring Aneityum and Erromango were more hierarchical than Tanna. One way this is reflected is in the land divisions, referred to as 'canoes' on each island (Tanna *niko/neteta*, Aneityum *nelcau*, Erromango *lo*). Tanna's more egalitarian chiefdoms are reflected in roughly 116 land divisions (some areas are still contested so the number fluctuates) over an area of 550 km². Aneityum is divided into seven main divisions for 159 km², each of which has a paramount chief. Erromango, the largest of the three islands (855 km²), has the smallest number of divisions, six. Each of the Erromangan *lo* is led by a paramount chief called the *fan lo*, whose title is usually passed down through the male lineage (Humphreys, 1926, pp. 128–134; Spriggs and Wickler, 1989, pp. 83–85).

However, there are similar patterns on Erromango in terms of competitive feasting and consensus-led decision making. The pinnacle of Erromangan feasting cycles involved the construction of a massive tower on which pigs, yams, kava and other produce were displayed, called the *nevsem*. These towers were built during feasts (*nisekar*) and other ceremonial occasions. While the feasts involved competition between rival chiefs, they are also referred to as an alternative and deterrent to warfare or a peacekeeping mechanism (Naupa, 2011, pp. 24–26).

One of the other main communal structures in Erromangan society was the men's meeting house or *siman lo*. One of the key activities in the *siman lo* was the nightly consumption of kava by chiefs and their followers, but this was also the place where important community decisions were made. Decision making was arrived at through a consensus of chiefs and involved community members, though Erromangan *fan lo* did have some kind of veto power if they thought the community was going astray (Humphreys, 1926, pp. 156–158, 178; Naupa, 2011, pp. 26–30). Even though Erromango was more hierarchical than Tanna, chiefs still relied on a cadre of friends and supporters as the foundation of their authority and were generally expected to follow the will of the people. The *nisekar* and other ceremonies were cooperative endeavours, built from the grassroots up rather than resulting from a coercive decree of the chiefs.

While Tanna and Erromango subsistence was primarily based on rain-fed agriculture with yams as the staple, Aneityum was a site of intensive taro production in irrigated systems of stone terraces (Spriggs, 1981; 1986). In places, erosion from these systems resulted in the creation of new alluvial deposits. Spriggs argues,

> Where the new alluvium built up, farmers constructed large agricultural complexes with irrigation canals, creating an engineered landscape in which chiefs could claim ownership and mobilize staples as rent. The result was the emergence of territorial chiefdoms like those in Polynesia.
>
> *(Earle and Spriggs, 2015, p. 523)*

Whether a 'bottom up' approach might allow for different interpretations on Aneityum (as has been suggested for Hawai'i, see Dye, 2010), island society certainly appears to have developed along a more hierarchical trajectory than its neighbours.

The small Polynesian Outlier Futuna, intervisible with both Tanna and Aneityum, is linguistically distinct from the neighbouring islands as a result of Polynesian colonisation late in the island's pre-European history. Despite the linguistic difference, Futuna's social and agricultural systems appear to be an interesting synthesis of the two differing pathways to social complexity and productive landscapes represented on Tanna and Aneityum. The other Polynesian Outlier in southern Vanuatu, Aniwa, not discussed in detail here, is quite close to Tanna and appears to be even more heavily influenced by its larger neighbour (Flexner et al., 2018).

Futuna is divided into seven wedge-shaped districts, though in this case the small number is related to the size of the island, which is only about 12km² in area. Futuna has extensive stone terracing (called *ropae*) for rain-fed agriculture on the dry (northern and western) districts, and irrigated taro pondfields in the wet (southern and eastern) districts (Flexner et al., 2018, pp. 251–252). Archaeologically, we can date these terraces to the last 1,000 years along with associated ancestral villages. But if the agricultural system looks similar to that on Aneityum, especially on Futuna's windward side (which faces Aneityum), the chiefly system is much more similar to Tanna. Futuna had numerous chiefs who were responsible for particular resources, ceremonies or knowledge. The chiefs were divided into two 'moieties': *Namruke*, which is wise and subtle, and *Kaviameta*, aggressive and strong in battle (Keller and Kuautonga, 2007, pp. 61–64). Tanna's two moieties have almost identical names (*Koyometa* and *Numrukuen*) and characteristics (Bonnemaison, 1994, pp. 152–153).

What is interesting here from the perspective of an 'anarchist' approach to this history is whether Futuna's Polynesian language and intensified agricultural systems, combined with the more horizontal Tannese-style chiefly system represents a triumph of the arts of resistance in the Polynesian Outlier. One question is how far back the current chiefly system might be projected. Futuna's oral traditions point to origins of the Polynesian population in Tonga, or at least close connections (Keller and Kuautonga, 2007, pp. 146–165). Tonga was the most hierarchical chiefdom in the western Pacific, led by a paramount chief, the 'Tu'i Tonga', who presided over a vast maritime empire (Clark et al., 2008; 2014).

Is it possible that for some reason (geographic circumscription, small population size, influence of the much larger neighbour), no paramount chief could hold authority on Futuna, and thus heterarchy carried the day? Or indeed were Futuna's Polynesian settlers in fact people who chafed under the Tongan maritime empire, and sought out new islands, finding the more egalitarian chiefly society of the Tannese more amenable? Unfortunately, it may not be possible to settle the matter definitively. However, the archaeological evidence suggests the creation of a monumental stone landscape. This landscape was either constructed in the absence of a coercive authority, or if there was a more hierarchical chiefdom involved to begin with, what evolved subsequently was more egalitarian. The apparent lack of large chiefly houses or ritual structures in Futuna suggests the former situation is completely possible. While I do not want to overdetermine conclusions about resistance in the past, it remains a tantalising possibility for understanding Futuna's cultural sequence.

Archaeological evidence and anarchist theories

The other side of the anarchist archaeology dynamic is what archaeology offers to anarchist theories (e.g. Angelbeck and Grier, 2012; Borck, 2016; Wengrow and Graeber, 2015). As always, the strength of our discipline lies in its use of material evidence to forge understandings of the past through hypothesis testing and theory building. Basically, archaeology as a discipline has a unique opportunity to contribute to discussions about anarchism because we have access to evidence not afforded by the documentary record.

As James C. Scott (2009, p. 34) notes, non-state societies do their best to 'stay out of the archives'. Archives are generally kept by states, and where non-state societies appear, it is as a source of irritating social disruption, or as resistance to be crushed. Minor acts of everyday resistance generally go unremarked upon. Returning to Kropotkin:

> The epic poems, the inscriptions on monuments, the treaties of peace – nearly all historical documents bear the same character; they deal with breaches of peace, not with peace itself. So that the best-intentioned historian unconsciously draws a distorted picture of the times he endeavours to depict; and, to restore the real proportion between conflict and union, we are now bound to enter into a minute analysis of thousands of small facts and faint indications accidentally preserved in the relics of the past; to interpret them with the aid of comparative ethnology; and, after having heard so much about what used to divide men, to reconstruct stone by stone the institutions which used to unite them. Ere long history will have to be re-written on new lines, so as to take into account these two currents of human life and to appreciate the part played by each of them in evolution.
>
> *(Kropotkin, 1902, pp. 116–117)*

Archaeology of course is the perfect discipline to offer the 'thousands of small facts and faint indications' to which Kropotkin alludes, both in societies with no written documents and on the margins of those societies that did.

I wouldn't consider myself or my work as central to any contemporary anarchists' movements in the Western world or elsewhere, so I am limited in what I can say about the value of archaeological work for anarchists. However, the Vanuatu examples point to the potential of using our archaeological understandings of the past to inform contemporary knowledge. The balancing and distribution of authority through diversification of roles involving both competition and cooperation (Tanna), the importance of feasting and consensus-based decision making (Tanna and Erromango), and the possibility of intensive agricultural systems functioning in the absence of a coercive authority (Futuna) all suggest ways to think about how these dynamics compare with those operating in contemporary societies.

Anarchism can be for everyone

In a recent manifesto on the topic (Black Trowel Collective, 2016), one of the main points is that archaeologists might come to anarchist ideas for a variety of reasons and from a variety of perspectives. To engage with these materials does not mean necessarily committing to a life of revolutionary action. There are many ways of 'building a new society in the shell of the old'. As a reader, you may or may not see this is a worthwhile endeavour. I hope, though, that some of these ideas offer a compelling argument for reasons to at least engage generally with anarchism from a philosophical and practical perspective. In terms of practice, many of us are already working in ways that align with anarchist ideals, particularly in the consensus-based collaborative work we do with communities.

In Vanuatu this is certainly true. Archaeologists, like other outside cultural researchers, are required to enter the field via the network of indigenous *filwokas* (fieldworkers), who ensure that projects are developed with community input, and that they are perceived as offering some benefit to local people (Bedford et al., 2011). Indeed, without the consensus of what are often very horizontally organised communities, it is not possible to work in very remote areas that might be classified in some cases as 'non-state space' (Flexner, 2018). As a result, archaeological work in Vanuatu, as in many parts of the Pacific, proceeds in collaboration with the communities whose pasts we are exploring, and who have an active interest in shaping the narratives that emerge about that past.

There are, of course, hierarchies and tensions inevitable to these interactions, which rest largely on the colonial and capitalist legacies of modern history that separated 'haves and have nots' (see Errington and Gewertz, 2010). There is also a difference between an arbitrary authority (which anarchists aim to avoid or undermine; see Scott, 1985) and the kinds of earned or achieved authority that result from different kinds of expertise (Maximoff, 1953, pp. 249–255): technical skills and knowledge for archaeologists; and the intimate understanding of island environments and traditional knowledge of Pacific Islanders. For an anarchist archaeology of the Pacific, one of the essential goals is to do what is possible to build consensus-based, non-coercive relationships that often cross the boundaries of culture, language and capital.

Many of us working in the Pacific have experienced the great feeling of working alongside local people with deep knowledge and interest in the past, who understand how our discipline can be used to build connections and expand ideas about island heritage. While we cannot erase the realities of deep inequalities in wealth, access to resources and education, we can find a common ground in the passionate and often joyful exploration of the traces of past societies. We can carry out this activity with our Pacific Islander contacts as equal partners, at least at some level. Even minor acts like acknowledging our local collaborators not as informants or research subjects, but as authors and colleagues in their own right, represents a step in the right direction (e.g. David et al., 2012; Flexner et al., 2016; 2018). It is not exactly storming the castle, but revolutionary projects happen over the long as well as the short term. What seem like small actions now can be the beginnings of a much larger wave with the potential to forge bigger changes down the line.

The principles of mutual aid, consensus-building and cooperation might sound a bit less radical when described in this way, and can offer a way forward when thinking of ways to use our work on the past towards building a brighter future. The idea that we can fight authoritarianism with a trowel and keyboard may sound hopelessly optimistic, even naïve. Yet optimism and idealism are precisely what an anarchist perspective necessitates. If prefiguration is a goal, it would be cynical to imagine a future society solely in terms of negatives, what we can be critical of in the present. A future orientation, built on knowledge of the past, focuses on what was and is positive and what we can build on, whether we are archaeologists, anarchists, Islanders or all of the above.

Notes

1 Bettinger is not explicitly drawing on anarchist thinkers, but his research does support the larger point, which is that hierarchies are not needed for complex, ordered social life.
2 This phrase, often quoted in anarchist literature, is drawn from the preamble to the Constitution of the International Workers of the World.
3 As a recent example of how deeply ingrained the idea of cultural superiority remains, even in a supposedly progressive democracy, media coverage of the discovery of the oldest edge-ground axe in northern Australia (Hiscock et al., 2016) provoked a sadly predictable deluge of disparaging commentary about Aboriginal people and their technical and cultural accomplishments.
4 A critique of this analysis, and one that I acknowledge, is that it privileges men and male roles. A large part of this bias reflects the very real gender segregation that still exists in Melanesian villages. As a male, I am largely excluded from the female perspective of life in the Vanuatu communities where I work, as knowledge tends not to cross gendered divides. A feminist perspective would certainly be of value here and could add much additional richness to our understanding of how these chiefdoms and communities functioned.

References

Angelbeck, B. and Grier, C., 2012. Anarchism and the archaeology of anarchic societies: resistance to centralization in the Coast Salish region of the Pacific Northwest Coast. *Current Anthropology*, 53(5), pp. 547–587.

Bakunin, M., 1950[1872]. *Marxism, Freedom and the State*. London: Freedom Press.

Ballard, C., 2016. The legendary Roi Mata. *Connexions*, 4, pp. 98–111.

Bedford, S., 2019 The complexity of monumentality in Melanesia: mixed messages from Vanuatu. In: M. Leclerc and J.L. Flexner, eds. *Archaeologies of Island Melanesia: Current Approaches to Landscape, Exchange, and Practice*. Canberra: ANU Press.

Bedford, S., Spriggs, M., Regenvanu, R. and Yona, S., 2011. Olfala histri we i stap andanit long graon. Archaeological training workshops in Vanuatu: a profile, the benefits, spin-offs, and extraordinary discoveries. In: J. Taylor and N. Thieberger, eds. *Working Together in Vanuatu: Research Histories, Collaborations, Projects and Reflections*. Canberra: ANU Press, pp. 191–213.

Bettinger, R.L., 2015. *Orderly Anarchy: Sociopolitical Evolution in Aboriginal California*. Berkeley, CA: University of California Press.

Black Trowel Collective. 2016. Foundations of an anarchist archaeology: a community manifesto. *Savage Minds*. http://savageminds.org/2016/10/31/foundations-of-an-anarchist-archaeology-a-community-manifesto/ (accessed Nov. 2019).

Bonnemaison, J., 1991. Magic gardens in Tanna. *Pacific Studies*, 14(4), pp. 71–89.

Bonnemaison, J., 1994. *The Tree and the Canoe: History and Ethnogeography of Tanna*. Honolulu, HI: University of Hawaii Press.

Borck, L., 2016. *Lost Voices Found: An Archaeology of Contentious Politics in the Greater Southwest, A.D. 1100–1450*. Tucson, AZ: Anthropology, University of Arizona.

Borck, L. and Sanger, M.C., 2017. An introduction to anarchism in archaeology. *SAA Archaeological Record*, 17(1), pp. 9–16.

Brunton, R., 1979. Kava and the daily dissolution of society on Tanna, New Hebrides. *Mankind*, 12(2), pp. 93–103.

Brunton, R., 1989. *The Abandoned Narcotic: Kava and Cultural Instability in Melanesia*. Cambridge: Cambridge University Press.

Clark, G., Burley, D.V. and Murray, T., 2008. Monumentality and the development of the Tongan maritime chiefdom. *Antiquity*, 82, 994–1008.

Clark, G.R., C. Reepmeyer, C., Melekiola, N., Dickinson, W.R. and Martinsson-Wallin, H., 2014. Stone tools from the ancient Tongan state reveal prehistoric interaction centers in the Central Pacific. *Proceedings of the National Academy of Sciences*, 111(29), pp. 10491–10496.

Clastres, P., 1987. *Society Against the State*. New York: Zone Books.

Crumley, C.L., 1987. A dialectical critique of hierarchy. In: T.C. Patterson and C.W. Gailey, eds. *Power Relations and State Formation*. Washington, DC: American Anthropological Association, pp. 155–169.

Darwin, C., 1849[1982]. *On the Origin of Species*. New York: Penguin.

Darwin, C., 1871. *The Descent of Man*, vol. 1. London: John Murray.

David, B., Lamb, L., Delannoy, J.-J., Pivoru, F., Rowe, C. Pivoru, M., Frank, T., Frank, N., Fairbairn, A. and Pivoru. R., 2012. Poromoi Tamu and the case of the drowning village: history, lost places and the stories we tell. *International Journal of Historical Archaeology*, 16(2), pp. 319–345.

DeMarrais, E., 2016. Making pacts and cooperative acts: the archaeology of coalition and consensus. *World Archaeology*, 48(1), pp. 1–13.

Denham, T., 2006. Envisaging early agriculture in the highlands of New Guinea. In: I. Lilley, ed. *Archaeology of Oceania: Australia and the Pacific Islands*. Oxford: Blackwell, pp. 160–188.

Denham, T., 2018. Collective action and wetland agriculture in the highlands of Papua New Guinea. *Journal of Contemporary Archaeology,* 5(2), pp. 259–267.

Douglas, B., 1996. *Across the Great Divide: Journeys in History and Anthropology,* Amsterdam: Harwood Academic Press.

Dye, T.S., 2010. Social transformation in old Hawai'i: a bottom-up approach. *American Antiquity,* 75(4), pp. 727–741.

Earle, T. and Spriggs, M., 2015. Political economy in prehistory: a Marxist approach to Pacific sequences. *Current Anthropology,* 56(4), pp. 515–544.

Errington, F. and Gewertz, D., 2010. Excusing the haves and blaming the have-nots in the telling of history. In: P.A. McAnany and N. Yoffee, eds. *Questioning Collapse: Human Resilience, Ecological Vulnerability, and the Aftermath of Empire.* Cambridge: Cambridge University Press, pp. 329–351.

Flexner, J.L., 2014. The historical archaeology of states and non-states: anarchist perspectives from Hawai'i and Vanuatu. *Journal of Pacific Archaeology,* 5(2), pp. 81–97.

Flexner, J.L., 2016. *An Archaeology of Early Christianity in Vanuatu: Kastom and Religious Change on Tanna and Erromango, 1839–1920.* Canberra: Australian National University Press.

Flexner, J.L., Willie, E., Lorey, A.Z., Alderson, H., Williams, R. and Ieru, S., 2016. Iarisi's domain: historical archaeology of a Melanesian village, Tanna Island, Vanuatu. *Journal of Island and Coastal Archaeology,* 11(1), pp. 26–49. doi: 10.1080/15564894.2015.1052865.

Flexner, J.L., 2018. Doing archaeology in non-state space. *Journal of Contemporary Archaeology,* 5(2), pp. 254–259.

Flexner, J.L. and Gonzalez-Tennant, E., 2018. Anarchisms in contemporary archaeology. *Journal of Contemporary Archaeology,* 5(2), pp. 213–219.

Flexner, J.L., Bedford, S., Valentin, E., Shing, R., Kuaotonga, T. and Zinger, W., 2018. Preliminary results of the South Vanuatu archaeological survey: cultural landscapes, excavation and radiocarbon dating. *Asian Perspectives,* 57(2), pp. 244–266.

Garanger, J., 1972. *Archéologie des Nouvelles Hébrides.* Paris: Musée de l'Homme.

Garanger, J., 1996. Tongoa, Mangaasi and Retoka – history of a prehistory. In: Bonnemaison, J. Huffman, K., Kaufmann, C. and Tryon, D., eds. *Arts of Vanuatu.* Honolulu: University of Hawaii Press, pp. 66–73.

Goldman, E., 1969[1910]. *Anarchism and Other Essays.* New York: Mother Earth Publishing.

Golson, J. 1977. *The Ladder of Social Evolution: Archaeology and the Bottom Rungs.* Sydney: Sydney University Press for the Australian Academy of the Humanities.

Golson, J., Denham, T., Hughes, P., Swadling, P. and Muke, J., eds. 2017. *Ten Thousand Years of Cultivation at Kuk Swamp in the Highlands of Papua New Guinea.* Canberra: Australian National University Press.

Gosden, C., 2010. When humans arrived in the New Guinea Highlands. *Science,* 330, pp. 41–42.

Graeber, D., 2004. *Fragments of an Anarchist Anthropology.* Chicago, IL: Prickly Paradigm Press.

Graeber, D., 2013. *The Democracy Project: A History, a Crisis, a Movement.* New York: Spiegel & Grau.

Graham, R., 2005. *Anarchism: A Documentary History of Libertarian Ideas,* vol. 1, *From Anarchy to Anarchism (300CE–1939).* Montreal: Black Rose Press.

Graham, R., 2015. *We Do Not Fear Anarchy, We Invoke It: The First International and the Origins of the Anarchist Movement.* Edinburgh: AK Press.

Guiart, J., 1956. *Un siècle et demi de contacts culturels à Tanna,* Paris: Musée de l'Homme.

Hiscock, P., O'Connor, S., Balme, J., and Maloney, T., 2016. World's earliest ground-edge axe production coincides with human colonisation of Australia. *Australian Archaeology,* 82(1), pp. 2–11.

Humphreys, C.B., 1926. *The Southern New Hebrides: An Ethnological Record*. Cambridge: Cambridge University Press.

Keller, J.D. and Kuautonga, T., 2007. *Nokonofo Kitea, We Keep on Living This Way: Myths and Music of Futuna, Vanuatu*. Adelaide: Crawford House Publishing.

Kropotkin, P.A., 1902. *Mutual Aid: A Factor of Evolution*. London: William Heinemann.

Layard, J., 1942. *Stone Men of Malekula: Vao*. London: Chatto & Windus.

Lindstrom, L., 1990. *Knowledge and Power in a South Pacific Society*. Washington, DC: Smithsonian Institution Press.

Lindstrom, L., 1996. Arts of language and space, south-east Tanna, In: J. Bonnemaison, C. Kaufmann, K. Huffman and D. Tryon, eds. *Arts of Vanuatu*. Honolulu, HI: University of Hawaii Press, pp. 123–128.

Lindstrom, L., 2011. Naming and memory on Tanna, Vanuatu, In: E. Hermann, ed. *Changing Contexts, Shifting Meanings: Transformations of Cultural Traditions in Oceania*. Honolulu, HI: University of Hawaii Press, pp. 141–156.

Lydon, J. and Rizvi, U., eds. 2010. *Handbook of Postcolonial Archaeology*. Walnut Creek, CA: Left Coast Press.

Macleod, J., 2015. *Merdeka and the Morning Star: Civil Resistance in West Papua*. St Lucia: University of Queensland Press.

Marshall, Y., 2002. What is community archaeology? *World Archaeology*, 34(2), pp. 211–219.

Maximoff, G.P., ed. 1953. *The Political Philosophy of Bakunin: Scientific Anarchism*. London: Free Press.

McGuire, R.H., 1992. *A Marxist Archaeology*. New York: Academic Press.

Naupa, A., ed. (2011). *Nompi en Ovoteme Erromango (Kastom and Culture of Erromango)*. Port Vila: Erromango Cultural Association.

Proudhon, P.-J., 1994. *What is Property?* Tr. D.R. Kelley and B.G. Smith. Cambridge: Cambridge University Press.

Rappaport, R.A., 1984. *Pigs for the Ancestors: Ritual in the Ecology of a New Guinea People*, New Haven, CT: Yale University Press.

Rappaport, R.A., 1992. The anthropology of trouble. *American Anthropologist*, 95(2), pp. 295–303.

Rathbone, S., 2017. Anarchist literature and the development of anarchist counter-archaeologies. *World Archaeology*, 49(3), pp. 291–305.

Sand, C., 2015. Prehistory and its perception in a Melanesian archipelago: the New Caledonia example. *Antiquity*, 77(297), pp. 505–519.

Scott, J.C., 1985. *Weapons of the Weak: Everyday Forms of Peasant Resistance*. New Haven, CT: Yale University Press.

Scott, J.C., 1998. *Seeing Like a State: How Certain Schemes to Improve the Human Condition have Failed*. New Haven, CT: Yale University Press.

Scott, J.C., 2009. *The Art of Not Being Governed: An Anarchist History of Upland Southeast Asia*. New Haven, CT: Yale University Press.

Scott, J.C., 2012. *Two Cheers for Anarchism: Six Easy Pieces on Autonomy, Dignity, and Meaningful Work and Play*. Princeton, NJ: Princeton University Press.

Shanks, M. and Tilley, C., 1987. *Social Theory and Archaeology*. Albuquerque, NM: University of New Mexico Press.

Smith, C. and Wobst, H.M., eds. 2005. *Indigenous Archaeologies: Decolonizing Theory and Practice*. London: Routledge.

Spriggs, M., 1981. Vegetable kingdoms: taro irrigation and Pacific prehistory, Unpublished PhD thesis, Canberra: Australian National University.

Spriggs, M., ed. 1984. *Marxist Perspectives in Archaeology*. Cambridge: Cambridge University Press.

Spriggs, M., 1986. Landscape, land use, and political transformation in southern Melanesia. In: P.V. Kirch, ed. *Island Societies: Archaeological Approaches to Evolution and Transformation.* Cambridge: University of Cambridge Press, pp. 6–19.

Spriggs, M., 2008. Ethnographic parallels and the denial of history. *World Archaeology*, 40(4), pp. 538–552.

Spriggs, M. and Wickler, S., 1989. Archaeological research on Erromango: recent data on southern Melanesian prehistory. *Bulletin of the Indo-Pacific Prehistory Association,* 9, pp. 68–91.

Summerhayes, G.R., Field, J.H., Shaw, B. and Gaffney, D., 2016. The archaeology of forest exploitation and change in the tropics during the Pleistocene: the case of Northern Sahul (Pleistocene New Guinea). *Quaternary International*, 448, pp. 14–30.

Tomlinson, M. and Tengan, T.P.K., eds. 2016. *New Mana: Transformations of a Classic Concept in Pacific Languages and Cultures.* Canberra: ANU Press.

Turner , G., 1861. *Nineteen years in Polynesia: missionary life, travels, and researches in the islands of the Pacific.* London: J. Snow.

Wengrow, D. and Graeber, D., 2015. Farewell to the 'childhood of man': ritual, seasonality, and the origins of inequality. *Journal of the Royal Anthropological Institute*, 21(3), pp. 597–619.

10

OPENING DISCURSIVE SPACE

New Guinea's contribution to the history of early agriculture

Tim Denham

The New Guinea region has some of the oldest archaeological evidence for cultivation in the world. The agricultural chronology at Kuk Swamp in the highlands of Papua New Guinea is suggestive of nascent forms of shifting cultivation during the early Holocene, with mound cultivation dating to 7000–6400 cal BP and the digging of ditches to delineate wetland field systems from c.4400–4000 cal BP (Golson et al., 2017; Denham, 2018a). Several globally important subsistence and cash crops, including bananas (*Musa* cvs.), taro (*Colocasia esculenta*) and some yams (*Dioscorea* spp.), trace part of their ancestry back to the broader Island Southeast Asian-New Guinea region (Lebot, 2009; Perrier et al., 2011) and are associated with early cultivation practices at Kuk (Denham et al., 2003; Fullagar et al., 2006). The New Guinea research has fostered the development of new concepts and methods for the investigation of early agriculture, which are relevant for other wet tropical regions.

Agricultural practices on New Guinea exhibit several characteristics that provoke us to reorient our thinking about early cultivation, human–plant domesticatory relationships and broader social processes. Foremost, plants are typically reproduced through asexual propagation, or vegetatively, under cultivation. The wide array of plants cultivated vegetatively, as well as the different ways in which they are propagated, has implications for the character of domesticatory processes and the ways in which cultivated plants accumulate distinctive phenotypic and genotypic attributes associated with human exploitation, namely for the emergence of domestication traits.

The attributes of early, as well as later, agricultural practices on New Guinea have motivated shifts in lines of argumentation away from more orthodox perspectives. In the New Guinea region, the primary diagnostics of agriculture in the past are archaeological and pedogenic evidence of cultivation practices (Denham, 2007), which can then be interwoven with archaeobotanical evidence for plant use and cultivation (Denham, 2009) and palaeoecological evidence of environmental transformations (Denham and Haberle, 2008). Practices are more fundamental, or ontologically prior, to domestication traits in the investigation of early agriculture (Denham, 2018a).

The significance of early agriculture in the New Guinea region is much more than adding another place to the map of early agricultural centres and inserting a few species in the table of global crop plant domestication. These substantive contributions are important, especially as they have been accompanied by major conceptual and methodological developments of broader relevance to the investigation of early agriculture globally. However, these findings also bring forth reflexive questions about the study of early agriculture and its significance. Certainly, the adoption or invention of agriculture marks a major technological transition for a society, yet the significance given to this transition arguably reflects the present as much as the past.

In this chapter, the character of domestication under vegetative forms of cultivation is discussed and contrasted to that of sexually reproducing crops, such as cereals and legumes. Domestication processes for most vegetatively propagated crops in the Island Southeast Asia-New Guinea region are poorly understood, morphogenetically ambiguous, and probably multilinear and decentred. These processes challenge dominant models of crop domestication applied in archaeological debates concerning early agriculture globally; indeed, they spur a rethink of the evidential bases for the investigation of early agriculture away from a reliance on archaeobotanical remains suggestive of domestication and towards multidisciplinary evidence for cultivation practices in the past. In turn, these methodological considerations raise conceptual questions regarding the importance of plant domestication and early agriculture as signposts for understanding the long-term past.

Domestication under vegeculture

Agricultural practices based on vegetative propagation have been termed vegeculture (e.g. Yen, 1973). The cultivation of plants using vegetative propagation is ancient and some have speculated that it predates other forms based on sexual reproduction from fertilised seed (Sauer, 1952). A vegetative orientation is exhibited by foragers as well as farmers (Barton and Denham, 2018); for instance, some Australian Aboriginal people were known to leave sufficient viable material underground when exploiting tuberous plants (Berndt and Berndt, 1993).

Vegetative propagation in the New Guinea region is primarily associated with the cultivation of 'root crops', such as giant taro (*Alocasia macrorrhizos*), gingers (*Zingiber* spp.), taro (*Colocasia esculenta*) and yams (*Dioscorea* spp.) (Hather, 1996), as well as more recently introduced manioc/cassava (*Manihot esculenta*), sweet potato (*Ipomoea batatas*) and English potato (*Solanum tuberosum*) (Lebot, 2009). Yet, in the Pacific, a broad range of plants is cultivated vegetatively, including bananas (*Musa* spp.), beans (*Psophocarpus tetragonolobus*), cane grasses (*Saccharum officinarum, Saccharum edule; Setaria palmifolia*), leafy vegetables (*Abelmoschus manihot, Rungia klossii*), sago palm (*Metroxylon sagu*), pandanus (*Pandanus conoideus, P. julianettii*) and some trees, such as breadfruit (*Artocarpus altilis*). Furthermore, most trees are usually reproduced through the transplantation of germinated seedlings rather than from planting of seed.

Early and later agricultural practices in the New Guinea region and the Pacific were predominantly vegetative (Denham, 2004; 2018a), as they were across Island Southeast Asia before the adoption of wet-field rice cultivation (Denham, 2013). These vegecultural practices enabled the colonisation of widely dispersed island groups, from Madagascar to Eastern Polynesia, by Austronesian language speakers. Arguably, several plants of traditional Pacific agriculture – principally bananas, taro and the greater yam (*Dioscorea alata*) – had the greatest longitudinal distribution of any cultivated plants before the age of European exploration from the 15th century CE onwards; for example, bananas were cultivated from West Africa and Iberia to Eastern Polynesia (Rangan et al., 2015).

The character of human–plant domesticatory relationships under vegeculture has led to some distinctive signatures, ranging from the biological (domestication traits) to the social (vegetative social forms). Biological domestication under vegeculture can be characterised as management of plastic responses in plants under cultivation to produce desired phenotypes; this type of management may, or may not, lead to the emergence of genotypic transformations in managed populations that correspond to, or 'fix', desired phenotypes. By contrast, in cereals and legumes phenotypic transformations often have corresponding genetic transformations that 'fix' domestication traits (Fuller et al., 2014). Social forms and practices reflecting the embedded character of vegetative crops and modes of reproduction recur throughout the New Guinea region, as well as in parts of Southeast Asia and northern Australia (Barton and Denham, 2018), and in regions to which these crops have been introduced and have become important staples, such as bananas (*Musa* cvs.) in Africa (Rangan et al., 2015).

Domestication traits are not necessarily as distinctive in vegetative plants as they are in sexually reproduced plants. Foremost, in sexually reproducing plants, the seed is the primary element of the plant selected for and eaten, as well as the means of reproduction. Human-mediated selection of seeds has led to phenotypic transformations in the seed itself, which have fixed genetic markers. Morphological transformations often occur in other elements of the plant to enhance seed production and reproduction, such as apical dominance, as well as to aid ease of harvesting, processing, consumption and palatability. Consequently, domestication traits in sexually reproduced plants can be tracked in archaeobotanical assemblages through seed size and shape, spikelet base morphologies, as well as using ancient and modern genes.

Although growing experiments suggest cereals could feasibly be domesticated over decades (Hillman and Davies, 1990), archaeobotanical assemblages indicate increases in seed size and the emergence of non-shattering actually occurred over millennia (Fuller et al., 2014). The domestication episode connotes the period over which transformations in plant morphology were initiated and concluded to 'fixation', thereby occurring in all derived cultivars. Extended domestication episodes likely reflect multiple factors, ranging from discontinuous periods of cultivation (intermittent directed selection) to continual interbreeding between more abundant wild plants and small populations of cultivars (lack of genetic isolation). Fixation of domestication traits likely followed sustained periods of cultivation, which entailed increasingly larger populations of crop plants and concomitantly smaller populations of wild plants within increasingly degraded agrarian landscapes. Fixation suggests irreversible changes to larger seed sizes and non-shattering forms, which presumably became genetically controlled over extended periods of selection under cultivation and eventual genetic isolation from wild forms. Although the domestication process for cereals and legumes is often characterised in these terms, it is not always so linear or clear-cut between 'wild' and 'domesticated' forms (Crawford, 2012).

In vegetatively propagated plants, domestication appears to be more ambiguous for some plants despite extended periods of cultivation. Whereas some plants are clearly domesticated, such as triploid banana and taro cultivars and sterile polyploids of sugarcane, Yen (1985) pointed to the 'semi-domesticated' character of several crop plants in the New Guinea region, including numerous vegetables and some banana and taro diploid cultivars (Denham, 2004; Kennedy and Clarke, 2004). Problems in delineating the domestication process for some vegetatively propagated plants partly stem from the character of cultivation practices (Denham, 2018a, p. 65):

- interbreeding or gene flow between wild and cultivated populations within the natural range of plants, with subsequent incorporation of sexually reproduced offspring into the vegetatively propagated stock;
- recurrent propagation of many vegetables and greens from wild or feral (abandoned or garden escapees) plants growing within disturbed forest and old garden sites, as opposed to solely from vegetatively cultivated stock;
- prolonged clonal reproduction of plants that are selected on the basis of phenotype and which accumulate genetic traits through somaclonal mutation rather than through sexual combination; and
- phenotypic plasticity of many plants under cultivation, most notably documented among tuberous crops such as taro and yams, leads to a lack of clear correspondence between phenotypic and genetic diagnostics for wild and cultivated plants, thereby hindering the ready identification of domestication traits.

As well as problematising the character of domestication under vegetative propagation, these observations also require a consideration of crop plants other than major, starch-rich staples. In New Guinea and neighbouring regions, a vast range of plants are used for food and other purposes (Powell, 1982; Kocher Schmid, 1991). Consideration of the various ways people used a broad range of plants in the recent ethnographic past provides a window on the texture of plant use in the distant past. It may also bring to light practices that were fundamental or significant in the emergence of the earliest forms of cultivation. The fixation on starch-rich plants, and to a lesser degree oil- and protein-rich plants, in the study of early agriculture is potentially misleading, yet likely to continue because of the large amount of multi-disciplinary data that can be drawn upon in the investigation of the past, including agronomic, botanical, ecological and genetic information. The relative abundance of information for starch-rich crops reflects the economic importance of these staples for subsistence and commercial agriculture today.

Multilinear and decentred domestication scenarios

The domestication of cereals and legumes has tended to be viewed as a linear pro-cess, namely progressing from 'wild' to 'cultivated' (Fuller et al., 2014), as well as geographically centred, namely, wild plants were brought under cultivation and domesticated in a particular region from which they spread (Bellwood, 2005; cf. Harris, 1990; Barker, 2006). Such scenarios have been proposed for a range of cereals and legumes in Southwest Asia (Zohary et al., 2012), rice (*Oryza sativa*) in the Yangtze River Valley in China (Zhao, 2011), and maize (*Zea mays*) in the highlands of Mexico (Piperno et al., 2009). It has long been recognised, however, that the domestication histories of many vegetative crops are likely to be different, especially in the Indo-Pacific region, where they seem to exhibit non-linear and decentred characteristics (Sauer, 1952; Li, 1970; Yen, 1985; Denham, 2018b).

   The importance of the New Guinea region to the domestication of several globally significant, vegetatively propagated crops has only been taken seriously since the 1990s (e.g. Yen, 1995; Lebot, 1999). Formerly, the major domesticates of Indo-Pacific agriculture were considered to be of East Asian and Southeast Asian derivation (Burkill, 1935; Sauer, 1952; Li, 1970; Yen, 1973), with allowance for the domestication of several minor or regionally significant crops in New Guinea (Barrau, 1965; Yen, 1973; Bayliss-Smith, 1985). However, caution is needed in the interpretation of claims for domestication of several globally significant crops in the New Guinea region; most are hampered by limited sampling coverage throughout Southeast Asia and the Pacific, and most were undertaken using old generation genetic analyses. Rather than advocating the primacy of one region over another (i.e. New Guinea over Southeast Asia) it is more sensible to consider the ways in which numerous crop plants were initially brought into cultivation in a wide trop-ical and subtropical band from India to the Solomon Islands (following Li, 1970). For instance, although part of the genetic ancestry of domesticated bananas (Perrier et al., 2011) and sugarcane (Grivet et al., 2004) can be traced to New Guinea, the geodomestication pathways for both crops are complex; they entail movements to and hybridisations within Island Southeast Asia to produce the groups of cultivars that are globally significant today.

   Based on current multidisciplinary evidence, it seems plausible that numerous genera and species of root crops, cane grasses, bananas and other plants were ini-tially exploited, managed and 'domesticated' in various ways across a broad region from India to the Solomon Islands (Denham, 2018b). The degrees of exploitation of genera and individual species, hence the intensity of selective pressure exerted, varied greatly temporally and geographically, partly reflecting biogeographical distributions and partly reflecting the types of exploitation practices and reasons for use of a plant in a given locale. These practices resulted in regional mosaics of domesticatory relationships for individual crop plants: these plants underwent decentred domestication. From this perspective, these practices yielded numerous locally and regionally important cultivars, many of which have become minor or 'lost' because, through time, they have been replaced by the sequential dispersal of more successful cultivars of the same species or genera.

To expand, individual species were enmeshed in different types of plant exploitation practices – including forms of foraging, fodder production and cultivation for food – in multiple locales. For example, archaeobotanical evidence for the exploitation of taro and yams has been documented in multiple locales for the Pleistocene (Barton and Paz, 2007; Loy et al., 1992), as well as being associated with early cultivation in highland New Guinea (Fullagar et al., 2006). In some places the degree of human-directed selection was more intense than in others. Against such a mosaic of plant exploitation practices, multiple types of domesticatory relationships and loci of 'domestication' can be hypothesised for some widely dispersed species, such as taro (*Colocasia esculenta*) and banana (*Musa acuminata*), and genera, such as yams (*Dioscorea* spp.). Some local domesticates became regionally significant cultivars and a few of these became the more widespread antecedents of today's major cultivar groups.

Individual cultivars became widely dispersed and more prevalent for multiple reasons, ranging from the functional (agronomic and dietary) to the cultural (colour, shape and taste). As some cultivars spread and were widely adopted, others remained locally significant and many would have been replaced, marginalised or forgotten. For instance, multiple local domestications of diploid taro cultivars can be envisaged, with subsequent widespread dispersals of specific diploids and, more recently, triploids.

Comparable scenarios can be envisaged for genera that contain multiple useful species, such as yams (*Dioscorea* spp.), bananas (*Musa* spp.) and cane grasses (*Saccharum* spp.). Yam is a pantropical genus and multiple species having been exploited for food by humans for millennia on different continents (Coursey, 1967; 1972). Foragers in Australia exploited 'wild' yams, whereas some yam species have undergone millennia of cultivation and have become heavily dependent upon people for propagation and dispersal, such as the greater yam (*Dioscorea alata*). The different character of human–yam domesticatory relationships in different places and times has influenced the degrees to which individual yam species were domesticated.

Different species and subspecies of banana (*Musa* spp.) were exploited within the natural range of the genus from eastern India to the Solomon Islands (Stover and Simmonds, 1987; Arnaud and Horry, 1997). Although widely cultivated for fruit, multiple species of banana have different local or regional uses; for instance, different parts of banana plants are eaten and used for fodder, medicine, ornamentation, rituals, textiles, utensils and wrappings (Kennedy, 2009). Two key banana species have emerged from this heterogeneity and become intensively selected and widely translocated – *Musa acuminata* ssp. *banksii* from the New Guinea region and *Musa balbisiana* from Southeast Asia (Perrier et al., 2011). Two of the most significant cultivar groups are triploid (AAB) introgressive hybrids derived from these two species: West African plantains and maoli-popo'ulu in the Pacific (De Langhe et al., 2015). The geodomestication histories for these groups of food crop have entailed multiple stages of selection for parthenocarpy, seed sterility and suppression, as well as hybridisation and triploidisation; different stages of the domestication process occurred in different places (De Langhe and de Maret, 1999; Perrier et al., 2011).

Comparably, numerous cane grasses were exploited for food, as well as construction, medicine and weaving from India to the Solomon Islands (van Dillewijn, 1952; Simmonds, 1976). The sugar-rich pith is eaten in some cultivars, while others are grown as vegetables. In the New Guinea region, several cane grasses are cultivated vegetatively, including sugarcane (*Saccharum officinarum*). Sugarcane domestication likely involved human-mediated translocation of two species – *Saccharum robustum* and *Saccharum spontaneum* – within the ISEA-New Guinea region, with introgressive hybridisation to yield *Saccharum officinarum* polyploids (Daniels and Daniels, 1993; Grivet et al., 2004), referred to as the 'Saccharum complex' (Premachandran et al., 2011).

Given the complexity of the geodomestication scenarios for bananas and sugarcane, it makes little sense to identify a locus of domestication for a particular crop plant. Rather, it makes more sense to propose a scenario in which these crops were plausibly domesticated across a vast region extending from India to the Solomon Islands (Li, 1970). At various times and places within this tropical and subtropical region, people enmeshed different lineages of subspecies, species and genera within their vegetative practices. The mosaic of plant exploitation practices yielded comparable mosaics of selection, or gradients of domestication. Through time, certain cultivars came to prominence at the expense of pre-existing cultivars of the same or equivalent species.

Here, it is only possible to sketch potential domestication scenarios for several crops that are cultivated vegetatively in the New Guinea region. At present, there is insufficient archaeobotanical evidence to track the domestication of any crop plant through time in the Indo-Pacific region. In part, this reflects limited preservation of macrobotanical remains of many tropical cultivars in wet tropical and subtropical environments, excepting nut shells and fruit stones. In part, though, this reflects uncertainties regarding the microbotanical (primarily phytolith and starch granule) diagnostics of domestication for most crop plants in the region, with bananas being a possible exception (Lentfer, 2009; Vrydaghs et al., 2009).

A priori, morphological diagnostics of domestication may be difficult to identify in the archaeobotanical record for many vegetatively propagated crops. In cereals and legumes, morphological changes such as the proportions of shattering and non-shattering spikelet bases, as well as potentially grain size, have been used to track domestication; these changes appear to be 'fixed' and genetically controlled. By contrast, in root crops and some other vegetatively propagated crops, morphological changes under cultivation may be more plastic, reflecting growth environment to a greater degree. For instance, the size and shape of many root crops reflect nutrient availability and compaction of the soil. As yet, the potentially confounding effects of phenotypic plasticity (West-Eberhard, 2003) on the archaeobotany of domestication for vegetatively propagated plants are not well known.

Furthermore, the basic ecology and genetic histories of many crop plants in the Indo-Pacific are poorly understood. Genetic investigations of modern cultivars, feral and wild types are skewed towards the dominant cultivar lineages of today; they are unlikely to include marginal or lost lineages. Genetic traces of initial historical processes are likely to be obfuscated by sequential human–mediated dispersals and resultant replacement of older genetic stock, or genetic reshuffling (e.g. Roullier et al., 2013). The poor preservation of genetic material in archaeobotanical remains in the perhumid tropics and subtropics makes it unlikely that aDNA will resolve these issues anytime soon.

Practices are ontologically prior to domestication

At first glance, problems associated with the character of vegetative propagation and the identification of plant domesticates would seem to problematize the investigation of early agriculture in the New Guinea region. However, if we step back and consider agriculture more broadly, in an everyday sense the term refers to the cultivation of the soil to grow plants; it does not refer to domestication per se. The fetishisation of domestication within archaeological debates concerning early agriculture has reified one epiphenomenon of cultivation practices to the level of primary diagnostic (e.g. Harris, 2007; Smith, 2001). As a result, early agriculture has been claimed based on the identification of domesticated crop morphotypes in archaeobotanical assemblages, even though there is no associated evidence of cultivation practices (e.g. Piperno et al., 2009). In what sense does such archaeobotanical evidence represent early agriculture?

If we reorient debate, an understanding of early agriculture requires exposition of the practices of plant exploitation and cultivation before detailed consideration of human–plant domesticatory relationships (Harris, 1990). We need to understand the multifaceted ways people engaged with or influenced plants before we can begin to understand how these practices affected plant phenotypes and genotypes. Various practices have intended and unintended consequences for the way people intervened in the life histories of plants; they range from deliberate planting and transplantation to the cumulative effects of gathering, landscape burning and tending. Practices are ontologically prior because they are the precondition for the phenotypic and genotypic changes characterised as domestication, as well as attendant social and environmental transformations. Practices are also methodologically prior because they emplace plants in the past.

In an everyday sense, practices are what people do, or did. In the consideration of early agriculture, they are constitutive for many different forms of plant exploitation, including gathering, management and cultivation:

> A focus on practices enables the continuities and discontinuities between forms of plant exploitation to be traced in space and time, and illustrates the ways practices were 'bundled', or deployed in conjunction with one another, by people living in specific landscapes in the past. … Essentially, a practice-based framework is intended to reflect the porous and fluid character of early cultivation practices as they are reconstructed in the multidisciplinary record for a given locale.
>
> *(Denham, 2018a, p. 5)*

The adoption of a practice-based approach softens the sharpness of 'monolithic' categories such as foraging, swidden cultivation and intensive cultivation. Although this perspective has been developed and applied in the New Guinea context (Denham, 2018a; also see Latinis, 2000; Terrell et al., 2003), it has broader applicability.

Archaeology lends itself to a practice-based method for the investigation of early agriculture because it is concerned with the material cultural evidence of people's actions in the past. By adopting a practice-based framework to investigate the emergence of agriculture, the analytical focus shifts away from archaeobotanically grounded narratives that emphasise domestication traits towards an understanding of how people exploited, managed and cultivated plants in the past. Some forms of cultivation, such as shifting cultivation, present ambiguously in the archaeological record; namely, it is difficult to differentiate shifting cultivation from plant exploitation in a patch or cultivation within a plot (Denham, 2018a). However, most forms of cultivation using mounds, furrows, ditches and pits are more visible archaeologically and more readily characterised in terms of analogous practices from the recent past (Bourke and Harwood, 2009).

Archaeological evidence includes tools, features and palaeosols associated with former cultivation. These are relatively direct lines of evidence associated with cultivation that can ground archaeobotanical and palaeoecological lines of evidence associated with plant exploitation and environmental manipulation, respectively (Denham and Haberle, 2008). Without grounding in archaeological evidence of former cultivation practices, the significance of other archaeobotanical and palaeoecological evidence in terms of past agriculture can be uncertain and unfounded.

The interpretation of practices-in-the-past is often not so clear cut as domestication traits in archaeobotanical (and zooarchaeological) assemblages. Perhaps morphological changes in plants and animals associated with domestication have come to the fore as a shorthand means to identify agriculture in the past primarily because they are so readily preserved and differentiated in many species. By contrast, the interpretation of past cultivation, as well as other forms of plant exploitation, requires consideration of the often ambiguous multidisciplinary evidence for a range of practices within demarcated plots, as well as across a landscape, respectively. Such a perspective reorients interpretation from a sequential and successive development from foraging to farming, to consideration of the expanding repertoire of plant exploitation practices through time, as employed in different parts of the landscape. From this perspective, the emergence of agriculture is gradational and represents a high degree of continuity from pre-existing practices.

Lines of argument and lines of evidence

The chronology from the highlands of New Guinea highlights how the history of agriculture and character of human–plant domesticatory relationships need to be considered for each region in its own terms (Harris, 1996). There is no universal model of how to measure early agriculture. Rather, the identification of early agricultural practices requires consideration of multiple lines of evidence, often in different combinations, that are then calibrated against recent agricultural practices from that particular region (Denham, 2011). There is a necessary interplay, or resonation, between the past and present in the interpretation of early agriculture, although this does not negate the potential identification of novel forms of cultivation in the past.

For instance, the interpretation of early agriculture in the New Guinea region is based on a particular combination, or hierarchy, of multidisciplinary evidence. Most fundamental is the archaeological evidence of former cultivation practices at sites of wetland production, such as Kuk Swamp, including: topographical manipulation (pits, runnels and stakeholes) of the wetland margin at c.10,000 cal BP; the bases of mounds at 6400–7000 cal BP; and, artificial drainage ditches from 4400 to 4000 cal BP (Golson et al., 2017; Denham, 2018a). Associative lines of evidence grounded by the archaeological evidence comprise archaeobotanical finds for the presence, use and cultivation of crop plants; palaeoecological records of contemporary environmental changes; and microstratigraphic traces of soil formation, digging and tillage (Denham, 2007; 2018a). The social implications of the earliest agricultural practices, especially before the advent of early house structures around 4500–4000 cal BP, are largely unknown and can only be inferred.

By contrast, early agriculture in Southwest Asia has primarily been grounded in archaeobotanical evidence for plant exploitation and domestication at occupation sites where foods are stored, processed and consumed (Zohary et al., 2012). Archaeobotanical remains document the exploitation and cultivation of morphologically wild plants and the generation and cultivation of domesticated morphotypes, as well as indicate the reliance of people upon cultivated foods for subsistence (Willcox, 2007). Palaeoecological evidence of environmental transformations potentially associated with early cultivation are relatively sparse and less significant for inferring the extent and character of practices. The archaeology of sites of agricultural production, such as former fields and cultivation practices, is largely inferred from crop plant assemblages and agricultural tools. The emergence of agriculture in Southwest Asia is sometimes characterised as marking a break from pre-existing practices (e.g. Bellwood, 2005). However, earlier lines of evidence from the Upper Palaeolithic site of Ohalo II, as well as Natufian and PPNA sites suggest considerable regional complexity and a greater continuity in terms of practices over millennia preceding early forms of agriculture (Weiss et al., 2004; Kuijt and Finlayson, 2009; Snir et al., 2015).

Other types of material cultural evidence that are often implicated in debates concerning the emergence of agriculture are not highly prominent in the archaeological record from New Guinea (Florin and Carah, 2018). These lines of evidence are often referred to as 'Neolithic' cultural traits that are sometimes bound together into a 'Neolithic package'. For example, early agriculture marked by the emergence of animal and plant domesticates in Southwest Asia is associated with, although not necessarily contemporaneous with, the adoption of ceramics, stone-built settlements and storage facilities, as well as a suite of polished stone tools. Only the prevalence of edge ground axe-adzes (Christensen, 1975) characterises early agriculture in the highlands of New Guinea, where indigenous animals were not domesticated, societies were aceramic and people lived in dispersed homesteads. There was no need for large-scale or long-term storage structures, as climates were largely aseasonal in the central highlands and many plant foods could be effectively stored in the ground, namely left to grow *in situ*. Even in the more seasonal climates of the eastern highlands, only limited above-ground storage was required (Feil, 1987).

Relatively small groups cleared and cultivated plots on a semi-permanent or shifting basis in the interior of New Guinea in the recent past (Bowers, 1968; Clarke, 1971; Powell et al., 1975). Groups came together to engage in the coordinated and integrated drainage of wetlands (Ballard, 2017), as well as to harvest and process *Pandanus* nuts, but such projects could also be pursued by relatively small groups independently. The social rhythms of agriculture and economic life did not require the emergence of large-scale or hierarchical societies.

The emergence of egalitarian societies

Societies in the interior of New Guinea were, until recently relatively, small-scale and egalitarian. Cohabiting groups could range in size from an extended family (Riebe, 1974) to several hundred within a nucleated settlement (Gardner and Heider, 1969) or communal longhouse (Shaw, 1996). In most areas, group membership was overtly based on descent, primarily patrilineal and patrilocal (Strathern, 1972), although often large numbers of non-agnates were incorporated (Feil, 1984); whereas in other areas group membership was more overtly based on co-residence (Riebe, 1974). Social landscapes of alliance and enmity enabled some groups to draw on much larger coalitions to engage in warfare, ceremonies, feasts and large-scale exchanges (Muke, 1992).

Most leaders, or big-men, did not rule with absolute power or through dictate, rather they were considered leaders due to their abilities, whether singly or a combination, such as orator, warrior, control of exchange networks or keeper of ritual knowledge. Most often, the attribution of leader status was acquired through an individual's life (Strathern, 1971), whereas in other groups inheritance was significant (Godelier, 1986). Big-men ordinarily led through persuasion and their ability to marshal others in the pursuit of an objective.

Although egalitarian, New Guinea societies are not utopian. Life expectancy was low due to a combination of disease, malnutrition and warfare. Internecine killings, warfare and beliefs in witchcraft, sorcery, animist spirits and ancestral spirits were endemic. Women had limited rights and could be subjected to high rates of domestic violence. Some groups practiced endo-cannibalism, namely, eating of deceased members, whereas others engaged in exo-cannibalism, namely, raiding and the eating of the killed and captives (Sanday, 1986).

Individuals identify with a sliding hierarchy of affiliations, from lineage or clan, to clan-cluster, named group and alliance partners. In recent decades, multiple new layers of affiliation are increasingly being drawn upon, including speakers of the same language, region of origin and being citizens of Papua New Guinea. These identities are variably mobilised in social networks depending upon context. For instance, a named group will often fight together in warfare with other named partners in an alliance, whereas individual clans and clan-clusters within that named group may engage in more circumscribed 'fights with sticks' to resolve disputes with each other (Muke, 1992).

New Guinea societies bear many similarities to small-scale societies in other parts of the world, as well as many differences. There is nothing implicit in the character of agricultural practices or social forms, nor the geography and available resources, to indicate why societies in New Guinea have remained relatively small-scale and egalitarian (Modjeska, 1982; Golson and Gardner, 1990). Demographic growth and the expansion of social scale have not been limited by agricultural capacity: throughout the Holocene there has been the potential capacity to intensify or expand agricultural production based on the available land, practices and plants.

The characteristics of early agriculture and social history in New Guinea are sometimes contrasted with those for other regions of the world (Diamond, 1997). In doing so, the New Guinea evidence can be shoe-horned into explicit or implicit models of social evolution, in which the emergence of early agriculture is considered a motor of history, demographic expansion and sociopolitical stratification. From this perspective, New Guinea is an aberration; it does not fit. Such narratives echo 19th-century evolutionary and unilinear thinking (critiqued in Golson, 1977). Such macroscale histories are normalising discourses that seek to justify the current world-order, in which early agriculture is effectively a cipher for something else, most often the rise of 'civilisation'.

Measuring the past

As well as the substantive contributions to global debates concerning early agriculture and plant domestication, research in the New Guinea region has generated new concepts and methods that have broader global relevance. The orientation of research has shifted from domestication as prime marker of early agriculture to a focus on practices. Practices are ontologically prior, while methodologically the archaeological record of former practices provides the essential context for interpreting archaeobotanical and palaeoecological lines of evidence.

The New Guinea record has opened up discursive spaces for understanding what early agriculture means in the present. The character of New Guinea societies documented ethnographically and historically shows there is no teleological imperative towards expanding societies, increasing sociopolitical hierarchies and 'civilisation' following the inception of agriculture. A priori there need not be; these are all assumptions derived from specific regional histories. Taken in its own terms, the New Guinea record fits within the spectrum of diverse social histories following the inception of early agriculture, especially in the wet tropics.

References

Arnaud, E. and Horry, J.P. eds. 1997. *Musalogue: A Catalogue of Musa germplasm. Papua New Guinea Collecting Missions, 1988–1990*. Montpellier: International Network for the Improvement of Banana and Plantain.

Ballard, C., 2017. The wetland field systems of the New Guinea highlands. In: J. Golson, T.P. Denham, P.J. Hughes, P. Swadling and J. Muke, eds. *Ten Thousand Years of Cultivation at Kuk Swamp in the Highlands of Papua New Guinea*. Terra Australis 46. Canberra: ANU E Press, pp. 65–83.

Barker, G., 2006. *The Agricultural Revolution in History*. Oxford: Oxford University Press.

Barrau, J., 1965. Witnesses of the past: notes on some food plants of Oceania. *Ethnology,* 4(3), pp. 282–294.

Barton, H. and Denham, T.P., 2018. Vegecultures and the social-biological transformations of plants and people. *Quaternary International,* 489, pp. 17–25.

Barton, H. and Paz, V., 2007. Subterranean diets in the tropical rain forests of Sarawak, Malaysia. In: T.P. Denham, J. Iriarte and L. Vrydaghs, eds. *Rethinking Agriculture: Archaeological and Ethnoarchaeological Perspectives*. Walnut Creek, CA: Left Coast Press, pp. 50–77.

Bayliss-Smith, T., 1985. Pre-Ipomoean agriculture in the New Guinea Highlands above 2000 metres: some experimental data on taro cultivation. In: I. Farrington, ed. *Prehistoric Intensive Agriculture in the Tropics*. Oxford: British Archaeological Reports, International Series 232, Part I, pp. 285–320.

Bellwood, P., 2005. *First Farmers*. Oxford: Blackwell.

Berndt, R.M. and Berndt, C.H., 1993. *A World that Was: The Yaraldi of the Murray River and the Lakes, South Australia*. Melbourne: Melbourne University Press.

Bourke, R.M. and Harwood, T., eds. 2009. *Food and Agriculture in Papua New Guinea*. Canberra: ANU E Press.

Bowers, N., 1968. The ascending grasslands: an anthropological study of ecological succession in a high mountain valley of New Guinea. Unpublished PhD thesis, Columbia University. Ann Arbor, MI: University Microfilms International.

Burkill, I.H., 1935. *A Dictionary of the Economic Products of the Malay Peninsula*. 2 vols. London: Crown Agents.

Christensen, O.A., 1975. Hunters and horticulturalists: a preliminary report of the 1972–4 excavations in the Manim Valley, Papua New Guinea. *Mankind,* 10, pp. 24–36.

Clarke, W.C., 1971. *Place and People: An Ecology of a New Guinea Community*. Berkeley, CA: University of California Press.

Coursey, D.G., 1967. *Yams*. London: Longmans.

Coursey, D.G., 1972. The civilizations of the yam: interrelationships of man and yams in Africa and the Indo-Pacific region. *Archaeology and Physical Anthropology in Oceania*, 7(1), pp. 215–233.

Crawford, G.W., 2012. Early rice exploitation in the lower Yangzi valley: what are we missing? *The Holocene*, 22, pp. 613–621.

Daniels, J. and Daniels, C., 1993. Sugarcane in prehistory. *Archaeology in Oceania*, 28, pp. 1–7.

De Langhe, E. and de Maret, P., 1999. Tracking the banana: its significance in early agriculture. In: C. Gosden and J. Hather, eds. *The Prehistory of Food: Appetites for Change*. London: Routledge, pp. 377–396.

De Langhe, E., Perrier, X., Donohue, M. and Denham, T.P., 2015. The original banana split: multidisciplinary implications of the generation of African and Pacific plantains in Island Southeast Asia. *Ethnobotany Research and Applications*, 14, pp. 299–312.

Denham, T.P., 2004. The roots of agriculture and arboriculture in New Guinea: looking beyond Austronesian expansion, Neolithic packages and Indigenous origins. *World Archaeology*, 36, pp. 610–620.

Denham, T.P., 2007. Early to mid-Holocene plant exploitation in New Guinea: towards a contingent interpretation of agriculture. In: T.P. Denham, J. Iriarte and L. Vrydaghs, eds. *Rethinking Agriculture: Archaeological and Ethnoarchaeological Perspectives*. Walnut Creek, CA: Left Coast Press. pp. 78–108.

Denham, T.P., 2009. A practice-centred method for charting the emergence and transformation of agriculture. *Current Anthropology*, 50, pp. 661–667.

Denham, T.P., 2011. Early agriculture and plant domestication in New Guinea and Island Southeast Asia. *Current Anthropology*, 52(S4), pp. S379–S395.

Denham, T.P., 2013. Early farming in Island Southeast Asia: an alternative hypothesis. *Antiquity*, 87, pp. 250–257.

Denham, T.P., 2018a. *Tracing Early Agriculture in the Highlands of New Guinea: Plot, Mound and Ditch*. Oxford: Routledge.

Denham, T.P., 2018b. Origin and development of agriculture in New Guinea, Island Melanesia and Polynesia. In: R. Hazlett, ed. *Oxford Encyclopaedia of Agriculture and the Environment*. Oxford: Oxford University Press. DOI: 10.1093/acrefore/9780199389414.013.171

Denham, T.P. and Haberle, S.G., 2008. Agricultural emergence and transformation in the Upper Wahgi valley during the Holocene: theory, method and practice. *The Holocene*, 18, pp. 499–514.

Denham, T.P., Haberle, S.G., Lentfer, C., Fullagar, R., Field, J., Therin, M. Porch, N. and Winsborough, B., 2003. Origins of agriculture at Kuk Swamp in the highlands of New Guinea. *Science*, 301, pp. 189–193.

Diamond, J., 1997. *Guns, Germs and Steel*. London: Norton & Co.

Feil, D., 1984. Beyond patriliny in the New Guinea highlands. *Man*, 19, pp. 50–76.

Feil, D., 1987. *The Evolution of Highland Papua New Guinea Societies*. Cambridge: Cambridge University Press.

Florin, S.A. and Carah, X., 2018. Moving past the 'Neolithic' problem: the development and interaction of subsistence systems across northern Sahul. *Quaternary International*, 489(30), pp. 46–62.

Fullagar, R., Field, J, Denham, T.P. and Lentfer, C., 2006. Early and mid Holocene processing of taro (*Colocasia esculenta*) and yam (*Dioscorea* sp.) at Kuk Swamp in the highlands of Papua New Guinea. *Journal of Archaeological Science*, 33, pp. 595–614.

Fuller, D.Q., Denham, T.P., Arroyo-Kalin, M., Lucas, L., Stevens, C., Qin, L., Allaby, R.G. and Purugganan, M.D., 2014. Convergent evolution and parallelism in plant domestication revealed by an expanding archaeological record. *Proceedings of the National Academy of Sciences (USA)*, 111, pp. 6147–6152.

Gardner, R. and Heider, K.G., 1969. *Gardens of War: Life and Death in the New Guinea Stone Age*. New York: Random House.

Godelier, M., 1986. *The Making of Great Men: Male Domination and Power amongst the New Guinea Baruya*, tr. R. Swyer. Cambridge: Cambridge University Press.

Golson, J., 1977. *The Ladder of Social Evolution: Archaeology and the Bottom Rungs*. Sydney: Sydney University Press.

Golson, J. and Gardner, D., 1990. Agriculture and sociopolitical organisation in New Guinea Highlands prehistory. *Annual Review of Anthropology*, 19, pp. 395–417.

Golson, J., Denham, T.P, Hughes, P.J., Swadling, P. and Muke, J., eds. 2017. *Ten Thousand Years of Cultivation at Kuk Swamp in the Highlands of Papua New Guinea*. Terra Australis 46. Canberra: ANU E Press.

Grivet, L., Daniels, C., Glaszman, J.C. and D'Hont, A., 2004. A review of recent molecular genetics evidence for sugarcane evolution and domestication. *Ethnobotany Research and Applications*, 2, pp. 9–17.

Harris, D.R., 1990. Vavilov's concept of centres of origin of cultivated plants: its genesis and its influence on the study of agricultural origins. *Biological Journal of the Linnean Society*, 39, pp. 7–16.

Harris, D.R., 1996. Introduction: themes and concepts in the study of early agriculture. In: D.R. Harris, ed. *The Origins and Spread of Agriculture and Pastoralism in Eurasia*. London: University College London Press, pp. 1–9.

Harris, D.R., 2007. Agriculture, cultivation and domestication: exploring the conceptual framework of early food production. In: T.P. Denham, J. Iriarte and L. Vrydaghs, eds. *Rethinking Agriculture: Archaeological and Ethnoarchaeological Perspectives*. Walnut Creek, CA: Left Coast Press. pp. 16–35.

Hather, J.G., 1996. The origins of tropical vegeculture: Zingiberaceae, Araceae and Dioscoreaceae in Southeast Asia. In: D.R. Harris (ed.) *The Origins and Spread of Agriculture and Pastoralism in Eurasia*. London: UCL Press. pp. 538–550.

Hillman, G.C. and Davies, M.S., 1990. Measured domestication rates in wild wheats and barley under primitive cultivation, and their archaeological implications. *Journal of World Prehistory*, 4, pp. 157–222.

Kennedy, J., 2009. Bananas and people in the homeland of genus *Musa*: not just pretty fruit. *Ethnobotany Research and Applications*, 7, pp. 179–197.

Kennedy, J. and Clarke, W.C., 2004. *Cultivated Landscapes of the Southwest Pacific*. Resource Management in the Asia-Pacific (RMAP) Working Paper 50, Canberra: RMAP, Australian National University

Kocher Schmid, C., 1991. *Of People and Plants: A Botanical Ethnography of Nokopo Village, Madang and Morobe Provinces, Papua New Guinea*. Basel: Verlag.

Kuijt, I. and Finalyson, W., 2009. Evidence for food storage and predomestication granaries 11,000 years ago in the Jordan valley. *Proceedings of the National Academy of Sciences (USA)*, 106, pp. 10966–10970.

Latinis, K., 2000. The development of subsistence system models for island Southeast Asia and Near Oceania: the nature and role of arboriculture and arboreal-based economies. *World Archaeology*, 32, pp. 41–67.

Lebot, V., 1999. Biomolecular evidence for plant domestication in Sahul. *Genetic Resources and Crop Evolution*, 46, pp. 619–628.

Lebot, V., 2009. *Root and Tuber Crops: Cassava, Sweet Potato, Yams and Aroids*. Crop Production Science in Horticulture, 17. Wallingford: CABI Publishing.

Lentfer, C.J., 2009. Tracing domestication and cultivation of bananas from phytoliths: an update from Papua New Guinea. *Ethnobotany Research and Applications,* 7, pp. 247–270.

Li, H.-L., 1970. The origin of cultivated plants in Southeast Asia. *Economic Botany,* 24(1), pp. 3–19.

Loy, T., Spriggs, M. and Wickler, S., 1992. Direct evidence for human use of plants 28,000 years ago: starch residues on stone artefacts from northern Solomon Islands. *Antiquity,* 66, pp. 898–912.

Modjeska, C.M., 1982. Production and inequality: perspectives from central New Guinea. In: A. Strathern, ed. *Inequality in New Guinea Highland Societies.* Cambridge: Cambridge University Press, pp. 50–108.

Muke, J., 1992. The Wahgi Opo-Kumbo. An account of warfare, Central Highlands, New Guinea. Unpublished PhD thesis, University of Cambridge.

Perrier, X., De Langhe, E., Donohue, M., Lentfer, C., Vrydaghs, L., Bakry, F., Carreel, F., Hippolyte, I., Horry, J.-P., Jenny, C., Lebot, V., Risterucci, A.-M., Tomekpe, K., Doutrelepont, H., Ball, T., Manwaring, J., de Maret, P. and Denham, T.P., 2011. Multidisciplinary perspectives on banana (*Musa* spp.) domestication. *Proceedings of the National Academy of Sciences (USA),* 108, pp. 11311–11318.

Piperno, D.R., Ranere, A.J., Holst, I.. Iriarte, J. and Dickau, R., 2009. Starch grain and phytolith evidence for early ninth millennium B.P. maize from the Central Balsas River Valley, Mexico. *Proceedings of the National Academy of Sciences (USA),* 106, pp. 5019–5024.

Powell, J.M., 1982. The history of plant use and man's impact on the vegetation. In: J. L. Gressitt, ed. *Biogeography and Ecology of New Guinea,* vol. 1. The Hague: Junk, pp. 207–227.

Powell, J.M., Kulunga, A., Moge, R., Pono, C., Zimike, F. and Golson, J., 1975. *Agricultural Traditions in the Mount Hagen Area.* Occasional Paper, 12. Port Moresby: Department of Geography, UPNG.

Premachandran, M.N., Prathima, P.T. and Lekshmi, M., 2011. Sugarcane and polyploidy. *Journal of Sugarcane Research,* 1, pp. 1–15.

Rangan, H., Alpers, E.A, Denham, T.P., Kull, C. and Carney, J., 2015. Food traditions and landscape histories of the Indian Ocean World: theoretical and methodological reflections. *Environment and History,* 21, pp. 135–157.

Riebe, I., 1974. '… And then we killed': an attempt to understand the fighting history of the Upper Kaironk Valley Kalam from 1914–1962. Unpublished MA thesis. Sydney: Department of Anthropology, University of Sydney.

Roullier, C., Benoit, L., McKey, D.B. and Lebot, V., 2013. Historical collections reveal patterns of diffusion of sweet potato in Oceania obscured by modern plant movements and recombination. *Proceedings of the National Academy of Sciences (USA),* 110, pp. 2205–2210.

Sanday, P.R., 1986. *Divine Hunger: Cannibalism as a Cultural System.* New York: Cambridge University Press.

Sauer, C.O., 1952. *Agricultural Origins and their Dispersals.* New York: American Geographical Society.

Shaw, R.D., 1996. *From Longhouse to Village: Samo Social Change.* Fort Worth, TX: Harcourt Brace.

Simmonds, N.W., 1976. Sugarcanes: Saccharum (Gramineae-Andropogoneae). In: N.W. Simmonds, ed. *Evolution of Crop Plants.* London: Longman, pp. 104–108.

Smith, B.D., 2001. Low-level food production. *Journal of Archaeological Research,* 9, pp. 1–43.

Snir, A., Nadel, D., Groman-Yaroslavski, I., Melamed, Y., Sternberg. M., Bar-Yosef, O. and Weiss, E., 2015. The origin of cultivation and proto-weeds, long before Neolithic farming. *PLoS ONE,* 10(7), e0131422. doi:10.1371/journal.pone.0131422

Stover, R.H. and Simmonds, N.W., eds. 1987. *Bananas,* 3rd edition. Tropical Agriculture Series. Harlow: Longman.

Strathern, A., 1971. *The Rope of Moka: Big-Men and Ceremonial Exchange in Mount Hagen, New Guinea.* Cambridge: Cambridge University Press.

Strathern, A., 1972. *One Father, One Blood: Descent and Group Structure among the Melpa People.* Canberra: Australian National University Press.

Terrell, J.E., Hart, J.P., Barut, S., Cellinese, N., Curet, A., Denham, T.P., Haines, H., Kusimba, C.M., Latinis, K., Oka, R., Palka, J., Pohl, M.E.D., Pope, K.O., Staller, J.E. and Williams, P.R., 2003. Domesticated landscapes: the subsistence ecology of plant and animal domestication. *Journal of Archaeological Method and Theory,* 10, pp. 323–368.

van Dillewjn, C., 1952. *Botany of Sugarcane.* Waltham, MA: Chronica Botanica.

Vrydaghs, L., Ball, T., Volkaert, H., van den Houwe, I., Manwaring, J. and De Langhe, E., 2009. Differentiating the volcaniform phytoliths of bananas: Musa acuminata. *Ethnobotany Research and Applications,* 7, pp. 239–246.

Weiss, E., Wetterstrom, W., Nadel, D. and Bar-Yosef, O., 2004. The broad spectrum revisited: evidence from plant remains. *Proceedings of the National Academy of Sciences (USA),* 101, pp. 9551–9555.

West-Eberhard, M.J., 2003. *Developmental Plasticity and Evolution.* Oxford: Oxford University Press.

Willcox, G., 2007. Agrarian change and the beginnings of cultivation in the Near East: evidence from wild progenitors, experimental cultivation and archaeobotanical data. In: T.P. Denham and J.P. White, eds. *The Emergence of Agriculture: A Global View.* Abingdon, Oxon: Routledge, pp. 217–241.

Yen, D.E., 1973. The origins of Oceanic agriculture. *Archaeology and Physical Anthropology in Oceania,* 8, pp. 68–85.

Yen, D.E., 1985. Wild plants and domestication in Pacific islands. In: V.N. Misra and P. Bellwood, eds. *Recent Advances in Indo-Pacific Prehistory.* New Delhi and Oxford: IBH Publishing, pp. 315–326.

Yen, D.E., 1995. The development of Sahul agriculture with Australia as bystander. *Antiquity,* 69(special number 265), pp. 831–847.

Zhao, Z., 2011. New archaeobotanic data for the study of the origins of agriculture in China. *Current Anthropology,* 52, pp. S295–S306.

Zohary, D., Hopf, M. and Weiss, E., 2012. *Domestication of Plants in the Old World: The Origin and Spread of Domesticated Plants in Southwest Asia, Europe and the Mediterranean Basin.* Oxford: Oxford University Press.

11

SETTLEMENT PATTERNS AND NETWORKS

Secondary centres and elite ritual-political power in the Society Islands chiefdoms

Jennifer G. Kahn

Archaeologists in Polynesia commonly use the spatial patterning of monumental architecture and other elite structures to infer political boundaries and changes in social organisation. When integrated with ethnohistory, such proxy data can be utilised to identify socio-political territories and their degree of political central-isation. Yet such territorial approaches imply fixed boundaries and obviate periodic cycles of centralisation, decentralisation and rotating centres of political power that are expressed in the historical records. In this chapter I present a case study that utilises settlement pattern data and landscape analyses to identify these sorts of organisational changes in the ritual-political centres of the 'Opunohu Valley. I argue that the identification of inland secondary ceremonial centres dramatically changes our perception of Society Islands political history. Network analysis provides added insights into how the Mā'ohi conceptualised landscapes and social relations. Examining temporal changes in the distribution and centralisation of elite political power highlights the creation of materially inscribed relationships between Mā'ohi elites in minor ritual-political centres. Such analyses effectively chart organisational changes in socio-political networks through the Classic period (1650–1767 CE) and point towards the important role that religious ideology had in ongoing political centralisation in Polynesian chiefdoms and other middle-range societies.

Settlement pattern analysis, landscape archaeology and community organisation in Polynesia

While archaeologists have long been interested in documenting Polynesian[1] monu-mental architecture, most notably temple sites (*marae* in the Society Islands, *meae* in the Marquesas Islands, *heiau* in the Hawaiian Islands), mound sites and tombs, early studies took a decidedly descriptive and culture historical approach (see Emory, 1933; Stokes, 1991). In the first decades of the 20th century, archaeologists (commonly with their Polynesian informants) documented and described only the largest and most elaborate site types including temples, *ahu* (upraised platforms and altars), *tiki* (sculpted god figures), shrines and other elite structures such as archery platforms, star mounds, burial platforms and *tohua* (dance and feasting grounds). In Eastern Polynesia, temples were treated as a form of material culture that could illuminate links between island societies, thereby allowing for migration sequences to be defined (Bennett, 1931; Emory, 1924, 1928, 1933; McAllister, 1933). A corollary goal was to use monumental architecture as a *fossil directeur* that exhibited temporal variation, permitting for the relative dating of Polynesian landscapes (see Emory, 1933, pp. 3–4).

The 1960s ushered in a period of significant change in how Polynesian archaeologists conceptualised archaeological sites and their distribution in broader physical landscapes. By asking questions such as 'How did the village plans in various Polynesian societies fit with the social organization of these groups?' Suggs's (1961, p. 122) Marquesan research was one of the first to tackle questions of social transformations in Polynesian chiefdoms with settlement pattern-like data. In 1960, Roger Green carried out a pioneering, intensive settlement pattern survey in the Society Islands (Green, 1961; Green et al., 1967), having been mentored by Gordon Willey, an innovator of settlement pattern studies, at Harvard (Willey, 1953). Yet Green's settlement pattern analysis differed from the dominant functional, evolutionary inspired analyses common in the 1950–1960s (for the latter see Parsons, 1972). Douglas Oliver, a pre-eminent Polynesian anthropologist at Harvard, pushed Green to inventory Māʻohi settlement patterns as a means of reconstructing pre-contact socio-political organisation, namely status differences and hierarchies existing among and between socio-political districts and communities (Green, 1996).

Green's intensive analysis of 'Opunohu Valley landscapes documented site types of all kinds; not only were the largest and most elaborate temples recorded, but so too were house sites, agricultural terraces, shrines and enclosures (1961; Green et al., 1967; Green and Descantes, 1989). Ultimately, Green's settlement pattern analysis was organised not only to see how the Māʻohi interacted with, adapted to and intensified the natural environment, but also to identify how social groups were distributed across cultural landscapes, thereby inferring aspects of social organisation and hierarchy. A suite of other regional settlement pattern analyses followed in Polynesia, some focused on functional adaptation to diverse environments, others focused more broadly on intra- and inter-community variability in social organisation (Allen, 2009; Campbell, 2001; Green and Davidson, 1969, 1974; Jennings et al., 1982; Kirch et al., 2004; Ladefoged et al., 2011; Maxwell and Smith, 2015; Morrison, 2012; Quintus et al., 2016; Verin, 1969; for New Zealand see discussion in Phillips and Campbell, 2004).

Investigating social variability

While archaeologists in Polynesia can thus be viewed as eager adopters of settlement pattern analyses, the region is also distinctive for inspiring studies aimed at the analysis of social inequality and hierarchy. Examples include innovative analyses of domestic structures, including house sites, *paepae* (raised stone platforms), and their associated middens, as a window into rank and status and patterns of political centralisation through time (Dixon et al., 2008; Field et al., 2010; Field et al., 2011; Gosser and Dixon, 1998; Kellum, 1968). Allen (2009) studied variability in house platform size, height, elaboration and change in the Anaho Valley (Nuku Hiva, Marquesas) to argue for displays of status, wealth and power during a period of climatic instability in the 17th century. In Hawai'i, Dixon and colleagues identified walled habitation compounds as traditional men's houses, arguing that structures these might have had a communal role for redistribution of items such as stone tools and pigs in the mid-17th century, a function which was later superseded by state or polity temples (2008, p. 282). Polynesian studies follow worldwide themes in regional survey where analysis of local-scale and community-scale domestic architecture is employed to infer regional processes of political centralisation and integration (Guengerich, 2014; Hutson, 2010; Steadman, 2015; Van Gijseghem and Vaughn, 2008). Such studies recognise that the built environment is inherently a social landscape.

As in other parts of the world, Polynesian settlement pattern research exploring rank and status has most commonly focused on monumental architecture, particularly ritual and ceremonial structures (Burley, 1996; Herdrich, 1991; Kahn, 2016a; Kahn and Kirch, 2014; Kennett and McClure, 2012; Martinsson-Wallin and Thomas, 2014; Maric, 2016; Molle, 2016; Sutton et al., 2003). For example, Maric's (2012) recent investigation of Tahitian settlement patterns utilised historical land records and site distribution analysis to document the number and placement of temples (*marae*) and other specialised sites (*fare 'arioi* [houses for fertility cult], *fare manihini* [elite meeting houses]) within traditional socio-political districts. Maric then compared the historical and archaeological data with chiefly genealogies to construct a relative chronology of temple construction and chiefly ascendancies on Tahiti in the late prehistoric period.

Economic control, territorial boundaries and political centralisation

Other studies of Polynesian landscapes have focused on identifying elite economic control, theorising that some monuments, such as temples, served as loci of tribute collection, while all monuments served as visual symbols of chiefly supported labour investments. A recent meta-synthesis of the Hawaiian archaeological sequence (Kirch, 2010) utilised the size and spatial position of temples (*heiau*) to infer specific types (e.g. temples for fishing, fertility and crop production, war) and hence modes of chiefly control linked to the regulation of tribute. In another study Martinsson-Wallin and Wallin (2014) theorised that the Rapanui *moai* statuary were symbolic capital, arguing that competition between junior and senior lineages was materialised in the built environment. Finally, analysis of fortified sites on Rapa (Kennett and McClure, 2012) documented the construction of two early fortified ridgetops during the 14th–15th centuries associated with rivalry between two major chiefly polities. A proliferation of Rapan fortifications in the 18th century, with strategic positions and defensive features including storage of surplus foodstuffs, signalled the advent of fortified hilltop villages, ultimately a result of increased inter-group rivalries, warfare and competition over the most highly productive agricultural lands.

Researchers have often utilised a combination of natural referent features, archaeological sites such as temples and altars, and historic documents to demarcate political boundaries on particular islands (Kolb, 1997; Mulrooney and Ladefoged, 2005; Shepardson, 2005; Orliac and Orliac, 1996). Hawaiian case studies have utilised common bifurcation points of territories, walls and trails to relatively date *ahupua'a* (third-tier territorial land units) boundaries (Ladefoged and Graves, 2006), noting that such boundaries appear to have been less fixed than district boundaries. Maric (2012) innovative use of Society Island historical documents, place names and archaeological survey data demonstrated that, during the 15th century, chiefly temples (*marae*) were situated at the mouths of principal valleys, where inland and coastal zones met. Yet in the 17th–mid-18th centuries, chiefly centres shifted to coastal promontory, where the largest and most elaborate *marae* were built. Both archaeological data (Maric, 2012; 2016; Sharp et al., 2010) and ethnohistorical documents (Salmond, 2009) suggest that proto-historic district boundaries could shift in the Society Islands as the result of diverse social factors – after times of war, with new chiefly alliances and with usurping chiefs.

As a corollary to the analysis of Polynesian pre-contact territories and political districts, a renewed interest in documenting elite ritual centres and central places has come to the fore (Clark and Martinsson-Wallin, 2007; Kahn and Kirch, 2014). Clark and colleagues' (2016) recent analyses of Lapaha, the central place of the Tongan archaic state, demonstrated an initial focus on community integration and secular building, with a shift through time to the construction of monumental elite tombs. These trends suggest that Tongan chiefs increasingly underwrote their power and authority through ideology (see also Clark and Reepmeyer, 2014). Kirch's (2010) synthesis of the Hawaiian archaic state sequence argues for a three-tiered settlement hierarchy. The king, along with his family, retainers and other high-ranked chiefs, lived in 'royal centres', or clusters of elaborate house sites, temples, places of refuge and specialised structures such as canoe sheds, storage houses and *hōlua* slides. District-level chiefs also lived in elite centres, while *ahupua'a* chiefs and land managers lived in elaborate specialised residences within larger communities. While Kirch reasons that royal centres developed gradually through time, their pronounced use in the mid-17th century suggests increasing political centralisation and elite socio-ritual and economic control.

Beyond primary centres: new thoughts on territoriality, networks and nodes

While Polynesian studies often focus on identifying the largest and most elaborate of elite ritual-political centres, international studies suggest that much is to be gained by studying secondary centres outside primary cores (Hendrickson and Evans, 2015). Such analyses have yielded new appreciation of the capacity for communities living outside political centres to shape regional dynamics (Smith and Janusek, 2014). Qualitative and quantitative studies of minor centres provide more accurate models of polity size, their horizontal and vertical integration, and the pathways leading to regional political centralisation (Chase and Chase, 2003; Connell, 2003; Iannone, 2003). Building chronological frameworks for minor centres can illustrate how communities fissioned as a result of demographic growth and agricultural intensification (Rosenswig and Mendelsohn, 2016) or how different factions competed within one another, requiring complex social strategies to promote and sustain integration across landscapes (Connell, 2003). Comparisons of site size, site types, and degree of interconnectivity (often identified through artefact provenance analysis) can illuminate how symbols of elite and sub-elite authority differed at the local and regional scales (Masson, 2003). Site distribution, site function, and the specific activities represented can also index the degree to which secondary centres served as important nodes in larger social and administrative networks (Millaire, 2010). Taken as a whole, such studies highlight the need for multi-scalar analyses of settlement patterns and landscapes in order to understand the dynamic nature of pre-contact political units.

Schortman and Ashmore (2012) argue that political formations are best understood by applying a network approach. They define social networks as being 'composed of people devoted to pursuing specific political projects through manipulation of resources that are conceptual (including ideas and the symbols that instantiate them) and material, as well as the rules by which such assets are acquired' (2012, p. 3). The goal is to identify the cultural entities that were connected (nodes such as individual households, settlements, mid-sized centres) and to examine flows of information and resources between these entities. Social network analyses (SNA) highlight similarities between site types or concentrations of site types, whether in architectural styles, site density, or artefact frequencies, as a means of defining flows of information and resources (Ostborn and Gerding, 2014; Peeples and Roberts, 2013). These interrelationships are then placed within a broader context (Mills, 2015), through regional settlement pattern analysis or other means (modelling, simulations). Such analyses emphasise horizontal and vertical relationships and connections between nodes (Mills et al., 2013), theorising that social power is generated by how such entities are situated in the network and connected to one another (Mizoguchi, 2009).

Network approaches support a view that political formations were rooted in the interaction of social, ritual and economic factors through time, moving away from idealised notions of formally circumscribed political types (Smith and Janusek, 2014). The paradigm offers a novel way for understanding how political power was actively negotiated and constructed by social actors operating within local and regional structures of resources, rules and events (Schortman and Ashmore, 2012). Flows or connections between network nodes are defined by similarities in empirical data, such as shared site types or architectural styles, or common types and sources of artefacts, and quantified through statistical analyses, network graphs, simulations, and agent-based modelling (Golitko and Feinman, 2015; Mills, 2015; 2017).

The only archaeological application of SNA to Eastern Polynesia at the time of writing is a recent case study identifying New Zealand 'site communities' and 'source communities', as inferred from obsidian sourcing data (Ladefoged et al., 2019). The study utilised social network analysis to define patterned interactions of trade and exchange and hence 'analytical site communities', or relational identities resulting from indirect or direct social connections. These were found to partially correspond to the identities of current Māori tribal territories and argued to have coalesced sometime after 1500 CE.

'Opunohu Valley networks and nodes: landscape analyses of secondary ritual-political centres

My case study from the Society Island chiefdoms centres on the materialisation of ideology at the community level. I utilise settlement pattern data and landscape analyses to identify secondary ritual-political centres in the 'Opunohu Valley, on Mo'orea Island (Fig. 11.1). As I will argue, Mā'ohi political power was realised, in part, through

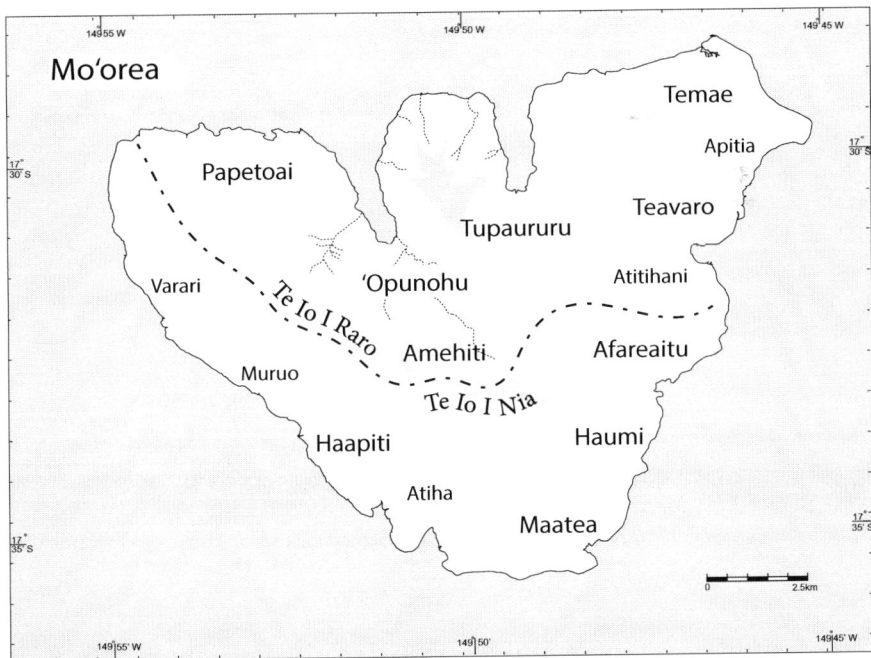

FIGURE 11.1 Map of Mo'orea showing districts and tribes.

Source: map by Jennifer Kahn, using districts depicted by Handy (1930, fig. 4).

socio–religious ceremonies at temples and shrines involving the gods and the ancestors. Like other complex societies (Demarrais et al., 1996; Moore, 1996), ideologies were materialised in public, monumental architecture, effectively supporting Mā'ohi chiefs' economic and socio-political power (Kahn and Kirch, 2011, 2014).

The Society Islands have been classified as a complex chiefdom with a high degree of stratification based on such criteria as: (1) the presence of at least three socially ranked echelons (commoner, low chief, high chief); (2) evidence for strict social restrictions/regulations (*tapu*) heavily affecting everyday life and access to resources; (3) intensification of production and economic specialisation; (4) large overall population size; and (5) large polity size (Oliver, 1974). Yet several lines of evidence indicate that status in ancient Mā'ohi society was even more complex than such models suggest. Ethnohistoric documents do reveal three main social classes: the *ari'i* (chiefs), the *ra'atira* (sub-district and district-level economic leaders), and the *manahune* (commoners) (Oliver, 1974), however, gradations in rank and status also existed within each social class. For example, the *ari'i* class held varied hereditary titled offices, such as those for principal or paramount chiefs (*ari'i rahi* or *ari'i nui*) and those for lesser-ranked lower chiefs (*ari'i ri'i,* such as *'iatoai* and *to'ofā*). Considered to be divine, *ari'i rahi* held the highest titles linked to prestigious *marae*; they also served as rulers over the largest and most influential political districts. At the time of European contact, *ari'i rahi* lived in coastal chiefly centres where elite residences, ceremonial structures, and related sites were clustered on promontories (Maric, 2012).

Lesser ranked chiefs lacked the absolute power of paramount chiefs, and as with other social classes, they likely had their own pattern of residence. *'Iotoai* served as inferior chiefs or underchiefs (Adams, 1976, p. 8; Oliver, 1974, p. 761), positions that were probably hereditary. *To'ofā* were another set of inferior chiefs and included junior chiefly lineages, 'near relatives … or younger brothers' of the paramount chiefs (Morrison, 1935, p. 167). *Ra'atira* had an administrative role, serving as land managers. *Manahune* were commoners, members of the lowest marriage class who lacked land-holding rights. Ethnohistoric documents and archaeological data suggest secondary chiefs, land managers and commoners lived primarily, but not exclusively, in inland contexts from c.1400 CE onwards (Descantes, 1990; Eddowes, 1991; Kahn and Kirch, 2014; Maric, 2012).

In trying to relate Mā'ohi gradations of rank and status to archaeological settlement patterns, the fact that most primary coastal centres have been destroyed by modern development leaves analyses of *ari'i rahi* settlement hierarchies difficult at best. Yet large clusters of elaborate *marae* found in interior valleys present the possibility of defining secondary centres or minor centres where junior chiefly lineages (*'iotoai, to'ofā*) and *ra'atira* held sway over local communities (*'āti,* sub-divisions of larger socio-political districts known as *mata'eina'a*).

Monumental architecture, ritual-political centres and community organisation

In Polynesian chiefdoms, temples or *marae* are the main forms of elaborate 'public architecture' of a monumental nature. Ethnohistoric accounts suggest that religious or ceremonial rituals carried out at temple sites were part of the ideological framework of elite control over labour and production. The positioning of temples in the landscape was also an avenue for territorial marking, facilitating territorial disputes, and strengthening the elites' all-important ties to the gods and ancestors (Kahn and Kirch, 2014). Temples were places used by chiefs and priests to lead formalised corporate rituals, arenas where commoners and women participated only from outside the temple walls (Kahn, 2016a).

As a means of understanding community-scale organisation in the Society Islands, I focus on the scale and temporality of aggregate site clusters, or what Green first referred to as 'focal point[s]' and 'principal locations' (Green et al., 1967), in inland valleys to pinpoint the presence of junior elites in these contexts. By documenting similarities between clusters of monumental temples and shrines and their association with other elite structures commonly used by chiefs and high-status ritual specialists, I outline the presence of inland ritual-political secondary centres. My data derive from landscape analyses in the 'Opunohu Valley (Fig. 11.1) where over 220 temples and shrines have been mapped and described (Green, 1961; Green and Descantes, 1989; Kahn, 2005; Kahn and Kirch, 2014). Landscape-scale mapping in the Tupauruuru sector of the valley has facilitated the identification of these centres.

I define Māʻohi ritual political centres as locations including two or more aggregated temple sites, often with a high degree of architectural elaboration (Kahn, 2011). Aggregated temple complexes are typically found in association with other ritual features, such as *ti'i* (god figures) and shrines, and with other specialised elite structures, such as archery platforms for elite sport and council meeting platforms for political activities. Everyday-use sites such as sleeping houses are uncommon in these locations, highlighting their specialised nature. Use patterns of aggregate temple complexes are restricted to the ceremonial activities of high-ranked elites, such as feasting, tribute collection and sport; these vary significantly from smaller ritual-residential complexes where domestic, subsistence and ritual activities are associated with a range of social statuses (Kahn and Kirch, 2014). Since the primary ritual centres of the *ariʻi rahi* and *ariʻi nui* were centred on the coast, these inland complexes likely defined the landed estates of secondary chiefs (*ariʻi riʻi*) (Oliver, 1974) and may have also been in close association with residences of the *raʻatira* (land managers).

Based on currently available archaeological data, I have argued that the pace of construction of specialised-use inland centres increased from the 17th century onwards. Their construction materialised the power strategies of rival Māʻohi junior elites (i.e. secondary chiefs) and high-status occupational specialists (i.e. high priests) (Kahn, 2011, 2015; Kahn and Kirch, 2014). Such bounded ritual zones allowed for manipulation of the political economy and integration of economic practices within the regional ritual calendar. From a network analysis perspective, these complexes can be viewed as secondary ceremonial nodes – the material correlates of junior ranking lineages that segmented and differentiated through time. I reason that increasing competition between these lineages was one of the factors leading to more formalised socio-political hierarchies in the archipelago. As such, communities living outside primary centres had the ability to shape regional dynamics.

Secondary ritual-political centres in the 'Opunohu Valley

Regional-scale analyses illustrate that there were five secondary ritual-political centres in the 'Opunohu Valley, four of which were situated in the Tupauruuru District and one of which was situated in the Amehiti District. Landscape analyses of 'Opunohu Valley centres (Kahn, 2018) confirm previous settlement pattern data suggesting that the Tupauruuru District had more abundant and elaborate ritual sites than those found in Amehiti (Green, 1996; Green et al., 1967; Kahn, 2005). Green (1996) interpreted the settlement pattern data as representing a more complex social hierarchy in Tupauruuru than Amehiti, as site density and types varied considerably between the two sectors.

However, chronological data suggest at least one secondary elite lineage moved into the most productive Amehiti agricultural lands and constructed ritual and residential sites there early on in the inland expansion sequence, c.1250–1350 CE (Kahn and Kirch, 2013). Later construction events in Amehiti's only secondary ritual centre included transforming a simple temple into a more elaborate war cult temple dedicated to the God 'Oro in the mid-17th to 18th century (Kahn, 2013). This was a material manifestation of this secondary lineage's efforts to maintain political alliances to ruling elites on coast of Mo'orea, on the neighbouring island of Tahiti, and to the more distant Leeward Island chiefdoms (e.g. Huahine, Ra'iātea, Bora Bora), (Kahn, 2010; see also Maric, 2012). Ethnohistoric documents record how, in late prehistory in the Windward Islands (Tahiti and Mo'orea), 'Oro type *marae* and the religious rites carried out at them were closely linked to the growing socio-political domination of the *ari'i rahi* (Newbury, 1967; Maric, 2012; Robineau, 2009; Salmond, 2009). New coastal temples consecrated to 'Oro, along with ownership and rites to ritual paraphernalia, became the source of political legitimisation and domination by the highest chiefs.

Similar patterns are found elsewhere in contexts suggestive of the power strategies of secondary chiefs. Construction of 'Oro style war cult temples (Fig. 11.2) is found at the same time in two of the four aggregate ritual centres of the Tupauruuru District (Kahn, 2010; Kahn and Kirch, 2014). Such events illustrate shifting ritual-political alliances through time and hint at cycles of centralisation, decentralisation and rotating centres of political power. They are also indicative of social networks between paramount and secondary chiefly lineages at the local scale (inland valley, inter- and intra-district), at the island scale (inland versus coastal), and at the archipelago scale (Windward chiefdoms of Mo'orea and Tahiti versus Leeward chiefdoms).

If we examine the constellation of aggregate ritual centres in the lowlands of the Tupauruuru District, we see that three centres are in close proximity (Fig. 11.3). Each centre has major temple sites with fronting terraces that were the loci of elaborate seasonal rituals, as well as *rites de passage* for the elites. Each has elite structures such as council platforms, archery platforms and specialised houses, structures which were used for varied socio-political activities (alliance building, elite sport, craft production). In addition, some centres have evidence of communal feasting in the second half of the 17th century (Kahn, 2016b; Kahn and Kirch, 2014).

FIGURE 11.2 Select structures typically associated with secondary centres, examples from the 'Opunohu Valley. Top: ScMo-129, Marae *Mahine*, 'Oro style *marae* with stepped *ahu* fashioned from worked loaf stones and rows of uprights and backrest stones on the paved court; Middle: ScMo-164b, rectilinear *paepae* (upraised stone platform) interpreted as a council platform; Bottom: ScMo-165, shrine with a rectangular stone pavement, backrest and uprights.

Source: Drawings and photographs by Jennifer Kahn.

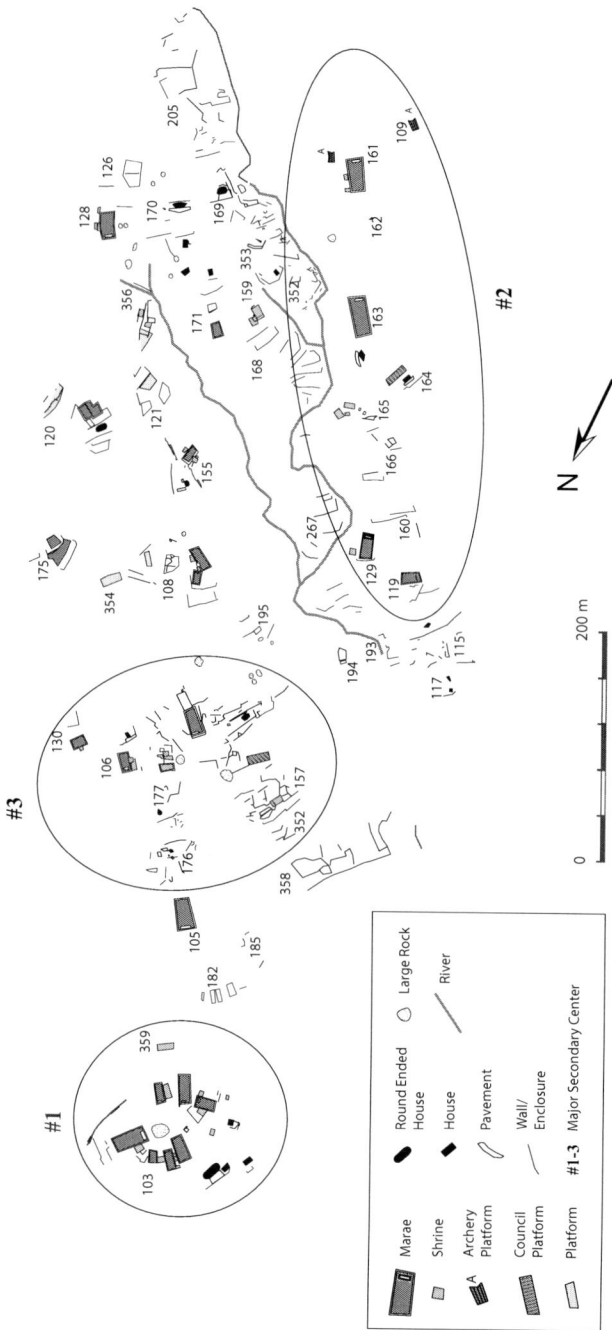

FIGURE 11.3 Section of the Tupaururuu District, 'Opunohu Valley with all surface sites depicted and major secondary centres delineated and numbered.

Various characteristics of the post-1650 CE 'Opunohu Valley secondary centres suggest the elaboration of community rituals and their relationship to exclusionary practices linked to social hierarchies. A case in point is the ScMo-103 complex which includes seven elaborate temples, in addition to round-ended and rectangular house structures and raised platforms. Excavations revealed that house sites within the ScMo-103 complex were not ordinary sleeping houses, but rather were specialised houses serving a range of socio-political functions, including sacred houses used by priests to store ritual sacra and others used as feasting locales (Green, 1996). In addition, an archery platform for sacred sport is found upslope of the complex and is associated with another large round-ended house and a chief's council platform (Green and Descantes, 1989). Archery platforms and the structures surrounding them served as places for communal gatherings of political and ritual elites coming from local sub-districts, other districts on the island and potentially the greater island context. Council platforms, like the one found upslope of ScMo-103, are also identified as specialised structures for chiefly activities. At these stone platforms, elites, including chiefs, priests and warriors, hosted political deliberations on matters such as warfare. Taken as a whole, the spatial configuration, types of structures, and activities represented at the ScMo-103 complex, like other 'Opunohu Valley aggregate ritual complexes, indicate that secondary centres had corporate ceremonial, political and socio-economic functions.

The fact that each of 'Opunohu Valley's five ritual-political centres was expanded and elaborated in similar ways in the late 17th century speaks to their integrated role at the regional level. It also speaks to the late 17th century as an intense period of political centralisation. As Emerson (1997) has noted for Mississippian ranked societies, ancestor cults that emphasise exclusiveness are politically manipulative. This certainly seems to be the case in the Society Islands. Across the archipelago secondary inland centres were expanded and elaborated after 1600 CE to accommodate large corporate rituals and community-scale economic events (Kahn, 2016a; Kahn and Kirch, 2014). Multiple lines of evidence suggest increasing socio-ritual elite power during this period (Lepofsky and Kahn, 2011).

Mā'ohi minor centres, or secondary ritual-political centres as networks and nodes

The 'Opunohu Valley sites can be conceived of as minor centres utilising Chase and Chase's (2003, p. 109) terminology, as 'small nodes of architectural concentration … with distinct non-residential architecture'. Here, chiefly lineages of high status, but of lower status than the most-high ranking lineages living on the coast, led their communities in a range of political, economic, social and ideological roles. Certainly, the high frequency of elaborate temples and shrines speak to the important ritual events (first fruits, rites of passage, mortuary rites) carried out at such centres. We can infer from the archaeological and ethnohistoric evidence that inland centres were political arenas where chiefs and other social elites conducted strategic meetings at council platforms. Other important social interactions revolved around watching elite sport and attending music and dance performances. Such places also served as economic centres where elites appropriated tribute during annual first fruit ceremonies on elaborate terraces facing the massive *marae*. In these ways, inland secondary centres served as political, economic and ritual nodes at multiple scales, linking neighbourhoods to communities, and inland areas to the coast.

I contend that such centres also served to create, and map onto the landscape, an exclusionary elite 'high culture' quite separate from commoner daily social life. Archaeological data suggest that from c.1650 CE onwards, elite feasts were integrated into political events and rites, and were provisioned by commoner labour and tribute (Kahn, 2016b). Feasting in and around elaborate temples, priests' houses, council meeting platforms and specialised eating houses (*fare tama'ara'a*) (Green et al., 1967, p. 138; Kahn, 2016b; Kahn and Kirch, 2014) was an exclusionary practice related to the consumption of high-status foodstuffs. Archery competitions likewise were the exclusionary creations of an elite high culture, as only the *ar'i* and the *r'atira* could participate (Corney, 1918, p. 45; Henry, 1928, p. 276), and also involved feasting and dancing. Historical accounts suggest that festivities at primary centres attracted *ari'i rahi* and district-level chiefs alike (Ellis, 1829, p. 301; Henry, 1928, p. 279); they also likely attracted sub-district chiefs from surrounding communities.

To summarise, minor centres have much to add to our regional understanding of ancient Mā'ohi social organisation, including insights into polity size and integration. All five minor centres in the 'Opunohu Valley have recognisable central areas that are hierarchically scaled in relation to the surrounding residential communities. They demonstrate, in Duffy's (2015) terms, 'regional functional specialisation' where a few large sites with specialised architecture and ritual spaces perform important functions for a region. These secondary inland centres are surrounded by smaller sites that do not have this specified function. Similarities in the timing, construction, and elaboration of each minor centre suggest a context of intensifying competition. In particular, the evidence for surplus food storage and intensive feasting, which are ubiquitous at such centres (Kahn, 2016b; Kahn and Kirch, 2014), indicate their important socio-political roles, particularly as loci for lavish entertaining and community building. We can envision how, at such places, local elites constructed alliances with neighbouring chiefly lineages and maintained ties to higher ranked lineages on the coast and on other islands in the archipelago. Yet, secondary centres also served important ideological roles by delineating specialised spaces for elite interactions and corporate rituals. *Tapu* (sacred, prohibited) regulations designated such places as having access restricted to elites. Thus, secondary centres effectively structured inland valley landscapes of power where access to specific zones was restricted to specific individuals based on their rank, gender and occupation.

Our regional maps often minimise the nature of contested social landscapes in their focus on fixed socio-political territories and well-delineated political boundaries (Fig. 11.1). I argue that secondary inland centres can be seen both as territorial markers of landed estates of secondary chiefs of *'āti* (sub-divisions of larger socio-political districts), and as resource rich and ceremonially rich nodes in networks of contested social relations. If we think of these secondary centres as parts of networks, they can be seen as the materialisation of political negotiations and alliances at the sub-district level. Such centres were joined to one another through internal and external social relations as well as elements of the natural landscape, such as paths and rivers. Next, I apply social network analysis to adze assemblages from one 'Opunohu secondary centre and several surrounding neighbourhoods to show how we might begin to discover these internal and external social relations.

Case study: social network analysis of 'Opunohu Valley sites and access to local and non-local adze sources

In the following analysis, sites in the 'Opunohu Valley have been grouped into five neighbourhoods based on proximity (Table 11.1). Data from excavations at nineteen sites has provided firm functional categories for these neighbourhoods (see Kahn, 2003; Kahn and Kirch, 2011, 2013, 2014; Kahn et al., 2013). They include: residential complexes (sleeping houses and cookhouses in association with agricultural sites and family-level temples), specialised ritual complexes (shrines, temples) which are sometimes concentrated into secondary ceremonial centres, and other types of specialised complexes (houses with specialised use, such as meeting houses, priests' houses, houses to store sacra and council meeting platforms). Sites with the 124 affix include those associated with the valley's largest secondary centre (see Kahn and Kirch, 2014).

Forty-six basalt artefacts from nineteen sites within these five neighbourhoods were identified to source by WDXRF. In a previous publication (Kahn et al., 2013), I suggested that the distribution of local versus non-local stone tools in the 'Opunohu Valley conformed to expectations of a localised elite prestige-goods economy. In the network graph (Fig. 11.4), we visualise the adze counts via lines of connection between each neighbourhood assemblage and the off-island and island sources. As the graph illustrates, higher frequencies of adzes manufactured from off-island sources were found at ritual or specialised use sites, spaces that were the purview of elites. This begs the question – were adzes perhaps part of gift exchanges that took place at socio-political gatherings of junior elites at secondary centres and did these spaces serve as nodes in the local prestige-goods economy?

Additional social network analyses will be required to tease out the specific patterns of access to adze sources, site type and social connections. Teasing out social or political interactions in different, yet perhaps overlapping economic realms (tribute, prestige-goods exchange, gift exchange), in different, yet overlapping functional contexts (ceremonial, specialised), as well as their association with specific elite social statuses (high chief, low chief, high priest, etc.) will be significant for modelling social transformations in late prehistoric Polynesian chiefdoms. In future network analyses, investigating other measures, such as how a variety of elites materially signalled 'high culture' in the architecture and layout of temples, sleeping houses and specialised house sites might be a fruitful path. Nevertheless, the 'Opunohu case study provides a glimpse into how socio-political power was

TABLE 11.1 Site descriptions for five 'Opunohu Valley neighbourhoods used in the network analysis

Neighbourhood	Structures	Function	Comments
ScMo-120	7 structures: one round ended house, several faced and paved or partially paved stone terraces, one temple, one raised stone platform	Specialised	Specialised locale where priests and craftsmen stored and manufactured ritual sacra used at temple ceremonies
ScMo-123	5 structures: rectangular house and adjacent pavement, one terrace, two temples	Specialised	Specialised locale, likely a temporary residence for priests and other ritual attendants; perhaps used during ritualised renewal ceremonies and other community-wide rituals
Zone A	13+ structures: three oval-ended houses, one rectangular house, two temples with attached shrines, seven agricultural complexes	Residential	Domestic complex for an extended residential group of moderately high status
Zone B	13+ structures: seven probable house sites, mostly of rectangular form, one cookhouse, one temple with attached shrines, one detached shrine, three agricultural complexes	Residential	Domestic complex for an extended residential group of moderate status
ScMo-124	31+ structures: One rectangular house, one round ended house; numerous faced and paved or partially paved stone terraces; nine temples; nineteen detached or attached shrines; three raised stone platforms; one council meeting platform	Specialised within Ceremonial Centre	Highly sacred ritual centre with evidence for ceremonial events, economic events (presentation offerings) and political events (meeting of elite councils).
ScMo-170–171	7 structures: one oval ended house, three rectangular houses, two stone faced terraces, one temple with two attached shrines	Residential	Domestic complex for an extended residential group of moderately high status; perhaps headed by a low ranked chief (to'ofa) or a land manager (ra'atira'a)

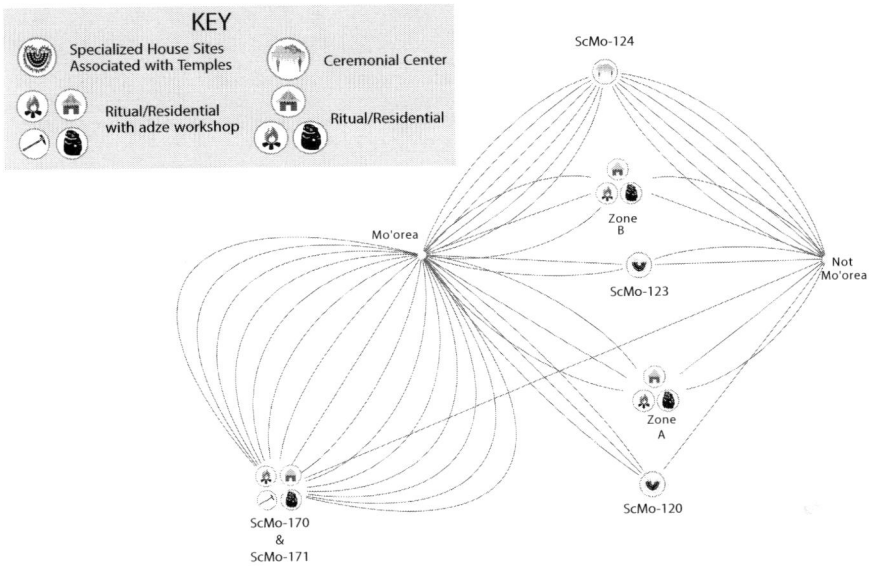

FIGURE 11.4 Social network graph of Upper Tupauruuru neighbourhoods, 'Opunohu Valley, Mo'orea and access to non-local and local adzes. Lines between the neighbourhoods represent the number of imported and local adzes found at the archaeological sites.

Source: drafted by Stefani Crabtree.

generated, transformed and centralised through time. It begins to establish how particular site complexes functioned within the overall settlement hierarchy and emphasises that the residents of such complexes may have played numerous diverse roles (see Mills, 2017).

Discussion

Viewing inland ritual-political centres as embedded within social networks highlights the dynamics of elite power strategies in the late prehistoric Society Island chiefdoms. Highlighting the activities of chiefs of secondary lineages works to tease apart the monolithic 'elite' category and allows for an understanding of varied gradations in rank and status that existed within complex chiefdoms. A network approach also shifts our attention to cycles of centralisation, decentralisation and rotating centres of political power expressed in the later historical records. For example, the fact that just over half of the local neighbourhoods associated with 'Opunohu Valley ritual centres modified temples in the war cult style is indicative of secondary chiefs' efforts to align themselves with members of the expansionist 'Oro war cult derived from Huahine and translocated to Mo'orea and Tahiti in the late Classic period. Perhaps the three lineages who constructed 'Oro style war cult temples post-1650 CE were led by chiefs with greater power at the local level in the century prior to European contact. Or perhaps these lineages were actively trying to establish and consolidate power at the local level by participating in coastal and regional-wide religious transformations during a period of increasing political centralisation. In either case, emphasis is placed on the role social networks played in political relations (see Lulewicz and Coker, 2018).

Conclusions

Minor centres have much to teach us about the process of political centralisation in the past. In the Society Island case study, landscape-scale mapping and excavation facilitated the identification of minor ritual-political centres and their surrounding communities. In conjunction with refined chronological sequences, such analyses highlight how secondary ritual-political centres emerged in the late Classic period, confirming that 1650–1767 CE was a period of intense political centralisation at multiple scales, including the sub-district, district, island and region. In the 'Opunohu Valley, the local and community scales provide a portrait of shifting and competing secondary chiefly lineages, each vying for political power through internal and external social alliances.

Viewed through a diachronic lens, we can begin to narrate the forces behind Society Island political centralisation. As major chiefly lineages with settlements on the coast fissioned after 250 years of rapid demographic growth following initial island colonisation, secondary lineages of some rank moved inland and took possession of the most highly desired lands in the 13th century. Through time, these secondary chiefly lineages intensified interior agricultural production and developed their own local communities replete with ritual structures, diverse agricultural complexes and houses for domestic and specialised activities. Like high-ranked lineages on the coast, the 17th century onwards saw the rapid advent of increasing competition between secondary lineage chiefs in interior valley complexes. Secondary ritual-political centres likely appeared as the material manifestations of inter- and intra-community chiefly competition, representing shifting and fluid alliances at the local level. Such complexes also created community-based identities centred in space and place in a context where even inland valleys were now experiencing close to 'full-land' situations. At a broader scale, secondary inland centres also played important roles as nodes in regional social, religious and administrative networks, creating links between nested settlement hierarchies of sub-districts and larger socio-political territories.

Ongoing integrated landscape-scale mapping and excavation will be critical for determining why these minor inland centres were established, how they functioned and what role they played in broader regional systems. As I have argued, landscape-scale analyses can effectively chart organisational changes in socio-political networks. Detailed settlement pattern data from minor ritual-political centres point towards the important role that religious ideology had in ongoing political centralisation in Polynesian chiefdoms. Framing these minor centres as nodes in a wider centralising network, we can better see the flux of political relationships common to other complex societies worldwide (Lulewicz and Coker, 2018; Schortman and Ashmore, 2012; Smith and Janusek, 2014). Such approaches offer fresh insights into how political power was actively negotiated and constructed, where social actors such as secondary chiefs operated within local and regional structures of resources, rules and events. Given that ethnohistoric sources in middle-range societies often emphasise the dynamic and fluid nature of chiefly political power, network concepts offer benefits to understanding how socio-political power was generated, transformed and centralised through time.

Acknowledgements

Funding for the development of the 'Opunohu Valley base map was provided by the Service de la Culture et du Patrimoine and Le Secrétariat Général de la Communauté du Pacifique, European Union (INTEGRE project). Permission to conduct archaeological survey and excavation on Mo'orea was obtained from Heremoana Maamaatuaiahutapu, Le Ministèrè de la Promotion des Langues, de la Culture, de la Communication, et de l'Environment; Teddy Tehei, le Chef de Service, Service de la Culture et du Patrimoine; Jean-Yves Meyer, Délégué à la Recherche de la Polynésie française; Lionel Beffre, Haut-commissariat de la Republique en Polynésie française; and the Director of the Service du Développement Rural. Belona Mou, Tamara Maric and Joany Hapaitahaa facilitated the permit granting process. The archaeological field work was completed with the assistance of Heinui Maitea, Phineas Maruhi, Angela Maruhi, Teamo Papa and Raimanu Maitea. Franck Ruédas directed the technical mapping. Stefani Crabtree performed the social network analysis, compiled the data seen in Table 11.1, and drafted Fig. 11.4, in addition to consulting on the interpretations. Diana Izdebeski is thanked for redrafting many of the final figures. Final thanks to Tim Thomas and an anonymous reviewer for their careful reading of an earlier draft of this manuscript.

Note

1 While my chapter briefly references some classic settlement pattern studies in Western Polynesia, as well as new archaeological research on Tongan elite central places, I focus to a greater extent on settlement pattern analyses, central places and ritual centres in Eastern Polynesia. As a recent synthesis of Polynesian settlement pattern studies offered a focus on Samoa and Hawai'i as regional case studies (Morrison and O'Connor, 2018), I have made an effort here to focus on studies carried out in French Polynesia, despite the fact that a large number of Eastern Polynesian projects have been completed in Hawai'i, Easter Island and New Zealand.

References

Adams, H., 1976 *Memoirs of Arii Taimai*. Reprint of the Clements Library Copy 1901. Paris.
Allen, M.S., 2009. Morphological variability and temporal patterning in Marquesan domestic architecture: Anaho Valley in regional context. *Asian Perspectives*, 48(2), pp. 342–382.

Bennett, W.C., 1931. *Archaeology of Kauai*. Bernice P. Bishop Museum Bulletin 40. Honolulu, HI: Bernice P. Bishop Museum.

Burley, D.V., 1996. Sport, status, and field monuments in the Polynesian chiefdom of Tonga: the pigeon snaring mounds of northern Ha'apai. *Journal of Field Archaeology*, 23(4), pp. 421–435.

Campbell, M., 2001. Settlement and Landscape in Late Prehistoric Rarotonga, Southern Cook Islands. PhD, University of Sydney.

Chase, A.F. and Chase, D.Z., 2003. Minor centers, complexity, and scale in lowland Maya settlement archaeology. In: G. Iannone and S.V. Connell, eds. *Perspectives on Ancient Maya Rural Complexity*. Monograph 49. Los Angeles, CA: Cotsen Institute of Archaeology, pp. 108–118.

Clark, G. and Martinsson-Wallin, H., 2007. Monumental architecture in West Polynesia: origins, chiefs and archaeological approaches. *Archaeology in Oceania*, 42(1), pp. 1–30.

Clark, G. and Reepmeyer, C., 2014. Stone architecture, monumentality and the rise of the early Tongan chiefdom. *Antiquity*, 88(342), pp. 1244–1260.

Clark, G., Reepmeyer, C. and Melekiola, N., 2016. Rapid emergence of the Archaic Tongan state: the royal tomb Paepaeotelea. *Antiquity*, 90(352), pp. 1038–1053.

Connell, S.V., 2003. Making sense of variability among minor centers: the ancient Maya of Chaa Creek, Belize. In: G. Iannone and S.V. Connell, eds. *Perspectives on Ancient Maya Rural Complexity*. Monograph 49. Los Angeles, CA: Cotsen Institute of Archaeology, pp. 27–41.

Corney, B.G., 1918. *The Quest and Occupation of Tahiti by Emissaries of Spain during the Years 1772–1776: Told in Despatches and other Contemporary Documents,* vol. 2. London: Routledge.

DeMarrais, E., Castillo, L.J. and Earle, T., 1996. Ideology, materialization, and power strategies. *Current Anthropology*, 37(1), pp. 15–31.

Descantes, C., 1990. Symbolic stone structures: protohistoric and early historic spatial patterns of the 'Opunohu Valley, Mo'orea, French Polynesia. MA, University of Auckland.

Dixon, B., Gosser, D. and Williams, S.S., 2008. Traditional Hawaiian men's houses and their socio-political context in Lualualei, Leeward West O'ahu, Hawai'i. *Journal of the Polynesian Society,* 117(3), pp. 267–295.

Duffy, P.R., 2015. Site size hierarchy in middle-range societies. *Journal of Anthropological Archaeology,* 37, pp. 85–99.

Eddowes, M., 1991. Ethnohistorical perspectives on the Marae of the Society Islands: the sociology of use. MA, University of Auckland.

Eddowes, M., 2003. Prospection archéologique de l'île de Huahine dans les Iles de la Société. *Dossier d'Archéologie Polynésienne,* 2, pp. 55–68.

Ellis , W., 1829. *Polynesian researches, during a residence of nearly six years in the South Sea Islands.* London: Fisher, Son, & Jackson.

Emerson, T.E., 1997. *Cahokia and the Archaeology of Power.* Tuscaloosa, AL: University of Alabama Press.

Emory, K.P., 1924. *The Island of Lanai.* Bernice P. Bishop Museum 12. Honolulu, HI: Bernice P. Bishop Museum.

Emory, K.P., 1928. *Archaeology of Nihoa and Necker Islands.* Bernice P. Bishop Museum 9. Honolulu, HI: Bernice P. Bishop Museum.

Emory, K.P., 1933. *Stone Remains in the Society Islands.* Bernice P. Bishop Museum Bulletin 116. Honolulu, HI: Bernice P. Bishop Museum.

Fang, H., Feinman, G.M. and Nicholas, L.M., 2015. Imperial expansion, public investment, and the long path of history: China's initial political unification and its aftermath. *Proceedings of the National Academy of Sciences,* 112(30), pp. 9224–9229.

Field, J.S., Kirch, P.V,. Kawelu, K. and Ladefoged, T.N., 2010. Households and hier-archy: domestic modes of production in leeward Kohala, Hawai'i Island. *Journal of Island and Coastal Archaeology*, 5(1), pp. 52–85.

Field, J.S., Ladefoged, T.N. and Kirch, P.V., 2011. Household expansion linked to agricultural intensification during emergence of Hawaiian archaic states. *Proceedings of the National Academy of Sciences*, 108(18), pp. 7327–7332.

Gijseghem, H. van, and Vaughn, K.J., 2008. Regional integration and the built environment in middle-range societies: Paracas and early Nasca houses and communities. *Journal of Anthropological Archaeology*, 27(1), pp. 111–130.

Golitko, M. and Feinman, G.M., 2015. Procurement and distribution of pre-Hispanic Mesoamerican obsidian 900 BC–AD 1520: a social network analysis. *Journal of Archaeological Method and Theory*, 22(1), pp. 206–247.

Guengerich, A., 2014. The architect's signature: the social production of a residential land-scape at Monte Viudo, Chachapoyas, Peru. *Journal of Anthropological Archaeology*, 34, pp. 1–16.

Gosser, D. and Dixon, B., 1998. An organizational analysis of Kaunolū, Lāna'i, Hawai'i. In: G. Lee, C.M. Stevenson and F.J. Morin, ed. *Easter Island in Pacific Context: South Seas Symposium*. Los Osos: Easter Island Foundation, pp. 260–266.

Green, R.C., 1961. Moorean archaeology: a preliminary report. *Man*, 61, pp. 169–173.

Green, R.C., 1996. Settlement patterns and complex society in the Windward Society Islands: retrospective commentary from the 'Opunohu Valley, Mo'orea. In: M. Julien, M. Orliac and C. Orliac, eds. *Mémoire de Pierre, Mémoire d'Homme: Tradition et Archéologie en Océanie*. Paris: Publications de la Sorbonne, pp. 209–228.

Green, R.C. and Davidson, J.M., 1969. *Archaeology in Western Samoa*, vol. 1. Auckland Institute and Museum Bulletin, 6. Auckland: Auckland Institute and Museum.

Green, R.C. and Davidson, J.M., 1974. *Archaeology in Western Samoa*, vol. 2. Auckland Institute and Museum Bulletin 7. Auckland: Auckland Institute and Museum.

Green, R.C. and Descantes, C., 1989. *Site Records of the 'Opunohu Valley, Mo'orea*. Auckland: Green Foundation for Polynesian Research.

Green, R.C., Green, K., Rappaport, R.A., Rappaport, A. and Davidson, J., 1967. *Archeology on the Island of Mo'orea, French Polynesia*. Anthropological Papers of the American Museum of Natural History, 51(2). New York: American Museum of Natural History.

Hendrickson, M. and Evans, D., 2015. Reimagining the city of fire and iron: a landscape archaeology of the Angkor-Period industrial complex of Preah Khan of Kompong Svay, Cambodia (ca. 9th to 13th centuries AD). *Journal of Field Archaeology*, 40(6), pp. 644–664.

Henry, T., 1928. *Ancient Tahiti*. Honolulu, HI: Bernice P. Bishop Museum.

Herdrich, D.J., 1991. Towards an understanding of Samoan star mounds. *Journal of the Polynesian Society*, 100(4), pp. 381–435.

Hutson, S. R., 2010. *Dwelling, Identity, and the Maya: Relational Archaeology at Chunchucmil*. Lanham, MD: Alta Mira Press.

Iannone, G., 2003. Rural complexity in the Cahal Pech Microregion: analysis and implications. In: G. Iannone and S.V. Connell, eds. *Perspectives on Ancient Maya Rural Complexity*. Los Angeles, CA: Cotsen Institute of Archaeology. pp. 13–26.

Jennings, J.D., Holmer, R. and Jackmond, G., 1982. Samoan village patterns: four examples. *Journal of the Polynesian Society*, 91(1), pp. 81–102.

Kahn, J.G., 2003. Maohi social organization at the micro-scale: household archaeology in the 'Opunohu Valley, Mo'orea, Society Islands (French Polynesia). In C. Sand, ed. *Pacific Archaeology: Assessments and Prospects*. Nouméa: Le Cahiers de l'Archéologie en Nouvelle-Calédonie, pp. 353–367.

Kahn, J.G., 2005. An archaeological survey of the Upper Amehiti Sector, 'Opunohu Valley, Mo'orea, Society Islands. In: H. Marchesi, ed. *Bilan de la recherche archéologique en Polynésie française 2003–2004*. Dossier d'Archeologie polynésienne 4. Punaauia: Service de la Culture et du Patrimoine, pp. 33–40.

Kahn, J.G., 2010. A spatio-temporal analysis of 'Oro Cult *Marae* in the 'Opunohu Valley, Mo'orea, Society Islands. *Archaeology in Oceania,* 45, pp. 103–110.

Kahn, J.G., 2011. Multi-phase construction sequences and aggregate site complexes of the prehistoric windward Society Islands (French Polynesia). *Journal of Island and Coastal Archaeology*, 6, pp. 24–50.

Kahn, J.G., 2013. Temple renovations, aggregate marae, and ritual centers: the ScMo-15 complex, lower Amehiti District, 'Opunohu Valley, Mo 'orea (Society Islands). *Rapa Nui Journal*, 27(2), pp. 33–49.

Kahn, J.G., 2015. Identifying residences of ritual practitioners in the archaeological record as a proxy for social complexity. *Journal of Anthropological Archaeology*, 40, pp. 59–81.

Kahn, J.G., 2016a. Public versus corporate ritual in the prehistoric Society Islands (French Polynesia): a multi-scalar analysis of religious practices. *Séances de la Société Préhistorique Française*, 7, pp. 141–161.

Kahn, J.G., 2016b. The functionality of feasting at late prehistoric residential and ceremonial sites in the Society Islands. *Journal of the Polynesian Society*, 125(3), pp. 203–238.

Kahn, J.G., 2018. The archaeology of the 'Opunohu Valley, Society Islands, Eastern Polynesia. In: C. Smith, ed. *Encyclopedia of Global Archaeology*. [online] Cham: Springer International Publishing, pp. 1–15. https://doi.org/10.1007/978-3-319-51726-1_2714-1

Kahn, J.G. and Kirch, P.V., 2011. Monumentality and the materialization of ideology in Central Eastern Polynesia. *Archaeology in Oceania,* 46, pp. 93–104.

Kahn, J.G. and Kirch, P.V., 2013. Residential landscapes and house societies of the late prehistoric Society Islands (French Polynesia). *Journal of Pacific Archaeology,* 4(1), pp. 50–72.

Kahn, J.G. and Kirch, P.V., 2014. *Monumentality and Ritual Materialization in the Society Islands*. Bishop Museum Bulletin in Anthropology, 13. Honolulu, HI: Bishop Museum Press.

Kahn, J.G., Sinton, J., Mills, P.R. and Lundblad, S.P., 2013. X-ray fluorescence analysis and intra-island exchange in the Society Island Archipelago. *Journal of Archaeological Science,* 40(2), pp. 1194–1202.

Kellum, M., 1968. Sites and settlement in Hane Valley, Marquesas. MA, University of Hawai'i.

Kennett, D.J. and McClure, S.B., 2012. The archaeology of Rapan fortifications. In: A. Anderson and D.J. Kennett, eds. *Taking the High Ground: The Archaeology of Rapa, a Fortified Island in Remote East Polynesia*. Canberra: Australia National University Press, pp. 203–234.

Kirch, P.V., 2010. *How Chiefs Became Kings: Divine Kingship and the Rise of Archaic States in Ancient Hawai'i*. Berkeley, CA: University of California Press.

Kirch, P.V., Hartshorn, A.S., Chadwick, O.A., Vitousek, P.M., Sherrod, D.R., Coil, J., Holm, L. and Sharp, W.D., 2004. Environment, agriculture, and settlement patterns in a marginal Polynesian landscape. *Proceedings of the National Academy of Sciences of the United States of America*, 101(26), pp. 9936–9941.

Knappett, C., 2013. Introduction: why networks? In: C. Knappett, ed. *Network Analysis in Archaeology: New Approaches to Regional Interaction*. Oxford: Oxford University Press, pp. 3–16.

Kolb, M., 1997. Labor, ethnohistory, and the archaeology of community in Hawai'i. *Journal of Archeological Method and Theory*, 4, pp. 265–286.

Lepofsky, D. and Kahn, J.G., 2011. Cultivating an ecological and social balance: elite demands and commoner knowledge in ancient Ma'ohi agriculture, Society Islands. *American Anthropologist,* 113(2), pp. 319–335.

Ladefoged, T.N., McCoy, M.D., Asner, G.P., Kirch, P.V., Puleston, C.O., Chadwick, O.A. and Vitousek, P.M., 2011. Agricultural potential and actualized development in Hawai'i: an airborne LiDAR survey of the leeward Kohala field system (Hawai'i Island). *Journal of Archaeological Science*, 38(12), pp. 3605–3619.

Ladefoged, T.N. and Graves, M.W., 2006. The formation of Hawaiian territories. In: I. Lilley, ed. *Archaeology of Oceania: Australia and the Pacific Islands,* Malden, MA: Blackwell, pp. 259–283.

Ladefoged, T.N., Gemmell, C., McCoy, M., Jorgensen, A., Glover, H., Stevenson, C. and O'Neale, D., 2019. Social network analysis of obsidian artefacts and Māori interaction in northern Aotearoa New Zealand. *PloS One*, 14(3), e0212941.

Lulewicz, J. and Coker, A.B., 2018. The structure of the Mississippian world: a social network approach to the organization of sociopolitical interactions. *Journal of Anthropological Archaeology*, 50, pp. 113–127.

Maxwell, J.J. and Smith, I.W., 2015. A reassessment of settlement patterns and subsistence at Point Durham, Chatham Island. *Archaeology in Oceania*, 50(3), pp. 162–174.

McAllister, J.G., 1933. *Archaeology of Oahu*. Bernice P. Bishop Museum Bulletin 104. Honolulu, HI: Bernice P. Bishop Museum.

Maric, T., 2012. Dynamiques de peuplement et transformations sociopolitiques à Tahiti, Iles de la Société. PhD dissertation, Université de Paris–Panthéon Sorbonne.

Maric, T., 2016. From the valley to the shore: a hypothesis of the spatial evolution of ceremonial centres on Tahiti and Ra'iatea, Society Islands. *Journal of the Polynesian Society,* 125(3), pp. 239–262.

Martinsson–Wallin, H. and Thomas, T., 2014. *Monuments and People in the Pacific*. Uppsala University Studies in Global Archaeology 20. Uppsala: Uppsala University.

Martinsson–Wallin, H. and Wallin, P., 2014. Spatial perspectives on ceremonial complexes: testing traditional land divisions on Rapa Nui. In: H. Martinsson–Wallin and T. Thomas, eds. *Monuments and People in the Pacific*. Uppsala: Uppsala University. pp. 317–342.

Masson, M.A., 2003. Economic patterns in northern Belize. In: M.E. Smith and F.F. Berdan, eds. *The Postclassic Mesoamerican World*. Salt Lake City, UT: University of Utah Press, pp. 269–281.

Millaire, J-F., 2010. Moche political expansionism as viewed from Virú: recent archaeological work in the close periphery of a hegemonic city-state system. In: J. Quilter and L.J. Castillo, eds. *New Perspectives on moche Political Organization*. Washington, DC: Dumbarton Oaks, pp. 221–249.

Mills, B., 2015. Challenges and opportunities for network approaches to interregional interaction: perspectives from the North American Southwest. In: S. Chiu, C. Sand and N. Hogg, eds. *Lapita Cultural Complex in Time and Space: Expansion Routes, Chronologies, and Typologies,* Archaeolgia Pasifika, 3. Noumea: Institute of Archaeology of New Caledonia and the Pacific, and the Center for Archaeological Studies, and Academia Sinica, pp. 207–219.

Mills, B., 2017. Social network analysis in archaeology. *Annual Review of Anthropology,* 46, pp. 379–397.

Mills, B., Clark, J.J., Peeples, M.A., Haas, W.R., Roberts, J.M., Brett Hill, J., Huntley, D.L., Borkck, L., Breiger, R.L.,. Clauset, A. and Shackley, M.S., 2013. Transformation of social networks in the late pre-Hispanic US Southwest. *Proceedings of the National Academy of Sciences*, 110(15), pp. 5785–5790.

Mizoguchi, K., 2009. Nodes and edges: a network approach to hierarchisation and state formation in Japan. *Journal of Anthropological Archaeology*, 28(1), pp. 14–26.

Molle, G., 2016. Exploring religious practices on Polynesian atolls: A comprehensive architectural approach towards the 'marae' complex in the Tuamotu islands. *Journal of the Polynesian Society*, 125(3), pp. 263–288.

Moore, J.D., 1996. *Architecture and Power in the Ancient Andes: The Archaeology of Public Buildings.* Cambridge: Cambridge University Press.

Morrison, A.E., 2012. An archaeological analysis of Rapa Nui settlement structure: a multi-scalar Approach. PhD, University of Hawaii.

Morrison, A.E. and O'Connor, J.T., 2018. Settlement pattern studies in Polynesia: past projects, current progress, and future prospects. In: T. Hunt and E. Cochrane, eds. *Handbook of Prehistoric Oceania.* Oxford: Oxford Press, pp. 450–468.

Morrison, J., 1935. *The Journal of James Morrison, Boatswain's Mate of the Bounty, Describing the Mutiny and Subsequent Misfortunes of the Mutineers, Together with an Account of the Island of Tahiti,* ed. Owen Rutter. London: Golden Cockerel Press.

Mulrooney, M.A. and Ladefoged, T.N., 2005. Hawaiian *heiau* and agricultural production in the Kohala dryland field system. *Journal of the Polynesian Society,* 114(1), pp. 45–67.

Newbury, C., 1967. Aspects of cultural change in French Polynesia: the decline of the ari'i. *Journal of the Polynesian Society,* 15, pp. 1–20.

Oliver, D.L., 1974. *Ancient Tahitian Society.* Canberra: ANU Press.

Östborn, P. and Gerding, H., 2014. Network analysis of archaeological data: a systematic approach. *Journal of Archaeological Science,* 46, pp. 75–88.

Orliac, C. and Orliac, M., 1996. L'écrit, le dit et l'enfoui. Considérations sur l'histoire d'une vallée de Tahiti. In: M. Julien, M. Orliac and C. Orliac, eds. *Mémoire de pierre, mémoire d'homme. Tradition et archéologie en Océanie. Hommage à José Garanger.* Paris: Publications de la Sorbonne, pp. 229–243.

Parsons, J.R., 1972. Archaeological settlement patterns. *Annual Review of Anthropology,* 1(1), pp. 127–150.

Peeples, M.A., and Roberts, J.M., Jr., 2013. To binarize or not to binarize: relational data and the construction of archaeological networks. *Journal of Archaeological Science,* 40(7), pp. 3001–3010.

Phillips, C., and Campbell, M., 2004. From settlement patterns to interdisciplinary landscapes in New Zealand. In: L. Furey and S. Holdaway, eds. *Change Through Time: 50 Years of New Zealand Archaeology.* Auckland: New Zealand Archaeological Association, pp. 85–104.

Prufer, K.M., Thompson, A.E., Meredith, C.R., Culleton, B.J., Jordan, J.M., Ebert, C.E., Winterhalder, B. and Kennett, D.J., 2017. The Classic Period Maya transition from an ideal free to an ideal despotic settlement system at the polity of Uxbenká. *Journal of Anthropological Archaeology,* 45, pp. 53–68.

Quintus, S., Clark, J.T., Day, S.S. and Schwert, D.P., 2016. Landscape evolution and human settlement patterns on Ofu Island, Manu'a Group, American Samoa. *Asian Perspectives,* 54(2), pp. 208–237.

Robineau, C., 2009. Marae, population et territoire aux îles de la Société. Le réseau ma'ohi. *Journal de la Société des Océanistes* 128, pp. 151–161.

Rosenswig, R.M. and Mendelsohn, R.R., 2016. Izapa and the Soconusco Region, Mexico, in the first millennium AD. *Latin American Antiquity,* 27(3), pp. 357–377.

Salmond, A., 2009. *Aphrodite's Island: The European Discovery of Tahiti.* Berkeley, CA: University of California Press.

Sharp, W.D., Kahn, J.G., Polito, C.M. and Kirch, P.V., 2010. Rapid evolution of ritual architecture in central Polynesia indicated by precise 230Th/U coral dating. *Proceedings of the National Academy of Sciences,* 107(30), pp. 13234–13239.

Schortman, E.M. and Ashmore, W., 2012. History, networks, and the quest for power: ancient political competition in the Lower Motagua Valley, Guatemala. *Journal of the Royal Anthropological Institute,* 18(1), pp. 1–21.

Shepardson, B.L., 2005. The role of Rapa Nui (Easter Island) statuary as territorial boundary markers. *Antiquity,* 79(303), pp. 169–178.

Sinoto, Y., 1962. A preliminary report on the excavations at Vairai, Tahiti and Afareaitu, Moorea. Unpublished report, Bernice P. Bishop Museum archives.

Smith, S.C. and Janusek, J.W., 2014. Political mosaics and networks: Tiwanaku expansion into the upper Desaguadero Valley, Bolivia. *World Archaeology*, 46(5), pp. 681–704.

Stokes, J.F.G., 1991. *Heiau of the Island of Hawaii: A Historic Survey of Native Hawaiian Temple Sites*. Honolulu, HI: Bishop Museum Press.

Suggs, R.C., 1961. *The Archeology of Nuku Hiva, Marquesas Islands, French Polynesia*. Anthropological papers of the American Museum of Natural History 49(1). New York: American Museum of Natural History.

Steadman, S., 2015. Archaeology of Domestic Architecture and the Human Use of Space. Walnut Creek, CA: Left Coast Press.

Sutton, D.G., Furey, L. and Marshall, Y.M., 2003. *The Archaeology of Pouerua*. Auckland: Auckland University Press.

Verin, P., 1969. *L'Ancienne civilisation de Rurutu: La période classique*. Mémoires Office de la Recherche Scientifique et Technique Outre-Mer 33. Paris: ORSTOM.

Willey, G.R., 1953. *Prehistoric Settlement Patterns in the Virú Valley, Peru*. Bureau of American Ethnology Bulletin, 155. Washington, DC: Government Printing Office.

12

GENDER ARCHAEOLOGY IN POLYNESIA

Past, present and future

Cynthia L. Van Gilder

Introduction

Despite the existence of many detailed ethnographic and ethnohistoric reports including information on gender and gender systems in the Pacific, archaeological studies that take as their focus understanding this vital and important dynamic of society and personal identity in the past are few and far between. An overwhelming interest in macroscale processes such as Pacific colonisation, environmental adaptation, political economy and the development of sociopolitical complexity, has dominated the archaeology of this region. In this chapter, I give a brief overview of archaeological gender theory (and its relationship to gender anthropology), review the most significant studies of gender and women's lives in Polynesian archaeology to date and demonstrate the potential of a 'gender as practice' approach in a case study from the Hawaiian islands.

Gender archaeology in the past

Sparking a conversation

The history of an explicitly gendered approach to archaeology is usually traced to Margaret Conkey and Janet Spector's publication of *Archaeology and the Study of Gender* (Conkey and Spector, 1984). Prior to that, archaeologists had dealt with gender in one of three ways – by ignoring it, by projecting contemporary Western gender norms into the past or by substituting an equally uncritical vision of 'prehistoric gender' based on modern fantasies. Insofar as there was a tradition of theorising gender in the human past, it belonged more to cultural anthropologists, whose work on the origins of gender stratification sought to determine whether female 'second-class citizenship' was indeed a human universal through time and space. Studies in this vein include Ortner (1972), hypothesising that a rise in gender stratification, as manifested in an obsession over female virginity before marriage, could be linked with the development of private property and the rise of the state (see also Rapp, 1977, Leacock, 1983; Barstow, 1978). Even though such evolutionary and materialist arguments seem, in retrospect, to have obvious resonance with processual approaches to thinking about the past, they did not become the subject of archaeological investigation. Elsewhere (Van Gilder, 2005), I have hypothesised that most archaeologists in the 1970s and 1980s were strongly wed to the ideas encapsulated in Christopher Hawkes's 'Ladder of Inference' (1954), the logic of which suggests that the reconstruction of gender, beyond the most basic sexing of a skeleton, lies on a rung beyond the archaeologist's reach.

Having been anthropology students during the height of second-wave anthropological feminism, Conkey and Spector saw the potential for feminist approaches to reinvigorate archaeological theory and practice, as it had for cultural anthropology. They argued that there were at least three avenues of action available to archaeologists wanting to take up a feminist approach to the practice of their discipline. These included engaging in critiques of existing androcentric research, undertaking original research explicitly focusing on women in the past and developing new methods and theories that would allow more robust modelling of gender (and other forms of social inequality) in the past (Conkey and Spector, 1984). This article inspired the first wave of explicitly gender-focused research in Polynesia (see below).

Joan Gero quickly answered the call to illuminate currently existing androcentric biases in archaeological interpretation and practice by publishing articles on the socio-politics of archaeology (Gero et al., 1983; Gero 1985; 1988). Yet despite this initial flurry of activity by a small group of practitioners, philosopher of science Alison Wylie wrote an article titled, 'Gender theory and the archaeological record: why is there no archaeology of gender?' (1991). After examining and subsequently rejecting the idea that there are no methodologies available, Wylie advanced three basic reasons for there being no archaeology of gender. These were: (1) for androcentric and sexist reasons archaeologists uncritically project onto the past 'natural' gender roles, and thus suppose that there are really no interesting or dynamic questions to be asked about gender; (2) due to a long-term commitment to models of culture and change that rest in large-part on 'eco-systems theory', gender is perceived to be irrelevant, or at best secondary, to questions of causality and social development; (3) there are not enough female archaeologists in positions of high visibility and influence within the field (Wylie, 1991, pp. 32–35). Arguably, all three of these conditions have been, and continue to be present in Polynesian archaeology.

The publication of *Engendering Archaeology: Women and Prehistory* (Gero and Conkey, 1991), was a landmark. This edited volume made available to a wide audience of archaeologists a collection of outstanding essays in all three of Conkey and Spector's (1984) avenues for further development. Archaeologists could now turn to one place to find examples of critiques of androcentric research (e.g. Conkey and Gero, 1991; Wylie, 1991), remedial research 'adding' women back into accounts of prehistory (e.g. Brumfiel, 1991; Watson and Kennedy, 1991), and new and exciting practical ideas for engendering archaeology (e.g. Conkey, 1991; Spector, 1991). Additionally, readers confronted a variety of methodologies and voices in these articles, from the relentlessly empirical contribution of Christine Hastorf's research on changing women's roles in the Inka Empire (Hastorf, 1991), to the imaginative narrative of Ruth Tringham's Neolithic household research (Tringham, 1991).

Two years later saw the publication of the first explicitly feminist monograph detailing an engendered archaeological study, *What This Awl Means: Feminist Archaeology at a Wahpeton Dakota Village* (Spector, 1993). In her project at the village of Little Rapids, Minnesota, a Native American site occupied in the 1800s, Spector sought to implement many of the ideas she and Margaret Conkey (1984) had formulated in the abstract. She called her initial approach to understanding gender at the site 'the task differentiation approach', the first step of which was to 'examine the relationships between material and non-material aspects of gender in known or documented cases where we could learn about gender-specific tasks, behaviours, and beliefs and their material/spatial dimensions' (Spector, 1991, p. 390). In other words, she hoped that through such comparative studies, she 'could eventually isolate some material regularities or patterns about different types of task systems which then could be identified archaeologically' (1991, p. 391). Spector had adopted the task differentiation approach to archaeological materials because she thought it would help illuminate gender relations in the archaeological record and add representations of women to accounts of the Dakota past.

However, Spector reveals that, as she began to work at Little Rapids, she decided that while providing certain insights, the task differentiation approach actually inhibited her ability to express what she had learned about the Wahpeton men, women, and children who had lived at Little Rapids during a particularly disruptive period, when American colonial expansion was rapidly accelerating in Minnesota (1991, p. 393). Spector subsequently 'began to experiment with a new way of presenting the archaeological and ethnohistoric knowledge [she] had acquired' (1991, p. 394). She adds that one of her primary dissatisfactions with the methodology was that, although taking into consideration both men and women in the past, it still treated the Dakota as groups of people following rules and living out patterns without any individuality or spirit of their own.

In short, Spector concluded that just as androcentric views of the past had flattened and stereotyped women in the past as stay-at-home baby-machines, she was now in danger of 'reinforcing Eurocentric stereotypes and images' of Native Americans as simple, unchanging, undifferentiated, and unmotivated as individuals (1991, p. 393). How could she bring the past to life in a way that respects and humanises the men, women and children who lived it, while simultaneously preserving a place for 'hard' archaeological data?

As Spector pondered this theoretical conundrum, she proceeded on her project, striving to involve local descendants of the Wahpeton in the process more and more. She found that her Native American collaborators had different types of research questions, different types of interpretations of archaeological record and different final conclusions than those her background in academic archaeology had taught her to ask and expect. She describes in her book how, just as the inclusion of feminist perspectives fundamentally altered archaeological questions and conclusions, so did the involvement of members of another culture (Spector, 1993). This insight has continued to be a concern of feminist archaeologies.

Spector's own solution to vivifying her Wahpeton data was to focus on a single artefact, the awl of the title, and create a fictionalised narrative of its owner and the object's loss and subsequent deposition. While this may not be every archaeologist's preferred writing style, several insights undeniably emerge from her study. One very significant one is the relationship between feminism, humanism and indigenism, and how intertwined these theoretical perspectives are. A second is the power of an inspired feminist perspective to break the hold of technological narrative so often dominating archaeological interpretation. Awls are composite tools, consisting of a handle and a tip. It is the tip that 'does the work' of an awl (piercing) and had always been the focus of archaeological typologies of awls. In Spector's work the handle was revealed to be potentially the more culturally significant piece for its owner, a repository of important cultural meaning, whereas the ends that had attracted so much archaeological attention were likely impersonal, replaceable and uninteresting in their utilitarian role.

Spector's work is worth revisiting in detail in this context for two reasons: (1) although the idea of an indigenous–engaged, or community-based, archaeology has been embraced in parts of Polynesia (especially New Zealand and Hawai'i, see Van Gilder, 2005; Kawelu, 2014) the other insights of feminist-inspired archaeology have largely been ignored; and (2) specifically, Spector's insight into the emic cultural valuing of the handle of the awl over the 'business end', is worth consideration by Polynesian archaeologists who, while intellectually aware that much of the material culture we (ethnographically) know was vitally important to islanders is not archaeologically preserved, have not spent much time theorising how that awareness might shape archaeological interpretation, particularly of microscale dynamics.

Polynesian archaeologists join the conversation

It is often noted that the mid-late 20-century processualist push for scientific rigour, systems modelling and functionalist explanations led archaeologists to ignore or forget that non-materialist aspects of past cultures existed. The hard line drawn between processualism and the 'soft science' of culture history, and the rejection of anthropological perspectives that foregrounded cultural particularity in preference for those that sought universals and regularities, led to a dehumanised past. Historical archaeologists, surrounded, as they often are with written documents containing names, and sometimes even the faces and words of specific individuals, retained an interest in the humanistic aspects of our discipline, even at the height of the New Archaeological furor. Archaeologists working in Polynesia, albeit to a lesser extent, have also retained an interest in the more humanistic questions of archaeology, largely due to the availability of ethnographic and ethnohistoric traditions in the region and a longstanding interest in their integration with archaeological data (Van Gilder 2003; 2005). For the same reasons, many of the questions, concerns and methodologies of culture history were retained in the Pacific context, and processual questions regarding cultural evolution and adaptive processes were simply added to the repertoire.

Arguably the first Pacific archaeological research to consider gender as a primary subject of inquiry was Yvonne Marshall's (1985) investigation of gender roles in pot production, focusing on the Lapita period. Marshall noted that pioneering examples of social archaeology utilising ceramics, such as the work of Hill (1968) reconstructing activity areas, or Deetz (1968) seeking to reconstruct community residence patterns and descent rules, assumed prior knowledge about who made and used pottery, thus perpetuating the assumption that division of labour by sex is obvious and does not require explicit examination. After considering the nature of analogy in archaeological thought, Marshall relies on a historical analogy to develop her ethnographic model of pottery making, utilising observations from societies with 'some degree of direct cultural relevance [to Lapita] by being restricted to the Oceanic region' (Marshall, 1985, p. 206). After surveying ethnographic accounts, Marshall defines generalised trait lists characterising three types of gendered pottery production (made only by women, only by men or shared). Her goal was to isolate the determining factors that predict division of labour in a known context, before proceeding to the unknown prehistoric cultural context. This interesting and ingenious approach is not unlike other searches for predictive archaeological correlates made popular in the heyday of New Archaeology (e.g. Peebles and Kus, 1977). What is unique (and arguably, feminist) is the sophistication of Marshall's understanding of gender and the nuanced way she interprets her model. As she states:

> What is actually being examined is not, in fact, 'Who made the pots, men or women?' but rather, 'How was labour divided between the sexes? In what situations were women or men allocated, or did they take upon themselves, the task of pottery manufacture?'
>
> *(Marshall, 1985, p. 209)*

Her analytical categories include: the context of pottery manufacture and distribution; vessel function (e.g. domestic food consumption, ceremonial); the nature and elaborateness of decoration; whether being a good potter confers high material rewards or respect; if the pottery is involved in local or long-distance trade networks; and which gender(s) control ceramic production, use and distribution (1985, pp. 209–221). For example, in the ethnographically known pottery traditions located in coastal or off-shore island communities, female potters produced ceramics for use in maritime trading networks dominated by men (1985, pp. 214–215). Synthesising the available archaeological data on Lapita sites and pottery distribution, Marshall develops a model of the Lapita pottery tradition and compares it against the components of her ethnographic model, asserting that 'the close similarities between the Lapita situation and the conditions in which women's potteries predominate is evident' (1985, p. 221).

Marshall then turns her attention to how engendering the practice of Lapita pottery manufacture and use might shed light on one of the most fascinating questions in Pacific archaeology, 'how or why Lapita lost its pots' (1985, p. 222). Using linguistic and archaeological evidence, she develops an argument that several social changes underlie, and/or co-occur with the disappearance of pottery in many areas of the Lapita distribution. These include the breakdown of communications systems and trade networks, the shift of ceremonial attention to male-produced artefacts made of wood, the development of new cooking techniques not requiring domestic pottery and the migration of 'female artistic expression … into a new medium – fine mats and tapa cloth' (1985, p. 224).

However, despite demonstrating the interesting potential of utilising rich ethno-historic/ethnographic records to generate models for gendered practices in the past, Marshall's article only inspired scattered following studies. Three years later, in an article whose title was clearly designed to evoke Marshall (1985), Jocelyn Linnekin (1988) asked, 'Who made the feathered cloaks? A problem in Hawaiian gender relations'. This article and the research behind it are significantly different from Marshall's study, though both clearly address a specific instance of a potentially gendered division of labour. First, Linnekin is a cultural anthropologist conducting ethnohistoric research on an artefact class that is not found archaeologically. The fact that it would later come to be associated as a companion, or parallel piece to 'Who made the Lapita pots?' is a testament to how closely intertwined ethnological and archaeological research has been in Pacific archaeology, and how little gender research using substantially archaeological materials has been undertaken in the region (Parslow, 1993). Linnekin positions her research broadly under the umbrella of understanding the 'incongruity between women's [inferior] ritual status and [significant] sociopolitical importance', noting that 'perhaps nowhere else in Polynesia were women as active politically as in Hawai'i' (1988, p. 265). Feathered cloaks were a form of woven material culture (generally considered women's work), that were imbued with tremendous spiritual power (*mana*) and subject to male chiefly taboo (*kapu*).

Linnekin explores the ethnohistoric literature, examining the various accounts of feather work and weaving generally, as well as references specifically dealing with the cloaks' manufacture, ownership and role in *ali'i* (chiefly) politics and reciprocity. She concludes that there is no particular evidence that the cloaks or the materials used to make them were sacred before they were worn by (and thereafter associated with) a chief who was himself sacred (1988, p. 277). This fact, along with several ethnohistoric accounts that explicitly state that women made the cloaks (e.g. King, 1967; Freycinet, 1978), leads her to conclude that, while men may have been the primary bird catchers (procurers of feathers), and primary cloak wearers (conveyers of sacredness), women were likely the actual artisans.

Linnekin's article was later revisited by Ross Cordy (2003), who contributed information on feathered capes found while 'conducting archival research in the late 1980s and early 1990s' (2003, p. 157). Much of this data takes the form of testimony in the 19th-century Hawaiian land courts, and includes references to bird catchers, feathers being supplied as a form of tribute for local chiefs, and families who specialised in feather work (e.g. capes, helmets). Although an archaeologist, Cordy's short communication does not address what, if any, implications this information regarding gendered labour distribution may have for archaeological studies of household space or for other ways of modelling gender, that could be visible in the archaeological record.

Further work in the 1980s and 1990s on gendered divisions of labour in pre-European Polynesia utilised bioarchaeological data. Dirk Spennemann's (1996) research on 'prehistoric and historic' Tonga was framed as a contrast to previous approaches, such as task differentiation, based on ethnographic analogy. Instead, Spennemann relied on skeletal analysis (1996, pp. 101–103). Activity pattern analysis by Philip Houghton, had previously determined that many male skeletons 'showed clear use of the arm in a highly specific manner, i.e., a strong, forcefully conducted, downwards and backwards directed movement of the upper arm' in association with osteoarthritis in the neck vertebrae, and these were surmised to be indicative of a lifetime of canoe paddling (Houghton, 1980, in Spennemann 1996, p. 103). Spennemann noted that human remains excavated by Janet Davidson on Tongatapu at the 'Atele College burial mounds also showed evidence of osteoarthritis, but in a different patterning (1996, p. 103). Male sexed skeletons exhibited significant arthritis in the neck area, while female sexed skeletons showed evidence of arthritis in their lower spine (1996, p.103). Spennemann proposes that the patterns seen in female backs were 'almost certainly due to carrying heavy loads and frequent bending', undertaken during four possible 'work patterns' associated with gardening, tapa production, shellfish gathering, and carrying heavy loads (1996, p. 104). Through analysis of the site's setting (inland) and other factors, he concludes that the female arthritic patterns were primarily the result of gardening work and 'carrying the produce back home' while that of the men was primarily due to fishing responsibilities (1996, p. 105).

These activities were considered to reflect a potentially different division of labour from that observed during the early period of European contact. Spennemann compiles a table (1996, p. 107) showing Tongan gender roles in manufacturing tasks and food production as witnessed by William Mariner in the early 1800s. Mariner's account appears to show that by the beginning of that century women did not do gardening work, however other reports suggest this only applied to women of rank. Spennemann concludes by adding that questions remain: if we interpret the data to mean that in earlier periods Tongan women were the primary gardeners (supported by osteological data) and then at some time post-contact, they stopped doing that work (supported by Mariner's observations), when and why did the change occur? Alternatively, social rank may have also been an important influence. Spennemann's methodology, while useful, rests on a theoretical base of simple task differentiation that problematically conflates biological sex with gender.

Perhaps the first articulation of an explicitly feminist perspective underlying an archaeology of gender in Polynesia, Parslow (1993) reviewed the identification of gender in New Zealand Māori archaeology. She begins by noting that the well-documented androcentric bias in historical and ethnographic accounts of Pacific societies presents a real challenge for archaeologists who regularly make use of these materials (1993, p. 41). Another of her primary points is to stress that researchers have a tendency to gloss over, or ignore altogether, variations in Māori society through space and time (1993, pp. 41–42). She aligns herself with 'anthropologists, sociologists, and women politicians' who revisit historical sources, including oral tradition, with an eye to correcting androcentric bias, highlighting internal and temporal differences in Māori culture and reinterpreting pre-contact gender systems to reclaim a Māori vision of female agency (1993, p. 42).

Parslow states, 'In Māori archaeology to date, there have been no published examples of practical applications involving the methodological theories offered in the archaeology of gender' (1993, p. 42). She suggests that one way forward is to target existing data from sites that show 'good evidence for internal functional differentiation and spatial separation' for possible reinterpretation (1993, p. 42). To demonstrate this potential, she then reviews three case studies where gendered analysis was undertaken after the fieldwork had been completed. The first is a spatial analysis of the Cross Creek site by Brenda Sewell (1984), which uses an ethnographic structuralist analysis (from Salmond, 1978) contrasting concepts of *right/male/west/front/tapu* with *left/female/east/rear/noa* to interpret activity areas at the site. Parslow's second example has to do with sex ascription and burial goods analysis in mortuary sites. She details how the original researchers of burials recovered from Wairau Bay made the assumption that any burial with grave goods must be male (Duff, 1956). Subsequent analysis by Leach (1977) revealed that ten of twenty-nine burials with grave goods were female, including one that had been evaluated as being of the highest rank marked. Parslow argues that data from burials and settlement patterns suggest that during the earliest period of Māori settlement, 'gender roles … are not as strictly defined as ethnohistorians would suggest' whereas after 1500 CE a 'more rigid organisation of labour and gender roles' developed (Parslow, 1993, p. 44).

The third example described by Parslow is a study of five houses at Lake Owhareiti (Marshall, 1990), which argued that one area, distinguished by evidence of wood and stone working, was likely dedicated to men's production activities, while another may have been dedicated to women's activities, such as processing of material for food and clothing (Parslow, 1993, p. 44). Parslow concludes the article by saying that attention to gender is a means of 'putting the "people" back into archaeology,' and thus is part of a larger archaeological mission of trying to 'distinguish between individuals' (1993, p. 44).

Marshall, Spennemann and Parslow's case studies, all explicitly cite Conkey and Spector (1984) as an important influence on their work. All three of these articles represent variations of the task differentiation approach, although in every case, it is clear that the authors had an eye to the broader potential of their work.

Spennemann saw that, where the archaeological evidence pointed to one direction (women gardening) and the ethnohistoric evidence disagreed (women not involved in gardening), there was potential to push the next phase of the investigation to questions of task differentiation by rank or other social identity category, or a consideration of changing gender roles over time. Marshall did not stop once she had identified women as the likely makers of the Lapita pots, but rather showed how a 'simple' task differentiation exercise could in fact lead to new insights and potential hypotheses to what had been judged a central mystery of Pacific prehistory: why stop making pottery? Lastly, Parslow demonstrates that Polynesian archaeologists of this era had begun to push beyond the process of 'looking for women and men in the archaeological record' to trying to investigate *gender* as a system in the past that structured identity and behaviour.

Moving the conversation forward

In her summary review of gender and archaeology in Australia, Papua New Guinea and the South Pacific, Cherrie De Leiuen states that, 'after substantive publications and multiple conferences on the issue throughout the 1990s there has been a general failure to incorporate gender into archaeological research in Australia' (2013, p. 612). The situation in Polynesian archaeology is even more desolate. The main research De Leiuen cites for the region are those studies by Marshall, Spennemann and Parslow just discussed. Sidsel Millerstom's work on rock art and settlement patterns in the Marquesas Islands is identified as a more recent continuation of gender research, although it is not entirely gender focused (Millerstrom, 2006). Millerstrom does have a short section asking, 'Were women allowed on the tribal ceremonial complexes?' (2006, p. 293) but this mostly reviews ethnohistoric sources. These offer conflicting answers, and Millerstrom concludes, 'that the *tohua* [tribal ceremonial complex] was divided into a strict *tapu* place and a more communal or public space' (2006, p. 295). She further opines that there may have been differing rules for women depending on social class, the specific ceremony being undertaken and/or a special status such as being a priestess (2006, p. 295).

De Leiuen also points to research concerned with gender at a much broader scales of analysis, including research on patterns of population interaction during episodes of Pacific colonisation. Per Hage and Jeff Marck (2003) speculated on the possible relationship between matrilineal social organisation and gendered population admixture during Lapita colonisation episodes, adding a social dimension to DNA analyses. These indicate that, while Polynesian mitochondrial DNA (inherited maternally) shows a predominantly Asian origin, Polynesian Y chromosomes (inherited paternally) show a dominant haplogroup of Melanesian origin (2003, p. S121). Hage and Marck address various models of Austronesian expansion across the Pacific, but also weigh in on the possible gender composition of voyaging canoe crews (2003, p. S125). Since most ethnographically known Polynesian cultures followed cognatic descent rules, these findings could also imply social reorganisation from earlier matrilineal-matrilocal house societies. This would likely mean a significant shift in marriage patterns and household composition – in other words, a reorganisation of the primary social loci that engender the lives of men and women. Hage and Marck's research conflates sex and gender, but it does situate sex/gender in social systems of kinship, which opens up possibilities for further development. Genetic evidence certainly has the potential to trace biological lineages across the Pacific, but as Hage and Marck demonstrate, it will be up to theoretically robust archaeological and historical linguistics to untangle the cultural, or gender, implications of these biological data.

De Leiun closes her review with a discussion of the potential impact of gender archaeology on the politics of the present, as well as its interrelatedness to indigenous rights and heritage management (2013, pp. 521–622). She notes a decline in explicitly feminist political motivations to the refinement of gender theory tied to broader social trends, but perhaps encouraged by an increasing emphasis on practical skills and training for CRM research in the region. She also notes that many archaeologists have yet to come to grips with the notion that sex and gender invoke fluid and interdependent categories rather than a binary male/female dichotomy, and that this is often reinforced by over-reliance on the ethnographic present. While indigenous societies in the region may divide their activities into 'male business' and 'female business', this has tended to be read as a dichotomous justification for reliance on male sources by male archaeologists. This has marginalised women's roles, but also neglects that, in indigenous frameworks, men's and women's business is 'always dynamic, interactive, interrelated, and complementary' (2013, p. 621).

The task differentiation approach to gender archaeology perhaps contributes to this dichotomous understanding of the problem, but it is only one of many gender-theory inspired research trajectories. Conkey and Gero (1997, p. 416), for example, identified six 'theoretically anchored positions' in gender archaeology. Each 'represents a different way to connect empirical archaeological study with theoretical resources and arguments'. I would argue that four of these theoretical anchors can profitably extend the historical focus on task differentiation in the Pacific: gender as social construction; gender as political economy; gender as agency; and gender as performance (Conkey and Gero, 1997, pp. 416–421).

The idea of gender as a social construction, as distinguished from the biological notion of sex, is a well-established vein of inquiry in cultural anthropology. Engagement with social constructivist perspectives requires us to keep at the front of our minds the dynamism of culture, its constantly negotiated state, and reminds us that archaeological assemblages are the results of myriad processes that can be obscured by the clumsy terms of anthropology. I reject more extreme, nihilistic versions of the constructivist position, for as Conkey and Gero assert, one of archaeology's important contributions to constructivist conversations 'is to probe the best means of analyzing the dialectic between human life as socially constructed and the very materiality of human life' (1997, p. 418).

Similarly, understanding gender systems as a fundamental part of the political economy of human societies has a long history in cultural anthropology. As discussed in the following section on Hawaiian gender relations, I believe that it is crucial to consider the ways in which gender relations both sustained and challenged economic bases of political power. The role of women's labour in the establishment and maintenance of socially stratified economies has only just begun to be understood, and it remains critically important that gender and social status be considered as interwoven variables unless proven otherwise.

To understand gender as agency is to engage with the body of literature in social theory known as practice theory (Bourdieu, 1977; Ortner, 1984). When Conkey and Gero assert that, 'gendered subjects are produced, not born' (1997, p. 420), they are recognising the ways in which agents, in their daily cultural practices, engage with structures to produce meaning and identity, including gender. This avenue of inquiry draws attention to the processes that constitute lived experience, sustain cultural traditions and bring about cultural change. Household archaeology has much to offer here as a way of accessing the praxis of everyday life and its role in reproducing gendered behaviours (see below).

Approaches emphasising the performative aspects of gendered identities are closely related to those emphasising gender as a facet of 'embodied subjectivities' (Bulgar and Joyce, 2012; Joyce, 2008). As Conkey and Gero point out, most recent works that self-consciously adopt a performative approach draw heavily on the works of Judith Butler (1988; 1990; 1993), who has been one of the most articulate theorists problematising universal definitions of sex or gender (see Conkey and Gero, 1997, pp. 420–421; Bulgar and Joyce, 2012, p. 75). As I have argued elsewhere, this approach has a great deal of resonance with Polynesian theories of personhood, which did not share Westerners' notions of gender essentialism, but rather emphasised behaviour and practice as an indication of identity (Van Gilder, 2005).

Gender as practice: a Hawaiian case study

One way of moving this conversation forward and bringing these theoretical themes together, is to focus more closely on community and household archaeology, informed by a deeper understanding of indigenous spatial orders, and gender roles. The archaeology of gender and household archaeology have enjoyed a close relationship in many regional traditions of archaeology. This is also the case in Polynesia. Jennifer Kahn (2016) provides an excellent, comprehensive review of household archaeology in the region. Kahn (2016, p. 332) cites an early phase of research, in which the household was primarily conceived of as a building block of settlement pattern archaeology (see also Van Gilder and Kirch, 1997). In this approach, 'the material correlates of primary residences and their auxiliary structures' are identified and investigated (Kahn, 2016, p. 332).

Early examples of such studies in Hawai'i mention gender in passing. Weisler and Kirch (1985) examine the settlement space of household clusters on the south coast of Moloka'i, Hawai'i, through the lenses of environmental, social, economic and political, and semiotic paradigms (1985, p. 151). In their consideration of social factors, they suggest that 'variable aspects of household clusters presumably reflect such factors as the size and *age-sex composition* of individual households, and presence of craft specialists' (1985, p. 153, my emphasis). The specific ways in which various age-sex compositions might affect household space are not investigated, but gender becomes a topic of some consideration in their discussion of the semiotics or 'symbolic order' of settlement space (1985, p. 154). They put forward the idea that Polynesian and Hawaiian ethnohistoric sources suggest a 'semiotic code' of east:west, sacred:profane, male:female, noting that structures interpreted as shrines lie to the east of other structures in the household cluster, and go so far as to suggest that an 'outlying ancillary structure to the west of the main complex appears to be a *hale pe'a*, or hut for menstruating women' (1985, pp. 154–155).

This article represents a slightly more sophisticated version of the way the phenomenon of gender has been treated as an extension of the functional approach to spatial analysis. My own research has aimed to understand how gender was 'lived', or practiced, during daily life by commoners in Hawai'i. I identify three important ways gender was embodied, or practiced, in late pre-contact Hawai'i. These were: (1) task differentiation, including men taking primary responsibility for agricultural work; (2) the spatial separation of men's and women's cooking and eating activities; and (3) men and women eating different foods, as prescribed by the *'ai kapu* or eating taboo, where, for example, pig was categorically a male food, and dog a female food (Van Gilder, 2001; 2005). I consider the information gleaned from the written sources and oral tradition not as inviolable truth, but rather as a working model of orthodox, or hegemonic gender practices. Each of these practices, through daily repetition, reinforced (and created) local understandings of masculinity and femininity. Each of these practices also offers a potential locus for heterodoxy, or even resistance.

Ethnohistoric sources have described Hawaiian households as being structured to accommodate gender-based taboos, including the *'ai kapu* (Handy and Pukui, 1972). One of the structures most commonly identified as being integral to a household cluster is the men's house (*hale mua*), often within a walled compound where men socialised and presented offerings to family spirits, often at an adjacent *heiau* or temple. Several archaeological studies in Hawai'i have identified prospective men's houses, using fairly disparate criteria (see Van Gilder, 2018, for examples). Complementary female spaces included the *hale 'aina*, or women's eating house, and *hale pe'a*, the menstrual retreat. Common houses, *hale noa*, where men and women could freely associate together, along with a variety of other structures, occurred nearby and made up the *kauhale* residential complex or household. Norms for pre-contact gender roles also included task specialisation; such as men having primary responsibility for agriculture and deep-sea fishing, and women focusing on textile production (i.e. woven baskets and mats, as well as beaten bark-cloth).

Gender was clearly a pervasive device for the organisation of spatial activity in Hawaiian society, and its inscription in the categorisation and use of architecture and food production reflects its performative character, in that the maintenance of gender categories was achieved in part through spatially structured daily praxis. Bulgar and Joyce cite Clark and Wilkie (2007) in defining 'embodied personhood' (Bulgar and Joyce 2012, p. 74) as the ways the body is involved in carrying out the activities expected of a certain aspect of personhood [such as gender or class] or socially recognised role' (2013, p. 74). To the extent that Hawaiian archaeologists have been interested in households as loci for the formation, 'performance' and negotiation of social identity, their questions have primarily been associated with the identification of the material correlates of social hierarchy in the archaeological record (e.g. Kirch and O'Day, 2003).

In my own work, three households in the leeward, windswept district of Kahikinui, Maui, were selected for intensive areal excavations with the idea of examining internal organisation and activity areas to illuminate the rhythms of family life in commoner households (Van Gilder, 2001; 2005; 2018; Kirch and Van Gilder, 1997). I particularly hoped to understand how gender identities, and possibly other social identities, were structured/practiced/constructed on a daily basis in these three households.

I noted a recurring pattern of side-by-side hearths in individual structures, within discrete households, reflecting a local variant on practices of cooking separation stipulated by the *'ai kapu*. That is, rather than segregating cooking in distinct men's and women's buildings, commoner households with insufficient resources for two buildings, maintained carefully separated ovens within the same structure. This hypothesis received corroboration in the form of faunal remains recovered from the hearths in site 752, where one hearth was found to contain the remains of pig (*Sus scrofa*), and the other of dog (*Canis familiaris*). These are two of the foods most widely cited as being subject to gender *kapu* (taboos). Pig was reserved for males, except at certain ritual occasions, and dog was primarily for females.

However, such meats were high-status products, and probably difficult to sustain or procure in the marginal, dry habitat occupied by commoners of Kahikinui. Instead diet was highly dependent on marine resources and sweet potato. In leeward regions the prohibition on women working in the fields was not enforced because extra agricultural labour was necessary (Van Gilder, 2005). In these dry areas, the highest status domesticated crop (taro) was of secondary importance in the daily subsistence regimen, having been supplanted by the more drought-hardy and reliable sweet potato as the main source of daily calories. Interestingly, traditional gender divisions may have also been modified with regard to fishing practices. Excavations recovered only one bone definitively identified as a benthic genus. Instead, 99.9% of the marine fauna represented in the remains recovered were in-shore species. Ethnographic and ethnohistoric sources indicate that women and children were usually primarily responsible for the collection of such in-shore resources. Since these are clearly important elements of the local diet, represented in relatively large quantities, it is probable that males were participating in the collection and distribution of these in-shore food items. This presents the possibility that in Kahikinui, rather than being separated, men and women may have been working side-by-side both to cultivate the primary crop, sweet potato, and to collect in-shore seafoods.

Thus, it is likely that commoner men and women usually consumed very similar meals. The practical realities or lived experiences of gender were consequently different from not only the idealised descriptions of gender systems described by ethnohistoric sources, but also from neighbouring communities whose subsistence base drew on wet-field cultivation and other food sources. Gender as such may be seen as a heterodoxic practice. Bourdieu's model of cultural negotiation within a culture's doxa, or beliefs, involves two 'universes' – that of the 'undiscussed' (or undisputed) and that of the 'discussed' (or disputed) (1977, p. 168). He suggests that change occurs at moments of crisis or conflict between interest groups, such as during culture contact or class warfare (1977, p. 169), rendering the undiscussed, naturalised, aspects of doxa a subject of dispute and potential heterodoxy. Based on the ethnographic and ethnohistoric records, the extension of settlement into leeward areas of Maui created such a cultural crisis; a moment where the doxa surrounding gendered food production was revealed as arbitrary due to economic circumstance, and thus subject to discussion and opinion. The practice of gender in these areas was different from that in other parts of the archipelago, and thus represents a heterodoxy in Bourdieu's terms.

A more complex view of the lived reality of gender in different contexts, and the links between gender, economic base and status, has implications for understanding core–periphery or hinterlands dynamics in the Hawaiian chiefdoms before unification, and indeed for our understanding of the 1819 dismantling of Hawaiian traditional religion, including the *'ai kapu,* after unification (Van Gilder, 2005). Dixon, Gosser and Willliams (2008), for example, explore the changing role that *hale mua* played in unifying one local community, Lualualei, O'ahu, and its role in regional politics over time. As part of their investigations, the authors identified prospective household clusters and tentatively identified their functionally differentiated components. They identified sites as prominent men's houses based on a combination of structural attributes such as their 'exceptional size and quality of construction', as well as excavated finds, such as debitage from stone-tool making and the presence of food items traditionally forbidden to women (e.g. pig) (2008, pp. 272–274). Men's houses played an important role in the region's religious and political organisation before the first half of the 18th century, serving as centres of communal redistribution within each extended family or between local residential groups. After this time their central role was eclipsed by polity or state temples, and their influence shrank to become highly localised. The authors link these changes to the political consolidation of the island, increased tribute demands by the paramount chief, and consequent intensification of dryland agriculture. Later, integration of the entire archipelago during the post-contact creation of the Kingdom of Hawai'i, led to the demise of the gendered eating taboo and other aspects of the *kapu* system. This is reflected in the subsequent virtual abandonment of *hale mua* and ultimately the fragmentation of the Lualualei *ahupua'a* itself (2008, pp. 282–283). In this study, then, *hale mua* stand as proxies for male head-of-household political efficacy and their integration in the wider political system.

These studies show that the way gender was performed in Hawai'i was structured by trends in political economy, economic affordances and contradictions and debates stemming from those arenas in dialogue with existing norms. It was a contextual, emergent facet of practice rather than a fixed or predetermined state.

Future directions

Polynesian archaeologists have barely begun to scratch the surface of feminist and gender archaeology approaches to invigorate our modelling of past lifeways and subjectivities. From the simple realisation that every rising and falling demographic curve represents real men and women making reproductive decisions in the context of living, loving, giving birth and raising families, to more complex and nuanced modelling of identity, as mediated and embodied in the material world, there is much this theoretical corpus has to offer. For example, there has been little or no discussion of an archaeology of childhood in Polynesia (e.g. Baxter, 2005). We know that sexuality was the subject of many great chants, as well as much Hawaiian humour and games (Van Gilder, 2018). And, despite the ethnographically known existence of third gender individuals in multiple Polynesian societies, there have been no published discussions of an archaeology of sexuality or third gender, which has shown great potential in other parts of the world (e.g. Schmidt and Voss, 2000).

Back in 1985, Marshall argued that 'division of labour by sex' is 'the most basic principle by which societies are socially differentiated', and that if we were able to understand how 'people divided labour between the sexes we will then be in a stronger position to address other, more complex, social issues' (1985, p. 205). Beyond this, only by taking gender, and other aspects of social identities, as a social construction that represents a dynamic historical practice that needs to be problematised (rather than treated as a given) will we be able to apprehend local cultural variants we have not yet recognised or comprehended.

Elsewhere, I have argued that, in my experience, studies that illuminate the microscale aspects of the lives of their ancestors have tremendous, intimate human appeal to all descendant communities, including indigenous Polynesians, in a way that macroscale evolutionary schemes do not (Van Gilder, 2005). As anthropological archaeologists, one of our ethical responsibilities is to explore approaches that illuminate the humanity of ancient Polynesians, and by extension their descendants. Indeed, only when the fullness of the human experience is taken into consideration in theoretical modelling, will Polynesian archaeology reach its full potential.

Acknowledgements

Many thanks are due to my family for their patience as I took on this writing as my fourth full-time job. I appreciated encouraging comments from Jenny Kahn and Scarlett Chiu along the way, and Anthony Talo and Dana Herrera had my back as usual, in material, as well as, ideal ways. Thanks for helping me create a productive dialectic. Finally, I can never say enough about what a critical source of support and inspiration Meg Conkey continues to be to my intellectual work as an anthropological archaeologist and woman in academia.

References

Barstow, A., 1978. The uses of archaeology for women's history: James Mellaart's work on the Neolithic goddess at Çatal Hüyük. *Feminist Studies*, 4(3), p. 7.

Baxter, J., 2005. *The Archaeology of Childhood: Children, Gender, and Material Culture*. Walnut Creek, CA: Rowman Altamira.

Bolger, D., 2012. Gender, labor, and pottery production in prehistory. In: D. Bolger, ed. *A Companion to Gender Prehistory*. Oxford: Wiley, pp. 161–179.

Bourdieu, P., 1977. *Outline of a Theory of Practice*. New York: Cambridge University Press.

Brumfiel, E.M., 1991. Weaving and cooking: women's production in Aztec Mexico. In: J.M. Gero and M.W. Conkey, eds. *Engendering Archaeology: Women and Prehistory*, Oxford: Blackwell, pp. 224–251.

Bulger, T. and Joyce, R., 2012. Archaeology of embodied subjectivities. In: D. Bolger, ed. *A Companion to Gender Prehistory*. Oxford: Wiley, pp. 68–85.

Butler, J., 1988. Performative acts and gender constitution: an essay in phenomenology and feminist theory. *Theatre Journal*, 40(4), pp. 519–531.

Butler, J., 1990. Gender trouble, feminist theory, and psychoanalytic discourse. In: L. Nicolson, ed. *Feminism/Postmodernism*. London: Routledge, pp. 327–340.

Butler, J., 1993. Critically queer. *GLQ: A Journal of Lesbian and Gay Studies*, 1(1), pp. 17–32.

Clark, B.J. and Wilkie, L.A., 2007. The prism of self: gender and personhood. In: L. Nelson, ed. *Identity and Subsistence: Gender Strategies for Archaeology*. London: Rowman & Littlefield, pp. 1–31.

Conkey, M.W., 1991. Contexts of action, contexts for power: material culture and gender in Magdalenian times. In: J.M. Gero and M.W. Conkey, eds. *Engendering Archaeology: Women and Prehistory*. Oxford: Blackwell, pp. 57–92.

Conkey, M.W. and Gero, J.M., 1991. Tensions, pluralities, and engendering archaeology: an introduction to women and prehistory. In: J.M. Gero and M.W. Conkey, eds. *Engendering Archaeology: Women and Prehistory*. Oxford: Blackwell, pp. 3–30.

Conkey, M.W. and Gero, J.M., 1997. Programme to practice: gender and feminism in archaeology. *Annual Review of Anthropology*, 26, pp. 411–437.

Conkey, M.W. and Spector, J.D., 1984. Archaeology and the study of gender. *Advances in Archaeological Method and Theory*, 7, pp. 1–38.

Cordy, R., 2003. Who made the feather cloaks in the Hawaiian Islands? Some additional information. *Journal of the Polynesian Society*, 116(2), pp. 157–161.

Deetz, J., 1968. The inference of residence and descent rules from archaeological data. In: S. Binford and L. Binford, eds. *New Perspectives in Archaeology*. Chicago, IL: Aldine Publishing Co., pp. 41–48.

Dixon, B., Gosser, D. and Williams, S.S., 2008. Traditional Hawaiian men's houses and their socio-political context in Lualualei, leeward West O'ahu, Hawai'i. *Journal of the Polynesian Society*, 117(2), pp. 267–295.

Duff, R., 1956. *The Moa-Hunter Period of Maori Culture*. Wellington: NZ Government Printer.

Freycinet, L. de, 1978. Hawaii in 1819: a narrative account by Louis Claude de Soules de Freycinet. *Pacific Anthropological Records*, 26, pp. 1–36.

Fulkerson, T.J., 2017. Engendering the past: the status of gender and feminist approaches to archaeology in the Pacific Northwest and future directions. *Journal of Northwest Archaeology*, 51(1), pp. 1–36.

Gero, J., 1985. Socio-politics and the woman-at-home ideology. *American Antiquity,* 50(2), pp. 342–350.

Gero, J., 1988. Gender bias in archaeology: here, then and now. In: S. Rosser, ed. *Feminism within the Science and Health Care Professions: Overcoming Resistance.* Oxford: Pergamon Press, pp. 33–43.

Gero, J.M. and Conkey, M.W., eds. 1991. *Engendering Archaeology: Women and Prehistory.* Oxford: Blackwell.

Gero, J.M, Lacy, D.M., and Blakey, M.L., eds. 1983. *The Socio-Politics of Archaeology.* Research Reports, 23. Amherst, MA: University of Massachusetts.

Hage, P. and Marck, J., 2003. Matrilineality and the Melanesian origin of Polynesian Y chromosomes. *Current Anthropology,* 44(suppl.), pp. S121–S127.

Handy, E.S.C., and Pukui, M.K., 1972. *The Polynesian Family System in Ka'U, Hawaii.* Rutland, VT: Tuttle Publishing.

Hastorf, C., 1991. Gender, space and food in prehistory. In: J.M. Gero and M.W. Conkey, eds. *Engendering Archaeology: Women and Prehistory.* Oxford: Blackwell, pp. 132–159.

Hawkes, C., 1954. Archeological theory and method: some suggestions from the old world. *American Anthropologist,* 56(2), pp. 155–168.

Hill, J. N., 1968. Broken K. Pueblo: patterns of form and function. In: S. Binford and L. Binford, eds. *New Perspectives in Archaeology.* Chicago, IL: Aldine Publishing Co., pp. 103–142.

Houghton, P., 1980. *The First New Zealanders.* Auckland: Hodder & Stoughton.

Joyce, Rosemary A., 2008. *Ancient Bodies, Ancient Lives: Sex, Gender, and Archaeology.* New York: Thames & Hudson.

Kahn, J.G., 2016. Household archaeology in Polynesia: historical context and new directions. *Journal of Archaeological Research,* 24(4), pp. 325–372.

Kawelu, K., 2014. In their own voices: contemporary native Hawaiian and archaeological narratives about Hawaiian archaeology. *The Contemporary Pacific,* 26(1), pp. 31–62.

King, Captain J., 1967. Supplement to Cook's Journal. In: J.C. Beaglehole, ed. *The Journals of Captain James Cook on His Voyages of Discovery,* vol. 3, pt. 1. Cambridge: Cambridge University Press for the Hakluyt Society, pp. 493–718.

Kirch, P.V. and Green, R.C., 2001. *Hawaiki, Ancestral Polynesia: An Essay in Historical Anthropology.* Cambridge: Cambridge University Press.

Kirch, P.V. and O'Day, S.J., 2003. New archaeological insights into food and status: a case study from pre-contact Hawaii. *World Archaeology,* 34(3), pp. 484–497.

Leach, B.F. 1977. Sex and funeral offerings at Wairau Bar: a re-evaluation. *New Zealand Archaeological Association Newsletter,* 20(2), pp. 107–113.

Leacock, E., 1983. Interpreting the origins of gender inequality: conceptual and historical problems. *Dialectical Anthropology,* 7(4), pp. 263–284.

Leiuen, C., 2015. Discourse through the looking glass: gender in the language of archaeological journals. *Archaeologies,* 11(3), pp. 417–444.

Linnekin, J., 1988. Who made the feather cloaks? A problem in Hawaiian gender relations. *Journal of the Polynesian Society,* 97(3), pp. 265–280.

Marshall, Y., 1985. Who made the Lapita pots? A case study in gender archaeology. *Journal of the Polynesian Society,* 94(3), pp. 205–233.

Marshall, Y., 1990. A complex open settlement at Lake Owhareiti, N15/505. In: D.G. Sutton, ed. *The Archaeology of the Kainga: A Study of Precontact Maori Undefended Settlements at Pouerua, Northland, New Zealand.* Auckland: Auckland University Press, pp. 56–83.

Matisoo-Smith, E., 2015. Ancient DNA and the human settlement of the Pacific: a review. *Journal of Human Evolution,* 79, pp. 93–104.

Millerstrom, S.N., 2017. *Te Henua Enana: Images and Settlement Patterns in the Marquesas Islands, French Polynesia.* Contributions of the Archaeological Research Facility, 67. Berkeley, CA: University of California, Berkeley.

Millerstrom, S.N., 2006. Ritual and domestic architecture, sacred places and images: archaeology in the Marquesan Archipelago, French Polynesia. In: I. Lilley, ed. *Archaeology of Oceania; Australia and the Pacific.* Oxford: Blackwell Publishing, pp. 284–301.

Ortner, S., 1972. Is female to male as nature is to culture? *Woman, Culture, and Society*, 1(2), pp. 5–31.

Ortner, S., 1984. Theory in anthropology since the Sixties. *Comparative Studies in Society and History*, 26(1), pp. 126–166.

Parslow, B., 1993. The identification of gender in Māori archaeology. In: H. Du Cros and L. Smith, eds. *Women in Archaeology: A Feminist Critique.* Canberra: Department of Prehistory, Research School of Pacific Studies, Australian National University, pp. 41–45.

Peebles, C.S. and Kus, S.M., 1977. Some archaeological correlates of ranked societies. *American Antiquity*, 42(3), pp. 421–48.

Rapp , R., 1977. Gender and class: An archaeology of knowledge concerning the origin of the state. *Dialectical Anthropology*, 2(1), pp. 309–316.

Salmond, A., 1978. Te ao tawhito: a semantic approach to the traditional Maori cosmos. *Journal of the Polynesian Society*, 87(1), pp. 5–28.

Schmidt, R.L and Voss, B.L., eds. 2000. *Archaeologies of Sexuality.* London: Routledge.

Sewell, B., 1984. The Cross Creek Site, N40/260, Coromandel Peninsula. Unpublished MA thesis, University of Auckland.

Spector, J.D., 1991. What this awl means: toward a feminist archaeology. In: J.M. Gero and M.W. Conkey, eds. *Engendering Archaeology: Women and Prehistory.* Oxford: Blackwell, pp. 388–406.

Spector, J.D., 1993. *What This Awl Means, Feminist Archaeology at a Wahpeton Dakota Village.* Saint Paul, MN: Minnesota Historical Society Press.

Spennemann, D.R., 1996. Changing gender roles in Tongan society: some comments based on archaeological observations. In: P. Herda, J. Terrell and N. Gunson, eds. *Tongan Culture and History: Papers from the 1st Tongan History Conference held in Canberra, 14–17 January 1987.* Canberra: Journal of Pacific History, pp. 101–109.

Tringham, R., 1991. Households with faces: the challenge of gender in prehistoric architectural remains. In: J.M. Gero and M.W. Conkey, eds. *Engendering Archaeology: Women and Prehistory.* Oxford: Blackwell, pp. 93–131.

Van Gilder, C.L., 1997. Household archaeology in Kipapa and Nakaohu, Kahikinui. In: P.V. Kirch, ed. *Na Mea Kahiko o Kahikinui: Studies in the Archaeology of Kahikinui, Maui.* Special Publication 1. Berkeley, CA: Oceanic Archaeology Laboratory, University of California, pp. 45–60.

Van Gilder, C.L., 2001. Gender and household archaeology in Kahikinui, Maui. In: C. Stevenson, G. Lee and F.J. Morin, eds. *Proceedings of the Fifth International Conference on Easter Island and the Pacific.* Los Osos, CA: Bearsville Press, pp. 135–140.

Van Gilder, C.L., 2005. Families on the Land: Archaeology and Identity in Kahikinui, Maui. Unpublished PhD, University of California, Berkeley.

Van Gilder, C.L., 2018. In the sea of night: ancient Polynesia and the dark. In: N. Gonlin and A Nowell, eds. *Archaeology of the Night: Life After Dark in the Ancient World.* Boulder, CO: University Press of Colorado, pp. 155–176.

Van Gilder, C.L. and Charles, D., 2003. Archaeology as cultural encounter: the legacy of Hopewell, In: R Jeske and D Charles, eds. *Theory, Method, and Practice in Modern Archaeology.* Westport, CT: Praeger, pp. 114–129.

Watson, P.J. and Kennedy, M.C., 1991. The development of horticulture in the Eastern Woodlands of North America: women's role. In: J.M. Gero and M.W. Conkey, eds. *Engendering Archaeology: Women and Prehistory.* Oxford: Blackwell, pp. 255–275.

Weisler, M. and Kirch, P.V., 1985. The structure of settlement space in a Polynesian chiefdom: Kawela, Molokai, Hawaiian Islands. *New Zealand Journal of Archaeology,* 7, pp. 129–158.

Wylie, A., 1991. Gender theory and the archaeological record: why is there no archaeology of gender? In: J.M. Gero and M.W. Conkey, eds. *Engendering Archaeology: Women and Prehistory.* Oxford: Blackwell, pp. 31–54.

13

ENTANGLED HISTORIES

Oral history and archaeology in the Pacific

Peter J. Sheppard

Introduction

Prior to the development of radiocarbon dating and scientific field archaeology, the rich oral traditions of the Pacific provided the basis for academic study of the history of its peoples. In the first issue of the *Journal of the Polynesian Society* the Editors noted upon publication of *Genealogies and Historical Notes from Rarotonga* in the Cook Islands that:

> It is upon these genealogies that all dates in Polynesian history must rest, and hence the interest attaching to them. Information is gradually accumulating which will allow of a comparison and correlation of the genealogies preserved by the New Zealanders, Rarotongans, Tahitians, Hawaiians, Samoans, and Tongans, in nearly all of which the names of common ancestors are preserved. When this has been done, the relative dates of events in the history of Polynesia will be placed on a firm footing.
>
> *(Nicholas, 1892, p. 21)*

However, with the coming of modern fieldwork and dating methods, Pacific archaeology developed an uneasy relationship with oral tradition and historical reconstructions dependent upon it. In an early statement of intent, Jack Golson, a pioneer of professional Pacific archaeology, noted that: 'Tradition and archaeology are concerned with appreciably different aspects of prehistoric activity and the degree of overlap between them is often surprisingly small' (1960, p. 380). Archaeology and oral tradition were argued to be different fields of study requiring separate methods and careful evaluation before any attempt at their incorporation into a single narrative. 'Again the writer must insist that he is not *necessarily* questioning the validity of the … traditions, but only their usefulness for organising and interpreting the archaeological data of … prehistory' (Golson, 1960, p. 397).

Since Golson's statement, the use of tradition, and more broadly ethnography, has waxed and waned given changing fashions in archaeological theory, methods and goals. Yet oral tradition has always had an important role in the Pacific, and in the last twenty-five years it has again become an important component of research. I will review some of this history and show what lessons have been learnt, as a contribution to recent calls for ways to again pull together the strands of anthropology (Fuentes and Wiessner, 2016).

Oral tradition and archaeology

In his evaluation of Maori tradition and its relation to archaeology Jeffrey Sissons states: 'Traditional accounts are from the outset intentional constructions related in specific contexts for specific reasons, and it is quite possible for them to begin life as abstract symbolic statements' (Sissons, 1988, p. 200). The same might be said of histories of all kinds including archaeology. We work within a theoretical frame, both explicit and implicit, which sets our questions and goals, defines relevant data and provides a methodology for generating valid or respected answers accordingly. Our socio-cultural context shapes this knowledge framework, and as contexts change over time so do frameworks. The archaeology of today differs greatly from that of 1917, just as all academic and popular histories of past events have changed with new questions and goals. Similarly, traditional and indigenous histories sit within changing social and cultural frameworks that foreground certain goals and questions and define useful data. The goals and questions of indigenous people in post-settler societies (Sissons, 2005) today may vary considerably from cultures in the third world or from indigenous goals and questions 100 years ago. In the Pacific the modern role of 'traditional' histories for Maori may be considerably different than they are for Samoans or Solomon Islanders or Hawaiians.

Although constructivist views of oral tradition (e.g. Hanson, 1989) may emphasise the current forces structuring and using tradition in the 'invention of tradition' paradigm, this is not something unrecognised by those who study oral tradition (Vansina, 1985). In the Pacific, considerable effort has gone into revealing and evaluating the forces shaping the form in which oral tradition has been recorded and synthesised, particularly for those recorded in the late 19th and early 20th centuries (e.g. Sorrenson, 1979; Gunson, 1993; Simmons, 1976; Adams, 1992; Anderson et al., 2015). More generally, Sahlins (1983; 1985; 1995) has shown how cultural structures in conjunction with events work to create histories in a process that is both replicative and potentially transformative. He has argued for an Anthropology of History, and a more constrained view of tradition in which narrated history conforms to cultural logics. History is not simply invented, as it must make sense within the logics of the people to whom it is relevant. It is on this basis that it can be judged valid by the audience for whom it is constructed (including of course recorders of tradition). This suggests that we should see in oral tradition histories constructed from events according to fundamental cultural logics (structure) which may generally produce consistency in form, but a form subject to change upon radical transformation of the underlying logic and through the situational interests of the actors (Sahlins, 1985, pp. 144–145). Understanding the 'data' requires understanding the theory or logics that define it, and understanding major changes requires understanding the significant challenges to those logics or their operation involving a paradigm shift. What then are the master logics operating in the Pacific and how might archaeologists benefit from the data they shape as reproduced in oral tradition?

Pacific cultural logics and oral tradition

One of the advantages of research in the Pacific is a widely shared cultural history. All of the people of Remote Oceania (Green, 1991), both in island Melanesia and Polynesia, have a shared ancestry based on their descent from the archaeological culture known as Lapita (Kirch, 1997), which represents the first settlement of the area some 3,000 years ago (Sheppard et al., 2015). This is also attested to by the fact that all of the languages spoken in Remote Oceania are closely related members of the Austronesian family. In contrast, Near Oceania to the west was first settled in the late Pleistocene by people ancestral to the Papuan language speakers of New Guinea. In the mid-third millennium, Austronesian languages and culture moved from island southeast Asia into the coastal margins of New Guinea and the Solomon Islands, where these new languages and cultural forms replaced, merged with or established themselves alongside Papuan forms. Influence may also have run in the opposite direction with Papuan speakers influencing or replacing Austronesians within Near Oceania.

The emergence of Lapita-era cultural structures, based on food production and new technologies including long-distance voyaging, was pervasive, being adopted even by many populations retaining their Papuan languages (Sheppard et al., 2010). Consequently, cultures throughout Near and Remote Oceania share many core cultural schema (Fox, 1995) that form the core logics found in the oral traditions of the region. Foremost among these are particular notions of origins, ancestry, alliance (Fox and Sather, 1996) and systems of social differentiation based on precedence (Fox, 1996, pp. 5–8), which in the Austronesian world rests on cultural values of *mana* and *tabu* [*tapu*].

Pacific people have for the most part truly heroic histories involving journeys of discovery and settlement, over sailing distances of many hundreds and often thousands of kilometres. Concepts of ancestry accordingly link genealogical descent to place, and ancestral narratives form core components of Pacific identities. Formal statements of identity, such as those recited during ceremonial greetings and rituals, narrate lineages of both ancestors and places to which persons affiliate.

Rights to land and social support depend on the ability to affiliate in this way. Therefore as Fox states:

> Together all of these notions imply an attitude to the past: that it is knowable and that such knowledge is of value, that what happened in the past has set a pattern for the present, and that it is essential to have access to the past in attempts to order the present.

(1996, p. 5)

Remembered history matters in the Pacific world.

Genealogy is important in the Pacific, but 'precedence' (Fox, 1995, p. 230) is what matters politically. In many strongly bilateral societies the older/younger distinction serves to rank, but also creates a line of fission whereby a younger sibling may move away to found a new settlement and a new line of precedence (see also Bellwood (1996, p. 20) for a discussion of founder ideology and the settlement of the Pacific). These systems of *lateral expansion* (Fox, 1995) tend to be found where there is room to expand, such as on larger islands. In contrast to these, in strongly unilineal societies, we find a tendency to 'restrict social reckoning in an ever-more-exclusive mode' (Fox, 1995, p. 223) in systems of *apical demotion*. These tend to be found on smaller islands or on the coasts of larger islands among communities concerned with trading and raiding. 'In such a system, only one line retains status; and within that line, in each generation, ultimately one individual. All other individuals are automatically demoted and thus lose status relative to a single apical point' (Fox, 1995, p. 223). This promotes hierarchy and such systems tend to have kings, rajas, sultans and sacred chiefs. Classic Pacific examples of this sort are found in the highly stratified societies of Samoa, Tonga, Tahiti and Hawaii.

Precedence is also expressed through place, and Fox (1997, see also Thomas, 2009) uses the concept of topogeny to refer to sequences of place as opposed to genealogy. Both principles can operate in Austronesian societies with the travels of ancestors forming part of many foundation traditions. More generally, topogeny may refer to the movement of ancestor groups or objects. Fox notes that a focus on topogeny is often associated with systems of *lateral expansion*, for example in the Solomon Islands many societies on large islands describe history as a series of movements between places (e.g. Oliver, 1955, pp. 46–60); while systems of *apical demotion* focus on the person and genealogy. Association with places thus materialises relationships and rights to land.

Through genealogies people locate themselves in terms of relationships with both the living and the dead. The depth of a genealogy is related to the uses to which it is to be put. In societies where status is inherited, knowledge of deep genealogies can validate status. In the Pacific status and rank are generally important and associated with leadership, although the extent to which this is elaborated varies. Chiefship is pervasive in Polynesia (Marcus, 1989) and linguists (Pawley, 1982; Lichtenberk, 1986) have reconstructed early proto-Oceanic terms that indicate status differentiation has great antiquity (c.3400 BP) in the Austronesian world, and that leaders were drawn from the senior branches of a lineage (Kirch and Green, 2001, p. 227).

Of particular importance in understanding Austronesian ancestry, leadership and status differentiation is knowledge of the pervasive concepts of *mana* (efficacy) and *tapu* (off-limits) (Kirch and Green, 2001, p. 240; Shore, 1989; Keesing, 1985). These terms are ways of expressing and structuring agency in the social world, which included both the living and ancestors. Extending agency to the ancestors can in English give the sense of 'sacred' to the use of these terms. The expression of sacredness in the Austronesian world varies considerably, but, arranged by scale, can include: descent from efficacious or successful close ancestors who bestow *mana*; descent from ancestors with supernatural qualities; descent from deified ancestors; and descent from gods whom the chief embodies. Ultimately chiefs are vehicles for *mana* (Shore, 1989, p. 139). In the simplest case chiefs can demonstrate *mana* through efficacious acts, while in other societies chiefs of high-status lines, or divine lineages, are marked by elaborate *tapu* and embody gods (Sahlins, 1985). In Hawaii, this led to a fundamental transformation and creation of a class system, whereby chiefly genealogies were highly maintained while commoner genealogies only extended to immediate kindred (Sahlins, 1992, p. 33).

In an ideal system of descent from a sacred ancestor, one line would be senior and inherit supreme status in a very ordered manner. In practice, many Austronesian societies have competing lines whose status is based on different principles. This seems to involve incorporating conquering or efficacious foreign lineages into an established system. Accounts of origin often recount a significant intervention from outside – an encounter between an indigenous presence and the coming of an outsider or an outside group. Generally this outsider alters the structure of the society, often introducing new political or religious dimensions. An origin narrative of the coming of the outsider often forms part of a narrative series of installations and displacements (Fox, 2008, p. 202). Sahlins has written extensively about the stranger-king duality in Remote Oceania, particularly in Fiji (Sahlins, 1985) but it is common elsewhere in Oceania. The themes noted constitute core cultural logics that play out within oral tradition in the Pacific, shaping both what is conveyed and why; and how it should be read by archaeologists interested in incorporating it in their narratives.

Pacific archaeology and oral tradition

Pacific archaeologists of the 1960s (see also Trigger, 1989, p. 356) were concerned by the uncritical use of oral tradition and believed archaeology and oral tradition to be fields with different methods and goals not easily accommodated in a processual archaeology. In the late 1980s reaction to this positivist approach foregrounded cultural tradition and structural logics in the move to a post-processual archaeology founded on a more relativist philosophy. In the Pacific, renewed interest in the rich corpus of oral tradition and ethnography amongst archaeologists was influenced by the theoretical development of historical anthropology (Sahlins, 1985; Kirch, 1992).

This led ultimately to an archaeology seeking to use oral tradition to add culturally specific meanings to the evolutionary approaches of Pacific archaeology, in what Trigger (1991) and Green (2000) called a holistic archaeology. The questions being asked were very similar to those of the early collectors and synthesizers of oral tradition. How did people settle the Pacific? When did they arrive in the islands? Can we identify specific historical events in the past? Can we explain the origins of cultural variety and the rise of complexity? I will use these various questions to briefly review how Pacific archaeologists have created and used data from oral tradition, recognising the role cultural logics play in its shaping, to inform the archaeology of settlement process, chronology, specific events and social transformation.

Settlement process

Traditions of Oceania speak of ancestors moving between islands, sailing off for adventure, searching for exotic goods, settling new lands and marrying into distant chiefly lineages (Dening, 1962). In East Polynesia tradition often begins with an ancestor discovering or 'fishing up' a new island, or a period of return voyaging and settlement (Simmons, 1976). Hawaii, like New Zealand, provides a tradition of early discovery by voyagers from a homeland (Kahiki) who then made numerous return voyages (Kirch, 2010, pp. 84–85; Emory, 1959; Cachola-Abad, 2000). In Western Polynesia, tradition speaks of voyaging between the islands of Tonga, Samoa and Fiji as part of the development of the Tongan maritime empire. On the Polynesian Outlier of Tikopia people complained that their chiefs were always away voyaging (Firth, 1961, pp. 150–152). In the 19th and early 20th centuries there was debate over the 'truth' of these accounts (Parsonson, 1972) with 'traditionalists' accepting them while others argued that settlement was the result of accidental voyages and drift. This line of debate ultimately carries on into the constructivist arguments of anthropology in the late 20th century (e.g. Hanson, 1989).

In 1957 Sharp argued that Polynesia:

> comprised a number of little worlds, inaccessible except by accidental migration. The limit of effective navigability was the distance which could be achieved in off-shore voyages of several days between islands where the conditions of wind and current were convenient for such journeys.
>
> *(Sharp, 1957, pp. 30–31)*

Without modern instruments, he argued it would have been impossible to make the long-distance two-way voyages required for the purposeful settlement of distant locations such as New Zealand and Hawaii (Sharp, 1961).

At issue was the ability to make purposeful return voyages of discovery and settlement. The ability of archaeology to investigate purposeful settlement is limited, although our capability to demonstrate the extent of inter-island movement has improved significantly. Levison et al. (1972) using computer simulation, found the probability of successful settlement of the Pacific by drift voyages to be very low.

Subsequently Irwin has shown how purposeful voyaging strategies hypothesised to have been used in Pacific settlement would have been effective (Irwin, 1992). Today this work, plus experimental voyaging (Finney, 1991), strongly supports the ability of Polynesians to conduct the voyaging described in the traditions (but see debate in Irwin and Flay, 2015; Anderson, 2008).

Direct evidence of material transport between islands provides strong support for the regular voyaging indicated by tradition. Dening (1962, pp. 122–123) reported the common finding of igneous stone adzes on Pacific atolls along with traditions of voyaging to obtain stone. Geochemical sourcing of adzes (Best et al., 1992; Weisler, 1997) provides considerable evidence for widespread voyaging. Early work on rock from a quarry in American Samoa showed distribution of adzes to the Cook Islands, Western Samoa, Tonga, Fiji, Tokelau and the Polynesian Outlier of Taumako (Best et al., 1992). The majority were transported after 1100 CE when distribution started or became important. Six adzes of a Samoan form were excavated on Rarotonga in the Cook Islands at the site of Ngati Tiare (Bellwood, 1978, p. 348). Oral tradition identifies this site with Karika, a chief from Manu'a in Samoa, who settled at Avarua some twenty-five generations before 1857 (Nicholas, 1892, pp. 21, 28). Geochemical and petrographic analysis (Walter and Sheppard, 1996) confirmed these adzes are Samoan and match samples from Manu'a as indicated by tradition. Assuming twenty-five years per generation the tradition would suggest settlement around 1350 CE. The four radiocarbon dates from the Ngati Tiare site range (1 sigma) between 1250 and 1450 CE (Walter and Sheppard, 1996, table 1).

Evidence for material transport in East Polynesia is now abundant (Weisler et al., 2016) and although quantities suggest two-way voyaging it could be argued to be the result of early one-way voyaging. Two-way voyaging has been shown, however, by New Zealand obsidian flakes excavated from sites in the Kermadec Group located 1200 km north of the source, presumably deposited on a return voyage to tropical Polynesia (Leach et al., 1986; Furey et al., 2015). Most recently Collerson and Weisler (2007) sourced an adze from an atoll in the Tuamotus to Kaho'olawe in Hawaii which they suggest represents a 4040 km return voyage (Collerson and Weisler, 2007, p. 1911; see also Anderson, 2008, and Kirch, 2010, p. 87).

Oral traditions describe an early period of two-way interaction after which islands became isolated from outside influences. In Hawaii genealogies suggest this period dates between 1270 and 1510 CE (Cachola-Abad, 2000, p. 300) with Kirch (2010, p. 87) proposing no more long-distance voyaging after 1400 CE. Similarly Anderson suggests Maori genealogies indicate a migration period from 1300 to 1400 CE (Anderson et al., 2015, p. 54). Recently Walter et al. (2017) argue that the New Zealand archaeological evidence supports settlement by a mass migration in keeping with Maori oral traditions of organised large-scale settlement events following periods of exploration. Archaeologists have regularly indicated cessation or significant reduction in distribution of foreign adze material around the Pacific after settlement, in the period 1400–1450 CE (Best et al., 1992; Collerson and Weisler, 2007; Allen and Johnson, 1997).

This model of exploration and then purposeful settlement, as provided by oral tradition, has been suggested by archaeologists as a way of considering settlement of the Pacific as a process, rather than an event (Graves and Addison, 1995; Irwin, 1992) allowing movement away from simple consideration of the earliest radio-carbon dates to modelling distributions of dates. Using oral tradition Cachola-Abad (1993) examined the temporal distribution, frequency and direction of voyaging traditions in Hawaii to evaluate archaeological models of Hawaiian settlement. This led her to conclude that a model of continuous interaction in an early migratory period was supported, over a broader area of central East Polynesia than previously proposed (Cachola-Abad, 1993, p. 26). Similarly in New Zealand Walter and Reilly (2018, p. 65) use both oral tradition and archaeology to provide a 'nuanced, multi-layered representation of the past' focusing on the process of migration and early settlement.

Why people took dangerous voyages, in seemingly rapid pulses of movement, is perhaps unknowable, however oral history again provides some hypotheses. Anderson (2006) has proposed that traditions of Polynesia indicate exile was an important factor and he links this to possible religious schisms described in some traditions. Firth (1961, pp. 147–151) reports a variety of factors motivating voyaging by Tikopians including exile and shame but also involving junior lineages seeking to escape the authority of seniors and a desire for simple adventure and new social contacts. During the early period much return voyaging seems to have been motivated simply by the desire to visit those left behind at a time when most remembered ancestors or relatives were still to be found in the home islands.

Settlement dates

Percy Smith famously argued that New Zealand was visited by Kupe in 950 CE, followed by Toi in 1150 and settled around 1350 by a fleet of six canoes from Rai'atea carrying 500 people (Smith, 1910, p. 89). The date of 1350 was arrived at by averaging a large number of genealogies, using a generation length of twenty-five years and counting twenty-two generations from 1900 (Simmons, 1976, p. 108). Similarly, Hawaiian tradition indicated settlement from Tahiti (Malo, 1951) thirty to forty generations before 1900, providing estimates between 900 and 1200 CE (Suggs, 1960), while the settlement of the Marquesas was suggested to be 950 (Handy, 1923).

Dating using genealogies is beset with many problems. Data quality can vary considerably and studies need to take care to determine authenticity or authority of the source. In New Zealand, Smith's work has been criticised as a synthesis and reformulation of disparate traditions by a biased Western scholar (Simmons, 1976). There is also concern that the accuracy or historicity of genealogies declines with age, with the oldest generations being mythical. In Hawaii the earliest recorded ancestors may not have been resident in Hawaii but in the homeland. Finally there is an assumption about generation length needed to calculate dates. Despite these issues, as radiocarbon dates have accumulated we see increasing convergence between oral tradition and archaeology, especially in New Zealand and Hawaii.

Reanalysis of 156 Maori *whakapapa* (genealogies) by Anderson et al. (2015, pp. 54–56), using a generation length of 29.5 years, notes significant convergence:

> the whakapapa can be set into a chronological framework that indicates that the migrations occurred in the interval AD 1200–1400 (the peaks in the combined canoe data would be at about AD 1290 and 1378). … Therefore, Maori whakapapa that reach back to the traditional migration canoes are consistent with scientific evidence of the age of initial human settlement.
>
> *(Anderson et al., 2015, fig. 5)*

Evidence from palynology dated by tephra provides evidence of widespread Maori occupation c.1350 CE (Lowe et al., 1998) and recent evaluation of dates indicates settlement in the range 1230–1282 CE (Wilmshurst et al., 2011).

In Hawaii Kirch considers: 'The mo'olelo [traditions] do not offer historically reliable information regarding initial colonization of the Hawaiian archipelago by Polynesians' (Kirch, 2010, p. 82). However using a generation length of twenty he estimates the Oahu genealogy starting with Māweke to be twenty-three generations from 1750 to 1770 CE, providing an age of 1310 CE. Wilmshurst et al. (2011) suggest a Hawaiian settlement radiocarbon range of 1219–1266 CE while Reith et al. (2011) estimate 1220–1261 CE for Hawaii island. The convergence with genealogy is striking, especially given the possible error factor in the generation length used. Although we should note if we used the 29.5 years preferred by Anderson the date would be 1027 CE, significantly earlier than recent archaeological argument.

The genealogies of East Polynesia record historical events of great importance to descendants by marking social relationships and rights to land. Through the growth of these relationships islands were settled and new social worlds created out of the old. To the west of East Polynesia, settlement occurred two thousand years earlier, but there early genealogies did not play the same role or have simply been forgotten, perhaps because other major events displaced their importance. Traditions for Tonga describe the origins of the chiefdom some 1,000 years ago (Burley, 1998) while early Fijian traditions are autochthonous (Williams, 1982, p. 1). Chiefly genealogies of West Polynesia mostly relate to events of the last 500–750 years when these islands along with Futuna and Uvea began a period of interaction. The development of the Tongan maritime empire began c.1450 CE with the political unification and reorganisation of Tongan society under the 24th Tu'i Tonga (Clark et al., 2008). Such major events have come to dominate historical discourse in these islands.

Events

Oral traditions are generally constructed as a series of events. Pacific traditions describe voyaging, exploring and naming, warfare, births and deaths of chiefly individuals, political conflict and intrigue involving usurpation of social order among many other types of events. In Melanesia, where topogenies, as opposed to genealogies, are important (Denoon and Lacey, 1981; Oliver, 1955), specific events with large impacts have received particular interest. Of note are dated volcanic eruptions and unusual social events tied to specific well-defined locations.

One of the largest Pacific events is recorded in the 'Time of Darkness' traditions of New Guinea (Blong, 1982), which refer to an eruption impacting 100,000 square kilometres of the Highlands. Tradition describes ash-fall on crops and the event serves as a temporal marker with people denoting other events, such as the introduction of kumara, as being prior to or after that time (Blong, 1982, p. 169). Genealogy would suggest it occurred some four to five generations before 1980 CE with dates clustering in the period 1840 to 1890 CE. Evidence for the actual eruption (of Long Island) thought to be linked to these traditions indicates, however, that it occurred around 1645 CE (Thornton, 2001). It might be suggested that in this case topogeny rather than genealogy was the core cultural logic of importance to the creation of oral tradition.

An important tradition from Vanuatu, collected by the ethnologist Guiart, is that of Roy Mata. According to Garanger (1997) Roy Mata came to Efate with several companions in a canoe possibly from the south (but see Luders, 2001). He became a prominent chief who transformed the social structure of the region and was buried with great ceremony on the small island of Retoka in a grave marked by upright stones. Excavation by Garanger (1972, pp. 59–77) revealed a central grave of an old man accompanied by many (46) other men and women, possibly sacrificed (Valentin et al., 2011). The detailed description in tradition was verified by the results of the excavation. Dating has proved problematic (Bedford et al., 1998) as has the traditional association of the burial as occurring before or after the nearby Kuwae eruption of c.1450 CE. Artefacts in the burials show an abrupt change in material culture at the time and show affiliation with West Polynesia which suggests (Spriggs, 1997, p. 212; Garanger, 1997) Roy Mata represented an intrusion from that area possibly leading to significant social change. This may have been part of the ongoing movements after 1000 CE into Island Melanesia from West Polynesia which created the Polynesian Outliers.

Debate over Roy Mata speaks to how historic events can be made use of in tradition. Garanger (1972) spoke of the importance of inter-disciplinary research and particularly that between ethnologists and archaeologists such as his collaboration with Guiart (1996). He argued that, although the structuralist interpretation of myth as conducted by Levi-Strauss (Guiart's mentor) was valuable, there was more to Oceanic myth than structure.

> Sans denier leur value en tant que matériaux que l'on puisse traiter par la méthode structural, les traditions et les mythes sont aussi sur un plan plus pragmatique pour les Océaniens, une atlas historique, un code civil et un cadastre

> [Without denying their value as materials that can be treated by the structural method, the traditions and myths also exist in a more pragmatic sense for the people of Oceania, a historical atlas, a civil code and a cadastral record]
>
> *(Garanger, 1972, p. 136)*

Subsequently he argued that the formal structural rules, coding social structure, themselves limited variation (Garanger, 1997, p. 328).

Luders (2001) has published a critique and revision of Garanger's presentation of the Roy Mata burials, partly based on additional oral tradition. In response Guiart (2004) argued that Luders was naive to seek history in the Roy Mata tradition. Prestige competition over ranked titles was an important component of Efate societies and the creation of variants for advantage was normal.

> Manipulating oral tradition is part of this game and has been for ages. Archaeology cannot validate this or that tradition as a whole. It can only confirm that a certain person, bearing a specific prestigious name, truly existed at a certain date in time, and therefore was a real person and not a mythical figure. This does not prevent the same, single or multiple, person to be illustrated in all kind of myths which fit into wider traditional and symbolic systems and which cannot have anything to do with any historical events. Archaeology cannot pretend to have the capacity of verifying any extraneous details of any myth. It came into this situation because there was an uncommon burial site and the people knew who was inside.
>
> *(Guiart, 2004, p. 379)*

This is a reminder that events and history are not the same thing. Just as many stories can be told about an artefact or site, depending on the interests of the researcher and questions asked, so people can make use of past events to construct different formulations of history given the nature, as Guiart puts it, of the 'game'. Major events, widely witnessed, like eruptions or finding and arriving at new islands, may serve as the stuff of tradition while other events of interest to archaeologists, such as the introduction of sweet potato or the arrival of the first European explorers, while necessary to understanding subsequent events, may pass unmarked as they did not relate in any way to the current 'game' of local people at the time (Salmond, 1991, pp. 122, 431). Understanding the 'game' or cultural logics working within specific structures of the conjuncture (Sahlins, 1985) is important in using oral tradition to complement archaeology in the study of cultural change.

Transformation – development of complexity

In recent years the use of tradition to complement archaeological narratives, as an independent line of evidence, or as a way of incorporating agency into materialist explanations of change (Kirch, 2010, p. 78), has become commonplace in the

Pacific. Where deep genealogies supporting social relationships and status are of limited importance, the absence of chronology limits what can be done. Elsewhere, deep genealogies provide a political history and chronology which can be put against archaeology, but care needs to be exercised in understanding the forces operating to create competing histories. In the Solomon Islands topogenies where the migration history of groups is recounted are common (Scott, 2007, p. 166), although long genealogies are also recorded in some locations (e.g. Ivens, 1927, p. 110). These topogenies relate to movement as garden land is exhausted but are also a function of social conflict over land rights. Miller (1980) has argued, based on early archaeological surveys, that Solomon Islands traditions have a recurring pattern with the oldest sites in the interior of island, generally associated with high hills, and younger sites closer to the coast. He also noted the distinction between 'bush' and 'saltwater' people. In both cases he argued that these distinctions were part of a symbolic structure or cultural geography which facilitated decisions of where to locate settlement (Miller, 1980, p. 458) although people were, in his view, creating 'linearly conceived series of sites' from the interior to the coast, chosen from a more or less continuous distribution of sites and not reflecting 'real' history *per se*.

In the past the interiors of the islands of the Western Solomons were occupied, however with the cessation of head-hunting at the end of the 19th century, population collapse and missionisation, populations all moved to the coast. Therefore for most people the history of movement is from the interior to the coast, whereas prior to the 20th century many people lived in the interior, seeking refuge from coastal raiders. The coast–interior tension has always been a part of life in the islands of the Solomons, where coastal people exchanged resources with those of the interior (Roe, 2000). We should not discount the real historical forces operating within what may be mythologised. Over the last twenty-five years research in the Western Solomons has integrated archaeology and oral tradition in our understanding of the recent past (Sheppard et al., 2004). This was driven by local people who had a strong interest in recording traditional sites, since that knowledge was related to the distribution of land rights. Social and genealogical relationships plus knowledge of the land serve as testimony supporting claims. Thomas (2009) provides a most insightful consideration of topogeny as a principle in New Georgia debates over land and construction of Roviana tradition.

In Roviana Lagoon we found a dense archaeological landscape, which subsequent research elsewhere in the New Georgia group has shown to be unique. Oral tradition states the Roviana chiefdom descends from a woman called Roviana, some fifteen generations before 1900 CE (Sheppard et al., 2002; Aswani and Sheppard, 2003; Sheppard et al., 2004; Aswani, 2000; Nagaoka, 1999). People at that time lived inland in an area known as Bao. At the time of the chief Ididubangara (twelve generations before 1900 CE) the people came down to the coast, as the chief desired the fossil shell (food waste of the gods) used in the manufacture of shell valuables, establishing through warfare the current Roviana chiefdom based at Nusa Roviana. Ididubangara made a shrine at the base of the central ridge of Nusa Roviana.

Subsequently a hillfort was constructed on the ridge, and included within its walls a series of named shrines dedicated to chiefly ancestors and their role in ensuring efficacy in warfare.

The archaeology of Roviana aligns well with tradition. Despite considerable survey the earliest shrine we have dated is the largest shrine located inland in the area of Bao, associated with Roviana origins and dating to c.1200 CE. The shrine (Site 79) on the island of Nusa Roviana, associated with Ididubangara, and incorporating considerable amounts of basalt slabs transported to the coralline island from the mainland, dates to the mid-14th century and is one of the earliest shrines on the island (Sheppard et al., 2004), a date in keeping with the genealogical estimate of c.1500 CE and the radiocarbon dating of hillfort construction.

Alignment with the archaeology leads us to have confidence in the historicity of the tradition. The extent to which it enriches the history of the place, and reinforces the telling of traditions of great interest and importance (Thomas, 2009) to Roviana people, is satisfying. How the traditions enhance archaeological data is a separate issue. Traditions link the coast and the interior, which is perhaps only shown archaeologically by the distribution of basalt from the mainland. Traditions suggest a motive of resource competition and conflict otherwise missing from the archaeology except for the presence of the hillfort. Traditions indicate a linkage between the supernatural ancestor shrines in the hillfort, the importance of shell valuables and the strengthening of chiefly authority through association with the supernatural, in a process of apical demotion (Aswani, 2000). Working between tradition and archaeology (Wylie, 1993) we can make linkages between the elements of the archaeological record, create a joint chronology and a more powerful narrative or theory of Roviana history.

The Roviana narrative describes late prehistory, and oral tradition touches only on the last dramatic sequence of events. In East Polynesia traditions may go back to initial settlement, but involve only a few or just one major societal transformation. In New Zealand, Anderson describes such an event.

> Whether or not the claims and encounters in the early history of terrestrial acquisition occurred precisely as they were described, the narratives indicate how the earliest terrestrial rights of major lineages were established in new lands. Within a few generations, the more usual means of territorial acquisition involved planned marriages, since the children of these brought access to the lands and resources of both parents. Some tribal narratives refer to fighting against earlier inhabitants – the first '*tangata whenua*' – but not as a major concern. Otherwise the process of population expansion and alliances continued peacefully for a number of generations after arrival. Then, quite quickly, circumstances seemed to have changed quite dramatically.
>
> *(Anderson, 2015, p. 98)*

Around 1500 CE traditions become more detailed and become conquest traditions concerning changing social relationships between hapū (related descent groups) and land. This has been described by Jones and Biggs (1995, p. 95) for Tainui in Waikato, and by Sissons (1988) for Ngapuhi in Northland. As Anderson notes one of the primary roles of tradition is to relate people to land and possessions both current and claimed (Anderson, 2015, p. 99). Sissons argues further that it is at this time that hapū known historically become named entities (Sissons, 1988, p. 202). It seems probable that this change, which is common to East Polynesia, reflects population growth such that the landscape is fully claimed or occupied, or at least the best land is occupied, after which we see growing competition. Sissons noted a correspondence between the change in tradition and the establishment of a fully defended fighting pā or fortification at Pouerua and discussed in Ngapuhi tradition. The development of the pā at Pouerua occurs in the early 1600s CE. Dating of pā construction indicates construction starts c.1550 CE (Schmidt, 1996) closely converging with changes in tradition. More generally these changes correlate with significant changes in the archaeological record described as a transition from the Archaic to the Classic period.

In Hawaii we see intensified competition at the same time, c.1550 CE (Kirch, 2010, p. 92). We also see a major transformation of social structure – the development of an Archaic state, divine kinship and a class system which severs the genealogical relationships of kinship. Patrick Kirch (2010) has recently made a masterful effort to bring together archaeology and the rich oral tradition of Hawaii, which he accepts is for the most part based on 'real' history (2010, p. 123).

Kirch (2010, pp. 77–82) describes bringing together the emic perspective of tradition with the etic approach of archaeology (see also Graves et al., 2011; Cachola-Abad, 2000; Cordy, 2000). He argues that the two lines of evidence are independent and, when mutually reinforcing, lend additional support to interpretations. They also provide different kinds of evidence. Oral tradition recounts 'births, deaths, wars, conquests, usurpations, marriages, and amorous affairs of the ruling ali'i and their kin' described in terms of personal motivations – a history grounded in individual human agency (Kirch, 2010, p. 78). This agency is subject to cultural structure as shown by repetitive patterns of behaviour in the context of similar social and economic conditions. Rupture of structure can occur however: 'from time to time some ali'i broke out of their cultural bonds to innovate entirely new structures. This is contingent, individual agency at work' (Kirch, 2010, p. 78). Understanding the long-term dynamics that underlie structural continuity and change requires the history of the longue durée provided by archaeology. This provides the ultimate drivers or constraints of economy, demography and environmental context, within which chiefs formulated their strategies and acted out their plans, and these in turn form proximate explanations of change.

Kirch employs tradition first to summarise the political histories of the different islands, noting periods when the transformation of social structure is evidenced. In the 16th century tradition indicates that the roles of the *ali'i nui* (great chiefs) were transformed and the 'Ancestral Polynesian socio-political system was sundered, and … the first manifestations of an archaic state emerged' at a time when archaeology indicates peak population, agricultural intensification and the construction of monumental architecture (Kirch, 2010, p. 103). Looking at the traditions for agency, Kirch (2010, p. 121) identifies a series of themes that emerge from close analysis, providing 'critical insight' into how chiefs become kings.

Beyond these (Kirch, 2010, p. 122) the traditions provide evidence for the shift of 'historical dynamism' over time to the islands of Hawai'i and Maui where the first large-scale political unifications occur. They also implicitly provide evidence for the expansion of elites over time and most probably the most recent traditions indicate the limits to growth of this state as rulers struggled to maintain control of the large island of Hawai'i, something not easily determined by archaeology.

Hawaiian traditions (Kirch, 2010, p. 176) indicate the start (around the late 16th century) of the major transformation of the ancient Polynesian cultural structures. This did not happen suddenly but over a period of time by chiefs employing five culturally specific strategies revealed through analysis of tradition. Without articulation with archaeology this history is simply an independent narrative, albeit a very rich one, which describes events and agency unknown(able) from archaeology. Direct connection with archaeology involves linkages between sites and figures identified in tradition, identification of changes which can be seen in the material record and creation of hypotheses which can be tested through archaeology. In many ways the relationship is much like that between reconstruction of cultural forms and meaning through linguistics and archaeology, where Kirch and Green (2001, pp. 42–44, 278) have argued triangulation of independent lines (Wylie, 1993) provides a more robust construction or interpretation of the past. In Hawaii sites and events such as the construction of large temples or irrigation systems can be linked to individuals in the traditions, providing evidence of transformation of religious practice or development of the means of production. Study of the frequency of events through time in tradition, such as the evidence for usurpation or warfare, can also be matched against the archaeology to look for concordance (Kirch, 2010, pp. 204–210; e.g. Cachola-Abad, 2000) and test materialist hypotheses. However it is the evidence of individual agency, often hypothesised to explain changing practices in archaeology (Joyce and Lopiparo, 2005) but rarely demonstrated, that oral tradition can uniquely provide. In Hawaii Kirch argues that without this we have a limited understanding of the development of this archaic state. 'there is no single "smoking gun" no universal "prime mover" or causal agent' (Kirch, 2010, p. 218).

I have focused on the use of tradition to examine the development of complexity in Hawaii however there is also considerable work on similar developments in Tonga (Burley, 1994; 1998; 1995) making use of the rich Tongan oral tradition. Comparison of the two sequences shows interesting similarities and differences. Of particular interest is the expansion of the Tongan chiefdom into the Tongan Maritime Empire (Burley, 1998). Traditions of Tongan influence and conquest, beginning shortly after the establishment of the genealogical chiefdom, are found from southern Island Melanesia throughout West Polynesia and archaeologists in those areas have regularly noted the coherence between tradition and the archaeological record (Sand, 1999; Clark et al., 2014).

Conclusion

Golson (1960, p. 380) did not completely rule out finding facts in tradition – but they were not archaeological facts and therefore hard to integrate into the scientific archaeological method and theory of 1960. Today we must join with David Burley and agree that: 'Few archaeologists – from McKern to the present – have ignored these types [traditional histories] of data when available. The task for future archaeologists is to view these data not as supplementary, but as just as integral to any interpretation as our excavated assemblages and features' (Burley, 1998, pp. 381–382). Today Pacific archaeologists are virtually unanimous in their agreement. This relates both to the growing body of oral tradition which is confirmed or supported by archaeology, affirming Golson's view that there is 'factual' evidence in Pacific tradition, and to the development of theory which leads us to the view that, without an understanding of agency, our explanations of cultural change ignore how people construct culture within material constraints. Agency is hard to monitor archaeologically, despite the rise of theories of 'materiality'. Oral tradition provides an insight into agency as recognised by the creators of the archaeological record, including both indigenous theories of agency and accounts of individual actions. This interaction of agency with material constraints is, however, both structured and historically contingent, for as Sahlins (2017) argues, although structure empowers agency in culturally specific ways it does not definitely determine the historical outcome which is contingent on the conjuncture of specific events. Understanding and making use of oral tradition requires understanding or consideration of the cultural logics or structure which empowers the recording and transmission of histories, and defines both the importance of events and the form in which they are recalled.

Archaeology can gain much from the use of tradition; yet doing so involves making use of indigenous histories whose creation and transmission may serve significantly different goals both in the past and present and great care must be taken in our reception and understanding of such compiled tradition. Just as we must treat archaeological materials with respect, so must we respect oral tradition and understand how our efforts may both preserve and alter it, given our distinctive interests and emphasis. In much of the world oral history is alive and working with those communities is a privilege. Use of oral tradition is one means by which archaeology can honour that privilege and form a mutually beneficial relationship with the descendants of the people whose remains we study.

Acknowledgements

I would like to thank Tim Thomas for inviting me to consider this fascinating topic. I would also like to acknowledge the almost thirty years of support offered to me by the people of the Solomon Islands who have taught me to appreciate the uses of oral tradition.

References

Adams, R., 1992. 'Good stories': the epistemological status of oral traditions on Tanna, Vanuatu. In: D. H. Rubinstein, ed. *Pacific History: Papers from the 8th Pacific History Association Conference*, Mangilao Guam: University of Guam Press and Micronesian Area Research Center Mangilao, pp. 433–437.

Allen, M. and Johnson, K., 1997. Tracking ancient patterns of interaction: recent geochemical studies in the southern Cook Islands. In: M. Weisler, ed., *Prehistoric Long-Distance Interaction in Oceania: An Interdisciplinary Approach*. Dunedin: New Zealand Archaeological Association, pp. 111–133.

Anderson, A., 1998. *The Welcome of Strangers: An Ethnohistory of Southern Maori AD 1650–1850*. Dunedin: University of Otago Press.

Anderson, A., 2006. Islands of exile: ideological motivation in maritime migration. *Journal of Island and Coastal Archaeology*, 1, pp. 33–47.

Anderson, A., 2008. Traditionalism, interaction, and long-distance seafaring in Polynesia. *Journal of Island and Coastal Archaeology*, 3(2), pp. 240–250.

Anderson, A., 2015. Te ao tawhito: the old world. In: A. Anderson, J. Binney and A. Harris, eds. *Tangata Whenua: A History*. Wellington: Bridget Williams Books, pp. 16–187.

Anderson, A., Binney, J. and Harris, A., eds. 2015. *Tangata Whenua: A History*. Wellington: Bridget Williams Books.

Aswani, S., 2000. Changing identities: the ethnohistory of Roviana predatory headhunting. *Journal of the Polynesian Society*, 109(1), pp. 39–70.

Aswani, S. and Sheppard, P., 2003. The archaeology and ethnohistory of exchange in precolonial and colonial Roviana: gifts, commodities and inalienable possessions. *Current Anthropology*, 44(suppl.), pp. S51–S78.

Bedford, S., Spriggs, M., Wilson, M. and Regenvanu, R., 1998. The Australian National University-National Museum of Vanuatu archaeology project: a preliminary report on the establishment of cultural sequences and rock art research. *Asian Perspectives*, 37(2), pp. 165–193.

Bellwood, P., 1978. *Man's Conquest of the Pacific*. Auckland: Collins.

Bellwood, P., 1996. Hierarchy, founder ideology and Austronesian expansion. In: J. Fox, and C. Sather, eds. *Origins, Ancestry and Alliance: Explorations in Austronesian Ethnography*. Canberra: Australian National University, pp. 19–42.

Best, S., Sheppard, P., Green, R. and Parker, R., 1992. Necromancing the stone: archaeologists and adzes in Samoa. *Journal of the Polynesian Society*, 101, pp. 45–85.

Blong, R., 1982. *The Time of Darkness: Local Legends nd Volcanic Reality in Papua New Guinea*. Canberra: Australian National University.

Burley, D., 1994. As a prescription to rule: the royal tomb of Mala'e Lahi and 19th-century Tongan kingship. *Antiquity*, 68(260), pp. 504–517.

Burley, D., 1995. Mata'uvave and 15th century Ha'apai. *Journal of Pacific History*, 30(2), pp. 154–172.

Burley, D., 1998. Tongan archaeology and the Tongan past, 2850-150 B.P. *Journal of World Prehistory*, 12(3), pp. 337–392.

Cachola-Abad, K., 1993. Evaluating the orthodox dual settlement model for the Hawaiian Islands: an analysis of artefact distribution and Hawaiian oral traditions. In: M. Graves, and R.C. Green, eds. *The Evolution and Organisation of Prehistoric Society in Polynesia*. New Zealand Archaeological Association Monograph, 19. Dunedin: New Zealand Archaeological Association, pp. 13–32.

Cachola-Abad, K., 2000. An analysis of Hawaiian oral traditions: descriptions and explanations of the evolution of Hawaiian socio-political complexity. PhD, Anthropology, University of Hawaii, Honolulu.

Campbell, I., 1982. The Tu'i Ha'atakalaua and the ancient constitution of Tonga. *Journal of Pacific History,* 17(4), pp. 178–194.

Campbell, M., 2002. History in prehistory: the oral traditions of the Rarotongan Land Court records. *Journal of Pacific History,* 37(2), pp. 221–238.

Clark, G., Burley, D. and Murray, T., 2008. Monumentality and the development of the Tongan maritime chiefdom. *Antiquity,* 82(318), pp. 994–1008.

Clark, G., Reepmeyer, C., Melekiola, N., Woodhead, J., Dickinson, W. and Martinsson-Wallin, H., 2014. Stone tools from the ancient Tongan state reveal prehistoric interaction centers in the Central Pacific. *Proceedings of the National Academy of Sciences,* 111(29), pp. 10491–10496.

Collerson, K. and Weisler, M., 2007. Stone adze compositions and the extent of ancient Polynesian voyaging and trade. *Science,* 317(5846), pp. 1907–1911.

Cordy, R., 2000. *Exalted Sits the Chief.* Honolulu, HI: Mutual Publishing Co.

Dening, G., 1962. The geographical knowledge of the Polynesians and the nature of inter-island contact. In: J. Golson, ed. *Polynesian Navigation: A Symposium on Andrew Sharp's Theory of Accidental Voyages.* Auckland: Reed, pp. 102–131.

Denoon, D. and Lacey, R., eds. 1981. *Oral Tradition in Melanesia.* Port Moresby: University of Papua New Guinea.

Duff, R., 1956. *The Moa-Hunter Period of Maori Culture.* 2nd ed. Wellington: Government Printer.

Emory, K., 1959. Origin of the Hawaiians. *Journal of the Polynesian Society,* 68(1), pp. 29–35.

Finney, B., 1991. Myth, experiment, and the reinvention of Polynesian voyaging. *American Anthropologist,* 93(2), pp. 383–404.

Firth, R., 1961. *History and Traditions of Tikopia.* Wellington: Polynesian Society.

Fox, J., 1995. Austronesian societies and their transformations. In: P. Bellwood, J. Fox and D. Tryon, eds. *The Austronesians: Historical and Comparative Perspectives.* Canberra: ANU Press, pp. 229–243.

Fox, J., 1996. Introduction. In: J. Fox and C. Sather, eds. *Origins, Ancestry and Alliance: Explorations in Austronesian Ethnography.* Canberra: ANU Press, pp. 1–17.

Fox, J., 1997. Genealogy and topogeny: towards an ethnography of Rotinese ritual place names. In: J. J. Fox, ed. *The Poetic Power of Place: Comparative Perspectives on Austronesian Ideas of Locality.* Canberra: ANU Press, pp. 89–114.

Fox, J., 2008. Installing the 'outsider' inside: the exploration of an epistemic Austronesian cultural theme and its social significance. *Indonesia and the Malay World,* 36(105), pp. 201–218.

Fox, J. and Sather, C., eds. 1996. *Origins, Ancestry and Alliance: Explorations in Austronesian Ethnography.* Canberra: ANU Press.

Fuentes, A. and Wiessner, P., 2016. Reintegrating anthropology from inside out: an introduction to Supplement 13. *Current Anthropology,* 57(S13), pp. S3–S12.

Furey, L., Ross-Sheppard, C. and Prickett, K., 2015. Obsidian from Macualey Island: a New Zealand connection. *Bulletin Auckland Museum,* 20: 511–518.

Garanger, J., 1972. *Archéologie des Novelles-Hébrides: contribution à la connaissance des îles du Centre.* ORSTOM, 30, Publications de la Société des Oceanistes. Paris: Musée de L'Homme.

Garanger, J., 1997. Oral traditions and archaeology: two cases from Vanuatu. In: R. Blench and M. Spriggs, eds. *Archaeology and Language I: Theoretical and Methodological Orientations.* London: Routledge, pp. 321–330.

Golson, J., 1960. Archaeology, tradition. and myth in New Zealand prehistory. *Journal of the Polynesian Society,* 69(4), pp. 380–402.

Golson, J., 1972. Foreword to the third edition. In: J. Golson, ed. *Polynesian Navigation: A Symposium on Andrew Sharp's Theory of Accidental Voyaging.* Auckland: Reed.

Graves, M. and Addison, D., 1995. The Polynesian settlement of the Hawaiian Archipelago: integrating models and methods in archaeological interpretation. *World Archaeology,* 26(3), pp. 380–399.

Graves, M., Cachola-Abad, K., and Ladefoged, T., 2011. The evolutionary ecology of Hawaiian political complexity; case studies from Maui and Hawai'i island. In: P.V. Kirch, ed. *Roots of Conflict: Soils, Agriculture, and Sociopolitical Complexity in Ancient Hawaii'i.* Santa Fe, NM: SAR Press, pp. 135–162.

Green, R., 1991. Near and Remote Oceania: disestablishing 'Melanesia' in culture history. In: A. Pawley, ed. *Man and a Half: Essays in Pacific Anthropology and Ethnobiology in Honour of Ralph Bulmer.* Auckland: The Polynesian Society, pp. 491–502.

Green, R., 2000. Trigger's holistic archaeology and Pacific culture history. In: M. Boyd, J. C. Erwin and M. Hendrickson, eds. *The Entangled Past: Integrating History and Archaeology.* Calgary: Archaeological Association of the University of Calgary, pp. 127–137.

Guiart, J., 1996. Archéologie et ethnologie. In: M. Julien, M. Orliac and C. Orliac, eds. *Mémoire de pierre, mémoire d'homme: Tradition et archéologie en Océanie, Hommage à José Garanger.* Paris: Publications de la Sorbonne, pp. 31–64.

Guiart, J., 2004. Retoka revisited and Roymata revised: a retort. *Journal of the Polynesian Society,* 113(4), pp. 377–382.

Gunson, N., 1993. Understanding Polynesian traditional history. *Journal of Pacific History,* 28(2), pp. 139–158.

Handy, E., 1923. *The Native Culture in the Marquesas,* vol. 9. Honolulu, HI: Bernice P. Bishop Museum Bulletin.

Hanson, A., 1989. The making of the Maori: culture invention and its logic. *American Anthropologist,* 91(4), pp. 890–902.

Irwin, G., 1992. *The Prehistoric Exploration and Colonisation of the Pacific.* Cambridge: Cambridge University Press.

Irwin, G. and Flay, R., 2015. Pacific colonisation and canoe performance: experiments in the science of sailing. *Journal of the Polynesian Society,* 124(4), pp. 419–443.

Ivens, W., 1927. *Melanesians of the South-east Solomons.* London: Kegan Paul.

Jones, P. and Biggs, B., 1995. *Nga iwi o Tainui: The Traditional History of the Tainui People.* Auckland: Auckland University Press.

Joyce, R. and Lopiparo, J., 2005. Postscript: doing agency in archaeology. *Journal of Archaeological Method and Theory,* 12(4), pp. 365–374.

Keesing, R., 1985. Conventional metaphors and anthropological metaphysics: the problematic of cultural translation. *Journal of Anthropological Research,* 41(2), pp. 201–217.

Kirch, P., 1990. Monumental architecture and power in Polynesia: a comparison of Tonga and Hawai'i. *World Archaeology,* 22(2), pp. 206–222.

Kirch, P., 1992. *Anahulu: The Anthropology of History in the Kingdom of Hawaii,* vol. 2, *The Archaeology of History.* Chicago, IL: University of Chicago Press.

Kirch, P., 1997. *The Lapita Peoples: Ancestors of the Oceanic World.* Cambridge: Blackwell.

Kirch, P., 2010. *How Chiefs Became Kings Divine Kingship and the Rise of Archaic States in Ancient Hawai'i.* Berkeley, CA: University of California Press.

Kirch, P. and Green, R., 2001. *Hawaiki, Ancestral Polynesia: An Essay in Historical Anthropology.* Cambridge: Cambridge University Press.

Leach, B.F., Anderson, A., Sutton, D., Bird, R., Duerden, P. and Clayton, E., 1986. Origin of prehistoric obsidian artefacts from the Chatham and Kermadec Islands. *New Zealand Journal of Archaeology,* 8: 143–170.

Levison, M., Ward, R. and Webb, J., 1972. The settlement of Polynesia: a report on a computer simulation. *Archaeology in Oceania*, 7(3), pp. 234–245.

Levison, M., Ward, R. and Webb, J., 1973. *The Settlement of Polynesia: A Computer Simulation*. Minneapolis, MN: University of Minnesota Press.

Lichtenberk, F., 1986. Leadership in Proto-Oceanic society: linguistic evidence. *Journal of the Polynesian Society*, 95: 341–356.

Lowe, D., McFadgen, B., Higham, T., Hogg, A., Froggatt, P. and Nairn, I., 1998. Radiocarbon age of the Kaharoa Tephra, a key marker for late-Holocene stratigraphy and archaeology in New Zealand. *Holocene*, 8(4), pp. 487–495.

Luders, D., 2001. Retoka revisited and Roimata revised. *Journal of the Polynesian Society*, 110(3), pp. 247–287.

Malo, D., 1951. *Hawaiian Antiquity*. Bernice P. Bishop Museum Special Publication, 2. Honolulu, HI: Bernice P. Bishop Museum.

Marck, J., 1996. The first-order anthropomorphic gods of Polynesia. *Journal of the Polynesian Society*, 105(2), pp. 217–258.

Marcus, G., 1989. Chieftainship. In: A. Howard and R. Borofsky, eds. *Developments in Polynesian Ethnology*. Honolulu, HI: University of Hawai'i Press.

Marshall, Y., 1987. Antiquity, form and function of terracing at Pouerua Pa. MA, Anthropology, University of Auckland.

Miller, D., 1980. Settlement and diversity in the Solomon Islands. *Man*, 15: 451–466.

Nagaoka, T., 1999. *Hope Pukerane*: a study of religious sites in Roviana, New Georgia, Solomon Islands. MA, Anthropology. University of Auckland.

Nicholas, H., 1892. Genealogies and historical notes from Rarotonga. Part I. *The Journal of the Polynesian Society*, 1(1), pp. 20–29.

Oliver, D., 1955. *A Solomon Island Society*. Cambridge, MA: Harvard University Press.

Parsonson, G., 1972. The settlement of Oceania: an examination of accidental voyage theory. In: J. Golson, ed. *Polynesian Navigation: A Symposium on Andrew Sharp's Theory of Accidental Voyages*. Wellington: A.H. & A.W. Reed.

Pawley, A., 1982. Rubbishman, commoner, big-man, chief? Evidence for hereditary chieftainship in Proto-Oceanic. In: J. Siikala, ed. *Oceanic Studies: Essays in Honour of Aarne A. Koskinen*. Helsinki: Finnish Anthropological Society, pp. 33–52.

Quintus, S. and Clark, J., 2016. Space and structure in Polynesia: instantiated spatial logic in American Sāmoa. *World Archaeology*, 48(3), pp. 395–410.

Rieth, T., Hunt, T., Lipo, C. and Wilmshurst, J., 2011. The 13th century Polynesian colonization of Hawai'i Island. *Journal of Archaeological Science*, 38(10), pp. 2740–2749.

Roe, D., 2000. Maritime, coastal and inland societies in Island Melanesia: the bush-saltwater divide in Solomon Islands and Vanuatu. In: S. O'Connor and P. Veth, eds. *East of Wallace's Line: Studies of Past and Present Maritime Cultures of the Indo-Pacific Region*. Rotterdam: A.A. Balkema, pp. 197–222.

Sahlins, M., 1983. Other times, other customs: the anthropology of history. *American Anthropologist*, 85(3), pp. 517–544.

Sahlins, M., 1985. *Islands of History*. Chicago, IL: University of Chicago Press.

Sahlins, M., 1992. *Anahulu: The Anthropology of History in the Kingdom of Hawaii*, vol. 1. *Historical Ethnography*. Chicago, IL: University of Chicago Press.

Sahlins, M., 1995. *How 'Natives' Think: About Captain Cook, For Example*. Chicago, IL: University of Chicago Press.

Sahlins, M., 2008. The stranger-king or elementary forms of the politics of life. *Indonesia and the Malay World*, 36(105), pp. 177–199.

Sahlins, M., 2017. Alterity and autochthony: Austronesian cosmographies of the marvellous. In: E. Gnecchi-Ruscone and A. Panini, eds. *Tides of Innovation in Oceania: Value, Materiality and Place*. Canberra: Australian National University, pp. 37–76.

Salmond, A., 1991. *Two Worlds: First Meetings between Maori and Europeans 1642–1772.* Auckland: Viking.

Sand, C., 1999. Empires maritimes préhistoriques dans le Pacifique: Ga'asialili et la mise en place d'une colonie tongienne à Uvea (Wallis, Polynésie occidentale). *Journal de la Société des Océanistes,* 108(1), pp. 103–124.

Sand, C., 2008. Prehistoric maritime empires in the Pacific: Ga'asialili ('Elili) and the establishment of a Tongan colony on 'Uvea (Wallis, Western Polynesia)'. In: A. Di Piazza, E. Pearthree and C. Sand, eds. *French Contributions to Pacific Archeology.* Noumea: Département Archéologie Direction des Affaires Culturelles et Coutumiètes de Nouvelle-Calédonie, pp. 73–105.

Schmidt, M., 1996. The commencement of pa construction in New Zealand prehistory. *Journal of the Polynesian Society,* 105(4), pp. 441–460.

Scott, M., 2007. *The Severed Snake: Matrilineages, Making Place, and a Melanesian Christianity in Southeast Solomon Islands.* Durham, NC: Carolina Academic Press.

Sharp, A., 1957. *Ancient Voyagers in the Pacific.* London: Penguin.

Sharp, A., 1961. Polynesian navigation to distant islands. *Journal of the Polynesian Society,* 70(2), pp. 219–226.

Sheppard, P. and Walter, R., 2013. Diversity and networked interdependence in the Western Solomons. In: G. Summerhayes and H. Buckley, eds. *Pacific Archaeology: Documenting the Past 50,000 Years, Papers from the 2011 Lapita Pacific Archaeology Conference.* Dunedin: University of Otago Studies in Archaeology, pp. 138–147.

Sheppard, P., Aswani, S., Walter, R. and Nagaoka, T., 2002. Cultural sediment: the nature of a cultural landscape in Roviana Lagoon. In: T. Ladgefoged and M. Graves, eds. *Pacific Landscapes: Archaeological Approaches,* Bearsville: Easter Island Foundation Press, pp. 37–61.

Sheppard, P., Chiu, S. and Walter, R., 2015. Re-dating Lapita movement into Remote Oceania. *Journal of Pacific Archaeology,* 6(1), pp. 26–36.

Sheppard, P., Walter, R. and Aswani, S., 2004. Oral tradition and the creation of late prehistory in Roviana Lagoon, Solomon Islands. *Records of the Australian Museum,* Suppl. 29: 123–132.

Sheppard, P., Walter, R. and Roga, K., 2010. Friends, relatives, and enemies: the archaeology and history of interaction among Austronesian and NAN speakers in the Western Solomons. In: J. Bowden, N. Himmelmann and M. Ross, eds. *A Journey through Austronesian and Papuan Linguistic and Cultural Space: Papers in Honour of Andrew Pawley.* Canberra: Pacific Linguistics Press, pp. 95–112.

Shore, B., 1989. Mana and tapu. In: A. Howard and R. Borofsky, eds. *Developmenst in Polynesian Ethnology.* Honolulu, HI: University of Hawaii Press.

Simmons, D., 1976. *The Great New Zealand Myth: A Study of the Discovery and Origin Traditions of the Maori.* Wellington: A.W. Reed.

Sissons, J., 1988. Rethinking tribal origins. *Journal of the Polynesian Society,* 97(2), pp. 199–204.

Sissons, J., 2005. *First Peoples: Indigenous Cultures and their Futures.* London: Reaktion Books.

Smith, S., 1910. *History and Traditions of the Maoris of the West Coast, North Island of New Zealand, Prior to 1840,* vol. 1. New Plymouth: Memoirs of the Polynesian Society.

Sorrenson, M., 1979. *Maori Origins and Migrations: The Genesis of Some Pakeha Myths and Legends.* Auckland: Auckland University Press.

Spriggs, M., 1997. *The Island Melanesians: The Peoples of South-East Asia and the Pacific.* Oxford: Blackwell Publishers.

Suggs, R., 1960. Historical traditions and archeology in Polynesia. *American Anthropologist,* 62(5), pp. 764–773.

Thomas, T., 2009. Topogenic forms in New Georgia, Solomon Islands. *Sites: A Journal of Social Anthropology and Cultural Studies,* 6(2): 92–118.

Thornton, I., 2001. Colonization of an island volcano, Long Island, Papua New Guinea, and an emergent island, Motmot, in its caldera lake. *Journal of Biogeography,* 28(11–12), pp. 1299–1310.

Trigger, B., 1989. *A History of Archaeological Thought.* Cambridge: Cambridge University Press.

Trigger, B., 1991. Distinguished lecture in archeology: constraint and freedom – a new synthesis for archeological explanation. *American Anthropologist,* 93(3), pp. 551–569.

Turner, G., 1983. *Samoa, a Hundred Years Ago and Long Before: Together with Notes on the Cults and Customs of Twenty-Three Other Islands in the Pacific.* Papakura: R. McMillan.

Valentin, F., Spriggs, M., Bedford, S. and Buckley, H., 2011. Vanuatu mortuary practices over three millennia: Lapita to the early European contact period. *Journal of Pacific Archaeology,* 2(2), pp. 49–65.

Vansina, J., 1985. *Oral Tradition as History.* Madison, WI: University of Madison Press.

Walter, R. and Sheppard, P., 1996. The Ngati Tiare adze cache: further evidence of prehistoric contact between West Polynesia and the Southern Cook Islands. *Archaeology in Oceania,* 31: 33–39.

Walter, R., Buckley, H., Jacomb, C. and Matisoo-Smith, E., 2017. Mass migration and the Polynesian settlement of New Zealand. *Journal of World Prehistory,* 30(4), pp. 351–376.

Walter, R. and Reilly, M., 2018. Ngā Hekenga Waka: migration and early settlement. In: M. Reilly, S. Duncan, G. Leoni and L. Paterson, eds. *Te Koparapara: An Introduction to the Maori World.* Auckland: Auckland University Press, pp. 65–85.

Weisler, M., ed. 1997. *Prehistoric Long-Distance Interaction in Oceania: An Interdisciplinary Approach.* Auckland: New Zealand Archaeological Association.

Weisler, M., Bolhar, R., Ma, J., St Pierre, E., Sheppard, P., Walter, R., Feng, Y., Zhao, J. and Kirch, P., 2016. Cook Island artifact geochemistry demonstrates spatial and temporal extent of pre-European interarchipelago voyaging in East Polynesia. *Proceedings of the National Academy of Sciences,* 113(29), pp. 8150–8155.

Williams, T., 1982 [1852]. *Fiji and the Fijians: The Islands and their Inhabitants,* vol 1. Suva: Suva Musuem.

Wilmshurst, J., Hunt, T., Lipo, C. and Anderson, A., 2011. High-precision radiocarbon dating shows recent and rapid initial human colonization of East Polynesia. *Proceedings of the National Academy of Sciences,* 108(5), pp. 1815–1820.

Wylie, A., 1993. A proliferation of archaeologies: beyond objectivism and relativism. In: N. Yoffee and A. Sherratt, eds. *Archaeological Theory: Who Sets the Agenda?* Cambridge: Cambridge University Press, pp. 20–26.

14

TAKING INDIGENOUS THEORY SERIOUSLY

Whakapapa and chevron pendants

Yvonne Marshall

At dawn on the morning of 10 September 1984 a group of Māori elders flanked by United States and New Zealand dignitaries assembled on the front steps of the New York Metropolitan Museum of Art. Bleary-eyed but curious onlookers watched as the Māori elders proceeded slowly up the stairs calling to their *tūpuna*, their ancestors, in *kōrero* and *waiata*, traditional chants and songs. The elders had travelled to New York to facilitate the journey of 174 treasured Māori objects or *taonga* from their resting places in New Zealand museums as part of a touring exhibition known as Te Māori. Crucially, these objects 'were selected according to their importance in Māori eyes' (Maihi, 2012) and they travelled not as objects of art, nor as archaeological objects, but as *he taonga tuku iho*, highly prized objects or treasures handed down from Māori *tūpuna* (Mead, 1984a, p. 21).

As *taonga*, the Te Māori objects did not – could not – travel alone. They were accompanied by songs, stories, texts, representatives of their living custodians including Māori elders, curatorial staff from New Zealand Museums and *kaiārahi*, Māori gallery guides who helped interpret the objects to the 200,000 New York visitors who came to see them (McCarthy, 2007; 2011). A *taonga* is not then simply an object, an artefact or piece of art. It is a cultural treasure composed of the object itself and associated songs, stories, rituals, performances, histories. In Sidney Meads's (1984b, p. 20) phrase, a *taonga* comes 'clothed in' or 'covered with' words. Through manufacture and social engagement 'more and more words' are added, so that 'over time an object becomes invested with interesting talk' (Mead, 1984b, p. 21). This talk is integral to the object, its meaning, the persons whose lives are woven with it, and thereby its *whakapapa*, genealogy.

Among the Te Māori *taonga* were three of the approximately eighteen known *rei niho*, pendants with chevron designs carved from whale ivory (Fig. 14.1). These were among the oldest, most powerful, objects in the exhibition; three of only twenty-six objects chosen to showcase *Te Tipunga*, the time of growth in Māori art,

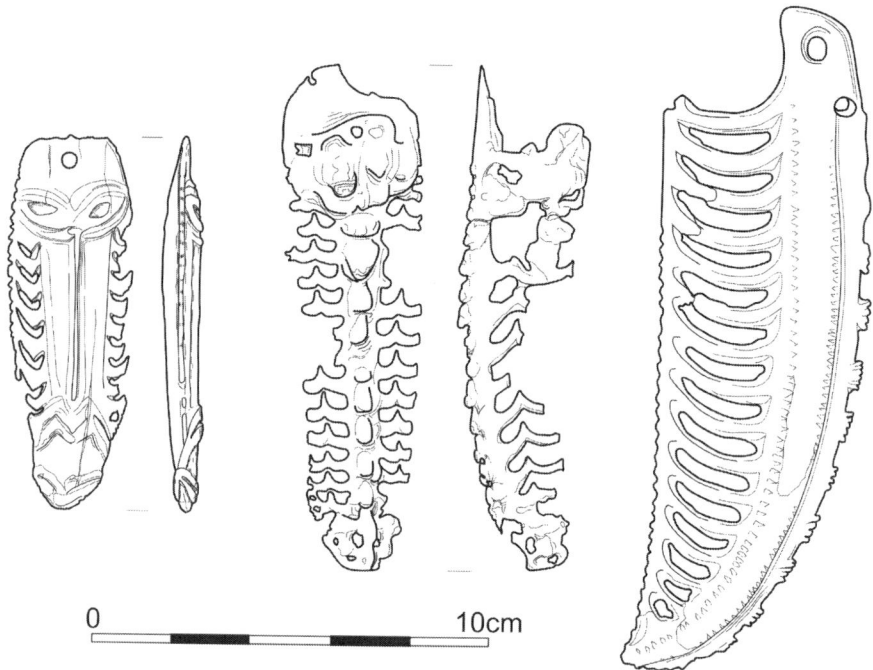

FIGURE 14.1 The three chevron pendants selected for the Te Maori Exhibition (Mead, 1984). From the left they are numbers 6, 1 and 15 in Table 14.1.

Source: Drawing by Penny Copeland.

approximately 1200–1500 CE (Mead, 1984c, p. 73). None of these pendants have been passed directly down to their present custodians in an unbroken line from the ancestors who created them. This creates uncertainty 'for who can possibly know what the tohunga [priest] of the early period said, what spells he recited, what curses he may have placed on certain items' (Mead, 1984b, p. 23) – in short, what talk these pendants might hold and what *whakapapa* they might weave.

The Te Māori exhibition was a watershed event in the promotion and resurgence of Māori pride and identity (McCarthy, 2011, p. 59). It was also a watershed moment in emerging archaeological and wider heritage practices of engaging 'worlds otherwise', and of taking indigenous theory seriously (Alberti and Marshall, 2009; Alberti et al., 2011; Marshall and Alberti, 2014). The visitors who flocked to the New York exhibition were invited by Māori into a world which was 'otherwise' to anything they had previously known or imagined (Roberts, 2013). Te Māori extended a serious invitation to engage an ontological other. Dismissal of the other as merely 'mistaken epistemologies' was refused (cf. Alberti and Marshall, 2009, p. 345).

In this chapter I have three objectives. First, I will show how taking indigenous theory seriously can enhance and expand our understanding of archaeological objects and potentially archaeology more generally. Secondly, to do this I explore and employ the Māori concept of *whakapapa*, a concept both superficially similar to, yet fundamentally different from, the genealogical and evolutionary concepts so pervasive in archaeological thinking. Finally, using the concept of *whakapapa* I explore the eighteen known *rei niho*, chevron pendants.

In previous papers I have developed ideas based in Western feminist and ontological theories (Marshall and Alberti, 2014; Alberti et al., 2011; Marshall, 2000; 2008a, b; 2013). Like others (Bell, 2017), I have found Western theories sometimes resonate in unexpected ways with indigenous theories and have responded by tentatively drawing on *whakapapa* to think about the Māori chevron pendants (Marshall and Alberti, 2014; Lyons and Marshall, 2014). But in this previous work indigenous theory remained secondary to Western theories. In this chapter my aim is to step up; to take *whakapapa* seriously as the central conceptual tool in framing my argument.

Whakapapa

Makere Rika-Heke (2010) and Gerard O'Regan (2010) open their accounts of being and becoming indigenous archaeologists with a *whakapapa*, a short Māori oration which sets out in personally selected terms who they are and where they belong. As Rika-Heke (2010, p. 268) explains, 'In any given setting, Maoris are expected to recite their *whakapapa* either in short or long form, so as to place themselves in our world and amongst the people. Not to do so is the utmost form of disrespect.' This is because for Māori it is not possible for a person to speak until they have made themselves known. A voice is always embodied in that it speaks from somewhere in particular. *Whakapapa* is then 'a way of knowing, a way of locating a person or a thing in time and space' (Roberts et al., 2004, p. 4). 'Hence for something to exist and be known, it must have a whakapapa: put another way, in order to "know" about a thing (or a person) one must know its whakapapa' (Roberts, 2010).

The concept of *whakapapa* is commonly translated into English as genealogy (Mahuika, 2019). While *whakapapa* does encompass some of the ideas that Europeans consider genealogy, such as drawing family trees, laying claim to ancestors and the construction of family histories from kin connections, it is much more than this. 'In its totality, Māori use of whakapapa and narrative creates a "metaphysical gestalt" or whole, integrated pattern, for the oral communication of knowledge' (Patu Hohepa quoted in Roberts et al., 2004, p. 1). For Māori, *whakapapa* is the backbone of history, a skeleton around which persons, families (*whanau*) and tribal groups (*hapu* and *iwi*) weave and present themselves as social entities (Binney and Chaplin, 1986, p. 1; Mahuika, 2019; Roberts, 2006). *Whakapapa* in its most complete sense encompasses talk, stories, places, landscapes, animals, objects and houses, as well as people both living and dead. It encompasses both blood and culture but is restricted to neither. It draws out political, economic, spiritual, religious and family histories. When presenting a *whakapapa,* a person or group may be said to draw their *whakapapa* around them, as one draws on a garment such as a kiwi feather cloak. In the process of drawing out and wrapping in *whakapapa* a person creates themselves as a socially appropriate, recognisable person within a specific delineated group.

Although *whakapapa* is embedded in genealogy and kinship, when practiced it operates quite differently to Western genealogical method (see also Ingold, 2000; 2007; 2011). Unlike the formally structured ordering of persons in Western genealogies, *whakapapa* is dynamic and relational, 'a cosmological system for reckoning degree of similarity and difference, determining appropriate behaviour, and manipulating existing and potential relationships to achieve desired effects' (Henare, 2007, p. 57). In any *whakapapa* each strand is formed in response to others; no strand can be understood except in relation to others. Consequently, *whakapapa* are not essentialist schemas that determine who a person is or their membership of a group. They do not fix identities. *Whakapapa* frame possibilities for who a person or group might be, who and what they might consist of, and what gives them their place in the world, a place in which they can stand and legitimately be, a place from which they can speak, a *tūrangawaewae*. They set out differences and commonalities in contingent, positioned, rather than categorical, terms. They are contextually constitutive; produced in social action not in advance of it. As a result, each rendition of *whakapapa* speaks to the requirements and desired outcomes of the specific persons, context and situation in which it is presented.

A single *whakapapa* may draw on many forms of relating (Roberts et al., 2004, pp. 18–19). In *whakapapa* 'the emphasis is on identification of relationships, but these are based on spatial and temporal associations (which may include both inanimate and animate things) as well as morphological resemblances' (Roberts et al., 2004, p. 20). While the content of a Western genealogical relationship is understood to precede our knowledge of it, *whakapapa* relationships cannot be known in advance. The word *whakapapa* brings together 'papa', meaning ground, foundation and the very earth itself, with 'whaka' meaning becoming. 'Therefore whakapapa can be thought of as "creating a foundation"' (Hudson et al., 2007, p. 44). Used as a verb *whakapapa* means to lay flat, to lay out in proper order or to place in layers (Roberts, 2006). Used as a noun, *whakapapa* names the outcome of this laying out, layering and ordering. An orator, carver or weaver creates a *whakapapa* in the process of revealing it through the performance of words, actions, art or other media. Neither relations nor *whakapapa* precede this process. They emerge together.

To draw out more clearly the incompatibilities of Western notions of genealogy with Māori *whakapapa*, it is helpful to consider the imagery each employs. Western genealogy is conceptualised as a tree, literally a family tree, with a thick, self-supporting, central trunk from which many strong, then increasingly fine branches diverge and spread. The entire edifice is rigid, self-supporting and of singular form. The tree is a metaphor of increasing differentiation and increasing distance from a central defining trunk. The rigidity of the tree structure stems from the use of a single criterion to define similarity and difference, for example blood, genetics or DNA. Only one criterion for relating is permitted for any tree and it must be specified in advance of drawing a tree. This image of the family tree is today largely synonymous with the concept of evolution as understood through genetics.

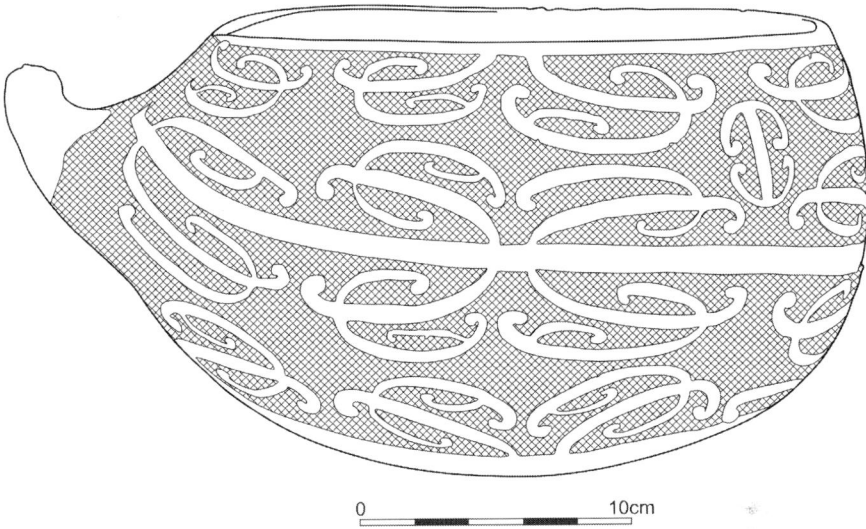

FIGURE 14.2 Gourd or *hue* decorated with *kowhaiwhai* style designs. The background fill in the illustration has been simplified to highlight the formline or *manawa* lines. Collection of the British Museum (Starzecka et al., 2010, p. 42, pl. 52, no. 187).

Source: Drawing by Penny Copeland.

The gourd plant is a common image for *whakapapa* (Fig. 14.2). The gourd is a vine with a strong central stem from which numerous branching tendrils spread out. It resonates closely with Ingold's (2007, pp. 117–118) imagery of the wayfarer's interlaced trails weaving a braid of life, and with Deleuze and Guattari's (1988, p. 5) concept of the rhizome. Unlike the free-standing, tidily diverging tree, the tendrils of a gourd coil back around themselves, knitting up a mass of interconnecting branchings in which main stems mesh with and become indistinguishable from minor ones. The gourd trails along and over the ground, not under the ground like a rhizome, growing up, and over any surface or structure, thus taking shape and direction from its environment. Significance paths are not self-evident in the manner implied by the branching of a tree, rather they emerge from selection and emphasis in telling. In performance, whether narration, carving, weaving or some other forum, *whakapapa* 'describes the context and brings into focus the most relevant of the myriad of layers of relationships that exist' (Hudson et al., 2007, p. 44; see also Roberts et al., 2004).

These features give *whakapapa* a flexible, pragmatic character, a point made explicit in the *whakapapa* of non-human entities (Roberts, 2013; Roberts et al., 2004). For example, the *whakapapa* of kumara, the Māori sweet potato (*Ipomea batatas*), describes the transgressions of the god Rongo-maui who steals the plant from his elder kin, gives it to humans and instructs them to cook it to remove its celestial power (*tapu*). So Rongo-maui 'flouts the rules and engages in disrespectful conduct' by stealing the kumara tubers, then adds insult to injury by cooking the tubers. These transgressive acts 'invite a reciprocal response in order to restore balance' (*utu*). 'However, although Rongo-maui's wrong-doing does not go completely unpunished [the gods send plagues of caterpillars to eat the kumara grown by humans] it could be argued that the eventual benefits (a valuable new food crop) outweigh both the risk and the subsequent penalty' (Roberts et al., 2004, p. 21). It is precisely this weighing of risk against the need to be cautious, of the imperative to respect established social customs and practices while remaining open to new needs and changing circumstances that makes *whakapapa* powerful as theory.

Roberts et al. (2004) highlight four significant features in their discussion of *whakapapa* of the non-human world. First, *whakapapa* of all plants and creatures is tribe specific. There is no generally agreed cross-tribal master lineage for either specific plants or plants in general. So, for example, those tribes who lived in the colder south outside the range of the tropical kumara might offer less detailed *whakapapa* for kumara than tribes in the north because their engagement with this plant is more distant and of less economic importance. Secondly, relations defined in a *whakapapa* are located in diverse of forms of connectedness, including place, event, utility to humans, morphology and stars. As a result, a kumara lineage for example, may draw in a wide variety of animals, plants and inanimate entities (Roberts et al., 2004, pp. 10, 20, 23). Thirdly, all organisms may be part of multiple 'realms' and therefore multiple lineages. There is never one definitive line of descent or fixed set of relations. Fourth and finally, everything has *whakapapa,* and whether object, plant, human or some other entity, all require narrative explanation. Lineage diagrams are only a starting point, the backbone, but the flesh of *whakapapa* lies in its covering talk. The narrative is where meaning is drawn out and understanding is established.

Whakapapa-informed approaches have been employed by Māori and non-Māori researchers working in diverse fields. They have been used to evaluate Māori positions with respect to Genetically Modified Organisms (Roberts et al., 2004); as a foundation to guide culturally sensitive genetic research (Hudson et al., 2007); to provide a framework for understanding the epidemiology of tuberculosis in the Pacific; to develop New Zealand immigration policy (Park et al., 2011); and to develop a model for understanding how oral societies make sense of their worlds through 'mind-maps' articulated in 'performance cartography' (Roberts, 2010). The foundation for these projects is Roberts et al., (2004) who makes the case that *whakapapa* constitutes a mental construct – a mind-map (Roberts, 2010). *Whakapapa* is a way of perceiving and ordering the world, as well as a way of being in that ordered world. It is both epistemology and ontology; a way of seeing and knowing (Roberts, 2013; Roberts et al., 2004, p. 4), a way of making the world known (Roberts et al., 2004, p. 7), and a basis for making decisions for living in that world.

The capacities of *whakapapa* that draw me to use it for archaeological analysis are similar to those highlighted by these researchers – interpretative openness, valuing multiple forms of relating and the contextualising of interpretation in specificities. There is also a desire to hold onto ambiguity and thereby highlight complexity, something that is always an issue when dealing with fragmentary archaeological materials (Gero, 2007; 2015). Each of these qualities has ethical, even moral, implications and these are central to the researchers' choice, including my own, to use *whakapapa* as an analytical tool (Park et al., 2011; Roberts, 2013, p. 97; Roberts et al., 2004). The chevron pendants are, however, a different kind of subject to those discussed so far in the sense that they are themselves, as Mead (1984b) emphasised, materialised *whakapapa*. In addition, each pendant has *whakapapa*, and the pendants as a group have *whakapapa* much as a person has personal, family (*whānau*) and tribal (*hapū* and *iwi*) *whakapapa* (Mahuika, 2019; Roberts, 2006).

This is more immediately evident for contemporary examples. Brian Flintoff is a carver of *kura koiwi*, bone treasures, many of which can be understood as materialised *whakapapa*. One of Flintoff's carvings, Te Puoro Hou, resides in the British Museum (Starzecka et al., 2010, p. 143). From even a cursory glance it is evident that Te Puoro Hou is related to the Okains Bay pendant (Fig. 14.3). But Te

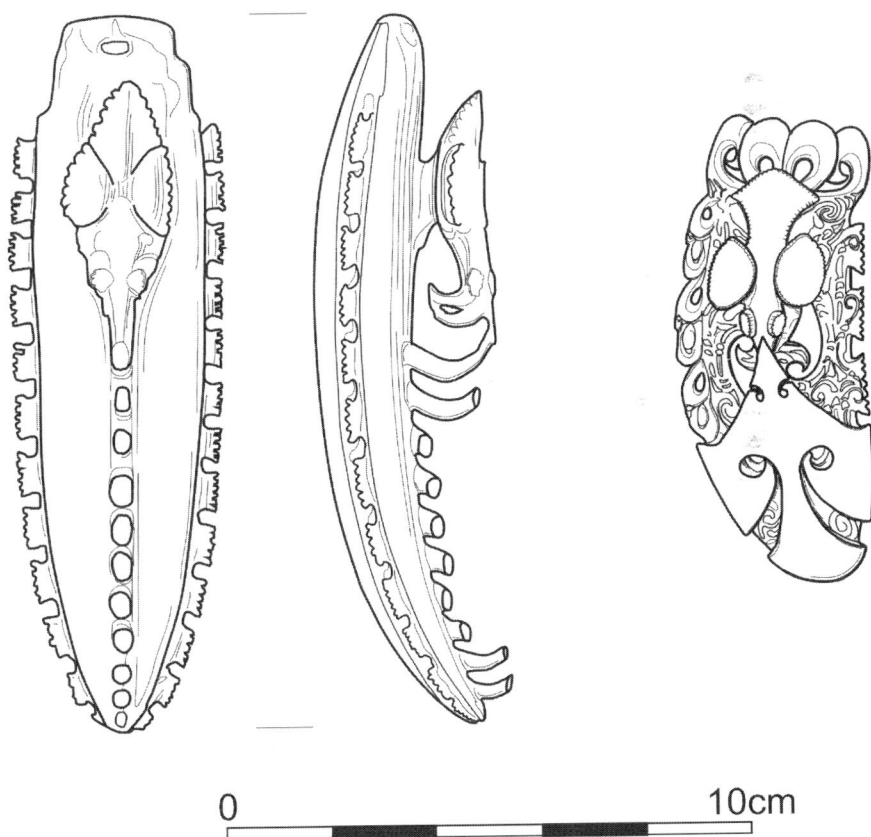

0   10cm

FIGURE 14.3 An old and new bird design chevron pendant. *Left:* the Okains Bay pendant, no. 7 in the assemblage. *Right:* contemporary pendant with a design including two stylised birds, carved by Brian Flintoff in 1994. Collection of the British Museum (Starzecka et al., 2010, p. 143, pl. 200, no. 2324).

Source: Drawing by Penny Copeland.

Puoro Hou is neither copy nor variation even though it draws from and speaks to the Okains Bay pendant. The upper bird and the chevrons along one side are carved in the ancient style of the Okains Bay pendant, they are *whakapapa* of words, while the lower bird and opposite side are carved in contemporary forms, *whakapapa* of tunes (Starzscka et al., 2010, p. 143). Te Puoro Hou, like the ancient pendants, holds onto ambiguity – could the lower bird be Kokako (Starzscka et al., 2010, p. 143) or is it a giant sea eagle (Flintoff (2011, pp. 64–65)? Perhaps neither, or both?

On one occasion Flintoff was given an especially large whale tooth and commissioned to carve 'a presentation pair of pendants' for Sir Tipene O'Regan and his close friend Bill Solomon, founder of Whalewatch Kaikoura (Flintoff, 2011, p. 77). Like the ancient chevron pendants and inspired by the paired Aniseed pendants (Fig. 14.4), Flintoff's pendants would be weavings of people. They would be *Taonga kōrero*, 'a personal pendant that tells a story' (Flintoff, 2011, p. 120). The pendants would gather, bundle and wrap the stories of the two men, their ancestry, their persons, their friendship (Flintoff, 2011, pp.6–7, 120–2). In this chapter my focus is on drawing out *whakapapa* of ancient chevron pendants as specific entities and as a group, rather than on the ways they materialise *whakapapa*.

What is a *rei niho* or a chevron pendant? Of boundaries, ambiguities and complexities

Archaeologists conventionally start artefact analyses by defining an assemblage. The usual procedure is to classify objects according to selected criteria (Bowker and Star, 2000). To create my archaeological assemblage of eighteen *rei niho* I have drawn together all the objects I know of that meet three defining criteria: manufactured from whale ivory (usually sperm whale), a design that includes chevron motifs in some form and the presence of at least one suspension hole. Importantly, these holes show the object was once attached to a cord, allowing it to be hung on the body, presumably around the neck. Such cords were commonly made of *muka*, fine flax fibre and possibly human hair (Lander, 2012). My three criteria create the chevron pendant as an artefact type.

Beginning with Skinner (1934), artefacts of this type have been referred to as chevron amulets, but I will follow Prickett (1999) and use the more neutral term pendant to avoid any Western overtones implying protective charm or magic. The group of objects meeting these three criteria forms an archaeological assemblage, a set of objects united by their possession of common elements or characteristics and comprising a bounded group marked off and set apart from objects which do not meet the defining criteria. Of these eighteen, eleven retain the original symmetrical form of the whale tooth (Skinner, 1934). These are referred to as tongue-shaped. The other seven are of asymmetrical form, made by splitting the whale tooth and opening it out to create paired pendants (Table 14.1; Fig. 14.4).

Archaeologists define assemblages of objects in order to address questions such as age and origins, or commonalities of form or function. This has certainly been the case for previous studies of Māori chevron pendants. The questions asked include the following. What other objects share similar elements of style? How are the

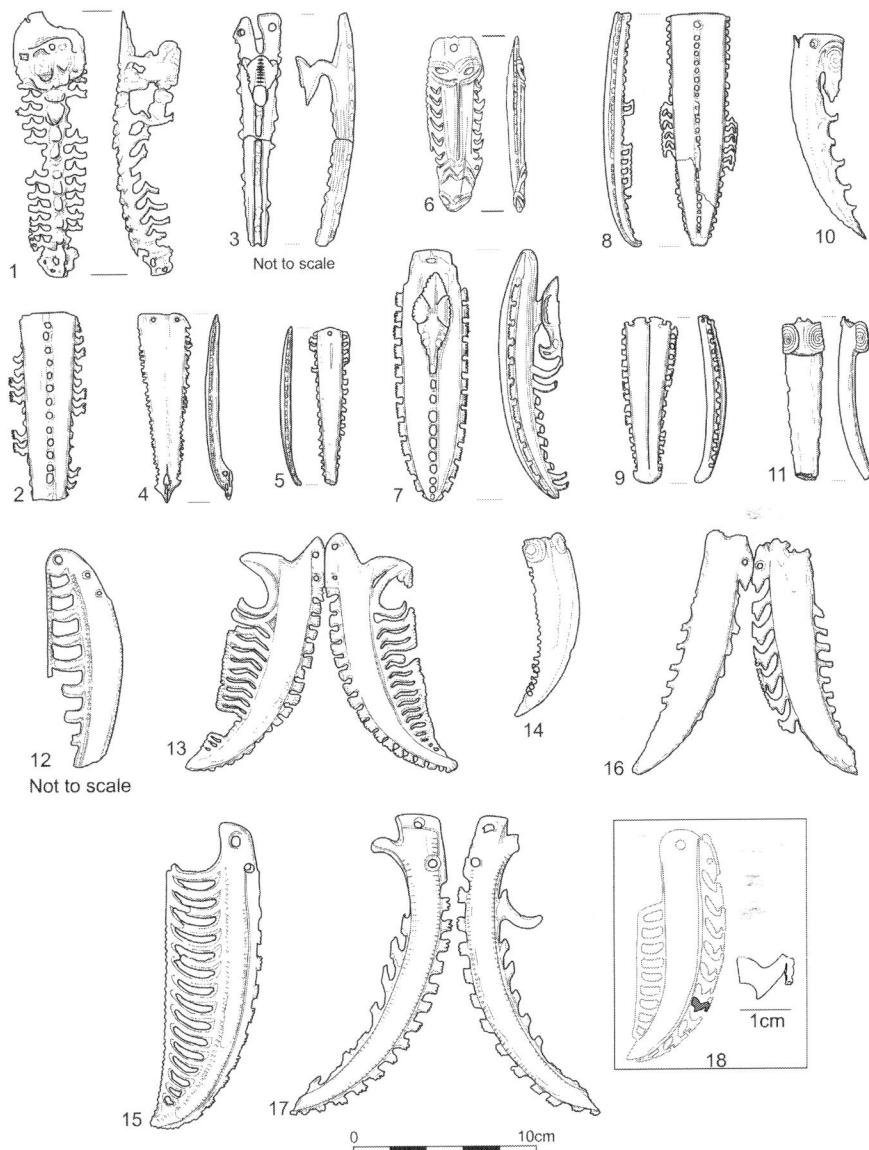

FIGURE 14.4 The selected assemblage of eighteen chevron pendants. Details in Table 14.1. Reported in Arvidson Smith (1986); Jacomb, (2012); Skinner, (1974); Walter et al. (2018).

Source: Drawing by Penny Copeland.

TABLE 14.1 The selected assemblage of eighteen chevron pendants, illustrated in Figure 14.4

No.	Length (cm)	Context	Name	Island	Type	Features	References
1	14.6	beach	Whangamumu, Northland	North	Tongue	Vertebrae chevrons; 2 figures; bird	Arvidson Smith 1986; Skinner 1974; 1934; 1943–4
2	11.3	Cave burial	Mercury Bay, Coromandel	North	Tongue		Arvidson Smith 1986; Skinner 1974
3	?	?	Mercury Bay Museum	North	Tongue	Possible bird	Jacomb 2012
4	11.1	Beach burial	Otoroa, Horowhenua	North	Tongue	bird	Arvidson Smith 1986; Skinner 1974
5	8.7	Beach burial	Lake Grassmere, Nelson	South	Tongue		Arvidson Smith 1986; Skinner 1974
6	9.7	Cave burial	Little Okains Bay, Banks Peninsula	South	Tongue	Two faces	Arvidson Smith 1986; Duff 1977
7	13.8	Cave burial	Okains Bay Bird, Banks Peninsula	South	Tongue	bird	Arvidson Smith 1986; Skinner 1974
8	12.9	beach	Shag River Mouth, Otago	South	Tongue		Arvidson Smith 1986; Skinner 1974
9	9.2	Beach burial	Hooper's Inlet, Otago Peninsula	South	Tongue		Arvidson Smith 1986; Skinner 1974
10	11.3	Cave burial	Whare Creek, Outram, Otago	South	Tongue	Spiral	Arvidson Smith 1986; Skinner 1974
11	9.03	beach	Chew Tobacco Bay	Stewart	Tongue	Spiral	Arvidson Smith 1986; Skinner 1974

No.	Length	Context	Location	Island	Paired	Survival	References
12	?	Cave burial	Rakautara Kaikoura	South	paired	Both found Only a sketch survives	Arvidson Smith 1986; Skinner 1974
13	13.15	unclear	Aniseed, Kaikoura	South	paired	Both survive	Arvidson Smith 1986; Skinner 1974
14	10.75	cave	Goat Cave, Banks Peninsula	South	Paired? No median ridge	One found Spiral	Arvidson Smith 1986; Skinner 1974; Duff 1977
15	16.8	beach	Little Papanui, Otago Peninsula	South	paired	One found	Arvidson Smith 1986; Skinner 1974; Skinner 1960
16	13.4	Beach burial	Wickliffe Bay, Otago Peninsula	South	paired	Both survive	Arvidson Smith 1986; Skinner 1974
17	?16.6/16.1	cave	Green Island, Otago	South	paired	Both survive	Arvidson Smith 1986; Skinner 1974
18	1.2	midden	Kahukura	South	?	Limb fragment	Walter et al 2018:29

Items listed from north to south within the categories of 'tongue' and 'paired' forms. All length measurements from Arvidson Smith (1986) except pendant 18. No measurements are available for pendants 3 and 12.

pendants distributed in time and space? What does this distribution suggest with respect to their age and origins? These questions have directed academic enquiries into chevron pendants (Arvidson Smith, 1986; Hamilton, 1901; Duff, 1977; Mead, 1975; 1986, pp. 146–155; Prickett, 1999; Skinner, 1934; 1943; 1974). In archaeological accounts the selected attributes are understood to be intrinsic to the objects. Both individual artefacts and the collective assemblage are cut off and held apart, they are bounded by their proscribed similarity and difference from other objects. The critical point is that the definition of the artefact and assemblage, the point of analytical departure, is independent of the analytical contexts in which they will subsequently be examined. Both artefacts and assemblage are 'objectively' defined and apprehended in advance of further analysis and contextual exploration (Marshall, 2013; Marshall and Alberti, 2014). Because they are pre-determined they cannot be subjectively engaged within the analytical process. The aim is to place the object of study, in this case chevron pendants, within a temporally calibrated, absolute sequence of change – an evolutionary or historical timeline, and to distinguish this sequence of change from confounding patterns of regional differentiation. In short, the analytical purpose is to produce a genealogical tree.

In taking a *whakapapa* approach, my assemblage of eighteen chevron pendants exists only within the terms I have set out. The objects I draw together, and the criteria of similarity on which the assemblage is based are of my choosing; they are designed to facilitate my archaeological project. The assemblage emerges in response to specific archaeological objectives and questions. My point is not that this procedure is wrong or inappropriate but that it is particular to me and my chosen project and speaks specifically to my chosen questions. The method employs selected criteria to produce the assemblage; but neither the assemblage as a whole nor the individual pendants that comprise it are independent of that method – they are a contingent set of objects brought together with a specific archaeological purpose in mind and they do not transcend that purpose and project. There is no essential character to an object which necessarily makes it a chevron pendant, and therefore no fixed boundary enclosing what is, from what is not, a chevron pendant. This conceptual difference is comparable to a distinction drawn by Peter Wilson (1989) between open and closed living spaces. Open living is conducted in relation to a central focus whereas closed living is conducted within formally bounded spaces such houses with walls. Open living has a centre whereas closed living has an edge or boundary. Similarly, while a conventional classification creates a circumscribed assemblage defined by its boundaries, a *whakapapa* assemblage takes its shape from a defined centre or focus.

The eighteen pendants have many characteristics beyond the three defining them. Some of these characteristics are unique, some are shared with others (but not all) in the assemblage, and all share characteristics with objects outside of the assemblage. There is a wide range of objects which meet some of the criteria but not others. With only a slight relaxing of any one of my three criteria – a different material, notches rather than chevrons, no suspension hole – the twelve objects listed in Table 14.2 and shown in Fig. 14.5 are drawn into my assemblage. With

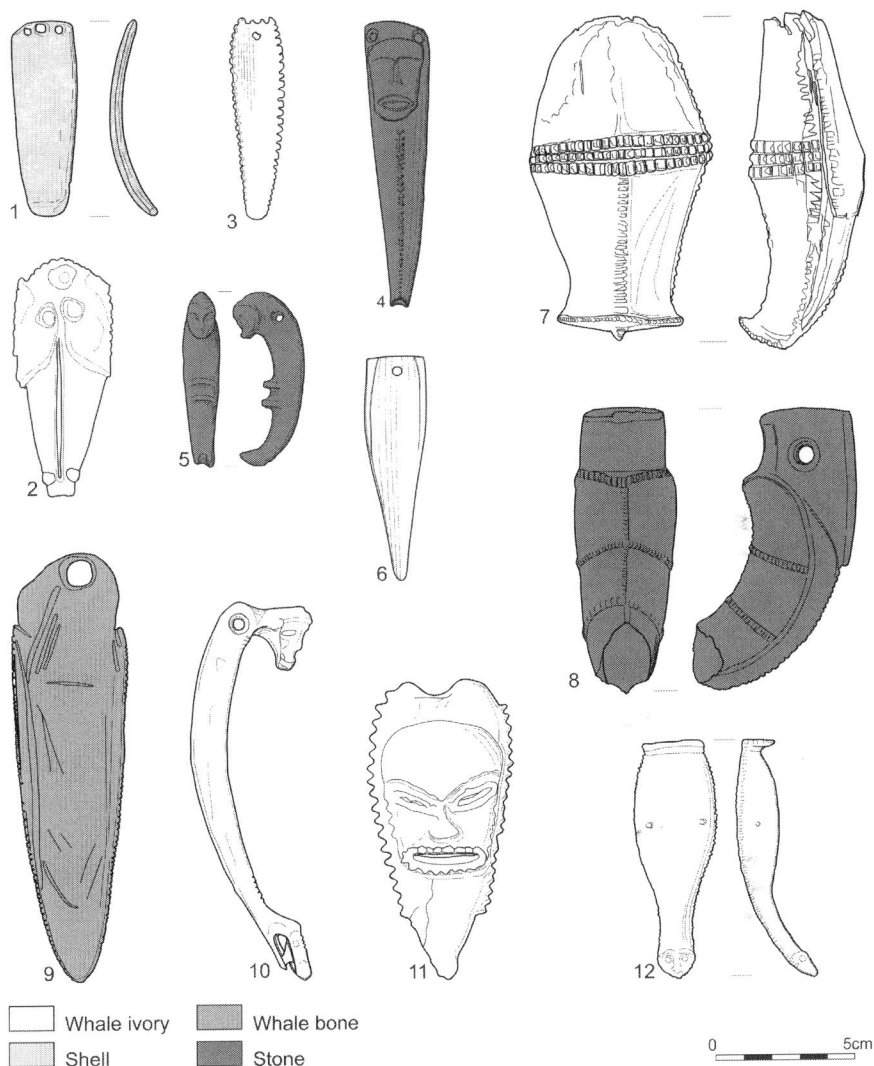

FIGURE 14.5 Twelve pendants of various materials with at least one key feature relating them to chevron pendants. Details in Table 14.2. Reported in Allingham (1989); Arvidson Smith (1986); Duff (1977); Prickett (1999); Skinner (1974).

Source: Drawing by Penny Copeland.

slightly different changes to the criteria many further objects come into my assemblage, notably the currently excluded *rei-puta*, whale ivory pendants which have eyes, sometimes faces, but not chevrons (Fig. 14.6). In *whakapapa* diverse 'boundary objects' can become part of the assemblage as appropriate during analysis without compromising the integrity of that assemblage by breaching its boundaries. We can hold onto the ambiguities of all these objects and others beyond.

TABLE 14.2 Diverse 'related' pendants sharing at least one of the three defining features of chevron pendants, illustrated in Figure 14.5

No.	Length (cm)	Context	Name	Island	Type	Features	References
1	7	?	Cape Maria	North		Shell; very simplified. One of two from same location.	Skinner 1974:83 1934:271
2	8.5		Tom Bowling Bay, Northland	North	Tongue	Bone, moa?	Arvidson Smith 1986; Prickett 1999
3	7.2	?	Howick, Auckland	North	Tongue	Whale ivory Notch chevrons	
4	10.2	Beach	Waitotara, Whanganui	North	Tongue	Stone; serpentine	Skinner 1974:70; Prickett 1999:16; Duff 1977: Plate 19A
5	6.2	?	Pukearuhe, Taranaki	North	Tongue	Stone Andesite?	Skinner 1974:70 Skinner 1934:212
6	8		Castlepoint Wairarapa	North	Tongue	Whale ivory, no notching	Duff 1977:433
7	12.7	?	Mikonui, Oaro, Kaikoura	South	Tongue	Whale ivory; No hole	Duff 1977: Plate 20 Trotter and McCulluch 1989:15
8	10.2	?	Laverique Bay, Pelorus Sound, Marlbouorgh	South	Tongue	Serpentine Orca tooth form	Skinner 1974:90 Prickett 1999:17
9	15.3	Beach Habitation-excavation	Tumbledown Bay, Banks Peninsula	South	Tongue	Whale bone; notch chevrons	Duff 1977: Plate 19B Allingham 1989
10	11.5	Cave?	Little Papanui reptile, Otago Peninsula	South	Tongue?	Whale ivory; Two faces; Notch chevrons	Skinner 1974:69 Skinner 1960:193–5
11	10.7	?	Te papa Museum	?	Tongue	Bone/ivory? Face; burnt	Skinner 1974:70
12	8.5	?	Te papa Museum	?	Tongue	Whale ivory, notched; face	Skinner 1974:69

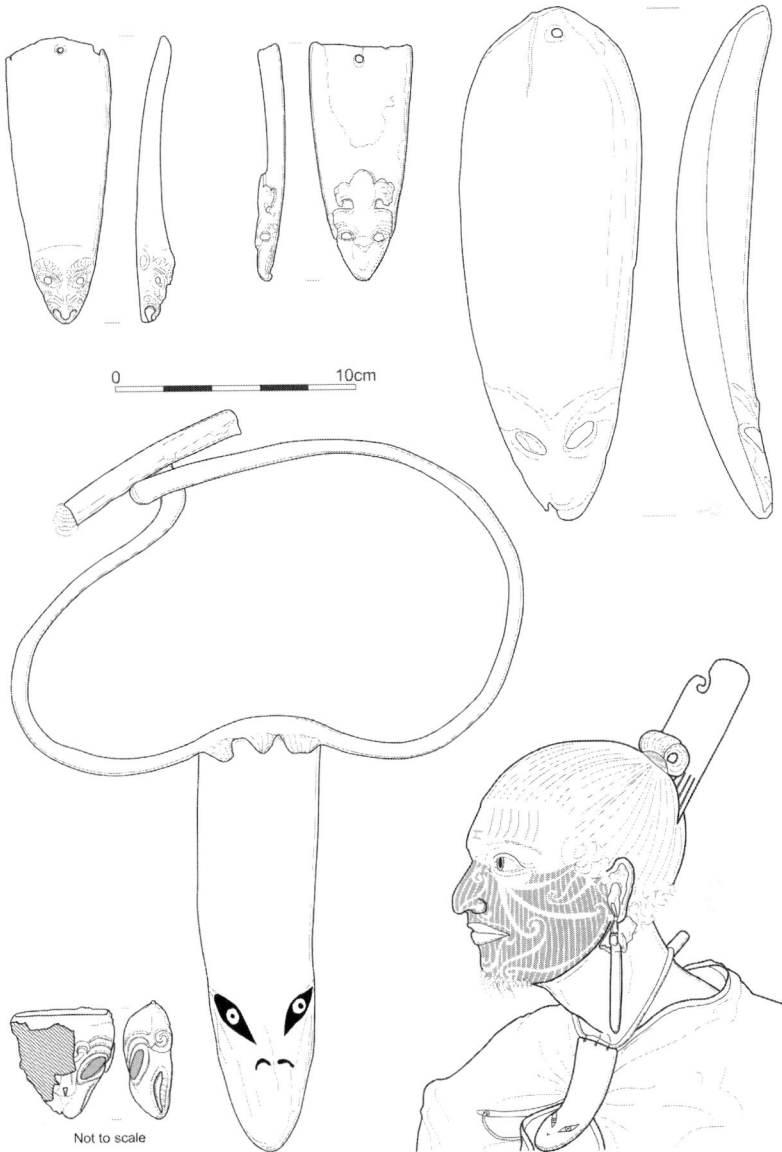

FIGURE 14.6 A selection of *rei-puta* pendants, all of whale ivory. Four archaeologically recovered pendants with carved faces: Clutha, Lake Forsyth, Orepuke and Woodbank pa (Skinner, 1974). *Rei-puta* with original cord, bird bone toggle and a simplified incised face dominated by blackened, angled eyes. Probably collected during Cook's first voyage and now in the Hancock Museum, Newcastle-upon-Tyne (Skinner, 1974). Maori chief, possibly Te Kuukuu, wearing a rei–puta pendant. Drawn from a photograph of the 1769 pen and wash portrait by Sydney Parkinson. Original in the British Library.

Source: Drawings by Penny Copeland.

Whakapapa assemble in order to draw out connections across diverse attributes or things – people, objects, gods, heroes, events, landscapes, all of which are understood to be co-present whatever their apparent separation in time and space. In *whakapapa*, the nature of relating is not pre-determined; it is outcome rather than stipulation. In thinking about the pendants using *whakapapa* we can look beyond object–object relating which is the basis of conventional classification, to object–person relating and potentially also person–person relating. Even though we cannot know the names, intentions or lives of specific persons, we can recognise and hold onto their presence within the object.

Crossing time and space

Whakapapa 'comprise knowledge concerning the origin and relationships of material things … visualised as a network of time-space co-ordinates arranged upon a genealogical framework' (Roberts, 2013, p. 97). Broadly speaking this is not so different to archaeological aspirations. However, in *whakapapa* relating can 'extend beyond the biological to material objects such as stars, as well as spiritual and historical things which are all perceived as somehow related in space-time', because 'all things ultimately trace descent' from 'one set of primal parents or ancestors' (Roberts, 2013, pp. 93, 97). Thus, while *whakapapa* employs many of the time-space forms of knowledge making that an archaeologist would conventionally employ, in *whakapapa* different kinds of relating across time and space may be considered together in ways that would not be acceptable in conventional archaeological accounts.

The age of the pendants is uncertain. Only one chevron pendant, a tiny limb fragment from Kahukura, has been recovered during formal excavations. It came from midden in Layer 4 which is dated to 1399–1659 CE – between the early 15th and early 17th centuries (Walter et al., 2018, pp. 65–66). All the other pendants are chance finds, for which only a few details concerning find location and circumstances have survived. Some pendants were found in association with objects that suggest an early date. For example, the Lake Grassmere pendant was found on a coastal sandpit 'in immediate association with moa bones' (Skinner, 1974, p. 78). Moa is a large flightless bird hunted to extinction well before the arrival of Cook in 1769, so the pendant must have been buried at least 300 years ago. Two other pendants, those from Shag River Mouth and Little Papanui, were recovered in the vicinity of sites with evidence of moa hunting. The Otoroa pendant came from a burial ground that included early adze forms among the grave goods (Adkin, 1948), and the find location for the Okains Bay pendant also contained a shell of *Dentalium nanum*, usually associated with early sites. Finally, the stylistic attributes of the pendants, particularly the chevrons themselves, are widely regarded as indicators of early manufacture (Mead, 1984a; Prickett, 1999; Skinner, 1974).

New Zealand was first colonised some 600–800 years ago by people from the eastern central Pacific region, probably the Cook Islands. Chevron pendants of this form are not found outside New Zealand, nor are they present in any New Zealand site believed to date to the very earliest years of colonisation. Nor are chevron pendants present in the distinctive late Māori assemblages of 300–400 years ago. Captain Cook and other European newcomers arriving in the late 1700s observed, recorded and collected *rei-puta,* but not chevron pendants.

So, we can confidently say that chevron pendants are an indigenous artefact form and are likely to have originated not long after initial colonisation. They were probably manufactured for only a brief period, possibly one or two hundred years, but at least some examples remained in circulation for longer. There is a disputed account that the Aniseed paired pendants were recovered as a bark wrapped package from a hollow tree (Arvidson Smith, 1986; Skinner, 1974, p. 82), and if this is accurate some chevron pendants may have still been in circulation when Europeans arrived. However, chevron pendants had fallen out of general use before the emergence of Māori society as described by European newcomers in the late 18th century (Mead, 1984a; Prickett, 1999, p. 26; Skinner, 1974).

The distribution of find locations is shown in Fig. 14.7. Their centre of gravity clearly lies in the south with numbers falling away to the north. All seven paired pendants, including the limb fragment and probable Goat Bay example, were recovered in the south, and cluster in two locations. In contrast, what little we know of the find locations of the twelve related pendants suggests a rather more scattered distribution around New Zealand.

With one exception all came from coastal locations. At least eight were recovered from beaches – sand spits, sand hills or dunes, and seven from cave locations – rock shelves, clefts, cervices or shelters. At least nine were found in association with human remains and several others were recovered from locations where burials are known to occur. As bodily ornaments it is fairly safe to assume that all pendants were originally deposited in deliberate acts of 'burial' even when there is no record of human remains. In almost all cases human remains found with a pendant are incomplete, indicating either a secondary burial or that the burial was in some way disturbed. Both male and female skeletal remains have been identified. Two pendants were found in association with multiple burials: the Mercury Bay pendant with four skulls and the Whare Creek pendant with skeletal parts from six individuals. Six pendants were found in association with other objects including nephrite objects, bone objects, dentalium shell, seal skin and human hair.

Although incomplete the collective picture of burial context is distinctive in two striking ways. First, most if not all pendants come from comparatively isolated burials and, secondly, with the exception of the Otoroa pendant none are confidently associated with a primary inhumation burial. These burial contexts are not unusual, as a wide range of burial practices are documented for all periods, however, during the earlier period human remains were commonly interred close to and within settlements, sometimes even beneath house floors, and the chevron pendants are notably absent from such contexts. Smaller, less formal burial grounds with primary inhumations and valuable grave goods are also documented at early sites but none has turned up a chevron pendant (Furey, 2002; Leach and Leach,

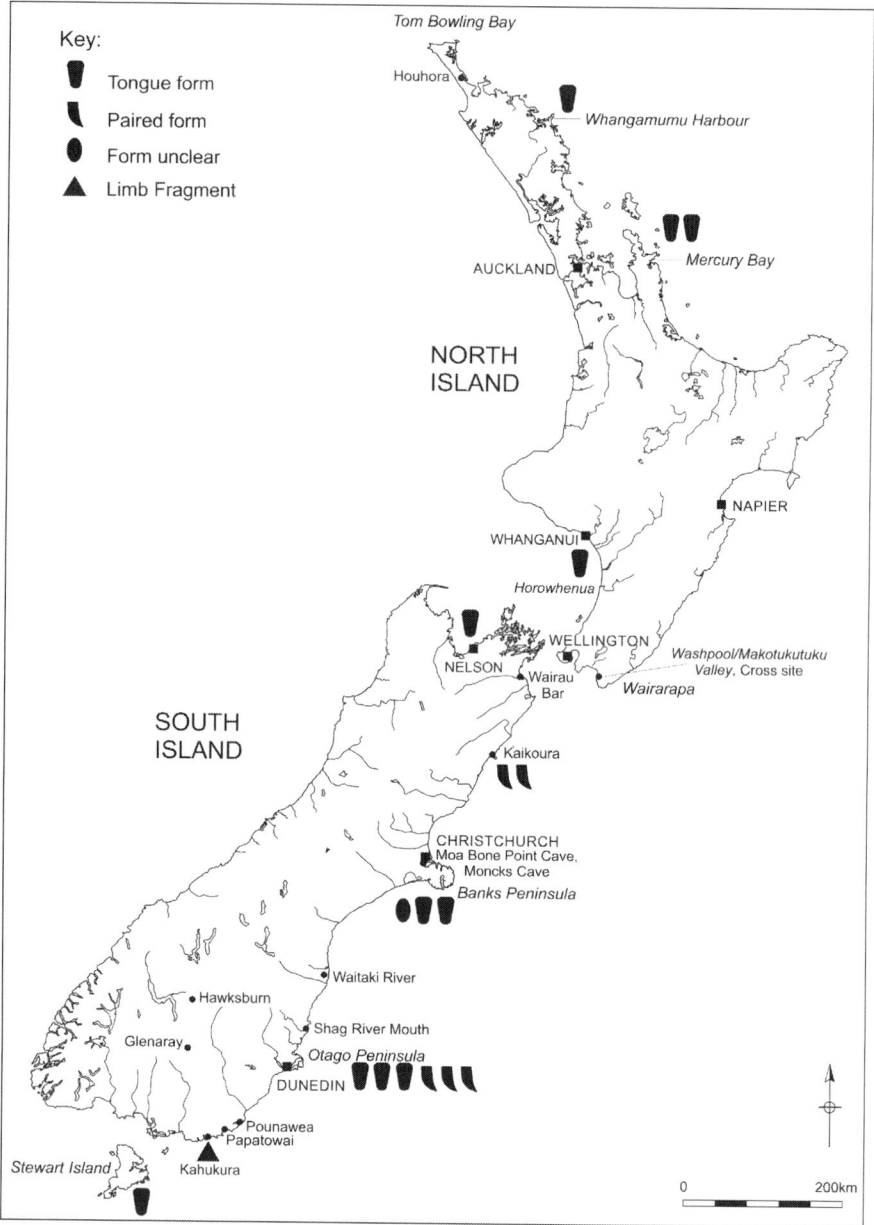

FIGURE 14.7 Distribution of the eighteen chevron pendants across New Zealand.

Source: Map by Penny Copeland.

1979; Anderson et al., 1996). The overall trend is for informal burial practices to become more common over time, while ordered burial grounds decline (Davidson, 1984, p. 173). So, although the pendants were probably manufactured soon after colonisation, they were not interred in any of the currently known early burial grounds. Instead they were placed with incomplete human remains in hidden or singular locations, suggesting they were kept with the living for some time before being 'put away'.

Archaeological research has largely explored how the pendants connect to other objects, particularly with respect to form, composition, design motifs and decorative features. The objective has been to identify stylistic variation in time and space, in order to distinguish patterns in regional variation and sequences of stylistic change over time (Davidson, 1984, pp. 213–214; Furey, 2004; Prickett, 1999; Skinner, 1974). Underlying this work is the idea that each object is a representation of some ideal form or norm presumed to be present in the mind of the maker and of society. Each artefact is a variation on a theme, a version of that ideal or core type. Change over both time and space occurs through gradual, largely unconscious drift away from the 'original' ideal form. Sudden step changes indicate the introduction of a new type. Typically, narratives of stylistic connectedness take the form of genealogical lineages, often presented in a branching tree diagrams – 'like forms share common historic origins' (Prickett, 1999, p. 6).

The tongue-shaped pendants have been viewed as variations on one ideal form, while the paired pendants are a considered a step-change in form with variation from both the tongue form and within the paired theme. One form is assumed to be an earlier, 'original' form and the other a later 'derived' form (Allingham, 1989; Arvidson Smith, 1986; Prickett, 1999, p. 28; Skinner, 1934; 1943, p. 135). Related pendants (Figs. 14.5 and 14.6) are tied into developmental sequences of change as derived, precursor or geographical variants. They are explained by reference to their 'lack' of the full complement of features present in the 'proper' chevron pendant forms. The exquisite Waitotara pendant, for example, is understood as a 'precursor' tongue-shaped chevron pendant executed in a variant material – a chevron pendant in stone (Duff, 1977). It is described by Prickett (1999, p. 16) as 'developed from the imitation whale tooth form and has clear links with chevroned ornaments'. Its comparatively simple form is taken to indicate an early date prior to the emergence of the more elaborate, fully formed chevron pendants (Prickett, 1999, p. 14).

The *rei-puta* is widely argued to derive from the older tongue pendant form, a return back to simpler forms (Prickett, 1999, p. 28). However, even the *rei-puta* has its variations including a preference for fuller featured faces in the south and a reduction of the face to eyes alone in the north, although these differences could be, at least in part, temporal with the more elaborate fuller faces earlier than the simpler eye form (Graham, 1923, pp. 31–32; Skinner, 1974, p. 84). A shift from stylistically complex chevron pendants toward a simpler *rei-puta* form is also suggested to have been part of a wider shift in ornament types from an emphasis on necklaces in earlier periods to pendants in later periods (Davidson, 1984, pp. 77, 90–1; Duff, 1977, p. 83; Furey, 2004, p. 41).

A prominent feature of these accounts is the use of language indicative of copying, suggesting a lack of authenticity. Any reel form not made in bone, or pendant of whale tooth form, which is not an actual whale tooth, is likely to be described as an 'imitation' (Furey, 2004, pp. 30–41; Prickett, 1999, pp.8, 28), a copy or 'hybrid' (Duff, 1977, pp. 100, 108) or as 'aberrant' (Duff, 1977, p. 119). The pervasiveness of this language of the inauthentic is reductive in the way it takes intriguing creative difference and through comparison identifies absence and lack. It is not a way of thinking objects and their materials which contemporary artists would recognise, as the exploration of form and material is usually integral to their work (Maihi, 2012).

A *whakapapa* approach is just as interested in connectedness over time and space when drawing on this archaeological knowledge. But it seeks connection in different ways. For example, chevron pendants are a key artefact defining a stylistic complex of Māori 'archaic decorative elements' (Prickett, 1999, pp. 22, 26) which is itself part of a wider archaic or early East Polynesian assemblage of stylistically related objects. The presence of 'archaic' form objects is character-istic of colonising and early sites across Eastern Polynesia (Walter, 1996; 2004). Chevron designs, notching more generally, and the use of whale ivory are among the defining features of objects found in archaic assemblages. The most abundant artefacts in early New Zealand assemblages are reels and whale tooth pendants manufactured in a range of materials including stone, moa bone, whale bone, whale tooth, and fossil *Dentalium*, both *nanum* and *giganteum*. Some of the reels, particu-larly those made in stone, and occasionally whale tooth pendants were grooved or notched along their edges. Duff (1977, p. 85) records that 'one Māori authority' thought they might be 'genealogical mnemonics (*whakapapa*)', and quoting a letter from Mr Graham reported that some Māori thought the reels themselves to be 'conventionalized *iwi tuara* (human vertebrae) and connected with genealogical matters' (Duff, 1977, p. 86). A similar view was also put forward by Hamilton (1901, pp. 406, 414) and Skinner (1960, p. 194).

Stylistic elements also link the chevron pendants to objects made in recent centuries across the wider Pacific. Notching and chevron decorative elements are very widespread across the Pacific and occur on a range of whalebone and ivory pendants (Prickett, 1999, p. 24), on reels as far afield as Tikopia (Duff, 1977, p. 87), and on many carved wooden objects, particularly in the Cook, Austral and Marquesas Island groups (Duff, 1977, p. 124; Hooper, 2006). One of the more extraordinary examples is a 200-year-old necklace from Fiji or Tonga (Hooper, 2006, p. 249; Kaeppler, 2008, p. 129). It is composed of eight figures and nine tiny notched whale tooth pendants carved in whale ivory. The similarity of these tiny whale tooth pendants to the much larger and older New Zealand examples is striking.

The number, variety and geographical extent of stylistic connections between the chevron pendants and both historical and contemporary objects found across the wider Pacific is astonishing (see e.g. Hooper, 2006; Kaeppler, 2008; Skinner, 1974). To give a flavour of these linkages consider the remarkable similarities in design elements between the chevron pendants and ethnographically known 'tongue-shaped turtle-shell terminals' from the Marquesas Islands (Skinner, 1934, p. 214). These objects have further stylistic links to hairpins of similar manufacture from New Guinea (Skinner, 1934, pp. 271, 273; Skinner, 1960; Reichardt, 1932). What is so compelling about these connections is that they link the chevron pendants across vast reaches of time and space. As Neich (1998, p. 93) points out, such linkages are impossible to explain in simple evolutionary terms or with reference to conventional time-line explanations. We know that these artefacts and design elements have common ancestors, which potentially reach back in time to artefacts made 3,000 years ago by Lapita colonisers, but the commonalities are so extensive and diverse and they resist strict temporal explanation.

In summary, an extraordinarily complex array of space-time connections links the chevron pendants with each other, with objects made much earlier, objects made much later, and with objects made not only in New Zealand but pretty much anywhere in the Pacific from Rapa Nui to New Guinea and Taiwan. Striking resonances occur between objects very distant in time and/or space and these have, unsurprisingly, captured our imagination and academic attention. However, deeper understanding of these tantalising linkages has proven intransigent in the face of conventional analyses. While it is undisputed that the pendants have ancestors in common with other diverse objects, many apparent connections cannot be comfortably accommodated in accounts framed by single attribute timeline sequences and regional differentiation patterns – by genealogical trees. A *whakapapa* framework, based in open 'scrolling' connections (Fig. 14.2), because it draws in a wider and more diverse range of evidence, is potentially more insightful – a key point also made in the analysis by Park et al. (2011).

Drawing people–object connections

Henry Skinner (1934, p. 212) long ago observed that the paired pendants from Little Papanui and St Clair 'have such a strong family resemblance as to suggest the work of a single carver'. In contrast, he goes on, the Wickcliffe Bay pendant 'is much more elaborate, and suggests the work of a different artist'. Skinner's observations direct us to the people who made, and remain part of, those pendants. He reminds us that the geographical distribution of pendants arises from the distribution, movement and engagement of people. To what extent we might ask, did the carver of any pendant know other pendants or their carvers directly, or know of other pendants indirectly through talk, or through having seen objects made in other media which speak to a pendant in some way?

Even a few generations after colonisation when the pendants were probably made, New Zealand was still a very sparsely populated place. A few thousand people thinly dispersed across an extensive new homeland. There may still have been people alive whose grandparents arrived in a colonising canoe. People had already penetrated into almost all corners of the new land – this happened very quickly – establishing the locations of resources and assessing their possibilities.

Even so people continued to move around, searching and experimenting (Walter et al., 2010). Clusters of people were living in large, permanently occupied, but transient villages primarily located along the east coast and on the banks of major rivers – places accessible to canoes (Anderson and Smith, 1996). This was an open, mobile taskscape (Ingold, 1993). People could and did move often, forging and reforging social connections, creating and redrawing their relations with people, objects, land, ancestors and gods.

Amidst this dispersed geography and shifting weave of intimate social relations the chevron pendants became players. How closely might one pendant know another, and how closely did the people who made, held, wore, valued and transacted the pendants know each other and other pendants. Consider the paired pendants (Fig. 14.4). Most were found in two tightly circumscribed areas, small enough for all people to know and be known to each other on some terms (Fig. 14.7). The pendants are intricately carved in a distinctive design but while each pendant is unique, their designs recall and echo each other closely. There is here a dense weave of connectedness. It is difficult to imagine how, given their tight distribution and closely referenced designs, these objects could have been made without each carver having knowledge of at least one of the others. Possibly a single carver made more than one of these pendants as Skinner suggests. Possibly a single person commissioned several of them. The purpose of their making and meaning, was to bring together into a specific object multiple forms of relating and lines of connectedness – much as Brian Flintoff has done in his contemporary carving. Each pair of pendants bundles into itself selected people, stories, talk, histories. At the same time each pendant also reaches out, making connections to other paired pendants, objects, places and people.

Of the eleven tongue pendants, eight are very alike in general form even though their state of preservation means it is impossible to know the details of their intricate designs. Like the paired pendants, these eight speak to each other and echo each other's designs so closely it is difficult to imagine that any of them could have been made without knowledge of at least one other. They reference each other as though the presence of any one of them presumes and anticipates the presence of others. Five of these eight pendants come from circumscribed areas close to those of the paired pendants. Three were recovered from sites in the north. Their distribution suggests they were made, and at least initially circulated, within the same social circle as the paired pendants. The striking stylistic resonances between the Mercury Bay Museum pendant and the Okains Bay pendant (Fig. 14.4, nos. 3 and 7) points to the possibility of a close social connection between people living in the north on the Coromandel Peninsula and people much further south in Banks Peninsula. Such a link would be likely in the early generations after colonisation. Another possibility is that the northern pendants stayed in social circulation for longer than the southern pendants and had time to travel further across wider social and geographical landscapes before being put away in burial.

The final three pendants (Fig. 14.4, nos. 1, 10 and 11) are different to any of the others in general form in that they maintain the full rounded profile of the whale tooth. Their specific designs do not echo each other closely, nor do they directly reference any of the other pendants. These are the most 'individual' of the chevron pendants in the sense that they might have been made without direct reference to, or knowledge of, any other pendant among those we still have with us. Interestingly, two of these pendants were recovered from the farthest reaches of New Zealand. Perhaps they were made on the edges of the social world from which the others emerged, or perhaps their lives took them far from their place of manufacture by the time they were put away.

The 'related' pendants are highly 'individual' in that each seems to tell its own story in its own terms (Fig. 14.5). While they do speak directly to other objects, including the chevron pendants, the carving of their bodies is not densely inscribed in the striking manner of the paired and tongue pendants – although in life of course webs of connectedness woven in social transactions may have become equally dense and extensive. The Waitotara pendant, for example, so singular in its stoniness, so introspective in mood, so arresting in design, cannot be dismissed as a contingent 'copy' in stone simply because whale ivory was not to hand. Rather than diminish its stoniness as 'lack' we should value its stoniness as central to its purpose and to the argument it presents to the world. Also of interest is the recovery of a small hank of braided human hair suggestive of cordage from the Waitotara cave (Lander, 2012). Such cordage is in itself a form of *whakapapa* and a significant connector because it 'completes' a pendant by tying it into the wearer's body (Lander, 2012; Maihi and Lander, 2005). In contrast, the Tumbledown pendant makes its argument very simply. Most of the *rei-puta* are also simple in design. However, even amongst *rei-puta*, the most tightly styled of the pendant forms, there are some highly inscribed examples.

The possibility that the chevron pendants, or more particularly the design elements of notching and chevrons, relate to genealogy or *whakapapa* is not new. Hamilton (1901) suggested 'that these lines or groups of notches are genealogical mnemonics' although Skinner (1960, p. 194) did not seem convinced. Prickett (1999, p. 2) picks up the idea that notching could have been a 'whakapapa memory aid' and Duff (1977, pp. 86–7) suggests archaic bone reels are metaphorical vertebrae. There is no question that the Whangamumu pendant resembles a backbone of articulating vertebrae (Fig. 14.1). These ideas have not been taken up or explored by archaeologists, although contemporary bone carver Brian Flintoff (2011, p. 77) has noted: 'I observed when copying this style that the notching adds life and movement to the design'.

Whakapapa draws out social connections that weave together people, places, myths, gods and objects. This weaving may be accomplished in many ways. It may employ open or dense weaves, just as a gourd may form open branching tendrils or it may become folded and entangled. Two recently developed archaeological concepts, sets, nets, lived and inscribed objects resonate with a *whakapapa* in their focus on building connectedness. First, building on Chapman's theories of fragmentation, which suggest that some objects were deliberately broken and distributed to create social networks, Gamble has developed the concept of sets as social 'containers', and nets as social instruments that effect social enchainment (Chapman, 2000; Gamble, 2007). The second is a distinction between plain, lived objects whose social meanings are covert and complex, and inscribed objects whose social engagements are spelt out explicitly (Marshall, 2000; 2008b). I developed these concepts using the work of Elizabeth Grosz (1994) and by extending Alfred Gell's distinction between the sacred, unmarked bodies of some divine Polynesian chiefs and highly tattooed bodies of other less divine chiefs, including Māori. With these distinctions in mind, consider the Māori chief painted by Sydney Parkinson in 1768 (Fig. 14.6). His faced is densely wrapped with images literally inscribed into his flesh, but he also wears, incorporated around and against his body a plain, minimally inscribed *rei-puta* pendant. The manner of telling *whakapapa* is always contextual, not simply temporal.

A loose, open weave, archaeological *whakapapa* could be understood as a set, while nets are drawn together closely into bundles held firmly in a dense entanglement of connectedness. Chevron pendants are nets – complex, closely woven narratives of connectedness bundled into small, intricately carved objects, pieced so they can be worn directly on the body – or perhaps more accurately as part of the body. A net may become bundled so tightly, wrapped so completely into itself that the many connections it holds become incorporated within the one. A *rei-puta* can be thought of as a wrapped chevron pendant in which the specific connections of the chevron pendant, whether concepts, ideas, talk, people, landscapes have been folded into each other such that the explicitly inscribed designs of a chevron pendant are presumed, already known and can therefore be presented inside the smooth contours of the *rei-puta*. Rather than the *rei-puta* 'losing' the complexity of a chevron pendant, we can imagine that complexity as being wrapped into the simpler form of a *rei-puta* body. The many has been folded into the one.

As Morphy (1991, p. 6) observed in the very different context of Yolnga art, while objects are a communication system, they are not simply a system for the transmission of information. Sometimes information is deliberately obscured so that only those who already have knowledge can see 'inside' an object. A wrapped net is a material memory in which the specifics of its *whakapapa* have been hidden, perhaps put away to be kept safe or to limit its accessibility to unknowing audiences. But however 'plain' a wrapped object body may be, it is not thereby closed off, bounded or fixed. Its apparently simple, unmarked form can at any time, through 'telling' in talk or other avenues, spring open and reveal its contents.

What does it mean to suggest that over time necklaces give way to pendants? Do necklace sets become wrapped into singular pendant bodies? Perhaps to some extent this does happen. But mostly there is ebb and flow. Lived contingent connections may be condensed into intricately carved objects with complex imagery. Similarly, complex inscribed imagery can be wrapped into simpler, plainer object bodies. All these *whakapapa* forms are repeatedly created, but the importance of each and the media in which they are presented are contextual and shifting. As ideas and objects become increasingly immersed in talk, they become more known and more can be assumed. There is less need for explicit accounting, and therefore more and more talk can be wrapped. At the same time new ideas emerge and new actions are taken so wrapping can be opened and contents reinscribed. There is no rigidly directional movement to this flow of change. It does not stride along a timeline.

Chevron pendants, however they are defined, present themselves and their narratives of connectedness in compressed, non-linear arguments – what I have previously characterised as 'tellings' (Lyons and Marshall, 2014). Like a painted *kowhaiwhai* design that stretches and twists itself around a gourd, a chevron pendant weaves its historical alchemy in a 'timeless space' composed of 'ancestors set in an ideal non-specified space'. The composition of a pendant is a *whakapapa* 'continually recreating the timeless, ever-present world of the ancestors' (Neich, 1998, pp. 91–2). It is atemporal, but nevertheless historical (cf. Massey, 2005). There is only relative time positioning the persons, events, ancestors which populate the narrative in relation to one another within a compressed, miniature landscape. Each pendant-landscape is delivered all at once, as 'a piece', a temporally flat singularity, a unique oratorical rendition of *whakapapa*. Every one of the pendants displays 'some difference, some new design touch that made it unique and individualised', and perhaps each also held 'a personal name, connecting them to the ancestor which gave them mana', which gave them power (Neich, 1998, p. 83).

Conclusion

In this chapter I have attempted to step up – to take *whakapapa* seriously as my central conceptual tool. I have found this more challenging than my work exploring Western theories as taking indigenous theory seriously means accepting the inevitability of being wrong-footed. The reward is new ways of thinking and doing archaeology. My exploration of chevron pendants has in many ways returned to an 'old-fashioned' kind of artefact analysis favoured in the early 20th century – an approach concerned with following objects' connections through time and space. The interpretative power of these early studies was I argue restricted by a perceived need to employ single lines of connectedness informed by a single selected attribute. *Whakapapa* is not restricted in this way. It permits multiple lines of enquiry following multiple forms of relating. In this chapter I have chosen to explore these possibilities by examining Māori chevron pendants. However, as shown in my discussion of *whakapapa* informed research, this approach could be extended to analyse non-Māori objects, and non-object entities. It has discipline wide potential for archaeological analysis.

Three concepts have emerged as significant analytical themes: ambiguity, selective knowledge making and memory. Archaeology as *whakapapa* remains open and it therefore actively engages with its ambiguities (Gero, 2007; 2015). In *whakapapa* meaning is not based in defining boundaries but works from focus to connectedness (cf. Wilson, 1989). Connections may be drawn in multiple ways and remain contingent and context specific. While we select and highlight links of specific significance to a selected event or argument our selections do not close down other possibilities. Connections are made, not discovered; they are drawn out, not revealed. This is vital because social life is never finished, so objects that participate in creating and making social lives are never complete (Gamble, 2007, p. 152). At best, completion can be contingent, fleeting and momentary. I am not suggesting we should abandon conventional archaeological analyses based in typology, classification and pattern recognition. Nor am I arguing that we should abandon the chronological rigour that so characterises archaeology as a discipline. I am, however, arguing that we must explicitly acknowledge the partiality of these established methodological and conceptual frameworks and therefore the partiality of the knowledge they produce.

A chevron pendant is *whakapapa* presented in a specific form. It is a specific knowledge-making event, which will subsequently be remade as it is repeatedly remade known. A chevron pendant is an account of the world which acts on and composes its world through its interventions. A chevron pendant makes accountings of the world in the form of presentation. As Morphy (1991) argued for Yolnga art, an inclusive account of the pendants, that draws in chevron, 'related' and *rei-puta* forms, highlights the selectiveness in what is made explicitly known and what left implicit. Over time the balance ebbed and flowed. Earlier examples were inscribed with knowledge and wrapped in images (Gell, 1993; 1998; Marshall, 2008b). In later examples knowledge is deliberately enclosed, wrapped inside simplified or abstracted images. Meaning and hidden knowledge could only be 'told' in appropriate contexts or for specific audiences who already possess particular kinds of knowledge. The knowing gives them insight into apparently simple objects while excluding the uninformed. The power of 'wrapped into', unmarked pendants begins to supersede that of 'wrapped around', inscribed pendants. A *whakapapa* approach acknowledges, even presumes, this selectiveness in form and context of telling.

Memory also plays its part in selective telling. Whether telling a pendant in a process of making, or in a context of speaking, what is made known is largely drawn from personal and collective memory. As discussed above this may be memory or direct knowledge of other pendants, but it will also be memory and knowledge of people, events and other connections with the world. So, knowledge does not flow directly from object to object; it is always mediated by people – by social relations past and present. There will then inevitably be 'spaces' between objects as we can know them today. It is not just that archaeologically we will never have a complete assemblage composed of all the pendants ever made to work from. Even if we did have such an assemblage it would still be full of stylistic jumps and gaps, 'retrospective' references, mixes of old and new elements, and unique components unexplainable by reference to other pendants.

Above all, *whakapapa* directs us to social relationships. Conventional archaeological analyses seek to identify time-space patterning in object = object relating. *Whakapapa* does not conclude here; it goes on to seek patterns of object = human relating and human = human relating. Fundamentally, *whakapapa* produces social archaeologies.

Acknowledgements

I would like to thank the following people for their comments, conversations and encouragement during the development of this chapter, and for their efforts to help me improve earlier drafts: Ben Alberti, Brian Flintoff, Chris Jacomb, Maureen Lander, Sue Loughlin, Toi te Rito Maihi, Julie Park, Tim Thomas and an anonymous reviewer. Thank you to Penny Copeland for her excellent line drawings.

References

Adkin, G.L., 1948. *Horowhenua: Its Maori Place Names and their Topographical and Historical Background*. Polynesian Society Memoir 26. Auckland: The Polynesian Society.

Alberti, B., Fowles, S., Holbraad, M., Marshall, Y. and Witmore, C., 2011. World's otherwise: archaeology, anthropology and ontological difference. *Current Anthropology,* 52(6), pp. 896–912.

Alberti, B. and Marshall, Y., 2009. Animating archaeology: local theories and conceptually open-ended methodologies. *Cambridge Journal of Archaeology,* 19(3), pp. 344–356.

Allingham, B., 1989. *Preliminary Report on Salvage Excavations at Tumbledown Bay, Banks Peninsula*. New Zealand Historic Places Trust, Permit 1987/9. Wellington: New Zealand Historic Places Trust.

Anderson, A. and Smith, I., 1996. The transient village in southern New Zealand. *World Archaeology,* 27, pp. 359–371.

Anderson, A., Allingham, B. and Smith, I., eds. 1996. *Shag River Mouth: The Archaeology of an Early Maori Village*. Canberra: ANH Publications.

Arvidson Smith, C., 1986. A catalogue of chevron amulets. Paper compiled for Archaeology 03.418. Auckland: Anthropology Department, University of Auckland.

Bell, A., 2017. Co-existing indigenous and settler worlds: ontological styles and possibilities. *Journal of New Zealand Studies,* NS 24, pp. 15–24.

Binney, J. and Chaplin, G., 1986. Nga *Morehu, the Survivors*. Auckland: Oxford University Press.

Bowker, G.C. and Star, S.L., 2000. *Sorting Things Out: Classification and its Consequences*. London: MIT Press

Chapman, J., 2000. *Fragmentation in Archaeology: People Places and Broken Objects in the Prehistory of South Eastern Europe*. London: Routledge.

Crosby, A., 2004. Ritual. In: L. Furey and S. Holdaway, eds. *Change through Time: 50 Years of New Zealand Archaeology*. Auckland: New Zealand Archaeological Association Monograph 26, pp. 105–124.

Davidson, J., 1984. *The Prehistory of New Zealand*. Auckland: Longman Paul.

Deleuze, G. and Guattari, F., 1988. *A Thousand Plateaus: Capitalism and Schizophrenia*, trans. B. Massumi. London: Athlone Press.

Duff, R., 1977. *The Moa-Hunter Period of Maori Culture*. Wellington: Keating, Government Printer.

Flintoff, B., 2011. *Kura Koiwi: Bone Treasures*. Nelson: Craig Potton Publishing.

Furey, L., 2002. *Houhora: A Fourteenth Century Maori Village in Northland*. Auckland: Bulletin of the Auckland Museum 10.

Furey, L., 2004. Material culture. In: L. Furey and S. Holdaway, eds. *Change through Time: 50 Years of New Zealand Archaeology*. Auckland: New Zealand Archaeological Association Monograph 26, pp. 29–54.

Furey, L. and Holdaway, S., eds. 2004. *Change through Time: 50 Years of New Zealand Archaeology*. Auckland: New Zealand Archaeological Association Monograph 26.

Gamble, C., 2007. *Origins and Revolutions: Human Identity in Earliest Prehistory*. Cambridge: Cambridge University Press.

Gero, J.M., 2007. Honouring ambiguity; problematizing certitude. *Journal of Archaeological Method and Theory*, 14(3), pp. 311–327.

Gero, J.M., 2015. *Yutopian: Archaeology, Ambiguity and the Production of Knowledge in Northwest Argentina*. Austin, TX: University of Texas Press.

Gell, A., 1993. *Wrapping in Images: Tattooing in Polynesia*. Oxford: Clarendon Press.

Gell, A., 1998. *Art and Agency: An Anthropological Theory*. Oxford: Clarendon Press.

Graham, G., 1923. 'Rei-Puta'. A maori pendent. *Journal of the Polynesian Society*, 32(125), pp. 29–34.

Grosz, E., 1994. *Volatile Bodies: Towards a Corporeal Feminism*. Indianapolis, IN: Indiana University Press.

Hamilton, A., 1901. *Maori Art: The Art Workmanship of the Maori Race in New Zealand*. Dunedin: Ferguson and Mitchell for the New Zealand Institute.

Henare, A., 2007. *Taonga Maori*: encompassing rights and property in New Zealand. In: A. Henare, M. Holbraad and S. Wastell, eds. *Thinking through Things: Theorising Artefacts Ethnographically*. London: Routledge, pp. 47–67.

Hooper, S., 2006. *Pacific Encounters: Art and Divinity in Polynesia 1760–1860*. London: British Museum Press.

Hudson, M.L., Ahuriri-Driscoll, A.L.M., Lea, M.G. and Lea, R.A., 2007. Whakapapa – a foundation for genetic research? *Bioethical Enquiry*, 4, pp. 43–49.

Ingold, T., 1993. The temporality of the landscape. *World Archaeology*, 25, pp. 152–174.

Ingold, T., 2000. *The Perception of the Environment: Essays on Livelihood, Dwelling and Skill*. London: Routledge.

Ingold, T., 2007. *Lines: A Brief History*. London: Routledge.

Ingold, T., 2011. *Being Alive: Essays on Movement, Knowledge and Description*. London: Routledge.

Jacomb, C., 2012. Personal communication. Notes taken on the Mercury Bay Museum Chevroned Amulet in 2010. University of Otago, Oct.

Kaeppler, A.L., 2008. *The Pacific Arts of Polynesian and Micronesia*. Oxford: Oxford University Press.

Lander, M., 2012. Personal communication. Oct.

Leach, B.F. and Leach, H.M., 1979. Burial positions and orientations in Palliser Bay. In: B.F. Leach and H.M. Leach, eds. *Prehistoric Man in Palliser Bay*. National Bulletin, 21. Wellington: Museum of New Zealand, pp. 205–213.

Lyons, N. and Marshall, Y., 2014. Memory, practice, telling community. *Canadian Journal of Archaeology*, 38, pp. 496–518.

Mahuika, N., 2019. A brief history of whakapapa: Maori approaches to genealogy. *Genealogy*, 3(32), pp. 1–13.

Maihi, Toi Te Rito, 2012. Personal communication. Oct.

Maihi, Toi Te Rito and Lander, M., 2005. *He Kete He Korero: Every Kete has a Story*. London: Penguin

Marshall, Y., 2000. Reading images stone B.C. *World Archaeology*, 32(2), pp. 222–235.

Marshall, Y., 2008a. Archaeological possibilities for feminist theories of transition and transformation. *Feminist Theory*, 9(1), pp. 25–45.

Marshall, Y., 2008b. The social lives of lived and inscribed objects: a Lapita perspective. *Journal of the Polynesian Society*, 117(1), pp. 59–101.

Marshall, Y., 2013. Personhood in prehistory: a feminist archaeology in ten persons. In: D. Bolger, ed. *A Companion to Gender Prehistory*. London: John Wiley & Sons, pp. 204–225.

Marshall, Y. and Alberti, B., 2014. A matter of difference: Karen Barad, ontology and archaeological bodies. *Cambridge Journal of Archaeology*, 24(1), pp. 19–36.

Massey, D., 2005. *For Space*. London: Sage.

McCarthy, C., 2007. *Exhibiting Maori: A History of Colonial Cultures of Display*. Oxford: Berg.

McCarthy, C., 2011. *Museums and Maori: Heritage Professionals; Indigenous Collections; Current Practice*. Walnut Creek, CA: Left Coast Press.

Mead, S.M., 1975. The origins of Maori art: Polynesian or Chinese. *Oceania*, 45(3), pp. 173–211.

Mead, S.M., ed. 1984a. *Te Maori: Maori Art from New Zealand Collections*. Auckland: Heinemann.

Mead, S.M., 1984b. *Nga Timunga me Nga Paringa o te Mana Maori*: the ebb and flow of Mana Maori and the changing context of Maori art. In: S.M. Mead, ed. *Te Maori: Maori Art from New Zealand Collections*. Auckland: Heinemann, pp. 20–36.

Mead, S.M., 1984c. Ka Tupu te Toi Whakairo Ki Aotearoa: becoming Maori art. In: S.M. Mead, ed. *Te Maori: Maori Art from New Zealand Collections*. Auckland: Heinemann, pp. 63–75.

Mead, S.M., 1986. *Te Toi Whakairo: The Art of Maori Carving*. Auckland: Reed.

Morphy, H., 1991. *Ancestral Connections: Art and an Aboriginal System of Knowledge*. Chicago, IL: University of Chicago Press.

Neich, R., 1998. Wood carving. In: J. Davidson, N. To Awekotuku, A.T. Hakiwai, R. Neich, M. Pendergrast, D.C. Starzecka and R, Jahnke, eds. *Maori Art and Culture*, 2nd edition. London: British Museum Press, pp. 69–113.

O'Regan, G., 2010. Working for my own. In: G. Nicholas, ed. *Being and Becoming Indigenous Archaeologists*. Walnut Creek, CA: Left Coast Press, pp. 235–245.

Park, J., Littleton, J., Chambers, A., and Chambers, K., 2011. Whakapapa in anthropological research on tuberculosis in the Pacific. *Sites: New Series*, 8(2), pp. 6–31.

Prickett, N., 1999. *Nga Tohu Tawhito: Early Maori Ornaments*. Auckland: David Bateman & Auckland Museum.

Reichardt, G.A., 1932. *Melanesian Design: A Study of Style in Wood and Tortoise Carving*, 2 vols. New York: Columbia University Press.

Rika-Heke, M., 2010. Haere Tika Tona Atu – keep going forward. In: G. Nicholas, ed. *Being and Becoming Indigenous Archaeologists*. Walnut Creek, CA: Left Coast Press, pp. 267–276.

Roberts, J., 2006. *Layer upon Layer, Whakapapa*. Cambridge: Wotz Wot Ltd.

Roberts, M., 2010. Mindmaps of the Maori. *GeoJournal*, 77(6), pp. 741–751.

Roberts, M., 2013. Ways of seeing: whakapapa. *Sites: New Series*, 10(1), pp. 93–120.

Roberts, M., Haami, B., Benton, R., Scatterfield, T., Finucane, M.L., Henare, M. and Henare, M., 2004. Whakapapa as a Maori mental construct: some implications for the debate over genetic modification of organisms. *The Contemporary Pacific*, 16(1), pp. 1–28.

Skinner, H.D., 1934. Maori amulets in stone, bone, and shell. *Journal of the Polynesian Society*, 43(171), pp. 198–215; (172), pp. 271–279.

Skinner, H.D., 1943. Maori amulets in stone, bone, and shell. *Journal of the Polynesian Society*, 53(3), pp. 132–152.

Skinner, H.D., 1960. Excavations at Little Papanui, Otago Peninsula. *Journal of the Polynesian Society*, 69(3), pp. 186–198.

Skinner, H.D., 1974. *Comparatively Speaking: Studies in Pacific Material Culture 1921–1972*. Dunedin: University of Otago Press.

Starzecka, D.C., Neich, R. and Pendergrast, M., 2010. *The Maori Collections of the British Museum*. London: British Museum Press.

Tapsell, P., 1997. The flight of Pareraututu: an investigation of *Taonga* from a tribal perspective. *Journal of the Polynesian Society*, 106(4), pp. 323–374.

Walter, R., 1996. What is the East Polynesian 'Archaic'? A view from the Cook Islands. In: J. Davidson, G. Irwin, B.F. Leach, A. Pawley and D. Brown, eds. *Oceanic Culture History: Essays in Honour of Roger Green.* Dunedin: Journal of New Zealand Archaeology, pp. 513–529.

Walter, R., 2004. New Zealand and its Polynesian Connections. In: L. Fureyand S. Holdaway, eds. *Change through Time: 50 Years of New Zealand Archaeology.* Auckland: New Zealand Archaeological Association Monograph 26, pp. 125–146.

Walter, R., Jacomb, C. and Bowron-Muth, S., 2010. Colonisation, mobility and exchange in New Zealand prehistory. *Antiquity,* 84, pp. 497–513.

Walter, R., Brooks, E., Greig, K. and Hurford, J., 2018. Excavations at Kahukura (G47/128), Murihiku. *Journal of Pacific Archaeology,* 9(2), pp. 59–82.

Wilson, P., 1989. *The Domestication of the Human Species.* London: Yale University Press.

INDEX

Note: Page numbers in *italics* indicate figures and in **bold** indicate tables on the corresponding pages.

Deleuze, G. 303
de Mendaña, A. 11
Denham, T. 114, 225
de Perthes, B. 15
Descent of Man, The 205
Dewar, R. 80
Diamond, J.M. 43, 44, 151, 159
Diderot, D. 12
diffusionism 17, 23, 25
dispersal models 156–158, *157*; seafaring
  politics and 163–165
diversity in networked world 113–116, *115*
Dixon, B. 236, 271
domestication: multilinear and decentred
  221–224; practices ontologically prior
  to 224–226; under vegeculture in
  New Guinea 218–221
domestic mode of production (DMP) 106
Donohue, M. 114
Douglas, B. 11
drift 66–68
Duff, R. 18, 321
Duffy, P.R. 246
Dunnell, R. 26
Durkheim, E. 104–105
d'Urville, D. 13, *14*, 15

Earle, T. 62, 70, 106, 184, 186–187, 189
Early Papuan Pottery (EPP) complex
  125–126
Easter Island, Earth Island 2
ecodynamics, human–island 46–47
egalitarian societies, emergence of 227–228
Eggan, F. 83
Ekholm, K. 181, 183–184
El Niño-Southern Oscillation (ENSO) 154
*Engendering Archaeology: Women and
  Prehistory* 259
Esoteric Efflorescence in Easter Island 39
ethnogenesis 79
Ethnographic Atlas 62
Ethnography of the Neolithic, An 6
Evans, J.D. 41–42, 45
evolutionary archaeology 66–68; case study
  of two approaches in 68–71, *69*
evolutionary theory 25–26, 71–72;
  introduction to 58–59; ladder-like
  cultural evolution 58–62, *60*; in the
  Pacific 59–68, *60*; phylogenetic history
  and adaptation and 63–66; population
  dispersal and 156–158; selection, drift,
  and other mechanisms in 66–68
*Evolution of the Polynesian Chiefdoms,
  The* 63

farming-language dispersal hypothesis
  (FLDH) 107
feminism 259, 262; *see also*
  archaeology, gender
Fernández de Quirós, P. 11
fishhooks 65, 67
Fitzpatrick, S.M. 38
Flannery, K.V. 62, 82, 85, 106
Fleisher, J. 4, 5
Flenley, J.R. 2
Flintoff, B. 305, *305*, 305–306
formalism 111
Fornander, A. 16
Forster, J.R. 12, 13
Fosberg, E.R. 46
Fowler, C. 6
Fox, J. 280
Friedman, J. 62, 181, 183–184, 186
Frobenius, L. 16
Fyfe, A. 108

Galton's problem 65
Gamble, C. 149
game-theory methods 64
Garanger, J. 286–287
gender archaeology *see* archaeology, gender
*Genealogies and Historical Notes from
  Rarotonga* 277
genealogy: dating methods using 277, 283,
  284–285, 288; historical models as 24,
  27, 86, 170; oral traditions and 171, 279;
  social rank and 162, 280–281; *see also
  whakapapa*
genetic comparative method 86
genetic model 84–85
Gero, J.M. 259, 267, 268
Gifford, E.W. 18
global island archaeology 38, 47–49
Goldman, E. 202
Goldman, I. 62, 81–82
Golson, J. 18–19, 277–278, 292
Gómez Bellard, C. 41–42
Goodenough, W. 40, 79; on controlled
  studies in Oceania 81
Gosden, C. 42, 140
Gosser, D. 271
Gould, S.J. 86
Graeber, D. 202
Graves, M.W. 149
Gray, R.D. 65, 95
Green, R.C. 18, 20–22, *21*, 23, 26, 66,
  151; on gradual process of network-
  breaking 92; on holistic archaeology
  282; on mechanisms of divergence 87;

settlement pattern analysis of 234–237; theories of origins of 15–16
positivism 3
Posth, C. 24
postprocessualism 3–4, 5
post-war social theory 105–106
pragmatism 4
preceramic shell artefacts: assemblage of 130–135, **131**, *132–133*; in Circum-New Guinea Archipelago space and time 138–139; excavation and identification of 126–128, *127*; shell identification and analytical methods for 128–130, *129*; Tanamu 1 worked shell within context of Circum-New Guinea Archipelago 135–138
prehistoric social life: archaeological network analysis and relational past in 110–113, *112*; continued debate over conceptualising 117–118; diversity in networked world and 113–116, *115*; early importance of Pacific ethnography to social theory of 104–105; introduction to ethnography of 102–104; language, material culture and human history in 107–110; in Near Oceania 109–110; the Pacific and post-war social theory of 105–106; testing the 'myth of the primitive isolate' of 107–109
pre-Māori people, theories of 15–16
prestige practices: conclusions on 194–195; end of Lapita 191–194; evidence for Lapita 185–187; introduction to 180–182, *182*; Pacific societies and 181–187; from prestige goods to 187–191, *190*
Prey Choice Model 63
Prickett, N. 321
Proudhon, P.-J. 202
proximal point analysis 111, *112*
proximate processes 59

races in the Pacific 12–16, *13*
Rainbird, P. 43
Ransfield, T. 8
Rapa Nui/Easter Island 12, 40; evolutionary processes and 63; isolation and interaction of people of 92–93
Rappaport, R.A. 41, 106
Ratzel, F. 16
reciprocal causation 148
rei niho 306
rei-puta 317–318, 322
relationality 8

relativism 3
Renfrew, C. 39, 107
Rieth, T.M. 49
Rika-Heke, M. 301
ritual-political centres *239*, 239–245, *243–244*; Mā'ohi minor centres 245–250, **248**, *249*
ritual practice 164
Rivers, W.H.R. 17, 23
Roberts 304
Roberts, J.M., Jr. 108
Romney, K. 82, 83–84, 85
Roscoe, P.B. 117
Rouse, I. 44
Roviana Lagoon 288–289
Rowlands, M. 181
Roy Mata tradition 286–287

Sahlins, M. 39–40, 61–63, 292; controlled comparisons by 81; on oral traditions 278; post-war social theory and 106
Sapir, E. 81
scale and colonisation 147–148
Schortman, E.M. 238
Schwartz, T. 111
Scott, J.C. 201, 202, 210
seafaring politics 163–165
secondary ritual-political centres, 'Opunohu Valley 242–245, *243–244*; Mā'ohi minor centres 245–250, **248**, *249*
selection 66–68
selection-based explanation of Lapita movement 70–71, 160
Seligman, C.G. 16
settlement dates, oral tradition on 284–285
settlement patterns and networks, Society Islands: analysis of 234–237; beyond primary centres 237–239; conclusions on 250–251; economic control, territorial boundaries and political centralisation in 236–237; investigating social variability in 235–236; Mā'ohi minor centres 245–250, **248**, *249*; monumental architecture in 240–241; 'Opunohu Valley networks and nodes in *239*, 239–245, *243–244*
settlement process 149; oral traditions of 170, 282–284
Sewell, B. 265
shared innovations 86
Sharp, A. 282
Sheehan, O. 95
Shennan, S. 108

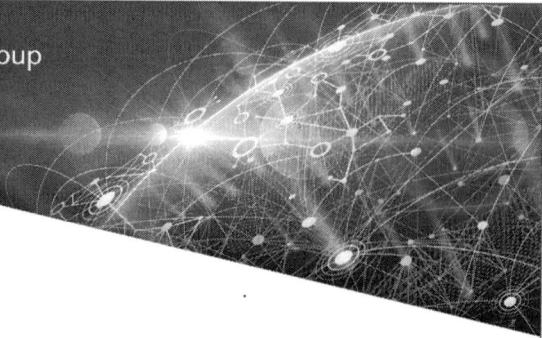